25%

BEM

PORTRAIT OF WYNDHAM LEWIS, 1913-14
HENRI GAUDIER-BRZESKA
CRAYON. 38 x 25 CM
COURTESY ANTHONY d'OFFAY

BLAST 3

EDITED BY SEAMUS COONEY

CO-EDITED BY
BRADFORD MORROW, BERNARD LAFOURCADE
AND HUGH KENNER

BLACK SPARROW PRESS • 1984

BLAST 3. Copyright © 1984 by Black Sparrow Press.

Previously unpublished letters by Ezra Pound, Copyright © 1984 by the Trustees of the Ezra Pound Literary Property Trust; used by permission of New Directions Publishing Corp., agents.

All rights reserved. Printed in the United States of America. No part of this book may be used or reproduced in any manner whatsoever without written permission except in the case of brief quotations embodied in critical articles and reviews. For information address Black Sparrow Press, P.O. Box 3993, Santa Barbara, CA 93130.

This project was supported in part by matching grants from the Santa Fe Arts Council, Santa Barbara Arts Services, and the National Endowment for the Arts.

ISBN 0-87685-591-5 (paper edition)
ISBN 0-87685-592-3 (deluxe cloth edition)

ACKNOWLEDGEMENTS

This compendium in honor of Wyndham Lewis embodies the efforts of many people. First there are the various contributors, who deserve thanks not only for their work but also for their patience in the face of the unforeseen delays in bringing the volume to publication. Second, for the inception of the project, credit goes to that devoted Lewisite, John Martin of Black Sparrow Press, and for the initial eliciting of contributions to him and Bradford Morrow. Hugh Kenner and Bernard Lafourcade, the other Associate Editors, also encouraged the project and elicted valuable contributions. At various stages thereafter, Sasha Newborn, Leena Bell, Beverley Endersby, Peter Sibbald Brown, and Barbara Martin all gave significant help in striving towards the ideals of liveliness, accuracy, and elegance which the volume aims for. Responsibility for what imperfections remain must be laid at the feet of the General Editor.

SEAMUS COONEY

LIST OF PLATES

Henri Gaudier-Brzeska ▲ **Portrait of Wyndham Lewis, 1913–14** ▲ Frontispiece
Henri Gaudier-Brzeska ▲ **Composition With Three Figures, 1914** ▲ 39
Wyndham Lewis ▲ **Drawing Of Ezra Pound, 1919** ▲ 58
Wyndham Lewis ▲ **Head Of Ezra Pound, 1939** ▲ 59
Henri Gaudier-Brzeska ▲ **Stooping Male Nude, 1912–13** ▲ 114
Wyndham Lewis ▲ **The Duc De Joyeux Sings, 1920s** ▲ 134
Henri Gaudier-Brzeska ▲ **Portrait Of Ezra Pound, 1914** ▲ 157
Michael Ayrton ▲ **Wyndham Lewis, 1955** ▲ 197
Wyndham Lewis ▲ **The Starry Sky, 1912** ▲ 231

A PORTFOLIO OF WYNDHAM LEWIS COLOR PLATES After Page 236

▲ **Lovers, 1912**
▲ **Centauress, 1912**
▲ **Composition III, 1914–15**
▲ **The Psychologist, 1917**
▲ **Walking Wounded, 1918**
▲ **Figure Composition, c. 1921**
▲ **Archimedes Reconnoitring The Enemy Fleet, 1922**
▲ **Vorticist Composition, 1922**
▲ **Figures In The Air, 1927**
▲ **The Immortality Of The Soul, c. 1933**
▲ **Red And Black Principle, 1936**
▲ **Landscape With Northmen, c. 1936–37**
▲ **Mexican Shawl, 1938**
▲ **Day Dream Of The Nubian, 1938**
▲ **Stephen Spender, 1938**
▲ **The Island, 1942**

Wyndham Lewis ▲ **Nude (Seated), 1919** ▲ 257
Wyndham Lewis ▲ **Abstract Figure Study, 1921** ▲ 293
Wyndham Lewis ▲ **Nude (Kneeling), 1919** ▲ 301
Henri Gaudier-Brzeska ▲ **Still Life With Mask Of Sophie Brzeska, 1912** ▲ 339

TABLE OF CONTENTS

Bradford Morrow ▲ **History of an Unapologetic Apologia: Roy Campbell's Wyndham Lewis** ▲ 11
Roy Campbell ▲ **Wyndham Lewis** ▲ 15
Reed Way Dasenbrock ▲ **Vorticism Among the Isms** ▲ 40
William C. Wees ▲ **Wyndham Lewis and Vorticism** ▲ 47
Michèle Poli ▲ **BLAST** ▲ 51
Ezra Pound ▲ **BLAST (radio speech #30: April 26, 1942)** ▲ 60
Giovanni Cianci ▲ **Pound and Futurism** ▲ 63
Timothy Materer ▲ **Wyndham Lewis the Soldier** ▲ 68
Guy Davenport ▲ **The Bowmen of Shu (illustrated by Henri Gaudier-Brzeska and the author)** ▲ 77
Daniel Schenker ▲ **Homo ex Machina: Wyndham Lewis on the Definitions of Man** ▲ 96
E. W. F. Tomlin ▲ **Wyndham Lewis the Emancipator** ▲ 109
B. W. Powe ▲ **The Hunter, Laughter, and the Surgical Blade** ▲ 115
C. H. Sisson ▲ **Lewis's Study of Himself** ▲ 122
Paul Edwards ▲ **"Clodoveo" and "Belcanto": Wyndham Lewis and James Joyce** ▲ 126
Jean Guiguet ▲ **Jeu de miroirs: jeu de massacre (Virginia Woolf et Wyndham Lewis)** ▲ 135
Jean-Jacques Mayoux ▲ **L'Amour puni** ▲ 141
Reno Odlin ▲ **Intellectus Possibilis, or Jên^2** ▲ 150
Bryant Knox ▲ **Ezra Pound on Wyndham Lewis's Rude Assignment** ▲ 158
Ezra Pound ▲ **Letters on Rude Assignment: Transcription, Notes and Facsimile Letters** ▲ 163
Seamus Cooney ▲ **Ezra Pound on Wyndham Lewis's The Hitler Cult** ▲ 183
Ezra Pound ▲ **Letters on The Hitler Cult: Transcription, Notes and Facsimile Letters** ▲ 184
Reno Odlin ▲ **From Thus to Revisit: Lewis in 1956** ▲ 198
Bernard Lafourcade ▲ **Creativity en famille: a study in genetic manipulations** ▲ 201
Wyndham Lewis ▲ **Creativity** ▲ 205
Mina Loy ▲ **"The Starry Sky" of Wyndham Lewis** ▲ 232
Seamus Cooney ▲ **Notes on the Color Plates** ▲ 233
Joyce Carol Oates ▲ **Frissons** ▲ 237
Clayton Eshleman ▲ **Lemons** ▲ 258
Aimé Césaire ▲ **Lay of Errantry (translated by Clayton Eshleman and Annette Smith)** ▲ 261
Ed Dorn ▲ **"The Party"** ▲ 264
Tom Clark ▲ **War and Other Poems** ▲ 265
Creeley/Olson ▲ **Letters** ▲ 272
George Butterick ▲ **Notes to the Creeley/Olson Letters** ▲ 292
Charles Olson ▲ **The Mast** ▲ 294
Fielding Dawson ▲ **Goodnight Irene** ▲ 297
Kenneth Gangemi ▲ **Six Poems** ▲ 302
John Sanford ▲ **The Leo Frank Case, 1913–1915** ▲ 309
John Sanford ▲ **Eugene V. Debs, 1855–1926** ▲ 316
Paul Bowles and Edouard Roditi ▲ **Open Letters to Le Journal de Tanger** ▲ 322
Gerard Malanga ▲ **Edward Albee's Ear in the Manner of Allen Ginsberg** ▲ 331
K.R. Campbell ▲ **The Maker of the Sound** ▲ (phono-disc, recording—loose insert)
K. R. Campbell ▲ **A Necessary Supplement to "The Maker of the Sound"** ▲ 334
Gilbert Sorrentino ▲ **John Gardner: Rhinestone in the Rough** ▲ 340
Alan Munton ▲ **Fredric Jameson: Fables of Aggression: Wyndham Lewis, the Modernist as Fascist** ▲ 345

▲ Notes on Contributors ▲ 353

BRADFORD MORROW

HISTORY OF AN UNAPOLOGETIC APOLOGIA:

ROY CAMPBELL'S WYNDHAM LEWIS

GHOST-BOOK

For the past fifty years Roy Campbell's study of Wyndham Lewis was thought not to exist. It has been deemed by bibliophiles and Lewis scholars to be a ghost-book. Although the book was completed sometime in 1931, and Campbell had contracted with a publisher and had read at least one set of proofs, *Wyndham Lewis* was never published. The original manuscript apparently was lost, and to this day its whereabouts are unknown. But the recent discovery of a set of page proofs (now housed at The Humanities Research Center, the University of Texas) makes this first publication possible.

Wyndham Lewis: An Essay—the original title for the piece—was to have been the fourteenth volume in the uniform series of Dolphin critical books, published by Chatto & Windus. The "Dolphins" were mostly brief, often favorably disposed studies of various contemporary novelists and poets. Campbell's *Lewis* was announced as being "in preparation" on the dustjacket flap of Louise Morgan's *Writers at Work* (London: Chatto & Windus, 1931—Dolphin Series, No. 11). *Wyndham Lewis* follows the unwritten premise of the series: it is a self-avowed panegyric, and its publication would have profited both publisher and author since most of Lewis's in-print books were also available from Chatto & Windus at that time. However, a remarkable string of misfortunes combined to ruin the project.

Raucous controversy followed the publication of *The Apes of God* in 1930. Those who were satirized in Lewis's novel were sufficiently powerful and wealthy that their extreme displeasure was translated into howls which resonated in the ears of literary London for many months. Lewis's editor at Chatto & Windus, Charles Prentice, had failed just a year before to come to terms with Lewis about publication of *The Apes of God*, forcing Lewis to undertake production of the massive work under his own imprint: The Arthur Press. This was a bitter disappointment to Prentice, and in effect marked the beginning of the end of their long-standing relationship. Indeed, only two years later Lewis left Chatto & Windus, after a further succession of nightmarish problems and misunderstandings: bad press on Lewis's *Hitler*, Prentice's reluctance to publish *Filibusters in Barbary*, the withdrawal and pulping of *Doom of Youth* (after Alec Waugh threatened to sue both Lewis and Chatto & Windus for libel in 1932), and so forth. Just months after *Doom of Youth* was withdrawn—and *Doom* was the last book Lewis was to publish with Chatto & Windus—*Filibusters in Barbary* was suppressed by his new publishers, Grayson, under the threat of another writ of libel.

Lewis had become what stockbrokers call a "bad risk."

Because of Campbell's close alignment with Lewis, his fortunes fell as Lewis's did. It is probable that since Lewis had left his longtime publishers, Chatto & Windus felt the need to promote Lewis was no longer a pressing matter. Furthermore, the suppression of two books in a row coupled with the hysterical press which haunted Lewis during the early thirties contributed to a slump in sales of his books.

The triumphs of the late twenties, triumphs which included generally favorable critical response to *The Art of Being Ruled, Time and Western Man, The Wild Body, The Childermass, The Lion and the Fox*, were temporarily forgotten in the critical-legal-popular scared-cat hullabaloo. This most likely made Campbell's study still less appealing to its publishers, though they had once been Lewis's staunchest allies.

The dustjacket blurb on *Writers at Work*, viewed from this perspective, attempts to shed a favorable

11

light on what was obviously a deteriorating public situation; but note the undercutting tone of phrases like "baffling talents" and "prominent controversialist" in the ad copy:

> In this essay—an estimation by one modern of another—Mr. Campbell endeavours to assess at their true value the baffling talents, creative and critical, which have made Mr. Lewis the most prominent controversialist of our time and one of its most original writers and artists.

In the brash arena of blurb-writing, adjectives like "baffling" and verbs like "endeavours" are not hard-sell terms: punches were already being pulled.

Besides the simple business angle of dropping the book because of possible poor sales or a general loss of interest in its subject in the editorial offices of the publishers, Campbell's very Lewisian description of Lytton Strachey in the essay probably made Chatto & Windus's shell-shocked libel lawyers quiver:

> Lewis's analysis of Joyce should be compared with his analysis of Strachey's *Elizabeth* (*Doom of Youth*)—this is a Freudian day-dream of an inferior and very different type, in which the author who (as nearly all good Bloomsburies are) is obsessed with the idea of Matriarchy, more-or-less identifies himself (as he did also with Queen Victoria) with the elderly female, especially in her admiration of beautiful young men, as long as they are very, very *young*—but execrates the idea of the ordinary grown-up male.

In the reactionary climate which had by then settled into London salons and gentlemen's clubs—especially near the precincts of Bloomsbury—Campbell's claim that Strachey suffers Freudian daydreams (i.e., has sexual fantasies) about identifying himself with an elderly female (i.e., wishes he were an old Queen/quean/queen) because he could then safely tender his affections to beautiful young men (but very, very young, please), simply begged for a threatening letter from a well-paid Bloomsbury solicitor in the morning mail.

RESPECTFULLY BACKWARD IN COMING TOO RAPIDLY FORWARD

Had Campbell's *Wyndham Lewis* been published in 1931 or 1932, it probably would have contributed much to the understanding of Lewis's books. It might have improved Lewis's career as perceived by an interested but mostly uninformed public (even today it is not uncommon to find oneself defending Lewis in conversation with an incensed neophyte who wrongly insists that *The Jews: Are They Human?* is an antisemitic tract: it helps when one reads the text).

Where Hugh Gordon Porteus's *Discursive Exposition* and John Gawsworth's *Apes, Japes and Hitlerism* maintained scholarly distances and critical trappings while sometimes missing the point, Campbell casts objective appearances to the four winds, but is often more exacting and accurate while discussing Lewis's work than his more sober fellow critics. Rather than adopting a standard, dryly disinterested posture—a practice historically used by critics to seduce the reader by hiding a subtle stance of pro or con behind a *tone* of empirical objectivity—Campbell leads us to a remarkably clear view of a number of Lewis's ideas and concerns. His paragraphs about Lewis's satire and the "sex-war" theories are among the most insightful any of Lewis's critics have written. In the unusual process of observing an intellectual "disciple" explain his reasons for discipleship we learn much about the subject of Campbell's adoration.

Campbell's incisive discussion of *The Art of Being Ruled* and *Doom of Youth* touches upon what may have been Lewis's most prophetic politico-economic notions about the sex-war and rise of the youth-cult. Citing Cato's imperative—divide and conquer—Lewis predicted in the late 1920s that a collusion between big business and government would ultimately result not in equality of the sexes (the prime objective of the sex-wars) but rather in a vast political/economic division between the sexes. This would make the boys as easy to rule as the girls and would therefore benefit both those who govern and those who run Business with a capital B. Campbell tracks this idea through its complex labyrinth better than any of Lewis's other commentators during the period. But Lewis and Campbell could never have guessed at the monsters such political genetics would breed.

The kingpins, the bully-boys and the Brown-shirts who expropriated the apparatus of government benefited from this equation even more than Lewis dreaded. The original equation is simple: when people are set to fighting among themselves they are less inclined, or able, to struggle with their rulers . . . a principle about the art of being a ruler which Machiavelli articulated early on. Business benefits from the equation as millions of women, seeking equality, enter the labor force. Wages are thus kept low since the supply of labor exceeds the demands of industry for workers. The collapse of the family unit, another progressive side effect of the sex-wars, helps reconstitute that massive labor force on an ongoing basis, as divorced couples commonly earn two wages rather than one. Pride increasingly eschews alimony blitzes. And naturally, a high percentage of joblessness in the populace provides a happy cushion for the employer: "Don't whine about these wages, you're lucky to have a job at all." A general swelling poverty among the unemployed keeps them essentially powerless. In the yawning gap which opens between those who rule and those who are ruled, rise Lewis's half-breeds: the revolutionary simpletons.

The media (which Lewis never lived to see in their post-1957 high-tech, ranging glory) have served boldly as messengers, and very often as interpreters, for government and big business. And the permutations of Lewis's sex-and-youth wars have been seen in strange places that Lewis never guessed at but would find both comical and terrifying. The *new* apes of god, not having inherited fortunes from old landed families with which to purchase paint, canvas and ateliers in Chelsea, Montparnasse, SoHo, Tribeca, are now given yearly grants by—governmental agencies. Lewis had not predicted the rise of the National Endowment for the Arts in America but it probably would not have surprised him. The more writers, painters, musicians, dancers, artists of mediocre talent are given funding—either from paternal sugar-daddies, as in *The Apes of God,* or from corporate-governmental sugar-daddies—to publish and distribute and show their work, the harder it becomes for the true artist to be heard above the ensuing din (cf. Nathaniel Tarn's letter to Eliot Weinberger, *Montemora* 5). The Republican administration in America, Lewis would suggest, erred by cutting back federal funding to the arts.

APOLOGIA PRO VITA SUA

On occasion Campbell's boundless enthusiasm sets him eagerly rushing after an impossible claim. His suggestion that Wyndham Lewis was somehow responsible for killing—"of a broken heart"—the periodical *transition* with the publication of *The Diabolical Principle and the Dithyrambic Spectator* seems farfetched now even to the most fervent Lewisite. But for the most part, Campbell-the-apologist steers a gratifyingly wide course around the temptation to make false claims for his master. Indeed, his proposal that Lewis slew the Goliath-like *transition* is an excess which is allowable in the tradition of the apologia. We may have a difficult time believing Emerson, for instance, when he tells us the trout in Walden Pond willingly swam to shore whenever Thoreau walked by, so that he might more easily make scientific examinations of them. But such passionate indulgence is reasonable within the context: it is an overstatement purposely geared to startle, giving the reader some sense of the "magnificence" or "greatness" or "larger-than-life" quality of the subject.

This method of public posturing Lewis used even on himself at times, from the earliest days when he stole into Ford Madox Hueffer's bathroom with a black cape and sombrero guaranteeing anonymity as he delivered the manuscript of a new short story, to the days of The Enemy persona. Lewis also employed a similar sleight-of-hand in the narratives of his fictions and in his polemics. Overstating one's case is the surest way of making one's case understood at all. And Campbell avoids raptures for the most part.

That Lewis was grateful for Campbell's friendship and his willingness to jump into the post-1930 *Apes of God* fray is evident from his letters to Campbell. When Augustus John warned Lewis about the dangers of Campbell's too uncritical praise—"I think Roy Campbell's flurry rather unnecessary. . . . just imagine our cumbersome and overcharged poet in the BULL RING! (at Nimes) farting a volley of epithets as he vaults to safety. Quelle blague!"—Lewis is uncharacteristically defensive and supportive of his friend:

> Campbell is a very fine fellow *and* a great bullfighter. He was quite right to make a fuss. What happened [when Campbell's review of *The Apes of God* was rejected] in the offices of the *New Statesman* happened (no doubt) in at least half-a-dozen other editorial offices. . . . Something had to be done about it and it was a good thing that I had a pugnacious matador (a credit to the Camargue) to take up the banderillo for me! Vive le Roy![1]

Lewis himself verges into the apologist's tone here when he makes claims about Campbell's deftness as a matador.

Indeed, Campbell is one of the few writers/artists with whom Lewis maintained an unbroken, supportive friendship throughout his life (they both died in 1957, within a month of one another). Lewis's affection for Campbell is best shown in a remarkable passage from a letter written to him in 1932, in which Lewis explains his intentions in having modeled the ill-fated character, Rob McPhail, after Campbell in his novel *Snooty Baronet:*

> Lastly, always remember this. At a point in my career when many people were combining to

defeat me (namely upon the publication of the *Apes of God*) you came forward and with the most disinterested nobleness placed yourself at my side, and defended my book in public in a manner that I believe no other work has ever been defended. And you can accept it as the most hundred per cent true statement that I would consider myself as the last of the ruffians, and the most ungrateful, if I ever by act or word did anything to harm or offend you. (*LWL*, 206)

Their relationship was obviously stimulating, and invigorated both. Lewis used Campbell as his model for the character "Zulu" Blades in *The Apes of God* (one of a *very* small number of sympathetic characters in the novel). Campbell, for his part, made numerous favorable references to Lewis in his autobiography, *Light on a Dark Horse*. Campbell's *Wyndham Lewis*, though, is perhaps the most significant document of this master-disciple relationship.

THE PROOF

The proof copy from which the following text is set has several corrections in Lewis's hand, and Lewis has written the author's name on the first page. It is possible that this copy was Lewis's reference proof. Throughout, British idioms, punctuations and spellings have been maintained. I have made only a few corrections of obvious typos and misspelled words; otherwise the text is printed without emendation.

1. W. K. Rose, ed., *The Letters of Wyndham Lewis* (Norfolk, Conn.: New Directions, 1963), p. 194. (Hereinafter cited as *LWL*.)

ROY CAMPBELL

WYNDHAM LEWIS

I

Individual genius is never merely original. It does not reject the past on principle or out of prejudice; it does not discard tradition; but consults what is eternally actual in itself. So Wyndham Lewis unites himself with classic tradition. The artist in him is balanced by the critic, and the philosopher is reinforced by the individual. He is an individual living in a literary republic of interdependent 'originals,' in an age when the superficial effects of novelty are encouraged to the prejudice of individuality. As any of our leading reviews of art or literature will show, nearly all contemporary mental activity is a sort of team-work, and consists in mutual exhortation 'towards the new this' and 'towards the new that.' More and more it tends to become a painfully self-conscious *folk-lore* in the evolution of which the individual is entirely subservient to the mass, and the present to a theoretical future. It is haunted with the idea of a 'goal'; and it has the playground of liberal 'reform' and communal progress for its entire Universe, a universe of only one dimension in which spatial, transversal, or static values do not exist; and in which there is no line of intellectual vision or movement save along the single meridian of time. It is because Lewis's vision can cut at right angles across this universally-accepted line, along which all contemporary literary, social, and artistic activity moves, that we are enabled in his work to get an objective view of modern thought and society.

If none of our other thinkers have been able to present us with such a view, it is because they have automatically accepted the main tendencies of modern thought, and cannot regard it from the outside, but only longitudinally in the direction in which they 'progress.'

As Lewis demonstrates in *The Art of Being Ruled*, the vulgarisation of Science as a popular religion has more or less stereotyped a revolutionary state of mind. Science, as knowledge, discovery, intellectual activity, can only be the privilege of a few; but in its politicised form as dogma, it rules the masses and corrupts, when it does not threaten, those more privileged people who, under normal conditions, would be independent of it. A numerous clergy of middle-men and interpreters have commercialised the emotional and dramatic aspects of scientific invention, as 'Progress,' and invested it with all the ritualistic awe and mystery which human nature requires of its priests. Beyond the everyday rigmarole and routine of change, the conception of Progressive Man (as phantasmal a figure as any in ancient mythology) is made to parade up and down as its mystical justification and goal. This abstraction, though lacking the convincing lineaments of a thoroughgoing god, devil, or umtagati, such as would have been required to impress a more practical and less theoretical age, is easily imposed upon a generation which has completely lost sight of the obvious in the theoretical; and which has accepted change as an end in itself, and as its native condition, not to be questioned or even regarded from an external point of view. The dramatisation of evolution by its great dogmatists such as Bergson, Shaw, and Nietzsche has succeeded in inducing a universal state of mind in which all values are immolated on the altar of the supreme deity, Time. To the general mind, therefore, no value exists so much in what it actually *is*, as in what it is theoretically *about to be*: and even what-it-is-about-to-be is again subservient to what-it-is-in-its-turn-about-to-be. Yet none of these thinkers seem to have stopped to ask themselves why God-in-the-Future should be any more real than God-in-the-Present: or why what-is should be subservient to what-it-is-theoretically-about-to-be—*i.e.* what-is-not. Yet this great What-is-not is the god of the Bergsonian universe and of the popular imagination. In speaking of the obvious material world most of our philosophers lower their voices as if reluctantly coerced into discussing some objectionable and indecent fact. Though it might easily be worked out that in nature there is quite as strong a tendency to stabilise forms and types as to change them or evolve new ones; this aspect of nature cannot be exploited from the dramatic-emotional point of view and it has been neglected, while the contrary aspect has been violently exaggerated. A state of mind has therefore been artificially induced which, when it cannot misinterpret, will do its best to obliterate any intellectual work which is evolved independently of its impositions. The result is that a great deal of modern philosophical and scientific activity which should be purely intellectual has been vitiated by emotional and dramatic standards; whereas art and literature have been vitiated by scientific standards. The emotional standards imposed upon the scientific theorist (as may be seen in Whitehead, Alexander, Smuts, and others) lead them to the back doors of romantic pantheistic poetry, and they end up at Meredith or the vaguer swirling 'cosmic' passages that Shelley wrote when he was tired. In the same way our literature, as may be seen in Shaw, Wells, Huxley, and others, ends up at the back doors of amateur economics, bacteriology, sanitation and psycho-analysis. Science and Literature tend more and more to become one and the same thing; vitiating one another and culminating both in scientific and literary philistinism. There are several shining exceptions: but the growing tendency of modern art and science is to steal from one another those qualities which muddle them most, and to resolve themselves into one chaotic dead-level. It amounts to a suicide of the intellect, a negation on the one side of scientific values and on the other of artistic values. It confuses the two opposite poles of human thought. For scientific and artistic values, even by studiously muddling them, cannot be made to tally. Science is concerned with classification, generalisation, and with the *sameness* between things. Art is solely concerned with particularising, with resolving things into their separate identities, and with the *differences* between things. These two principles can only balance one another when they act in their natural places in *opposite* scales of the balance.

Accepted, then, as an article of faith, this ideal perfected 'Man in the Street,' the new Messiah of contemporary religion whose parthenogenesis is to be brought about by a continuous automatic rejection of present values for new, has completely dominated all literary, scientific, and social activity for the last fifty years. In all these activities the revolutionary habit has been hypnotically imposed on every performer both by his public and by himself as the sole *raison d'être* upon which he can claim to be an artist, thinker, or philosopher. No matter who he is, he is dunned for an explanation as to how his work will change, alter, benefit, or damage society—even if he is an independent artist of no political or social importance there is always the progressive impresario near at hand to discover some 'revolutionary' import in his work: by which the scientist or artist will usually profit if he has any commercial *nous*, or sense of self-preservation, and do his best to cultivate it. Even in the field of psycho-pathological research intended primarily to cure patients, the impresario has exploited and dogmatised pathological discoveries until his propaganda has resulted (at least in literary and aesthetic circles) in setting up a more oppressive and narrow-minded form of morality than that which it claims to have supplanted, though in many ways it is the logical conclusion and supreme expression of Victorianism—with which it is still deeply involved and mentally obsessed. Victorian prudery certainly had a great deal to do with the sexual antagonism that culminated in the sex-war, and it remains unchanged in those more 'refined' aesthetic circles which dictate most contemporary fashions, and in which the impact of such dogmas (easily assimilated and puritanised) has in no way changed that anglican-liberal consciousness which since the death of Byron has dominated British thought. It is a strange philistinism compounded of humanitarian-altruism, protestantism, and a sort of arts-and-craftsy, amateur attitude towards life and art. As a vegetarian gets far more pleasure out of reading up in text-books about various pepsins, proteins, and vitamins than out of eating them, and more satisfaction out of eschewing meat than out of swallowing lentils, so in its attitude to life, art, and sex, this liberal-protestant consciousness lives more fully in what it lacks, eschews, or denies than in what it possesses or enjoys. This is well expressed, or confessed, by Mr. Strachey in a passage which I cannot quote exactly; but he says that though some may find the supreme pleasure in creating great works of art and things of beauty, others (meaning himself) look in another direction and find it 'in detachment.' Though Mr. Strachey's is often the breathless 'detachment' of a servant girl at a keyhole, yet he has here expressed an aspiration, an ambition—'to be detached.' This is where that nineteenth-century liberal-protestant consciousness must inevitably land when it gets tired. Unfortunately in the less 'refined' spheres of literature and science it is far from tired. Scientists of the Haldane type have dogmatised Science for Science's sake, and issue from the laboratory every now and then to show how their discoveries will change or alter humanity, whether for better or for worse it does not matter, as long as we can ultimately produce people from test-tubes, etc. Scientists of this type, whether primarily actuated by the protestant consciousness or not, have the same hatred of the normal, of the natural, and, above all, of the organically physical. Less cynical, perhaps, than the 'refined' Stracheys, yet their attitude is in many ways similar; for to wish at all costs to *change* one's existence and organic functions implies as great and unnatural an alienation from them, and as great a bias against them, as is implied (paradoxically) in Mr. Strachey's 'detachment.' Unless this bias underlay most contemporary thought, its activity would be directed to establishing and perfecting rather than to continually changing and innovating.

Recent mental activity has been therefore rather nomadic than civil—a processional wandering of tribes who (for far vaguer promises than the Canaan of their prototypes) have been wandering mentally for no other motive than a communal wanderlust which forbids them to camp for two nights on the same site—let alone to undertake the foundation of a habitable city. The holy scriptures of modern dogma promise them a New Jerusalem ready-made on the sole condition that they must go on revolving till they find it, encouraged of course by the daily thunders from the Sinai of the B.B.C. and the T.S.F.

There is not one among our great popular priests who does not hold the main idea that human life must necessarily fulfil itself as a communal transition (as rapid as possible) from one condition to another: and not as it consummates itself in each individual separately. Yet this main conception, upon which all modern Utopianists and prophets agree, is absent from, or at the most only plays an insignificant part in, the thought of all other civilisations past or present. The only result of its acceptance as gospel has been to precipitate the whole of modern life into a breathless transitional race with time as aimless as it is frantic.

'Revolution'-as-a-habit entirely defeats the ends of *revolution* as a substitution of new, stable values for old and useless ones; and, while assailing many values (which it cannot substitute with better ones) because they are solid and resist its flux, yet it is apt to drag along with it, because they yield and drift without resistance, many useless, outworn values, without questioning them. If we accept the definition of revolution as the introduction of new and reliable values for outworn values, then Lewis, in his revolt against automatic 'revolution-as-habit,' may be the most thorough revolutionary living. In our age the general 'revolutionary' consciousness is, above all other things, hostile to thought at the expense of which it exalts the feelings, the unconscious, and the emotions. The very word 'intellectual' is used as an insult in the polite literary-artistic salons: and it is dreaded by all save a few who have committed the crime of thinking outside the hypnotic range of fashionable revolutionary routine. The act of thinking, itself, is like the explosion of a bomb to the conventional 'revolutionary simpleton'—as may be seen from recent attempts by various editors to smother, boycott, and misinterpret Lewis's work.

To think at all, unless one uses one's thought to subvert the authority of the intellect, as Lawrence did, is a sin against contemporary morality. To think as Lewis does is to cause a panic in the camp of the stereotyped revolutionaries-by-habit. As Lewis's work becomes more widely known it exerts a growing influence in crippling the activities of the collective revolutionary-simpleton, and in laying the foundations of a new *order* of thought.

Whatever is revolutionary in Lewis is concerned only with essential values. He is the first of the moderns to discard the obligatory make-up, uniform, and manner in which most contemporary prophets conventionally parade their lack of individuality. He emerges as the ruthless enemy of these superficialities and the redoubtable antagonist of revolution as habit, as sentiment, and as melodrama: spreading terror among those swarming dilettantes of whom this sort of revolution is the favourite parlour game. It has become far too easy to buy a cheap 'revolutionary' uniform ready-made: and the swarm of flunkeys who parade in this uniform both retard and obscure the real issue.

Nowadays it suffices for anybody to have a bee in his bonnet, to see in Lewis the marauder of his own particular hive, and to leave it at that. But it has proved impossible to ignore him. The once redoubtable sigh of weariness and the patronising shrug, with which the dilettantes of Bloomsbury and Chelsea were able to dispose of anything that excelled their easy-going standards, or momentarily disconcerted their comfort, have now given place to less graceful movements. The weary sigh has devloped into a form of asthma: and the gentle shrug into a perpetual St. Vitus shimmy of the shoulders. For Lewis is magnificently armed, as every individual artist has to be nowadays if he is to survive (without taking part in them) the intrigues, deals, and boycotts with which the great central Lumber-Syndicate of logrollers govern contemporary literary life.

It is natural that the morality of the collective literary amateur should exalt all those qualities in human nature or art which are within the reach of a majority. One of the strangest effects of modern education has been this influx of leisured and moneyed amateurs into literature and art. It is to be expected that, having paid for their right to paint, read, and criticise, they should exalt such qualities as the naïf, the polite, the skittish, the exotic, or the 'naughty' (which are in everybody's reach) at the expense of intellect, genius, or individuality, which savour of privilege and authority and to which, above all (not having paid for them), their possessors have no civil right. This exaltation of common qualities above the rarer ones is useful, for it is as flattering and ingratiating to their public as it is to the mass of writing and painting amateurs. Since Mr. Strachey, by far the best of them, first patented his cheap, ready-made shot-gun for the hunting down of the 'great,' an epidemic of biographers has broken out. They have armed themselves with the same facile weapon and made war against every figure in history or literature who could possibly be suspected of having been privileged above the average.[1] Even Mr. Strachey has been peppered severely (with his own shotgun) by a disciple who seems to have suspected him of some outstanding quality; all the big game has been 'bagged,' but the arms and ammunition, we observe, will now be used (for want of better sport) on the smaller fry by their own species—since it is not in the nature of the Bloomsbury to make an attack (unless collectively) on any outstanding man who is capable of defending himself while he is alive. I shall go more thoroughly into the question of the literary amateur in dealing with Lewis's *Dithyrambic Spectator*. I have introduced the amateur here in order to focus the position of Lewis in relation to contemporary literary-artistic life: and it is necessary to focus his position if we are to comprehend the true significance of his work as a polemist, which I shall deal with first before going on to his more important creative and philosophical work. For it is primarily as a polemist that Lewis presents himself to the startled imagination of the public: and in Lewis the polemist there is quite enough to dazzle, disconcert, and distress average reviewers; and to keep them busy, without bothering about his other work. It is the fashion in private conversation to dismiss Lewis as 'merely destructive.' Destructive he certainly is—nobody has ever shattered so many popular idols in so short a time. It is possible that Scipio Africanus or Leonidas may have seemed merely destructive to the invading barbarians whose only contact with them was through their destructive powers. As it has the dramatic interest of a prizefight, Lewis's polemical activity attracts more notice than his constructive work. Besides, it is far easier to read; and since his creative work is not only addressed to the intellect but exerts a considerable strain on it, like a fiery racehorse on the rein, it is only likely, for the present, to appeal to the more adventurous minds of a generation which is more addicted to ambling pads than racehorses. It would be too much to expect that the great passages of the *Childermass* should sink at once into the consciousness of a generation whose toughest mental food is the easy pattering journalese of Huxley, Arlen, Strachey, and others of the same class of polite entertainers, who are undistinguishable from one another in style, outlook, ideas, and in their general attitude, which is not that of any individual mind but of a class and a period.

Literature has become so easy through low and pusillanimous standards of criticism that whole families go in for it, aunts, uncles, brothers, and sisters, just as if it were a family business. When a man of genius who has to work alone, besides earning his living, has to climb through this seething mass of family picnics, camping parties, and Cook's-tours-to-Parnassus, it is not surprising if he upsets a few lunch-baskets on his way up: and Lewis himself is represented as being wantonly destructive, with a rage for annihilation. Yet it may be questioned whether any of his victims have been anything but violently destructive in intention: and whether he has attacked any but fanatical destroyers. When Middleton Murry, in the rôle of a benevolent Thersites, or malevolent Santa Claus, with the greatest human sympathy, attacked his dead friend D. H. Lawrence, he earned universal praise for it. But when Lewis far more effectively attacked the destructive and barbarian side of Lawrence, the latter was in the prime of his powers. Lewis's attack in *Paleface* was a Mithraic act of strength and skill in which the powers of light (the intellect itself) completely destroyed the powers of 'darkness' in the person of the most fanatical and powerful, self-avowed enemy of the human 'spirit' and intellect that this age has produced. It was a clean estocade delivered without shedding any crocodile's tears. It was accompanied rather by a brain-cleansing, side-splitting crackle of laughter, and it was that very laughter that made it unpopular. The idea of an open intellectual enemy attacking his enemy openly is not relished: and a man who, like Lewis, can do so with such deadly effect is not to be encouraged in a literary society so pusillanimous that it even requires that insults should be delivered in the form of compliments. In his attack on Lawrence Lewis was scrupulously fair, and he did not stray an inch outside that part of Lawrence's work in which he attacks and derides the consciousness of the European white, and exalts the blind tom-tom beating instincts of the savage. Yet Lewis is decried for this attack as being wantonly ferocious, though he thereby vindicated the white intelligence: while those more frenzied dervishes whose activity has been chiefly to undermine and destroy for destruction's sake, and who in many cases have perverted magnificient gifts to that end, are regarded as martyrs to Lewis's rage.

Let us consider those other writers who have received destructive treatment at his hands—Spengler, for instance. Is not his theory of chronological fatalism more or less calculated to hypnotise our classical culture into a state of disintegration?

The French Surrealistes of whom he makes hay in *The Diabolical Principle* are avowedly destructive in their intentions at any rate. As for our English Utopianists—though they are avowedly philanthropists—they can found nothing that does not imply a universal negation, ban, or denial of the human body, of human nature, and even of life itself. The Earthly Paradise of Shaw seems in every way to have been dictated by the fear of pain, discomfort, and death, and a horror of human nature rather than out of any love of life or humanity. In *Back to Methuselah* there seems to be nothing enjoyable in life or sex that Shaw would not sacrifice in order to obtain a vegetable immunity from emotional strain and physical discomfort; and a long dispensation from the agony of death. The only signs of human nature which appear in Shaw's paradise of centenarians are immediately punished with death or humiliation. Only negative qualities, such as fear, receive any respect from the dehumanised puppets of the Shavian millennium. 'Thou shalt not' is writen over every gate of the Shavian Heaven.

Bertrand Russell, too, can only found his happiness on arbitrary bans and negations of the most deeply-rooted human instincts.

Nothing strikes one more in all this literature of protestant-liberal reform than the amount of destruction and mutilation it involves: and the dreary howling puritanism in which it invests itself. If Lewis as polemist is to be disposed of as merely destructive for attacking such writers, let his accusers examine the fanatical amount of destruction, mutilation, and castration implied in the Utopias of our great puritan prophets who are commonly regarded as creative in their outlook. I hope to show in the course of these notes that Lewis is perhaps the only important English writer whose work is in any way compatible with a creative outlook.

The acceptance of life-as-progress is as closely implicated in the 'literature of disillusion' as in that of the Utopianists. The disillusionment depends upon one's having believed that life is in some way honour-bound to progress nicely and pleasantly and finding that it does not do so. This seems to be the main preoccupation of those writers who have best expressed the predicament of the post-war generation. Lewis begins where they have left off.

It is impossible to imagine that Lewis ever regarded existence from the point of view of an alien or a foreigner. While most writers are in the position of interned aliens dying of homesickness for the customs of some theoretical fatherland, the sigh, the groan, and the comment-from-behind-the-barbed-wire are entirely absent from Lewis's work. His radii of vision shoot out from a central core of reality, whereas nearly all his contemporaries focus the core from the circumference and comment upon that core as something external to themselves, something from which both their inclinations and their centrifugal natures keep them far off. Even those more joyously bouncing poets who exult in being 'one with nature' and tell us that 'life' is good, and real, and earnest, are in the same position—their comments come from outside. If not to interned aliens, they can be compared to enraptured tourists in a foreign country who have to pinch themselves, when confronted with reality, to see if they are really awake or dreaming. 'Now we are really in Spain! So the Alhambra is after all real! How marvellous!' Snap goes the mental kodak, a momentary emotional contact is established—'So this is really Nature and I am here—*in* Nature, and a part of life itself. How marvellous!' The violence of the jerk with which they realise this argues how alien they are to reality. Whitman never got over the fact that he really was actually alive. He insists on the fact so violently, with such emphasis, and so repeatedly, that one wonders from what peculiar exterior angle he regarded his relationship to the visible, sensible world. The streak of philistinism that runs through Wordsworth is entirely traceable to the same external attitude. All his poetry is an attempt to establish a contact between the natural, visible world and the mental fatherland which he describes in his 'Ode on the Intimations': it was that fatherland where he really dwelt. All education for a hundred years or so has been romantic. Its aim has been to provide us all with comfortable nightcaps from which, when we peep out into the world, we see its difference from our own mental domestic-interior, and are only too delighted or surprised to find any point of similarity. The spectacle of a Russell with the air of an infatuated entomologist chasing after happiness as after some rare, unclassified butterfly could not have been imagined before the nineteenth-century romantic era. Our literature tends more and more to treat the abstract, the infinite, and the undefinable with the same clumsy material familiarity as a cook her pots and pans: while towards common, visible material or organic objects its attitude becomes more and more 'mystical' and emotional. This tendency can be traced throughout nineteenth-century literature, and it culminates in contemporary literature.

Between the century we are in the habit of calling the artificial century and our own, the obvious world may be said to have ceased to exist as far as English literature is concerned. This visible world at least served more fortunate generations as a sort of mirror by which one could regulate one's reflections to proportion, elegance, and style. Most modern literature is merely an attempt to veil this mirror of reality: but it remains uneasily conscious of its existence which obtrudes itself from time to time with the callous indifference of a fact.

Lewis has explained that his main source of experience is his eye. In this he is in open revolt against the current fashion of mediumistic and ventriloqual literature. Every one of Lewis's novels is concerned almost entirely in the visual image. The visual image is the language of all great poetry. The classical muse is the muse of vision: the eye is the most intellectual of all the organs of perception and the most closely implicated with the imagination. Even blind poets like Homer and Milton work almost exclusively in the visual image. The nature and essence of a person or thing is, to Lewis and to every true artist, more implicit in its complete form than in any hidden ganglion, or gland, or combination of elements. Any attempt to analyse things into their component atoms or elements simply destroys, in its very process, their essence and nature. Theoretically, the man who cut open his nugget-laying goose was quite right, but artistically his operation was a failure. While nearly all other writers arbitrarily introduce themselves into their characters (like Lawrence who ventriloquises in turn from the womb of a woman, the stomach of an Indian, or the bowels of a horse) Lewis isolates his characters into vivid, separate identities and *forms*. While modern literature gropes inward towards the unconscious, Lewis's thought radiates outwards into the visible and the conscious. While Lawrence at his best succeeds in setting up in his readers a mild sympathetic erethism, a muscular rhythm, or a crepuscular kind of fear or longing, Lewis on the other hand gives one a shock of terrific voltage which immediately translates itself into an orgasm of laughter or into a sudden dazzling realisation of an idea. In Lewis's work we leave the fluid world of semi-organic dreams and enter a world of vivid ideas, hard contours, and momentous impacts.

If Lewis had lived in a heroic age he might very likely have been an epic poet: but in a non-heroic age his vision has operated none the less heroically on its environment, creating out of our modern life the unforgettable effigies by which future generations shall recognise our time, and galvanising those effigies with violent red laughter. Lewis's characters are Titans of extravagant mirth, like the grinning giants of the carnival, but they are so terribly vital and charged with such energy that they carry us outside the ordinary limits of comedy and tragedy, into the world of epic realities that is peopled by such figures as Panurge, Don Quixote, Sganarelle, Tartuffe, Doctor Johnson, Falstaff, and Volpone, as well as by the thundering kings of great Tragedy. It is a world where the figures transcend those of ordinary natural existence in *reality* and in vitality: where they become eternal symbols and live on a higher plane than that of human life—in a world of *ideas*, only just below the gods and prophets of religion. Panurge and Quixote and Doctor Johnson (as seen by Boswell) are far more than men, they are actual Dæmons: and Lewis has conjured up dæmons of the same kind in his satirical work. They inhabit a world of ideas; a world that is flooded with brilliant intellectual daylight; a world in which the *mind* becomes a terrific gymnastic force, winged with supernatural laughter and electrified with vivid ideas, and resumes its proper empire as the *sun* of the visible world.

II

In *Tarr* (1918), the earliest and least satirical of Lewis's novels, he presents us with a picture of life in Paris immediately before the War. The central figure, Tarr, is an artist at grips with his environment, and through this figure Lewis seems to make a declaration of his creed as an artist. The 'Vie de bohème' is here seen in all its shabby futility—not perhaps in such an advanced state of decomposition as in the post-war Montparnasse, but on the way to it. The intrusion of the disguised amateur and tradesman into the sphere of creative Art had by that time begun on a grand scale: and there is in *Tarr* a glorious specimen of this type of gregarious artistic flunkey, Hobson. In a conversation with this figure Tarr analyses the whole amateur movement in art. The main theme of the book is concerned with Tarr's efforts to find a foothold in the shifting sands of this disintegrating society. His love affair with Bertha is told with consummate skill: the gradual unwinding of the hero's perplexities into a sane, sincere, and satisfactory solution of the warring claims of his personal pride, his devotion to his art, and his normally sexed human nature, is worked out with wisdom and humour.

As in Dostoevsky, the main characters of *Tarr* move with a kind of accelerating velocity to their respective destinies. The unforgettable and sinister figure of Kreisler (a titanic conception in itself) reacting to circumstances in a perfect logical coherence with the lineaments of his character, is hurled (by a force as actual as the force of gravity itself) through a series of terrific situations of farce and horror, to find degradation and death. This character alone would have sufficed to make *Tarr* an outstanding novel in any age. But *Tarr* is more than 'fiction,' it is a prophetic and inspired book, and belongs to that category in literature which for want of a better word one might call apocalyptic: for in it Lewis seems to have consciously realised himself as a new intellectual force in the world, and his whole system of thought is embryonically present in this first novel. Tarr seems, like the later Lewis, to centre his chief strength in the impregnable citadel of laughter: and if his philosophy is not intended for Everyman, it is certainly a great gift to his future leaders and rulers. *Tarr* not only foresaw the disruption of our society but answers it with a sane, constructive, and individual philosophy.

Tarr was followed shortly after by *The Caliph's Design*—an analysis of fashions in art and literature, with special regard to the modern movement. Though a pamphlet in form and size, it is of permanent constructive value, and contains a sample of Lewis's polemical powers at their best: for it ends with a splendid attack on the 'philandering flapper-sensibility which transpires in every sentence of our indigenous English aesthetes when they write anything affecting to be critical of French art.' *The Caliph's Design* was a blow struck in defence of a serious attitude to painting, at a time when the more bouncingly irresponsible interpreters and popularisers of modern art were waltzing through London with the importance of prophets. Lewis's psychological insight into the workings of the mass mind is strikingly conspicuous in his analysis of the operation of fashion on art and literature: and though it is here confined mostly to these two subjects, it is evident that his mind is capable of applying itself to a far wider field of activity: for already in *The Caliph's Design* he has begun to enquire into the workings of those great social forces and principles which form the subject of *The Art of Being Ruled.*

The Art of Being Ruled is a colossal work which focuses from an entirely new point of view the whole modern social world in a state of transition, and the whole history of the modern social revolution from the time of Rousseau. The first part of it, as we have seen, deals with the vulgarisation of science and the dangerous obsession of the human consciousness with mechanical betterment as centred in the religious abstraction of the Progressive Man. In the second part Lewis compares the two great conflicting political principles in Europe—that of liberal democracy on the one hand and that of authority (as evinced in leninism and fascism) on the other hand. The european system is no longer ascendant in the world-wide accommodation of ideas which is now going forward: and the liberal-democratic european ideal is doomed, for in its inherent tendency towards petty franchises and nationalisms and in its superficial idea of 'freedom,' it is anarchistically hostile to the organisation of the white race as a whole, and is one of the chief causes of the decline of european power.

Lewis contrasts the indirectness of liberal-democratic rule (giving the public 'what it wants') with the directness of Soviet and Fascist rule (*i.e.* the government of the masses by a dictatorship of the most vigorous and intelligent). If anything so definite as a public *will* exists, it could be resolved into a few simple appetites. But a luxurious hypothetical surplus of wants is being forced on to it.

'As a result of the dogma of *What the Public Wants* and the technical experiences of the publicist, a very cynical idea of what the Public *is*, is widely held to-day. And indeed the contemporary public, corrupted and degraded into a semi-imbecility by the operation of this terrible canon of press and publicity technique, by now confirms its pessimism. It has learned to live *down* to its detractor. It is inevitable that men who had escaped or resisted the general dementia should, surveying the fruits of liberal enlightenment and Press control, at last formulate a counter-doctrine. "Why turn yourself into the eternal servant of an imbecile," they then exclaim, "or condemn yourself to teach the alphabet to an infant class for ever? Why not *rule*—would not that be simpler?" That is the natural reaction of the best contemporary statesmanship to the fruits of What the Public Wants', as we have seen in Russia and Italy where the inevitable chaos resulting from years of mystical and liberal drifting has been so swiftly and triumphantly organised.

Though such prophets as Russell may hope that education can still save the public, yet we witness daily a constant deterioration in the quality of what the public gets as 'education.' The very principle of liberal democracy carries in itself the seeds of a deterioration which must in the end be as fatal to itself as to the public which it is ruining. If the public only knew *at what a cost to itself* it is fed on '*What the Public Wants*,' it would clamour perhaps for a more efficient rule than its own self-flattery. Lewis clearly shows that the illusion of personal 'freedom' and 'independence' exists no more in the liberal-democratic state, such as England, than it does under the perfectly open dictatorial rule of leninism or fascism. The only difference is in the efficiency and style of the rule. The dictatorial rule of a vigorous and intelligent minority is the only possible ultimate answer to the ever-growing chaos consequent upon liberal democratic reform, which is perhaps in Britain and America the true self-expression of the Anglo-Saxon race now for the first time breaking through the traditional culture of its aristocracy of French or celtic overlords.

Lewis goes very deeply into the psychology of the small man and the plain man: and he deals very brilliantly with the vulgarisation by Nietzsche, Sorel, and others of disgust and hatred into a weapon for the use of the small man against the signs of authority and privilege. The 'sex-war' and the wholesale feminisation of the european male are also fruits of the liberal-democratic principle, and Lewis goes into this aspect of the social revolution very thoroughly. He deals with the war against the intellect on the part of politicised artists: and sees in most fashionable literary movements (as exemplified by Stein, the later Joyce, and others) an organised attack on the intellect. The sex-war itself is the outcome of this hostility to the intellect—a hostility which naturally puts the female on an equal, if not on a superior plane to the male, and forces the male to effeminise hmself or to remain as childish as possible.

Lewis deals here also with the whole history of the social revolution and compares the ideas of all the great social reformers, from Rousseau down to Shaw and Russell. He is especially brilliant where he compares the Federalised peasant socialism of Proudhon with the Social Contract of Rousseau.

It is impossible in the course of so brief an essay to do more than touch on a few of the salient points of such works as *The Art of Being Ruled*. It is a book that makes the whole state of the modern world clear. It breaks through a thousand fallacies that we accept out of mere force of habit: and it reveals to us the whole machinery of modern society, not as we are taught to regard it, in pieces, but in its whole operation, relating all its parts to one another, and showing every movement in its entire scope and operation. It is the greatest intellectual gift which has been given to our generation: it clears a space in the ruins of our society where a growing number of independent spirits may share in a few of the advantages of the future society that this book prognosticates.

All Lewis's other philosophical works are intricately interwoven with the central idea of *The Art of Being Ruled*, and they ramify this idea triumphantly into every sphere of art, science, literature, and philosophy. In modern thought as in modern politics, there is absolutely no *Opposition*. Modern thought in England, till Lewis arrived, was simply the elaboration of one super-structure on top of another super-structure, a whole-hearted, fanatical tendency to improve the top-heavy by making it even more top-heavy. And like modern politics the whole structure is rotten and crazy from about a quarter of the way up. Lewis is the *Opposition*, and the only one we have. Russell's pessimism is only an emotional opposition. Lewis's destructive activity is an intellectual and practical opposition to a principle which is in itself so top-heavy that it would be bound to come down with a far bigger and more fatal crash, if he did not take it down scientifically. He is engaged in pulling down a whole row of condemned sky-scrapers whose very architects themselves are for the most part in a panic at the sight of their own crazy constructions. Where Lewis pulls any one of them down he leaves solid foundations for habitable structures. He has opposed wholesale collective hysteria and dementia in the only possible way in which it can be opposed, namely by individual sanity and wisdom.

With *The Art of Being Ruled* should be read *Doom of Youth*, as it is a continuation of Lewis's brilliant analysis of the class and sex-wars begun in the former. In the liberal-democratic state, it is 'big business' that rules the state. Instead of centralising itself in the state it rules the masses impersonally and indirectly through the Press, which for all the 'freedom' and 'independence' of the individual democratic can turn him into cannon-fodder in two seconds. The English people have been fed with 'humour' as a sort of dope. Spoken to in the Drage manner, and in a hearty uncle-ish way, the Englishman or the American can be precipitated by the press into any state of mind: and he is more at the mercy of that kind of persuasion than any Russian or Italian is at the hands of dictatorial coercion: he will react with a blind, unreflecting stupidity to any suggestion, and can be propelled at will into any attitude no matter how unreasonable. Big business, of course, with the gradual unification of trusts and cartels, becomes more and more like a dictatorial government, as in the bolshevik state—but not being identified with the life of the state, it operates independently of the welfare of the state, and quite irresponsibly, though it adopts the benevolent manner and mask of an uncle or a Mr. Drage.

The great factor that had to be destroyed in the total subjection of the masses was the unity of the family, a comparatively aristocratic institution, which is both economically and socially opposed to the principle of big business. The economic possibilities of a Sex War are obvious. It cheapens labour and it breaks up the family unit. It is enough to make persons conscious of their *category* whether it be sex, nationality, generation, size (tall or short), colour (dark or fair), or the shape of his nose (snub or aquiline), and by a brief press campaign one can set the whole country at war one half with another. The more the masses are divided amongst themselves the easier they are to rule. Clive and Dupleix easily ruled over India by setting the nabobs against one another. 'Divide et Impera,' said Cato—encourage your slaves to quarrel, foster hatred amongst them, and then they will not conspire against their master. The Sex War and the Age War have been fostered on the same lines, and the intelligentsia have been the first to fall into this trap. The youth racket is a marvel of the politicisation of a thing which has in itself no more political significance than a boiled egg. Yet people are passionately worked up about it. 'Youth' is cheered on as it bashes into middle age: controversies rage in the papers—all of whom have their professional 'youths' (Winn, Waugh, Beverley Nichols, Raymond Mortimer), they are trained to make generalisations comparing the younger generation with the older, and more-or-less anthropomorphically personifying the two generations as if they were each a *type* (the one a pleasant, and the other an unpleasant type). Some of these 'youths' are men of forty or fifty years old. Others are recruited almost as soon as they leave the nursery.

If people can be made to feel hostile about the number of years they have lived, there is nothing so unreasonable that they cannot be made to quarrel about. As soon as the youth racket has been exploited there will be a snub-versus-aquiline racket, or a blond-versus-dark racket. Both the Sex War and the Age War are very closely related: and big business, however unconsciously or impersonally it works, has not been slow to profit through them. The Sex War lowered the cost of and doubled the supply of labour. The youth racket has hypnotically induced a feeling of inferiority on people of middle age; they are not encouraged in these huge public controversies except as *targets*: only a few of the stupider generalisations of angry old colonels are ever printed (from the other side) so as to look silly: the effect of this politicisation of Youth against Age is to humble the adult male or female: they can be made through this feeling of inferiority to accept wage reductions and are put still more under the *power* of that huge, smiling, Drage-like, impersonal, occult Ruling Power; while the youth *employed* in the racket are equally in its power, and have more or less pledged their own middle-age to the same humiliation.

Doom of Youth and *The Art of Being Ruled* reveal a hundred such unreasonable and stupid expenses of energy as the Youth Racket. It is through expending its energy so uselessly to itself that 'youth' is *ruled* by 'big business' and helps it with that energy to grind down and rule the other half of the community. Nothing more was necessary than the arbitrary division of the community into young or old. The energy of one half of the community is then used to paralyse the other half. Lewis, in revealing the workings of these sex-wars, class-wars, and age-wars, gives us a new technique of living and saves one from allowing oneself to be manipulated as a pawn in these manoeuvres; or of having one's energy quite unconsciously harnessed to work some unreasonable and ridiculous machine against our own interests and those of humanity.

A notable feature of all these sex and youth wars, and of the whole mental and social revolution, is that they all aim at the adult male or 'head-of-the-family,' and they are organised with most destructive force against the sign and cause of his authority—the intellect, for that is the only quality which distinguishes the adult male from the others of his species.

In this attack on the intellect even the finest contemporary intellects have been politicised. Nearly all modern writers are out to humiliate the conscious white 'self' in favour of the savage, the woman, the child, or even the animal (as in *St. Mawr* and the *Roan Stallion*). It is a curious fact that the intellect of the white man, perhaps the finest and most victorious force that the world has seen, has hypnotised itself into a feeling of 'inferiority'— an inferiority which, moreover, does not exist at all apart from the hypnotically induced 'feeling.' Modern philosophy, exalting the intuitive animal instincts above the mind, and deifying Time, as in Bergson and Spengler, has *educated* the contemporary white into a state of mind which is suicidal. We observe in the modern consciousness a wholesale reversion, a tendency to *return* to the unconscious, to go back to the womb, to childhood, and to get as near to the original matrix as possible. There are few modern writers who would not sooner *be* women, to judge from their work; most modern literature and philosophy is an attempt to identify oneself with the female principle. So the white man has begun to 'look back towards that feminine chaos, from which the masculine principles have differentiated themselves, as more perfect. As the Child is more perfect than, and the conditions of its life are more desirable than those of the Man, so the mind of the Woman is more perfect than, and the lot of Woman—in league with, or immersed in Nature—more to be desired than the lot of the Man. So the contemporary Man has grown to desire to be a woman and has taken obvious steps to affect this transformation (cf. pages on the shamanistic cult, *The Art of Being Ruled*). Then Power or Wealth has been represented as not only evil in itself, but not at all to be desired (cf. the "higher type" of collective man of communism according to René Fülöp-Miller). And so on through all the series of backward-cults from primitivism or naturalism to fairyhood.'

The exotic obsession is one of the main channels of the Great Trek from consciousness; it is more than a mere cult: it has become a sort of religion, and forms, with the feminist, child, and nancy movements, the vanguard of the Crusade against the intellect. In *Paleface* Lewis deals with this attempt at suicide on the part of the white intellect. In this book it seems as if the white intellect itself, as derided by Lawrence, Sherwood Anderson, and others, springs like an armed Minerva to revenge itself on those whites who have tried to betray their intellectual inheritance. The revenge is deadly, and it blows into smithereens both the anti-white propaganda on the part of sentimentally-politicised whites and their superstitious reverence for the savage. The exotic sense flourishes most strongly in a time of 'decadence.' It is a defeatism: and in its result it provides only for a superficial parasitic existence, trying to sample and taste things which we can never make on our own. *Paleface* should be read along with *Hitler* where, in contrasting the Blutsgefühl of the german national socialists with the exotic ramp, of which the former is in some ways a radical corrective, Lewis shows us that the racial solution indicated in Hitlerism is not entirely to be despised (if not necessarily to be swallowed whole) whereas the exotic sense is an entirely despicable and crass form of sentimentality.—'No very active man could experience it—he would be too absorbed with the satisfactions of his own personal activity to wish to transfer his attentions so far from his vital and effective centre—his own creative principle of life. Essentially it is non-creative: it possesses the characteristics of the traditional feminine surrender rather than of the male insurgence and egoism. At its heart, it can be nothing but a pathetic diffusive expansion towards some Otherness, which will, it is felt, satisfy, where the thing-we-know does not. The ego is discredited when such a state of mind exists as causes the individual to fling himself at the feet of one alien Ego after another in flight from his own, in a feverish centrifugalism.'

Of course the exotic sense draws a great deal of its life from the chronological fatalism of Spengler and the Time theories of Bergson. The wholesale exaltation of animals, as we see, in the Press surpasses in the actual passion anything that the Hindus can exhibit in its way of cow-worship. In England the dog is almost the king of the emotional universe, and canine qualities have come to be regarded as social virtues. In papers like the *Observer* reviews of the biographies of puppy-dogs are given precedence over the biographies of statesmen, poets, and artists. This is another side of the Bergsonian exaltation of intuition over the mind and a far more degraded form of the craving for 'otherness.' There is nothing wrong with dogs as animals, nor with negroes as people. It is only when some mystical significance beyond what they are actually able to support is laid upon them by sentimentalists that they both become blatantly ridiculous[2]: and so, to a lesser degree perhaps, does the ordinary petit-bourgeois of Europe as idealised by Kipling and others of the older imperialistic school. But surely, even from the point of view of magic and 'strangeness,' and above all from the barbarian point of view, with his extraordinary valour and physical prowess, the ordinary white philistine with his watch and chain, his looking-glass, and his trousers is a more interesting phenomenon (if one takes an impersonal point of view) than the bourgeois of the Congo or the Zambezi who is only too ready to shed his own tribal paraphernalia for the first pair of European breeches he can get hold of, and who, *luckily for the European*, has an even more pronounced 'exotic sense,' generally speaking, than the most Spenglerised and Bergsonised of our softened white prophets.

The significance both of *Paleface* and of *Hitler* lies in verities which are entirely invulnerable to the abstract sexual or racial sages of writers like Lawrence: verities which were first inimitably and gloriously stated by Cervantes: and which in Lewis's hands, as applied to our age and time, are given a new polish and reveal our modern knights-errant and crusaders in a more laughable light. The very principle of the comic character is the principle of seeking passionately for *unreal*, second-hand experience—as the 'exotic' tries to live on the experience of the savage, as the nancy tries to live on the borrowed experience of the woman or the child: as the average 'suffragette' tries to live on the experience of the male: as the moneyed bohemian philistine tries to live on the experience of the un-moneyed apache, the worker, the underdog; all seeking passionately to attach themselves by imitation, parasitically, to some class, sex, group, or period to which they do not belong, as a result, generally, of defeat and failure to *be successfully* what they are. In the modern world this class of people who seek to live on fictitious or imitative experience of different creatures from themselves is enormous. In their very desire to be different, they only become more ridiculously similar to one another, and as they form the majority of European society, the modern world (in spite of the tragic fact of the war, and the fact that our generation *sees itself as tragic*) is really and actually a *comic* world, and the accepted leaders of the modern consciousness are, in fact, burlesque comic figures acting and thinking farcically. The seriousness with which it is done intensifies the farce. Quixote would have had less comic significance if he had laughed at himself. A world in which the whole four quarters of the population are trying, each one, to become one of the others, is a sham world, a world of farce. It was left for Lewis to discover this, as it was left for Cervantes to discover that the consciousness of his time was comic, and that it was impossible to deal with it otherwise than satirically. His contemporaries did not take to this view any more than Lewis's do—but he was right. By far the majority, in fact more than 90 per cent., of the European population is engaged in this gigantic farce. The worker wishes to become a rich bourgeois: the idle rich bourgeois, especially of the bohemian type, passionately tries to identify his aims with that of the poor starving worker: the adult white tries to identify himself with children or animals, as is envinced in the average plain man's hatred of what is 'highbrow' or intellectual, in 'Kids of Sixty' joining the 'League of Youth,' and in the amount of detective literature and Sheik literature (twenty years ago this was only to be read in the *Boy's Own Paper*) that is devoured by the adult population; the man who tries to feel like a lady; the lady who feels like a man; 'soggy people'; the white who identifies himself in his imagination with the savage: etc., etc.—these are all types in the world-wide movement towards *'otherness,'* a huge wholesale

Bergsonian flux which has as its chief unconscious aim the destruction of all vertical contours and distinctions and a return to primitive chaos. The *failure* of Don Quixote was in trying to identify himself with a principle which was far higher than himself, the conception of a strong, invincible, and valiant warrior—that failure is the comic motive of Cervantes but it is also a *heroic* motive. In Lewis's work the comic motive is the failure of certain equally stereotyped classes (for Don Quixote represented also a contemporary literary type) to identify themselves with principles which are not in any way higher than themselves, but simply physiologically, racially, or sexually *different* from themselves—and only because they *are* different. The actual motive is more *comic* in Lewis's work because it is not only a fact, but because it is more illogical and incomprehensible—the desire simply to *differ* from oneself is far more illogical, in the abstract, than the desire to appear better than, or to excel oneself. It is more comic than actual Tartuffe-hypocrisy, or the hypocrisy of the moral-minded Victorian Pecksniff, for that implies a certain amount of *amour-propre*—just like that sort of hypocrisy which causes people to wear wigs, false hair, and false teeth. That sort of hypocrisy is at least humanly pathetic. But that which causes a person to stampede *away* from his own image, his own face, his own lineaments, and his own nature passes the bounds of the humanly pathetic—it passes into the giant vacuous Chaos in which humour is the only creative principle that can live at all, or operate on this dehumanised material as an organising *Fiat Lux*. For in renouncing oneself personally, and in attempting to identify oneself with something contradictory to oneself, one ceases to be human at all: one becomes a clown and a puppet. In dealing with this great centrifugal stampede as represented by its intellectual leaders, Lewis's ordinary method is simple enough. After carefully separating the person in his sham form, or in his transformed centrifugal state, from the person in the native form which he is *trying to differ from*, Lewis suddenly confronts the one with the other as in a mirror. The effect is as highly comic as it would be to see a person confronted in a mirror by some other face than the one he thinks he possesses (or Gogol's major when he found *his own nose* walking about in a uniform of superior rank to his own). There is no attempt here to distort: each portrait is logically worked out as in a theorem of Euclid. It is simply a case of *reductio ad absurdum* on a human plane ruthlessly worked out, without any possibility of appeal even to one's own self-indulgence.

In this way Lewis killed (of a broken heart) the periodical *Transition*: the organ of the vast parisian colony of leisured and moneyed aesthetes who grouped themselves round the banner of Lautréamont, Sade, and the surrealistes. In his essay on the Diabolical Principle, Lewis analyses a form of philistinism peculiar to our age which draws its chief strength from an obsession with protestant, nineteenth-century morality (especially in regard to sex), a passionate obsession which is kept alive by means of a sort of mental 'artificial respiration' (long after the morality with which it is preoccupied has ceased to operate); and which gives the *illusion* of daring, of wickedness, and riskiness without incurring the risks of anything. Elsewhere (*Time and Western Man*—'Romance and the Moralist Mind') Lewis had already traced the course of the Diabolical Principle. ' . . . There is nothing abstruse,' he wrote, 'in the ethical code of the "puritan" produced by the Reformation and his descendants to-day. For its spirit and various ordinances are to be found in the Old Testament. Our use of that primitive code, framed as it is for conditions totally different from ours, is symbolic of our incurably romantic outlook. . . . '

'Our civilization is more artificial than that of Greece or Rome; and the main cause of that is the christian ethic. Where Romance enters the sphere of morals is at the gate of sex;

and nearly all the diabolism (helping itself to the traditional masochistic and invert machinery) springing up so eagerly in a puritan soil, can be traced to a sex-root. It is even extremely easy in the modern West to *sexify* everything in a way that would have been impossible in the greek world, for instance. To see this you have only to consider the fact that the Athens of Socrates was notorious, as his dialogues witness, for what is (for us) the most obsessing sort of sex-cult. Yet it did not interfere at all with greek philosophy; the life of the intellect and that of the senses co-existed harmoniously: and philosophic speculation, for the men who disputed with Socrates, was evidently as exciting as any of their other occupations. The dialogues of Plato have not an alexandrian effluvia of feminine scent; nor do they erect pointers on all the pathways of the mind waving back to the gonadal ecstasies of the commencement of life. They are as loftily detached from the peculiar delights in fashion, as it is possible to be . . . The psychological composition of the mind of such a philosopher as Socrates, or Democritus, showed no bias whatever, such as you would inevitably find in a Wilde or a Pater, that alexandrian softening and enervation of all the male chastity of thought. . . .'

Attacking the politico-aesthetes of the Diabolical Principle, Lewis shows that they are simply inverted moralists condemned to live and die under a puritan obsession. The philistine *politicisation* of art in Modern Europe takes one of two forms either resulting in its milder benevolent form, in a Tolstoyan puritanic bias (Tolstoy half-killed his own genius with it): or in the form of blood-and-thunder *à la Lautréamont*, and in incitements to violence, as in the hands of the surrealistes and their evangelically-bred American disciples.

It has often been objected against Lewis (as Colley Cibber objected against Pope, and Shadwell against Dryden) that he occupies himself with 'trivial' movements such as that of *Transition*: but these movements are continual—as soon as one dies another springs up: they explain and represent our times as well as bestsellers, and these are the most exact social thermometers that we have. What Pope wrote about Grub Street remains true of all commercial journalism to this day. What Lewis wrote of the sentimental diabolism of Paul, Jolas, and Co. is likely to remain true of all subsequent revivals of it, as it is true of all preceding attempts at it, and as *The Caliph's Design* has remained true of all subsequent art-movements.

In *The Dithyrambic Spectator*, in the same volume, Lewis deals with the growing tendency, in modern life, of the audience to participate in the performance of the arts—it deals with the entrance of Everyman on to the stage, as in the primitive festivals before the days of individual dramatists and actors. This tendency is welcomed by the erudite Miss Harrison (in her popular book, *Ancient Art and Ritual*) as a great 'return to life.' Miss Harrison seems to have the idea that there is something more valuable and desirable in a crowd of yokels dancing around a maypole than in a trained and intelligent crowd watching some performance by a supreme expert: that it is better to go into a field and clumsily kick a ball about oneself than to watch (with certain powers of appreciation) a game perfectly played. She is not only the announcer of this return to the primitive (which she regards as a progress), but she is a perfect example of the performing spectator herself. Art is her 'football' in this case—and this is the way she kicks it about. (The italics are mine.)

'We English are not supposed to be an artistic people, yet art, in *some form or another* (*does it matter what?*) bulks large in the national life. We have theatres, a National Gallery, we have art schools, our *tradesmen* provide for us "art-furniture," we even hear, absurdly enough, of "art colours." Moreover, all this is not a matter of mere antiquarian interest . . . a movement *towards* or *about* art is all alive and astir among us. We have new developments of the theatre, problem plays, Reinhardt productions, Gordon Craig Scenery, Russian Ballets. We have new schools of painting treading on each other's heels *with breathless rapidity*: Impressionists, Post-Impressionists, Futurists. Art—or at least the desire for, the interest in, art—is assuredly not dead.—Moreover, and this is very important, we all feel about art a certain *obligation*, such as some of us feel about religion. There is an "ought" about it. Perhaps we do not really care much about pictures and music and poetry but we feel we *ought* to.'

Here the dithyrambic spectator, as invading or 'moving *towards*' art, gives a portrait of herself or himself. Omnivorous, with the digestion of an ostrich, the power of discrimination of a dog, and the swallow of a hippopotamus, this huge collective spectre (dowdy, woolly, and of a mental *greyness* and inelegance that would have been criminal in any other age) advances with its mouth open (and its eyes shut, of course) to devour 'art' ('furniture,' 'colours,' and all)—not from any natural appetite, but as a sort of conscientious obligation, such as that which forces the traditional religious hypocrite to church. Whatever chance there could be for the survival of art, when threatened with this open maw, this huge, all-devouring, collective compromise between a matrix and a stomach, would depend, if not on the actual emetic power of that art, at least on its hardness and insolubility in the feelings, the instincts, and the other gastric juices of this great digestive system, which suffers from elephantiasis of the unconscious; and that hardness, emetic power, or insolubility can only be supplied by the individual intellect.

In *Time and Western Man* Lewis launches out on a comprehensive study of the obsessions with Time as reality, which in one form or another have gained an undisputed ascendancy in the intellectual world. The object of this book is ultimately to contradict and if possible to defeat, these particular conceptions upon the popular, the concrete plane where they present themselves, as it is, *in a misleading form.* He begins with analysing the romantic principle in general and finds that the general spirit of all modern art is romantic—that is to say popular, sensational, and 'comically' confused as distinguished from the classical which is the rational, aloof, and aristocratical. Romance and reality are two terms that we most often employ to contrast what we regard as dream and truth respectively.[3] We have that in our age, even Commerce and the Romantic spirit are closely allied. Nothing from hair oil to boot polish is even marketable unless it has been romanticised, given an unreal glitter, and sensationalised by Advertisement. The unreality with which modern life is drugged, through and through, is obvious in the huge amount of sensationalism and romance which surrounds even a special brand of tooth-brush, soap, or sanitary paper. The force of romance can be seen even in its operation on the obsession of morality (an abstract thing enough) but one through which it succeeds in physiologically transforming the relation of the sexes not for any desirable end, but merely for the satisfaction of the romantic idea of sensationalism, and by literary and scientific systems which are entirely comparable with and analogous to the methods of ordinary commercial advertisement—that is to say, methods which employ sensationalism for its own sake. Lewis succeeds in showing that a greater part of modern science and philosophy (far from being unimpersonal, unemotional thought) is dictated by this inherent romanticism; or politically calculated to appeal to it; or at least (as in the case of the popularisation of Freud) that it depends for its popularity and success on the stimulation and excitement of the romantic consciousnes; and that, in many cases, the actual methods employed are not radically different from the methods employed by best-sellers or soap advertisers. He shows that especially in modern art and literature there is a general appeal (on the lines of advertisement) to the vanity of the reader as well as to sensationalism, emotion, or sex. He brilliantly analyses and compares the appeal of Charlie Chaplin, Gertrude Stein, and Anita Loos as different forms of the flattery of the small by the small, and he attacks the system upon which *Ulysses* and the later works of Joyce are based showing how the time-basis, in spite of Joyce's powerful impressionism, is an unsatisfactory basis for the creation of *real* art (though he admits that *Ulysses* is a masterpiece of *romantic* art); and he shows how the basing of art on the fluid material gushing of undisciplined life, dating from the publication of *Matière et Mémoire* or of the earliest psycho-analytic tracts, leads (and is probably intended to lead) to a physical disintegration and a formal confusion. It becomes a highly personal day-dream, culminating in the phantasmagoria of the pure dream. Lewis's analysis of Joyce should be compared with his analysis of Strachey's *Elizabeth* (*Doom of Youth*)—this is a Freudian day-dream of an inferior and very different type, in which the author who (as nearly all good Bloomsburies are) is obsessed with the idea of Matriarchy, more-or-less identifies himself (as he did also with Queen Victoria) with the elderly female, especially in her admiration of beautiful young men, as long as they are very, very *young*—but who execrates the idea of the ordinary grown-up male, as in the case of Raleigh: and who was politically passionate in this attitude in spite of his idealisation of 'detachment.' His choice of 'Eminent Victorians' shows him not only to have been hypnotised by the idea of 'time' but also to have been politically prejudiced against the male principle, which he not only chose to write about in its uglier forms, but to which he chose to add deformities and vices which (in some cases) were not warrantable upon any other grounds than those of the ordinary excited pre-war suffragette. If one compares Lewis's work on Joyce with that on Strachey, in which, from the same attitude, he deals with both the noblest and the least noble type of 'time'-politics, one sees how his whole attitude on this question has become crystalised in a perfect form, like a diamond, and how the knife-edge of each separate facet, going in a different direction, cuts the different methods of Joyce, and Lawrence, and Strachey, and the whole Huxley-and-Arlen school, not with an ordinary assassin's knife (as generally supposed), but in each case with a brilliant ray of intellectual vision which will endure in most cases long after the cause that incited it.

The greatest part of *Time and Western Man* is the attack on Spengler. Lewis shows how Spengler's whole view of the past is more-or-less concerned with the manœuvres of the second-rate (politicians, kings, and soldiers), and how his whole vision of history is rather confined to elections, fights, and riots, than to permanent achievements. Lewis is better formed for attacking this gigantic type of polypus, with its chronological fatalism, than for attacking any other type, and his attack on the chronological fatalism of Spengler is final and mortal. On his way, he takes the Behaviourists, too, and laughs them into the next world, without any trouble to himself.

In *Time and Western Man* he has shown that modern science, art, and politics, whether consciously or not, all conspire mutually to create an *unreal* state of mind in which the Sentimental and the Illusory can flourish better than anything else. But at the same time he has dynamited great holes in the subterranean corridors of literary and scientific experience, from which anybody with the courage of a rabbit can walk out into the fresh air, asking himself why he ever took this carefully-built, underground world so seriously. The aim of *Time and Western Man* is to show how almost every step that we regard as 'progressive' in modern philosophy and art, is actually *retrogressive*, towards the original savage, intuitive, or matriarchal state of the prehistoric world, but without having any necessary *reason* to be so retrogressively directed. Lewis opposes to this religion of 'time' as concerned especially with the future or the past (and its homing instinct is more concerned with the primitive past) a spatial conception of existence. He opposes to the Bergsonised idea of the intuitive, fluid, living nature of matter, and to the Berkeleyan idea that it consists mostly of mere façades, the idea that matter is mostly solid and dead—it amounts to the opposition of the living human individual, and whatever ideas can be abstracted from him, against the clock and the microscope (which depend as much on the human eye as does the human individual himself) and whatever deities can be extracted from *them*. But it is not to be thought that Lewis opposes the *machine*, as machine, except when it is made to oppose the human being. Unlike most modern writers he does not identify our civilisation with machines: for he knows very well that the life of every stage of human being is entirely involved with machines,[4] and that the more 'savage' one is, the more one is ruled by machines. Canoes, huts, ploughs, traps, fish-traps, fish-nets, clothing, snow-shoes, weapons, etc.—are all machines. The life of the 'savage' is more dependent upon actual mechanical *routine* than that of a bank clerk—and he is actually more tied up to his machines and dominated by them than we are. The actual power or otherwise of one's machines has nothing to do with one's state of culture or civilization or barbarism. *That* depends entirely on ideas. That the general trend of modern philosophy and science is in the opposite direction from that of culture, as far as its final results go, no one who reads *Time and Western Man* will be left a chance of doubting. Even though Lewis attacks 'Relativity' (*not* as expounded by Einstein, but as interpreted by his popular impresarios in the interests of their particular politics) his final championship of his own spatial conception of life does not oppose it in any way: it is in fact a sort of application of many of the principles of relativity, in a human way, to human life.

In *The Lion and the Fox* Lewis departed a little from his main scheme as the poet, historian, and analyst of the great centrifugal stampede. Nevertheless it is his most perfect prose work outside his three great novels and *The Wild Body*. In it Lewis studies the rôle of the hero in the plays of Shakespeare. In dealing with the usual attempts to conjure up the personality of Shakespeare, Lewis writes (explaining also the scope of his book) '... interest in his personality or impersonality which is much the same thing—obscures the very active features of the wonderful mind exhibited in his plays. I am setting out to show how—with all the noble proportion and harmonious adjustments that made his achievement so incomparable—bellowing at you from the windy corner of every scene in his great tragedies, is a human personality for whom such playful, theatrical or finicking disguises as are thrust upon him by his interpreters, would have been pushed aside with as much distraction as Charles, Duke of Byron, at the moment of his pathos, would have shown a laundry-bill. Each of the figures of his tragedies, Timon, Lear, Coriolanus, are vast keys to unlock a giant's meditative fastness. It is because the scale of his mature creations is so superhuman that it has been possible to describe them as standing aside from Life, or as arabesques of unwieldy passion dispassionately projected. They are, it is true, immense shadows rather than realities in a cheaply concrete sense; and their roar is muffled by the great lines that interpret it. And it is true that in this control of these creatures Shakespeare showed all the sangfroid that we associate with the great technician in the tactical transference of individual experience into a series of prepared puppets. But such puppets are born, not made, by a most painful gestation. It will be my business here to relate the spasms of these scowling and despairing monsters to a particularly concrete figure, or to a mind experiencing things according to identifiable personal laws. ... It will also come into my scheme to show how, contrary to the

33

aristophanic function the comic spirit in Shakespeare was Puck-like and anarchic, and not at the service of reactionary superstition. For the curses of Caliban and Thersites are Shakespeare's curses: and far from being a feudal poet, the Shakespeare that *Troilus and Cressida, The Tempest*, or even *Coriolanus* shows us, in much more a bolshevik (using this little word popularly) than a figure of conservative romance. . . . '

Lewis shows how in the supposed 'Sweet Will,' as in the good-natured Ford, there was that wild subversive matter that fermented and broke out in the personal life of Marlowe. He shows once and for all that there was a profound feminine principle (not only revealed in the sonnets) but also present in the plays. Frazer has shown how the idea of the king or the god is always implicated with the idea of sacrifice—as in the case of the Christians, the Aztecs, and the Bull-god Apis. Lewis's idea of Shakespeare is as a universal priest (or executioner) who performs the same sacrifice. He shows the impact of Machiavellianism on the idea of Chivalry, as it violently obsessed every Elizabethan besides Shakespeare, and the conflict of these two principles in Shakespeare himself. Shakespeare was more positivist than Cervantes but less than Rabelais. The main preoccupation in Shakespeare is the struggle between the simpleton (generally a 'colossal' type) and the Knave, often a 'small' Machiavellian, 'Fox' type—Coriolanus, Hotspur, Ajax, and Hector are instances of *simpletons* with whom Shakespeare has, in varying degrees, little or no sympathy.

Lewis sees Shakespeare as a *critic* of action, and wherever the man of action is involved, to be rather opposed to him than for him, as he is certainly opposed to the heroes of the Homeric Saga. He shows that Thersites and Lear say the same things though one croaks and the other bellows. He shows how Falstaff is rather Shakespeare's Quixote than his Sancho Panza, and that in Shakespeare's *criticism of action* Falstaff is made to play a similar rôle to that of Thersites. Here for the first time, certain contours in the mind and outlook of Shakespeare are delineated, leaving very little room for mystifiers, merrie-Englanders, Lambs, and Hazlitts to put the 'merry twinkle' in Shakespeare's eye, etc., etc. It is the profoundest study of Shakespeare yet written in English and the only one which constructs without the aid of conjecture or sentiment.

We now come to *The Wild Body*. This is a collection of short stories (written over a period of many years), most of which are told through the lips of a hypothetical 'Soldier of Humour,' Kerr-Orr, a comic expert and a wandering adventurer in search of the comic who describes himself as follows:—

'I am a large blonde clown, ever so vaguely reminiscent (in person) of William Blake and some great american boxer whose name I forget. I have large strong teeth which I gnash and flash when I laugh. But usually a look of settled and aggressive naïveté rests on my face. I know much more about myself than people generally do. For instance I am aware that I am a barbarian. By rights I should be paddling about in a coracle. My body is large, white and savage. But all the fierceness has been transformed into laughter. . . . Everywhere where formerly I would fly at throats I now howl with laughter.' Using this fanciful figure as his mouthpiece or showman, to whom the antics and solemn gambols of people are a source of strange delight, Lewis reveals his astounding dance of stupefying, brilliantly-coloured automatons. Galvanised into superhuman velocity, they hurtle across his pages, amazing us, exasperating us into that sort of laughter which is perhaps the most profound of all the mysterious spasms of *The Wild Body,* that stark apparatus in which Lewis set out on his adventures.

'The fascinating imbecility of the creaking men machines that some little restaurant or

34

fishing boat works, was the original subject of these studies, though the nautical set never materialised. The boat's tackle and dirty little shell, or the hotel and its technique of hospitality, keeping the limbs of men and women involved in a monotonous rhythm from morning till night, that was the occupational background, placed in Brittany or Spanish Galicia.

'A man is made drunk with his boat or restaurant as he is with a merry-go-round: only it is the staid, everyday drunkenness of the normal real, not easy always to detect. The wheel at Carisbrooke imposes a set of movements upon the donkey inside it . . . but in the case of a hotel or a fishing boat it passes as open and untrammelled life. This subtle and wider mechanism merges for the Spectator in the general variety of nature. Yet we have in most lives the spectacle of a pattern as circumscribed and complete as a theorem of Euclid. So these are essays in a new human mathematic. But they are each of them simple shapes little monuments of logic. . . . '

Lewis's whole theory of laughter is explained in 'Inferior Religions' (printed in *The Wild Body*), the most profound and the richest in poetry of all his essays. . . .

'The chemistry of personality (subterranean, in a sort of cemetery, whose decompositions are our lives) puffs up in frigid balls, soapy Snow-men, arctic carnival masks, which we can photograph and fix. . . . Upwards from the surface of existence a lurid and dramatic scum oozes and accumulates into the characters we see. The real and tenacious poisons and sharp forces of vitality do not socially transpire. Within five yards of another man's eyes we are on a little crater which if it erupted would split up as would a cocoa tin of nitrogen. Some of these bombs are ill made, or some erratic in their timing. But they are all potential little bombs. Capriciously, however, the froth-forms of these darkly-contrived machines twist and puff in the air, in our legitimate and liveried masquerade.' . . . Again he explains, 'The finest humour is the great play-shapes blown up or given off by the tragic corpse of life underneath the world of the camera': and elsewhere in the same essay occurs this passage which illuminates Lewis's attitude:

'It is often part of our own organisation to become a Fetish. So Boswell's Johnson or Sir John Falstaff are minute and rich religions. That Johnson was a sort of god to his biographer we readily see. But Falstaff as well is a sort of English god, like the rice-bellied gods of laughter in China. They are illusions hugged and lived in: little dead totems. Just as all gods are a repose for humanity, the big religions an immense refuge and rest, so are these little grotesque fetishes. One reason for this is that, for the spectator or participator, it is a world within the world, full of order, even if violent.

'All these are forms of static art, then. There is a great deal of divine olympianship in English humour and its delightful dreams. The most gigantic spasm of laughter is sculptural, isolated, and essentially simple.'

Lewis, in opposing his aesthetic against the 'poetic' or 'beautiful' view, has many fine things to say: and he champions the humourist point of view triumphantly. Henri Fabre was in every way a superior being to a salon artist and he knew of elegant grubs which he would prefer to a salon painter's nymphs. We have in Lewis a writer who compares to our best naturalistic novelists as Henri Fabre would to such painters: as Swift would compare to Ambrose Phillips, or Jonson to Shirley.

Modern English fiction is by far the most dully photographical of all the arts: it remains in the same state as English painting was in the time of Millais. We have at least five hundred first-rate *copiers* from Life. The number of people of whom it could be said quite truthfully by

MacCarthy, Nicolson, Gould, Walpole, Priestly, and others in their weekly writings, 'he is one of the most brilliant of our younger novelists,' etc., runs well into three if not four figures. They are all equally *good*, and their success depends not on their style, which is similar and only distinguishable by mannerisms, but largely on the novelty or sensationalism of the 'situation,' the sex interest, or the crime interest; or having visited some exotic country that has not been '*done*' before—all of these are not literary considerations and have nothing to do with fiction, *as fiction*, or invention. Yet it is to these purely external details that nearly all modern criticism devotes most attention. Lewis is first concerned with *creating*, and his work is entirely different from any one else in this one respect, that one would have to find some other word than fiction, as applied to modern novels, in order to describe it. The only book of our time comparable to *The Childermass* is *Ulysses*, but that if satirical in part, has rather the *effect* of a long narrative lyrical poem, and Lewis's mind is not lyrical but heroic. Compared with the slightly Celtic mist and *greyness* of *Ulysses*, *The Childermass* is all vivid reds, yellows, and whites.

Lewis is, of course, a painter, and it was as a painter that he first won fame. The peculiar vivid quality of what he writes is certainly due to this fortunate fact. *The Childermass* is a poetic vision on a very grand scale indeed, and it utilises the symbolic machinery of Epic poetry. The terrific strain with which Lewis compresses his fiery imaginative vision in his other novels (utilising it rather to intensify and vitalise his realism) is here relaxed and his vision is powerfully exerted to create both the element and the setting in which the interplay of the spiritual forces with which he is concerned can be logically embodied and displayed. The quality of his imagination can be judged from the fact that when it is working allegorically and independently of the tangible and visible world it creates another world as tangible, logical, and visible without begging the aid of the dark, the mysterious, and the mystical. As Dante visually *created* the Heaven, Hell, and Purgatory that was emotionally and mentally inhabited by his contemporaries, Lewis has here visually created space-and-time as emotionally and mentally inhabited by the modern consciousness. It is a stupendous feat, and the only thing in modern literature which attempts anything on this epic plane—for it is a part of the function of epic poetry to visualise and bring into spiritual focus the contemporary conception of the world—as Dante did, as Milton did, both basing their heavens and hells on the contemporary doctrines, and as Lewis does here satirically. Yeats has compared this first part of *The Childermass* to *Gulliver*, and not without reason.

The Childermass is still to be completed. But the first part deals with a quarantine or immigration camp of souls on the outskirts of the magnetic city (of heaven). Here we meet the types of modern consciousness such as we meet them in life. Under the charge of the '*Bailiff*' they are kept as it were marking time, day after day, in expectation of entering the City. Lewis manages to suggest in quite an uncanny way that they will never get there. We see in the Bailiff the whole personification of that anonymous occult power which operates on modern democratic life, which in the spirit of a Pelman or a Drage, points at you from every advertisement, slaps you on the back in every column of the newspapers, feeds you with 'humour' in order to turn you into tame cannon-fodder, talks to you 'as man to man': a mixture of the sporting parson, Punch, and the gentleman who says good-night (twice) on the wireless—but drawn with such mastery as to be unforgettable, and to take on a superhuman significance like the character of Mephistopheles. The dismal plight of the great 'sporting' boy-man type, his helplessness and nullity are wonderfully brought out in the person of Sattersby, who suddenly finds himself 'on the other side' where he meets his old school-friend Pullman, one of the earnest *John-o'-London*-reading type. They wander about the outskirts of the camp discussing their position (the small Pullman piloting his unwieldy pal)—a sort of Quixote and Panza of a contemporary kind. Their adventures bring out all the extravagance of Lewis's imaginative humour. The assemblies of appellants, over which the Bailiff procrastinatingly presides, are the pandemonium of modern life. *The Childermass* is the poetical realisation of the philosophical attitude already crystallised in *The Art of Being Ruled* and *Time and Western Man*.

This first part is a complete poem in itself: it is one of those rare philosophical novels that are the glory of any language in which they are written, and of which *Dead Souls, Don Quixote, Gulliver, Pantagruel,* and *Hudibras* are, in their different ways, representative. Lewis's humour, in its *kind*, is nearest to that of the Butler of *Hudibras*, but it is of a superior quality, and the resounding roll of his prose is Olympian. There is no prose or poetry being written at this time that is at once so densely packed with thought, meaning, and vision, and at the same time moves with such velocity. It is electric; and it is refreshing, in this age of heavy entrails and organic gush, to see a man whose passion is a white-hot spiritual flame, operating his material and his style, not as if he were manipulating or straining his own guts, but as if he were driving some clean, external hundred-horsepower motor, which he dominates, but which does not dominate *him* though it keeps every nerve of the driver taut and attentive.

With *The Apes of God* Lewis crashes finally and triumphantly through the barriers of modern social and literary shams. Our period is notorious for patronising and ridiculing other periods, but there has never been a period so sensitive (and with as much reason to be) as ours, to criticism by contemporaries. Every possible attempt was made to suppress and misinterpret *The Apes of God* on its first appearance. The history and the victory of this battle were both recounted and achieved in the pamphlet *Satire and Fiction*, which completely silenced the opposition as far as it was articulate in print.

The author describes the book as 'reflecting the collapse of English social life in the grip of post-war conditions. Its theme is the confusion of the intellect and of the emotions in a society beneath the shadow of a revolutionary situation. It shows that society groping back to its childhood, and how beneath the threat of a future whose significance it is too exhausted to grasp, it calls loudly for its Mamma, and returns to the bibs and bottles of its Babyhood.' The origin of the title is in the early Christian belief that the world swarmed with small devils who impersonated the Deity.

Lewis, in this colossal novel of 650 pages, excels all his previous performances. The changing scenes follow one another with the harsh electric brilliance of the best comedies of Jonson: but the stage is vaster and the action more varied. We are reminded of Petronius more than any one else. *The Apes* is a human encyclopedia besides being a social drama and a great poem; and it places Lewis as the first, if not the only, genius writing in England at the present day.

I am aware that these notes are not written in the fashionable way—'on the one hand,' and 'on the other hand.' It is entirely partial, if you like: but not for any other reason than that Lewis's work itself inspires me with whole-hearted admiration. A casual reference to my other writings will show that, unlike other English critics, I am not in the habit of paying or returning compliments, and I do not remember having bestowed such terms as 'genius' on any other contemporary: my use of superlatives in this essay should therefore be compared with my general attitude to contemporary literature, as expressed, for instance, in *The Georgiad*.

1. This war upon the privilege of genius is implicit in the passionate controversies that surround Homer and Shakespeare: in which it is determined to prove that Homer was a sort of co-operative society; and that Shakespeare at all costs was anybody but himself in spite of all the testimonies of Jonson, Fuller, and others of his contemporaries. The great thing is to cast a doubt on the authenticity of the outstanding individual, even if it is only to prove that he may be somebody else. We may be thankful that record has been kept of the actual existence and activity of Virgil, Dante, Camoens, Cervantes, and Milton as public figures—the slightest biographical obscurity would be an excuse to prove that, if not co-operative groups, they were at least other persons than themselves.

2. Tables and chairs (another type of quadruped) quite sensible in their place, immediately become comic figures when credited with almost 'human' feelings by Russell and other philosophers.

3. This distinction must broadly suffice here as we have no room to go into Lewis's reservations.

4. Even that of animals, too, is involved with the working of machines—bird's-nests, beehives, ant's-nests, etc., are all machines, and occupy as much of the time and care of their owners in almost every stage of life, as do any of our own machines. Lewis does not attack our machines but our tendency to 'poeticise' and romanticise them.

COMPOSITION WITH THREE FIGURES, 1914
HENRI GAUDIER-BRZESKA
CRAYON. 48 x 31.5 cm
COURTESY ANTHONY d'OFFAY

REED WAY DASENBROCK

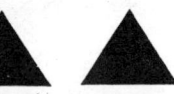

VORTICISM AMONG THE ISMS

Though BLAST is principally thought of today as the magazine of Vorticism, it was planned and announced before the birth of Vorticism, and, indeed, most of the first issue was laid out before the Vorticist manifestos which open and close that issue were conceived. Pound wrote to Joyce on April 1, 1914, that "Lewis is starting a new Futurist, Cubist, Imagiste Quarterly," and the advertisement for BLAST which appeared in *The Egoist* on April 15, 1914, announced it as a "Discussion of Cubism, Futurism, Imagisme and all Vital Forms of Modern Art."[1] The most telling evidence that BLAST preceded Vorticism is in BLAST itself. In one of Lewis's notes, "The Melodrama of Modernity," he is willing, despite the critique of Futurism in the same article, to accept the label Futurist for his own art. He does say, however, that "we may hope before long to find a new word."[2]

Only some time in May or June of 1914 did Pound and Lewis come up with that new word, Vorticism, which would describe their art in contradistinction to the other *isms* of modern art, Cubism, Futurism, Imagism, and Expressionism. The launching of their own movement caused a decided change in their attitude towards those *isms*. As late as April, Cubism and Futurism were vital forms of modern art, but in the first issue of BLAST, dated July 2, 1914, they were the objects of extended and hostile critiques.

This abrupt volte-face raises some doubts about these critiques: were they a sincere expression of the Vorticists' differences with Cubism and Futurism, which can be seen in their art as well as their propaganda? Or were these polemics merely worked up quickly so that Vorticism would seem to have an original position? Lewis had been willing to accept the label English Cubist at the "Exhibition of the Camden Town Group and Others" held in Brighton six months before. Then he had accepted the label Futurist in "The Melodrama of Modernity." Can one therefore truly distinguish Vorticism from the other *isms* which were springing up at such a rate all over Europe in this period? Was Vorticism original, and if so what was original about it?

Pound, though he named Vorticism, never distinguished it sharply from its fellow art movements on the Continent. In "Vortex Pound" he referred to "Picasso, Kandinski, father and mother, classicism and romanticism of the movement" (BLAST 1, 154), and in the September 1914 article, "Vorticism," Pound identified Vorticism with Continental art more sweepingly and tendentiously: "now you have vorticism, which is, roughly speaking, expressionism, neo-cubism, and imagism gathered together in one camp and futurism in the other."[3] Pound would not have been unaware of the differences among these movements he has tied together, but here as always he stressed the continuity in the movement of the avant-garde more than the discontinuities. In other words, Pound was less interested in showing Vorticism's originality than in denying its isolation.

But Lewis drew sharp distinctions between the Vorticists and everyone else, and it is to the writings of Lewis that we must turn to find Vorticism defined. The process of definition is essentially negative: one learns what Vorticism is by learning what it is not, by learning what Lewis found lacking in the 1914 avant-garde. But a genuine and fascinating position is worked out, one reflected in Vorticist art, which shows that the distinction between Vorticism and the Continental art movements is not a paper one. Though one can see Lewis scrambling to find and define the individuality of his hastily assembled group, the evidence of BLAST shows that he did succeed. The heart of the Vorticist position, put simply, is that Vorticism accepted Futurism's critique of Cubism, but criticized Futurism in turn from a standpoint indebted to Cubism. Following these two vectors one arrives at Vorticism.

The Futurist painters on the occasion of their first

Paris exhibition in February 1912 declared themselves to be "absolutely opposed" to Cubist painting. They objected primarily to what they considered the lack of energy or dynamism of Cubist painting. According to the catalogue to this exhibition (which also went to London), the Cubists

> are furiously determined to depict the immobility, the frozenness and all the static aspects of nature. They worship the traditionalism of Poussin, of Ingres, of Corot, ageing and petrifying their art with a passéist obstinance that remains, for us, absolutely incomprehensible.[4]

In opposition to this "static art," the Futurists painted objects in motion. Among their favorite subjects were trains, automobiles, and people engaged in physical activity or in demonstrations or riots. They associated static art with a concern with the past largely because they associated their own dynamic art with a concern with the modern. They painted modern urban and industrial subjects, not simply because these lent themselves to the dynamic treatment the Futurists advocated, but also because in their view art had a responsibility to respond to and incorporate these new forces which were transforming society. From this perspective, they attacked the subject matter of Cubist painting. To work in the traditional genres of individual portraiture, landscape, or still life, no matter how revolutionary one's treatment of those genres might be, was to be, as far as the Futurists were concerned (in one of their favorite phrases), "fatally academic."

Lewis's view of Cubism is very similar. Cubist art for Lewis was static and heavy, and its subject matter was embarrassingly trivial:

> HOWEVER MUSICAL OR VEGETARIAN A MAN MAY BE, HIS LIFE IS NOT SPENT EXCLUSIVELY AMONGST APPLES AND MANDOLINES. Therefore there is something to be explained when he foregathers, in his paintings, exclusively with these two objects. (BLAST 2, 41)

But to accept the Futurist critique of Cubism is not to accept Futurism: Lewis criticized Futurism more fiercely than Cubism. This countercritique was not indebted explicitly to Cubism, as the Cubists never responded to the Futurist attack on them. (Cubism was not an organized movement in the way Futurism and Vorticism were, and only the lesser Cubists, Gleizes and Metzinger, formulated principles of Cubism in writing.) But there is an implicit debt to Cubism in Lewis's critique, as the faults he saw in Futurism he sought to guard against in his own art through borrowing from Cubism.

First, Lewis criticized Futurism as the latest form of Impressionism. Its art was too formless and blurred. In trying to be dynamic the Futurists succeeded merely in being fluid and imprecise. Their aim was to be faithful to the sensations they received in the presence of the subject they painted, and they went so far as to claim "that painting and sensation are two inseparable words."[5] For Lewis those two words must be separate, and he would claim the support of Cubism and Cézanne for his contention that the artist must organize and form his material. He should dominate his subject matter; the Futurists were dominated by theirs.

Second, Lewis considered that the fuss that the Futurists made about their subject matter was quite ridiculous. He accepted that subject matter—the modern mechanistic environment—but did not want to treat it with their sentimentality and romance. The Futurists gushed about machines, according to Lewis, only because mechanization was new to Italy. His contrasting ideal was to treat the Futurists' subject matter with the objectivity and analytic perspective of Cubism. The Futurists were right, according to Lewis, in trying to get away from apples and mandolins, but wrong in replacing the coldness and hardness of Cubism with, in his words, sentimental Latin romance.

The program of Vorticism was therefore to combine (what Lewis saw as) the strengths of these two movements. The subject matter of the Vorticists was modern, but they did not identify with that subject matter in the manner of Futurism. The Vorticists did not paint the mechanistic world they lived in because they found it better or more beautiful than the past. Nowhere in Vorticism can one find the inanities of Futurist propaganda, the urging of the destruction and transformation of Venice into an industrial port, the claim that a speeding automobile is more beautiful than the *Victory of Samothrace*, or the reference to the art of the past as a great joke.[6] In fact, Lewis argued in "The Exploitation of Vulgarity" in BLAST 1 that a pessimistic attitude towards the modern world dominates modern art and that it was precisely the vulgarity, ugliness and insanity of the modern world which offered art a great opportunity.

This fits in with his idea that England is "just now the most favourable country for the appearance of a great art" (BLAST 1, 33). The English have by and large created "this bareness and hardness" of the modern world, and, as familiarity with mechanization breeds detachment if not contempt, it should be easier for them to adopt a cold and unromantic attitude towards the machine. The great art, Lewis obviously hoped, would be Vorticism, which would be distinguished for its detached attitude towards its modern subject matter. As he put it in "Our Vortex":

> In a Vorticist Universe we don't get excited at what we have invented. . . .
> We hunt machines, they are our favourite game.
> We invent them and then hunt them down.
> This is a great Vorticist age, a great still age of artists. (BLAST 1, 148)

Nothing separated the Vorticists more sharply from the Futurists than this ideal of "a great still age." Yet it seems an odd ideal for them to hold. The paintings of the Cubists are much more obviously still, which is what sparked the Futurist critique of the "static forms" of Cubism. Vorticism sought to reconcile these static forms with Futurist dynamism through painting dynamic forms, such as the vortex, which is in constant motion but has a stable form and a still center. The art in this view is not still; the Vorticist artist is, as he occupies that still center and, looking out with detachment at the chaos whirling around him, he sees that it is really formed, by and around his still point.

This dynamic formism represented by the vortex was central to Vorticist art.[7] Abstract dynamic forms like the vortex were more prominent in the Vorticist polemics than in its painting, but concrete equivalents, human activities which are dynamic yet formed or patterned, are found everywhere in Vorticist art. The subject of the dance, taken up by David Bomberg, William Roberts, Gaudier-Brzeska, and Lewis, in Richard Cork's words, "ran like a connecting thread through the convoluted imagery of Vorticist art."[8] David Bomberg's two great Vorticist canvases, *In the Hold* and *The Mud Bath*, portray human activity in rhythmic motion, the first, laborers handling cargo in the hold of a ship and the second, men in a bath, which is expressed on the canvas as a pattern of interlocking geometric forms.

The human figure was depicted as a machine in Vorticist art, as well as a pattern or rhythmic form, particularly in Lewis's drawings of the period around 1914 and in Jacob Epstein's *Rock Drill*. This mechanization of the human figure was part of the (pessimistic) response of these artists to the modern world: their art was portraying the dehumanization they saw around them. But this response was articulated through the style of dynamic formism. These figures are dynamic and in motion, usually engaged in combat or in physical labor. But the non-naturalistic way in which these figures are portrayed stylizes them, making them seem like machines or robots. The rounded contours of the human figure have been replaced by crisp, harsh diagonal lines, representing their movement in a formed geometric manner.

Probably the central Vorticist subject and certainly Lewis's central subject in this period was the city. In contrast to the cityscapes of Futurism which are characteristically warm and dynamic, filled with chaotic masses of people, Lewis's cityscapes reveal his Vorticist preoccupation with finding the order of that chaos. These paintings are cold and still, depicting bleak and austere shapes which suggest buildings. Yet a kind of dynamism is present: the planes and the colors of the forms are manipulated to generate a sense of motion. The thrusting diagonal lines and extreme color contrasts in the painting *Workshop*, for instance, create a sense of dynamism appropriate to the modern city. [And see Color Plate 3 in the present volume.—*Ed.*]

This concern with dynamic forms was thus both an important Vorticist subject and an important part of the style of Vorticist art. Other paintings of the period, Marcel Duchamp's *Nude Descending a Staircase* (1912), Kasimir Malevich's *Knife Grinder* (1912), and Francis Picabia's series of paintings of dancers of 1912-13, tried to reconcile form and motion in ways parallel to Vorticism. But these are isolated works: no other movement tried to effect a synthesis of Cubist form and Futurist movement, and this synthesis unifies many of the disparate subjects of Vorticist art.

But subject matter itself was coming under attack in the years just before World War I. Cubism and Futurism were not the only art movements to which a fledgling art movement in 1914 felt compelled to respond. Both (by and large) retained an element of representation in their paintings, whereas other painters and movements were renouncing representation between 1910 and 1914. The chronology of this development is both complex and confused, but Kandinsky in Munich seems to have been the first to paint non-representational works around 1910.[9] He was closely followed in 1911 by a Czech painter who worked in Paris, Kupka, in 1912 by the Orphist Delaunay, the Futurist Balla, and the Russian Rayonist Larionov, and in 1913 by Léger, Severini, and Malevich.

Most discussions of Vorticism have situated it in this movement towards total abstraction which swept over Europe just before the War. Richard Cork, in the major study of Vorticism revealingly titled *Vorticism and Abstract Art in the First Machine Age*, frankly confesses that Vorticism interests him primarily as "an indigenously English form of abstraction."[10] Elsewhere, Anthony d'Offay has claimed that "certainly our interest in the [Vorticist] movement today must be centered on the degree of abstraction it achieved."[11] D'Offay's claim is easily countered: my interest in Vorticism has nothing to do with the degree of abstraction it achieved. But, more to the point, abstraction was not an important goal of Vorticism. The Vorticists did do some totally abstract works, largely drawings and preparatory sketches, but they returned to a subject in their major works, because, I think, they agreed with the Futurists that art must respond to the society surrounding it. They willingly retained subject matter in their art because only with a subject could their art have the kind of significance they intended.

Lewis drew a clear distinction between abstraction and the aesthetic of Vorticism. His "A Review of Contemporary Art" in BLAST 2 discussed three groups of artists in detail, Cubism and Futurism (in ways already discussed) and Expressionism, by which he said that he meant the work of Kandinsky. His discussion of Kandinsky focused on the question of representation and abstraction, and in typically Vorticist fashion he arrived at his own doctrine about representation by attacking Kandinsky's. Lewis himself called attention to his discussion:

> In dealing with Kandinsky's doctrine, and tabulating differences, you come to the most important feature of this new synthesis I propose. (BLAST 2, 42)

Lewis focused his discussion on Kandinsky because he considered him "the only PURELY abstract painter in Europe" (BLAST 2, 40). BLAST 1 contained excerpts from and comments by Edward Wadsworth on Kandinsky's book *Concerning the Spiritual in Art.* Moreover, Kandinsky exhibited in London at the Allied Artists' Association in 1909, 1910, 1913, and 1914, where in 1913 and 1914 Lewis, Epstein, Gaudier-Brzeska, and other Vorticists showed. The works Kandinsky showed in 1913 and 1914 included some of his most advanced paintings (*Improvisations No. 29* and *No. 30*), so Lewis's critique was based on first-hand knowledge of Kandinsky's "abstract" work.

However, these paintings no longer seem abstract to us; *Improvisation No. 30*, in particular, is famous because it contains two cannons in the lower right which, according to Kandinsky, made their way into the work unconsciously.[12] Though Lewis discusses Kandinsky's work as if it were totally abstract, the presence of such veiled or unconscious imagery in these paintings actually supports his argument, which is that representation is unavoidable. To "attempt to avoid all representative element is an equal absurdity." It is absurd because

> If you do not use shapes and colours characteristic of your environment, you will only use some others characteristic more or less of somebody else's environment, and certainly no better. (BLAST 2, 45)

The artist works with shapes and forms, and it is impossible, whether or not it is desirable, to avoid using shapes which suggest objects in the material world. He repeats this over and again: "everything is representation, in one sense, even in the most 'abstract' painting" (BLAST 2, 45).

Lewis did not, however, advocate a naturalistic representation of the material world. He called imitative realism "an absurd and gloomy waste of time" (BLAST 2, 45). He advocated a synthesis of, or creative interplay between, abstraction and representation:

> We must constantly strive to ENRICH abstraction till it is almost plain life, or rather to get deeply enough immersed in material life to experience the shaping power amongst its vibrations, and to accentuate and perpetuate these. (BLAST 2, 40)

For Lewis, the key to art is its shaping power or formal organization. But it does not therefore follow that one must try to use forms without representational content, because it is the material world which suggests to the artist the shapes and forms he paints. Vorticist art is therefore not abstract in the sense of non-representational; the only sense in which it is abstract is that the Vorticist artist wants to extract or abstract the meaning or essence of his subject.

Lewis's cityscapes, for example, works such as *New York, The Crowd,* and *Workshop,* are not paintings of any particular location. Certainly to a beholder of 1914 they must have seemed completely abstract, just as Kandinsky's *Improvisations* seemed abstract to Lewis. But the shapes on the canvas ineluctably suggest modern buildings (and, in *The Crowd*, people in and around buildings), and virtually every other aspect of the paintings supports that suggestion.

These paintings try to represent the essence of the modern city which for Lewis can be seen in its huge, cold buildings, its seeming dynamism and activity and yet simultaneous deadness and inhumanity. Lewis wanted to express the mood of his urban subject as much as its appearance, but he would have argued that this mood is a function of that subject, not a projection of the artist.

This brief analysis could be extended to the work of the other Vorticists. Their work retained a subject, and they sought to express or represent the essence of that subject, using formal means inherited from Cubism and Futurism, and like those movements never renouncing the subject. This might not have been the *synthesis* of abstraction and representation Lewis desired; it might have been only an uneasy balancing act between them, but this balancing act, in my view, is central to Vorticism. Vorticism has no great importance in the development of abstraction: at least five separate groups on the continent were ahead of it and other movements pursued abstraction with more dedication and rigor. Its originality lies in that, among those who arrived at total abstraction (as it did sporadically), it was the first movement to turn back, retaining subject matter and developing a theory of representation concerned not with illusionistic representation but with schematic or diagrammatic representation.

Pound in his September 1914 essay, "Vorticism," is more explicit than Lewis about his Vorticist attitude towards subject matter. The center of his discussion is an elaborate analogy borrowed from mathematics. (I do not answer for Pound's mathematics.) After saying that Vorticism is "an intensive art," he says that mathematical expressions can be ranked according to intensity. Arithmetic contents itself with statements of fact such as $3^2 + 4^2 = 5^2$. This is true about itself, but does not say anything about any other numbers. A more intensive statement is $a^2 + b^2 = c^2$ because this applies to a lot of facts. More intense yet is to say that these equations govern the ratios of the length of the sides of a right-angle triangle. Pound compares this level of intensiveness to art criticism as it involves criticism of form, but not its creation (*G-B*, 91).

The final level of intensity is reached in analytical geometry. A statement that the equation $(x-a)^2 + (y-b)^2 = r^2$ governs the circle is not a statement about a particular circle but "any circle and all circles." This analytical statement is the form or essence of the circle itself. Pound then claims that "the difference between art and analytical geometry is the difference of subject-matter only" (*G-B*, 91). Great works of art similarly "cause form to come into being" (*G-B*, 92). They do not treat the accidental appearance of their subject, but its analytic form.

Pound's language differs from Lewis's, but there is an underlying agreement between them on the relationship between Vorticist art and its subject matter. This position is distinct from abstraction and is as uniquely Vorticist as the dynamic formism discussed above. Dynamic formism is Vorticism's synthesis of Cubism and Futurism; this theory of analytic intensity is its synthesis of the representationalism of these movements and Kandinsky's expressive abstractions.

To use the word synthesis is, however, to accept Vorticism's valuation of itself. If one looks at Vorticism from the standpoint of Cubism or that of Kandinsky, one is far more likely to say that Vorticism simply missed the point of the movements it sought to criticize. And it must be admitted that Lewis, obstinately bent on defining Vorticism *against* the other *isms*, could be extremely reductive in his presentation of other movements. His discussion of Picasso's constructions, collages and *papiers-collés* in "Relativism and Picasso's Latest Work" in BLAST 1 is an excellent case in point. These works were exploring an area of profound interest for Lewis and Vorticism, the possibilities of non-illusionistic representation.[13] But Lewis could only see that Picasso was blurring the distinction between art and life which was of such importance for Lewis. For this reason he utterly rejected these works of Picasso's, whereas someone with the same aesthetic stance but a greater interest in finding allies could have easily found things to praise in these seminal works.

This does not deny the originality of Vorticism; instead, it explains what impelled that originality. Lewis was never comfortable sharing any common ground with anyone, fearful that this would compromise his integrity. This is, one must note, a very curious frame of mind for the leader of a movement, and there was a movement of sympathy towards and identification with other art (and artists) foreign to Lewis running through Vorticism, found, for example, in Pound's criticism and in the Vorticist sculptors' primitivism. But Lewis's attitude dominated just as Lewis dominated Vorticism, which makes it ironic that Richard Cork and others should value and study Vorticism for the extent to which it anticipated and led to the purely abstract art that followed. Yet it is understandable that Cork would try to increase the visibility of Vorticism by ascribing to it an important role in the development of abstraction. For what did it lead to? Why should we study it today?

Lewis put out only two issues of BLAST. Vorticist art was exhibited in one group show in London and one in New York and then ceased to be produced. Gaudier-Brzeska died in the war. Epstein returned to a traditional style of portraiture. Most of the others retreated in style and were forgotten. Lewis turned primarily to figure painting which led to a series of masterful portraits in the 1920s and 1930s which are in my opinion Lewis's greatest paintings. These are also his influential works, for they helped to perpetuate a tradition of English figure painting which blossomed after 1945 in the work of such London-based artists as Michael Ayrton, Francis Bacon, David Hockney, R. B. Kitaj, and Frank Auerbach. Lewis welcomed what he saw of these painters, the work of Ayrton and Bacon, and arguably both his work and that of David Bomberg had an influence on them. But these figure paintings are quite removed from the concerns of Vorticism. Vorticism in art, we must conclude, was largely still-born, a promising movement killed by the war, that more imposing blast of 1914.

But what is lost in Cork's (or any) art historical view of Vorticism is that it was not just a movement in painting and sculpture but a program for all the arts. As Pound put it, "we wished a designation that would be equally applicable to a certain basis for all the arts. Obviously you cannot have 'cubist' poetry or 'imagist' painting" (*G-B*, 81). That this was not just Pound's personal notion is shown by Lewis's inclusion of literature, including his own play *Enemy of the Stars*, in BLAST. Lewis conceived of this play as the literary equivalent to his own painting, his attempt to show writers the way to a truly modern literature.[14]

Vorticism was not the isolated and abortive movement it might seem to be to an art historian, for its impact and influence was primarily on Modernist literature, not on the visual arts. Its detached modernism and willingness to use past styles showed Pound how to reconcile his "passéism" and his modernism. This reconciliation leads directly to the Modernist "mythic method" and the creative relationship the major Modernists had with past works of art. Moreover, the dynamic formism Vorticism advocated and represented became a formal pattern underlying central works of Modernist literature. Finally, Lewis's attack on narrative conventions in *Enemy of the Stars* prefigures later, more successful attacks by Eliot, Pound and Joyce.

I obviously cannot show all of this in detail, so I must let one representative moment suffice. Yeats's *A Vision*, in brief, is the delineation of a system of geometric patterns, predominantly gyres or vortices. At times Yeats claims that in the dynamic interaction of these gyres the essence of human history and personality is represented. But in his introduction to *A Vision*, "A Packet for Ezra Pound," Yeats displays a rather different attitude towards the content of *A Vision*:

> Some will ask whether I believe in the actual existence of my circuits of sun and moon. . . . To such a question I can but answer that if sometimes, overwhelmed by miracle as all men must be when in the midst of it, I have taken such periods literally, my reason has soon recovered; and now that the system stands out in my imagination I regard them as stylistic arrangements of experience comparable to the cubes in the drawing of Wyndham Lewis and to the ovoids in the sculpture of Brancusi.[15]

A Vision, then, is a system of geometric but dynamic forms which Yeats conceives of as comparable to the forms of Vorticist and other Modernist art, and which function as the kind of intensive analytics Pound prescribed as the Vorticist ideal. Modernist literature is full of these diagrams and of concrete images which represent them—axles embedded in mud, roses in steel dust, Chinese ideograms—which try to represent essential patterns as dynamic forms in a way parallel to and indebted to the forms of Vorticist art. The Vorticist program or ideal to a large extent becomes the ideal of Modernist literature in English.

Lewis moves away from this concern with representing forms like vortices in his painting, but, in a key passage in his 1922 "Essay on the Objective of Plastic Art in Our Time," the image of the vortex reappears in his thinking about art in a new and striking way. He quotes from what he calls "Schopenhauer's eloquent and resounding words" about art in *The World as Will and Idea*:

> While science, following the unresting and inconstant stream of the fourfold forms of reason and consequent, with each end attained sees further, and can never reach a final goal nor attain full satisfaction, any more than by running we can reach the place where the clouds touch the horizon; art, on the contrary, is everywhere at its goal. For it plucks the object of its contemplation out of the stream of the world's course, and has it isolated before it. . . . It therefore pauses at this particular thing; the course of time stops; the relations vanish

for it; only the essential, the Idea, is its object.[16]

Lewis calls this "a splendid description" of what art does. The result is that a "sort of immortality descends upon these objects. It is an immortality, which, in the case of the painting, they have to pay for with death, or at least with its coldness and immobility."[17]

Lewis here redefines the vortex in a manner which suggests the design of his major novels. Art plucks its subject out of life's stream, and analyzes it while it spins to a stop. That passage out of time, from the vitality of life to the deadness of art, is figured forth time and again in Lewis's novels (and his portraits). Groups of characters are isolated and analyzed while their doomed world slowly grinds to a halt. Characteristically, his novels end where they begin (Lady Fredigonde Follett's, Percy Hardcaster's Spanish prison), but with major characters dead and all possible motion blocked. Everything has seized up and the objects of Lewis's scrutiny have attained an immortality which they have paid for with death or its coldness and immobility.

This general pattern, of course, is merely that, and is not rigidly executed in all of Lewis's novels. But the fact that this pattern does shape *The Apes of God*, *The Revenge for Love*, and *Self Condemned* exemplifies both the impact of Vorticism on literature and the tenacity of a kind of Vorticism in Lewis's work. Vorticism did give rise to the Great English Art envisioned in BLAST, despite its short life and the dispersal of the London Vortex, but that art was not painting, the art for which Lewis was trained, but literature, that which he adopted and in which he ultimately did his greatest work.

---

1. Forrest Read, ed., *Pound/Joyce: The Letters of Ezra Pound to James Joyce, with Pound's Essays on Joyce* (New York: New Directions, 1970), p. 26; Hugh Kenner reprints the advertisement from *The Egoist* in *The Pound Era* (London: Faber & Faber, 1975), p. 237.
2. BLAST 1, p. 143 (1914; reprinted, Santa Barbara: Black Sparrow Press, 1981). All subsequent references will be incorporated parenthetically thus: (BLAST 1, 143).
3. Pound included this esay in *Gaudier-Brzeska: A Memoir* (New York: New Directions, 1970), p. 90. Subsequent references will be incorporated parenthetically: (G-B, 90).
4. Umbro Apollonio, ed., *Futurismo* (Milano: Mazzotta, 1970), p. 90. This invaluable and convenient collection of Futurist manifestos is available in an uneven translation in English, *Futurist Manifestos*, trans. Robert Brain et al. (New York: Viking, 1973). I have reworked their translation here.
5. Apollonio, *Futurist Manifestos*, p. 46.
6. The Futurist manifesto "Contra Venezia passatista" has been reprinted in Luigi Scrivo, *Sintesi del futurismo: storia e documenti* (Roma: Bulzoni, 1968), pp. 15-16; for the other remarks, see Apollonio, *Futurist Manifestos*, pp. 21 and 203.
7. An earlier version of this essay used the term "dynamic formalism." This sounds much better, but it was pointed out to me that the term is intended to refer to a concern with dynamic form, not with being dynamically formal, whatever that would be.
8. Richard Cork, *Vorticism and Abstract Art in the First Machine Age*, 2 vols. (Berkeley: Univ. of California Press, 1976), p. 392. This is perhaps the place to say that my various criticisms of Cork's study should not conceal my indebtedness to it; virtually every work of art mentioned here is reproduced and discussed by Cork.
9. The dating of Kandinsky's first abstract work is a matter of some controversy, which, however, does not affect my argument. See Rose-Carol Washton Long, "Kandinsky and Abstraction: The Role of the Hidden Image," *Artforum* 10, No. 10 (1972): 42-49.
10. Cork, from the unpaginated introduction.
11. In the introduction to the exhibition catalogue, *Abstract Art in England 1913-1915* (London, 1969), p. 6. Though exhibiting exactly the same group of artists that Cork calls Vorticist, d'Offay rejects the Lewis-centered term Vorticism, preferring to speak of "the abstract movement." William C. Wees and Timothy Materer also see Vorticism as essentially abstract, with exceptions; see Wees, *Vorticism and the English Avant-Garde* (Toronto: Univ. of Toronto Press, 1972), pp. 151 and 154, and Materer, *Vortex: Pound, Eliot, and Lewis* (Ithaca: Cornell Univ. Press, 1979), p. 87.
12. See Will Grohmann, *Wassily Kandinsky: Life and Work* (New York: Abrams, 1958), p. 128.
13. Clement Greenberg writes of Picasso and Braque having to "choose *between* illusion and representation," in his essay "Collage," reprinted in his *Art and Culture* (Boston: Beacon Press, 1961), p. 77.
14. Wyndham Lewis, *Rude Assignment* (London: Hutchinson, 1950), p. 129.
15. W. B. Yeats, *A Vision* (London: Macmillan, 1962), pp. 24-25. This passage is in the revised version of 1937, not the original of 1925; "A Packet for Ezra Pound" was first published separately in 1929.
16. Arthur Schopenhauer, *The World as Will and Idea*, trans. R. B. Haldane and J. Kemp (London, 1896), p. 239. This seems to be Lewis's text as well; he quotes what I do here, but not in order.
17. Walter Michel and C. J. Fox, ed., *Wyndham Lewis on Art: Collected Writings 1913-1956* (New York: Funk & Wagnalls, 1969), p. 208.

WILLIAM C. WEES

WYNDHAM LEWIS AND VORTICISM

In 1914 Wyndham Lewis devoted much of his time to what he described as his "undeniable political activity." In the space of half a year Lewis directed London's new Rebel Art Centre, led a widely reported campaign against the Italian Futurists, and edited and made most of the major contributions to BLAST, *Review of the Great English Vortex*. These activities attracted attention—exactly the purpose of art politics—and won for Lewis a reputation as, in the words of the *Daily News* (7 April 1914), "the extremely able leader of the Cubist movement in England."

Lewis's sly self-caricature in *Blasting and Bombardiering* describes "Mr. W.L., Leader of the 'Great London Vortex,'" who discovered in himself the "romantic figure [who] must always emerge to captain the 'group.'" In accordance with his role, he never passed up a chance to explain in articles, interviews and manifestos, "why life had to be changed, and how." "'Kill John Bull with Art!' I shouted. And John and Mrs. Bull leapt for joy, in a cynical convulsion. For they felt as safe as houses. So did I."[1] Exciting and inconsequential—Lewis's role as leader seemed little more than that, when measured strictly in political terms. Nevertheless, without the urge to captain a group, Lewis might not have produced the public pronouncements that were, certainly, propaganda for himself and his group. The pronouncements were critical and aesthetic documents as well, and they emerged from a concerted effort to find new art forms appropriate to the new times.

BLAST was the major document. It was the Vorticist group's statement, not Lewis's alone. In fact, it was one of the fruits of a four-year transformation of the English art world that had begun with Roger Fry's "Manet and the Post-Impressionists" exhibition in November 1910.

In 1910, as the art critic Frank Rutter said at the time, "Art in Paris had entered upon a stage practically unknown to us in Britain."[2] Two years later, however, at Fry's "Second Post-Impressionist Exhibition" there was an "English Group" including some English artists as "advanced" as any in Paris. December 1913 saw a large exhibition of "Post-Impressionists, Cubists and Others" at Brighton, with a separate "Cubist Room" for eight of the exhibiting artists. Most of those eight joined Wyndham Lewis at the Rebel Art Centre when it opened in April 1914.

Intended as a crafts workshop, atelier, gallery and lecture hall, the Rebel Art Centre in reality was little more than a meeting place for some of the English Cubists, who were soon calling themselves Vorticists. This group included Edward Wadsworth, Frederick Etchells, Cuthbert Hamilton, Lawrence Atkinson, William Roberts, Jessie Dismorr, Helen Saunders, Henri Gaudier-Brzeska, Wyndham Lewis and Ezra Pound. It was Pound who first applied the label "Vortex" to their particular phase of English Cubism, and in July 1914, BLAST appeared, defining and illustrating Vorticism as a movement in its own right.

"We worked separately, we found an underlying agreement, we decided to stand together," Pound said of the group.[3] "To stand together" was a political way of talking, and characteristic of a time when "avant-garde" had not lost all of its military connotations, when "revolutionary" or "anarchical" art was still regarded as a political threat to the Establishment, when "militant" was as readily applied to artists as to suffragettes, when artists joined "conspiracies" and "putsches," had "headquarters" and issued "manifestos." The format and predominant tone of BLAST derived from that state of the arts in England, and the way Pound, Lewis and others talked about Vorticism was strongly shaped by it.

The Vorticists' "underlying agreement" revealed itself in the strikingly similar phrases they used to convey their sense of intense artistic expression: "a mental-emotive impulse" (Lewis), "an intellectual and emotional complex" (Pound), "a vast intellectual emotion" (Gaudier-Brzeska). It appeared in the images with which they characterized art they admired: "sharpness and rigidity" (Gaudier), "hard light, clear edges" (Pound), "rigid reflections of stone and steel" (Lewis). It expressed itself most powerfully in the visual and literary styles of the movement, and in the theory and criticism included in BLAST.

The essence of the Vorticists' visual style lay in the kind of solutions those artists found to the problem of formally unifying abstract, geometrical shapes. The most forceful solutions came from Lewis, who had been working on the problem since 1911 or 1912. Lewis brought to his work an Expressionist fascination with strange, stark pictures with powerful psychological overtones; a Futurist desire to shatter his subjects into interpenetrating fragments locked together by dynamic "force-lines"; a Cubist refusal to make more than minimal reference to anything outside the picture's own formal, abstract framework. Perhaps the first fully successful synthesizing of these predilections appeared in his *Timon of Athens* drawings of 1912. There Lewis integrated mask-like faces, stylized limbs, truncated bodies, arcs, lines and wedges, to produce abstract designs with representational details. By the end of 1913, some of Lewis's work eschewed representational elements entirely.

In the "Cubist Room" at Brighton and in subsequent exhibitions of 1914 and 1915, he showed a number of totally abstract pictures. Interlocking lines, arcs, triangles, rectangles and other geometric forms drawn with mechanical precision and painted with flat, low-keyed hues (when colour appeared at all) had become characteristic of all the Vorticists' work by the time they exhibited together at the "Vorticists' Exhibition" in June 1915. But only Lewis seemed fully capable of conveying what the *Athenaeum* (19 June 1915) called "systems of interacting movement" and the "clash of opposing forces." In Lewis's work, the meeting and interpenetrating of abstract, geometric elements reshaped and energized the spaces they defined, so that the whole design and all of its parts, seemed forever locked in conflict, or in a highly aggressive embrace. Combat, dance and courtship had often served as subject matter for Lewis's pre-Vorticist pictures, and they continued to be reference points or analogies for the brutal and delicate, passionate and coolly precise relationships implicit in his abstract, Vorticist work.

Similar preoccupations were at work when Lewis tried to produce a literary counterpart to the Vorticist visual style. The diction and layout of BLAST's manifesto grew out of Lewis's efforts to bring literature up to the front ranks of the "visual revolution." Gaudier-Brzeska's "Vortex" essay in BLAST 1, and Pound's "Dogmatic Statement on the Game and Play of Chess (Theme for a Series of Pictures)" in BLAST 2, were also contributions to that effort, but the *pièce de résistance* of literary Vorticism was Lewis's "Enemy of the Stars" in the first issue of BLAST.

In that violent closet drama, character, setting and action emerge in glimpses and fragments. A characteristic passage presents a fight (strongly suggestive of the combat relationships in Lewis's visual art) between Argol and his disciple Hanp:

> Flushes on silk epiderm and fierce card-play of fists between them: emptying of "hand" on soft flesh-table.
>
> Arms of grey windmills, grinding anger on stone of the new heart.
>
> Messages from one to another, dropped down anywhere when nobody is looking, reaching brain by telegraph: most desolating and alarming messages possible.
>
> The attacker rushed in drunk with blows. They rolled, swift jagged rut, into one corner of shed: large insect scuttling roughly to hiding.
>
> Stopped astonished. (BLAST 1, 75)

The action and language are violent, but individual moments of action are strangely isolated and static. Events are broken down and reconstructed like the interrelated fragments in Vorticist pictures.

No single work, except BLAST itself, fully expressed the whole set of attitudes that constituted Vorticist doctrine. With its pinkish-purple cover crossed diagonally by the single word "BLAST" in three-and-one-quarter-inch-high black letters, its 160 nearly folio-sized pages of unusually heavy paper, its thick, blocky print, some of which was larger than newspaper headlines, its manifesto of "blasts" and "blesses," and its generally aggressive tone, BLAST 1 seemed exceedingly brash and in bad taste. Its sense of humour ("great barbarous weapon," as the manifesto called it) mixed with a tone of righteous indignation, gave BLAST the mien of a modern barbarian bent upon destroying an old, weak, decadent civilization. In the spirit of Nietzsche's declaration, "This universe is a monster of energy without beginning or end, a fixed and brazen quality of energy," BLAST set about establishing a new, virile civilization based on hardness, violence, and the worship of energy. "Will Energy some day reach Earth like violent civilization, smashing or hardening all?" Lewis asked in "Enemy of the Stars." BLAST was meant to be a harbinger of that Energy pursuing its self-appointed mission of, in Lewis's words, "blowing away dead ideas and worn-out notions."

The Vorticists intended to build—or rebuild—as well as destroy, and they regarded England as the proper site for their constructive efforts. "The Modern World is due almost entirely to Anglo-Saxon genius— its appearance and its spirit," they announced in their manifesto. "Machinery, trains, steam-ships, all that distinguishes externally our time, came far more from here than anywhere else." English artists should be the best equipped to bring "the forms of machinery" into modern art, for the English "are the inventors of this bareness and hardness, and should be the great enemies of Romance." By this line of argument the Vorticists accomplished two things at once. They emphasized the Englishness (and hence, uniqueness) of their movement, and they linked their movement—whether they intended to or not— with T. E. Hulme's crusade against softness, empathy, and other expressions of the "Romantic" point of view.

The Vorticists exceeded Hulme, however, in their invocation of a great, primitive "Art instinct" that used machinery for its models of "bareness and hardness." "Vorticism accepted the machine world," Lewis said later. "It sought out machine-forms."[4] In fact, in BLAST 2 Lewis insisted that all modern artists should strive to express "something of the fatality, grandeur and efficiency of a machine." The perfect Vorticist machine was the dynamo, whose work goes on out of sight, beneath a hard, implacable exterior. Internally dynamic and energy-producing, externally calm—that was the impression aimed for in Vorticist art, and evoked by the image of the Vortex appearing several times in the pages of BLAST 1: a solid cone whirling on an unshakeable axis, a symbol of primordial energy harnessed by the intellect and by art.

The broadest implications of the Vortex led to the division of all art into two categories essentially parallel to Hulme's "abstract" or "Classical" (of which the Vorticists approved) and "empathetic" or "Romantic" (of which they did not). Anything clear-cut, hard, rigid, and uncompromising gained the Vorticists' approval; conversely, blurred lines, softness, flexibility, and compromise were rejected and ridiculed. Speed, mass education, democracy, and all forms of sentimentality were attacked because they, too, seemed to blur lines of distinction and break down rigid demarcations.

Of all the Vorticists, Lewis was the most uncompromising. He praised the "disciplined, blunt, thick and brutal" designs he found in a display of German woodcuts, and he referred admiringly to the "savage" artist who prefers to "reduce his Great Art down to the simple black human bullet," rather than risk "dissolv[ing] in vagueness of space." Lewis prescribed a "course of egoistic hardening" for artists to save them from the diluting effects of a social life where men "overlap" and "intersect" and where "promiscuity is normal." "The Vorticist does not suck up to Life," Lewis proclaimed. The Vorticist uses "Life" for his "brothel," so that he can keep himself "pure for non-life, that is Art."

Lewis's "Vortex" was a whirling, arrogant monster of energy: "Our Vortex is fed up with your dispersals, reasonable chicken-men. Our Vortex is proud of its polished sides. Our Vortex will not hear of anything but its disastrous polished dance," Lewis wrote in BLAST 1. This Vortex symbolized the "Art instinct" that expressed itself in a few, distinct cultures. England, with its "iron Jungle [of] the great modern city," was one of those cultures, and Vorticist art, with its "rigid reflections of stone and steel," fulfilled the vigorous demands of the Vortex.

Lewis might have continued to think and work along these lines had war not broken out in August 1914. At first, he regarded the war as simply another expression of the Vortex, and, in itself, unlikely to change his own theory and practice of Vorticism. He wrote in BLAST 2, "All art that matters is already so far ahead that it is beyond the sphere of these disturbances." With equal confidence he promised that BLAST would accompany England into a postwar world of an even "more ardent gaiety." But no more issues of BLAST appeared, and while some of the Vorticists continued to work in the pre-war Vorticist style, Lewis rejected that style when he produced his war paintings and drawings, and he never returned to it. "The geometrics which had interested me so exclusively before, I now felt were bleak and empty," he said. "They wanted *filling*."[5] He had even deserted the Vorticist literary style by the time he published BLAST 2 in 1915 and *Tarr* in 1916. After writing "Enemy of the Stars" he concluded that "words and syntax were not susceptible of transformation into abstract terms, to which process the visual arts lent themselves quite readily."[6]

Some Vorticist ideas continued to be central to Lewis's concerns, but the Vorticist visual and literary styles were not. He just as decisively rejected his "leader" role after a brief regrouping with some of the pre-war Vorticists and a few other artists for the "Group X" exhibition in the spring of 1920. There was, in fact, no longer a movement for Lewis to lead.

"In the early stages of this movement," Lewis once wrote of Vorticism, "we undoubtedly did sacrifice ourselves as painters to the necessity to reform *de fond en comble* the world in which a picture must exist.... In the heat of this pioneer action we were even inclined to forget *the picture* altogether in favour of *the frame*...."[7] Though unfair, perhaps, to Vorticist art, Lewis's emphasis on the social commitment of Vorticism is proper. No matter how advanced an art movement may seem to be, no matter how new its art forms, it can make no serious claim to relevance unless it is bound, at some irrevocable point, to society. If it be truly avant-garde, the movement's reference points will be images of the future society embedded in the present one. The avant-garde movement will not so much lead the society, as show that society the direction it is going. Lewis believed that Vorticism had produced images of "a new civilization." The problem was to teach people how to see them. "It was more than just picture-making," he said; "one was manufacturing fresh eyes for people, and fresh souls to go with the eyes"[8]—which is to be political in the profoundest sense of that term.

1. Wyndham Lewis, *Blasting and Bombardiering* (London: Eyre and Spottiswoode, 1937; republished London: Calder and Boyars, 1967), pp. 32 and 36.
2. Frank Rutter, *Revolution in Art* (London: Art News Press, 1910), p. 46.
3. Ezra Pound, "Vorticism," *Fortnightly Review,* 573 (Sept. 1, 1914): 471.
4. Wyndham Lewis, *Wyndham Lewis the Artist: From 'Blast' to Burlington House* (London: Laidlaw and Laidlaw, 1939), p. 78.
5. Wyndham Lewis, *Rude Assignment: A Narrative of My Career Up-to-date* (London: Hutchinson, 1950), p. 129.
6. Ibid.
7. Wyndham Lewis, "Plain Home-Builder: Where Is Your Vorticist?" *Architectural Review,* 76 (November 1934): 156.
8. Lewis, *Rude Assignment,* p. 125.

MICHÈLE POLI

BLAST

BLAST connut l'existence éphémère des petites revues de son époque: en effet, deux numéros seulement parurent à un an d'intervalle, l'un en juin 1914, quelques semaines seulement avant la déclaration de guerre, l'autre en juillet 1915. Baroque, insolite et insolente, BLAST représente le type même du «canular» sérieux et, quelque soixante ans après sa naissance, sa verve et sa vigueur surprennent encore. La revue a le charme un peu irritant des enfants terribles et reflète la personnalité de Lewis jeune: rédacteur en chef, il se présente aussi comme le principal animateur du groupe des Vorticistes et le véhément défenseur d'une esthétique neuve opposée à l'académisme moribond d'une Angleterre encore engourdie dans un siècle révolu.

BLAST apporta à Lewis une soudaine célébrité. Lorsqu'il revint à Londres en 1909, après avoir étudié la peinture dans les capitales européennes, sa renommée dépassait peu les limites étroites d'une avant-garde littéraire et artistique où figuraient en bonne place Ezra Pound et les poètes imagistes, le philosophe bergsonien T. E. Hulme, théoricien complaisant des nouvelles conceptions esthétiques. Dans les réceptions qu'organisait Mrs. Kebblewhite en l'honneur de ce dernier, Lewis pouvait rencontrer des peintres dont les idées s'apparentaient avec les siennes: Spencer Gore, Harold Gilman, C. R. Nevinson et les sculpteurs Epstein et Gaudier-Brzeska. Depuis 1911, sa propre peinture s'orientait de plus en plus vers le cubisme. Il commençait à exposer ses œuvres et s'enorgueillissait de voir son ami Augustus John acquérir l'une de ses toiles. Il participait en 1911 à l'exposition post-impressionniste organisée par Roger Fry à la galerie Grafton, y présentait des tableaux abstraits et une série d'illustrations pour une édition de *Timon d'Athènes* qui allait paraître en portfolio en 1913. Il avait terminé en 1912 la décoration d'une boîte de nuit à la mode récemment ouverte par la seconde épouse de Strindberg, «The Cave of the Golden Calf». C'est dans cet antre de l'intelligentsia que, sous l'œil amusé de Ford Madox Hueffer: «les jeunes» allaient bientôt s'exercer aux danses vorticistes, le Turkey Trot et le Bunny Hug. En février 1914, la Comtesse Drogheda ouvrait à ses amis une salle à manger fraîchement décorée par les soins de Lewis, travail dont il semble avoir été satisfait puisqu'il figure en photographie parmi les illustrations de BLAST.

Ce faisant, Lewis cherchait à se rapprocher des artistes avec lesquels il se sentait le plus d'affinités et faisait partie des membres fondateurs du Camden Town Group qui rassemblait également Gilman, Sickert, John et Gore. Bien qu'il se tînt résolument à l'écart du milieu de Bloomsbury auquel appartenait Roger Fry, il entretenait avec ce dernier une correspondance suivie depuis 1912 et, lorsqu'en juillet de l'année suivante, Fry ouvrit ses Ateliers Omega, il participa à leurs activités. Moyennant un salaire modique mais régulier, les Ateliers Omega offraient aux artistes des travaux de décoration, de mobilier, d'étoffes et d'intérieurs. Les relations entre Fry et Lewis se détériorèrent très vite. Les deux hommes s'étaient heurtés dès 1912 sur le montant des commissions que Fry eût dû verser à Lewis à la suite de la seconde exposition post-impressionniste en septembre 1913; Lewis et Gore accusèrent Fry d'avoir commis une nouvelle indélicatesse à leur égard. En octobre, Lewis, Cuthbert, Hamilton, Edward Wadsworth et Frederick Etchells offrirent leur démission aux Ateliers Omega en expliquant leur mécontentement dans une lettre circulaire. A ces quatre amis liés par une même rébellion vint s'adjoindre peu de temps après le peintre C. R. W. Nevinson. Tous présentèrent leurs œuvres dans la «salle cubiste» de «l'Exposition des Post-Impressionnistes, Cubistes et autres» d'origine anglaise qui se tint à Brighton à la fin de 1913. Le catalogue de cette exposition comporte une note rédigée de la main de Lewis qui définit le groupe d'artistes auquel il appartenait alors comme «une île vertigineuse sans être exotique dans l'archipel placide et respectable de l'art anglais». Filant sa métaphore géographique, il constatait que «cette formation [était] sans conteste volcanique de par sa matière et son origine».

C'est en mars 1914 que ces mêmes artistes s'associaient pour fonder le «Rebel Art Centre» ou «Centre Cubiste» dont Lewis devint directeur et dont les fonds furent fournis par le peintre Kate Lechmere, amie de Lewis. Les prospectus annonçaient des conférences sur l'Imagisme par Pound, le Futurisme par Marinetti, chef de file du groupe milanais, la musique par Schoenberg et Scriabine. Le Centre se proposait d'offrir également des cours artistiques dans un esprit comparable à celui qui animait les ateliers des grands peintres de la Renaissance. Ce centre dont l'existence n'excéda pas quatre mois servit de lieu de rencontre à Lewis et ses amis et de ce fait favorisa la naissance de BLAST.

Conçu originellement comme moyen de faire connaître la peinture post-impressionniste, BLAST s'ouvrira très vite à la sculpture sous l'égide de Gaudier-Brzeska et à la nouvelle poésie avec Pound. Sa conception donna lieu à moult réunions et réjouissances dont un thé dans le studio de Lewis où une violente querelle força C. R. W. Nevinson à battre une retraite précipitée. C'est pendant cette réunion que fut dressée la liste des «Blasted» et «Blessed» dont nous parlerons plus loin. Des cartons d'invitations annonçaient peu après un soirée BLAST durant laquelle «le manifeste de l'Art des rebelles sera[it] lu avec accompagnement de trompettes soigneusement choisies». Enfin un dîner dans un restaurant de Percy Street, «The Eiffel Tower», devait permettre aux convives d'admirer une nouvelle décoration intérieure dûe au futur rédacteur en chef.

La naissance de BLAST est donc liée à la création du «Rebel Art Centre»; elle semble s'être accomplie dans une atmosphère allègre et chaotique. Pourtant les textes que rédigeait Lewis durant cette période témoignent de la force de conviction qu'il accordait à son projet. Création collective, confluent de discussions souvent houleuses entre amis animés d'idéaux voisins, BLAST n'en demeura pas moins l'œuvre de Lewis. Pound pourra écrire à l'artiste Gladys Hynes: «Il est certain que W.L. a créé le Vorticisme. C'est à lui seul que nous devons l'existence de BLAST».

D'ailleurs les contemporains de Lewis identifieront si bien la revue avec son créateur que l'effet de scandale qu'elle produira lors de sa parution rejaillira essentiellement sur lui. BLAST faisait naître une sourde inquiétude qui n'épargnait même pas les hommes politiques. Le premier ministre Asquith que Lewis rencontra alors dans des soirées mondaines interrogeait négligemment le chef de file des Vorticistes sur les mystérieuses activités de son groupe.

Peut-être avait-il peine à imaginer que les convictions artistiques pussent seules engendrer une telle ferveur séditieuse. En fait, Lewis pourra dire que «toute cette effervescence organisée, c'était les arts qui se comportaient comme s'ils étaient de la politique».

BLAST visait à l'effet de choc par son titre même. *Blast*—l'explosion d'une bombe, la déflagration qui, prophétiquement, en précédait de plus mortelles. «Blast! Blast it!», c'était aussi le juron gaillard et irrévérencieux lancé à la face des Philistins. Dans sa présentation, la revue semblait vouloir remettre en cause toutes les traditions de l'édition. Ses dimensions l'apparentaient à un annuaire téléphonique, objet maniable et usuel dont la familiarité bonhomme était démentie par la couverture. Sur un fond violet-prune, à la fois franc et raffiné, s'étalait grassement un titre largement déployé en diagonale. BLAST suggère l'art de l'affiche contemporaine: nombre de pages consacrées aux manifestes et déclarations de principes, ornées d'une typographie gigantesque, ponctuées du signe du Vortex (tourbillon d'hélice ou turbine stylisée) rappellent autant de placards publicitaires. Cette typographie généreuse, ludique, d'un narcissisme insolent séduit encore tant elle révèle d'humour ainsi qu'un amour artisanal du détail matériel. Rien ici du bon goût feutré des périodiques habituels de l'époque, rien non plus qui suggère la maigreur des moyens financiers. Un épais papier rêche où figurent les textes contraste avec les feuillets glacés qui présentent des illustrations en noir et blanc d'une qualité acceptable. Publié par John Lane à Londres, BLAST était imprimé en banlieue, à Harlesden, chez un artisan que Douglas Goldring, ami de Ford Madox Ford [Hueffer] et de Violet Hunt, avait été chargé de dénicher pour Lewis.

Annoncé comme périodique trimestriel dans le premier numéro, BLAST affirme sa parenté avec le «Rebel Art Centre» d'Ormond Street où Lewis se chargeait de l'écouler. Le studio de Pound, à Kensington, constituait un autre point de vente. Le second BLAST se contente d'annoncer deux autres numéros avant janvier qui ne verront jamais le jour. Il reflète des conditions d'existence difficiles, la maladie du rédacteur en chef au début de la guerre, le transfert des bureaux au 4 Phené Street, la perte d'une partie des archives de la revue.

BLAST 2, comme *The Egoist*, l'organe des Imagistes à la même époque, se refuse à adopter le ton martial ou nationaliste geignard. Les deux revues ont en commun le souci de proclamer la pérennité de l'art et de la littérature en dépit des à-coups de la politique internationale.

«Il se trouve qu'en tant qu'artiste», déclare Lewis,

je me situe à peu près là où se rencontrent et s'unissent la Probabilité et le Désir. Et il me semble qu'en ce qui concerne l'art, les choses en seront exactement au même point après la guerre qu'auparavant.

(I happen, as an artist, to be placed about where Probability and Desire harmoniously meet and mingle. And it seems to me that, as far as art is concerned, things will be exactly the same after the War as before it. [BLAST 2, 13])

Néanmoins le numéro de juillet 1915 porte l'empreinte du conflit qui secoue l'Europe. Sa présentation n'est plus aussi luxueuse que celle de son frère aîné et son ton est moin tonitruant. Sous la plume de Lewis, il devient en partie une sorte de méditation nerveuse sur la guerre. Le rédacteur en chef insiste sur la responsabilité de l'artiste de qui dépendra la renaissance d'un art plus vigoureux «lorsque l'Europe sera débarrassée de ses difficultés».

Nous ne cesserons pas de parler de la Culture lorsque la Guerre sera terminée».

(We will not stop talking about Culture when the War ends. [BLAST 2, 5])

Il envisage, avec un pessimisme malheureusement prophétique, une époque où les conflits mondiaux deviendraient une réalité permanente d'un caractère bien plus cynique et professionnel.

Cette saignée massive et soudaine est si impressionnante et consternante. Un filet de sang régulier, tout au long des années, d'abord dans un coin puis dans un autre, ne se remarquerait pas autant, et cependant le siècle écoulé, ces endroits respectifs auraient saigné tout autant.

(This blood-letting in mass, all at once, is so impressive and appalling. A steady dribble of blood, year by year, first in one corner and then in another, would not be noticed to the same extent, though at the end of a century it would have bled the respective areas as much. [BLAST 2, 15])

La sécheresse de ton de Lewis, dans l'ensemble des articles qui touchent à la guerre correspond sans nul doute à un désir de protection contre l'hystérie collective ou le sentimentalisme facile. Il lui semble indispensable de mettre la musique de Bach ou les écrits de Nietzsche à l'abri de la propagande nationaliste infantile. Bien que la guerre ne lui apparaisse pas comme un thème inférieur (pour lui, tous les thèmes se valent), il refuse l'optimisme béat qui attend d'un renouveau de conscience nationale ou d'un art engagé une moisson de chefs-d'œuvre. Son point de vue coincide ici exactement avec celui de Gaudier-Brzeska qui, dans un article rédigé dans les tranchées, rapporte son expérience de sculpteur confronté à une tragédie quotidienne:

Mes émotions naîtront seulement de *l'organisation des surfaces*, je présenterai mes émotions par l'organisation de mes surfaces, des plans et des figures qui les définissent.

(I SHALL DERIVE MY EMOTIONS SOLELY FROM THE ARRANGEMENT OF SURFACES, I shall present my emotions by the ARRANGEMENT OF SURFACES, THE PLANES AND LINES BY WHICH THEY ARE DEFINED. [BLAST 2, 34])

L'annonce de la mort de Gaudier-Brzeska, tué à Neuville-Saint-Vaast en juin 1915, qui suit cette déclaration ajoute une résonnance stoique à une affirmation de résistance esthétique.

Marqué par la guerre, le second BLAST constitue sans doute une mine de renseignements moins riche que le premier sur le mouvement vorticiste. Mais il est évident que le grand tourbillon dans lequel s'est engouffrée l'Europe n'a pas fait dévier Lewis et ses amis des principes énoncés un an auparavant. Bien au contraire, le signe du Vortex sous lequel ils se sont ralliés n'a jamais paru mieux choisi. C'était Ezra Pound, toujours inventif lorsqu'il s'agissait de baptiser une nouvelle formation littéraire, qui avait proposé cet emblème en mars ou avril 1914. Il avait déjà utilisé le symbole du Vortex quelques mois auparavant dans une lettre adressée au poète William Carlos Williams. L'arrangement et la pagination de BLAST indiquent clairement que la revue était sous presse lorsque le mot de Vortex y fut introduit.

Qui se rassemblait sous la bannière du Vortex? Lewis affirmera en 1956 qu'elle ne regroupait guère, en dehors de lui-même «que deux femmes et un ou deux hommes sur qui l'on pouvait compter». En fait, si nous nous reportons aux signatures apposées aux manifestes des Vorticistes, nous retrouvons certains membres fondateurs du «Rebel Art Centre»: Lewis, Hamilton et Wadsworth. S'y ajoutent Gaudier-Brzeska et Pound, W. Roberts, Jessie Dismorr et Helen Saunders (les deux éléments feminins auxquels Lewis fera allusion plus tard). D'autres signataires semblent avoir joué un rôle mineur de sympathisants. Ainsi le poète Richard Aldington, au demeurant fervent admirateur de BLAST, ne participa nullement à sa rédaction et continua à se déclarer Imagiste.

Le signe du Vortex semble en fait n'avoir guère eu

d'autre fonction que celle de métaphore et de révélateur commodes. Lewis et Pound en seront les plus ardents défenseurs. Gaudier-Brzeska jongle sans conviction avec ce vocable, le façonne et le déforme comme une boule de glaise.

Aussi plastique et malléable que puisse être le concept de Vortex, il recouvre cependant un ensemble d'opinions bien affirmées dont on peut suivre la permanence dans les deux numéros de BLAST. Les Vorticistes présentent la naissance d'un art national et désirent infléchir la direction dans laquelle celui-ci va s'engager.

«Nous sommes les premiers hommes d'un avenir qui ne s'est pas matérialisé. Nous appartenons à la «grande époque» qui n'a pas abouti», soupirera plus tard Lewis avec une amertume excessive. En 1914, il proclame que l'art doit avant tout s'appuyer sur l'individu ou le peuple. Dans son esprit, la notion de peuple exclut toute idée de paupérisme ou de classe spécifique. Le Vorticisme répugne à tout engagement politique et bannit aussi toute assimilation à une élite sociale ou culturelle: Honnis à tout jamais soient le gentleman et l'esthète! L'Angleterre pourtant accueillante à ces deux types humains, paraît offrir des conditions idéales pour qu'y fleurisse un art moderne. Elle a été jusqu'ici absorbée par une industrialisation rapide et d'ailleurs bénéfique. Mais, de ce fait, elle ne manifeste pas devant le monde de la machine le romantisme admiratif et béat qui caractérise, aux dires de Lewis, les peuples latins. La dureté des paysages industriels qu'elle a créés peut inspirer les artistes au même titre qu'une jungle tropicale ou des forêts américaines.

> La Volonté qui, en affrontant ses besoins, a déterminé la direction du monde moderne, a dressé des arbres d'acier là où la verdure faisait défaut.
>
> (. . . the Will that determined, face to face with its needs, the direction of the modern world, has reared up steel trees where the green ones were lacking. . . . [BLAST 1, 36])

De plus le goût du luxe, du sport, le snobisme, un amour mièvre de la nature domestiquée caractérisent la vie anglaise. Voilà bien ce qui peut provoquer chez ce primitif supérieur qu'est l'artiste, de saines réactions de rejet. Lewis affirme ainsi dans un paradoxe qui n'a rien d'absurde que le bon goût ambiant dans «l'architecture, le vêtement, l'ornement» n'est pas forcément favorable à l'épanouissement de l'artiste. Celui-ci risque de s'amollir dans l'harmonie, tandis qu'il se nourrit d' «un chaos d'imperfections, de discorde». Ainsi l'Angleterre, cette «Sibérie de l'esprit» doit, par contre-coup, engendrer un art raffiné. L'artiste qui choisit le Vortex pour emblème se situe au cœur même d'un mouvement dynamique qui accepte et exclut à la fois. C'est ainsi que même les erreurs d'une nation à laquelle il appartient, peuvent devenir pour lui fructueuses, tandis que ses vertus traditionnellement reconnues l'entravent et le handicapent. Ce n'est pas le «Non» tonitruant de Melville que le Vorticiste adresse au monde, il dit à la fois «Oui» et «Non». Il doit être habité par une conscience constante de la dualité. C'est dans ce domaine que les affirmations des Manifestes sont le plus convaincantes et le plus frappantes: «Nous sommes les mercenaires primitifs du monde moderne».

Les Vorticistes pourront donc se battre avec une égale vigueur dans des camps ennemis.

> Nous voudrions nous installer entre l'Action et la Réaction. . . .
> Nous voulons que l'Humour prenne l'Humour à la gorge.
>
> (Beyond Action and Reaction we would establish ourselves. . . .
> We set Humour at Humour's throat. [BLAST 1, 30–31])

Fidèles à ce principe les Vorticistes honnissent ce qu'ils déclarent adorer: la vérité pour eux coïncide avec un mouvement dialectique qui, indéfiniment repris, n'aboutit point, spirale du tourbillon où se heurtent et s'entrechoquent brutalement le «Oui» et le «Non», les bénédictions et les malédictions.

> Maudit soit l'humour anglais, médicament de charlatan pour la bêtise et l'engourdissement. Ennemi suprême du Réel . . . [qui] fige la souplesse du Réel en une féroce chimie du rire.
>
> (BLAST HUMOUR
> Quack ENGLISH drug for stupidity and sleepiness. Arch enemy of REAL . . . freezing supple REAL in the ferocious chemistry of laughter. [BLAST 1, 17])

Mais aussi:

> Béni soit l'humour anglais. C'est la grande arme barbare du génie parmi les races. Grandes montagnes russes déchaînées qui bondissent d'une idée à l'autre, dans la vieille foire de la vie.

(BLESS ENGLISH HUMOUR
It is the great barbarous weapon of the genius among races. The wild MOUNTAIN RAILWAY from IDEA to IDEA, in the ancient Fair of LIFE. [BLAST 1, 26])

Ainsi sont tour à tour portés au pinacle et ignominieusement condamnés l'Angleterre et la France et leurs diverses caractéristiques nationales. Accessoirement les coups d'encensoir sont allègrement distribués aux amis qui figurent dans une liste où se retrouvent dans une intimité inattendue Charlotte Corday, le Pape et l'huile de Ricin. Ce sont les «Blessed», les bienheureux du paradis vorticiste auxquels font face sur l'autre volet du diptyque les «Blasted», les damnés, les maudits: ennemis personnels, artistes connus, «l'évêque de Londres et toute sa postérité» (condamnation d'autant plus savoureuse que ledit évêque ne connaissait point les joies du conjugo).

Dans ce chassé-croisé entre les contraires, certaines valeurs se font jour cependant. Tout d'abord celle de la rigueur et de la dureté. L'artiste n'est vraiment créateur que tendu vers le but qu'il poursuit, échappant ainsi au mouvement alangui du temps qui risque de le noyer dans la nostalgie du passé ou de le propulser vers un avenir nébuleux.

Tout instant qui ne se détend pas dans la faiblesse, et qui ne glisse pas en arrière, ou, qui, d'autre part, ne rêve pas avec optimisme, est de l'Art. . . .
Notre Vortex est fier des ses flancs polis.

(Any moment not weakly relaxed and slipped back, or, on the other hand, dreaming optimistically, is Art . . . .
Our Vortex is proud of its polished sides. [BLAST 1, 148-9])

L'œuvre vorticiste idéale, fraîchement jaillie de l'élan de l'instant, refuse toute référence à des sources d'inspiration aussi floues que le sont les abstractions de la Nature ou de la Vie.

La Nature n'est pas plus inépuisable, neuve, débordante d'invention, etc . . . que ne l'est la vie pour l'homme moyen de quarante ans, avec sa routine, ses désillusions et son petit train-train de distractions habituelles.

(NATURE IS NO MORE INEXHAUSTIBLE, FRESH, WELLING UP WITH INVENTION, ETC., THAN LIFE IS TO THE AVERAGE MAN OF FORTY, WITH HIS GROOVE, HIS DISILLUSION, AND HIS LITTLE ROUND OF HABITUAL DISTRACTIONS. [BLAST 1, 129])

Le discrédit dont souffre la peinture naît de ses sources d'inspiration. Tant qu'elle choisit de n'être qu'un reflet dégradé de la vie, elle n'est que piètre palliatif à cette vie.

Il n'y a qu'une seule chose préférable à la Vie . . . et cela c'est quelque chose de très abstrus et de splendide, qui ne dépend en aucune façon de la «Vie». Ce n'est pas l'équivalent de la vie mais une *autre* vie, aussi nécessaire à l'existence que la précédente.

(There is only one thing better than "Life" . . . and that is something very abtruse and splendid, in no way directly dependent on "Life." It is no EQUIVALENT for Life, but ANOTHER Life, as NECESSARY to existence as the former. [BLAST 1, 130])

L'artiste doit donc se retirer en lui-même, c'est en lui que se niche la réalité, mais cette réalité n'appartient pas à la rêverie, elle doit se situer idéalement entre les deux pôles extrêmes de l'Abstraction et de la Vie.

L'Art le plus beau n'est pas pure Abstraction, il n'est pas non plus la vie inorganisée.

(The finest Art is not pure Abstraction, nor is it unorganised life. [BLAST 1, 134])

Le regard que l'homme moderne pose sur le monde extérieur n'est pas celui du primitif.

Nos regards balaient la vie horizontalement.

(Our eyes sweep life horizontally. [BLAST 1, 141])

Craignant de se dissoudre dans une réalité qu'il ne peut contrôler, le sculpteur africain s'attache à la représentation de la forme humaine individualisée. L'artiste du XXe siècle, pour Lewis, vit dans une société organisée dont il est capable de percevoir le chaos sans s'y laisser absorber, aussi s'oriente-t-il vers une déshumanisation où le corps humain ne joue plus le rôle primordial.

Rigoureux, exigeant, capable de se situer au centre du geste créateur, l'artiste vorticiste se définit surtout négativement: il sait d'abord ce qu'il ne veut pas être. Ainsi le Vortex, symbole de création dynamique, est aussi le tourbillon où viennent s'engloutir les gloires les plus confirmées. Les Impressionnistes n'ont rien fourni de neuf à la peinture si ce n'est une palette plus pure. Ils se sont contentés de répéter le réalisme de Daumier, réalisme auquel ce dernier parvenait à échapper et où eux-mêmes se sont laissés engluer. Les Cubistes français, en particulier Picasso, n'ont pas su abandonner l'asservissement à la Nature. Leurs toiles jouent avec un nombre de thèmes limités, sans refléter le chaos de la perception:

> Tout musicien ou végétarien que l'on puisse être, on ne passe pas sa vie exclusivement parmi des pommes et des mandolines.
>
> (HOWEVER MUSICAL OR VEGETARIAN A MAN MAY BE, HIS LIFE IS NOT SPENT EXCLUSIVELY AMONGST APPLES AND MANDOLINES. [BLAST 2, 41])

En revanche, les Expressionnistes, et même parmi eux, Kandinsky dont Lewis reconnaît pourtant le rôle de pionnier, mettent un entêtement excessif à éviter la représentation. Aussi leurs créations se diluent-elles dans une fluidité abusive. Enfin les Futuristes ne trouvent pas davantage grâce aux yeux du chef de file des Vorticistes. C'est contre eux que Lewis se déchaîne avec une ardeur qui pique notre curiosité. Sans doute leur troupe vociférante regroupée autour de Marinetti savait user de l'effet de choc qui ne déplaisait pas aux Vorticistes eux-mêmes. Peut-être ceux-ci craignaient-ils la fadeur dans laquelle, par comparaison, ils risquaient d'être rejetés. De plus, le vocable commode de Futuriste risquait d'être appliqué par un public mal initié à toutes les productions qui bouleversaient les habitudes mentales et annonçaient un XXe siècle aux délires inquiétants. Mais surtout, Marinetti et ses disciples professaient pour le monde moderne de la ville et de la machine une admiration qui n'était pas étrangère aux Vorticistes. Ceux-ci se devaient donc de définir soigneusement leurs buts par rapport à un mouvement rival, aux méthodes publicitaires éprouvées. Lewis s'incline devant la vitalité futuriste: Théoriciens, propagandistes, chevronnés, Marinetti et ses amis se sont malheureusement, pour Lewis, laissés engloutir dans l'effervescence de l'action où se dilue la pensée, leur culte de la machine, leur «Automobilisme» les entraîne dans un optimisme aveugle à vouloir concurrencer la Nature.

«Nous», déclarent en revanche les Vorticistes, «nous ne saurions pas fabriquer un éléphant».

Les Futuristes n'ont rien ajouté de nouveau à l'Impressionnisme sinon une confiance démesurée dans le modernisme et des idées nietzschéennes mal assimilées. Seuls Severini et Balla, dont Lewis a pu contempler les œuvres à l'Exposition Futuriste à la Galerie Doré en 1914, sont dignes d'éloge, encore convient-il de préciser que leurs mérites ne doivent rien au doctrinaire Marinetti.

Cette hargne (peut-être volontairement forcée) avec laquelle Lewis se déchaîne contre les Futuristes n'a d'égale que celle de Pound: «Marinetti est un cadavre». ("Marinetti is a corpse"—[BLAST 1, 154].)

Mais l'Expressionnisme de Kandinsky et le Cubisme de Picasso n'éveillent pas chez Pound les mêmes réserves que chez Lewis. De même Gaudier-Brzeska accorde son admiration à différents artistes (Epstein, Brancusi, Archipenko, Dunikowski, Modigliani) auxquels le rédacteur en chef de BLAST n'a pas donné sa bénédiction. Chacun ajoute au crédo vorticiste formulé par Lewis la marque de sa personnalité propre. Pour Pound, les arts, s'ils veulent renaître, doivent tendre à retrouver leur «forme primaire», ce que l'image est à la poésie. Citant sa propre définition de l'image comme «ce qui représente un complexe intellectuel et émotionnel dans un instant du temps», Pound établit une filiation entre l'Imagisme en poésie et le Vorticisme pour l'ensemble des arts. Toute expression artistique se doit de revenir à la structure fondamentale, élément premier, garant d'une totale efficacité. «Le Vortex est le point d'énergie maximal». L'image nichée au cœur du poème, est signe dynamique essentiel, intermédiaire unique entre l'écrivain et son lecteur. Ainsi l'émotion transmise n'est-elle point liée à la complaisance sentimentale du créateur, elle est fruit d'une technique économe et concentrée, spécifique à chaque forme d'art: «On s'intéresse à une certaine peinture parce que c'est un arrangement de lignes et de couleurs».

Quant à Gaudier-Brzeska, son langage s'apparente plus à celui de la parabole ou de la méditation poétique qu'à celui du théoricien. Bannissant les sculpteurs grecs trop absorbés dans une contemplation narcissique à reproduire la forme humaine, il souhaite que soit retrouvée la pureté d'expression plastique des chasseurs paléolithiques qui faisaient surgir des fresques de chevaux dans le gorges de Fonts-de-Gaume.

Autoritaires et dogmatiques lorsqu'ils énoncent les principes qui guident leurs recherches, les Vorticistes se montrent plus conciliants lorsqu'il leur faut nourrir les pages de leur revue. Certes BLAST, dominée par Lewis, accorde la part du lion aux artistes et écrivains qui prennent le Vortex comme signe de ralliement: C'est ainsi que les deux numéros présentent de nombreux poèmes de Pound dont la vigueur de ton devait, à leur époque, renforcer l'effet de scandale de la revue. Ainsi la «Troisième Salutation»:

Raillons la tranquillité niaise du *Times*:
Rire gras!

(Let us deride the smugness of "The Times":
GUFFAW!
[BLAST 1, 45])

S'en prenant aux «critiques baillonnés», il apostrophe ainsi le journal qui incarne la respectabilité britannique:

Toi, l'obstructionniste au ventre de catin,
Toi, l'Ennemi déclaré de la liberté d'expression et de la bonne littérature,
Toi, champignon, toi, perpétuelle gangrène.

(You slut-bellied obstructionist,
You sworn foe to free speech and good letters,
You fungus, you continuous gangrene.
[BLAST 1, 45])

Dans le second BLAST, les «Chroniques» de Pound attaquent avec la même âpreté l'«homo canis» qui n'a pas su apprécier la revue vorticiste de 1914. Pourtant, selon lui, «seule BLAST a osé montrer au monde moderne son visage dans un miroir honnête». Estoquant de droite et de gauche, il s'en prend sur le ton de l'anecdote acide au pasteur de Kensington dont les cloches perturbent le sommeil des paroissiens plus que ne le font «trois temples de Bacchus» et «un sanctuaire d'Aphrodite populaire».

Wadsworth, dont plusieurs toiles sont présentées en illustration des deux numéros de BLAST, y apparaît aussi comme traducteur et commentateur de ce même Kandinsky qui n'obtient pas tous les suffrages de Lewis. Les productions littéraires de Vorticiste fidèles mais mineurs comme Jessie Dismorr affadissent le second BLAST.

Quant à Lewis, sa présence est partout dominante. A l'ensemble des manifestes, articles critiques ou essais de sa main viennent s'adjoindre une pièce assez cryptique, *Enemy of the Stars* dans BLAST 1, et dans le second numéro le début d'un roman, *The Crowd-Master*.

Comme la plupart des «petites revues» de l'époque, BLAST accueille dans ses page des textes qui ne répondent apparemment pas aux critères définis par les manifestes. C'est ainsi que le début du roman de Ford [Hueffer], *The Good Soldier*, paraît dans le premier BLAST sous le titre *The Saddest Story*. Il semble bien que les liens d'amitié et de reconnaissance aient ici primé sur les impératifs catégoriques vorticistes. Des motifs similaires justifient sans doute la publication d'une nouvelle de Rebecca West, *Indissoluble Matrimony*, qui dépeint les tribulations d'un couple mal assorti. De même, au milieu des illustrations reproduisant des toiles ou des œuvres plastiques vorticistes, viennent s'insérer des créations de Spencer Gore auquel Lewis pouvait ainsi rendre un hommage posthume.

C'est dans le domaine des arts plastiques que BLAST a le plus vieilli, et c'est par un retour en arrière volontaire que nous pouvons apprécier aujourd'hui, par exemple, la hardiesse du «Portrait d'une Anglaise», un des meilleurs Lewis présentés dans la revue.

Dans son ensemble BLAST donne cependant une impression de vigueur et de jeunesse. L'emportement fébrile avec lequel les Vorticistes essayaient de briser le carcan des habitudes esthétiques garde tout son pouvoir de séduction. Ils avaient en fait épousé leur siècle avant que leurs contemporains n'y soient contraints par une série de cataclysmes internationaux. Arrogants et cruels, certes, ils l'étaient. Ford Madox Ford sera le premier à en pâtir qui, sous les invectives de Lewis tout enfiévré de Vorticisme, songera à renoncer définitivement aux lettres et à se retirer dans quelque campagne provençale. Mais leur révolte avait de la santé et de la gaieté. Douglas Goldring rapporte que, durant la lecture des manifestes vorticistes, Lewis et Pound échangeaient des fous rires et clins d'oeil de connivence. En effet, c'est bien le rire de Lewis que nous entendons à travers les pages de BLAST. Sérieux par la force de conviction qu'elle exprime, BLAST n'en demeure pas moins l'œuvre ludique par excellence: jeu social où la respectabilité se dégonfle comme ballon de baudruche, jeu intellectuel où l'œil et l'esprit se réjouissent. C'est le jeu que suggèrent l'équilibre acrobatique de la typographie, la fermeté élastique de l'écriture, l'insolence tranquille du paradoxe. La pensée paradoxale vient tout naturellement s'insérer dans le boomerang des contraires, dans cette dualité chère à Lewis, car ce jeu n'est jamais gratuit. Il semble répondre à quelque secrète exigence intérieure; le rire prend une valeur thérapeutique. L'ambiguité n'engendre pas d'irritation. Il semble qu'en retrouvant Lewis dans BLAST nous comprenions ce que recèle cette première phrase du «Wyndham Lewis Vortex No. 1»: «Il faut parler avec deux langues si l'on ne veut pas créer de confusion» ("You must talk with two tongues, if you do not wish to cause confusion."— [BLAST 2, 91]).

DRAWING OF EZRA POUND, 1919
WYNDHAM LEWIS
PENCIL ON PAPER. 35.6 x 25.5 cm
PRIVATE COLLECTION, PHOTOGRAPH COURTESY OF ANTHONY d'OFFAY
NOT IN MICHEL

HEAD OF EZRA POUND, 1939
WYNDHAM LEWIS
BLACK CHALK. 30.5 x 24 cm
FROM THE COLLECTION OF D. G. BRIDSON
MICHEL 937

EZRA POUND

BLAST

(RADIO SPEECH #30: APRIL 26, 1942)

It is gettin' on to be nigh thirty years since Mr. Wyndham Lewis, the vorticist painter, began rootin' round and prospectin' the publication of an art magazine called BLAST, the word meaning commonly explosion of dynamite, etc., but connected in the arcane recesses of Mr. Lewis's mind with blastoderms and sources of life. And this magazine or manifesto was in its way a harbinger (I am never quite sure about that word harbinger, but it does seem to be generally accepted as meaning a sign of something about to come). Well, the other war came and prevented its being a periodical or annual publication, got out a second number in 1915 and that ended it, Gaudier-Brzeska the sculptor havin' been killed in the interim.

And that manifesto was the best we could then do toward assertin' what has now become known to the world, or at least to the European continent as the crisis OF the system. Crisis OF, not IN the system; not a crisis inside the system. But of the SYSTEM, crisis OF the system, *DEL sistema*, not merely *nel sistema*.

Now the particulars about the art movement, insofar as they affect merely painting and sculpture, may not much matter in themselves, you will say. But the point is these things ONLY occur, changes like that in art and writin' ONLY occur when something moves deeper down, something gets going, something is workin' inside, and the LIVE artists, as distinct from exploiters and deadheads, get the itch to DO something about it, itch to do something LIKEWISE.

Anyhow, BLAST appeared, and somewhere inside it or in some contemporary explosion of Wyndham's there was the statement: "MATTER when there is not [a] certain amount of intelligence INSIDE it, decays and rots." It would have been a happier day for all England, if all England had looked at that sentence. Which marks the end of an era, marks the end of the Marxist era (if there was a Marxist era), marks the end of the XIXth century usurocracy and mercantilism. Matter in which there is not a certain amount of intelligence decays and ROTS.

Waal, BLAST made a bit of a stir, mebbe on the surface. It penetrated into society circles, etc., New Zealand attacked it. The stinking old *Manchester Guardian* took six months to discover that BLAST was satiric.

BLAST could have been RECONSTRUCTIVE, if the body of England hadn't been too far gone, too far descended into a state of flaccidity to be able to react to the medicine.

A copy of BLAST penetrated into the lofty purlieuws of the Beerbohm Tree family.

Yes, BLAST was out for publicity, it was not hidin' its head like a violet. It was made to be seen; it was said to be two foot square; which it wasn't but it was as large, and its typographic display was as impressive as Mr. Leveridge, the printer, could be induced to give credit for. And the STAGE in those days, as I suppose it still is in England, was esteemed far more than mere art, or mere intellect; so for an ART paper to penetrate into the upper reaches, as it were, of SIR Herbert's ambience, was already a proof of something or other, I won't say vitality but at least visibility. Cause Herb, SIR Herb, was not only IN the limelight, but OF it, he was as you might say, built out of limelight, constructed of limelight, made out of limelight, as stuff and substance.

Waaal, the Tree[s] and their circle were havin' tea on the lawn; as one did in the upper reaches, with due paraphernalia, large silver tea urns, etc. and up come a storm, thunder and lightnin', and the family naturally plunged indoors, and one of Sir Herbert's nieces described to me the scene, possibly prophetic scene, that resulted.

BLAST had been left solitary there on the lawn, and the niece and Sir Herbert gazed elegiacally from the drawingroom window on the scene of grass and wet dampness. A FLASH of lightning lit up the lawn. There in its solitude, huge on the flaring magenta cover, the black letters vivid, the word BLAST was written. Possibly someone ventured out to rescue the treasure, now valued of second hand book sellers, but more probably no one did. It was in many ways a languid era, so few DID.

I take it in retrospect that my tendency to action had effects, people who were bored with stagnation, and were relieved at the sight of ANY vitality, this must have been a TINY minority, and the vast majority of the small minority into contact with which I came, was uneasy, disturbed, horrified in fact: for that sign of action was also some sort of a harbinger.

SOMETHING was going on, or if not actually going ON, something might occur somewhere.

And DID.

Not only one war, but another, and the END of the materialist Era. The end of that particularly dirty *Anschauung*. Not merely the change of an IDEA, not the change of ONE idea, or notion, but the change of a WHOLE disposition toward life. Sloth, laziness, snobbishness, greed or whatever prevented the English from seeing what the change was to be, or what it was when it hit 'em. Also ignorance, also that part of the constructed snobbishness which had helped to blot out historic sense. (Not by accident. *That* was intended.)

However, the dichotomy, the division was an age-old division. When Mencius went to see King Huei of Liang, the King said, have you got something that will bring PROFIT? Profit motive, already known, two thousand five hundred years before BLAST; 2,400 years before Marx half swallowed Hegel. And Mencius said: why use that word, what I got is my sense of EQUITY. If you can't use that in your Kingdom, good morning, I have mistaken the address.

Well, now the sense of EQUITY, sense of justice, was what England had lost or mislaid. *Ben dell' intelletto* Dante called it, or something not very far from it. Homely English would get that down to "use of your wits," but I reckon Dante meant something nearer to Mencius's meaning. However BOTH the use of the wits, and the sense of justice or equity had gone out of fashion in England by 1914. And this is no subject for merriment. When a nation loses its sense of justice, sense of fair play to ALL comers and loses the use of its wits, it is the end of an era, or the end of the nation, or BOTH.

We have seen the Russian Empire come to an end. Grand Dukes sellin' the country, and thought not encouraged by the class that was then in power. We have seen the end of the Hapsburgs. You would think old W. Steed would have learned something from his study of the dealin's of the Hapsburgs, and that he would have applied it into his observation of England, but evidently he has not.

I dunno where you folks will come out, but I know you won't start toward coming out till you recognize the use of straight thinking. Till you stop bilking yourselves, till you get rid of the people who have encouraged you in the worst of your vices—opium of one sort or another, dumping one sort onto China, and using another sort for home consumption. Landor, Trollope, Hobhouse, Major Douglas, even ole William Yeats, plenty of your own wise men have told you.

And the Ta Hsüeh, the Great Learning, First book of confucian philosophy ends: Profits do not profit a nation. Lucre does not profit a nation. The sense of equity, sense of justice is that wherefrom a nation hath benefit.

The whole of your rulin' class has run plumb haywire on profits; [*FCC transcript*: run haywire on lucre; despised the use of the ——despised the good of the intellect; falsified everything.

I'm hep to your B.B.C., to your——advocate in India. India has already given way, that is,——and false promises. Now the B.B.C. comics and falsification of everything. Now the only point I've heard on the London Radio was what one Royal Canadian, who had swallowed all the ——swallowed all the lies you had told him. Still dreaming along in the years of Victorian (jubilee). Lucre does not profit a nation. Sense of justice is that where from a nation can benefit.

Ezra Pound speaking——or perhaps only an admonition. That is——is your only way out.]

From *"Ezra Pound Speaking": Radio Speeches of World War II*, ed. Leonard W. Doob. (Westport: Greenwood Press, [1978]), pp. 107-9. [A few minor emendations have been made—*Ed.*]

GIOVANNI CIANCI

POUND AND FUTURISM

The history of the English avant-garde in the years preceding World War I, particularly in 1913 and 1914, seems incomplete without a detailed account of the impact of Futurism on England, of which, so far, only a general outline is available. The consequences of the lack of a thorough investigation into this area (particularly in the field of literature) can be seen, for instance, in the treatment of Ezra Pound's Imagist and Vorticist phase. While Futurism has been ignored or passed over lightly, there has been too much emphasis on the influence that Fenollosa's manuscripts and the Chinese ideograms had on Pound's development, to the neglect of equally important factors which went to shape it.

Noel Stock's biography of Ezra Pound, published in 1970, conventionally dismisses the impact of Futurism on Pound. He writes that "Pound was never a Futurist and [was] either indifferent or opposed to most of their principles."[1] Even excellent Pound scholars take this for granted, to the point of contradicting themselves. Both Donald Davie and Hugh Kenner, in fact, agree that the turning point in the early Pound is his Vorticist phase of late 1913 and 1914. But they are singularly reticent about or oblivious of Futurism, although they stress the liberating experience of Vorticism. Donald Davie thinks that Vorticism can be explained through the formulations of an English theosophist, Allen Upward, especially in his book *The New Word*.[2] Hugh Kenner, with a view to throwing some light on Vorticism, draws instead a fascinating and at the same time remote genealogy which includes, among others, Transcendentalism, Whitehead, Darwin, Frazer, Gestaltists, Buckminster Fuller, Leibnitz, Chu Hsi, etc.[3]

How can we account for this silence or reticence about the impact of Futurism? If we look closely into this curious phenomenon, we shall see that Pound scholars (T. S. Eliot included) have been repeating almost verbatim what Pound and Wyndham Lewis said in 1914, after the break with Marinetti took place. As everyone knows, the various movements of the avant-garde were not only waging war against the establishment, but warring amongst themselves, too. It is easy to realize, then, that we can expect no disinterested or unbiased judgments in that period. BLAST was launched to counteract Futurism: so it is no surprise that in the *Review of the English Vortex* the criticism of Futurism is almost sectarian.[4] BLAST was bound to be as nationalistic as Futurism itself. It preached a Northern art opposed to the Mediterranean Futurism. T. E. Hulme had attacked Futurism as being "the deification of the flux, the last efflorescence of Impressionism."[5] Lewis and Pound repeated the definition with small variations.[6] Disparagement of Futurism or silence about its existence and the role it had played were only to be expected. This was Wyndham Lewis's strategy to erase even the slightest memory of the great debt Vorticism owed to Futurism. Pound himself, in his BLAST contribution, "Vortex"—which was to become one of the main sources of information for future literary historians—did not mention Futurism at all when he summarized the "Ancestry" of this new revolutionary movement. He listed instead Pater, Whistler, Imagism, Picasso and Kandinsky.[7] Yet anyone who knows what Futurism was about only has to think of the name BLAST itself (the title of the Vorticist review). Or, and this will convince him more quickly, let him take a look at the revolutionary typographical layout of BLAST. It will be enough to remind him of Apollinaire's Futurist *L'Antitradition futuriste*.[8]

Vorticism had a very short life. The catastrophe of the war put an end to it. And in 1917 T. S. Eliot's statement that

> Pound has perhaps done more than anyone to keep Futurism out of England. His antagonism

to this movement was the first which was not due merely to unintelligent dislike for anything new, and was due to his perception that Futurism was incompatible with any principle of form[9]

was destined to be more or less repeated in every account concerning Pound and Futurism, without anyone questioning it or bothering to look more closely at the facts.

Now, I think, it is high time that such crystallized judgments were put to the test. With our historical perspective, we can no longer maintain nowadays the distortions which Vorticism had necessarily to broadcast in the past in order simply to affirm itself and survive. The first move which it seems profitable to make is simply to point out, in a detailed analysis, how influential and widespread Futurist concepts were in 1913 and 1914, for a very short although extremely intense period.

William C. Wees, in his volume *Vorticism and the English Avant-Garde*, has done the groundwork. Although his book is mainly an account of events rather than a critical discussion and evaluation of them, it has been very helpful in correcting the picture of the impact of the Futurists. Wees has brought a lot of information to light. After reminding us of the great echo of the two Futurist exhibitions in London (in 1912 and in 1914), Wees tells us that between 1913 and 1914 Futurism became a fad. Evidence of the Futurist vogue was discernible everywhere in art galleries, music-halls, in men's and women's fashion, etc. More recently, Richard Cork, in his two-volume study *Vorticism and Abstract Art in the First Machine Age*, has shown us that it is difficult to overestimate the impact of Futurism on the rise of Vorticism. Along with Cubism, Futurism is the main force underlying Wyndham Lewis's paintings. But we would look in vain for an anticipation of explosive Vorticist militancy in cold and cerebral Cubism. It is to Futurism we must turn if we want to see the model for Pound's and Lewis's declamatory and belligerent attitudes. Lewis was quick in adopting the same technique as the Futurists used in order to make themselves heard, and to stir up and outrage public opinion. Without the example of Futurist radicalism, demonstrations, etc., the combative programs of the Rebel Art Centre would be hardly conceivable. Futurism gave indirect help in bringing about the break from the amateurish and too "passéist" Omega Workshop of Roger Fry. (The Rebel Art Centre, founded by Wyndham Lewis, had among its members Ezra Pound, the painters C. R. Nevinson, F. Etchells, H. Saunders, J. Dismorr, L. Atkinson, W. Roberts, C. Hamilton, E. Wadsworth and the sculptor Gaudier-Brzeska.) What we must keep in mind is the scandal and the extraordinary success of the physical presence of the Futurists in London in those years. What they were so exceptionally successful in making people see was how art could actually impinge strongly upon the environment. The Futurists were the first in Europe to exhibit this by employing a revolutionary strategy based on *soirées*, manifestos, proclamations, publicity stunts, expeditions and so on. Art was *praxis* and it could have a direct bearing on society. Furthermore, we have to bear in mind not only the practical results achieved by the Futurists (exhibitions, publicity campaigns, etc.) but also their formidable theoretical work which resulted in the famous manifestos, most of which were quickly translated into English in newspapers and in the most advanced literary reviews.[10] That the Futurists were the revolutionary leaders of the day, and that they were very influential is borne out by Wyndham Lewis himself when, significantly some months before the conflict between them, he defines Marinetti as "The Cromwell of our times."[11] It is hardly possible to explain Pound's decision to become militant and his aggressive campaign in support of the radicalism of the new art (especially in painting and sculpture) without connecting him with the contempt for bourgeois values and the revolutionary attitude so fervently preached by the Futurists. The war against the still largely Victorian English establishment was sparked by the radical and vociferous Futurists. The cherished Whistler was partly behind this, but the up-to-date figure who set up the model for the general attack against institutions was now Marinetti. If we go carefully through Pound's prose in 1913 and 1914, and particularly if we read the articles he wrote in *The New Age* in favor of the innovations of Wyndham Lewis and Jacob Epstein, we are struck by the many echoes of Futurist manifestos.

In those years Imagism as a cool and detached "critical movement" was laid aside or left behind. Literature was now involved along with all the arts (from painting to music) in a general revolution breaking away from any compromise or cautious attitude. Pound no longer believed in the "system," and his rebelliousness now echoes the tenets of Futurism. Defending Epstein's sculpture from the attacks of the press in February 1914, Pound writes in terms which are very akin to Marinetti's radicalism and iconoclasm. He praises primitivism, dissension and violence. He rejoices that

The artist has at last been aroused to the fact

that the war between him and the world is a war without truce.

With typical Futurist hyperbole, he says that "his [i.e., the artist's] only remedy is slaughter." Again: "His gods are violent gods." Futuristically, "those artists . . . whose work does not show [this] strife, are uninteresting." And Pound is impatient of "analysis." In the style of the Italian manifestos, he resorts to strong language when he expresses his dissatisfaction with the contemporary condition of art and society:

> We are sick to death of the assorted panaceas, of the general acquiescence of artists. . . . To the present condition of things we have nothing to say but "merde."[12]

Writing to Harriet Monroe in October 1913 he says that "the public can go to the devil" and suggests treating it in the Futurist manner, that is to say with a punch in the face.[13]

If we want to understand what nurtured Pound's radical stance in such poems as "Tenzone," "Salutation the Second" (October 1912, later collected in *Lustra*) we must go back above all to Futurism, and not to Shavian Ibsenism as some critics have suggested.[14] Vorticism is no mere change of name from Imagism. Between Imagism and Vorticism we have to take into account Pound's radical phase, his militancy, his subversion, his decisive and formative experience with the revolutionary avant-garde, in 1913-14 largely under Futurist influence.

It is misleading to suggest, as Davie does, that we must go back principally to theosophy in order to understand Vorticism. True, the name *vortex* itself can be explained partially in terms of occultist and esoteric thought (Pound uses the word *vortex* for the first time in his poem "Plotinus" in 1908; and, in a typescript note—where the vortex is identified with the cone—he says that "The 'cone' is I presume the 'Vritta' whirl-pool, vortex ring of the Yogi's cosmogony"[15]). But the crucial point to make is that in 1913 and 1914, as a symptom of Pound's decision to fight for the experimentalism of the new art, the concept of *vortex* undergoes a significant metamorphosis. The vortex now assumes a modernist and Futurist connotation. As in the Futurist painter Carlo Carrà, the vortex is no longer a purely metaphysical and esoteric word, but becomes a concrete symbol of urban life, with its noise and bustle. It stands for the chaos of the industrial metropolis, its frenetic activity, its din and its smells. In brief, it suggests the contemporary dynamism produced by modern mechanized life. Carrà uses the word *vortex* in his manifesto "La pittura dei suoni, rumori e odori" (September 1913). A propos of his painting *Funerale Anarchico* (which influenced Lewis) and *Sobbalzi di Fiacre*, he speaks there of a "ribollimento e turbine di forme e di luci sonore" ("bubbling and whirling of forms and lights"), and adds:

> Questo ribollimento implica una grande emozione e quasi un delirio dell'artista, il quale per dare un *vortice*, deve essere un *vortice* di sensazioni, una forza pittorica, e non un freddo intelletto logico. (my italics)

> (This kind of bubbling over implies a great emotion and almost a delirium on the part of the artist, who in order to achieve a vortex, must be a vortex of sensation himself, a pictorial force and not a cold reasoning intellect.[16])

Perhaps it is not coincidental that Pound makes use of the same word with the same connotations in connection with the poetry of Vildrac when he writes, in the same month of September 1913, that the poet becomes "a 'crater' or a vortex."[17]

We can gain an idea of this Futurist-inspired *vortex* by looking at the "dipinto parolibero" by Carrà entitled *Festa Patriottica* (June-July 1914). There the forceful spiral form aims at suggesting not so much mysticism as the "tumulto civico" ("civic tumult")[18] of actual reality, thanks to the whirling mass of the collage realistically mingling visual and aural impressions, suggesting references to trains, trams, automobiles and to modern technology.[19] So it seems true to say that in 1913 and 1914 the vortex leaves the sphere of theosophic speculation for the technological habitat of the industrial town. This technological habitat was being exalted, along Futurist propaganda lines, in BLAST, despite its anti-Futurist intentions.[20] I have shown elsewhere,[21] in much greater detail, how Futurism made its mark on Pound's writings of 1913 and 1914. Let me add here that, as B. W. Rozran pointed out some years ago, in poems such as "In a Station of the Metro" and "Game of Chess," Futurist suggestions may be discernible in "the visual arrangement of words, phrases and lines as an intrinsic part of a poem's communication."[22]

Let us not forget that in the very period when Pound is strengthening his links with the masters of the new art, both Epstein and Wyndham Lewis are strongly under the spell of Futurism. One of Lewis's most Futurist works—the drawings for *Timon of Athens*—is celebrated by Pound as the symbol of his generation's revolt. There is nothing more Futuristic than Epstein's sculpture entitled *Rock Drill*,[23] a striking example of what the Futurists called *macchinolatria*. It is well known that Pound's critical terminology teems with words derived from the language of sculpture and painting (the term "lines of force" seems to be particularly reminiscent of Futurism). It is to the aesthetics of the machine, over which (to quote Lewis) the Futurists "gushed," that Pound refers when, using technological similes, he defines Joyce's styles as "hard" and "metallic."[24]

Recent interpretations have given up the search for a single structure in the *Cantos*, emphasizing their fluidity. Donald Davie has commented upon certain passages of the *Cantos* which seem like vortices or waterspouts.[25] Ronald Bush has underlined the impact of the radical experiments of avant-garde painting and sculpture on the *Cantos*. In particular, Lewis's drawings for *Timon of Athens* with their "sense of movement" and their elements of "conflict and drama"—with, in other words, their narrative potentiality—may have been chosen as a model for Pound's "attempt at a major 'modern' narrative composition."[26]

This is not the place to discuss these critics' suggestions in detail. It is important to realize that if the turning point in the early Pound is centered on the new awareness of a common interaction between all the arts, and if it manifests itself in the search for dynamism, we have to give credit for this discovery to Futurism. Futurism, in fact, was in those years (especially 1913–1916) publicizing the need for abolishing the barriers between the arts, and pointing out the necessity for a dynamic art to match the challenge of the new dynamic world; and it was doing this not only theoretically in the manifestos but empirically in the artistic scene in London.

The epic organization of the *Cantos* is based on the rejection of static Imagism, which was connected with the somewhat decorative "one image poem" technique. Pound himself was to point out later that:

> The defect of earlier Imagist propaganda was not in misstatement but in incomplete statement. The diluters took the handiest and easiest meaning, and thought only of STATIONARY image. If you can't think of imagism or phanopoeia as including the moving image, you will have to make a really needless division of fixed image and praxis or action.[27]

It appears to me that if the crux of Pound's evolution lies in the shift from static Imagism to dynamic Vorticism, it is to Futurism that we must direct our attention. This is justified if we bear in mind not only the theory of Futurism but its widespread practice in the milieu in which Pound worked and acted. Dynamism was prominent, of course, in Vorticist paintings. It is interesting to note that, even after the break with Marinetti, Vorticism was blaming Cubism for lack of movement, etc., repeating literally what the Futurists had said against Picasso and Braque when they wrote that they painted

> ... l'immobile, l'agghiacciato e tutti gli aspetti statici della natura
>
> (... the immobile, the frozen and all the static aspects of nature).[28]

On the whole I think that the impact of Futurism on the form of Pound's poetry, in the sense of an overt imitation, is occasional and must be approached with due consideration for the interplay of other elements. The importance of Futurism is qualitatively different. As in the case of other avant-garde writers (Wyndham Lewis,[29] D. H. Lawrence[30] and James Joyce), Futurism exercised an exceptional stimulus towards a totally radical reconsideration of art and its function in contemporary society. It functioned both in England and throughout Europe as a powerful catalyst. The actual influence detectable in the short-lived imitations of the Futurists (which are nevertheless there to be seen) is less momentous than the extraordinary commotion successfully engineered by the Futurists, which helped the most restless and sensitive artists of those years to develop their own answer to their own problems. When we look at the turning point in the development of Pound's poetry leading to the composition of the *Cantos*, it is certainly right to take into account his experience of the Japanese *hokku* poetry and his study of Fenollosa's writings. But we can no longer neglect the by no means minor role played by Futurism, even if it led to a poetry which cannot be explained in terms of the Futurist impact alone. Of course, the reasons for which Pound was partially in disagreement with Futurism even before the break with Marinetti are very well known. Pound was deeply immersed in the past, so that he could not welcome the Futurists' famous *antipasséism*. Moreover, he could not bring himself to follow the Futurists in throwing overboard (as they seemed to suggest) the painfully acquired formal discipline of Imagism in order to create *parole in libertà* (words set free). Yet there is abundant evidence in Pound's decisive experimental phase of

1913 and 1914 that the impact of Futurism was far from superficial. It was, in fact, instrumental in the genesis of Pound's poetics, even though it merged with other important experiences, so that the final result came to have a distinctiveness of its own.

1. N. Stock, *The Life of Ezra Pound* (London: Routledge & Kegan Paul, 1970), p. 115.
2. D. Davie, *Pound* (London: Fontana-Collins, 1975), p. 44.
3. H. Kenner, *The Pound Era* (London: Faber & Faber, 1972), pp. 230-31.
4. As has been observed, it is only at a later stage that BLAST became decidedly anti-Futurist. In April 1914 an advertisement launched BLAST as a "Discussion of Cubism, Futurism, Imagisme and all Vital Forms of Modern Art," but just before its appearance, following the break with Marinetti, Lewis inserted the *Vortex* manifestos which attacked Futurism. So that in BLAST references to Futurism reflect contradictorily both the first phase of ideological agreement and the later phase of disagreement. See W. C. Wees (pp. 162-63) and R. Cork (pp. 236-37) in their books quoted later.
5. See T. E. Hulme, "Modern art and its philosophy" (January 1914) reprinted in *Speculations* (1924).
6. "Futurism, as preached by Marinetti, is largely Impressionism up-to-date" (W. Lewis in "Melodrama of Modernity," BLAST 1, 143). For Pound Futurism was "a sort of accelerated Impressionism": see his essay on "Vorticism" in *The Fortnightly Review*, 1 September 1914, p. 461.
7. E. Pound, "Vortex. Pound," BLAST 1, 154.
8. See W. C. Wees, *Vorticism and the English Avant-Garde* (Toronto: Univ. of Toronto Press, 1972), pp. 172-76; R. Cork, *Vorticism and Abstract Art in the First Machine Age* (London: Gordon Fraser, 1976), 1: 249-51. Apollinaire's manifesto was published in *Lacerba* (Firenze) on 15 September 1913. Carlo Carrà wrote that *L'Antitradizione Futurista* was given its typographical shape by Marinetti himself in Milano, after receiving the manuscript from Apollinaire. Marinetti sent it back to Apollinaire for approval. Apollinaire was happy with Marinetti's textual alterations and printing layout, so Marinetti proceeded to print it (see Carrà's letter to Prof. P. A. Jannini in P. A. Jannini's *Le Avanguardie Letterarie nell'Idea Critica de Apollinaire*, Roma, Bulzoni (1971) 1979, pp. 150-51). It is significant that the French poet referred to *L'Antitradizione Futurista* as "mon manifeste milanais" when he saw in BLAST an imitation of his manifesto (see *Œuvres Complètes* de Guillaume Apollinaire, Paris, ed. by A. Ballandes and J. Lecat, 1966, 2: 453).
9. T. S. Eliot, *Ezra Pound: His Metric and Poetry* (1917) reprinted in *To Criticize the Critic* (London: Faber & Faber, 1965), pp. 174-75.
10. See Patrizia Ardizone, "Il Futurismo in Inghilterra: Bibliografia 1910-1915" in *Futurismo/Vorticismo—Quaderno 9*, Istituto di Lingue e Letterature Straniere dell'Università di Palermo, maggio 1979, pp. 92-115 and the Supplement to the bibliography by V. Gioè in *Quaderno 16*, Palermo, 1982, pp. 76-83.
11. W. Lewis, "A Man of the Week—Marinetti," *The New Weekly*, 30 May 1914 (reprinted in *Futurismo/Vorticismo—Quaderno 9*, p. 124).
12. All quotations from E. Pound, "The New Sculpture," *The Egoist*, 16 February 1914, pp. 67-68.
13. D. D. Paige, ed., *The Selected Letters of Ezra Pound* (London: Faber & Faber, 1971), p. 13.
14. See K. K. Ruthven, *A Guide to Ezra Pound's Personae (1926)* (Berkeley: Univ. of California Press, 1969), p. 54.
15. See M. J. King, ed., *Collected Early Poems of Ezra Pound* (London: Faber & Faber, 1977), p. 296.
16. See Carlo Carrà, "The Painting of Sounds, Noises and Smells 1913" in *Futurist Manifestos*, ed. by U. Apollonio (London: Thames and Hudson, 1973), p. 115. I have slightly modified the translation to make it more literal.
17. See E. Pound, "The Approach to Paris—Vildrac," *The New Age*, 25 September 1913, reprinted in *Selected Prose (1909-1965)*, ed. by W. Cookson, (London: Faber & Faber, 1973), pp. 333-40.
18. See C. Carrà, *La Mia Vita*, p. 172 (quoted by Willard Bohn, see next note).
19. For a detailed and perceptive discussion of this painting, and its relationship with Apollinaire, Marinetti etc., see W. Bohn, "Circular Poem-Paintings by Apollinaire and Carrà," *Comparative Literature*, Summer 1979, pp. 246-71. Maurizio Calvesi touches on the spiral form and Orphism in *L'Arte Moderna* No. 40, Milano, Fabbri, 1975, pp. 225-26. See also, J. Purce, *The Mystical Spiral* (London: Thames and Hudson, 1974) and E. Gombrich, *The Sense of Order* (Oxford: Phaidon, 1979), pp. 137-38 and 243-46.
20. See for instance the pages "blessing" "restless machines of scooped out basins, heavy insect dredgers, monotonous cranes, stations, lighthouses" etc. and "Bless England, Industrial Island Machine," etc. (BLAST 1, 23).
21. See G. Cianci, "Futurismo e Avanguardia Inglese: il primo Pound tra Imagismo e Vorticismo" in *Futurismo/Vorticismo,— Quaderno 9*, pp. 7-66. Updated and slightly revised it has appeared in English in: *AAA—Arbeiten aus Anglistik und Amerikanistik* (Tübingen), vol. 6, No. 1, 1981, pp. 3-39.
22. See B. W. Rozran, "A Vorticist poetry with visual implications: the 'forgotten' experiment of Ezra Pound," *Studio International*, April 1967, p. 172.
23. See Cork, chap. 16 and J. Korg, "Jacob Epstein's *Rock Drill* and the *Cantos*," *Paideuma* No. 2-3, Autumn-Fall 1975, pp. 301-13.
24. See E. Pound, "Dubliners and Mr. Joyce," *The Egoist*, 15 July 1914, p. 267 and in *Future*, May 1918, p. 161.
25. Davie, pp. 62-74. Compare in particular: "As we start to read the *Cantos*, we float out upon a sea where we must be on the look out for waterspouts. These, when they occur, are ideas, the only sort that this poem is going to give us. And meanwhile we can forget about such much debated non-questions as whether this poem has a structure, and if so, what it is: or again, why the poem isn't finished, and whether it ever could have been. Does a sea have a *structure*? Does a sea finish anywhere?" (Ibid., pp. 73-74).
26. See R. Bush, *The Genesis of Ezra Pound's Cantos* (Princeton: Princeton Univ. Press, 1976), pp. 46-47.
27. See E. Pound, *ABC of Reading* (1936) (London: Faber & Faber, 1961), p. 52.
28. See "Prefazione al Catalogo della I° Esposizione di Pittura Futurista," February 1912 ("The Exhibitors to the Public 1912" in *Futurist Manifestos*, p. 46).
29. See G. Cianci, ed., *W. Lewis—Letteratura/Pittura*, Palermo, Sellerio, 1982.
30. See G. Cianci, "D. H. Lawrence and Futurism/Vorticism" in *AAA*, Vol. 8, No. 1, 1983, pp. 41-53.

TIMOTHY MATERER

WYNDHAM LEWIS THE SOLDIER

Ezra Pound described Wyndham Lewis as a "man at war" in June of 1914, two months before the First World War began and almost two years before Lewis left for the front lines in France. As the Vorticist artists responded to the spirit of violent change that preceded the War, Pound claimed that their generation would "sweep out the past century as surely as Attila swept across Europe."[1] The three disruptive movements that George Dangerfield credits with the destruction of the Liberal establishment in England before the War—the Labour Movement, the Ulster rebels, and the Suffragettes—all have their representatives "blessed" in the Vorticist journal BLAST. The only form of violent protest the Vorticists disapprove is the destruction of works of art by the Suffragettes. BLAST praises their movement but warns: "LEAVE ART ALONE, BRAVE COMRADES!"[2]

Pound celebrated the power of artists, "the antennae of the race," to anticipate the currents of change in society. Lewis, on the other hand, wrote in 1937 that he found it

> somewhat depressing to consider how as an artist one is always holding the mirror up to politics without knowing it. My picture called "The Plan of War" [BLAST 1] painted six months before the Great War "broke out," as we say, depresses me.... With me war and art have been mixed up from the start.[3]

In *Rude Assignment* (1950), Lewis shows how far back this mix of war and art goes in his life. He recalls that as a child of eight he stitched together his own war epics, which he describes as "no stupider than the Volsungensaga but in range even narrower, being confined altogether to war, instead of practically altogether to war." His first drawings were of primitive redskins and palefaces as illustrations for his stories:

> I was a denizen of the "Leatherstocking" world. I started life at eight as a war-chronicler therefore. It never ceases for me to be unpleasant that the tiny mind of a little animal like myself at eight and earlier should be filled by its elders with such pasteboard violence, initiating it into this old game of murder. Born into a military aristocracy life begins full of excited little bangs and falsetto war-cries.[4]

Although scarcely one of the "military aristocracy," Lewis's father was trained at West Point and served in the Civil War as a Captain in Sheridan's Cavalry. This military heritage certainly was a force in Lewis's life, even though it's likely that his desire to be as military as his father did not last much beyond his eighth year. In a fragment he wrote in 1914, his autobiographical protagonist "Cantleman" is astonished when a friend claims that a European War is imminent: "What was war? He had no idea.... His father had been a soldier. That was a reason to misunderstand war, or think little about it: what his father had done he would not do."[5]

We never learn why Cantleman reacts so decidedly against his father, but we know that Lewis himself disapproved of his father and perhaps even felt betrayed by him. Charles Edward Lewis married an Englishwoman, Anne Stuart, and then lived on both sides of the Atlantic until Percy Wyndham was ten, when they separated, and Anne Lewis and her son settled in England. Charles Lewis supported his son erratically. Lewis wrote to his mother in 1907: "I suppose, as you say, it's difficult to extract money, even one's due, from our fellow beings especially at Christmas time.—I didn't certainly think that the Parent over the Water would respond to my amiable letter: he's an old rip."[6] His feelings about his father surface in his autobiographical first novel *Tarr*. One of the novel's characters, Kreisler, is supported as an art student in Paris by his father. When his father cuts off his allowance and marries Kreisler's own fiancée, the artist begins a desperate series of actions that finally leads to his suicide. It is also significant that a character in Lewis's play *The Ideal Giant* (1914) asserts her identity by murdering her father. This deed inspires the Lewis figure in the play, who so far has merely theorized about the relationship of thought to action, to defend the murderess from the detective who attempts to seize her. These works were being written as Charles Lewis's support of his son dwindled to nothing. As late as 1937, Lewis complained that he felt "cheated of my patrimony."[7]

Yet Lewis's paternal heritage as well as his service in the First World War shaped his personality throughout his life. John Rothenstein wrote of Lewis as he was in the Thirties: "War played, I think, a considerable part in his imaginative life: he occasionally used military terms to describe his own operations, offensive or defensive, and he alluded more than once to his belonging by birth 'to a military caste.' "[8] Lewis's attitude toward his father eventually mellowed, and in 1940 he began but never finished editing selections from his father's war memoirs, wishing to preserve the memory of "this one-time captain in Sheridan's Cavalry—this fox-hunting, brigantine-owning, essay-writing *bum* . . . this odd-man-out in a society of go-getters." Lewis characterizes his father as a political naïf. Charles Edward Lewis left West Point in 1862 prepared to fight on the side of his friends at the Academy, who were Southerners. This decision horrified his family back in upstate New York, where he was soon convinced that he should fight on the Northern side. Lewis sees this vacillation as typical of his father:

> That he had any understanding, however rudimentary, of the true backgrounds of this great Civil disturbance, there is no evidence. To learn for instance that it was a war made by an industrial community upon an agricultural community . . . or anything abstractly political of that nature, would have surprised and abashed him very greatly I am sure. He might never have fought at all, for either side, had any notions of that sort been introduced into his already confused head.[9]

Lewis's own father is the first of the political "simpletons" that Lewis scorned throughout his life.

The son, however, was as big a "simpleton" as the father. When Lewis reflected on a photograph of himself in uniform, he compared the soldier to the child who wrote and illustrated war chronicles:

> I see the same self that was responsible for the booklets: but this time he is not a child, he is in uniform among belted, pouched, tin-hatted, fellow-soldiers of world war i. I perceive a sort of repetition—it is the same pattern, only the bangs and cries of battle had become real, for the figure in the photograph, not academic.— And I am ashamed to say that even then I still saw these things as a child does.[10]

Lewis admits elsewhere in *Rude Assignment* that he tends to exaggerate the naiveté of his early attitudes, and I believe that is the case here. Not even Ford Madox Ford could have foreseen how disastrous the first modern war would prove to be.

A conviction about his pre-war naiveté was in any event a cherished part of his personal myth, and he liked to compare his inexperienced opinions to what he asumed was the wisdom of older friends such as T. Sturge Moore and Ford Madox Ford. Ford is the model for the friend who predicts the war in the "Cantleman" fragment in which the protagonist reacts against his father's military career. The fictionalized scene is not as amusing as the actual one as remembered by Lewis in *Blasting and Bombardiering*. In August of 1914 Lewis was staying with Pound, Ford, and Violet Hunt at the countryhouse of Mrs. Turner— the novelist Mary Borden, who was one of Lewis's patrons. The Berwickshire setting was a strangely quiet one in which to hear of the outbreak of war, and Ford himself remembered that weekend as a "charmed occasion, a last, magical Edwardian pause before the crash of the war."[11] Lewis agreed with his hostess when she told Ford:

> "There won't be any war, Ford. Not here. England won't go into a war."
> Ford thrust his mouth out, fish-fashion, as if about to gasp for breath. He goggled his eyes and waggled one eyelid about. He just moved his lips a little and we heard him say, in a breathless sotto voce—
> "England will."
> "England will! But Ford," said Mrs. Turner, "England has a Liberal Government. A Liberal Government cannot declare war."
> "Of course it can't," I said, frowning at Ford. "Liberal governments can't go to war. That

would not be liberal. That would be conservative."

Ford sneered very faintly and inoffensively: he was sneering at the British Government, rather than at us. He was being the omniscient, bored, and sleepy Ford, sunk in his tank of sloth. From his prolonged siesta he was staring out at us all with his fish-blue eyes—kind, wise, but bored. Or some such idea. His mask was only just touched with derision at our childishness.

"Well, Ford," said Mrs. Turner, bantering the wise old elephant. "You don't agree!"

"I don't agree," Ford answered, in his faintest voice, with consummate indifference, "because it has always been the Liberals who have gone to war. It is *because* it is a Liberal Government that it *will* declare war."

About this talk of "liberal" and "conservative" Lewis said he knew as little as the "peacocks at the zoo." The "blasting" of England was such fun for the Vorticists because they felt secure themselves: "Life was one big bloodless brawl, prior to the Great Bloodletting."[12]

However naive or inexperienced Lewis may have been, he was not emotionally unprepared for the war. The fiction he wrote before he fought in France shows how far he was from conventional sentiments and expectations about the war. Lewis's fellow Vorticist Henri Gaudier-Brzeska, an avowed anarchist, praised the War as a "great remedy." Lewis expresses his more realistic view of the War in a story of 1915, when his character contradicts Lloyd George's famous description of the War: " 'This "great war" is the beginning of a period, far from being a war-that-will-end war, take my word for it.' "[13] Lewis's protagonist in this story, "The French Poodle," is so shocked by the way war reduces men to a level below the animals that he severs relations with those closest to him and transfers his affection to a dog, preferring to man's barbarity the "sanity of direct animal processes." Lewis traces the development of the gunner's "sullen neurasthenia" into a psychotic state in which he kills his dog rather than leave it among men. He wishes for death himself, in part because he has shot his dog, and is killed as soon as he returns to the Front. This sympathetic study of the impact of war on a sensitive mind resembles "The King of the Trenches" of 1916, in which another shell-shocked veteran is described.[14] But this later story he never published. Like Yeats in writing of Wilfred Owen, Lewis could not consider "passive suffering" a worthy response to the War. He felt a more aggressive and sardonic reaction was needed to the spectacle of mass slaughter. He attempts this harsher reaction in the same issue of *The Egoist* in which "The French Poodle" appears. Since it has never been reprinted, I quote this brief anecdote or parable, "The Young Soldier," in full:

> I asked Peach how he liked war. He seemed intoxicated with the notion of extinction. He winked at me as though to say "Hurry up and come and have a pinch!" I felt that military death was the latest dope. But he always winked like that, and he may have no very original feeling about his new experience. On the other hand, I saw a young soldier in the Tube yesterday. He was a born warrior, meant to kill other men as much as a woman is meant to bear children. I realised as I looked at him how there is only one thing a woman thoroughly understands in a man, of the things specifically his, and recognises of equal importance to her own functional existence. When he kills she feels that he is about a business as profound and sinister as her own. This young man was strung to a proud discipline. He was a youthful favourite of Death's, something like a sparring partner. He had the equivalent of chewing-gum, too, in the cynical glitter of his face, and his lazy posing. And I have seen many exalted and enthusiastic middle-class masks. The aristocrats have their old indifference, their adamantine Style. There are other styles, too, that come in handy. How young the world is, fortunately. It will certainly maul the Constellation of Hercules if that misguided organisation should come in our direction.

In departing from the sympathetic tone of "The French Poodle," Lewis adopts a cynical one that seems as much a pose or mask as the attitudes that he ridicules in "The Young Soldier." Yet the piece is a genuine attempt to find a response adequate to the fact of war and, for the soldier, the nearness of death. One can sense in the tone of this work the personal and intellectual crisis Lewis was suffering at the time. He had recently recovered from a long illness and was trying to settle his personal affairs, particularly the support of his two illegitimate children, before he would leave England. The intellectual crisis is seen in the exaggeratedly Nietzschean sentiment that the young soldier was "meant to kill other men as much as a woman is meant to bear children." This idea, more carefully expressed, inspires Lewis's best war story, "Cantleman's Spring-Mate."

Lewis wrote in *Rude Assignment* that Nietzsche's *Joyful Wisdom (Die Fröhliche Wissenschaft,* also known as *The Gay Science)* was among his favorite reading before the war. In that work, Nietzsche claims that "Hatred, delight in mischief, rapacity and ambition, and whatever else is called evil—belong to the marvellous economy of the conservation of the race." It would be naive to condemn the passions that animate the life of mankind. Nietzsche thinks that the proper response to man's violence is not pity or horror but laughter:

> When the maxim, "The race is all, the individual is nothing."—has incorporated itself in humanity, and when access stands open to everyone at all times to this ultimate emancipation and irresponsibility.—Perhaps then laughter will have united with wisdom, perhaps then there will be only "joyful wisdom." Meanwhile, however, it is quite otherwise, meanwhile the comedy of existence has not "become conscious" of itself.... [15]

Lewis attempts to place the War as a crucial episode in this "comedy of existence" and look upon the spectacle rationally. The "laughter" appropriate to this greatest of man's "evils" is of the type Lewis praises in BLAST, in which Swift is "blessed" for "his solemn bleak wisdom of laughter" and Shakespeare for "his bitter Northern Rhetoric of humour."[16] Captain Charles Lewis's response to war was instinctive; his son's would be "conscious" in this Nietzschean sense.

Is it possible, however, to keep this privileged consciousness in the midst of action? Can one look on the war as a comedy when one is part of the play? In a part of the "Cantleman" series called "The Code of a Herdsman," the master herdsman advises his disciples from his mountaintop: "—The terrible processions beneath are not of our making, and are without our pity." He tells his disciples: "Always come down with masks and thick clothing to the valley where we work. Stagnant gasses from these Yahooesque and rotten herds are more dangerous often than the wandering cylinders that emit them. See you are not caught in them without your mask." But the herdsman has been careful to retain the prerogative of the master: "—Do not expect *me*," he warns his disciples, "to keep in sufficiently good training to perform the feats I recommend.—I usually remain up on the mountain."[17] In Lewis's case, the herdsman joined the army, and his best short story responds to this paradox of a contemplative man entering the world of action.

"Cantleman's Spring-Mate" was finished and sent to Pound for *The Little Review* in May of 1917. The Cantleman of the story is in exactly Lewis's situation of waiting in a camp to be shipped off to fight in France. Cantleman like Lewis is thinking of what experience lies ahead: "In a week he was leaving for the Front, for the first time. So his thoughts and sensations all had, as a philosophic background, the prospect of death.... He was pretty miserable at the thought, in a deliberate, unemotional way."[18] Cantlemen's meditations have for background an English spring whose beauty he is able to appreciate:

> Cantleman walked in the strenuous fields, steam rising from them as though from an exertion, dissecting the daisies specked in the small wood, the primroses on the banks, the marshy lakes, and all God's creatures. The heat of a heavy premature Summer was cooking the little narrow belt of earth-air, causing everything innocently to burst its skins, bask abjectly and profoundly. (*CS-M*, 8)

The "dissecting" Cantleman does is mental rather than physical, though the momentary image of the soldier picking apart flowers is appropriate; his analysis of the spring mating season links, in the manner of "The Young Soldier," mating with death: "The only jarring note in this vast mutual admiration society was the fact that many of its members showed their fondness for their neighbour in an embarrassing way: that is they killed and ate them." Nature is at war also, or so it seems to Cantleman's imagination: "He saw everywhere the gun-pits and the 'nests of death.' Each puff of green leaves he knew was in some way as harmful as the burst of a shell"(*CS-M*, 8, 12-13). Like the protagonist of "The French Poodle," Cantleman prefers the "sanity of direct animal processes" to the universal brutality of men: "Human beings anywhere were the most ugly and offensive of the brutes because of the confusion caused by their consciousness.... In the factory town ten miles away to the right, whose smoke could be seen, life was just as dangerous for the poor, and as uncomfortable, as for the soldier in his trench" (*CS-M*, 8, 13).

Cantleman attempts to dissociate himself from the natural and unnatural mechanisms of death. He has a Nietzschean dream of a "new human chemistry," but concludes that "he must repudiate the human entirely, if that were to be brought off." He is therefore disturbed that he is attracted to a spring-mate of his own, a girl he has met on his walks to town. He admits he must give in to the "humiliating gnawing and yearning in his blood" (CS-M, 10, 12), but justifies this surrender by resolving not to romanticize the relationship. It will be a mating and not a love affair. When he seduces her, he is as callously brutal as he conceives Nature to be:

> On the warm earth consent flowed up into her body from all the veins of the landscape. The nightingale sang ceaselessly in the small wood at the top of the field where they lay. He grinned up towards it, and once more turned to the devouring of his mate. He felt that he was raiding the bowels of Nature: not fecundating the Aspasias of our flimsy flesh, or assuaging, or competing with, the nightingale. Cantleman was proud that he could remain deliberate and aloof, and gaze bravely, like a minute insect, up at the immense and melancholy night.... (CS-M, 13)

Cantleman imagines that he has outwitted nature, even when, after he has arrived in France, Stella writes to say she is pregnant. He ignores her letters and does not reflect that his part in her life "might be supremely unimportant as far as Stella was concerned." Nature betrays Cantleman by inducing him to bring another being in the world through Stella. Lewis uses the same theme in the last war story he wrote, "The War Baby" of 1918, in which a returning soldier, a less defiant and more responsible man than Cantleman, discovers the stupidities of his mistress developing in his own child. But Nature betrays Cantleman through the War even more thoroughly than it has through Stella. A description of the animal world, in which only the fittest survive, opens the story; it concludes by describing Cantleman fighting in the violent world of man at war, in which brute force and cunning prevail no less than they do in the animal world. Although Cantleman feels that he is defying Nature by destroying its prime product, man, he is really furthering Nature's scheme:

> And when he beat a German's brains out, it was with the same impartial malignity that he had displayed in the English night with his Spring-mate. Only he considered there too that he was in some way outwitting Nature; he had no adequate realization of the extent to which, evidently, the death of a Hun was to the advantage of the animal world. (CS-M, 14)

Cantleman is merely carrying on the evolutionary struggle. The Nietzschean moral is that "Hatred, delight in mischief, rapacity and ambition . . . belong to the marvellous economy of the conservation of the race. . . ." Whether seducing his mate or killing a Hun, Cantleman is furthering Nature's schemes. There are no exceptions; defiance is impossible.

The story of Cantleman and Stella resembles the plot of Lewis's pre-War novel *Tarr*, in which Tarr proclaims the artist a "new sort of person" who rises above merely human frailties. Yet the comedy of Tarr's story is that he spends his time, not creating works of art, but extricating himself from one mistress and acquiring another. The greater power of the Cantleman story derives from the bitterly comic perspective it takes of the war, and it was this perspective as much as the story's supposed "obscenity" that led to its suppression.

The October 1917 issue of *The Little Review*, which contained "Cantleman's Spring-Mate," was suppressed by the U.S. Post Office under a law which kept "every obscene, lewd, or lascivious" publication from polluting the mails. But Pound considered that the more likely ground for its suppression was the story's attitude toward the War (which the United States had entered in 1917), and he wrote to the judge who upheld the Post Office's decision on this issue. Pound cited his own efforts to educate the American people on the necessity of entering the war and Lewis's dangerous service in the front lines.[19] The judicial decision itself alludes to the story's anti-war tone even though the issue was supposed to be its obscenity. Judge Augustus N. Hand admits that the story "naturally causes a reflecting mind to balance the heroism and self-abnegation that always shines forth in war with the demoralization that also accompanies it. The very old question suggests itself as to the ultimate *values* of war."[20] If Lewis could prod Judge Hand into such a reflection, even for the brief time that he wanders from the obscenity issue, the story was indeed a threat to the "war effort."

"Cantleman's Spring-Mate" is one of the greatest pieces of literature to come not merely out of the war but (since it was written in 1917) directly from it. In recent years, many critics have examined the difficulty the wartime artists had in creating an "adequate response" to their experience, a response that was not merely pathetic or hysterical in tone.[21] Lewis's passionate but analytic response to the War was equal to this challenge. But his insight into the War did not make the experience of it any easier to bear.

A comment he sent to Pound soon after he arrived in France shows how ingrained the Nietzschean perspective was to him: "Life as you know is only justifiable as a spectacle: the moment at which it becomes harrowing and stale, & no aesthetic purpose is any longer served, War would be better exchanged for Diplomacy, Intelligence!—or something else!" (July 7, 1917).[22] He confesses to Pound in October of 1917 that the burden of his disillusion with the war is hard to bear and that his training as an artist only makes the spectacle harder to endure: "Nature & my training have made me curiously sensitive to ugly and stupid influences. The whole point of *Me* is that (& *not* that I don't happen to be over physically nervous). This causes me to suffer a great deal more than most people by my surroundings. Again, as I have cogitated a good deal throughout my days, the futility, trickery, the element in fact of despicable inhuman swindle in all this dreary & rotten business is borne in upon me more sharply than upon most people. This has its effect." He put a similar idea most succinctly in a letter to his mother of August 1916: "And I don't want to get killed for Mr. Lloyd George, or Mr. Asquith, or for any community except that elusive but excellent one to which I belong."

It is characteristic of Lewis's kind of sensitivity that the physical sufferings of trench warfare were no more burdensome than the personal relationships the army forced upon him. In "Cantleman's Spring-Mate," Lewis satirizes his own sensitivity in the person of Cantleman, who hates his fellow soldiers with a thoroughness that is comic: "A. he hated because he found him a sturdy, shortish young man with a bull-like stoop. . . . B. he disliked because . . . he stank, to Cantleman's peculiar nose, of Jack London, Summer Numbers magazines, bad flabby Surburban Tennis. . . . " and "C. he resented for the sullen stupidity with which he moved about, the fat having settled at the bottom of his cheeks, and pulled the corners of his mouth down, from sheer stagnation." Cantleman seizes one of Thomas Hardy's novels from B., "as though B. had no business to possess such books." He eventually steals the novel and "also tried to take a book away from A. (a book incompatible with A.'s vulgar physique)" (*CS-M*, 10-11). Lewis is here writing about his experience of training camp; the pressures of combat made this group existence still more trying.

Lewis tells Pound that he can bear the hardships of the Front, but adds that "there is one awful shadow over my existence here: and that is the too frightful incompatibility of my companions. I should go stark staring mad if I had to witness their awful archness, their abominable skittishness, and bathe in their banality for very long" (August 20, 1917). He is particularly sensitive, as he reveals in the same letter, to the "culture" of his associates: "A horrible phonograph played by my horrible brothers-in-arms renders intelligible writing difficult. The unspeakable, vulgar brutes have introduced The End of a Perfect Day and a score more obnoxious pieces into a dugout 12 by 8." Yet we mustn't conclude from these remarks from a man under fire that he hated all of his companions. In October 8, 1917, he tells Pound that "Three nights ago I had all my first-gun detachment except two men knocked out—the new sergeant among them. This is the second sergeant in six or eight weeks. I have lost, I am sorry to say, many a pleasant companion by this—Old Bill, amongst them. . . . He dreamt the night before that the whole detachment had been wiped out." He wrote truly when he told Pound on September 22, 1917, of his shelling a ruined church: "I was glad that it was a presumably *empty* ruin that I was guiding the bursts upon. I am truly not sanguinary except when confronted by an imbecile. . . . "

Lewis's openness to his new experience, and what he once called the "courage of one's sensations," saw him through his time at the Front. He ridiculed what the *Daily Mail* called the "great adventure" of the war but was not indifferent to what adventure there was. As he told Pound in an early letter of 1917, "what is the good of going to War if you never see war?" He tells Pound on August 20, 1917, of his rough life: "I am both glad and ashamed to say that I rather enjoy it." He intended to leave the Front only after he experienced whatever was unique to it. He wrote to Pound on June 19, 1917:

> I want to be in another battle or two, and get as much experience as I can, so that if necessary my knowledge of languages would be reinforced with knowledge of gunnery, & war conditions. In any case, I am glad I am here, and this experience is valuable. Unless I get knocked out, I don't intend to abridge it.

Lewis recorded these "valuable" experiences with the impersonal, understated style that was not only natural to him, as one sees from *The Wild Body* stories, but also to the experience of war. After writing of shell craters "big enough to put a horse and cart in," Lewis describes his encampment with the traditional litotes of war literature: "It is a bad spot." The following three excerpts give a good cross-section of

Lewis's understated style:

> This road for its own sake is being shelled constantly, & because the Bosche imagines that there are machine gun emplacements at the farther end. He also imagines that the wood is bristling with batteries; & is fatuous enough, in addition, to believe that his beautiful concrete dugouts are being used by our men. (You notice how guarded my language is.) (June 14, 1917)

> I put my head out of my dugout, and was shocked and flabbergasted to find the atmosphere whistling with machine-gun bullets. I withdrew, put on my tin-hat, and recovered from my amazement, once more protruded my person from my minuscule fortress, & looked towards the clouds. Imagine my indignation and interest on finding two of the abominable enemy flying at an insolently low altitude and pooping off in all directions. (June 19, 1917)

> The other side of the road is the weird desert alright. Shells rain on it all day. As you probably know, a shell is most dangerous when it falls on top of your head. It is next most dangerous at from 200 to 400 or 500 yards—a big one, that is. We get nothing but big ones. (August 20, 1917)

To gauge the power of Lewis's observations, however, one needs a long excerpt from his descriptions of the war. The following, from a letter sent to Pound on June 14, 1917, was written under difficult conditions at the Front, and yet it seems as profound and polished as his best work. The conclusion of the letter shows he considered it merely informal "chat," but its steady power to see without illusions is the style of one of the masters of descriptive prose:

> This morning is peaceful: the enemy is now much farther away, and we are temporarily derelict among 12" railway mountings, horse lines: senior Headquarters are even moving up among us. I expect we shall have to go pretty soon. Yesterday once more I took my way to the forward intelligence O[bservation] P[ost]. We were shelled out of it yesterday morning, the side of the dugout being disorganized by an 8" shell.——Imagine a stretch of land one mile in depth sloping up from the old German firstline to the top of a ridge, stretching to right & left as far as you can see. It looks very large, never-ending and empty. There are only occasional little groups of men round a bombdump, or building a light railway: two men pushing a small truck on which a man is being brought back, lying on his stomach, his head hanging over the side. The edge of the ridge is where you are bound for, at the corner of a demolished wood. The place is either loathesomely hot, or chilly according to the time of day at which you cross it. It is a reddish colour, and all pits, ditches, & chasms, & black stakes, several hundred, here & there, marking the map position of a wood. Shells never seem to do more than shave the trees down to these ultimate black stakes, except in the few cases when they tear them up, or a mine swallows them.
>
> The moment you get in this stretch of land you feel the change from the positions you have come from. A watchfulness, fatigue and silence penetrates everything in it. You meet a small party of infantry slowly going up or coming back. Their faces are all dull, their eyes turned inwards in sallow thought or savage resignation; you would say revulsed, if it were not too definite a word. There is no regular system of communication trenches yet. As a matter of fact it only becomes clearly unsafe as you approach the ridge. You get nearer to the shell bursts on the crest, until the nearest black cloud is only a hundred yards away, on the road at the skyline. Perhaps to your right, half way up, there has been heavy shelling, but not near enough to require craft, & the noise is inconsiderable. There are shrapnel bursts overhead almost continually, but for some reason absurdly high and ineffective.——As to the ridge: I have been there three times. Yesterday as we got within a hundred yards of the road there was suddenly a swooping whistle: my commanding officer shouted *down*: we crouched in a shell hole and a 5.9 burst about 15 or 20 yards away, between us & the wood—about 3 shell holes away, you could say, they were so regular thereabouts. Another came over about 15 yards nearer the wood, & at the third, actually in the wood, we concluded it was the wood corner they were after, & proceeded. The road at the top runs along the front of the wood for about 100 yds, the O.P. in the edge of the wood, being about 40 yards from where we struck the road.... As we reached this road, four black bursts came in succession halfway down the short stretch we could see. Straight for those

bursts we made: but I shall not repeat that often. Nothing else came over as it happened. But as soon as we had reached the handsomely concreted German dugout, three 5.9's dropped just outside the door. This goes on the whole while up there.——Shall I or shall I not ask to go up there again tomorrow? There is nothing there you cannot imagine: but it has the unexpected quality of reality. Also, the imagined thing and the felt are two different categories.

This category has its points. I will write you further on the subject of war. Do not expect my compositions to be well-worded, as letters (my letters) are only meant to be chat and slop.— Remember me to Mrs. Pound.

Yrs.

W.L.

---

1. Ezra Pound, "Wyndham Lewis," *The Egoist* 1 (June 15, 1914), 233, 234.
2. George Dangerfield, *The Strange Death of Liberal England* (New York: Capricorn Books, 1961). The representatives blessed are Sir Edward Carson, leader of the Ulster rebels; Robert Applegarth, a trade unionist; and Lillie Lenton, a suffragette who burned down the tea pavilion in Kew Gardens. See Appendix B of William C. Wees, *Vorticism and the English Avant-Garde* (Manchester: Manchester Univ. Press, 1972).
3. Wyndham Lewis, *Blasting and Bombardiering* (London: Eyre and Spottiswoode, 1937), p. 4.
4. Lewis, *Rude Assignment* (London: Hutchinson, 1950), p. 110.
5. Lewis, "The Country House Party," in *Unlucky for Pringle: Unpublished and Other Stories*, ed. C. J. Fox and Robert T. Chapman (London: Vision Press, 1973), p. 47.
6. W. K. Rose, ed., *The Letters of Wyndham Lewis* (Norfolk, Conn: New Directions, 1963), p. 33.
7. Lewis, *Blasting and Bombardiering*, p. 211.
8. John Rothenstein, *Brave Day, Hideous Night, Autobiography, 1939-1965* (London: Hamish Hamilton, 1966), p. 42
9. Lewis, "The Do-Nothing Mode," *Agenda*, 7-8 (Autumn/Winter, 1969): 217, 221.
10. Lewis, *Rude Assignment*, p. 110.
11. Arthur Mizener, *The Saddest Story, A Biography of Ford Madox Ford* (New York and Cleveland: World Publishing, 1971), p. 248.
12. Lewis, *Blasting and Bombardiering*, pp. 62-63.
13. Lewis, "The French Poodle," in *Unlucky for Pringle*, p. 56.
14. "The King of the Trenches" (pp. 60-72) and "The War Baby" (pp. 85-108) are included in *Unlucky for Pringle*.
15. Friedrich Nietzsche, *Joyful Wisdom*, trans. Thomas Common (London: T. N. Foulies, 1910), pp. 31-31.
16. BLAST 1, 26.
17. Lewis, "The Code of a Herdsman, *The Little Review* 4 (July 1917): 7.
18. Lewis, "Cantleman's Spring-Mate," *The Little Review* 4 (October 1917): 8. Subsequent page references are given parenthically: (CS-M, 8).
19. Pound sent this letter of protest via John Quinn on January 18, 1918. It is in the John Quinn Memorial Collection at the New York Public Library.
20. Margaret Anderson, "Judicial Opinion (Our Suppressed October Issue)," *The Little Review* 4 (December, 1917): 47.
21. For examples, see Arthur E. Lane, *An Adequate Response, The War Poetry of Wilfred Owen and Siegfried Sassoon* (Detroit: Wayne State Univ. Press, 1972); Paul Fussell, *The Great War and Modern Memory* (New York and London: Oxford Univ. Press, 1975); Bernard Bergonzi, *Heroes' Twilight* (London: Constable, 1965). The Fussell book credits the War with fostering in Lewis the "binary" cast of mind that actually was already fully developed before the War. The Bergonzi book contains a fine appreciation of Lewis's *Blasting and Bombardiering*.
22. I am grateful to Omar Pound for his assistance with Lewis's letters. Excerpts from Lewis's previously unpublished letters: © (1984). Estate of the late Mrs. G. A. Lewis by permission. The Wyndham Lewis Memorial Trust (a registered charity).

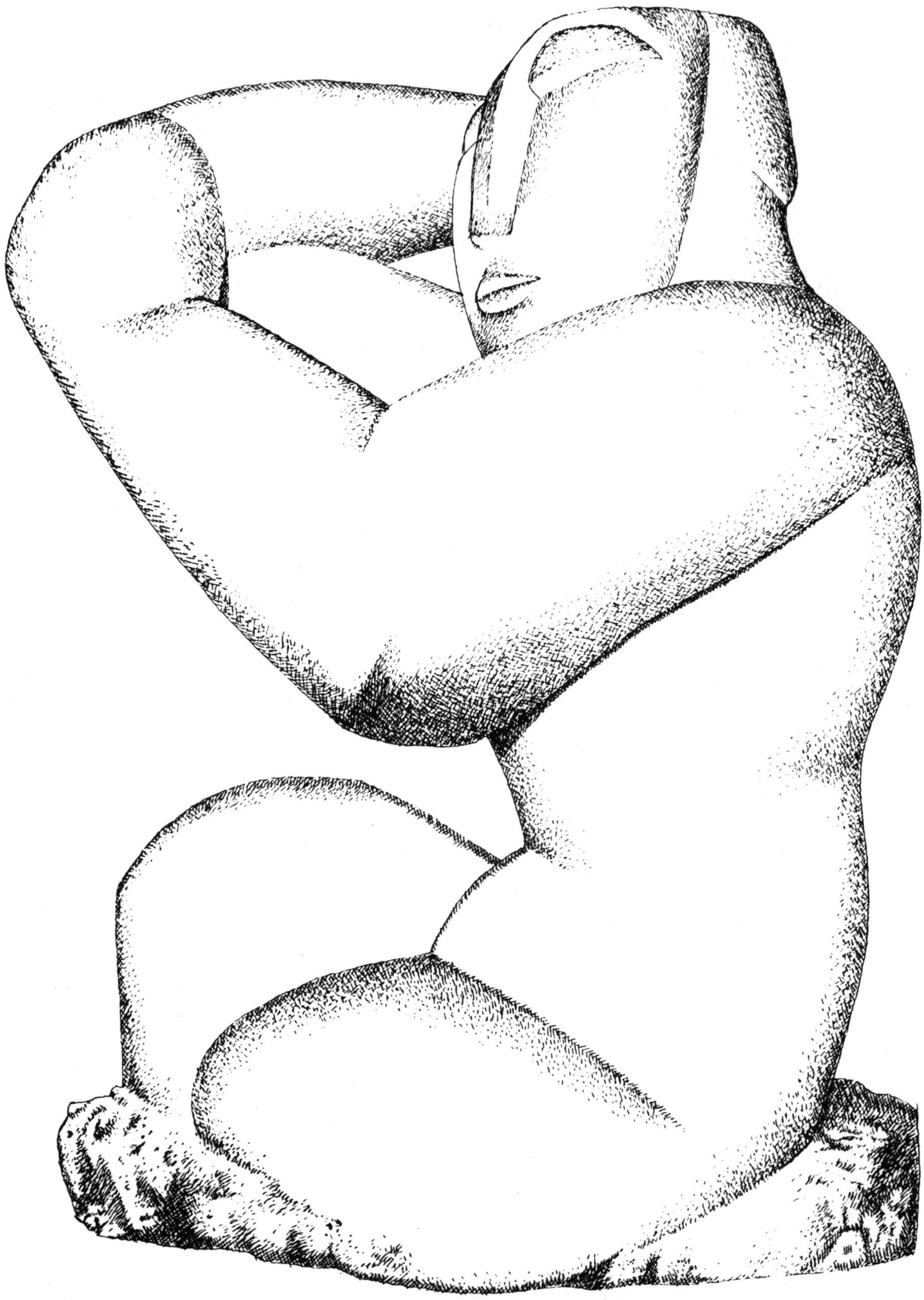

GUY DAVENPORT

THE BOWMEN OF SHU

ILLUSTRATED BY HENRI GAUDIER-BRZESKA AND THE AUTHOR

27 DECEMBER 1914

Here we are picking the first fern shoots and saying when shall we get back to our country, away from *das Trommelfeuer*, the gunners spent like winded dogs, white smoke and drizzle of sparks blowing across barbed wire in coils, the stink of cordite. 27 December 1914. Avalanches of shrapnel from fieldguns firing pointblank with fuses set at zero spray down in gusts, an iron windy rain. Here we are because we have the huns for our foemen. It's with pleasure, dear Cournos, that I've received news from you. We have no comfort because of these Mongols. You must have heard of my whereabouts from Ezra to whom I wrote some time ago. Since then nothing new except that the weather has had a change for the better. We grub the soft fern shoots, the rain has stopped for several days and with it keeping the watch in a foot deep of liquid mud, the crazy duckwalks, hack and spit of point guns.

HOOGE RICHEBOURG GIVENCHY

The smell of the dead out on the wire is all of barbarity in one essence. Also sleeping on sodden ground. The frost having set it, we have the pleasure of a firm if not warm bed, and when you have turned to a warrior you become hardened to many evils. When anyone says *return* the others are full of sorrow. Anyway we leave the marshes on the fifth January for a rest behind the lines, and we cannot but look forward to the long forgotten luxury of a bundle of straw in a warm barn or loft, also to that of hot food, for we are so near the enemy and they behave so badly with their guns that we dare not light kitchen fire within two or three miles, so that when we get the daily meal at one in the morning it is necessarily cold, but alike the chinese bowmen in Ezra's poem we had rather eat fern shoots than go back now, and whatever the suffering may be it is soon forgotten and we want the victory.

SCULPTURAL ENERGY IS THE MOUNTAIN

Sculptural feeling is the appreciation of masses in relation. Sculptural ability is the defining of these masses by planes. The Paleolithic Vortex resulted in the decoration of the Dordogne caverns. Early stone-age man disputed the earth with animals.

LES FALLACIEUX DETOURS DU LABYRINTHE

The rifles *crack! thuck!* whip at the bob of helmets of the *Boches* in the trenches across the desolation of an orchard. If they stir too busily at a point our *mitrailleuses* rattle at them, their tracers bright as bees in a garden even in this dead light. With my knife I have carved the stock of a German rifle into a woman with her arms as interlocked rounded triangles over her head, breasts triangles, sex, thighs. Like the Africans I am constrained by the volume of my material, the figure to be found wholly within a section of trunk. De Launay handles the piece with understanding eyes and hands. He is an anthropologist working on labyrinths, and has a major paper prepared for the *Revue archéologique*. I am, I tell him, a sculptor, descended from the masons who built Chartres. We have seen a cathedral burn, its lead roof melting in on its ruin. De Launay sees a pattern in this hell. We are the generation to understand the world, the accelerations of the turn of vortices, how their energy spent itself, all the way back to the Paleolithic (he tells me about Cartaihlac and Teilhard and Breuil). But our knowledge, which must come from contemplation and careful inspection, has collided with a storm, a vortex of stupidity and idiocy. His tracing of the labyrinth from prehistory forward has put him in a real labyrinth of trenches, its Minotaur the Germans, that cretinous monster of pedantic dullness. Yet, Henri, he says, we are learning the paleolithic in a way that was closed to us as *savant* and *sculpteur*. His smile is deliciously ironic in a face freckled with mud spatter, his eyes lively under the brim of his helmet.

MAÇON

How veddy interesting, Miss Mansfield said, sipping tea, when I told her I was descended from the craftsmen who carved Chartres. *I could have died of shame*, Sophie screeched at me as soon as we were outside. These people, she said, will have no respect for you. I am of the Polish gentry, which is hard enough to get them to understand. Very much the *pusinka*.

SMOKING RIVERS OF MUD

We say will we be let to go back in October. There is no ease in royal affairs. We have no comfort. Our sorrow is bitter. But we would not return to our country. What flower has come into blossom. We have time to busy ourselves with art, reading poems, so that intellectually we are not yet dead nor degenerate. Whose chariot, the General's horses, his horses even, are tired. They were strong. We have no rest. Three battles a month. By heaven, his horses are tired. The generals are on them, the soldiers are by them. If you can write me all about the Kensington colony, the neo-greeks and neo-chinese. Does the *Egoist* still appear? What does it contain? My best wishes for a prosperous and happy 1915. Yours sincerely Henri Gaudierbrzeska.

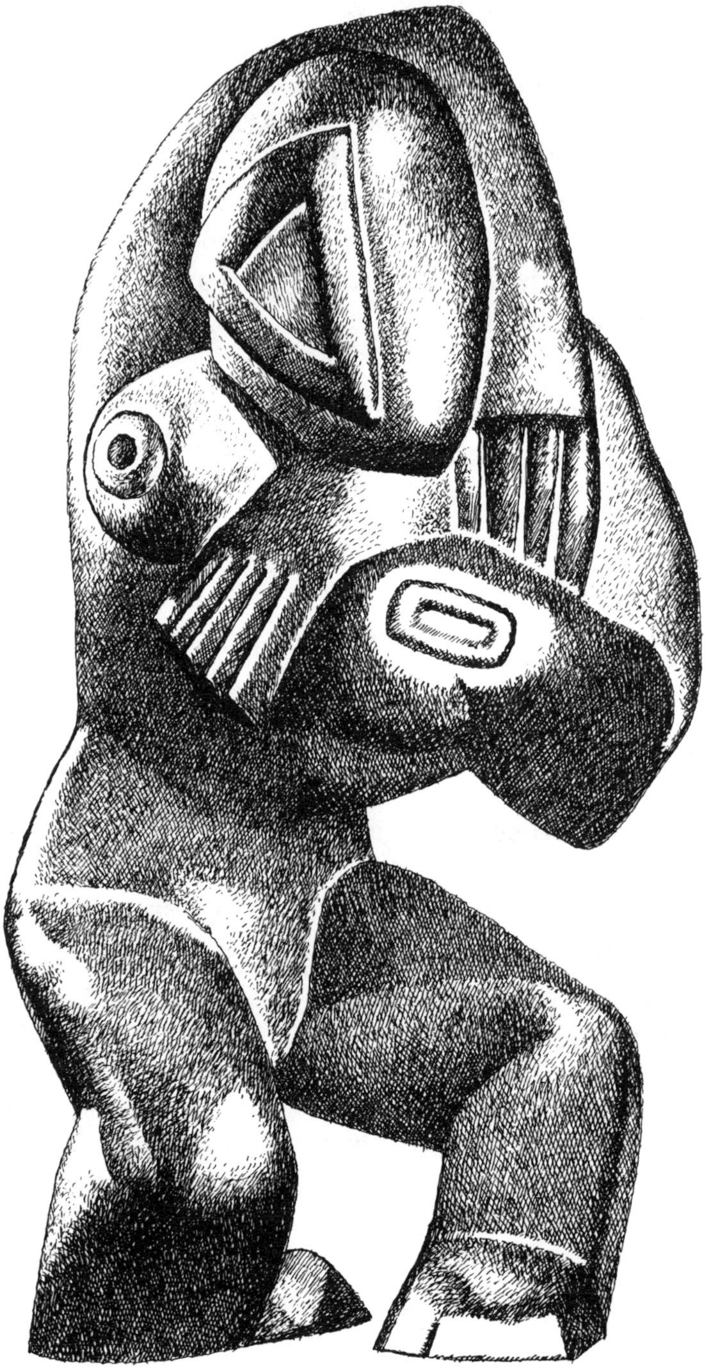

THE NORTH BORDER. BLUE MOUNTAINS. BARBARIANS.

The horses are well trained. The generals have ivory arrows and quivers ornamented with fishskin. The enemy is swift. We must be careful. When we set out, the willows were drooping with spring. We come back in the snow. We are hungry and thirsty, our mind is full of sorrow. Who will know of our grief? The newspapers say that our trench labyrinths are comfortable, that the British throw grenades with the ease of men accustomed to games of sport from their infancy. Tiger in the bamboo. Thunder from beyond the mountain. How and when we shall survive who knows? Stink of cordite. Rain of ash.

THE IMP

Stands in mischief, knees flexed to scoot.

DAS LABYRINTH

Between Neuville St.-Vaast to the north and Arras to the south, and Mt. St.-Eloi and Vimy east and west, lay the underground maze of tunnels, mines, fortresses in slant caves, some as deep as fifty feet, which the Germans called The Labyrinth, as insane a nest of armaments and men as military strategy ever conceived. Its approaches were seeded with deathtraps and minefields. It was invisible to aerial observation. Even its designers had forgotten all the corridors, an *Irrgarten* lit with pale battery-powered lights. Foch himself came to oversee its siege. The British hacked their way toward Lille, the French toward Lens, past The Labyrinth. The offensive began 9 May 1915. Out from Arras, past St.-Catherine, 7e Compagnie, 129e Infanterie, IIIe Corps, Capitaine Ménager the Commandant, marched on the road to Vimy Ridge, Corporal Henri Gaudier at the head of his squad. Except for mad wildflowers in sudden patches, their tricolor was the only alleviation in the grey desert of craters, burnt farms, a blistered sky.

THE SOLDAT'S REMARK TO GENERAL APPLAUSE

Fuck all starters of wars up the arse with a handspike dipped in tetanus.

BRANCUSI TO GAUDIER

Les hommes nus dans la plastique ne sont pas si beaux que les crapauds.

THE WOLF

Is my brother, the tiger my sister. They think *eat*, they think grass, bamboo, forest, plain, river. Their regal indifference to my drawing them, on my knees outside their cages, is the indifference of the stars. I feel abased, ashamed, worthless in their presence. But I close, a little, the gap between me and them, in catching some of their grace. And afterwards, they will say, *He drew the wolf, the deer, the cat. His sculpture was of stag and birds, of men and women in whom there was animal grace.*

THE CATHEDRAL BURNT IN FRONT OF MY EYES

Rheims. My Lieutenant sent me to repair some barbed wire between our trenches and the enemy's. I went through the mist with two fellows. I was on my back under the wire when *zut!* out comes the moon. The *Boches* could see me *et alors! pan pan pan!* Their fire cut through the tangle above me, which came down and snared me. I sawed it with my knife in a dozen places. The detail got back to the trench, said I was done for, and with the lieutenant's concurrence they blasted away at the *Boches*, who returned the volleys, and then the artillery joined in, with me smack between them. I crawled flat on my stomach back to our trench, and brought the repair coil of barbed wire and my piece with me. The lieutenant could not believe his eyes. When the ruckus quieted down, I went back out, finished the job, and got back at 5 a.m. I have a gash, from the wire, in my right leg, and a bullet nick in my right heel.

LA ROSALIE

The bayonet, so called because we draw it red from the round guts of pig-eyed Germans.

FONT-DE-GAUME

A hundred and fifty metres of blind cave drilled a million years ago by a river underground into the soft green hills at Les Eyzies-de-Tayac in the Val Dordogne, in which, some forty thousand years ago, hunters of Magdalenian times painted and engraved the immediate reaches with a grammar of horses and bison, and deeper up the bore, mammoths, reindeer, cougars, human fetuses, human hands, a red rhinoceros, palings of lines recording the recurrence of some event, masks or faces, perhaps of the wind god, the rain god, the god of the wolves, and at the utmost back depth, horse and mountain cat.

NIGHT ATTACK

We crept through a wood as dark as pitch, fixed bayonets and pushed some 500 yards amid fields until we came to a wood. There we opened fire and in a bound we were along the bank of the road where the Prussians stood. We shot at each other some quarter of an hour at a distance of 12 to 15 yards and the work was deadly. I brought down two great giants who stood against a burning heap of straw.

SOLDAT

I have been fighting for two months and I can now gauge the intensity of life.

DOGFIGHT

Enid Bagnold, horse-necked, square-jawed, nymph-eyed, finally came to sit, after weeks of postponing, Sophie sniffy with jealousy, suspicion, fright. The day was damp and cold. Gaudier lumped the clay on its armature and set to, nimble-fingered, eyes from the Bagnold to the clay. His nose began to bleed. He worked on. The Bagnold said, Your nose is bleeding. I know, said Gaudier. In that sack on the wall behind you there's something to stop it. She

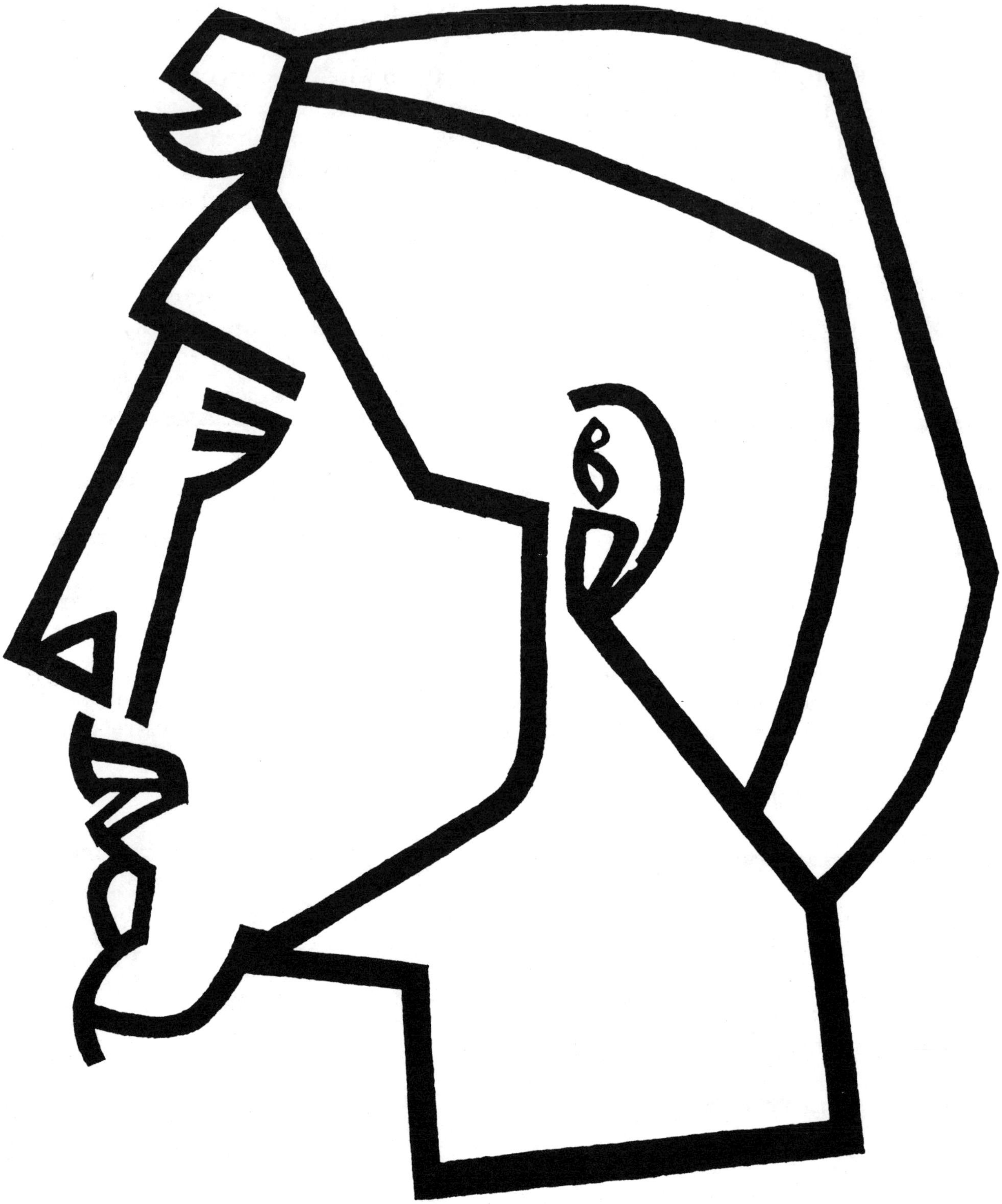

looked in the bag: clothes. Some male and dirty, some female and dirty. Rancid shirts, mildewed stockings. She chose a pair of Sophie's drawers and tied them around Gaudier's face, to soak up, at least, some of the blood, which had reddened his neck and smock. Lower, he said, I can't see. Take your pose again, quickly, quickly. She dared not look at him, wild hair, bright black eyes ajiggle above a ruin of bloody rags. The light was going swiftly, the room dark and cold. He worked on, as if by touch. And then a barrage of roars pierced the air. A dog fight outside. My God, she said. Tilt your chin, he said. Keep your neck tall. She tried the pose, wondering how he could see her in the dark. The dogfight raged the louder. Gaudier went to the window. The streetlamp at that moment came on, and she watched him with the fascination of horror, masked as he was in bloody cloth, staring out at the dogfight. He watched it with dark, interested eyes, his hands white with clay against the dirty window. Monsieur Gaudier! she said, are you quite in command of yourself? You may go, he said.

PARTRIDGES

Horses are worn out in three weeks, die by the roadside. Dogs wander, are destroyed, and others come along. With all the destruction that works around us, nothing is changed, even superficially. Life is the same strength, the moving agent that permits the small individual to assert himself. The bursting shells, the volleys, wire entanglements, projectors, motors, the chaos of battle do not alter in the least the outlines of the hill we are besieging. A company of partridges scuttles along before our very trench.

FRITH STREET

Sat on the floor at Hulme's widow's while he talked bolt upright in his North Country farmer's body and stuttered through his admiration and phlegmatic defense of Epstein's flenite pieces, so African as to be more Soninke made than Soninke derived, *feck undity in all its so to speak milky bovinity* (and Marsh clasping his hands, as if in prayer, and giving responses, *teddibly vital isn't it I mean to say* and *the phallic note*, with Ezra cutting his wicked eye at me from his Villon face). Sat with the godlike poet Brooke and the catatonically serious Middleton Murry, and the devout, Tancred, Flint, FitzGerald, and the fair-minded skeptics, Wadsworth and Nevinson. The ale was good and Hulme chose his words with booming precision and attack.

RODIN

Conceive form in depth. Under all the planes there is a center in the stone. All things alive swell out from a center. Observe relief, not outline: relief determines the contour. Let emotion stream to your center as water up a root, as sunlight into a leaf. Love, hope, tremble, live.

PARIS 1910

The chisel does not cut the stone, but crushes it. It bites. You brush away, blow away the dust the fine blade has crumbled. The mind drifts free as you work, and memories play at their richest when the attention is engaged with the stone. There was Paris, there was the decision,

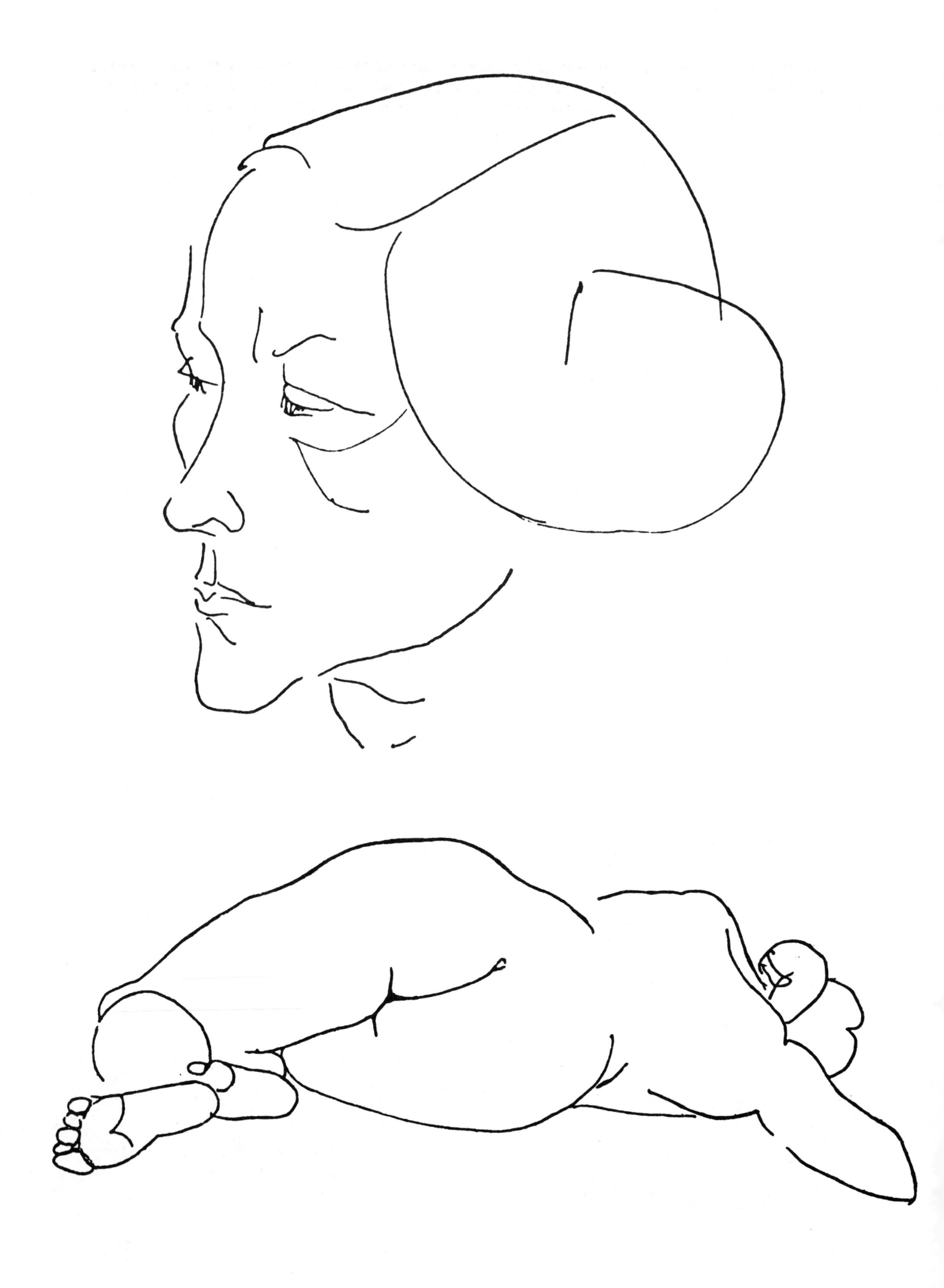

there was Zosik. England and Germany have nothing like the Parisian café where of a spring evening you sit outside making a glass of red wine last and last. It was at the Café Cujas that he met another stranger to the city, a poet, a Czech poet—Hlaváček? Svobodová? Bezruč? Dyk?—who, talking of Neruda, of Rimbaud, sorted out Gaudier's array of ambitions and focussed them upon sculpture. Rodin! Phidias! Michelangelo! It was the one art that involved the heroic, the bringing of a talent to its fullest maturity to do anything at all. It was an art that demanded the flawless hand, a sense of perfection in the whole, a pitiless and totally demanding art. But it had not been to the Czech that he had announced his commitment, but to the woman Sophie, not as an intention or experiment but as a road he was upon, boldly striding out. *Moi? Je suis sculpteur.* She, for her part, was a writer, a novelist. She had never shown anyone her work, it was too personal, too vulnerable before an unfeeling and uncomprehending world. Night after night he heard her story, not really listening, as it was her face, her eyes, her spirit that he loved, coveting her her maturity—she was 39, he a green and raw 17—and her story was a kind of badly constructed Russian novel. She was a Pole, from near Cracow. Her father threw away a considerable inheritance on gaming and shameless girls. She was the only daughter of nine children, and she was made to feel the disgrace of it, as she was useless as a worker, would have to be provided with a dowry in time. Her brothers called her names, and reproached her with her inferior gender. At sixteen she was put out to work, as her family was tired of supporting her as a burden. They found an old man, a Jew, and offered her to him as a wife. But he, like any other, demanded a dowry with her. This threw Papa Brzesky into a fit. A Jew want a dowry! There were three other attempts to marry her off. Two were likely business for the undertaker. The other was a sensitive young man of broken health whom she loved, the apple of his mother's eye. He came courting and played cards with Mama Brzeska, who one day accused him of cheating and chased him out of the house. Then her father went bankrupt. Sophie made her way to Cracow, hoping to study at the university, but she was neither qualified to enter it nor able to pay the tuition it asked. She came to Paris, took a nursemaid's job, and was driven away by the snide remarks of the other servants, who were ill bred. She went from menial job to menial job until her health, never robust, gave way. Then she was taken on as a nurse to a rich American family about to return to Philadelphia. She was to look after a ten-year-old boy and his sister. The boy died soon after. The sister begged to hear dirty stories, and when Sophie refused to tell her any, complained to her parents that the nurse bored her to tears. Entertain the child, commanded the parents, so Sophie told her dirty stories, and was promptly fired for moral turpitude and kicked out without a reference. She found refuge in an orphanage in New York run by nuns. They farmed her out as a nanny. Fathers made advances to her, which she could have accepted and got rich. But all this time she kept her body pure and virgin. What money she could manage to save she sent to her youngest brother in Poland, enabling him to emigrate to America. He came, was disappointed, worked as a garbage boy for a hotel, accused Sophie of having tricked him, and would not speak to her ever afterward. A nursing job came along that took her to Paris again. Here she was destitute, and returned to Poland, where she was taken in by a rich uncle. This uncle was a widower and lived in sin with her cousin, whom he had enticed into his bed by telling her that Sophie had often done so. The shock of this lie unstrung her nerves and made a wreck of her composure for the rest of her life. Her brothers taunted her with having gone to America and failed to come back rich. She took up a life of dissipation. If no one believed in her virtue, why keep it? But dissipation undermined her constitution, and she had to recuperate at Baden, little as she could afford it.

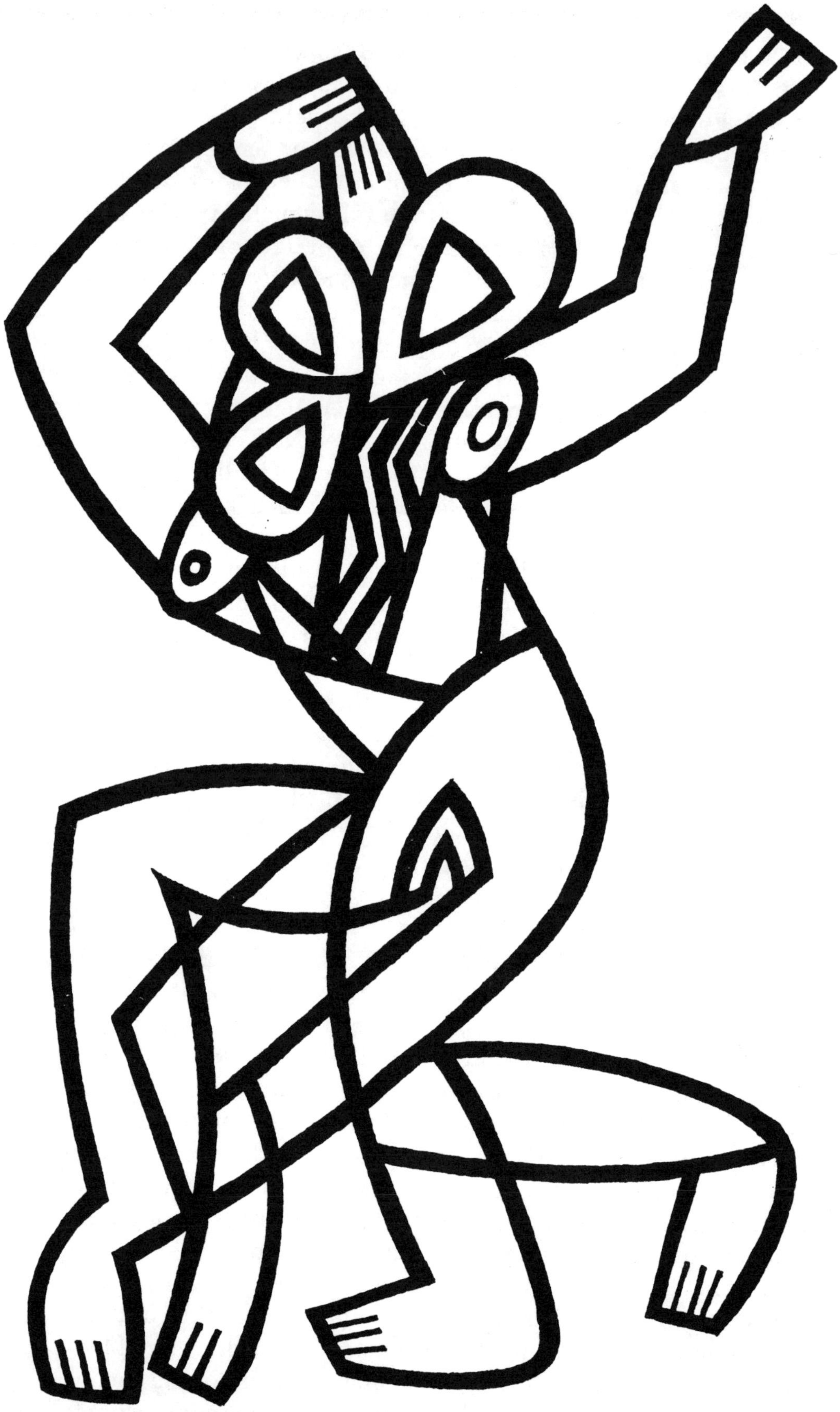

She then fell in love with a wealthy manufacturer aged fifty-three. He was witty, bright, kind, and in possession of a keen appreciation of the beauties of Nature. He courted her for a year without asking for her hand. When she tried to bring matters to a head, they had a fight that nearly sent them both to the hospital and thence to their graves. In this fracas he disclosed to her that he loved another, by whom he already had a son, and wished to remain free in case the other ever agreed to be his wife. She felt that her sanity was going. Her rich lover paid for her recuperation at a home in the country. She wrote him daily, he answered none of her letters. She would contemplate for hours the most painless means of doing away with herself. She returned to her family in Poland, where they taunted her with her failure, her age, her pretentions, her ugliness. She made her way to Paris again, and began to observe with fascination the faun-like young man who came every evening to the Bibliothèque Ste.-Geneviève to read books of anatomy. They met on the steps one evening at closing time, and walked along the Seine. She could scarcely believe it when he said he was in love with her.

THE BRITISH MUSEUM

Out of the past, out of Assyria, China, Egypt, the new.

EPSTEIN, BRANCUSI, MODIGLIANI, ZADKINE

Out of the new, a past.

VORTEX

From Rodin, passion. From John Cournos, courage. From Alfred Wolmark, spontaneity of execution. From Epstein, the stone, direct cutting. From Brancusi, purity of form. From Modigliani, the irony of grace. From Africa, the compression of form into minimal volume. From Lewis, the geometric. From Horace Brodsky, *camaraderie de la caserne*. From Ezra Pound, archaic China, the medieval, Dante, recognition. From Sophie, love, abrasion, doubt, the sweetness of an hour.

THE BRONZES OF BENIN

The Calf Bearer, T'ang sacrificial vessels, the shields of New South Wales, Soninke masks, the Egypt of *The Scribe* and *The Pharaoh Hunting Duck in the Papyrus Marsh*, Hokusai, Font-de-Gaume, Les Combarelles.

JE REVIENS D'UN ENFER

The young anthropologist De Launay, the student of mazes whose paper on labyrinths has been accepted for publication, has been shot through the neck outside the Labyrinth at Neuville-St.-Vaast, drowned in his own blood before the medics could see to the wound. *Je t'écris, cher Ezra, du fond d'une tranchée que nous avons creusée hier pour se protéger des obus qui nous arrivent sur la tête régulièrement toutes les cinq minutes, je suis ici depuis une semaine et nous couchons en plein air, les nuits sont humides et froides et nous en souffrons beaucoup plus que du feu de l'ennemi nous avons du repos aujourd'hui et ça fait bien plaisir.*

ST.-JEAN-DE-BRAYE

In the dry, brown October of 1891 there was born to Joseph Gaudier of St.-Jean-de-Braye, maker of fine doors and cabinets, descendant of one of the sculptors of Chartres, a son whom he baptized Henri.

CHARLEVILLE

Far to the south the one-legged Rimbaud lay dying in Marseilles, which he imagined to be Abyssinia. He was anxious that his caravan of camels laden with rifles and ammo should get off to a start before dawn, for the march was to Aden. *Armed with the fierceness of our patience*, he once wrote, *we shall reach the splendid cities at daybreak.*

TARGU JIU

In Craiova the fourteen-year-old Constantin Brancusi was learning to carve wood with chisel and maul. He was a peasant from Pestisani Gori across a larch forest from Targu Jiu, which he left when he was eleven, in the manner of the Roumanians, to master a trade. He would enter the national school for sculptors, and then walk from Roumania to Paris.

L'ENFANT DIFFICILE

He did not spank well, the child Henri. He doubled his fists, held his breath, and arched his back in an agony of stubbornness, until at an early age his parents began to reason with him before whacking his behind. He reasoned back. As he grew older, he kicked them when he was punished, and they reasoned the harder. *A very philosopher*, his father said, and his mother put her head to one side, crossed her hands over her apron, and looked at her son with complacent disappointment. *The rogue*, she said, *the darling little rogue.* He drew, like all children. His mother taught him to draw rabbits, and to surround them with grass and flowers. With his father's marking pencil, carefully sharpened for him with a pen knife, he drew ships, igloos, medieval trees, the cathedral at Orléans, and American Indians in their eagle-feather bonnets. At six he turned to insects. At first he drew gay fritillaries and gaudy moths. Only flowers had their absolute design and economy of form, which he thought of as *sitting right*. A roseleaf hopper was tucked into its abrupt parabola as if it were a creature all hat, and yet if you looked, it had feet and eyes and chest and belly just like the great dragonflies and damsels of the Loiret, or the mason wasps that built their combs under the eaves of the shed. But it was the grasshoppers and crickets that he drew most. From the forelegs of the grasshopper he learned the stark clarity of a bold design one half of which was mirror image of the other half. The wings of the moths were like that, but the principle was different. Wings worked together, the grasshopper's forelegs worked in opposition to the hindlegs, and yet the effort of the one complemented the effort of the other, like two beings jumping into each other, both going straight up. Earwigs, ants: nothing could be added, nothing subtracted. Who could draw a mosquito? In profile it was an elegance of lines, each at a perfect angle to the others. *Bugs*, his sisters said. Uncle Pierre gave him a box of colored pencils, and he drew pages of ladybirds and shieldbugs and speckled moths.

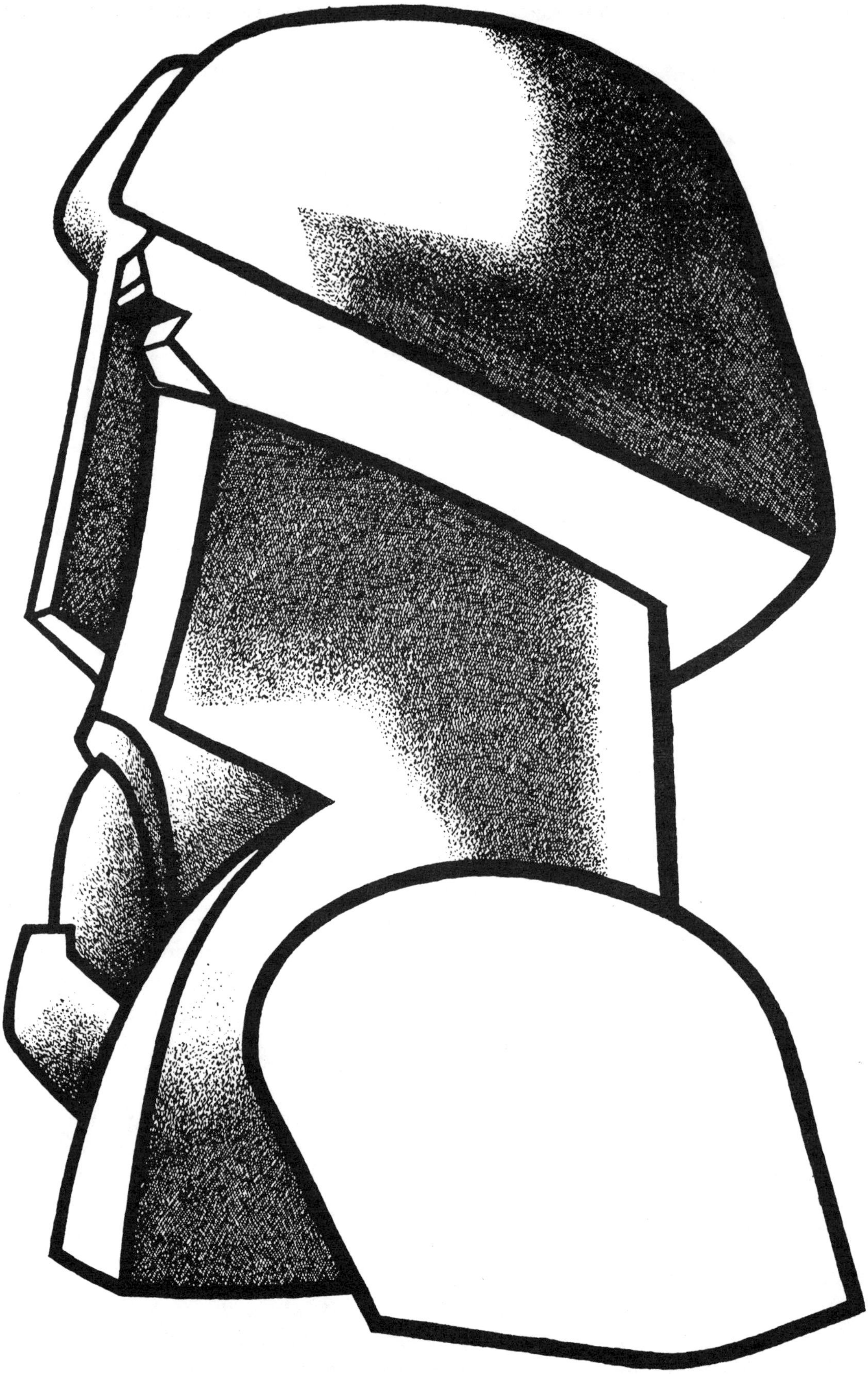

ARTILLERY BARRAGE. THE LABYRINTH. JUNE 1915.

Smoke boiling black, white underbelly, blooming sulphur, falling dirt and splinters. The daytime moon. Larks.

HENRI LE PETIT

The first day of school, his new oilcloth satchel in his lap, his new pencil box in his hands, he breathed the strange new smell of floor polish and washed slate blackboards in numb expectation. The upper half of the classroom door was glass, through which a bald gentleman in a celluloid collar came and peered from time to time. The teacher was a woman who handled books as he had never seen them handled before, with professional delicacy, grace, smart deliberateness. Down the front of her polka-dot dress she wore a necktie, like a man on Sunday, and a purple ribbon ran from her glasses to her bosom, anchored there by a brooch. The letter A was a moth, B was a butterfly, C was a caterpillar, D was a beetle, E an ant, F a mantis. G and H he knew: he had learned them the other way round, with a dot after each, to indicate who drew his drawings.

RAILWAY ARCH 25

His Font-de-Gaume. Planes, the surfaces of mass, meet at lines, each tilted at a different angle to light. The mass is energy. The harmony of its surfaces the emotion forever contained and forever released. Here he drank and roared with Brodsky, here he sculpted the phallus, the menhir, the totem called *Hieratic Bust of Ezra Pound. It will not look like you, you know.* It will look like your energy.

SOPHIE

All night by her bed, imploring her. It is revolting, unspiritual, she said.

PIK AND ZOSIK

Brother and sister. Even Mr. Pound believed it. Pikus and Zosiulik. The neurotic Pole and her sly fawn of a lover.

MON BON DZIECKO UKOCHANY

According to the little book which I am reading about Dante, the devil lived on very good terms with very few people, because of his terrible tendency to invective and reproach, and his extraordinary gift for irony and irresistible sarcasm—just like my own funny little Sisik. To be quite honest, Sisik, I love you passionately, from the depth of all my being, and I feel instinctively bound to you; what may often make me seem nasty to you is a kind of disagreeable horror that you don't love me nearly so much as I love you, and that you are always on the point of leaving me.

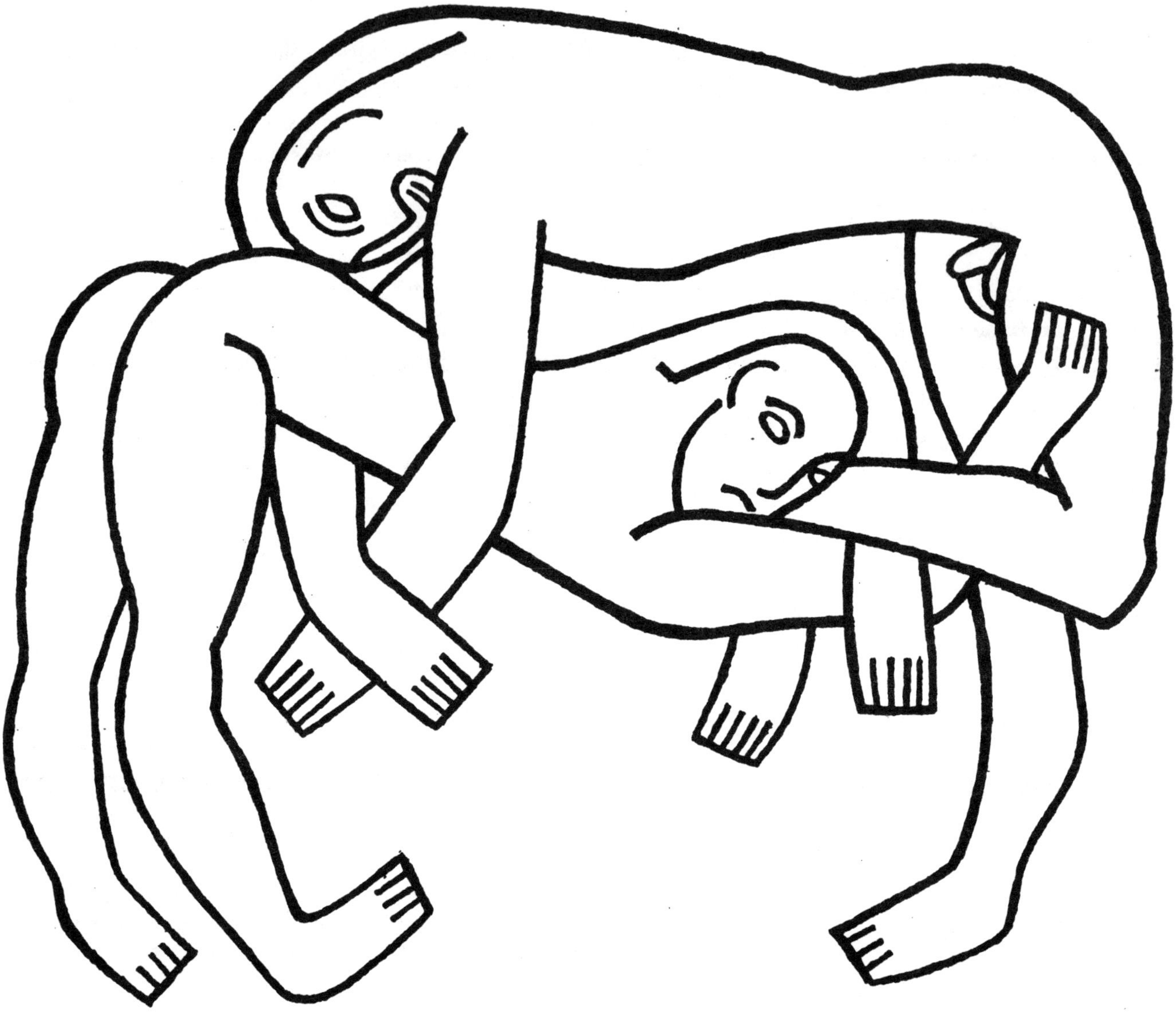

CAPITAINE MENAGER

Nous admirions tous Gaudier, non seulement pour sa bravoure, qui était légendaire, mais aussi et surtout pour sa vive intelligence et la haute idée qu'il avait de ses devoirs. A ma compagnie il était aimé de tous, et je le tenais en particulière estime car à cette époque de guerre de tranchées j'étais certain que—grâce à l'exemple qu'il donnerait à ses camarades—là où était Gaudier les Boches ne passeraient pas.

THE OLD WOMAN TO PASSERSBY

J'ai perdu mon fils. L'avez-vous trouvé? Il s'appelle Henri.

CHARGEZ!

One after another in those weeks of May and early June of 1915, the sugar refinery at Souchez, the cemetery of Ablain, the White Road, and the Labyrinth yielded to the fierce, unremitting blows of the French. The Labyrinth, all but impregnable, was a fortification contrived with tortuous, complicated tunnels, sometimes as deep as fifty feet below the surface, with mines and fortresses, deathtraps, caves and shelters, from which unexpected foes could attack with gas or liquid fire or knives. In the darkness and dampness and foulness of those Stygian vaults where in some places the only guiding gleams were from electric flashlights, men battled for days, for weeks, until June was half spent. What wonder that the Germans could scarcely believe the enemy had made it their own?

CORPORAL HENRI GAUDIER

Mort pour la Patrie. 4 octobre 1891–5 juin 1915.

THE RED STONE DANCER

Nos fesses ne sont pas les leurs. Il faut être absolument moderne.

▼ ▼ ▼

DANIEL SCHENKER

HOMO EX MACHINA:
WYNDHAM LEWIS ON THE DEFINITIONS OF MAN

SCIENCE AND SATIRE

Tarr's exotic woman-friend, Anastasya, catechizes him on the mysteries of art and life as they wade through a sumptuous meal at a restaurant off the Boulevard Clichy: "You say that actors on the stage are pure life, yet they represent something that *we* do not. But 'all the world's a stage,' isn't it? So how do we not also stand for something?" The dialogue proceeds with his response, and Anastasya's subsequent rejoinder:

> "Yes, life does generally stand for that something, too; but it only emerges and is visible in art."
> "Still, I don't know what art is!" (*Tarr*, 316-17)[1]

Tarr, however, refuses to provide a systematic definition of art, preferring instead to speak in metaphor —of the tortoise's hard shell and the plumage of birds. His ideas, as he unfurls them, are less original than brash, but remain to this day a frequently revisited oracle of twentieth-century aesthetics: "Deadness... is the first condition of art. The second is the absence of *soul*, in the sentimental human sense.... This is another condition of art; *to have no inside*, nothing you cannot see" (*Tarr*, 317).

If *Tarr*, however, survives the way many of the ancient classics have survived, as snippets of illustrative quotation in the commentaries, future historians will have a very misleading sense of the novel; for *Tarr* fails to observe these self-advertised standards. The novel is not *dead* (however that adjective might apply to fiction), it does traffic with the souls of men and women, and it often explores an inner landscape that the eye cannot see. Rebecca West, "by far the best book-critic at that time" in Lewis's estimation, described the first edition of *Tarr* as "a beautiful and serious work of art that reminds one of Dostoevsky only because it too is inquisitive about the soul..." (cited by Lewis in *BB*, 87). And the author himself, while urging that the parallel with Russian fiction not be exaggerated, admitted three decades later: "Its dynamism is psychological.... Although there is much action, it is the mind not the senses that provide it" (*RA*, 148). In *Tarr*, Lewis slowed the bustling pace of Dickensian narrative to the vicinity of absolute zero and managed to counter the "Dostoevsky diffuseness" with abruptness and a "strong visual notation" (*RA*, 148), but he had yet to purge himself of the Romantic legacy in art that values insides and origins at the expense of our superficial present.

That legacy infects even Tarr's polemical stance, which helps to explain why Lewis did not write the novel his chief "showman" (as he calls Tarr in the book's preface) might have demanded. A master of dialectic in his own right, Lewis subjects Tarr's aesthetic program to some careful scrutiny. Officially Tarr has set out on a crusade against the internalization of consciousness that has continued apace since some time after Homer and achieved orthodoxy in the late eighteenth and early nineteenth centuries. But during an impromptu lecture in the Luxembourg Gardens on the relation between genius and the crowd, Anastasya, his sole intellectual rival in the novel, mounts a challenge that goes to the very heart of his position: "Your philosophy reminds me of Jean-Jacques... your hostility to a tidy rabble, and preference for a rough and uncultivated bed to build on brings to mind 'wild nature' and the doctrine of the natural man. You want a human landscape similar to Jean-Jacques' rocks and water falls." He replies that, unlike Rousseau, he does not "poetize" [sic] wild nature nor set it forth as an ideal, but Tarr's insistence that crudeness and the isolation of the artist are prerequisite to the creative act has a distinctly Byronic ring. Visions of Manfred in the Alpine wilderness come to mind, or Shelley's reverie upon the seacoast from a poem about himself and Byron: "I love all waste/And solitary places; where we taste/The pleasure of believing what we see/Is boundless, as we wish our souls to be" ("Julian and Maddalo," ll. 14-17). Of course Shelley's lines betray as much love of self as love of nature and point up that characteristic Romantic desire to engulf the world with the soul. Tarr, however, fails to see that the hated impulse towards internalization often stems from a condition of embattled solitude like the kind he promotes. When Anastasya still cannot get Rousseau and Romanticism off her mind, he at last parries with, "An artist is a cold card, with a hide like a rhinoceros." But Anastasya will not be fooled, for even behind this warlike display she sees his little egoistic fire burning (with a hard, gemlike flame, no doubt): "You are poetizing him!" (*Tarr*, 246). Tarr has not yet learned to fully disentangle himself from the enemy.

Lewis's interest in Romanticism at this time extended only as far as his need to expose and exorcise the Romantic in himself. In *Tarr*, purgation took the form of Otto Kreisler's suicide (this boorish student incarnated nineteenth-century German philosophy and aesthetics) and Tarr's inability to leave behind the sentimental attachment to self apparent in his "cold card" manifesto. Sentimentality Lewis elsewhere defines as an unwillingness to take an idea to its inevitable conclusion. If one wants to play the role of Nietzschean Superman or Byronic hero, all well and good, but suicide and marriage (*Tarr*'s heroes' respective fates) are not the sign of genuine commitment to principle. Neither can much be said for the artist who isolates himself upon some lonely eminence only to repopulate his private universe with companionable extensions of his imperial soul. The entire Romantic age, which so often reeled in horror from the consequences of the revolutionary energies it had initially released, exemplified in history this species of hypocrisy. But Lewis's attack on Romanticism, both the historical period and its lingering ideology, had constructive as well as destructive aspects. Over against Lord Byron, Lewis would have opposed Chapman's Duke of Byron, a figure who stands for the stark and analytic genius of an age that men like Byron and Shelley tried feebly to revive: the Renaissance.

The Renaissance unquestionably holds the place of honor in Modernist historiography. Pound raided the past like a Jamesian millionaire hoping to acquire *objets d'art* for his intrinsically uninteresting native city; the more European and sophisticated Lewis overlooked things for the sake of controlling ideas and the people behind them. The fruits of these early labors are distilled into *The Lion and the Fox*, a book-length study that purports to examine "the role of the hero in the plays of Shakespeare." In 1937, he described the book as being "all about Shakespeare's politics." In fact it is sometimes difficult to say what Lewis's early nonfiction is about, since his arguments bear an unfortunate resemblance to the trajectory of buckshot, fanning out as you move away from the first line of a chapter or volume. But whatever its thesis, *The Lion and the Fox* presents an important meditation on two of the most influential personalities of the age.

While Lewis followed tradition by paying homage to da Vinci as the Renaissance man *par excellence*, his achievement, because it did not receive immediate and universal recognition, is not the occasion of Lewis's essay. Among the Italians, Machiavelli is singled out as having had the most significant impact on the thinking of Western Europe, for better and for worse. Lewis especially admired Machiavelli's candor, his "diabolical honesty," which unmasked "organized duplicity... giving away the whole position of the ruler, and revealing even the very nature of all authority" (*LF*, 76). Although written in a style as disarmingly simple as Defoe's, *The Prince* was ranked by Lewis with Darwin's *Origin of Species* as a book "that forces civilization to face about and confront the grinning shadow of its Past, and acknowledge the terrible nature of its true destiny" (*LF*, 76). The allusion to Darwin, and to the quasi-scientific prose of the eighteenth century, is intended to remind us that the modern science which gave us natural selection and other sundry de-mystifications had its origins in the Renaissance. If Machiavelli could be called typical of his age, it would be because he was first and foremost a man of science; his particular genius showed itself in application:

> The political science of Machiavelli was the first strictly *scientific* doctrine produced in Europe, the result of an inductive psychological method. It was the first political system to refuse to admit anything that it could not directly observe. (*LF*, 90)

The reader familiar with *Tarr* will hear in this a distinct echo of Tarr's insistence that art should treat "nothing you cannot *see*." Wyndham Lewis the artist will often characterize his work as scientific, arguing that both art and science spring from the same impulse towards an unvarnished truth. For empiric proof of this doctrine, he needed only to turn back to Renaissance Italy, and the time before new methods of production and reproduction had divided the world into "the sciences" and "the humanities." "Science," Lewis tells us, "was understood as a universal principle of exact experiment. As much in the painting of a picture as in the construction of a fortification, the artist *and* the man of science would appear" (*LF*, 51). Coluccio Salutati, secretary of the Florentine republic, wrote business documents like works of literature; the painter Leonardo designed engines of war. So just as Machiavelli was one of the first scientists in modern Europe, he was among its first artists, too: these talents were perfectly commutative.

Sometimes one senses in Lewis a lingering regret that as an artist in our own age, long after the divorce of art and science had been made permanent by Newton and the positivists, he could have no role in the practical affairs of his community; and that when he did speak out on politics or economics, he was not likely to be listened to precisely on account of his artistic credentials. The motif of the artist as man of action appears in many Lewis novels, but it takes on special poignancy near the end of his life in *The Human Age, Self Condemned,* and *The Red Priest*—and in the scenario for an unwritten historical novel, the only one he ever seems to have contemplated, set in the cinquecento Italy of Machiavelli.[2]

But at the same time that Lewis casts a wistful eye towards political power, he warns us of the dangers to the artist's (or scientist's) integrity from an involvement in worldly affairs. What finally tarnishes Machiavelli's reputation as an artist in politics is his tacit alliance with the "foxes"—the small and cunning men of the world—to whom, of course, *The Prince* had been originally addressed. In this respect he is overshadowed by Shakespeare, foremost representative of Anglo-Saxon culture (always the main region of Lewis's inquiry), who will eventually be brought forward as the nonfiction hero of *The Lion and the Fox*. This does not mean to say that Shakespeare escaped the tremendous influence of Italian political science on the Tudor imagination generally. The Italians at the very least set the terms of all future dissections of human nature with their simple but powerful dialectic: "The form this essay has been given," Lewis informs us in a chapter called "Shakespeare's Nihilism," "has been that of a hunt in the mind of Shakespeare, as exhibited in his plays, for the two symbolical animals, the lion and the fox, used by Machiavelli in the composition of his perfect human being" (*LF*, 177). The results of Lewis's hunt are sometimes difficult to figure out since he seems intent upon making Shakespeare into a kind of "Enemy" much like himself. But he does insist on one point: although plays such as *Othello* and *Antony and Cleopatra* carefully anatomize the inevitable power struggle between the hero with clay feet and his cunning if ignoble nemesis—between the two "symbolical animals" in all their diverse incarnations—Shakespeare, unlike Machiavelli, elects never to take sides. He understood too well the operation of these rigorous forces in nature. Thus:

> ... it would not be natural for Shakespeare to intervene in the eternal dispute of good and evil, or in the battles of the animal kingdom, where the foxes and lions perpetually manoeuvre. It is impossible to make a fox-hunter of him: and he showed no tendency to wish to be a lion. (*LF*, 178)

Shakespeare's almost total detachment from his material thus perfects the scientific analysis introduced first in Italy by Machiavelli and his fellow artists. Having arrived at this juncture, we must now introduce one or two caveats.

To begin, Lewis, in the same paragraph cited above, goes on in that inimitable manner of his to contradict himself. He says that certainly in the case of *Othello*, there can be little doubt that Shakespeare is *not* on the side of Othello's "small destroyer," Iago. What then has suddenly happened to Shakespeare's even-handedness? Nothing at all has happened to Shakespeare; however, our own expectations in this case have received quite a jolt. We are accustomed to think of scientific detachment as akin to the godlike indifference of Stephen Dedalus's artist (whose characteristics are enumerated in another Modernist oracle).[3] But here the godlike indifference of Joyce is supplanted by the *human* indifference of the Lewisian artist—who *as a man* cannot be wholly indifferent. Lewis maintained that enough of Shakespeare's personality emerges in his work to indicate his basic sympathy with his fallen heroes. (Claims to impersonality, Lewis argues elsewhere, are as phony as claims to indifference, since all human speech implies a person and a personality.) In the last analysis, Lewis saw Shakespeare, the exemplary artist, as a kind of shamanistic executioner who presides while the ritual of the "dying god"—the fated triumph of the small over the great that nourishes the Christian imagination—is enacted again and again, as necessity demands. His science, however, did not leave him unaffected by the spectacle:

> His *impassibility* was the professional mask of the hangman. For dramatic effect the dramatist, like the hangman, must be *impassible*. . . . But actually the [dramatic] mask was incessantly convulsed with the most painful unprofessional emotions; and it was apt to be tear-stained and fixed in a bitter grimace as he left the scaffold. (*LF*, 145)

That sudden tear coursing down the mask of the communist showmaster in the last scene of *The Revenge for Love* has its origins in this vignette of Shakespeare. In any event, this important distinction between godlike indifference and mere professional impassibility helps us to understand how Lewis, who insisted throughout his career that the artist had to remain an apolitical figure, spent most of his active life thinking and writing about politics.

A second check upon the scientific impulse behind the artist has to do with the dialectic of artist and audience. As a popular author, Shakespeare was beholden to the pennies of those who came to see his plays and, in some measure, had to satisfy their expectations. Against this social backdrop, the meaning of Shakespearean tragedy—his enactment of the "dying god" ritual—takes on an added dimension:

> The implication of those monotonous sacrifices is clearly non-heroic, and not engineered in favour of the titan; and in that sense tragic art is in its essence democratic and religious, the enemy of human energy and success, or such a check on them as to be that, and the opponent of action. (*LF*, 170)

But if tragedy favors the Many against the One and stands watch as the foeman of human energy, Lewis had nothing better to say for tragedy's smiling twin, and all that it represented. The raucous comic spirit of Aristophanes, exemplified in his attack on Socrates in *The Clouds*, militated against innovation and intelligence, "and served the conservative bourgeois spirit with its compelling laughter" (*LF*, 38). Comedy stands for smugness and the idolatry of success; and the comic artist in his turn pays the piper called aristocracy or despotism, which demand just such expressions.

Lewis's Shakespeare is an admittedly paradoxical creation, at once perfectly detached from and involved with his characters. He exists as part of a Utopian scheme—and all great art, Lewis tells us, *is* Utopian (*LF*, 114)—superimposed on a planet (our own) where the chance that an ideal can be fulfilled is so slight that the artist who seriously pursues one is justly placed, without a sentimental glimmer in the eye, in the company of the lunatic. Still, at odd moments, Shakespeare does seem able to mirror the world without quite touching it or declaring a stake in the eternal wars of lions and foxes:

> Shakespeare had an infinite love and compassion for the heroic figures of his art, or of anything naturally translatable into that world; but it is unlikely that the things of this world appeared to him to have any importance save as symbols of that. He recreated everything for himself, and his system balanced with nature to a nicety, and his work exhibited nature's system, too. (*LF*, 209)

In its broad outlines, Lewis has simply reproduced the eighteenth-century argument for Shakespeare as poet of Nature, with perhaps a more than eighteenth-century emphasis on the private character of Nature as refined and mediated by the Bard. Of greater significance for us is the work Lewis referred to at this point to illustrate Shakespeare's method at its finest: *Timon of Athens*.

The figure of Timon presents a kind of test case of Shakespeare's scientific ability. On the one hand, Lewis informs us, Shakespeare was fully capable of seeing in Timon the furious egotist, insane spendthrift, and dissipated fool—and this view does predominate in the first half of the play. But balanced against this is the organ music of a violent and mournful despair that "rises from a great nature, full of generosity in a time of awakening and immense astonishment at the vileness of the world" (*LF*, 209-10). Unlike tragedy with its democratic biases, *Timon of Athens* does not share in the "general delight" at the hero's fall (*LF*, 168); and the play expresses little of that comic spirit which above all values success and security. Instead, the noble and foolish Timon inhabits the sterile, and yet not dispassionate, environment of Shakespeare's personal system:

> That personal system had no ethical bias, but was entirely an aesthetic phenomenon. Its goods and bads were the beautiful and the ugly. As such it was necessarily noble and immaculate, removed from the sphere of Thersites or Iago, made of different clay, and contrasted always with the actual world of men, and its figures provided with a suitable *pathos* at the hands of the crowd. They are in this way much more "moral" in their *effect* than the most powerful sermon or display of "principle" can be. (*LF*, 210)

Scholars, incidentally, have never been able to agree whether *Timon of Athens* should be classified as a tragedy or a comedy. Lewis, who rejected both terms as inadequate for Shakespeare's most important work, had another name for the genre of *Timon*: he called it satire.

In Lewis's work of the decade following the First World War, as he tried to assimilate experience of art and war into a personal system of his own, we see the process, rather than the product, of his thought. This begins to change about 1930 after he had mapped, subjugated, and policed the contemporary intellectual scene in a series of theoretical books (one of which we will examine in some detail in the next section). *Paleface* accomplishes in sentences what it took *Time and Western Man* paragraphs to do. The pamphlet *Satire and Fiction*, hastily written (its author confesses) to promote *The Apes of God*, summarizes much that *The Lion and the Fox* had to say about what art can and should be.

The part entitled simply "Satire" furnishes a gloss on Lewis's earlier statement that Shakespeare's personal system, at its strongest in a play like *Timon*, had no "ethical bias." Here he asserts that whoever criticizes from an explicitly moral vantage is secretly the ally of the society he attacks. Where else did Juvenal, to cite the classic example of the moral satirist, learn morality but from the official ideals of the Roman state? An alliance with society means an alliance with the powers that be—democratic, aristocratic, or monarchic—and a surrender of the perfect equanimity that distinguishes satire from comedy or tragedy. The social consequences of one's art, as determined by its often unintentional political alignment, cannot be ignored by the conscientious man, though at all events Lewis maintained that no intelligent and wide-ranging mind had ever succumbed to "the crude injunctions of any purely moral code" (*SF*, 43).

The artist's detachment, in the limited sense that Lewis intended, never existed as an end in itself ("art for art's sake" died for Lewis in 1914), but was necessary to insure the scientific accuracy of the artist's observations—a prerogative that he inherits, as we have seen, from the Renaissance masters. Lewis makes this point on several occasions in *Satire and Fiction*: "Satire is in reality often nothing else but *the truth*, in fact that of Natural Science" (*SF*, 48). It is important to understand that by the phrase "Natural Science," he has in mind the strictly empirical investigations of the fifteenth through the early nineteenth centuries, before science itself upset the common-sense view of the world, and replaced the eye with electrodes and Geiger counters as the instruments of research. Therefore, when Lewis calls satire "scientific," he means that it is purely a work of the eye. But can a single eye—even the dispassionate eye of the satirist cum natural scientist—give us the complete picture? What about the possibility of distinct satiric and romantic truths about a person, or perhaps an unvarnished "non-satiric, non-romantic" truth underlying all? While Lewis concedes that these different views may stand upon an equal intellectual footing, he casts his vote for the accuracy of satire, if only because "the humanly 'agreeable' is more often false than the humanly 'disagreeable.'" And to this he adds sardonically: "That is unavoidable, seeing what we are" (*SF*, 49).

What we are, of course, is precisely the question in dispute. Throughout his career Lewis sought to describe, in fiction and non-fiction, the social and political relations that bind men to one another; but he followed Machiavelli and Hobbes (and not Proudhon and Marx) in his conviction that a study of politics must begin with an empirical survey of human nature. It is pointless to talk about reconstructing society along socialist lines, for example, if you believe that men are *inherently* selfish, or in some other way *irrevocably* flawed. Lewis, however, analyzed this problem in starker terms than the relative amount of good and evil in men; he asked instead whether or not it was even proper to think of most men as *men*.

In *Satire and Fiction* Lewis places himself in a tradition of satiric writing that runs back at least as far as Ben Jonson (although he did not necessarily think of him as an exemplary satirist). Jonson has never been as popular a writer as the Shakespeare of

A Midsummer Night's Dream or *The Tempest*, as witness the complaint of William Hazlitt in *The English Comic Writers*, which Lewis quotes at some length:

> Shakespeare's characters are men; Ben Jonson's are more like machines, governed by mere routine, or by the convenience of the poet, whose property they are. In reading the one, we are let into the minds of his characters, we see the play of their thoughts, how their humours flow and work.... His humour (so to speak) bubbles, sparkles, and finds its way in all directions, like a natural spring. In Ben Jonson it is, as it were, confined in a leaden cistern, where it stagnates and corrupts; or directed only through certain artificial pipes and conduits to answer a given purpose.... Sheer ignorance, bare-faced impudence, or idiot imbecility, are his dramatic commonplaces—things that provoke pity or disgust, instead of laughter. (*SF*, 45)

Lewis's response to this charge against Jonson, and by extension, against himself, is twofold. He first of all states that since no one expects the work of the surgeon to provoke bubbling laughter, why should one expect it from the artist who anatomizes man and his world as he ferrets for the truth about both? This repeats the "art as science" argument, and a bit further on Lewis again returns to the Italian Renaissance for a source authority: "Natural Science is a disagreeable study (this was acutely recognized by Leonardo da Vinci, himself both a scientist and a master of vitalist illusion)" (*SF*, 49). And while laughter does have a role to play in satire, it is rather the harsh and mocking laughter appropriate to the situation of a mortal and therefore tragic being. Secondly, Lewis questions the very premise upon which Hazlitt's distinction between Shakespeare's and Jonson's characters rests:

> But when Hazlitt speaks of the characters "like machines, governed by routine," there, I think, he gives himself entirely away. For what else is a character in satire than that? Is it not just because they are such *machines, governed by routine* —or creatures that stagnate, as it were "in a leaden cistern"—that the satirist, in the first instance, has considered them suitable for satire? (*SF*, 45)

The force of this declaration is not immediately certain, as we shall see in a moment, but it seems to suggest that some men should indeed be valued and treated as machines—the soulless automata that composed the animal kingdom for Descartes, and an entire array of servomechanisms that have otherwise bedevilled the literary imagination since the time of E. T. A. Hoffman and Mary Shelley.

The attentive reader may wish to quibble: Lewis says that characters *in satire* are machines, but doesn't this leave open the possibility that characters in some other genre are not? Practically speaking, no. In the wake of Lewis's huge claims for satire—it does, after all, capture "*the truth*" which eludes romance—little remains for other art forms to boast of. And if art does not express the truth, what reason is there to value it as art? Lewisian satire also takes under its protection works that up until then had not been considered as such: "The wind that blows through satire is as bitter as that that predominates in the pages of *Timon* or *King Lear*. Indeed the former *is* a satire. And *Hamlet*, for instance, is very much that too—a central satire developing now into tragedy, now into comedy" (*SF*, 46). So the identification in Lewis's mind is nearly complete: when he says that all men in satire are machines, he might as well be saying that all men in *art* are machines.

Should we from this conclude that men in *life*, for whom the art-men presumably stand in as counters, are machines, too? One might begin to formulate an answer by turning back to Lewis's author-to-the-reader apology in *The Wild Body*, "Inferior Religions," in which he speaks of "a new human mathematic" and of men "frozen and congealed into logic" (*The Wild Body*, 234, 236); or perhaps the reader should take up Lewis's biography to see how he actually treated his fellow man. However, the interesting question for us will not be what Wyndham Lewis *really* believed (the jaded modern critic no longer trifles with such matters), but why during the twenties and thirties he would be so insistently perverse— especially when this anti-humanistic position seemed to bring him into line with the Futuristic "Automobilism" at the base of all fascistic doctrines, whose mechanical hustle-bustle he had rejected as early as 1914.[4] What then might have been the calculated polemical reason of Lewis's argument in favor of the machine? For the answer to this we will have to turn to the chief theoretical book of the period.

FROM BERGSON TO BERKELEY

A quarter-century after its publicaion, Hugh Kenner placed the phrase "one of the dozen or so most important books of the twentieth century" in casual apposition to *Time and Western Man*.[5] Few people would have agreed with that pronouncement in 1954, and I doubt that many have been won over since then. Prima facie, *Time and Western Man* has *not* been an important book in the sense of, let us say, Heidegger's *Sein und Zeit* (published in the same year) which remains the subject of endless debate.[6] The most telling appraisal comes from Lewis's second autobiographical volume, *Rude Assignment*:

> Arriving as I do now at "Time and Western Man" I feel that I am standing before a substantial fortress, once full of vigorous defenders, but now silent, probably a place where bats hang upside down and jackals find a musty bed-chamber. To be frank, I have no desire to re-enter it.—What was it set there to defend? Obviously the Western World, which in less than two decades has fallen to pieces. (*RA*, 192)

Time and Western Man today lies in the archive like a modern *Paradise Lost*—a monument to dead ideas—a reactionary bill of particulars sworn out against the twentieth century.

Reactionary? Such at least is the term customarily used to describe the ideology of Modernism, but the word does get bandied about with a good deal of bogus self-righteousness. That Lewis stood recusant from liberal democracy, Marxism, the inevitability of history, and the tenets of orthodox humanism cannot be denied. However, in *Time and Western Man* he makes the following counter-assertion:

> What I have written—and I call to witness my book, *The Lion and The Fox*—should prove me exceedingly remote from what is generally termed a "reactionary." But I am entirely sick to death, like a great host of other people, of many of the forms that "revolution" takes, in art, sociology, science, and life: and I would, however modestly, hasten the day when "revolution" should become a more rigorous business, humanely and intellectually, if undertaken at all, and no longer be left only in the hands of people who do nothing but degrade and falsify it. (*TWM*, 135)

I might add that in an earlier volume of nonfiction, *The Art of Being Ruled*, Lewis actually expressed a certain admiration for the Bolshevik revolution in Russia which at least had the virtue of bringing about an honest and radical change in that country. He could never understand how in Western Europe and in England particularly many of the same people who were the loudest proponents of revolution also had the greatest stake in the preservation of the old social and economic order. *Time and Western Man*, however, goes after the related intellectual hypocrisy that falsified the work of numerous contemporary thinkers and artists, and which Lewis found exemplified in the writings of Henri Bergson.

This is not the place to undertake a complete exposition of Bergson's philosophy. However, it will be useful to begin with one or two generalizations which do not, I believe, misrepresent the spirit of his work. Bergson adopted Heraclitus' dictum, "all things flow," and raised it to the status of a theological principle. No point or axis, not even the human intellect, remains unaffected by this universal motion (which Lewis called *Time*—"Time, on the physical side, and apart from its discrimination in the hand of Bergson into mental and mathematical time, is merely change or movement" [*TWM*, 163]). As a corollary to this, Bergson suggested that there could be no dead tissue, as it were, anywhere in the universe. The motile impulse, almost a species of low-level consciousness, suffused every nook and cranny of God's creation. Lewis's broadside in *Time and Western Man* is leveled against these two main positions.

His first objection had less to do with the content of Bergsonism than with its advertisement—which in the modern world counts for as much, if not more. "Time," the philosophy of change, is paraded forth as a revolutionary doctrine; but as Lewis saw it, Bergson was at the head of a Romantic reaction against the materialistic world picture developed by natural science. We find early evidence of this despair in the face of materialism whenever we leaf through Tennyson, or when we read of Meredith's Prince Lucifer gazing bitterly upon the circling stars, "the army of unalterable law." Clearly this had been the result of three centuries of rationalistic probing by science since the Renaissance, which had chased soul and spirit out of all the individual members of creation, not excepting man himself. Lewis viewed Bergson's program for reform as a new animism which called for the taking of the inert and passive residue left by science and "pumping it full of time" to make it come to life once again. A vulgar interpretation of modern physics (which was itself caught up in the Time-cult mentality) was then brought in to lend an air of objective legitimacy to this wholesale conversion from product into process: even the stuffed chair in the living room had now been transformed from an unfeeling lump of substance into a veritable beehive of sub-atomic activity, not unlike ourselves in many respects.

When Lewis referred to Bergson's philosophy as part of a "Romantic" reaction, he wanted not only to convey his general impression of Bergson's writing (or of those he associated with Bergson) but to locate its theoretical origins in the early decades of the nineteenth century. One would expect, perhaps, an extended discussion of Hegel, father of the hated *Zeitgeist*, but in *Time and Western Man*, we find only a pair of references to him, one of these referring to his philosophy as a "repulsively technical one" (*TWM*, x). (When Lewis recalled his early exposure to German philosophy in *Rude Assignment,* he admitted, "Hegel... I could never read"—*RA*, 120.) Instead, he turns his attention for several pages to Arthur Schopenhauer and his "great book upon the subject of the Will." Lewis identifies Schopenhauer as the first philosopher to try to look natural science straight in the eye. He accepted its positivist insights and banished from his system all overtly theological principles: God, human freedom and responsibility, the great chain of being. Schopenhauer's new cosmos is simply a Newtonian machine without the super-addition of a First Principle. The machine itself, including the part labeled "Man," has only a tenuous phenomenal existence; the sole *Ding an sich* in the Schopenhauerian system is the Will whose representation is the visible world. Of course, the Will functions as a God in this secular pantheism, though it remains a kind of cipher-God, a brute and mindless power, that goes on representing itself without meaning or purpose.

The one virtue of Schopenhauer's philosophy was its "honest pessimism" (*TWM*, 434). For what else could be our response to the knowledge that our destiny is controlled by a blind, mechanical Will? Commented Lewis, "Despair is a stimulant, and as a doctrine of despair we are inclined to welcome the creed of Schopenhauer" (*TWM*, 327). He notes, however, that the absolute character of the Will so mocks human wisdom and endeavor that Schopenhauer is moved to counsel resignation and not rebellion—a logical conclusion for Schopenhauer, perhaps, but one that Lewis, who believed in an eternal struggle of opposites, could hardly accept. Still, this was preferable to Bergsonism, which he viewed as Schopenhauer turned sideways and presented in bad faith. In a word, Bergson re-christened the Will *élan vital*, which is equally mindless, but which he identifies with a happy animal energy that penetrates to every atom of existence, making it come organically alive. Instead of resigning ourselves to *élan vital*, Bergson urges that we joyously give ourselves to this newly discovered source of Life.

When reading Lewis on Bergson or any of the other Time-cult villains in *Time and Western Man* (the list includes Whitehead, Spengler, Russell, Croce, William James, and virtually all the major literary figures of Lewis's day), we have to keep in mind Lewis's assumption that the basic unit of existence is the individual. On one occasion he even speaks dourly of a "first law of being"—an injunction that a man preserve his own identity through all the shapes or forms that the self adopts as it attempts to express its innate vitality. So the idea of a wholesale merging into something other, no matter how warm and pleasant, was necessarily repugnant to him. Lewis also considered the individual the sole repository of value in human culture—not the group (as in socialist theory) or the natural world itself (as in Bergson). Let me illustrate further with reference to an author Lewis did not discuss but might well have, had not most of his critical energy been absorbed into contemporary literature. I place on exhibit the following lines:

> And what if all of animated nature
> Be but organic Harps diversely fram'd,
> That tremble into thought, as o'er them sweeps
> Plastic and vast, one intellectual breeze,
> At once the Soul of each, and God of all?
>
> (Coleridge, "The Aeolian Harp," ll. 44-48)

The interesting phrase here is "intellectual breeze." Obviously (assuming one shares Lewis's faith in the individual) the breeze cannot be intellectual; only human beings are capable of intellection. The Romantic imagination steals this uniquely human quality and distributes it, Prometheus-like, throughout the inanimate world. In the process, however, men are reduced along with everything else to an egalitarian community of "organic harps"—machines that make music, and organic ones, but machines none the less. Schopenhauer's displacement of the Will and Bergson's displacement of *élan vital* from their proper human owners to the world at large follow essentially this same paradigm.

But Lewis, who had an uncanny sixth sense for buried ideology, suspected there was more to this than a mere altruistic desire to play Prometheus to all the rocks and stones and trees. In the antiseptic workrooms of philosophic speculation Lewis caught a whiff of politics: "No doctrine, so much as the

Time-doctrine, lends itself to the purpose of the millennial politics of revolutionary human change, and endless 'Progress' " (*TWM*, 434). Behind the assault on the position of the individual he could see a more general attack upon all forms of authority in the name of democratic reform. But even admitting for the moment the need for more democracy and less authority (as though the two were mutually exclusive), who is after all intended to gain by these changes? Presumably the average man or woman. Certainly Bergsonism, which advertised itself as the enemy of the materialistic army of unalterable law, made "a considerable sentimental appeal"; but in the long run it rendered the plain man more insignificant that ever:

> For what the *benefit* to you, in this famous change from matter to mind, from "matter" to "organism," is going to be, it is very difficult to discover. For it is not *you* who become "organic"; *you* have been organic all along, no one has ever questioned that. It is your tables and chairs, in a pseudo-leibnizian animism, not you, that are to become "organic." (*TWM*, 170)

Throughout *Time and Western Man*, but more especially in the companion volume, *The Art of Being Ruled*, Lewis suggests that precisely such a philosophy, infecting in its more vulgar forms a subject population, actually facilitates rule by those parties in power. By ascribing the course of events to Will or History or *Zeitgeist*, for example, in which we all participate on equal terms, a ruler can effectively cloak his exercise of power behind an impersonal—and therefore irresponsible—device. Thus, in the long run, this "romantic reaction" was not only reactionary in itself, but failed to protect the individual against the encroaching mechanization and authoritarianism of modern life. If anything, it had made matters worse.

Bergson's philosophy also promised men what we today would call expanded consciousness. As one merges into the *élan vital*, his physical senses extend to infinity, and the gates of perception open wide to bring him into contact with vivid and concrete reality. Reality, however, no longer consists of the discrete and inert objects that were the creation of a classical mind biased in favor of the spatial dimension. Time and change must now be taken into account. This new object is neither absolute nor eternal, but rather a series of events (seamlessly joined) glimpsed at from a number of different perspectives. Thus reality should not be thought of as a thing (in space) but as a becoming or an impulse towards (in time).

With this emphasis on the extra-human power that continually informs the visible world, the "Time-school" presented itself as a novel variety of philosophical realism. The realist, of course, claims that the world exists independently of the mind, in opposition to the all-mental arrangements of the idealist camp. Naturally we should think that the descriptive adjective "concrete" more deservedly belongs to the realist's system than to that of the idealist. There is nothing very concrete about an idea, after all. But Lewis in one of his more dramatic gestures asserts that precisely the reverse is true: "[The reader] will perhaps think it is a strange thing that 'absolute idealism' should stand for the *concrete*, the *non-abstract*, whereas contemporary thought, which is surely highly 'realistic' and positivist, should stand for the *abstract* or the *non-concrete*." He goes on here to add that "such an extreme idealist doctrine as that of Berkeley . . . stood even fanatically for the *concrete*, as against the *abstract*" (*TWM*, 165).

I can hardly overemphasize the importance of this invocation of Bishop Berkeley, who is, in fact, one of the half-dozen or so writers to whom Lewis ever extended his unqualified endorsement. Because Lewis viewed himself as a kind of new Berkeleyan, we will better understand what all the fuss is about in *Time and Western Man* when we see that Lewis's quarrel with Bergson in many ways repeats Berkeley's falling out with John Locke.

In his search for an objective absolute, Locke recognized the unreliability of the human senses. The color of something, for example, changed according to the intensity of the light in which it was seen; objects will feel hotter or colder depending upon the body temperature of the observer. So one could not be wholly empirical in his approach to the world unless he was prepared to risk frequent deception. Locke therefore promulgated his famous separation of primary and secondary qualities. The latter were indeed contingent upon perception, but the primary qualities of something—mass, extension in space, volume—were inherent and functioned as a guarantee that the thing did *really* exist, regardless of what we thought about it. This is the crucial point at which Locke's empiricism intersects with philosophical realism.

The chief drawback to Locke's concrete entities, secure in their primary qualities, is that we can never have any direct knowledge of them. For how could we perceive something without the interference of those troublesome secondary qualities? "For my own part, I see evidently that it is not in my power to frame an idea of a body extended and moved, but I must withal give it some color or other sensible quality which is acknowledged to exist only in the mind" (*Principles of Human Knowledge*, I, 10).[7] Even if Locke's thing-in-itself did exist, it could never be concrete in any experiential way for a mind—the human mind—condemned never to step behind the curtain of appearances.

Back now to the twentieth century. Lewis notes that the Enlightenment realist was quite satisfied to have his real matter static and dead. (Locke discusses the world as if it were composed of differently shaped wooden blocks.) But the insights of modern physics will no longer permit this state of affairs:

> The materialist of today is still obsessed with the wish to make this dead matter *real*: only he is more subtle, and he knows very well that it cannot be "real" if it remains "dead" and "matter." So he brings it to life, by pumping it full of "time," until it is a quicksilver beneath his hand. Having done this, he proceeds to attempt its fixation, somehow and at some point, into an objective absolute: and . . . that is no easy matter. (*TWM*, 166)

The absolute or primary quality of modern realists is time or change: the process of becoming. But the volatilized objects of the Time philosophers (which are not of course objects at all, but ongoing clusters of events) are so elusive that the human mind can no more concretely perceive them than it could Locke's odorless, colorless, and tasteless entities. Time, according to Lewis, was one of a "new race of *things-in-themselves*, or noumena, which have all been invented to *physical ends*, to commence with, and are on the other hand exceedingly abstract and, according to the general use of the term, non-physical" (*TWM*, 165). Lewis, like Berkeley, could not see how the insistence upon a material absolute could do anything other than lead us from the physical world and into a realm of abstraction; and so, again following his eighteenth-century mentor, he abandoned any notion of primary qualities or the independent existence of things in favor of the position that our entire world is contingent upon our perception of it.

But hasn't Lewis just sawed off the polemical limb upon which he has been standing all the while? For how can he expect to argue on the side of the concrete if he says that everything is in the mind? Perhaps the difficulty lies in our interpretation of that word "concrete" which, although frequently heard in philosophical debate, is actually quite meaningless except as it carries some rhetorical or political force. It is equivalent to stamping your foot on the ground for emphasis, or employing that same foot to kick a stone when you tire of arguing and want to prove that your words correspond to reality, without putting it so abstractly as that. The occasion of its utterance is therefore the time to become a little suspicious of the man who uses it to make a theoretical point, as Lewis discovered in his examination of contemporary philosophy. At all events, when Lewis claims (ultimately for reasons less philosophical than political, as we shall see in a moment) that the idealist world is more concrete than the realist pretender, he means that our perception of it is more shocking and immediate. Realism always obliges you to take a step back and think about things by inference alone. When you walk out of a room (to use the philosophers' favorite example) your belief in the continued and independent existence of the furniture inside is wholly contingent upon an act of logical deduction, because once you have left their presence, direct perception of the objects in question comes to an end. Those tables and chairs back in the room—if you really believe they do still exist—are thus considered exceedingly abstract entities by the partisans of idealism: "It was *abstraction*, Berkeley said—the admission of inferences and fictions of the mind upon an equality with perception—that caused men to believe in the reality of the external world" (*TWM*, 168). In short, realism, in spite of the advertisement potential of its name, cannot distinguish fact from fiction.

But there remains a still more important reason to describe the objects that inhabit the idealist world as uniquely concrete. The modern realist knew, as Lewis pointed out, that matter could not be both real and dead; so he gave matter a kind of organic life by suffusing it with Will or the Unconscious or *élan vital* or any of those pervasive forces which Lewis placed under the general rubric "Time." Of course these powers which have now been apportioned throughout the material world rightfully belonged only to the human mind. As Lewis characterized this new status quo: "The 'psyche' disappears; but everything becomes psychic" (*TWM*, 349). The most important consequence of this enfranchisement is that matter and mind are conceived of as essentially the same substance: "Matter loses its alien and concrete integrity, so useful, and indeed necessary to the mind" (*TWM*, 349).

The extreme idealism of Berkeley, which Lewis wholeheartedly embraced, preserves if nothing else the radical distinction between the mind (the sole active principle) and its ideas (the passive material of the visible world). As Berkeley himself indicates in a passage Lewis quotes in *Time and Western Man*, the two cannot be united by any secret identity principle or commutative operation:

> There can be no idea formed of a soul or spirit: for all ideas whatever, being passive and inert, they cannot represent unto us, by way of images or likeness, that which acts.... Such is the nature of spirit, or that which acts, that it cannot be of itself perceived, but only by the effects which it produceth. (*TWM*, 179)

Behind Bishop Berkeley and Wyndham Lewis stands an injunction against the confounding of mind and matter that goes back to the origins of the Western civilization Lewis believed he was protecting from the "mongrel westernized-oriental" mysticism of the Time doctrines—back as far as the Old Testament where the separation of God from his material creation is insisted upon in the polemic against nature cults (cf. I Kings 19:11-12).[8] The religious or theological element in Lewis's thinking eventually comes into its own at the very end of his career in *The Human Age* and *The Red Priest*, but the importance of religion (not in any sectarian form, of course) as he formulated his positions during the twenties and thirties should not be completely overlooked. He even admitted to a cautious alliance with contemporary Thomistic philosophers who were as fervid as Lewis in their opposition to all varieties of mysticism: "So it is the 'materialism,' the pagan health, of the classical inheritance that I am thinking of when I invite you to fraternize with the catholic thinkers, in their high and nobly-ordered pagan universe" (*TWM*, 376). This uncompromising demand for a material world *of an alien order from man* is critical to our understanding of Lewis's views on politics and the arts, and deserves exploration in more detail. Suffice it to say for the present that he wanted a stubborn and intransigent reality that although (quite paradoxically) contingent upon perception, none the less manages to keep the perceiver in his place. Such is the force of his seemingly unidealistic pronouncement at the end of his chapter entitled "Analysis of the Mind of James Joyce": "I am for the physical world" (*TWM*, 113).

The curious relationship of opposites now established between man and his environment will help explain an apparent contradiction in Lewis's thinking that can in fact be illustrated by citing that last line of his Joyce chapter against some of the remarks in the chapter itself. For example, he attacks *Ulysses* because of its method of "telling from inside," quite as we should expect; but he then proceeds to complain about the "amount of *stuff*—unorganized brute material" that has found its way into the story, inhibiting the flow of the narrative:

> At the end of a long reading of *Ulysses* you feel that it is the very nightmare of the naturalistic method that you have been experiencing. Much as you may cherish the merely physical enthusiasm that expresses itself in this stupendous outpouring of *matter*, or *stuff*, you wish, on the spot, to be transported to some more abstract region for a time, where the dates of the various toothpastes, the brewery and laundry receipts, the growing pile of punched 'bus-tickets, the growing holes in the baby's socks and the darn that repairs them, assume less importance. (*TWM*, 91-92)

Why did Lewis, who bristled at any attempt to volatilize matter into abstraction, react so violently to the material plenitude of *Ulysses*, referring to the novel a few lines later as "a monument like a record diarrhoea"? Why? Because he understood that mind and matter are fundamentally at war; and that although the material world and the limits it imposes must be accepted as the conditions of our existence, it was nevertheless something that revolted and disgusted him.

At the base of this conflict lurks a rigorous economics of scarcity in which precious reality occupies the niche of a commodity in short supply. Lewis has all along rejected attempts to enfranchise the non-human world with human intelligence—the single guarantor of any kind of life we would care to term real (intelligence is in fact practically synonymous with reality). Since there is hardly enough reality to go around for men to begin with—the ghostly peons laboring in the wastes of *The Childermass* were perhaps intended to dramatize the point—the last thing we should do is squander what we have on the rocks and stones and trees. Indeed, Lewis insisted upon the utter deadness of matter as a means of preserving the life of the mind: "The main thing about this 'dead' nature was that it is impossible to conceive it as *acting*, as possessed of any agent principle whatever. That is the guarantee, as it were, of its *unreality*; nothing so thoroughly as that secures the ascendency of 'the mind'" (*TWM*, 179). Or as he restates his position in the "Conclusion," this time appending a colorful, fittingly eighteenth-century vignette:

The *more* static, the more solid, the more fixed, the *more* unreal; as compared with the vivacious, hot, mercurial broth of an object, that results in the alexandrian or bergsonian realism.... On a still day consider the trees in a forest or in a park, or an immobile castle reflected in a glassy river: they are perfect illustrations of our static dream; and what in a sense could be more 'unreal' than they? That is the external, objective, physical, material world ... to which we are referring. (*TWM*, 437)

Lewis's penchant for theatrical jargon and what I have earlier called the rhetoric of surfaces now acquires a kind of metaphysical rationale. When Lewis said, "All the world's a stage," he wasn't talking only about the way men play a number of roles in society (though he meant that, too); he was implying that the entire physical universe, including at least the bodily parts of mortal beings (our "wild bodies"), existed as devices for a grand stage spectacle produced and directed by, and yet, like a vaguely malevolent troupe of automata, not completely under the control of, mind. The very persistence of this bogus and unthinking world proves that it cannot be real, although it behaves towards us exactly as if it were: "that if there could be such a thing as an actual fire ... then it would *burn* us when we touched it, just as we now imagine that it burns" (*TWM*, 455). Indeed, the most generous thing Lewis has to say for matter is that "it is playing at *being*" (*TWM*, 461).

Certainly Lewis's metaphysics could not withstand the rigors of an analysis by a master logician—but that is quite beside the point. His interest in philosophy, as has already been suggested, extended no further than his concern for morality and politics. With particular relish, in fact, he quoted Berkeley's remark that a belief in abstract ideas was the sign of "a mind ... debauched by learning" (*TWM*, 409). It was Carlyle who said that the English were a dumb people ("I hope we English will long maintain our *grand talent pour le silence*"—*Heroes and Hero-Worship*), and without question Lewis fits into the tradition of Anglo-Saxon philosophers who hated philosophy in proportion to the distance it lead a man away from common sense. Accordingly, when we see a word like "real" in *Time and Western Man*, we should not berate Lewis for failing to provide a precise definition of his term (that would have made his writing, like Hegel's, "repulsively technical"), but instead should quietly substitute a word of equivalent moral force, something along the lines of "valuable" or "important."

For philosophical realism had confounded our priorities: it could not distinguish between what was important and what was not. Wyndham Lewis the artist rejected realism's valorization of matter at the expense of creative intelligence. The sheer stupidity of "*stuff*—unorganized brute material" disgusted him and made him long for a more abstract region where the mind could range at liberty (a Shelleyan or Byronic landscape, perhaps). On the other hand, when he complains that "the various attempts to impart reality to the world of appearance [have] the curious result of making it, in effect, less real" (*TWM*, 462), we should hear Lewis the hard-nosed political economist, who demands that men not lose sight of the material limitations forced upon them—limitations that melt away in the hothouse optimism of pantheistic or animistic systems. But perhaps strangest of all is the Lewis who, at the very end of his monumental defense of Western Man founded upon a number of Berkeleyan principles, has the audacity to announce: "Nothing, in a certain sense, more flippant has ever been invented than the gimcrack world of façades of Berkeley—that of tables and chairs that come and go, of hollow and one-sided mountains, like theatrical structures of stucco.... It is an extremist philosophy for *surface-creatures*: and it is as that, essentially, ... that we should, I believe, regard ourselves" (*TWM*, 462). In this peroration we hear, although it may be hard to accept at first, the voice of the reluctant humanist (just how reluctant will be made clear in *Snooty Baronet*). The realism of Bergson, Lewis felt, made impossible demands upon people; it insisted that men exist without ontological lapses—in the fullness of "Time"—much as the puritanical moralist requires a continuous semblance of divine perfection in men. These are the true enemies of mankind, as we learn when we meet the angelic governors of *The Human Age*. Lewis may have hated men for what they are, but he never hated them for what they could not hope to be. He preferred a definition of man that took account of his shortcomings—even his tendency to be a little hollow and machine-like—and did not make the species appear so fallen that the sight of him would elicit Swiftian revulsion. Lewis's claim that we are "surface-creatures" and that our world is an assemblage of "gimcrack façades" insures that we do not take man so seriously as to deprive him of all value whatsoever.

1. Parenthetical references to Lewis's works are to the following editions: *BB: Blasting and Bombardiering* (Berkeley: Univ. of California Press, 1967); *LF: The Lion and the Fox* (London: Methuen, 1951); *RA: Rude Assignment* (London: Hutchinson, 1950); *SF: Satire and Fiction* (London: Arthur Press, 1930; reprinted Folcroft Library Editions, 1972); *Tarr* (New York: Alfred A. Knopf, 1918, reprinted Jubilee Books, 1973); *TWM: Time and Western Man* (Boston: Beacon Press, 1957 [First published in 1927]); and *The Wild Body* (New York: Harcourt, Brace, 1928).

2. A typescript of this synopsis can be found among Lewis's papers at Cornell University.

3. James Joyce, *A Portrait of the Artist as a Young Man* (New York: Viking, 1964), p. 215.

4. Wyndham Lewis, "A Man of the Week: Marinetti" (*The New Weekly*, May 30, 1914), pp. 328-29 and "Automobilism" (*The New Weekly*, June 20, 1914), p. 13; both reprinted in *Quaderno 9: Futurismo/Vorticismo* (1979), pp. 123-31.

5. Hugh Kenner, *Wyndham Lewis* (Norfolk, Conn.: New Directions, 1954), p. 74.

6. Fredric Jameson points out the ironic synchrony in *Fables of Aggression: Wyndham Lewis, the Modernist as Facist* (Berkeley: Univ. of California Press, 1979), p. 123. He accurately notes that Heidegger's book might have furnished "the principal exhibit" of *Time and Western Man*.

7. George Berkeley, *Philosophical Works*, M. R. Ayers, ed. (London: Dent, 1975).

8. I enter the writings of Wyndham Lewis into evidence as proof "that we are a far more Biblical society than we admit." The quotation is from the preface to Herbert Schneidau's exceedingly useful book, *Sacred Discontent: The Bible and Western Tradition* (Berkeley: Univ. of California Press, 1976), in which it is argued that the jaundiced eye of criticism descends directly from the Old Testament prejudice against myth and high culture.

▼ ▼ ▼

E. W. F. TOMLIN

WYNDHAM LEWIS THE EMANCIPATOR

One can only wish that he had lived long enough to witness the turn of the tide: for this artist now promises to emerge as the most considerable figure of the age.
—Malcolm Easton, *Apollo*, February 1971.

I

In the now almost forgotten pamphlet *Satire ana Fiction* ("Enemy Pamphlets, No. 1"), published in 1930, we read: "Mr. Wyndham Lewis is not the man of any set or literary club. . . . No one has ever been less puffed or jockeyed into importance than Mr. Lewis. No circle or clique has 'imposed' him upon the public." This was true, and it remained true throughout his combative life.

Although Lewis spoke of himself as being in a situation of "solitary schism," he was in many ways a social man. By that I do not mean a sociable man, though he was likable enough. He could be very affable, and to some he was a loyal and affectionate friend. I refer rather to the fact that he believed in society, the society of men of intellect, the Republic of Letters. And he spent much time trying to encourage the formation of such a society in the London of his day. In doing so, he was fighting against heavy odds. When *The Apes of God* appeared in 1930, Bloomsbury was still very powerful. Indeed, we know that Bloomsbury *was* a reality, and that it could go so far as to excommunicate and to ostracize. When people express the view that Lewis's attack upon Bloomsbury was misconceived, that he was engaged in a "massacre of the insignificants," and that he had conjured up out of nothing his band of apes, we would do well to reflect upon the following, written by a man who knew what he was talking about:

> I doubt . . . whether more than a few people are even now aware how closely-knit an association "Bloomsbury" was, how untiring its members were in advertising one another's work and personalities. Most people who came into casual contact with members of this gifted circle recall its charm, its candour, its high intelligence; few of those who were impressed by the openness of mind and the humane opinions proclaimed by "The Nation," afterwards "The New Statesman and Nation," their parish magazine, suspected how ruthless and businesslike were their methods. They would have been surprised if they had known of the lengths to which some of these people—so disarming with their gentle Cambridge voices, their informal manners, their casual unassuming clothes, their civilized personal relations with one another—were prepared to go in order to ruin, utterly, not only the "reactionary" figures whom they publicly denounced, but young painters and writers who showed themselves too independent to come to terms with the canons observed by "Bloomsbury" or, more precisely, with the current "party line," which varied from month to month in accordance with what their leader considered the most "significant" trends of opinion prevailing in Paris. If such independence was allied to gifts of an order to provoke rivalry, then so much the worse for the artists. And bad for them it *was*, for there was nothing in the way of slander and intrigue to which certain of the "Bloomsburys" were not willing to descend. I rarely knew hatreds pursued with such malevolence over so many years; against them neither age nor misfortune offered the slightest protection. [1]

To stand out against this kind of opposition was not easy. Yet that was precisely what Lewis did, despite lack of funds and a refusal to throw himself on the mercy of "well-connected" persons. During the 1930s, when it was the fashion in Britain to assume a left-wing viewpoint, Lewis would have none of it. The difficulty in fighting extremes is that it compels the critic to assume an extreme position himself. I do not share the view that Lewis was at any time a fascist, and there is only one short passage (in *Count Your Dead, They Are Alive*) where he appeared to see some merit in Hitlerism, though even here his tongue may have been in his cheek. (And what about Yeats's *On the Boiler*?) When one reflects upon the radical political sympathies displayed by men who have since joined the Establishment, Lewis's own refusal to be badgered, jockeyed, or inveigled into alliance with the left-wing intelligentsia shows stoutness of character and independence of spirit. And now that a New Left has arisen, Lewis's work possesses fresh relevance, especially as today's radicalism combines its assault upon the "foundations of society" with the most pitiful essays in the scabrous. Never has a movement of reform, if it can be called such, been under such mindless and callow leadership. How Lewis would have trounced it all—the "raptures and roses of the erotic bookshelves", etc. (BLAST 1, 18)

To create a *vie littéraire* out of practically nothing: that was Lewis's aim, as it was that of Ezra Pound. The qualifications for assuming this role are, apart from literary eminence, great organizing ability and irrepressible spirits. Lewis, in his prime, possessed the latter; perhaps, unlike Pound, he was deficient in the former, or perhaps his work as both writer and painter left him insufficient time for action. The interesting fact is that Vorticism did play a not inconspicuous part in the intellectual life of London. Even Mr. Asquith, the Prime Minister, was aware of it:

> For a few months I was on constant exhibition. I cannot here enumerate all the sightseers, of noble houses or of questionable Finance, who passed me under review. They were legion. Coronetted envelopes showered into my letter-box. The editor of BLAST must at all costs be viewed; and its immense puce cover was the standing joke in the fashionable drawing-room, from Waterloo Place to the border-line in Belgravia. (*BB*, 46-47)[2]

Today, no equivalent link exists between the literary world and the "ruling class": the only "art" to permeate society from top to bottom is so-called Pop Art. (We may be sure that genuinely new talent will not be recognized by the present arbiters of taste, whose illiteracy goes beyond anything in the past.) For a time, until Lewis was driven into isolation and self-imposed exile, the high spirits had their moment, and added to the gaiety of at least one nation. Certain people who believed themselves to be pilloried in *The Apes of God* raised the alarm—one of them placing an advertisement in the *Times*, another threatening Lewis's life, many sending violent letters through the post, while "a certain poetess, who supposed herself an 'ape,' had a seizure as she caught sight of Mr. Lewis's advancing sombrero in a Bayswater Street, and had to be led into a chemist's shop—where the old-fashioned remedy of Arquebuscade Water was applied with marked success" (*SF*, 7).

There is nothing of that now, no comparable light-heartedness, the sign of renewal and creativity. At most, in a similar situation, the supposed victims would be solemnly questioned in a television studio, and the whole affair drowned in "comment." But more probably it would not excite any curiosity at all.

Strive as he might, therefore, Lewis made precious little mark with the periodicals he launched. *The Enemy* and *The Tyro* were short-lived affairs, though they were packed with talent, and today they rank as collectors' pieces. *The Enemy* was perhaps the last review of its kind: a one-man show, not even subsidized by a foundation or a benevolent person of wealth, but containing genuinely new and interesting material. Today, the little reviews continue to appear, but few are without a "grant," and behind none that we can at present see is there a powerful personality with his own programme or *œuvre*. Lewis's pamphleteering was both possible and necessary, because, as he said, he needed the firepower of these little gunboats to defend his cruisers. Admittedly, some critics derided the pamphleteering; but to those who remember their appearance, always strikingly jacketed and eccentrically printed, they still make good, if nostalgic, reading. Even so slight a work as *The Old Gang and the New Gang* has become a document of its time. The "trivial" surface aspect of this essay could have been the product only of a profoundly serious thinker, who, like many other serious men, knew how to write in light vein. To cite a larger work, a cruiser in fact: much of the beginning of *Time and Western Man* is on this level, but it is for that reason one of the parts that has worn best. There is what has been called "a fusion of the manners of casual chat with a stand-offish highbrowism of content."[3] The really superior mind can afford to take its days off. Blake, whom

Lewis resembles in so many ways, could write *An Island in the Moon*, which contains some excellent fooling. One of the signs that a writer in his major works is not fooling us is that in his slighter works or passages he obviously is. Wit, raillery, irony: these are the weapons of the man who has important things to say to his fellows, whereas solemnity is often the cloak for humbug and lack of invention. Laughter is a form of liberation. In short, the world needs a rebirth of wit, which Lewis had in abundance as he had the capacity for raillery and irony. That the current pornographic craze should be backed up by the claptrap of popular psychiatrists and even ecclesiastics is not an accident: it is all put forth in deadly earnest. Can we imagine a Voltaire or a Diderot approving such material? Intellect was what Lewis was defending: in other words, the adult, the mature.

The truth is that few writers have been so adult as Lewis. He seems to have arrived at maturity unusually early. His first publications were of remarkable finish. Some of the stories in *The Wild Body* are among the best in English of this century. Maturity implies a temperate skepticism. Eliot once said that he held his beliefs with a skepticism that he hoped would never leave him. This form of skepticism is not, and it certainly was not for Eliot, incompatible with deep conviction. When I stated that Lewis held such convictions, one of his supporters, Geoffrey Grigson, exploded in ridicule. There are supposed to be men who do not believe in anything; but if you examine their life and works, you find often that they care passionately about causes; and if you believe in causes, you believe in values. Bertrand Russell was such a man. His tirades against religion were made from a point of view difficult to distinguish from a religious one. The ethical neutralist, like his political counterpart, is using his title as a convenient cover for the espousal of what he believes to be the stronger party. The ethical neutralist will tend always to favor the weakening of the barriers against instinct. Lewis did not subscribe to any set of dogmas; but it was his belief that without intellectual and religious values, life became brutalized. Not that he favoured the birth of a new order "thick with a mediaeval gloom of bloodshot righteousness" (*P*, 5), any more than he approved of D. H. Lawrence's "universe full of 'abdominal' afflatus and hot, unconscious, 'soulless,' mystical throbbing" (*P*, 196). He was for sanity.

II

In any list of literary outsiders, Charles Doughty would have to be included. This calls to mind another passage in *Blasting and Bombardiering*: "When Colonel Lawrence visited Doughty, he asked him how he came to go to Arabia. The reply made by the author of *Arabia Deserta* was that he went there 'in order to rescue English prose from the slough into which it had fallen'" (*BB*, 13).

In *Tarr*, Lewis did something of the same kind, though from a sick bed in Percy Street, London, rather than from the desert. When he later visited the desert, or the *bled*, in Morocco, he produced another book containing passages of fine prose, *Filibusters in Barbary*. Lewis described the new prose of *Tarr* very aptly; and a new kind of prose implies a new kind of content:

> The *statement*—the narrative technique—was denuded of those rhetorical ornaments to which the English critic had become accustomed in a work of fiction. It was not a world of gentlemen and ladies that was unfolded in its pages, nor yet of love's young dream, nor of the "kindly" emotions. But it was not (if you cared to cross the Channel) the first book in European literature to display a certain indifference to bourgeois conventions, and an unblushing disbelief in the innate goodness of human nature.
>
> *Tarr* was not "constructed," as the commercial pundit calls it. It did not conform to the traditional wave length of the English Novel. There was not a lot of soft padding everywhere... (*BB*, 88)

By way of illustration, let me take two examples. In a few lines, where Henry James would have taken fifty and at the same time have *told* you what effect he was trying to create (and told you again, at greater length, in the Preface), Lewis pictures Tarr talking with Anastasya:

> Tarr had Anastasya in solitary promenade two days after this conversation. He had worked the first stage consummately: he swam with ease beside his big hysterical black swan, seeming to guide her with a golden halter. They were swimming at the moment with august undulations of thought across the Luxembourg Gardens on this sunny and tasteful evening about four o'clock. (*Tarr*, 227)

Then there is the new content, above all the polemic against the "romantic":

> "... Deadness is the first condition of art. The armoured hide of the hippopotamus, the shell

of the tortoise, feathers and machinery, you may put in one camp; naked, pulsing and moving of the soft inside of life—along with elasticity of movement and consciousness—that goes in the opposite camp. Deadness is the first condition for art: the second is absence of soul, in the human and sentimental sense. With the statue its lines and masses are its soul, no restless inflammable ego is imagined for its interior: it has *no inside*: good art must have no inside: that is capital." (*Tarr*, 303)

The whole of this chapter is full of remarks of xtreme interest about life and art:

> "What is art?—it sounds like Pompous Pilate!"
> "Life with all the humbug of living taken out of it..."
> "Very well: but what is life?"
> "Everything that is not yet purified so that it is art."

Of life, indeed, Lewis had many apt things to say. When he remarked of *Tarr* that it displayed no "unblushing belief in the innate goodness of human nature," he did not exaggerate. It was this disillusioned view of humanity which earned Lewis his reputation for coldness and negativity: a coldness which, as he said, characterized as a rule neither the English novel nor indeed the English philosophy of life. In modern English literature the nearest to a cynical view of the world was that expounded by Thomas Hardy; but in Hardy's novels it is heaven, or God, or the President of the Immortals, who is evil, or just simply blind or blundering, whereas man is the innocent victim. About Hardy there is always a touch of sentimentality; Tess is a rather more grown-up and robust Little Nell. That is perhaps why Hardy's popularity as a novelist has never waned, and why his bulky *Collected Poems*, most of which are concerned with the betrayal of innocence by a malignant Providence, is still a bestseller. Lewis has never reached a comparable popularity, nor is he ever likely to do so, because he refuses to flatter human nature:

> It does not require a gigantic intelligence to perceive that mostly life is ugly and foolish. This or that person, almost anyone (there are not in the nature of things many exceptions) regards himself as awfully "kind" or intensely "attractive": yet when the eye observing him is for some reason dispassionate, he does not look like that at all, but is mean—in both senses, for he is the stuff of the average. (*DP*, 94).

This is a dash of cold water indeed. In book after book, Lewis represents human beings as puppets. The only "living character" in *The Apes of God* is not strictly in the novel at all: he is Pierpoint, or Lewis himself (though it was pointed out at the time that Pierpoint was the name of Britain's official hangman, still living). Lewis was not trying to draw characters "in the round," with "minds of their own." He was pointing out how few people have minds at all independent of the herd; and the group or herd-mind had fascinated Lewis ever since he had written the passages about crowds in BLAST 2 based upon his experience of the collective displays of emotion at the start of the First World War. He resumed the subject in Part II, Chapter IV of *Blasting and Bombardiering*. Meanwhile, the desire of men to be types had already preoccupied him in *The Art of Being Ruled:*

> If [men] were watched in the act of expressing their personality, it would be found that it was somebody else's personality they were expressing. If a hundred of them were observed "expressing their personality," altogether and at the same time, it would be found that they all "expressed" this inalienable, mysterious "personality" in the same way. In short, it would be patent at once that they had only *one* personality between them to "express"—some "expressing" it with a little more virtuosity, some less. It would be a group personality they were "expressing"—a pattern imposed on them by means of education and the hypnotism of cinema, and wireless, and press. (*ABR*, 164-65)

Earlier still, in *The Wild Body*, he had made a similar point about the plain man and his supposed "nearness" to life:

> One of the great superstitions is that the plain man, being so "near to life," is a great "realist." In fact, he never gets close to reality at all, in the way, for instance, that a philosophical intelligence, or an imaginative artist, does. He looks at everything from the outside, reads the labels, and what he sees is what he has been told to see, that is to say, what he expects. What he does not expect, he, of course, does not see. For him only the well-worn and general exists. ("The Cornac and His Wife," (*CWB*, 102).

Naturally to take this view of the human being, with no warm soul inhabiting him and setting him aglow, was in appearance to dispose of free will. But then a puppet has no will at all: only the puppet-master has that, just as a crowd must have its "crowd-master." Lewis did not mean to suggest that men *were* puppets, but rather that they preferred to act as such, just as they preferred to be types. That is why they could be so easily manipulated. That, too, was why they were comic. Satire was not so much a distortion of human nature as the plain truth about most of it. Satire had for long been in eclipse because the writer, and especially the poet, had refused to face this truth. The bourgeoisie, to whom the writer catered, preferred those willing to kowtow to it. The "indifference to bourgeois conventions" of which Lewis spoke in connection with *Tarr* was a refusal to do just that. No wonder that he incurred the obloquy of this class, especially in its upper reaches; for it need hardly be said that European society in the twentieth century was essentially a bourgeois society, with bourgeois values reigning supreme.

What, indeed, could be more bourgeois than the intellectual revolutionary? "Revolutionary politics, revolutionary art, and, oh, the revolutionary mind, is the dullest thing on earth". We have had a good deal of all three since Lewis wrote these words. Few revolutionary spokesmen seem to care much about the kind of society they wish to put in place of the present one: indeed, we have great difficulty in discovering what precisely they are getting at, so difficult is it to penetrate beyond the jargon. How many wish to bring about the state of affairs described by the master himself: "Every emancipation is a restoration of the human world and of human relationships to man himself."[4] Indeed, it is those who wish to establish "socialism with a human face" who are, at all costs and with every ingenuity, accused of grave "errors" and "eliminated." It is the men of Lewis's type, supposedly inhuman, who fight for the higher values, and who are the real emancipators. Perhaps this is coming slowly to be realized. It is difficult to see in a Herbert Marcuse a similar force for emancipation; for with all his attacks on the "totalitarianism" of liberal society, he remains remarkably entrenched within it. It is not without significance that at the begining of his book *One-Dimensional Man* (1964), acknowledgement should be made to assistance given the author by the American Council of Learned Societies, the Louis M. Rabinowitz Foundation, the Rockefeller Foundation, and the Social Research Council. No such Establishment backing was afforded the author of *The Art of Being Ruled*, who was indeed in extreme financial straits when he wrote that volume.

With Lewis, therefore, we have that kind of "naked vision" of life which characterized Blake, and that cannot exist more than once in several generations. Of Blake, Eliot said: "He approached everything with a mind unclouded with current opinions. There was nothing of the superior person about him. This makes him terrifying." Of Lewis this was true too: he was whole and of complete integrity. That is why he was an emancipator.

Now integrity begins a long way down. In his *True Voices of Feeling* (1953), Herbert Read observed that "form is the natural effect of the poet's integrity" (he could have substituted for poet, any creative writer), and, to quote Eliot again, "a form grows out of the attempt of somebody to say something" ("The Music of Poetry"). We might add that form, true form, is a new way of being free. Lewis was one of the few writers of the century to have had something new to say, and to have consequently developed his own form. That is why he will continue to be read, even if only by a limited audience. A critic recently said that he was "on the skids and heading for limbo." Well, if it was *Dante's* limbo he was heading for, Lewis would find himself in good company. The truth is that Lewis is *emerging* from limbo. Today, we observe an enormous adulation of small figures, of whom posterity will hear nothing. Lewis, for his part, will become more relevant; for the true emancipator, as opposed to the iconoclast with his negative mission and hatred of form, is society's greatest friend.

---

1. John Rothenstein, *Modern English Painters: Lewis to Moore* (1956; rev. ed., New York: St. Martin's Press, 1976), pp. 14-15.
2. Parenthetical references to Lewis's works are to the following editions: *ABR: The Art of Being Ruled* (London: Chatto & Windus, 1926); *BB: Blasting and Bombardiering* (Berkeley: Univ. of California Press, 1967); *CWB: The Complete Wild Body* (Santa Barbara: Black Sparrow Press, 1982); *DP: The Diabolical Principle and The Dithyrambic Spectator* (London: Chatto & Windus, 1931); *P: Paleface* (London: Chatto & Windus, 1929); *SF: Satire and Fiction* (London: The Arthur Press, 1930); and *Tarr* rev. ed. (London: Chatto & Windus, 1928).
3. C. H. Sisson, *English Poetry, 1900–1950* (London: Hart-Davis, 1971), p. 223.
4. Marx, *Zur Judenfrage* (1844).

STOOPING MALE NUDE, 1912–13
HENRI GAUDIER-BRZESKA
CRAYON. 48.5 x 38 cm
COURTESY ANTHONY d'OFFAY

B. W. POWE

THE HUNTER, LAUGHTER, AND THE SURGICAL BLADE

Wyndham Lewis's literary criticism, in *Men Without Art, Paleface*, and "The Revolutionary Simpleton" portions of *Time and Western Man*, slices through the object of his attention—whether it is Hemingway, Lawrence, Faulkner, or Pound—with Lewis brandishing his surgical blade (his diagnostic insights, his therapeutic verbal overflow) with exuberance, scorn, wit, and always a commitment to cultural continuity and intellectual integrity. His method and intentions are satirical: he prods, he pokes, he jolts the writer and reader; he mixes high and low writing styles, mingling extensive quotations, informal chat, sudden savage description, and passages of caricature and burlesque. He is awake, keen, cool—the Enemy, blasting the formidable artists of his age.

But this smiling savagery is not done for fun or to provoke mere discussion. Lewis is concerned with what the effect of reading these writers will be:

> The principles of intellectual *detection*—the injunction to look *behind* everything, however trivial, in the art-field, as a matter of routine, and challenge all "face-values"—merely have to be restated every time, for the benefit of the inattentive, and the chronically "comfortable"—the inveterately "cosy."[1]

He tries to show how the "Stein-stutter" (*MWA*, 29) of Hemingway, or the gushing of the hot vitals (in Lawrence's novels), or the "record diarrhoea"[2] of an age, as in Joyce's *Ulysses*, will embody the tyrannical *zeitgeist* and affect the "Plain Reader" (*MWA*, 8). His essays and polemics work through conflict and provocation, as he hunts for the political significance of a writer and then forces the reader into a position of conscious choice. He is, as he repeatedly claimed, an outlaw who has gone outside for the sake of intellectual freedom: both his and ours.

Lewis's prescience, too, was usually uncanny. As he said, an artist is always engaged in writing a detailed history of the future because he is the only one conscious of the present. Who else foresaw in the late 1920s and early 1930s that the most mythologized and discussed artists of his time would be, today, Lawrence, Joyce, Faulkner, and Hemingway?

Yet for the generation of writers accustomed to the delicate locutions of T. S. Eliot's prose—the possum "disguising himself as a corpse," as Ezra Pound once snarled[3]—or the antiseptic patter and patterns of the structuralists—"The type of literary study which structuralism helps one to envisage would not be primarily interpretative; it would not offer a method which, when applied to literary works, produced new and hitherto unexpected meanings," sniffs Jonathan Culler[4]—Lewis's criticism seems so idiosyncratic and cruel that it has been either curtly dismissed, misrepresented, or defended in an orgy of apologies.[5] Irving Howe, for example, refers to Lewis as "that snarling authoritarian."[6]

Lewis's criticism is a unique and consciously developed style of penetration by deflation. His essays, on Faulkner, Stein, and Hemingway, especially, have a bitter comic surface, a surface of "laughter," and a wonderfully sophisticated tone (and that tone is surely one of the great creations of modern letters) which shapes an approach that is consistent throughout Lewis's œuvre. "Satirical criticism" is a method which illuminates, offering a key for the reader's detachment, at the same time as it mocks, lampoons, and vivisects.

Wyndham Lewis went to great lengths to define and defend his use of satire, particularly in *Men Without Art* and *Rude Assignment*. "Satire is *cold*, and that is good" (*MWA*, 121); satire is a kind of realism, looking at the Pure Present with a clear, harsh, outlaw's *eye*. It depends on blasting and seeing, not argument, on the encounter with "monoliths" (*MWA*, 14) (never hunt anything small), and the close observation of an author's social-political beliefs; in short, satire depends on being outside, on being literally an ex-centric, as it were. Yet satire, Lewis writes in *Men Without Art*, "refers to an 'expressionist' universe which is reeling a little, a little drunken with an overdose of the 'ridiculous'—where everything is not only tipped but *steeped* in a philosophic solution of the material, not of mirth, but of the intense and even painful sense of the absurd" (*MWA*, 288–89). *The Absurd*: that human life is... chaotic, sometimes crazed, indeed "ridiculous," capable of outrageous and dangerous twists. This is a comment which, incidentally, puts Lewis in some relation with Albert Camus, a writer he shows sympathy for in *The Writer and the Absolute*.

The quotation from *Men Without Art* cited above is probably as good a description as possible, but seeking greater precision, Lewis resorts to the dictionary in *Rude Assignment*:

> The dictionary describes *satire* as "a composition in verse or prose holding up vice or folly to ridicule... use of ridicule, irony, sarcasm, etc., in speech or writing for the ostensible purpose of exposing and discouraging vice or folly."[7]

Now, all this is really playing on that age-old difficulty in the defining of the word "satire," a complexity that has emerged out of two apparently distinct etymologies. The Greek word *satyros* means satyr—a Dionysian creature that is a combination of human and goat. In this case, satire would be a *tone* of approach—derisive, playful, scolding, ironic. The Latin "satira" or "satura" is a form, a mixture, or a medley (hence "per saturam," the OED informs us, meaning "in the lump," "indiscriminately"). This form is usually distinguished by a mixture of different styles, sometimes alternating prose and poetry.[8]

Satire for Lewis uses that mocking tone to investigate and lacerate hypocrisy and affectation and decadence; it is pre-eminently concerned with words and their magical, social impact; it is also a conscious form that achieves its effects through disjunction and surprise. As Ezra Pound writes, relevantly, in "The Serious Artist," "the cult of ugliness, Villon, Baudelaire, Corbière, Beardsley are diagnosis. Flaubert is diagnosis. Satire... is surgery, insertions and amputations."[9] For Lewis, in order to achieve maximum penetration, satire is *both*.

The consistent public persona he created, of the Enemy, is a part of this satirical technique. He made himself both a weapon and a target. "I expect retaliation," he says (*RA*, 52). And: "I have an obvious interest in what I am writing about! And if you should wish to retaliate upon me, there are the targets standing ready. All you need to be is a practised shot!" (*MWA*, 118) His outsider role, that of secular mythographer or "official of the flood,"[10] forced him to adopt the outlaw tone, the permanent "Loyal Opposition" stand. "But certainly I am issuing a 'challenge' to the community in which I live. I am 'criticizing all its institutions and modes of action and of thought'" (*TWM*, 5). The painting "Mr. Wyndham Lewis as a Tyro" (1920–21) shows this target and persona as sharp lines, hard and exact like iron girders buried deep in the flesh, the teeth like a white chewing machine, ready to snarl and gnash and rip, one eyebow raised, the eyes spectacularly sly and bright and (yet) unpredictable. ("I knew you'd like the Enemy," he starts the poem "If So The Man You Are.") As steely and aloof as this image is, you don't take on *that* character without considerable forethought.

This Lewisian figure—"A Lewisite begging your pardon"[11] he says in *The Diabolical Principle* (and I propose here that rather than "Lewisian," which to my ears sounds awkward, we use "Lewisite" which is, of course, a destructive nerve gas developed during the First World War)—this Lewisite figure is, however, no cranky or excessively solemn pose. He is capable of satirizing himself, as this excerpt from "What It Feels Like To Be an Enemy" shows:

> The telephone is an important weapon in the armoury of an "Enemy," a sort of deadly air-pistol. I don't know what I should do without the telephone.
>
> After breakfast, for instance (a little raw meat, a couple of blood-oranges, a stick of ginger, and a shot of Vodka—to make one see Red) I make a habit of springing up from the breakfast-table and going over in a rush to the telephone book. This I open quite at chance, and ring up the first number upon which my eye has lighted. When I am put through, I violently abuse for five minutes the man, or woman of course (there is no romantic nonsense about the sex of people with an Enemy worth his salt), who answers the call. This gets you into the proper mood for the day.
>
> You then throw on a stately Stetson, at the angle that intimidates, thrust a cigar between your teeth, and swagger out into the street, eyeing all and sundry as if they were trespassing on the pavement.[12]

Why Lewis chose this route has been so misunderstood as to constitute something of a literary scandal. His frequent quarries—Joyce, Pound, Eliot—unerstood the high order of the Enemy's attacks and its potential dangers. Pound's famous comment on Lewis being "prey to the furies"[13] was a tribute and a warning. If you seek intellectual independence, you risk more than just being shot back at by the "outraged nobodies or their buddies" (RA, 52), you risk losing yourself in the hysterical inferno you describe (the satirist satirized; becoming suddenly, shockingly, an Ape; or a harbinger of the very barbarism he fought —though "That is not what I meant at all. / That is not it, at all"); becoming eventually, tragically, the outlaw as outcast. We note: *Self Condemned* looms. However, the deliberate adoption of this Enemy persona, what Marshall McLuhan has called "fittingly," the "put-on," had, as I have mentioned, an essential relationship to the "Plain Reader" ("the inveterately 'cosy'"). The outlaw was concerned with "a system,"[14] as he often said, and this system was meant to offer to the reader a way out of the impositions of the fashionable present. It was a way to become distant, a way towards thinking.

So, *outside*, where the cold air is freedom, the hunter can employ his principal strategies for insight: observation of political significance, laughter, and the bitter hardness. As he writes in *Men Without Art*:

> He who wants a jolly, carefree, bubbling, world chock-full of "charm," must not address himself to the satirist! The wind that blows through satire is as bitter as that that predominates in the pages of *Timon* or *Kig Lear*. (113)

Yet:

> Laughter—humour and wit—has a function in relation to our tender consciousness; a function similar to that of art. It is the preserver much more than the destroyer. And, in a sense, *everyone* should be laughed at or else *no one* should be laughed at. (MWA, 109)

The Laugh is the essential reflex of the humane observer. It is the recognition of absurdity, of incongruity, of the strange density of human behaviour. As Lewis describes in *Blasting and Bombardiering*, there is the "*Ah-ness* of things," which is the sadness uttered in the face of the transience of experience. There is also the "*Ho-ho-ness*":

> And against the backgrounds of their sempiternal *Ah-ness* it is possible, strictly in the foreground, to proceed with a protracted comedy, which glitters against the darkness.[15]

For those who have asserted that Lewis's work is the product of a negative and brutal mind, this statement should reveal what is, I believe, a courageous stand against melancholy and meaninglessness, the tragic-laughter of "the enemy of the stars," brilliantly deriding the forces that seek to render us "chronically comfortable." "BLESS the solitude of LAUGHTER," he wrote in BLAST (1, 26). If you can still laugh, you can still breathe.

The outlaw stand and the laugh combine to form *the tone*. This tone goes to work on his first "monolith" in *Men Without Art*. Ernest Hemingway, "The Dumb Ox":

> Ernest Hemingway is a very considerable artist in prose-fiction (MWA, 17).

Admit him to a pantheon of sorts: the target is set up; Hemingway, we understand, is not trivial (he probably would not be here if he was):

> Beside this, or with this, his work possesses a penetrating quality, like an animal speaking.

The declaration of diagnostic intent follows, flushed with rhetorical flourishes that are aimed, entirely, at the "Plain Reader," to beg, borrow, or steal his indulgence:

> Let me attempt to isolate that quality for you, in such a way as not to damage it too much: for having set out to demonstrate the political significance of this artist's work, I shall, in the course of that demonstration, resort to a dissection of it—not the best way, I am afraid, to bring out the beauties of the finished product. This dissection is, however, necessary for my purpose here.

It is a neat balancing act—Mr. Wyndham Lewis ("'Personal-Appearance' Artist") on the podium, in front of a lectern, or, if you will, in your den, in some completely civilized place, casually, the worldly sophisticated tone in place, perhaps with pipe in hand (recall the congenial but ironic "Self-Portrait with a Pipe," 1938), at a leisurely pace, is about to ... dismember a lion.

"But *political significance!*"

It leaps out at you. This is Lewis's touchstone. He writes criticism, as he says in *Paleface*, "purely as investigations into contemporary states of mind..." (*P,* 97). This is his reason for satire. His description of Hemingway's style as embodying "the anonymous folk-rhythm of the urban proletariat" (*MWA,* 23) is a political insight. His concern is always for the work's impact on, and reflection of, the cultural and political values of the west.

Lewis now proceeds with increasing vigor and hardness. Quotations are marshalled. This is true in all that he writes on Faulkner, Joyce, Eliot, Spengler, or Bergson: generous chunks of an author's works are used for illustration; he even, quite notoriously, takes to extensively quoting himself. The effect is that of a collage or juxtaposition. This reveals another writer's manner by context. Lewis could expose an artist's excesses or ideas by merely quoting him in a different framework. He in no way distorts these quotations—his excerpts are generally lengthy—but they are shown in a light which instantly identifies their salient absurdities. His expert comic demolition of William Faulkner's inattention to diction—the repetition of "sourceless" and "myriad" in *Light In August* and *Sanctuary*—is accomplished by a mere list.

Lewis constantly swings back to that personal, colloquial tone, acknowledging the reader's presence ("You," out there) in a personable, intimate way that is sophisticated without being ostentatiously erudite. "I hope this does not seem irrelevant to you: it is not, let me reassure you, but very much the contrary" (*MWA,* 22). In "The Revolutionary Simpleton" parts of *Time and Western Man,* this tone is used with devastating effect against the jittery, romantic mannerisms of Pound and the "unreadable" repetitiveness of Gertrude Stein. "Come now, don't we know better?" he seems to say. Through this, Lewis achieves an effect of removal *on the reader's part* that could not be achieved if he were to proceed as an analytical, "toneless" (read: faceless) author.

The Lewisite comical tone can in no way be better represented than in the often quoted description of Hemingway's use of the first-person narrative technique:

> The sort of First-person-singular that Hemingway invariably invokes is a dull-witted, bovine, monosyllabic simpleton. This lethargic and stuttering dummy he conducts, or pushes from behind, through all the scenes that interest him. This burlesque First-person-singular behaves in them like a moronesque version of his brilliant author. He *Steins* up and down the world, with the big lustreless ruminatory orbs of a Picasso doll-woman (of the semi-classic type Picasso patented, with enormous hands and feet). It is, in short, the very dummy that is required for the literary mannerism of Miss Stein! It is the incarnation of the Stein-stutter—the male incarnation, it is understood.
>
> But this constipated, baffled, "frustrated"—yes, deeply and Freudianly "frustrated"—this wooden-headed, leaden-witted, heavy-footed, loutish and oafish marionette—peering dully out into the surrounding universe like a great big bloated five-year-old—pointing at this and pointing at that—uttering simply "CAT!"—"HAT!"—"FOOD!"—"SWEETIE!"—is, as a companion, infectious. (*MWA,* 29)

This is based on delivery: the outrageous exaggeration (and for Lewis exaggeration is elevated to High Art; he no doubt felt that he had to exaggerate: to make a point you have to pound hard), the compound words, and disjunctives all have a marvelous oral effect. You can hear this:

> But this constipated, baffled, "frustrated"...

Here, the confidential aside:

> yes, deeply and Freudianly "frustrated"...

And—*laughter*:

> this wooden-headed, leaden-witted, heavy-footed, loutish and oafish marionette...

Lewis is relishing his own pyrotechnics here, delighting in the kind of verbal abundance that Hemingway would never use:

> ...peering dully out into the surrounding universe like a great big bloated five-year-old—pointing at this and pointing at that...

This is caricature: Lewis is expanding an image to the point of an intense visual analogy. The rhetorical aim is to make the reader see; and what we see is a sort of Hogarth print coming to life:

> ...is, as a companion, infectious.

The voice drops, becomes fraternal. Lewis has memorably ridiculed the famous Hemingway manner, and yet has ended by winking at the reader, just to inform us how unique this style really is.

And Hemingway's retaliation?

The heads of several flowers were punched off in Sylvia Beach's bookstore. And in *A Moveable Feast*, the revenge:

> Wyndham Lewis wore a black hat, like a character in the quarter, and was dressed like someone out of La Bohème. He had a face that reminded me of a frog... It was embarrassing to see him... I do not think I have ever seen a nastier looking man. Some people show evil as a great horse shows breeding... Lewis did not show evil; he just looked nasty... Under the black hat, when I had first seen him, the eyes had been those of an unsuccessful rapist.[16]

Lewis has tour-de-force passages like the one from "The Dumb Ox" throughout his writing. They make exhilarating reading and repay close attention. His expansion of syntax, through adjectival lists, disjunctives, parenthetical asides, and imagistic elaboration to the point of caricature, is a result of a deep comprehension of verbal energy. There are stylistic echoes of Swift, Sterne, Nashe, and Dickens in the masterly managing of tone and rhythm. And as always, the passage is driven by the breaking, thrusting, muscular power of Lewis's intellect and humor.

William Faulkner receives rougher treatment in *Men Without Art*. However, the foray into Faulkner's "fecund" world inspires some deft critical perceptions. Lewis's attachment to the concrete, to definition, to common sense, revolts against the pretty obfuscations of Faulkner's florid style:

> But there is a lot of *poetry* in Faulkner. It is not at all good. And it has an in the end rather comic way of occurring at a point where, apparently, he considers that the *atmosphere* has run out, or is getting thin, by the passage of time become exhausted and requiring renewal, like the water in a zoological-garden tank for specimens of fish. So he pumps in this necessary medium, for anything from half a dozen to two dozen lines, according to the needs of the case. (*MWA*, 45)

This is also a well-known statement. The demolition is achieved by catching what is clearly, for Lewis, ridiculous. All Lewis needs to do is cite Faulkner's opacities ("whip-poor-wills, cicadas, lilac, 'seeping' moonlight, water-oaks, and jasmine") and it is unlikely that we will ever read those again without being acutely conscious of the "fluid" mannerisms.

Lewis's savage synoptic abilities are on brilliant display when he describes Faulkner's characters as being "an impressive company, in their hysterical way. All are demented: his novels are, strictly speaking, clinics" (*MWA*, 49). And: "Death is a bagatelle to a Sartoris—and indeed a Sartoris only becomes really effective after demise. As a ghost he is *some* ghost!" (*MWA*, 50) Again, "ah-ha-ing" and "ho-ho-ing" in the face of the artist's quirks. Though the laughter is, once more, not for fun and games: these comments are meant to reveal Faulkner's infatuation with extremes, with the flux, "romance," and a potentially diabolical fatalism.

Lastly, the whole joke of the chapter revolves around the never stated, but suggested, image of Faulkner, like his impotent creation Popeye in *Sanctuary*, achieving his moral impact "*with a corn-cob!*" (*MWA*, 64) That is, he prods the reader with a fake phallus. Lewis describes this with approval.

The satirical criticism in *Paleface* and *Time and Western Man* is less comic and more penetrating as political-social analysis. He always insists on the philosophical and political ramifications of both a theoretical bias and a distinctive writing style. The attacks on D. H. Lawrence in *Paleface*, while still offering the glowing verbal exuberance and the deflating sound of his vocal manner, is more obviously the work of an outsider who realizes that there is something immediate and dangerous at stake. While most of the "monoliths" of *Men Without Art* are clearly not without political significance—they are moralists, assaulting a trivial, puppet-ridden world—and though the vision of a world without art intimated in the later chapters is bleak, it is really in *Paleface* and *Time and Western Man* that the satire is presented at its hardest. This is explained in *Men Without Art*, when he writes, "Satire in reality often is nothing else but *the truth...*" (*MWA*, 121).

But the contrary methods in these great works of the 1920s are put to very pronounced ends:

> About the time of "Paleface" I began, with considerable exhilaration, to swim against the tide. The "tide" is usually going in the wrong direction anyway—or in the right direction in the wrong way...
>
> It had at the moment the name of *Lawrence*: for "tides" have names... (*RA*, 204)

Lawrence is attacked for "mindlessness" (*P*, 176) and sentimentality. Lewis defines sentimentality as '*Any idea... that is not taken to its ultimate conclusion*" (*P*, 248).

There is little discussion of the actual literary qualities, as such, though this is in fact linked to the examination of Lawrence's ideas—that is, *how* Lawrence writes is related to *what* he has to say:

> (1) The Unconscious; (2) The Feminine; (3) The Communist; those are the main principles of action of the mind of Mr. Lawrence, linked in a hot and piping trinity of rough-stuff primitivism, and freudian hot-sex-stuff. With *Sons and Lovers*, his first book, he was at once hot-foot upon the fashionable trail of incest; the book is an eloquent wallowing mass of Mother-love and Sex-idolatry. His *Women in Love* is again the same thick, sentimental, luscious stew. (*P*, 180)

It is difficult to imagine a more unfashionable criticism of Lawrence. Lewis is championing the "classical" approach, as opposed to the "romantic" (the classical being hard and precise, the romantic being soft and vague). The attack is based on Lewis's awareness of how these factors embodied in the very tissues of Lawrence's writing reflect and help propel the *zeitgeist*'s obsessions—the child-cult, fantasy, the doom of youth, homo-eroticism, primitivism, Freud, and "musicalization," the sensibility of the "ear."

"The Revolutionary Simpleton," in *Time and Western Man*, where Lewis blasts Pound, Stein, Joyce, and, of all people, Anita Loos, presents these qualities of tone and disjunction of form in what is the most vigorous defence of intelligence, the external, and visual attributes achieved in this century. Here the intentions are clear: the Enemy is observing and slashing open the "time" cults, leaving the large corpus of writings on that subject *as a corpse*, using his satirical style of exaggerating, lampooning, and invective to directly aid the bewildered and seduced, if not unconscious, Plain Reader. The message: never be a victim of the propaganda of the age, even if it is articulated by its greatest artists.

"Oh it is a wild life that we live in the near West, between one apocalypse and another!" (*P*, 100) As I have been arguing, Lewis undertook this task for the purpose of dealing with his audience, with what is left of western man. "You," to whom he constantly refers (and he does mean YOU), are his partner in this exposition and exposé:

> All forms of art of a permanent order are intended not only to please and to excite, believe me, Plain Reader, if you are still there, but to call into play the entire human capacity—for sensation, reflection, imagination, and will. (*MWA*, 8-9)

The intention is to make the Plain Reader not so plain anymore:

> In such a fluid world we should by all rights be building boats rather than houses. But this essay is a sort of ark; or dwelling of the mind, designed to float and navigate; and we should all be wise, with or without covenants, to provide ourselves with some such shell in everything, rather than rely on any conservative structures. For a very complete and profound inundation is at hand. After *us* comes the deluge: more probably than not, however, before that, and out of its epigrammatic sequence.
>
> Meantime, we have a duty where the *officials of the Flood*, as they might be called, are concerned. We have to serve them out with gas-masks, light navigable craft of a seaworthy and inconspicuous type, and furnish them with instructions as to currents, winds, head-swells, maritime effluvia, Saragossa [*sic*] seas, doldrums, sharks, water-spouts, and sea-serpents. The complete equipment of an inspector of the Flood would be of such a technical description that it is impossible, however, to more than hint at it.[17]

Lewis's satirical methods are a way of achieving what Kierkegaard called *indirect communication*:[18] the aim is to shatter fashions and façades and bring in a new perspective. Hence the commitment to the external, to the outside; for the outsider is always a stranger, "the voice of one crying in the wilderness."

> My main object in *Paleface* has been to place in the hands of the readers of imaginative literature, and also of that very considerable literature directed to popularizing scientific and philosophic notions, in language as clear and direct as possible, a sort of key; so that, with its aid, they may be able to read any work of art presented to them, and, resisting the skilful blandishments of the fictionist, reject this plausible "life" that often is not life, and understand the ideologic or philosophical basis of these confusing entertainments, where so many false ideas change hands or change heads. (*P*, 109)

If Wyndham Lewis had chosen the conventional methods of criticism, abandoning his "ho-ho-ho," machine-gun insights, mosaic techniques, his Swiftian explosions of unquestioned assumptions, and that colloquial tone, he would have been unable to carry out his commitments to diagnosis and surgery. (So, for example, the usually maligned appendix to *Men Without Art*, "The Taxi-Cab Driver Test for 'Fiction,'" is much more easily understood as a strategy for alerting the reader to shifting stylistic currents and muddied generical distinctions.) Rather than having axes to grind, or being obsessed with hatred and jealousy—as has been charged—Lewis was attempting nothing less than the wholesale regeneration of cultural values and perceptive integrity. This is why *Men Without Art*, *Time and Western Man*, *Paleface*, and *The Diabolical Principle* all fit together; why the tone— lively, bantering, hectoring, bombastic, congenial, wise, and absurd—is so unified throughout. Lewis was concerned with malaise. He saw the possibility of a world without art. He felt, rightly, that traditional methods were not useful because they were not forceful or immediate enough. Lewis insisted, again and again, that he had something to say, that art had meaning, and what he had to say was concerned with a defense of artistic and intellectual clarity, hardness, freedom, and stability. One of the great difficulties in writing about Lewis, I believe, is due precisely to this always present emphasis on the reader's awareness. The tendency of most readers of Lewis is to try and decide to what extent he is *right* in his literary judgments—that is, judge the content of his criticism. This is never the point. The satire is frequently directed *at the writer himself*, as we have seen. All this is accomplished for one extraordinary purpose: to permit the reader to experience and see the "flood," to understand where society, as portrayed and often initiated by literature, is quickly (too quickly) moving.

His point is moral. The paradox stated in *Men Without Art* that the greatest satire is non-moral should not confuse us : Lewis is referring there to a kind of moralism—to didacticism, and to the fact that you do not moralize with your targets. You present, offering a "key," "an ark," a guide.

Lewis set out, particularly from 1927 on, to establish a presence in letters (the Enemy) who would relate everything to his intelligence and savage laughter and awareness of change and creeping barbarism. This task was creative: to help bring a fresh perspective that would allow the great achievements of the west to continue. The characterization of the outlaw was the vehicle, the agent, the Lewisite medium for expressing "the rot."

As I have been stressing, the tendency with modern criticism (with a few notable exceptions) has been to nervously sidestep the outlaw's crashing, tearing energy, or, in the harshest censorship of all, to ignore it. But Lewis was performing a great service, and he did so with a passionate wholeness. Indeed, it is as if he ends each piece of critical prose with the unspoken last question directed at the audience: *who are you? and where do you stand?* The Enemy fought the apathy and the temporary enthusiasms and the triviality of all the readers he would never know.

---

1. Wyndham Lewis, *Men Without Art* (London: Cassells, 1934), p. 9 . Hereinafter cited as *MWA*.
2. Wyndham Lewis, *Time and Western Man* (London: Chatto and Windus, 1927), p. 109. Hereinafter cited as *TWM*.
3. Quoted in Timothy Materer, *Vortex, Pound, Eliot, and Lewis* (Ithaca: Cornell Univ. Press, 1979), p. 36.
4. Jonathan Culler, *Structuralist Poetics* (Ithaca: Cornell Univ. Press, 1975), p. viii.
5. William Pritchard, a noted Lewis critic, is, I believe, particularly guilty of this overly apologetic attitude towards Lewis's writings.
6. Irving Howe, "Beliefs of the Masters," in *The Decline of the New* (New York: Harcourt, Brace, and World, 1970), p. 42.
7. Wyndham Lewis, *Rude Assignment: A Narrative of My Career Up-to-date* (London: Hutchinson, 1951), p. 43. Hereinafter cited as *RA*.
8. See Robert C. Elliott, *The Force of Satire: Magic, Ritual, Art* (Princeton: Princeton Univ. Press, 1960), for a further discussion of this. I am also indebted to some as yet unpublished research done by Eric McLuhan.
9. Ezra Pound, "The Serious Artist," in *The Literary Essays of Ezra Pound*, ed. T. S. Eliot (New York: New Directions, 1968), p. 45.
10. Wyndham Lewis, *The Art of Being Ruled*, in *Wyndham Lewis: An Anthology of His Prose*, ed. E. W. F. Tomlin (London: Methuen, 1969), p. 95.
11. Wyndham Lewis, *The Diabolical Principle and the Dithyrambic Spectator* (London: Chatto and Windus, 1931), p. 22.
12. Wyndham Lewis, "What It Feels Like To Be an Enemy", in *Wyndham Lewis on Art*, ed. Walter Michel and C. J. Fox (New York: Funk & Wagnalls, 1969), p. 267.
13. Ezra Pound, *The Egoist*, August 1914, p. 307.
14. Wyndham Lewis, *Paleface* (London: Chatto and Windus, 1929), p. 109. Hereinafter cited as *P*.
15. Wyndham Lewis, *Blasting and Bombardiering* (London: Calder and Boyars, 1967), p. 8.
16. Ernest Hemingway, *A Moveable Feast* (New York: Scribner's, 1964), pp. 108-09.
17. *The Art of Being Ruled*, p. 95.
18. Soren Kierkegaard, *The Point of View for My Work as an Author: A Report on History*, trans. W. Lowric; ed. B. Nelson (New York: Harper and Row, 1962), p. 35.

C. H. SISSON

LEWIS'S STUDY OF HIMSELF

It was no doubt as a piece of modest effrontery, of the kind he was accustomed to employ for the purposes of publicity, that Lewis included among his studies of his literary contemporaries a chapter on himself. *Men Without Art* (1934) is one of the crucial works of twentieth-century criticism, and the necessary indignities it inflicts have even now not been absorbed by the public which claims to read books and certainly writes them. The T. S. Eliot who is the object of study in the schools of English Literature is not, generally speaking, the one from whom the bits pared off by Lewis in this volume have in fact been pared. It cannot be said that Lewis's study of himself is quite in the same style as what he wrote about others. This is inevitable, and no doubt the joke of giving himself an unfair advantage, for a moment, was not lost on him. For while Eliot, Hemingway, and Virginia Woolf were placed in the perspectives of *The Apes of God* and *Time and Western Man*, the subject of the chapter on Lewis was, naturally, seen from the point of view from which those perspectives were the only ones.

Lewis starts from the phrase—apparently intended to be derogatory—of a critic writing in the *Daily Telegraph*. "Mr. Wyndham Lewis could be described as a *personal-appearance* satirist." This is seized on with a sort of *Tyro* grin. "But that is a compliment," Lewis says. The author of *The Apes of God* "lays great store by that *externality*, in a world that is literally inundated with sexual viscera and the 'dark' gushings of the tides of *The Great Within*. Call him a 'personal-appearance writer' and he is far from being displeased!" (*MWA*, 123).[1] The subtitle of the chapter is "The Theory of the External, the Classical, Approach in Art."

A theory of the external, and a theory of time, are the two axes of Lewis's position as a philosopher—if that jealously guarded professional designation can be given to his somewhat home-made speculations. The two are related. The theory of *Time and Western Man* is developed explicitly from the point of view of "the plastic or the visual intelligence." And the preference for "the shield of the tortoise, or the rigid stylistic articulations of the grasshopper" expressed by Wyndham Lewis as artist is at the same time a revulsion from the flux conceived by the apologists of space-time. What Lewis disliked in Whitehead is summed up in this:

> He wishes to use, subjugate, invest and possess the concrete, in the interests of the abstract: and when so clothed, in his full panoply of "concreteness," to deliver an attack upon another sort of "abstract" that he does not like. The analysis of the contemporary time-philosophy is so fanatically directed to disintegrate and to banish the bogey of "concreteness," that it would be impossible not to receive the impression of a peculiar hostility to "the concrete," in its most inclusive sense, in favour of something abstract and mental.... (*TWM*, 164)

By a reversal of terms one can arrive at a fair statement of what Lewis himself is about in his writings on time. He uses the language of theory merely in order to defend the concrete against the abstract. He cannot be said to have made a philosophical discovery as, despite the element of mere restatement in all human thinking, a Descartes or a Berkeley may be said to have done. Indeed he can hardly be said, in his fat book on the time philosophy, to have succeeded in disengaging a philosophical notion of his own at all. He is rather a diagnostician or detective, tracing the effects of certain current notions on the human animal and finding them malign. There are dangers about such a proceeding. Having identified one's clues or symptoms, and having given a name to the crime or disease they are taken to indicate, one sees them everywhere, or everywhere except in oneself, so that one tends to set oneself against the whole world, which is not prudent and cannot be altogether accurate. A more subtle danger is that one comes to see certain phenomena as having no other significance than the one that one's own theory gives them. Lewis, however, perfectly recognized that the absolutes he proposes are, humanly speaking, relatives, and under the vast panache there is a remarkable humility before the objective world, nowhere more touchingly demonstrated than in the scene in *Malign Fiesta* where Pullman falls on one knee in contemplation of the form and structure of a flower.

Lewis's critique of the time-philosophy is not so much an exploration of reality as a sort of combat exercise against a vast unreality which overshadows our world with its wings. It is a defensive action, and what he is defending is a simple, common-sense view of what is actually there and can be seen. But, of course, the notion of what can be seen is not all that simple the moment one stops to think about it; the world of sense, with its evanescent impressions, retains its solidity only if one is prepared to plump for a certain dogmatism. Lewis is really an exponent of the view which he characterizes as that of "ancient philosophy, in the account given . . . by Bergson," that an object "realizes itself, working up to a climax, then it disintegrates. It is its apogee or perfection that is *it*," he adds, "for classical science. It is the rounded *thing* of common-sense" (*TWM*, 163). Both Berkeley and Dr. Johnson held, in their several ways, that any theorizing the tendency of which was to rob people of this common-sense world was, to say the least, suspect. Lewis was of the same mind. He had the special bias which came from his genius for the visual arts, but his passion for the ordinary world as it was made does not end there. There is a profound humanism implicit in all Lewis's critical writing, and in the clouds which gathered around him as he completed *The Human Age* he came to the traditional question as to whether it could be maintained, except under God. "Historically, I am a Christian," says Pullman in *Malign Fiesta*. "But I did not, for the major part of my life, practise my religion, and I died an agnostic." The main feature of the space-time doctrines was that they pretended to offer

> something *alive*, in place of "mechanism": "organism" in place of "matter." But the more you examine them . . . the more you will feel that you are being fooled. For what the *benefit* to you, in this famous change from matter to mind, from "matter" to "organism," is going to be, it is very difficult to discover. For it is not *you* who become "organic"; *you* have been organic all along, no one has ever questioned that. It is your tables and chairs, in a pseudo-leibnizian animism, not you, that are to become "organic." (*TWM*, 170)

What happens to you is that instead of being a distinct self, set over against the physical world, you are invited to merge into "the pantheistic immanent oneness of 'creative,' 'evolutionary' substance." This conjuring trick is suspect alike to the artist, the humanist, and the man of common sense.

> By this proposed transfer from the beautiful *objective, material* world of common-sense, over to the "organic" world of chronological mentalism, you lose not only the clearness of outline, the static beauty, of the things you commonly apprehend; you lose also the clearness of outline of your own individuality which apprehends them. (*TWM*, 171)

It was inevitable that, when Lewis came to the examination of his own work in the light of these principles, he should find it very satisfactory. As a matter of fact he does not examine it in any detail. He concentrates on *The Apes of God*, which had recently been published when *Men Without Art* was being written, and even as regards that work he contents himself with generalities. The theory may be said to have got the better of the critic. Indeed the whole of *Men Without Art* is really a testing of contemporary Anglo-Saxon literature in the light of the technical principles embodied in *The Apes of God*. That book was, "as you may recall," he says to the reader of his criticism, "a fiction-satire . . . of considerable proportions." He is saying what the reviewers had for the most part failed to say. What is of interest, however, is not the belated and self-constructed boost but the explanation of the method.

> . . . *the eye* has been the organ in the ascendant there. For *The Apes of God* it could, I think quite safely, be claimed that no book has ever been written that has paid more attention to the *outside* of people. In it their shells or pelts, or the language of their bodily movements, come first, not last. (*MWA*, 118)

The book was a counter-blast to the stream-of-consciousness school, to the methods of Joyce and

Gertrude Stein which professed to see everything from the inside—though that is a claim which Lewis perhaps takes a little too readily at its face value. In the euphoria of his apologia, Lewis lays it down that the *internal* method should be used only in dealing with the extremely aged, young children, half-wits, and animals—a piece of dogmatism which certainly leaves the subject less, rather than more clear than it was before. It is at such moments that one regrets that Lewis's discursive method has so much of the art of the picador about it. His shafts land with precision—and on sensitive spots—but he does not stay to come to grips with the beast he is attacking. "In my opinion," he says categorically, the internal method "should be entirely confined" to the four classes he has named. This is a clue to his own technique in *The Apes of God*. It does not throw light on any wider critical principle. There is no doubt that Lewis's habit of presenting the combative thought of the moment as a general truth—which it can often be shown not to be—has done harm to his reputation. The reader who is in general sympathy with Lewis's point of view can accept these absolute statements for what they are—provisional definitions of something which is never quite defined, and perhaps never can be, but which is felt subjectively as an absolute. In spite of the momentarily overbearing tone—which again has helped to make enemies for the *Enemy*—Lewis's approach to fundamental problems shows an engaging diffidence. "What is 'truth' regarding any person?" he asks, and goes on:

> It is difficult to see how the objective truth of much that is called "Satire" can be less true than the truth of lyrical declamation, in praise, for instance, of a lovely mistress. There is, in both cases, *another* truth, that is all. But both are upon an equal intellectual footing, I think—only the humanly "agreeable" is more often false than the humanly "disagreeable." That is unavoidable, seeing what we are. (*MWA*, 122)

The claim for the external method is really no more than that it is the vehicle of a truth. That is modest enough. And that satire partakes of the nature of scientific observation.

With this it would hardly be possible to disagree. But although Lewis returns frequently, in the course of his work, to such modest statements of his intentions, which obviously lay very near the root of his mind, his temperament did not allow him to rest on them for long enough for people to recognize this as a characteristic pose. In a nine-point summing up at the end of his study of "Mr. Wyndham Lewis: 'Personal-appearance' artist, he makes claims for the external method as the characteristic method of the future. Using the language of hoary controversy, he equates it with "the 'classical' manner of apprehending" (*MWA*, 126). This owes something, without a doubt, to the arguments of the pre-First World War period in which he set out. There is a little of T. E. Hulme, even of Sorel and Péguy, in all this. His real concerns—and they are a painter's—may be identified by the sudden illumination of his language when he says that for the external approach "even a crocodile's tears can be relieved of some of their repulsiveness." He relates the "romantic snapshotting of the wandering stream of the Unconscious" to the "naturalism of the Greek plastic"—which again recalls Hulme, though that is not to say that Hulme was more of an inventor than Lewis in this field. Indeed, the setting up of the "formalism of the Egyptian or the Chinese" against the plastic ideals of post-Renaissance Europe, and the positing of an *Umwertung aller Werte*[2] which will change the face of the world, if examined in the light of Lewis's own principles, may lead one to wonder whether Hulme himself was not a little infected by the Time disease, and whether Lewis is not here showing symptoms of it himself. Is a new "period" something with which we should really be concerning ourselves, and is the notion any the less suspect because the one here identified by Lewis is of global proportions? It is doubtful whether a change of the proportions suggested would anyhow be visible in contemporary perspectives. It is safer to assume that it is the same old world we are grubbing around in, and that we had better treat it with as much circumspection as technology allows.

It is an important critical fact about Lewis that his own theory of himself is incomplete. That this is so was perhaps due to his diffidence as much as to his taste for satiric overstatement and natural *panache*. But unquestionably, having noticed certain characteristics of his own art and found that they were unacceptable to large numbers of people most influential in the world of artistic and literary middlemen, he succumbed to the temptation to exaggerate their importance, sometimes, it would seem, out of an understandable pleasure in discomfiting those who valued him below his true worth. To some extent, however, he was no doubt the victim merely of his own belief in a theory which touched truth at so many points and produced such abundant seeming proofs of its own validity. Yet now that the time has come for a re-assessment of Lewis's work as a whole, it would be a pity if potential readers among a new generation were put off by a praise which would be merely an echo of his own stridencies. Lewis's greatness, it should now be understood, does not rest on the necessary correction he gave to various contemporary excesses. His work in that field tended to make him replace one overemphasis by another. It is worth pointing out that it is not when he is writing most persistently in accordance with his own canon that he writes best. If *Apes of God* has not the speed and freshness of *The Wild Body* or *Tarr* nor the profundity of *Self Condemned* or *The Human Age*, it is because of a relative lack of vitality in the observation and interest in the persons portrayed. The external method of course needs reinforcement from within. There was lurking under Lewis's much-advertised carapace not merely a humanism, but a humanity, without which, after all, there is no great work in literature, however one may be tempted to keep silent on the subject by the slop which generally passes for humanity. "To be a fool with a robust body can be no more pleasant for the person concerned than being an intelligent dwarf: yet no one scruples to laugh at the former, but parades a genteel sensitiveness regarding the latter." If "the greatest satire is non-moral," as Lewis claimed, it is because the variety and complexity of the world is such that a judgment of others is not our business. It is our *common* absurdities that Lewis laughs at. "*Freedom* is certainly our human goal, in the sense that all effort is directed to that end: and it is a dictate of nature that we should laugh, and laugh loudly, at those who have fallen into slavery and, still more, those who batten on it" (*MWA*, 116).

---

1. Parenthetical references to Lewis's works are to the following editions: *MWA: Men Without Art* (1934; repr. New York: Russell and Russell, 1964) and *TWM: Time and Western Man* (1927; repr. Boston: Beacon Press, 1957).

2. "Revaluation of all values"—*Ed*.

PAUL EDWARDS

"CLODOVEO" AND "BELCANTO":

WYNDHAM LEWIS AND JAMES JOYCE

"[Belcanto] is not one of the greatest of the great, you know, . . . though extremely self-conscious. But he is a most gentle humorous and nimble person with a fine nose for the mot juste and a rare tongue for an old brandy and a lovely melodiush tenor. . . . He becomes rather abusive sometimes when he discovers me talking about him—but as it's in his bellocanto cant it's as though you were being called no gentleman *or you're another* in singsong pedlar's french.*"*

—Wyndham Lewis, *The Childermass*, p. 278.

There was always an element of rivalry, not always friendly rivalry, between James Joyce and Wyndham Lewis. Joyce's casting of Lewis as Shaun against his own Shem in *Finnegans Wake* attests to it. At times it was almost as if Ezra Pound ran them against each other like a pair of racehorses. In some respects their careers ran parallel. Both had their first novels serialized by *The Egoist* and both got *The Little Review* suppressed on account of the indecency of their writings. Pound, in his criticism, compared *Tarr* with *A Portrait of the Artist as a Young Man* and, later, *The Apes of God* with *Ulysses*. The unusual relations between the two writers cannot really be understood unless the figure of Ezra Pound is included in the account. He was the impresario who got them both into *The Egoist* and *The Little Review*. In 1920 it was at Pound's urging that Lewis, Joyce, and T. S. Eliot assembled together, a meeting of titans, clustering round Pound's old shoes as if they were an emblem in a poem by Wallace Stevens. And when Lewis's criticism of Joyce was published seven years later, Pound was again an invisible presence.

In the years between their first meeting and Lewis's attack, their relations were amicable. There were numerous drinking sessions that made Lewis unpopular with Joyce's wife; but a few anecdotes show something of the background of their subsequent disagreements. The most famous is the one told by Lewis himself in *Rude Assignment*;[1] the two disagreed about the façade of Rouen Cathedral. Lewis at some length criticized the fussiness and purely quantitative expression of the front of the building, which he found boring. Joyce replied that he, on the other hand, liked that kind of art and used the same methods himself, in writing.

Richard Ellmann, in his biography of Joyce, also tells of how, when Lewis once suggested a breach of decorum with a couple of prostitutes the two writers often met in a bar, Joyce reminded Lewis that he was the author of "The Ideal Giant."[2] This anecdote supports Lewis's contention that Joyce was very familiar with his work, from which can be inferred that Joyce saw Lewis as a rival to be watched. Lewis wrote to his patron Sidney Schiff in 1922 saying that Joyce, having read "Bestre" regarded him as the contemporary English prose writer most worth taking seriously.[3] It is possible that "Bestre" influenced Joyce. It appeared just at the time Joyce was uncertainly starting out on *Finnegans Wake*, and its extravagant portrayal of an outrageous and almost metamorphic innkeeper who probably exposes himself to a woman could certainly have helped Joyce to define for himself the hero of the *Wake*: Humphrey Chimpden Earwicker, an innkeeper probably also prone to sexual exhibitionism.

There was obviously admiration on Lewis's side as well, though at the time of their first meeting Lewis was not familiar with Joyce's writing. The admiration can be seen in the pen and ink drawings Lewis made of Joyce at this period, which express more fully than his other portraits of the time, a varied and complex personality. By contrast, the Pound series, though in some ways more impressive, is characteristically impersonal. But Lewis also fixed the satirist's eye on Joyce and made the drawing "The Duc de Joyeux Sings," mocking Joyce for what Lewis regarded as his obsession with social status. [See p. 134 below]

From about 1925 Lewis began dissociating himself from his old allies, and emerged on the scene again as the "Enemy" in 1927. He had already, the previous year, criticized Joyce's use of the stream of consciousness in *Ulysses* in *The Art of Being Ruled*.[4] His main attack came in the first issue of *The Enemy* in January 1927: "An Analysis of the Mind of James Joyce," which was reprinted in *Time and Western Man* in September of the same year. Lewis's attack was the beginning of a public controversy between the two writers that became increasingly personal, and which, though amusing to read now, undoubtedly spoiled their friendship, however much they tried to patch it up. Joyce's first reply was published in *transition* 6, in September 1927, and in *Finnegans Wake*, Part I, Chapter vi, Professor Jones's lecture. In the same month, Lewis published *The Enemy* No. 2, in which he announced an Enemy campaign against *transition*, though he carefully dissociated Joyce from the movement he would be attacking: "Amongst these people the author of *Ulysses* is hardly at home, he belongs elsewhere."[5] As if trying to win Joyce over to the side of the Enemy, he described Joyce's genius as "of a character very different from, and even, I believe, the opposite of the character and beliefs of the people with whom he is associated."[6] In his original "Analysis," Lewis had expressed the hope that Joyce might be "won over" to the side of the Enemy. This was perhaps only slightly less naive than Joyce's own belief that Lewis's attack would have been moderated greatly if a copy of *Pomes Penyeach* had been available to him. In the October issue of *transition* Joyce made further allusion to Lewis ("cattlemen's spring meat" i.e. "Cantleman's Spring-Mate") in the revised version of Part I, Chapter vii of *Finnegans Wake*, on Shem the Penman, part of an earlier version of which Lewis had criticized in his "Analysis." In the December 1927 issue of *transition* appeared an editorial reply to Lewis's criticisms of Joyce, Gertrude Stein, and *transition*. This was called "First Aid to the Enemy," and was answered by Lewis in the final issue of *The Enemy*, issued in March 1929: "The Diabolical Principle." In this essay Lewis was less careful to dissociate Joyce from his Paris-based publishers and promoters, perhaps because it was now clear Joyce was not going to be "won over." In February 1928 Joyce published a version of the "lesson" in *transition* (*FW*, II, ii). This contains some mockery of Lewis, but is a less extended reply than the earlier lecture of Professor Jones (*FW*, I, vi). The next month Joyce renewed the attack in *transition* with the fable of the Ondt and the Gracehoper (*FW*, III, i). Joyce's replies consisted mainly of mockery and parody of Lewis, which prompted Lewis to retaliate with a parody of Joyce in *The Childermass*, published in June 1928.

It is entertaining to follow the controversy all the way through in the original texts, but from start to finish there's virtually no exchange of ideas, since both writers seem unable to see each other outside the perspective of their own particular concerns at the time. Joyce assimilated the disagreement to the Shem/Shaun archetype, for example, with him and Lewis as twins condemned to quarrel and fight each other. It is not possible to be sure what relation Joyce believed to obtain between the archetypes he included in *Finnegans Wake* and reality, but the myth under which he figured his own quarrel with Wyndham Lewis, whatever its aesthetic propriety within *Finnegans Wake*, does not answer to the real complexities of the event. Conversely, Lewis's criticism of Joyce's mind fails to do justice to the complexities of Joyce's art.

But if there is no fruitful exchange of ideas, there is an amusing exchange of insults and parodies. When Lewis writes, in *Time and Western Man*,

> There is not very much reflection going on at any time inside the head of Mr. James Joyce.

and

> It is a suffocating, moeotic expanse of objects, all of them lifeless, the sewage of a Past twenty years old, all neatly arranged in a meticulous sequence.[7]

Joyce parodies:

> And, an you could peep inside the cerebralised saucepan of this eer illwinded goodfornobody, you would see in his house of thoughtsam ... what a jetsam litterage of convolvuli of times lost or strayed, of lands derelict and of tongues laggin too. ...[8]

To that Lewis responded:

> Ant say too sumthin like dublinpubmumper on the rivolooshums-highbrow-lowneck-racket mit a bag full of tricks mun (for Arm scottish tew) full of wormeaten wordies infant-bitten and granfer-mumbled, scotched gutted scuttled and jettisoned in killeidoscoptic otts ents ant mitships upon the coasts of Barbaree. ...[9]

In this parody in *The Childermass* Lewis has Joyce,

whom he nicknames "Belcanto" in mockery of *Chamber Music* and *Pomes Penyeach*, use the phrase "on me giltedged giltie conshie of a playboy of westend letters," which naturally recalls Joyce's reference to *Time and Western Man* as *Spice and Westend Woman* "(utterly exhausted before publication, indiapepper edition shortly)." The controversy between the two writers is largely conducted on this level of mockery and abuse, though a genuine reply has been discerned in Joyce's fable of the Ondt and the Gracehoper. Lewis had made two major criticisms of *Ulysses*; first, that it was effectively without a formal structure, and second, that it was the work of a craftsman who was naively unaware of the implications of the ideology embodied in his art. So the Gracehoper tosses himself "in the vico."[10] The allusion is to the Viconian structure of *Finnegans Wake*, which Joyce no doubt considered adequately guaranteed against the formal deficiency Lewis complained of in his first criticism. But as far as Lewis was concerned, Joyce's use of Vico in this aesthetic manner laid Joyce all the more open to Lewis's second criticism. It is hardly surprising that Lewis considered Vico to be an over-historicist philosopher, similar to those whom he had criticized in *Time and Western Man*. Hence his reply in *The Childermass*:

> (with Vico the mechanical for guide in the musty labrinths of the latter-days to train him to circle true and make true orbit upon himself).[11]

Vico's cyclical view of history is mechanical, and Joyce's adoption of it makes his work mechanical also, Lewis is saying.

Similarly, when Joyce follows *transition*'s view of Lewis as a blimpish killjoy and a sensationalist philistine (the cheerless Ondt), while presenting himself as the "artist" (the light-hearted irresponsible Gracehoper, careless of the future), he is translating the disagreement into precisely the sort of large-scale cliché that Lewis believed vitiated his work.

Since Geoffrey Wagner's pioneering study of this controversy, it has been customary for critics to assume that Joyce's contributions are adequate as replies to Lewis's original attack and the arguments contained in it. But this assumption is unwarrantable, although it is made under cover of two other assumptions that are more plausible: first, that Joyce presents the matter in such a masterly fashion that it forms some of the most effective sequences in *Finnegans Wake*; and second, that after criticizing Joyce in such personal terms in *Time and Western Man*, Lewis was a worthy target for any satire and mockery that Joyce cared to direct his way. The common point of view is further reinforced by the literary brilliance of Joyce's parody of Lewis in his "knowall profoundly impressive role." He parodies one of Lewis's digressions on the "sex-question," for example, and exactly catches the rhythm and tone of Lewis's discursive style:

> Now there can be no question about it either that I having done as much, have quite got the size of that demilitery young female (we will continue to call her Marge) whose types may be met with in any public garden, wearing a very "dressy" affair, known as an "ethel" of instep length and with a real fur, reduced to 3/9, and muffin cap to tone (they are "angelskin" this fall), ostentatiously hemming apologetically over the shirtness of some "sweet" garment, when she is not sitting on all the free benches avidously reading about "it" but ovidently on the look out for "him" or so "thrilled" about the best dressed dolly pram and beautiful elbow competition or at the movies.... [12]

Compare this with the following, taken, almost at random, from *The Art of Being Ruled*:

> At all events, at the root of the mechanical, subconscious obsession that in the fashions takes such ridiculous forms that it is impossible not to suppose that there is a mind at the back of them capable of appreciating a joke, perhaps too well (though the "wisdom" of this comedian can be doubted), is the reflection of political decay, the stopping-up and closing-down of the great traditional vents for ambition, and the overthrow of any "public life" that could claim a significance beyond the function of office-boy and valet.[13]

Another factor which cannot be ignored is Joyce's stature as a great literary artist. This can only predispose critics to accept his arguments. It is worth pointing out here that Wyndham Lewis himself would not have argued with a very high valuation of Joyce's writing, and, further, did not consider his own attack on Joyce as an attack on such a valuation. He wrote in a letter to *The Listener* in 1935 that "Mr Wyndham Lewis, speaking in person, desires to say that he regards James Joyce as a great literary artist"[14] and in the comparatively unrestrained parody included in *The Childermas* Lewis went out of his way to deny the capacity of his attacks to ultimately damage Joyce:

No mortal organ is at the stake: except for immaterial injuries in borrowed plumes that do not matter it is O.K. and you're as safe with me as the licensed houses of Limerick at this moment.[15]

While I dispute the commonly agreed "score" for this literary tennis match, I think that arguing over the points is now less useful to anybody than examining some of Lewis's original criticisms in the hope that doing so will illuminate the positions of both Joyce and Lewis himself.

Briefly, the burden of Lewis's original attack is as follows; he accuses Joyce of having, where life is concerned, an entirely conventional outlook, and of uncritically incorporating ideas into his work without realizing their source or implications. *Ulysses* he considered a monument to triviality; the concerns of the characters are unimportant and provincial; the characters are anyway artificially constructed from hackneyed stereotypes; the fanatical inclusiveness of the naturalism at work in the narrative and the fluid technique of the internal monologue rob the book of internal structure, and so on.

Now most of these criticisms can be and have been answered in one way or another, and, obviously, Lewis's is not the idea of *Ulysses* that has prevailed. That book is now regarded as a masterpiece mainly because, from underneath all the triviality that Lewis could not see beyond, some of the deepest concerns of human beings emerge. A conviction is gained that human values can survive in the most barren and debased conditions, even when the only material they have in which to be embodied is the stray flotsam and jetsam of Dublin in 1904.

But this is not the way in which *Ulysses* was regarded in the earliest critical reactions to it, and it is necessary to place Lewis's ideas in the context of critical debate about the book.

> The history of *Ulysses* criticism can be viewed ... as an extended conversation—often amiable, occasionally irritable—between the spiritual descendants of Pound and Eliot.[16]

One of the main subjects of debate about *Ulysses* has been the function and importance of the mythical, symbolic, and stylistic framework. To a great extent, a critic's attitude to the mythological framework determines his reading of *Ulysses*, or is at least a crucial part of the reading and interpretation. Myth became important to both Pound and Eliot in their poetry, and it is clear that they both learned from Joyce's use of it in *Ulysses*. Pound and Eliot (and Lewis) agree about the way Joyce uses myth in at least one respect:

> Joyce emploie un échafaudage pris à Homère, et les restes d'une culture moyenâgeuse allégorique; peu importe, c'est une affaire de cuisine, qui ne restreint pas l'action, qui ne nuit pas à son réalisme, ni à la contemporanéité de son action. C'est un moyen de régler la forme.[17]

Although Eliot expressed dissatisfaction with this view of Pound's of the mythological structure of *Ulysses*, complaining that the structure "has been treated as an amusing dodge, or scaffolding erected by the author for the purpose of disposing his realistic tale, of no interest in the completed structure,"[18] he nevertheless himself sees it as an external imposition of form, a useful fiction:

> It is simply a way of controlling, of ordering, of giving a shape and significance to the immense panorama of futility and anarchy which is contemporary history.[19]

For both Pound and Eliot, the Homeric parallels are a device, though for Pound they have little to do with the meaning of the book, which is present entirely in its naturalistic content, while for Eliot it is precisely their presence that gives the naturalistic content its meaning. Pound can be seen as the first of the "naturalist" school of *Ulysses* criticism, and Eliot the first of the "symbolist" school (unless that title be reserved for Valéry Larbaud).

The other notable feature of the book's formal structure, its various styles, symbolic organs, colors, and so on, stands in somewhat the same relation to the naturalist material as does the mythological structure. A critic's attitude towards this is therefore similar to his attitude to the Homeric parallels, and the naturalist reader will either ignore them, or, more subtly, attempt to show how they support his reading.

Wyndham Lewis's discussion of *Ulysses* is firmly in the Poundian, naturalistic critical tradition:

> As to the homeric framework, that is only an entertaining structural device or conceit. (*TWM*, 104)

It is therefore primarily as a naturalistic novel that Lewis reads *Ulysses*, but his analysis is hostile and disputes many of Pound's ideas about the book. The disagreement takes place in the context of certain shared assumptions. Both take *Ulysses* to be a species of purge, or catharsis, in a sense more literal than Aristotelian:

> And if *Ulysses* has any existence, it exists as a great work of Katharsis.[20]

Lewis's description is more vivid than Pound's:

> So rich was its delivery, its pent-up outpouring so vehement, that it will remain, eternally cathartic, a monument like a record diarrhoea. (*TWM*, 92)

Pound's later statement of the cathartic nature of *Ulysses* is in almost the same terms as Lewis's, but was clearly conceived earlier:

> In 1912 or eleven I invoked whatever gods may exist, in the quatrain:
> Sweet Christ from hell spew up some Rabelais,
> To belch and ... and to define today
> In fitting fashion, and her monument
> Heap up to her in fadeless excrement.
> *Ulysses* I take as my answer.[21]

Both see *Ulysses* as a monument marking the end of an era; Lewis: "It is the sardonic catafalque of the victorian world" (*TWM*, 92); Pound: " 'Ulysses' is the end, the summary, of a period...."[22] The era Pound sees *Ulysses* as closing is the "age of usury," while Lewis emphasizes the pre-First World War nature of the book, and what he regards as its substantial irrelevance to modern life.

Lewis's first disagreement with Pound over Joyce's work is recorded in a letter from Pound to Joyce, dated by Forrest Read in *Pound/Joyce* circa April 1, 1914; Pound reports that Lewis, Hueffer, and others have called the novel *A Portrait of the Artist as a Young Man* "good stuff," and mentions that Lewis might accept a contribution from Joyce to the magazine he is about to start (BLAST): "He likes the novel but isn't very keen on the stories."[23] The disagreement over the *Dubliners* stories is not well-documented, but its cause is not difficult to discover, since, to a great extent, both Pound and Lewis saw *Ulysses* as another *Dubliners* writ large. Pound, in a 1914 article for *The Egoist*, presents Joyce as a meticulous realist, distinguished by a capacity for rigorous selection of the essential from the materials at hand. Maupassant, Stendhal, and Flaubert are writers whom Pound describes Joyce as resembling. These writers are part of a tradition often sketched by Pound in his critical writings, particularly in his essays on Henry James and James Joyce. The tradition's germinal point is in Pound's view the manifesto of "realism" written by the Goncourt brothers as a preface to *Germinie Lacerteux*. For Pound, the aim of these writers is to "get the record straight," in as concise and complete a form as possible. *Ulysses* thus becomes for him an expression of the same impulse. This impulse is naturalistic, but it is also fiercely satirical; Flaubert and Swift are cited to indicate this.[24]

One of Wyndham Lewis's major lines of criticism is to relate Joyce's writing to this tradition in a more nuanced and damaging way:

> So, to start with, Joyce is not a homologue of Swift. That is a strange mistake. There is very little of the specific power of that terrible personage, that *terribilità*, in the amiable author of *Ulysses*. Another writer with whom he has been compared, and whom he is peculiarly unlike, is Flaubert. (*TWM*, 76)

Lewis does not deny Joyce's affinity with the "naturalist" tradition sketched by Pound:

> No writing of his before *Ulysses* would have given him anything but an honourable position as the inevitable naturalist-french-influenced member of the romantic Irish Revival—a Maupassant of Dublin, but without the sinister force of Flaubert's disciple. (*TWM*, 75)

Lewis also denies this "sinister force" and intensity, a quality he valued highly, to *Ulysses* itself. Bloom is a dilute Bouvard and Pécuchet, and the "Circe" episode cannot compare in power with Flaubert's *Tentation*, however well it throws off the shackles of nineteenth-century naturalism.

What Joyce takes over from this tradition is, therefore, what Lewis considered to be only an empty shell. He sees *Ulysses* as a collection of data without a real vital principle animating it—only the sluggish tide of *élan vital*. Lewis analyzes the main characters of the book, and its first chapter, to show that there is in *Ulysses* only a "superficial appearance of life." Lewis's description of the opening of *Ulysses* shows him at the height of his comic powers, but it is also excellent literary criticism. After extensive mockery he concludes that

> all this has to be read to be believed—but read, of course, with a deaf ear to the really charming

workmanship with which it is presented. *Written on a level with its conception, and it would be as dull stuff as you could easily find.* (*TWM*, 97)

The effect of Lewis's critique is to undermine completely the Poundian perspective on *Ulysses* by showing that, if the book is the kind of book Pound said it was, it is so in a highly unsatisfactory way. The question we need to consider is whether Lewis actually thought that *Ulysses* was only the overdressed naturalism he treated it as. There are, in fact, crucial points where Lewis shies away from deeper investigation. He recognizes, for instance, in the above quotation, that there is a gap in *Ulysses* between the physical events described and the language describing them, but looks only at the first chapter; the gap becomes progressively wider as the narrative proceeds, until the physical events (the naturalist content) are almost inaccessible. The naturalism that the reader begins by trusting becomes at last only one literary convention among many, each dictating a highly restricted selection from an experience that can only find expression by means of convention. It is the tradition of criticism deriving from Eliot that has explored the possible ways we can interpret the effect on the "meaning" of *Ulysses* of such "formal" devices.

Yet Lewis did notice the "gap" I have spoken of. His remarks about the "Circe" episode being liberated from the restraints of nineteenth-century naturalism show that he could have discussed the matter if he had wanted to. It could be said that Lewis uses the context of his essay (an attack on the "time" philosophies) to justify his not coming fully to terms with *Ulysses*. This would be excusable if what were omitted from Lewis's account did not materially affect his case, and one naturally assumes that it did not (it seems as if he regarded the multiplicity of styles in *Ulysses* mainly as showpieces of craftsmanship), but it leaves Lewis rather open to the charge of equivocation. He appears to accept the main lines of discussion laid down by Pound, that *Ulysses* is *Dubliners* writ large, but,

> *Ulysses* was in a sense a different thing altogether. How far that is an effect of a merely technical order, resulting from stylistic complications and intensified display, with a *Dubliners* basis unchanged, or, further, a question of scale, and mechanical heaping up of detail, I should have only partly to decide here. But it places him—on that point every one is in agreement—very high in contemporary letters. (*TWM*, 75)

Lewis's analysis is based on his having made precisely that decision which he says he will not make. It is not unreasonable to complain that he should have explored his professedly ambivalent reactions to the book further, since he has destroyed by his analysis the grounds upon which it had been agreed to place Joyce "very high in contemporary letters." If Lewis wished to insist on this high place (as he did throughout his essay), some other grounds should have been discovered to justify it. This might have had the effect of swinging the critique more to the "Eliot" end of the critical spectrum.

On the other hand, it is unrealistic to attach much weight to the somewhat pedantic strictures on Lewis's criticism that I have made. Lewis's criticism still has life, and has an important place in the critical debate about *Ulysses*, and probably will continue to do so. A probable reason for the continuing life of Lewis's critique is that its prime purpose is not literary-critical. By this is meant that the aim of the writer was not to produce literary criticism as such, in the way that was the aim of, say Stuart Gilbert, or, more recently, Richard Ellmann. For such "pure" critics, the text studied can only be a "given," precisely an object of study. Certainly, whatever the importance of the work studied might be in the critic's own life, his engagement with a book will be different from that of a practising creative writer. In the case of *Ulysses*, it is precisely because so many creative writers felt it to be essential to come to terms with the book that it now looks so central in the history of modernism.

Ulysses seems to have opened up new ways forward for both Pound and Eliot, for each of whom the postwar years were difficult. Eliot's adaptation of Joyce's "mythical" method helped him escape from the personal and formal confines of his poetry (compare the quatrain poems of 1920 with *The Waste Land*), and his plays are also based on the kind of transposition of an ancient story that he found in Joyce. For Pound, *Ulysses* was important in reorienting *The Cantos*, in showing him the usefulness of the resourceful Ulysses persona for exploring the rag-bag of the modern world. The early versions of the first *Cantos* had been presided over by a rather limited dilettante figure, similar to the one Pound exorcised (though not as completely as he thought) in *Hugh Selwyn Mauberley*. The example of *Ulysses* seems to have given both Pound and Eliot (Pound especially) confidence in larger and looser structures for their poems.

For Lewis, as a writer of prose fiction, a more mixed response was inevitable, not only because he was bound to feel in competition with Joyce (thanks to Pound), but also because, working in the same medium as Joyce, too great an influence would rob him of his distinct individuality. But Lewis needed to discover a new way forward after the war just as much as Pound and Eliot did. *The Crowd-Master, Hoodopip,* and *Joint* were none of them brought to a satisfactory state of completion. Lewis was conscious of the difficulty of incorporating the innovations pioneered in *Enemy of the Stars* into any large-scale work of fiction. But, it must have seemed to him, this was exactly what Joyce, in "Circe," managed to do. With *The Childermass* and *The Apes of God* Lewis was eventually able to open up his fiction in both form and content in a way similar to Eliot and Pound. These works are certainly not under the shadow of Joyce, but they would have been very different books if *Ulysses* had never been written.

In *Joint*, Lewis's struggles with Joyce (and Pirandello) don't reach the stage of being creative. Joint's direct quotation from one of Bloom's internal monologues ("If a fellow gave them trouble being lagged they let him have it hot and heavy in the bridewell") and his reflection on that act show Lewis simultaneously trying to assimilate aspects of Joyce's technique and to keep his distance from the creator of Bloom:

> "If I lie here drivelling like this and allow the author to snapshot this mechanical reminiscent rubbish swishing about in my inane I shall find myself mixed up in people's minds with Mr. and Mrs. Bloom, that obnoxious couple over the road, or rather over there in Ireland."[25]

In *The Apes of God* Lewis is capable of presenting material that is recognizably "Joycean," yet preserves and projects his own creative personality. Although the scene in the Camden Distillery in Part II of *The Apes* originates in emulation of Bloom's disgusted visit to the Burton restaurant in *Ulysses*, it transcends its origin in a way the allusion in *Joint* does not and is completely integrated with its satirical context. The way Lewis repeatedly explained the stand-off he at last managed to achieve was that Joyce used the "internal" method, while he himself used the "external" method. That explanation will not satisfy anyone who attends to the way Joyce and Lewis actually wrote, but the technical independence it asserts was real.

Lewis's insistence on the great technical difference between himself and Joyce proves that such technical matters were important to him, but the main aim of his analysis was, I have argued, to show that *Ulysses* was an inadequate depiction of the modern world, in comparison with a hypothetically successful example of the genre of compendious satirical naturalism in which Pound had placed it. At crucial points where Lewis could have taken his critique of the book into areas that might have better illuminated what gives *Ulysses* enduring value, he did not do so. I think we can conclude from this that Lewis was ultimately more interested in a hypothetically successful example of Pound's genre than he was in *Ulysses*. Not surprisingly, after publication of *The Apes of God*, Pound welcomed it and in due course assigned it to a prominent place in the genre in which he placed *Ulysses*.

Lewis had failed to continue the Vorticist movement with any productive conviction after the war and was very conscious that the post-war world was very different from the one he knew before he left to fight on the Western front. By contrast, Joyce seemed to have carried on as if nothing had changed. Lewis's literary ambition was to depict in as compendious a form as possible the condition of the new world and the forces that made it what it was. Just as, on a technical level, *Ulysses* had to be engaged with, so Lewis had to reckon with its reputation as the depiction of the panorama of contemporary history that Eliot had described it as.

For Lewis, the world of *Ulysses* was not the contemporary world at all. It was "consciously the decay of a mournful province, with in addition the label of a twenty-year-old vintage, of a 'lost time,' to recommend it" (*TWM*, 83). Far from presenting the reader with the truth of the modern world, *Ulysses* actually masks the true nature of that world, Lewis contends. By devoting himself to depicting the colorful details of a remote enclave of time, Joyce can be seen as participating in a political process (involuntarily, no doubt) of diverting attention from the truth about the modern world, which is that there is now virtually a world hegemony. Lewis points a parallel with Fascist Italy:

> The adventitious stimulus given to the historic sense, the imposition of this little picturesque flourish or that, a patina like that manufactured for the faking of "antiques" (a good example is the "roman" veneer in fascist Italy), goes hand in hand and side by side with a world-hegemony, externally uniform and producing more every day a common culture. (*TWM*, 82)

The atavism of Joyce's mind led him to think in terms of the typical, yet the "types" in *Ulysses* are well-worn and cannot represent truly life as lived in the post-war world.

In an Appendix to Book I of *Time and Western Man*, Lewis makes it clear, then, why he has been analyzing, not *Ulysses*, but "the mind of James Joyce":

> If we turn to art, we find that experiment in the arts, or *revolutionary* experiment, if that word is desired, has almost ceased since the War. By experiment I mean not only technical exercises and novel combinations, but also the essentially new and particular mind that must underlie, and should even precede, the new and particular form, to make it viable. (*TWM*, 126)

And in the Preface to Book II, it is the negative example of "the mind of James Joyce" against which Lewis defines his notion of the truly revolutionary artist:

> To receive blindly, or at the best confusedly, from regions outside his own, all kinds of notions and formulae, is what the "creative artist" generally does. Without knowing it, he receives into the central tissue of his work political or scientific notions which he proceeds to embody, if he is a novelist, in his characters, if he is a painter, or a poet, in his technique or emotional material, without in the least knowing what he is doing or why he is doing it. But my conception of the rôle of the creative artist is not merely to be a medium for ideas supplied him wholesale from elsewhere, which he incarnates automatically in a technique which (alone) it is his business to perfect. It is equally his business to know enough of the sources of his ideas, and ideology, to take steps to keep these ideas out, except such as he may require for his work. (*TWM*, 140)

Lewis is of course defining the kind of creative artist he himself hoped to be. It was not until he, justifiably, felt he had achieved that ambition, and himself depicted the "immense panorama of futility" that was the modern world, that Lewis could admit, without anxiety, that his old drinking partner was "a great literary artist."

---

1. Wyndham Lewis, *Rude Assignment* (London: Hutchinson, 1950), p. 56.
2. Richard Ellmann, *James Joyce* (London: Oxford Univ. Press, 1966), p. 530.
3. The letter is among Schiff's papers at the British Museum.
4. Wyndham Lewis, *The Art of Being Ruled* (London: Chatto and Windus, 1926), pp. 400-02.
5. Wyndham Lewis, "Editorial Notes," *The Enemy*, No. 2 (1927): xxiii.
6. Ibid., xxvi.
7. Wyndham Lewis, *Time and Western Man* (1927; reprinted Boston: Beacon Press, 1957), pp. 90 and 91. (Hereinafter cited as *TWM*.)
8. James Joyce, *Finnegans Wake* (1939; reprinted New York: The Viking Press, 1966), p. 292. Cf. *transition*, No. 11 (Feb. 1928): 13.
9. Wyndham Lewis, *The Childermass: Section I* (London: Chatto and Windus, 1928), p. 171.
10. *Finnegans Wake*, p. 417.
11. *The Childermass*, p. 173.
12. *Finnegans Wake*, p. 166. For commentary on the controversy see Hugh Kenner, *Dublin's Joyce* (London: Chatto and Windus, 1955), passim; Geoffrey Wagner, *Wyndham Lewis: A Portrait of the Artist as the Enemy* (London: Routledge and Kegan Paul, 1957), pp. 168-88; Adaline Glasheen, "Rough Notes on Joyce and Wyndham Lewis," *A Wake Newslitter*, 8, No. 5 (Oct. 1971): 67-75; William F. Dohmen, " 'Chilly Spaces': Wyndham Lewis as Ondt," *James Joyce Quarterly*, 2, No. 4 (Summer 1974): 368-86. For a fuller bibliography, consult entry F638 in Bradford Morrow and Bernard Lafourcade, *A Bibliography of the Writings of Wyndham Lewis* (Santa Barbara: Black Sparrow Press, 1978).
13. *The Art of Being Ruled*, p. 180.
14. Wyndham Lewis, "Martian Opinions" (letter), *The Listener*, 14, No. 340 (July 17, 1935): 125.
15. *The Childermass*, p. 174.
16. A. Walton Litz, "Pound and Eliot on *Ulysses*: The Critical Tradition," in *Ulysses: Fifty Years*, ed. T. F. Staley, (Bloomington: Indiana Univ. Press, 1974), p. 16.
17. Ezra Pound, "James Joyce et Pécuchet," *Mercure de France*, 156, No. 575 (June 1922), reprinted in *Pound/Joyce: The Letters of Ezra Pound to James Joyce*, ed. Forrest Read, (New York: New Directions, 1970), p. 206.
18. T. S. Eliot, "*Ulysses*, Order and Myth," *The Dial*, 75 (Nov. 1923); reprinted in *James Joyce: The Critical Heritage*, ed. R. H. Deming (London: Routledge and Kegan Paul, 1970), 1: 268.
19. Ibid., p. 270.
20. Ezra Pound, "Le Prix Nobel," *Der Querschnitt* (Berlin) 4, No. 1 (Spring 1924), reprinted in *Pound/Joyce*, p. 220.
21. Ezra Pound, *Guide to Kulchur* (1938; reprinted London: Peter Owen, 1966), p. 96.
22. *Guide to Kulchur*, p. 96.
23. *Pound/Joyce*, p. 25.
24. Ezra Pound, "Paris Letter," *The Dial*, 72, No. 6 (June 1922), reprinted in *Pound/Joyce*, p. 194.
25. Wyndham Lewis, "From *Joint*" (written in mid-1920s), *Agenda* (Wyndham Lewis Special Issue), 7, No. 3–8, No. 1 (Autumn–Winter 1969–70): 201. See James Joyce, *Ulysses* (1922, reprinted New York: Vintage Books, 1966), pp. 162-63. Compare *Ulysses*, pp. 169-73 with Wyndham Lewis, *The Apes of God* (London: The Arthur Press, 1930), pp. 73-78.

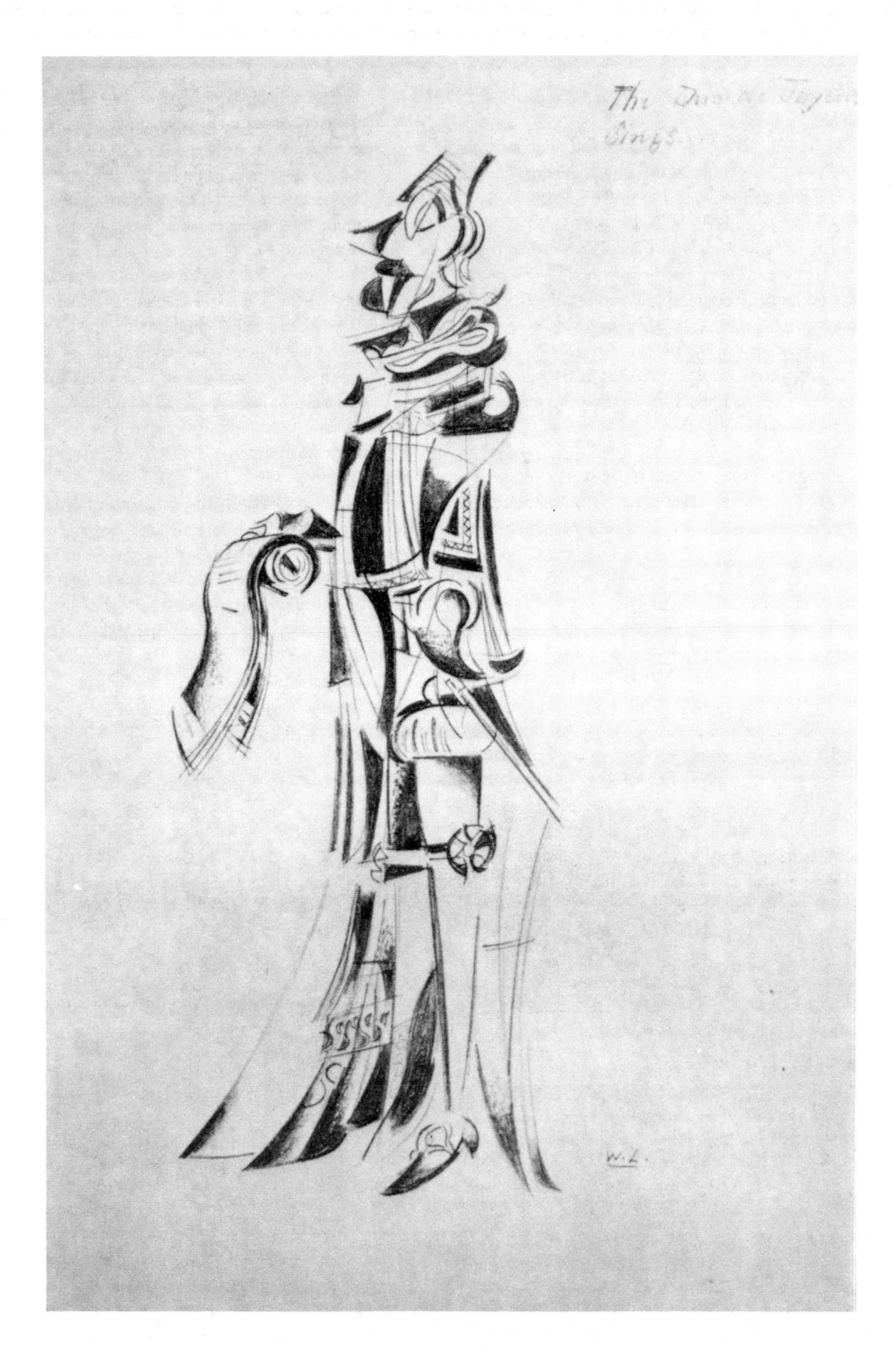

THE DUC DE JOYEUX SINGS, 1920s
WYNDHAM LEWIS
PENCIL 30.5 x 18 cm
FROM THE COLLECTION OF WALTER MICHEL
MICHEL 662

JEAN GUIGUET

JEU DE MIROIRS : JEU DE MASSACRE

VIRGINIA WOOLF ET WYNDHAM LEWIS

Quand, aux dernières pages de *Between the Acts*, ou plus exactement, au dernier acte de la pièce présentée à la kermesse, tous les acteurs réunis agitent des miroirs devant leur public tandis qu'une voix hurle dans un mégaphone sous différentes formes qu'ils ne sont que lambeaux, bribes et fragments,[1] les notables et leurs invités sont décontenancés. Littéralement mitraillés par cette volée d'images éclatées où ils se voient eux-mêmes mis en pièces et dispersés, ils ne savent quel sens donner à cette attaque inattendue. Toutefois, pour le lecteur graduellement préparé tout au long du roman, les intentions de Miss La Trobe, auteur de la pièce—et de Virginia Woolf— sont sans ambiguïté. Les habitants du village, transparents sous leurs costumes, renvoyaient déjà aux spectateurs, réfléchie sur les personnages de la pièce et leurs situations, l'image de leur quotidienne réalité. Et si la vie se joue entre le réel et l'imaginaire— comme la vraie pièce se joue entre les actes—leur lieu de rencontre et d'articulation, le miroir, dans lequel le réel se réfléchit et au travers duquel il est saisi comme image, n'est-il pas la surface magique où s'opèrent fusion et transmutation? Rappelons que les fenêtres de Virginia Woolf n'ont jamais de rideaux, des glaces sans tain pour ainsi dire, et ainsi, tout en accusant la séparation de l'en deçà et de l'au delà, n'assurent-elles pas leur continuité—et, qui sait, leur identité? Indépendamment de ceux du finale de *Between the Acts*, les miroirs sont des accessoires favoris dans la panoplie des instruments dont Virginia Woolf se sert pour capter la réalité qu'elle poursuit.[2] On en pourrait d'emblée déduire un certain narcissisme, mais ce penchant est vraiment trop répandu pour qu'il vaille qu'on s'y arrête. Le jeu du miroir, chez Virginia Woolf est infiniment subtil, et l'essentiel dont il explore les avatars est la présence-absence qu'il permet, la coïncidence du réel et de l'imaginaire, la superposition de l'être et du néant. De cette simultanéité destructrice, tout comme dans la mitraillade de *Between the Acts*, il ressort que le jeu de miroirs peut aussi être un jeu de massacre.

L'artiste n'a qu'une connaissance intérieure de son œuvre, de même nature, toutes choses égales d'ailleurs, que la connaissance qu'il a de lui-même: grevée d'intimité, d'adhérence, elle est plus sensation que pensée et n'accède jamais à la clarté intellectuelle qui pourrait déboucher sur une analyse impartiale. Le critique, la critique, est le miroir qui offre à l'artiste une image de son œuvre, lui révèle son apparence alors qu'il n'en connaît que l'existence. Mais du même coup, cette extériorité le choque, et il est prêt à récuser le critique en tant qu'étranger, comme la femme récuse son miroir au bénéfice de sa passion qui lui garde sa jeunesse et sa beauté. Isa, dans *Between the Acts*, scrute son miroir pour s'y chercher, mais aussi pour s'y fuir; il lui décoche les traits du temps: telle année a laissé cette marque, tel événement cette atteinte; mais cette vérité est mensonge puisqu'il suffit de détourner la tête pour l'effacer. Ces rapports de fascination et de crainte qui lient l'artiste et le critique peuvent être suivis avec assez de précision dans le cas des réactions de Virginia Woolf à Wyndham Lewis, telles que nous les restituent les lettres et le journal.

Il n'est pas indifférent de rappeler les circonstances qui amenèrent les deux artistes à être tangentiels au même cercle ayant pour centre, dans les années 1910–13, Roger Fry en tant qu'organisateur des expositions Post-Impressionnistes de 1910 et 1913 à la Grafton Gallery et des Omega Workshops. Wyndham Lewis a deux toiles acceptées pour la première exposition: il fait donc partie de ceux qui, dépassant l'ère victorienne et surtout son héritière immédiate, la période édouardienne, estiment, comme l'écrira Virginia Woolf un peu plus d'une décennie plus tard (précisément dans cet essai[3] dont Wyndham Lewis fera le centre de sa critique), que la nature humaine a changé vers 1910, et qu'en conséquence pour l'exprimer adéquatement les artistes doivent inventer des moyens différents de ceux auxquels avaient recours leurs prédécesseurs. Mais, en art comme en politique, les révolutionnaires, unis à l'origine d'un grand bouleversement, ne tardent pas à se séparer tant sur des questions de personnes que sur des points d'idéologie, les unes et les autres, comme les prétextes et les raisons fondamentales, se trouvant inextricablement mêlées. À la suggestion de Leonard Woolf, Roger Fry, pour faire face aux frais de l'exposition ayant demandé aux exposants une commission sur les ventes plus élevée que celle originellement prévue, Wyndham Lewis protesta; Roger Fry fit la sourde oreille. Par suite de l'érosion du temps et du télescopage des événements, Leonard Woolf écrivant ses mémoires dans les années soixante rapporte l'affaire en ces termes:

> Wyndham Lewis, at best of times a bilious and cantankerous man, protested violently. Roger was adamant in ignoring him and his demands. Lewis never forgave Roger, and as I was a kind of buffer between them he also never forgave me.[4]

En fait, les lettres échangées entre Wyndham Lewis et Roger Fry en 1912 et 1913 à propos de la formation du Grafton Group pour préparer la deuxième exposition et touchant à la collaboration de Lewis aux Omega Workshops, montrent bien, qu'en surface au moins, les deux hommes avaient décidé d'oublier leur brouille. Toutefois pas pour longtemps. Une autre affaire de pourcentage, encore une fois au détriment de Lewis, entraîna la rupture et des jugements dans diverses lettres de Roger Fry qui, d'octobre à décembre 1913 deviennent de plus en plus sévères:

> I have tried to treat Lewis with every consideration, but I fear nothing I can do comes up to his ideal of what is due to him.[5]

> I suspect that Lewis has never been in the Omega except for what he could get out of it. (*LRF*, 373)

> A quite absurd misunderstanding produced by Lewis's predisposition to believe himself the object of subtle antagonistic plots. (*LRF*, 374)

Et finalement:

> I think Lewis's vanity touches on insanity. (*LRF*, 375)

Si Leonard Woolf s'était trouvé impliqué dans la première querelle, Vanessa Bell et Duncan Grant furent aussi parties dans la seconde; on ne s'étonnera pas alors que Virginia Woolf ait quelque prévention envers Lewis. Cependant, elles ne sont pas uniquement affectives. En effet, à propos de T. S. Eliot que les Woolf commencent à voir davantage et à mieux connaître en septembre 1920, elle écrit dans son journal: «Unfortunately the living writers he admires are Wyndham Lewis & Pound.—Joyce too, but there's more to be said on this head.»[6] L'association des trois noms, assortie d'une réserve favorable pour Joyce, est significative. C'est l'avant-garde qui mène le même combat qu'elle, mais avec des tempéraments différents, des méthodes qu'elle n'approuve pas et peut-être des objectifs qu'elle récuse. Toujours au sujet de Wyndham Lewis, Roger Fry, dans une lettre à Duncan Grant, avait évoqué «the vindictive jealousy among artists» (*LRF*, 379). Virginia Woolf ne niera pas être accessible à ce sentiment, même vis-à-vis de ses amis, Lytton Strachey, E. M. Forster, T. S. Eliot ou Katherine Mansfield. «But jealousy is not a very bad fault is it? I am often jealous of other people's gifts» écrira-t'elle un jour à Ethel Smyth.[7] Du tour de certaines phrases du journal ou des lettres on peut sans crainte d'erreur déduire qu'elle en éprouve à l'égard d'un artiste qui non seulement n'appartient pas au clan, à Bloomsbury, mais se targue d'en être «l'Ennemi.»

Ce sentiment, surtout quand il reste inavoué, écarté du regard et de la conscience auxquels il ne pourrait paraître qu'absurde, impossible, simplement parce qu'il impliquerait une comparaison entre le jaloux et le jalousé, brouille d'une façon plus ou moins profonde l'image que Virginia Woolf découvre d'elle dans le portrait qu'a tracé son antagoniste. Toutefois, la nature et l'étendue de cette distorsion présente peu d'intérêt dans le cas de Wyndham Lewis, les deux écrivains travaillant sur des registres trop éloignés l'un de l'autre—l'analyse serait en revanche très rentable dans le cas de E. M. Forster et surtout de Katherine Mansfield. Mon analyse portera uniquement sur la tentative de redressement de l'image esquissée par Wyndham Lewis—ou du moins telle que la voit Virginia Woolf. Il s'agit de la satire de Bloomsbury autour de la figure de Lytton Strachey dans *Apes of God*, le roman de 1930 qui avait proliféré à partir de l'extrait du même titre publié en 1924.

Dans une lettre à Quentin Bell du 28 octobre 1930, reprenant les termes d'une lettre à Vanessa de la veille, Virginia Woolf écrit:

> Now if Wyndham Lewis instead of writing a Bloomsbury Black Book in which every sinner of either school [«every sod and every saph» dans la lettre à Vanessa] is to be pilloried were to write what is the truth—that we are merely *wild, odd, innocent, artless, eccentric* and *industrious* beyond words, there would be some sting to it. But to represent us as he does [as] one seething mass of correlated villainy is so beside the point... that it glances from the back. (*LVW*, IV, 238)

Chacun des six adjectifs (que j'ai soulignés) fait pendant aux traits que met en évidence la satire de Lewis; cette contre-évocation est caricaturale, c'est à dire conforme au genre, et en tant que telle empreinte d'exagération et de fantaisie telles que Virginia Woolf à cette époque a su les manifester avec brio dans *Orlando*. En ce qui concerne les rapports du critique et de sa victime, ce passage met en évidence le déclenchement du processus autocritique qui fonctionne comme un réflexe de défense. Mais encore faut-il pour qu'il fonctionne efficacement que l'accusé se reconnaisse, au moins partiellement, dans le réquisitoire. C'est seulement alors qu'il se sent piqué au vif et réagit positivement. Que l'accusation manque de crédibilité au point de devenir inacceptable, elle ne suscite qu'une réaction de rejet, instantanée et superficielle: les miroirs mal orientés ne renvoient qu'images incongrues et le tireur n'a descendu qu'une poupée de son.

Tout autre est la réaction à *Men Without Art*. On en trouve un examen minutieux dans une entrée du *Journal* en date du 11 octobre 1934. Que Virginia Woolf pressente l'hostilité de Wyndham Lewis avant d'avoir lu autre chose que l'annonce du livre dans le *Times Literary Supplement* n'a rien d'étonnant; mais il est intéressant de constater qu'elle distingue deux courants dans son intuition: «Now I know by reason and instinct that this is an attack»; je crois précisément que cette dualité explique la complexité de l'attitude de Virginia Woolf qui, clarifiée à propos de ce cas particulier, peut, sans grand risque d'erreur, être généralisée et considérée comme typique des rapports de l'artiste et de la critique. Instinctivement, du simple fait que c'est «l'Ennemi» qui écrit, sans même le lire, elle sent l'effet de l'attaque: elle voit son image détruite dans le public en général, et plus particulièrement dans les milieux universitaires d'Oxford et de Cambridge et là où les jeunes lisent Wyndham Lewis. L'Université: la tradition; la jeunesse: l'avenir; on retrouve ici toute l'ambiguïté de l'orientation de Virginia Woolf qui a suscité tant de jugements contradictoires, tant sur Bloomsbury dans son ensemble que sur elle-même d'ailleurs. Et pour résister à cet éreintement: «My instinct is not to read it.» C'est le retrait de la sensitive qu'elle tente d'expliquer un peu plus loin: «Why am I sensitive? I think vanity: I dislike the thought of being laughed at: of the glow of satisfaction that A., B. and C. will get from hearing V. W. demolished...» (11 Oct. 1934).[8] Le terme «ridicule» revient souvent quand elle parle de critique; comme si elle acceptait à cent pour cent l'opinion populaire sur la puissance destructrice du ridicule. La légende veut qu'elle suscitât l'hilarité des passants par ses vêtements, sa démarche, son regard. Leonard Woolf dans son autobiographie confirme le fait sans pouvoir l'expliquer avec certitude. Ce qui peut chez les proches ou les amis engendrer un amusement bienveillant où domine la sympathie, chez des étrangers indifférents ou hostiles suscite un réaction extérieurement analogue, mais dont la signification est totalement différente; elle exprime précisément l'indifférence et l'hostilité, rejette de la communauté des rieurs, isole et enferme la victime dans sa singularité qui du coup est prononcée—et ressentie—coupable. Enracinement d'un complexe d'infériorité dira-t-on dans un langage déjà démodé—avec pour seule défense possible le développement d'un complexe de supériorité. La conjugaison de la timidité et de l'orgueil, de la peur et du courage est aussi généralement acceptée que celle de la haine et de l'amour. Ces dualités contradictoires habitent Virginia Woolf.

Mais revenons à la dualité instinct-raison dont j'ai développé le premier terme; elle se confond d'ailleurs avec les autres couples auxquels j'ai abouti. En effet la fuite instinctive devant l'attaque qui témoigne d'une certaine lâcheté à l'affronter est compensée et même annulée par une démarche rationnelle où dominent l'orgueil et l'assurance. En faisant siennes, par une décision volontaire et réfléchie les raisons que Keats a de mépriser les critiques, Virginia Woolf se hausse au rang du poète et écrase son détracteur. Bien qu'alors au sommet et presque au terme de sa carrière, dans son identification avec Keats, elle rature ce qui touche à la prétention à la postérité: «Well: do I think I shall be among the English novelists after my death? I hardly ever think about it.» Tout l'accent est mis sur la conscience douloureuse et sans cesse à reconquérir que le véritable artiste a de sa valeur.

> Praise or blame has but a momentary effect on the man whose love of beauty in the abstract

makes him a severe critic on his own works. My own domestic criticism has given me pain beyond what Blackwood or Quarterly could possibly inflict.

de Keats, tel que le cite Virginia Woolf devient, en ce qui la concerne:

> perhaps I feel uncertain of my own gifts: but then, I know more about them than W.L.: and anyhow I intend to go on writing. . . . Already I am feeling the calm that always comes to me with abuse: my back is against the wall: I am writing for the sake of writing, etc. (*WD*, 11 Oct. 1934)

À l'image proposée par Wyndham Lewis et qu'elle projette directement et uniquement à partir de l'idée qu'elle se fait du critique puisqu'elle n'a pas encore lu le livre, elle substitue l'image de l'Artiste que rien ne peut atteindre. Les deux images—on s'en doute—sont aussi irréelles l'une que l'autre. Ce sont des simplifications pour ainsi dire archétypales nées de la crainte comme du désir. Quittant la scène épique, où l'Artiste et L'Ennemi s'affrontent, pour considérer le quotidien de l'écriture, non plus des images d'Epinal, mais l'entreprise terre à terre que constitue la patiente création d'une oeuvre, Virginia Woolf nous révèle une stratégie qu'à ma connaissance elle n'a discutée nulle part ailleurs, et qui témoigne d'une sagesse, d'une intelligence, d'un sang froid et d'une lucidité que d'autres traits de son caractère tendent à effacer des portraits que nous avons d'elle. «What I shall do is craftly to gather the nature of the indictment from talk and reviews; and, in a year perhaps, when my book is out, I shall read it.» En fait, trois jours après, le 14 octobre, livrée à elle-même par une de ces défaillance de l'inspiration qui interrompt périodiquement tous les artistes, elle lit le chapitre redouté: «This morning I've taken the arrow of W.L. to my heart: he makes tremendous and delightful fun of B. and B. ["Mr. Bennett and Mrs. Brown"]: calls me a peeper, not a looker; a fundamental prude but one of the four or five living (so it seems) who is an artist.» Ce dernier compliment suffit-il à anesthésier les blessures portées par les autres traits du critique? Est-il à l'origine de la générosité qui dicte l'épithète «delightful», ou celui-ci est-il une sincère et impartiale appréciation de la fantaisie de Wyndham Lewis? Il est difficile de le dire. En tout cas, la colère reprend vite le dessus: «Well: this gnat has settled and stung: and I think (12.30) the pain is over.» Lucidité, humour que cette mention de l'heure. Virginia Woolf sait bien que dans une heure, un jour, un mois . . . la douleur peut revenir aussi cuisante. Toutefois, plus intéressante que les réaction affectives est l'analyse de la position de l'écrivain et l'affirmation de son indépendance et de son intégrité:

> The danger of being attacked is that it makes one answer back—a perfectly fatal thing to do. I mean fatal to arrange *The P.s* so as to meet his criticisms. And I think my revelation two years ago stands me in sublime stead: to adventure and discover and allow no rigid poses: to be supple and naked to the truth. If there is truth in W.L., well, face it: I've no doubt I'm prudish and peeping. Well then live more boldly, but for God's sake don't try to bend my writing one way or the other. Not that one can. (*WD*, 11 Oct. 1934)

On saisit dans ce passage, trait après trait, nuance après nuance, comment la caricature critique de Wyndham Lewis a suscité la prise de conscience de Virginia Woolf et l'a amenée en quelque sorte à remplacer dans le miroir que lui tendait perfidement l'auteur de *Men Without Art* l'image qu'elle a trouvée d'elle par une autre dans laquelle l'accent, les rapports sont différents. Tout en reconnaissant la réticence prude et le voyeurisme de sa nature profonde dont Wyndham Lewis fait la source de toutes ses faiblesses d'écrivain et en se proposant même de vivre plus ouvertement, plus dangereusement, elle refuse catégoriquement d'infléchir son style—et il faut donner à ce mot (elle emploie, «writing») sa pleine valeur woolfienne qui est à la fois mode d'être, d'agir et de s'exprimer, car pour elle tout cela passe dans l'écriture. Et elle sait bien que tout cela qui est nous-mêmes est au delà de toute atteinte—et précisément, en discuter par rapport à une grille du bien et du mal ou du bon et du mauvais, n'a guère de sens.

Cette détermination inébranlable à persévérer dans l'être est en fin de compte le résultat final de toute critique, même lorsqu'elle s'attaque à des natures en apparence aussi vulnérables que Virginia Woolf—ou Keats. Là encore la romancière avec sa lucidité coutumière énumère quelques composantes de cette révélation de soi qui devient affirmation de soi. Elle parle du «queer» (ailleurs, elle écrit «odd») «disreputable pleasure in being abused, in being a figure, in being a martyr, and so on» (*WD*, 11 Oct. 1934). Deux jours plus tard, elle ajoutera: «and the feeling of being dismissed into obscurity is also pleasant and salutary» (*WD*, 14 Oct. 1934). Ces remarques aux harmoniques thérapeutiques font écho à des déclarations antérieures d'une douzaine d'années, quand Desmond MacCarthy fit un compte rendu élogieux de *Monday or Tuesday* in *The New Statesman* «which at any rate made me feel important (and it is that that one wants)» (*WD*, 9 Apr. 1921). Et quand Lytton Strachey se répandit en louanges hyperboliques sur *Jacob's Room*, elle note: «I want to be through the splash and swimming in calm water again. I want to be writing unobserved» (*WD*, 14 Oct. 1922). Cette complexité des réactions, ces contradictions qu'elles accueillent, ces fluctuations qui les portent de la vague déferlante à l'eau morte, témoignent des rapports infrangibles et profonds qui lient la critique à la personnalité tout entière bien plus qu'à l'écrit. Symptomatique à cet égard, et corroborant mon exploration, est l'analyse de Virginia Woolf lorsqu'elle lit la réponse de Wyndham Lewis à la critique de *Men Without Art* que Stephen Spender avait publiée dans le *Spectator* du 19 october 1934 et dans laquelle il avait pris la défense de ses amis de Bloomsbury. Cette page du journal, en date du 2 novembre 1934, fait le point avec un détachement, une telle sobriété, et en même temps une prise en compte de tous les éléments du problème, qu'elle pourrait me servir de conclusion.

Malgré tous les appels—intérieurs ou extérieurs—à l'indifférence, l'arme suprême, l'artiste ne peut être insensible à la critique. C'est comme une maladie plus ou moins longue selon les cas; et même si on sait qu'on va guérir, c'est assommant. La parade? Les deux tranchants de la même lame: le réalisme et la lucidité. «At the worst, should I be a quite negligible writer, I enjoy writing: I think I am an honest observer. Therefore the world will go on providing me with excitement whether I can use it or not». C'est à nouveau la fusion inconditionnelle de l'être et de la création artistique, indépendamment de la valeur de cette création. Mais comme le point de départ de ces réflexions reste la mise en cause de la valeur de l'oeuvre par le critique, c'est à ce jugement que revient Virginia Woolf pour en évaluer la validité et éventuellement le récuser. «Also, how am I to balance W.L.'s criticism with Yeats—let alone Goldie [G. Lowes Dickinson] and Morgan [E. M. Forster]? Would they have felt anything if I had been negligible?» La réponse vient comme une révélation indiscutable en pleine nuit: «And about two in the morning I am possessed of a remarkable sense of driving eyeless strength... And... if only for a time I could completely forget myself, my reviews, my fame, my sink in the scale—which is bound to come now and to last about 8 or 9 years—then I should be what I mostly am: very rapid, excited, amused, intense» (*WD*, 2 Nov. 1934). On aboutit une fois de plus à l'autoportrait qui dans le miroir efface le portrait présenté par le critique; mais cette fois, après deux semaines de maturation, à la première épreuve dans laquelle Virginia Woolf avait accepté de faire figurer quelques traits de la caricature de Wyndham Lewis, elle substitue un visage tout différent, l'opposé même de celui qu'avait dessiné Lewis.

Elle peut conclure: «Let all praise and blame sink to the bottom or float to the top and let me go my ways indifferent. And care for people. And let fly, in life, on all sides.» Cette résurrection, ce départ triomphant, n'est que l'ultime moment d'une épreuve qui passe par la souffrance, l'humiliation, la mutilation. En 1919, après *Night and Day*, ayant à peine achevé ses années d'apprentissage, Virginia Woolf ne semblait encore connaître que la phase négative de cette épreuve: la distorsion du miroir, l'impact des coups portés: "So all critics split off, and the wretched author who tries to keep control of them is torn asunder» (*WD*, 6 Nov. 1919). Au sommet de sa carrière et de sa maîtrise, sans être immunisée au malaise des images déformées ni au venin des intentions malignes, Virginia Woolf émerge du fantôme auquel on tentait de la réduire, plus clairement et plus volontairement elle-même qu'elle n'était auparavant—avant cette traversée des apparences: par le jeu des miroirs elle échappe au jeu de massacre.

---

1. *Between the Acts*, Uniform Edition (London: The Hogarth Press, 1941, réimprimé 1953), pp. 219, 220, 221, 225.
2. Vide particulièrement «The Lady in the Looking Glass», dans *A Haunted House and Other Stories* (London: The Hogarth Press, 1944), pp. 76-88. Assez curieusement, c'est une autre Isabelle qui, dans cette esquisse de 1929 s'insère entre sa réalité tangible et son image réfléchie dans son miroir.
3. «Mr. Bennett and Mrs. Brown», d'abord publié dans *The Criterion* en juillet 1924 sous le titre «Character in Fiction», puis dans la Hogarth Essay Series la même année. Repris dans *The*

Captain's Death Bed (London: The Hogarth Press, 1950).
4. Leonard Woolf, *Beginning Again* (London: The Hogarth Press, 1964), pp. 95-96.
5. *Letters of Roger Fry* (London: Chatto & Windus, 1972), p. 372. *LRF* dans les notes qui suivent.
6. Virginia Woolf, *The Diary of Virginia Woolf* (London: The Hogarth Press), Vol. II, p. 67. Il est assez curieux de constater qu'une lettre à Roger Fry du 18 nov. 1918 (pp. 295-96) parlant du premier dîner auquel T. S. E. fut invité par les Woolf évoque la même discussion et des opinions identiques.
7. *The Letters of Virginia Woolf* (London: The Hogarth Press), Vol. IV, 1978, p. 199 (15. Aug. 1930). *LVW* dans les notes qui suivent.
8. Virginia Woolf, *A Writer's Diary* (London: The Hogarth Press, 1953), pp. 227-28. *WD*, avec mention de la date, dans les notes qui suivent.

▼ ▼ ▼

JEAN-JACQUES MAYOUX

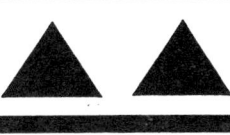

L'AMOUR PUNI

Wyndham Lewis fut en son temps un polémiste considérable. De l'aspect politique de cette activité, de l'attrait qu'eurent pour lui le fascisme et le nazisme, nous ne parlerons pas, si ce n'était une sorte de préalable à *The Revenge for Love*, comme à *Self Condemned*. Le fascisme à ses yeux joue le rôle de l'Ennemi qu'il se proclame lui-même. Il vous balaie mainte imposture. Wyndham Lewis est capable de trouver drôles les purges à l'huile de ricin. Il ne sent guère le besoin de postuler pour ces idéologies une vertu: il suffit que les autres fassent les vertueux. Les hommes sous leurs professions et leurs attitudes sont d'assez misérables animaux: il faut les dresser. On a pu dire que l'optimisme était de gauche et le pessimisme de droite: ce serait assez vrai de notre homme. En fait le pro-fascisme de Wyndham Lewis est tout de même important, parce qu'il est important pour un créateur littéraire—et sans doute même plastique—qu'il éprouve et qu'il manifeste du mépris pour l'homme, un double mépris pour la femme. «Mon éducation artistocratique», dit-il dans *Blasting and Bombardiering*, où il parle de ce père martial qui fit qu'il n'a point d'aversion pour les militaires.

Ses écrits politiques sont allés rejoindre ceux de Céline. Ils ne comptent plus. Mais ils comptaient pour lui quand il écrivait ses romans. On ne voit pas dans sa geôle espagnole de *politicos* qui soient des politiques: c'est «une bande cordiale d'idéalistes experts en hold-up.»

Par contre *Time and Western Man* fut sans doute l'événement, dans le domaine de la contestation politico-philosophico-littéraire, de l'année 1927. Sur un plan large, il s'agissait de mettre au point une critique de l'apocalyptisme de Spengler (*Déclin de l'Occident*); sur un plan plus resserré, de s'en prendre à ce qu'il tenait pour une mode—à l'inflation du sens du temps, de la temporalité, de la durée, dans les lettres contemporaines. Toute polémique littéraire est salutaire, en tant qu'elle dérange le confort des modes; toute polémique littéraire est néfaste en ce qu'à une éventuelle (mais possible) spontanéité créatrice elle substitue une conscience troublée.

Pope voulait définir tout être humain par sa passion dominante ("ruling passion"). Sans doute peut-on dire que la passion dominante de tout artiste est la création. Mais l'autre? comme dirait Harpagon. Et pour cet artiste-là? Même dans l'œuvre, c'est l'affirmation de soi, *contre*. L'agressivité est patente: asting». C'est sa mission, sa fonction, comme il les voit. Il est l'Ennemi. C'est un programme. Il s'y est tenu fidèlement, depuis ses débuts avant 1910 pendant près de vingt-cinq ans. Il y faut sans doute une sève de jeunesse: ne pressent-on pas que vers 1937 et le temps de *The Revenge for Love* la sève commence à circuler moins vivement, moins violemment?

Le théoricien est, je crois bien, moins original que l'artiste—plastique ou littéraire. Il a sans doute trop conscience de sa filiation futuriste—il a été l'un de ceux qui ont accueilli Marinetti à Londres en 1913— pour ne pas vouloir s'en dégager, maladroitement quand il déclare qu'il est contre leur culte des machines, alors que par ailleurs il déclare qu'en peinture le vorticisme (ainsi baptisé par Ezra Pound) se propose de construire un langage visuel aussi abstrait que la musique en s'appuyant sur «le monde des machines». La vue d'un pamphlet ou «manifeste» lewisien avec ses modulations menaçantes de capitales rappelle à s'y méprendre Marinetti:

> Bang! Bang!
> Ultimatum to you!
> Ultimatum to you!
> ULTIMATUM TO YOU!

Mais je ne vois rien dans le futurisme, ni par la suite dans le bien plus complexe Dada qui corresponde à la sévérité de langage, aussi bien plastique que littéraire, de la création lewisienne. Les théories, elles, ne nous concernent que dans la mesure où elles deviennent obsédantes et informent sa conception, donc sa création, du monde. Elles construisent, par exemple, un univers mâle, caractérisé par une prédominance de l'intellect, d'une activité mentale déployée dans l'espace qu'elle se donne, et opposé à un univers féminin, émotif et sensuel, fluide et obscur, flottant dans des brumes de mémoire, c'est à dire de temps. Ces données s'appliquent au créateur et à ce qu'il estime devoir à sa création—au créé—c'est à dire qu'elles devront se retrouver projetées dans les personnages et leurs rapports. Comme Hogarth, Wyndham Lewis a ses bêtes noires; comme Fielding et dans la bonne vieille tradition anglaise il pourfend l'affectation et l'hypocrisie soit dans les milieux littéraires et artistiques, qui le touchent de près, et dans leurs productions, soit parmi les politiques où il les tient pour particulièrement néfastes.

Entre théories et polémiques il est, pour un romancier, très contraint dans sa liberté créatrice. La satire peut être une bonne servante et une mauvaise maîtresse. *The Apes of God*, porté aux nues par ses amis, me paraît un échec aussi bien qu'un réservoir de bonnes pages, de trop bonnes pages: une sorte d'exercice de style satirique très aristophanesque, prenant dans la réalité des modèles aisément reconnus, les Sitwell, ou ce Sidney Schiff qui se prenait pour Marcel Proust. Les portraits ambulants qui peuplent le livre ont une force de présence extraordinaire. Mais ils ne vont nulle part. Marcel Schwob leur aurait reconnu ce génie anglo-saxon pour le réalisme fantastique qu'il trouvait à Stevenson décrivant «un visage comme un jambon». Les bajoues de Fredigonde «comme deux aigres œillères qui auraient glissé» battaient au fil de son discours. Hogarth n'aurait vu ni fait mieux.

Stendhal dans un climat froid: je suis à l'occasion tenté de qualifier ainsi Wyndham Lewis, mais on ne pourrait l'entendre que dans un sens partiel et restreint. Ce sont sans doute les deux égotistes les plus décidés, les plus articulés, de l'histoire des lettres. Stendhal farouchement tendu vers la réalisation artistique de lui-même, méditant les disciplines psychologiques enseignées par les idéologues, observe en lui-même avec sévérité les mouvements qu'il lui importe de contrôler, de maîtriser, d'utiliser, fût-ce l'amour. Wyndham Lewis ne dit-il pas que la nature d'un artiste, tel que Tarr, est de se construire, et non de se dépenser pour construire une idole féminine. La condition d'une jouissance durable, c'est de ne pas se laisser absorber en elle: «un homme est le contraire de son appétit.» La misogynie, le mépris de la sexualité, nous mettent rapidement bien loin de Stendhal. Il y aurait aussi pourtant la volonté de réaliser dans et par l'écriture une lucidité sans ornements ni fards. Mais à d'autres égards on serait proche au moins en théorie du nouveau roman par l'attention prêtée à l'installation des structures et par un refus radical des voies traditionnelles: «l'art valable ne doit pas avoir d'intériorité» ("good art must have no inside"). «Les gens», écrit-il dans *Blasting and Bombardiering*, «sont des propositions ambulantes» ("walking notions"). «J'aime la surface de la vie.»

«Le Temps est plus abstrait que l'Espace», remarquait-il dans *Time and Western Man*. Un artiste en quête des valeurs solides de la plastique, s'il écrit, aura la charge et le souci de les faire passer dans son écriture. Spatialiser le plus possible cet art dont on avait toujours convenu que c'est par essence et nature un art du temps, tel est le propos, tel est le défi de Wyndham Lewis. Il voit à ses contemporains l'obsession du cinéma, et d'abord de la séquence. Eh bien il prendra ses ciseaux, séparera chaque image, et à chaque pause d'immobilité il fera un sort. On a souligné l'emploi, dans la première version de *Tarr*, d'un signe affecté à une fonction particulière, dans la ponctuation, de point ou plutôt de surpoint: =. En vérité le signe qu'il lui fallait aurait dû être vertical: ||, une double paroi, et isolante.

En somme il lui appartient, il lui incombe de montrer la puissance du sensible, qui sera le visible avant tout autre: il doit disposer et construire de telle sorte son système du visible que, comme il n'arrive pas dans la vie, nous sachions le lire et y trouver une formule satisfaisante, une traduction du «réel.»

Cette vue des surfaces sera-t-elle pour autant impersonnelle? Pas le moins du monde; la description des apparences sera méchamment caricaturale, férocement satirique. On n'y portera pas la bonhomie de Shakespeare mais le venin de Pope. «La satire pour être valable doit être injuste et sans nuances.»

La satire refusera donc, entre autres gentillesses, tout effort de compréhension, toute ouverture d'imagination; elle s'emparera de ces «propositions ambulantes» et vous les fera ambuler de belle manière. Elles nous seront comiques parce que nous avons sur elles l'avantage d'exister, de n'être pas des pantins, des automates. Mais après tout si nous avions très bonne mémoire, nous nous rappellerions avoir entendu au Collège de France Henri Bergson, en même temps qu'il lançait dans le monde, pour une déplorable carrière, le temps et la durée, formuler une telle théorie du comique.

«La racine du comique», écrit en effet Wyndham

Lewis, «est à chercher dans les sensations qui résultent de l'observation d'une chose se conduisant comme une personne.» Mais de ce point de vue tous les hommes sont nécessairement comiques, car ils sont tous des choses ou corps physiques se conduisant comme des personnes.

Ce serait après tout assez simple: si nous avions le courage de ce que nous éprouvons, chacun de nous trouverait tous les autres, les ayant perçus comme réifiés absolument, comiques. Mais, dans une position beaucoup moins forte que ne lui donnait cette saine philosophie de l'universel dérisoire, ne se range-t-il pas, dans *The Writer and the Absolute*, derrière Goethe qui distingue parmi les *autres* hommes deux catégories, les *pantins* et les *natures*: n'est-il pas amené à oublier que chacun est pour les autres un pantin et pour lui-même une nature? Bref à un comique démocratique ne substitue-t-il pas un comique aristocratique? Le relativisme modeste du comique devient dès lors l'outrance absolue et, oui, l'injustice méprisante du satiriste. Au fond, entre l'idée d'être un oeil observant la surface des choses et construisant un simulacre efficient d'humanité sur un système de gestes et d'attitudes, et l'idée de ressusciter un grand art satirique, n'y a-t-il pas une contradiction qui finira par éclater? L'art de Swift est-il un art du monde extérieur?

Parlant de ses premières créations littéraires, les Bestre ou les Brotcotnaz, Wyndham Lewis leur confirme le titre de Wild Bodies, «corps sauvages», primitifs subsistant à même la vie sans émerger à l'existence. Que restera-t-il de ces natures obscures, en quelle mesure iront-elles vitaliser certains pantins par la suite?—Victor Stamp n'est-il pas corps sauvage et pantin?—que reste-t-il de «nature» une fois que Tarr ou le Pierpoint de *The Apes of God* sont sortis du roman? à ceci je pense qu'on peut répondre, la nature concentrée chez le romancier lui-même se fait à distance satirique des pantins.

Si on laisse de côté, faute de pouvoir honnêtement prendre la mesure de cet étrange monument, les gros volumes de *The Human Age*, l'œuvre romanesque de Wyndham Lewis comporterait, après les superbes esquisses du début, *Tarr, The Apes of God* et les deux romans de la maturité, *The Revenge for Love* et *Self Condemned*. Tarr est l'artiste réglant ses rapports avec le monde. Il doit se préserver pour se construire. Il doit sans cesse se poser des problèmes et toujours rester imperturbé, observant toujours froidement le jeu des chaînes causales: comme Joyce il pourrait dire que ses erreurs sont «volitionnelles»; plus arrogant que Joyce même il dirait plutôt qu'un artiste comme lui ne fait pas d'erreurs. Kreisler est l'anti-Tarr: il est voué à se détruire, bruyamment. Son diabolisme naît de son absence au monde: il est ressentiment total à l'égard d'une réalité qui l'ignore. Or justement on n'est réel que si on est dans le réel, à moins que plutôt, comme Tarr, triomphe du micro-contre le macrocosme, on ait tout son réel, tout le réel, en soi. Kreisler est en fait un moyen, cruel, pour Tarr de poursuivre *a contrario* la conscience de soi. Les gesticulations de Kreisler deviennent, à mesure que ce pantin se désarticule, de plus en plus amusantes pour Tarr, qui tire dédaigneusement quelques ficelles par manière de jeu.

Tournons-nous vers *The Revenge for Love*. Théoricien agressif, Wyndham Lewis a commencé son roman comme une démonstration: on ne le saurait pas qu'on serait frappé de l'aspect immédiat de l'œuvre: ce n'est pas un corps organique, c'est une armure tout en acier riveté, étincelant et dur. Cela dure cinquante pages et puis soit on s'habitue soit le romancier se détend; mais de toute façon l'effet est produit.

Si l'art doit éviter l'intériorité, il s'agira donc de construire froidement à partir de données sensibles, visuelles ou auditives, un système de signifiants qui se suffise. La scène d'ouverture dans la prison espagnole est peut-être à cet égard le triomphe du livre. Don Alvaro est ce qu'il fallait à Wyndham Lewis, un corps expressif, tout en mouvements et en langage gestuel, chaque mouvement épié et noté avec une précision moins gratuite que physionomique par l'observateur: «Don Alvaro, son corps basculant sur les hanches, cracha dans le caniveau disloqué.» Don Alvaro, assis sur une table, examine le panier qu'apporte à Percy une visiteuse, puis se relève en décomposant le mouvement, comme aurait fait Sterne par jeu et précisément pour séparer et isoler le monde extérieur: «il commença par déplier ses jambes avec une lenteur langoureuse qui suspendit la jambe transférée pour une appréciable succession de secondes...»— les mouvements et les gestes sont présentés sous un aspect mécanique, déshumanisé, réifié; et d'autant plus absurdes lorsque la mécanique individuelle est prescrite par le social: un code implicite prescrit à un homme dans la situation d'Alvaro l'attitude dans laquelle il doit attendre une femme comme la visiteuse, «le pied droit en avant, l'angle du coup de pied à 90°», etc.

La réification pure et simple, cependant, ne serait possible qu'avec l'emploi de mots *neutres*. Ceux de Wyndham Lewis sont loin de l'être. Ils sont aussi marqués que les lignes caricaturales de Hogarth: le gardien se racle la gorge «to the remotest mucinous crypt»: l'alliance ironique de la crypte et du mucus prépare le jaillissement exceptionnel du crachat violent qui va frapper le sol comme une balle. . . . La réification va avec le morcellement de ce qui aurait pu être une personnalité, dont émergent alors des fragments disjoints et privés de sens: le col de chemise d'un prisonnier est ouvert comme pour permettre à la pomme d'Adam de monter et descendre à volonté «comme si elle eût été quelque parasite familier domicilié dans son gosier.» Ici et ailleurs la métaphore caricaturale aboutit à une réduction, de l'homme à l'animal: «il cligna de l'oeil comme une chouette offensée». On voit à Alvaro «un mouvement de chat efflanqué», une moustache recourbée en dedans «comme des arêtes noires». «Entendant cette toux, il se rendit compte que c'était un bouc qui avait toussé.»

Une telle conscience du corps, du mouvement physique, de l'acte réflexe fait de la présence du personnage un jeu de l'auteur: comme ceux de Hogarth, ce personnage est un acteur tenu à jouer son rôle, ou plutôt à travers qui l'auteur qui le manipule joue des rôles. Car, bien entendu, il s'agit de pantins. Le langage du geste, parce qu'il les traverse et ne leur appartient pas, doit être non seulement explicite, mais encore en fait expliqué, commenté, qualifié. Il apparaît au bout du compte que le geste présenté est une singerie, une parodie de ce que serait le même mais spontané, commandé irrésistiblement par un sentiment éprouvé—et non choisi par un acte de jugement comme l'attitude convenable à la circonstance, exigé par ce que la vieille rhétorique appelait «le décorum».

A ce point—il était temps, véritablement—l'intériorité expulsée rentre par la fenêtre: le comportement gestuel, loin qu'il reste dans sa pureté fait sans cesse l'objet d'une métaphorisation éclairante, motivante: nous voyons, dès le tout début, Alvaro communiquer avec Hardcaster comme du haut du «pic socratique glacé de sa sagesse» avec un pic voisin. Plus loin il parle «d'un ton assez maître d'école— comme qui présenterait la loi à une classe arriérée». On retrouve plus loin sa voix qui prend «les intonations argumentatives d'un conférencier complaisant.» Ainsi quand on se lasserait de l'implacable surprécision du signe, un signifié plus subtil s'y insère; du jeu de clowns une réalité renaît: des prisonniers invectivant le geôlier nous lisons qu'il y avait dans leur flamme une sorte de malice: «c'était un simulacre, «une flamme creuse.»

Et puis quand on passe d'Alvaro à l'autre gardien, Serafín, nous avons une physionomie digne d'un Balzac où le caractère s'insère sans vergogne ni discrétion, mais avec une virulence comparable une fois de plus à celle qui crée les «villains» de Hogarth:

Sa lèvre inférieure pendait mollement en avant de son menton comme si elle eût été mise à jamais hors d'état par un homérique rhume de cerveau. En résultat la viande rouge de la gencive inférieure était généralement en évidence. Les gencives n'étaient pas saines, c'étaient de vilaines racines écarlates. Une petite moustache couleur moutarde collait moite à la lèvre supérieure. Le bas de sa figure, en fait, était en déclin, tout y croulait. . . . Il se fendit d'un formidable clin d'oeil, et découvrit toutes ses dents qui auraient pu passer telles quelles à un musée dentaire comme superbe modèle de carie, et qui suggéraient, par quelque détour, tous les réconforts et les avantages d'une extrême corruption, aussi bien sur le plan *de la morale*.

Le plus curieux est que c'est Wyndham Lewis qui met «*moral*» en italique.

Pourquoi ce roman? Wyndham Lewis n'en fait pas secret. C'est presque avec emphase qu'il présente, souligne et reprend le motif-symbole du double fond, le thème du faux, de l'inauthentique, du mensonge, qui est d'ailleurs le sien depuis toujours. L'annonce en est si gratuite, si hors de propos, qu'il faudrait être un lecteur bien distrait pour ne pas lui prêter attention. C'est à la douzième ligne de la première page que le gardien de prison déclare que «nous ne sommes libres qu'une fois dans notre vie, quand nous finissons par regarder dans le fond du coeur de la bien-aimée et que nous le trouvons»— false, dit l'anglais, double, disons-nous d'un fond— «double», donc, «*comme tout en ce monde.*» Treize pages plus loin, le fond du panier de la visiteuse lui vient dans les mains: il est double. Plus loin nous lisons, «il vit que cet homme était faux. Sa moustache était collée.» Puis nous voici au centre même de l'œuvre et de son espace, dans la maison O'Hara: «c'était une boîte à doubles parois, et peut-être à double fond.» O'Hara, qui s'y connaît, a déjà déclaré que les Fenians étaient un tas de faux bonshommes (littéralement, «de doubles fonds»). Dans cette maison creuse où tout sonne le creux, Victor Stamp finit par s'écrier, «Crois tu que ces gens soient réels!»

Et c'est plus loin le portrait de Freddie Salmon dont le visage présente «un vraiment énorme double fond»—avec un mâchoire inférieure visiblement fausse et surajoutée. Or il dirige un atelier de fausse peinture où pour le moment on fabrique de faux Van Gogh à la journée.

Et à huit pages de la fin, Victor explique à Margot que leur voiture est à double fond. Mais cette fois le comble d'humour noir de ce double-fond est que c'est une fausse cachette, un *faux* double-fond et que là où sont censées être des armes il n'y a que des briques et du papier. C'est le ricanement ironique des Dieux que l'on devrait entendre à travers les Pyrénées, et non pas le tonnerre.

L'imposture est la chose du monde la mieux partagée, dirait volontiers Wyndham Lewis. Nos sociétés «civilisées», dans leurs couches «cultivées», ne sont que cela. De faux talents falsifient les valeurs, de faux juges les apprécient, de faux amateurs les discutent, la vie sociale semble obliger chacun chaque jour à paraître ce qu'il n'est pas, à professer des sentiments, des émotions, des goûts qu'il n'a pas. On remarquera que le même ramassis d'imposteurs de toute nature groupés autour des prestiges de la culture se trouve de livre en livre chez Aldous Huxley, et particulièrement dans *Point Counter Point*. Un néophyte vraiment trop récent, et qui correspondrait à Jack Cruze dans l'œuvre présente, parle avec emphase du génie du grand peintre Bagosso. La culture est un plumage de parade où les attitudes politiques ont leur rôle de parure, ou au contraire. Wyndham Lewis rassemble joyeusement ses aversions: en 1935 l'intelligentsia est le plus souvent à gauche, les rapins et autres faux créateurs se croient volontiers communistes. S'il y en avait un véritable, ce serait, l'auteur est prêt à le concéder, l'ouvrier communiste. Il n'y en a pas parce qu'il n'y a pas un seul ouvrier dans cet ouvrage. Le plus proche est Percy Hardcaster, mais cet ancien ouvrier est devenu cette nature amphibie qu'est l'agitateur. Il n'est pas question qu'il devienne bourgeois, il ne le peut ni ne le veut—son auteur pour le montrer lui fait déboutonner sa braguette dès la cour de la prison, avant d'entrer aux cabinets: «pas de vergogne bourgeoise». S'agissant d'une cour de prison espagnole, on est bien tenté de penser que la vergogne de Wyndham Lewis est presque trop exigeante ou trop britannique.

Wyndham Lewis a voulu son livre résolument anticommuniste, mais dans cette optique où finalement seuls les faux semblants de sa classe sont en cause. Ce n'est pas une nouveauté si l'on songe à la tradition anglaise du genre: *The Princess Casamassima* de Henry James, *The Secret Agent* et *Under Western Eyes* de Conrad. Si l'on compare le dernier ouvrage nommé au nôtre, on mesure la résolution satirique et l'animosité de Wyndham Lewis par comparaison avec l'effort d'imagination de Conrad qui s'il jette un Peter Ivanovitch et un Necator dans un plateau de la balance met Sofia et Tecla dans l'autre, avec sur leur tête le poids de l'épreuve et de la souffrance équilibré par le courage. Le poids de la vie est absent par principe de toute œuvre de Wyndham Lewis; on peut cependant ajouter qu'en avançant dans l'œuvre l'écrivain a renoncé à isoler chaque personnage sous un feu de projecteur, ou qu'au moins il a été plus attentif aux rapports et aux échanges, à ce que l'espace commun comporte aussi un voile atmosphérique sinon un air respirable et chargé d'émotions. Il manquera toujours me semble-t-il un regard réciproque: un regard cela prend du temps, et le temps, c'est toujours l'ennemi.

Au surplus, il n'y a pas de coups bas dans cet affrontement. Wyndham Lewis qui dénonce la légende d'atrocités fabriquée par les communistes espagnols et leurs alliés britanniques, ne craint d'en proposer de son côté à ses lecteurs une double ration, le jésuite scié en deux dont les poumons sont vendus pour mou de chat, et cet autre dont les côtes pendent aux crocs d'une boucherie incendiée. De l'hôpital, Percy voit passer les funérailles du militant qui est mort d'une indigestion de mauvais caviar. Lénine, nous dit le romancier, détestait les violonistes, «parce qu'ils lui donnaient envie de leur caresser la tête alors qu'il savait que son devoir était de les décerveler.» Céline est-il jamais tombé aussi bas?—C'est de si mauvaise littérature que ce n'est même pas de bon pamphlet.

Un roman qui se veut au premier chef satirique doit chercher sa grande scène satirique, et Wyndham Lewis la place dans la soirée chez les O'Hara. Est-elle aussi forte qu'il le voudrait? De la verve, de la saveur langagière il n'y a pas de doute. Mais finalement, a-t-elle, cette scène, la force expressive et la *vis satirica* des deux scènes, de vingt ans plus anciennes, du «Café Pompadour» dans *Women in Love*: «Crème de menthe», et surtout «Gudrun at the Pompadour»? Ce n'est pas certain.

La scène de Wyndham Lewis est en forme d'ellipse. Elle n'a pas un centre, mais deux foyers: le héros Percy Hardcaster, qui a perdu une jambe dans sa tentative d'évasion, et qu'entourent les militantes en chaleur, donne sa version grotesquement héroïque de son martyre espagnol, allant pour le bien de la cause jusqu'à l'inversion pure et simple des événements réels. Le militantisme s'amenuise à mesure qu'on s'éloigne du héros, et l'ardeur des corps l'emportant sur celle des âmes, la *party* dégénère assez vite en médiocre partouze. L'autre foyer est formé par les deux faussaires O'Hara et Abershaw, imitant la signature de Victor Stamp et préparant déjà leur mauvais coup: sur eux se concentre le sinistre de l'œuvre, un sinistre de «thriller» dont l'aboutissement logique sera la mort de deux innocents sans importance. Il ne s'agit plus de la Cause, les armes pour la Cause n'étant elles-mêmes qu'un moyen, mais bien des affaires qui sont les affaires. La physionomie de l'agent double O'Hara est celle d'un gnome maléfique et nous éloigne sensiblement de l'art des surfaces.

Deux foyers, mais comme déjà telle grande scène collective dans *Tarr*, celle-ci n'est point bâtie, de façon relativement statique, d'une multitude de petits mouvements: un grand mouvement de quête touchant et ridicule comme tout ce qui touche à ce personnage, la traverse: Margot a, symboliquement, perdu Victor, et le cherche, dans une inquiétude qui a l'acuité du pressentiment.

Tel quel, Percy, le héros comique de l'histoire, Sancho Pança commis, bon gré mal gré dans le rôle de Don Quichotte, a une bonne tête derrière le masque, un bon fond sous le double, «un bon naturel», une portion indestructible de vérité humaine: «il n'y avait pas dans le parti de plus honnête garçon: ayant appris son rôle il le jouait vraiment con amore.» Wyndham Lewis le construit et le meut de façon à montrer non pas un communiste bon mais un homme qui parvient à préserver un peu de bonté de son communisme. Mais l'auteur identifie-t-il aussi clairement qu'il le croit ce «communisme»? Lorsque dans ce salon ces «communistes» s'agglutinent autour de lui, ce sont eux qui sont la cible, et non point tellement leur surface, mais plutôt leur secrète conscience: perdre une jambe comme ça, ça ne pouvait arriver qu'à un ouvrier: «il n'y avait qu'un ouvrier pour aller là où ce genre de chose risquait d'arriver à ses jambes. Eux, il leur incombait de rester la tête.» Parmi ces «militants» la plus détestable est la grande bourgeoise, Gillian, «Jill», qui finira par trouver le partenaire sexuel qu'il lui fallait, un «Jack» de *nursery rhyme*, un piètre valet de cartes (jack), un médiocre satyre de village déguisé en homme d'affaires. Cette fille de diplomate se situe en évoquant assez souvent les souvenirs de son enfance «en poste» et elle écrase de son dédain la petite bourgeoise Margot. Elle est de celles qui serrent de près le héros unijambiste: mouvement traditionnel de l'érotisme féminin. C'est chez elle que cette scène-ci, la symphonie devenue un trio à vrai dire assez stridente, aura son écho, son épilogue à quelque temps de là. Elle sera si outragée lorsque Percy en malencontreuse veine de franchise lui dira que le communisme n'a que faire de héros ni, finalement, d'admiratrices, que se trouvant ridiculisée elle se venge comme une fille: Jack survenant à point, ce mâle efficace et complet est chargé d'administrer à Percy une raclée qui l'enverra à l'hôpital. Avec de cruelles délices Wyndham Lewis hausse son art au niveau de la violence, qui crée certes les plus riches et les plus intenses surfaces vitales. Ici se déploie sa technique littéraire de la description objective et détachée des phénomènes, qui déshumanise au point qu'il semble s'agir d'insectes féroces, l'un bientôt sur le dos remuant faiblement ses pattes démantibulées, présentés dans le plus extrême détail. La scène soulève le coeur sans susciter la sympathie: déshumaniser, c'est le moyen de désentimentaliser. La douleur même, chez l'homme devenu pantin, est comique. La laideur est radicale, et pour ce qui est de l'objectif complémentaire: déshéroïser, radicalement efficiente.

Tout ce qui concerne Jill trouve un regain d'actualité de notre temps et dans cette lumière est peut-être plutôt à nuancer et à rectifier qu'à simplement annuler. En tout état de cause le socialisme, à plus forte raison le communisme, est pour un bourgeois, de naissance, de formation ou simplement de culture, un choix difficile à maintenir, et l'intellectuel qui se sentant «révolutionnaire» adhère brièvement au parti puis se reprend, ne fait guère que manifester des contradictions inéluctables et le plus souvent des sincérités successives. La prise de possession arrogante de l'idée révolutionnaire par de tels éléments, le surengagement dans «l'action» allant de pair avec un moindre engagement dans l'activité vitale, est un phénomène d'un ordre différent et que pour le meilleur ou pour le pire nous appelons gauchiste. Il y a ce que le romantisme bourgeois du pseudo-classique Lewis invente: le complot communiste sous toutes ses formes, et ce que Lewis observe, qui n'est point le communisme mais la comédie du pseudo-communisme. «Gillian Communist», ce n'est pas une communiste, c'est, grotesquement, une gauchiste, en qui l'appartenance de classe et les habitudes de vie, d'une part, le verbalisme idéologique d'autre part, font un ensemble d'une irréalité glorieuse. «Vous êtes dans ce jeu pour l'amusement», dit Percy. Mais elle finira par proclamer: «C'est nous, les soi-disant intellectuels des classes supérieures, qui sommes les seuls vrais communistes.» Ce que Wyndham Lewis ne voit pas finalement, c'est que tout en faisant de Percy Hardcaster une grosse caricature, il ne parvient pas à ne pas suggérer à travers lui que le communisme, même l'anglais, est quelque chose de sérieux, sinon, pour l'Ennemi, de respectable.

Mais enfin à lui qui n'avait cure de ces nuances il fallait un complot, et O'Hara, nain bossu comme tant de traîtres depuis le Frocin de Tristan et Iseult, est l'homme qu'il lui fallait. Mais si même un parti révolutionnaire voué à soutenir des actions secrètes croit devoir utiliser des agents secrets, il ne les confond pas avec les siens. L'agent secret O'Hara se trouve être un agent double. Un militant expédié en Allemagne par ses soins va lui devoir une fin désagréable. Encore que le cas des Stamp puisse être présenté comme «pour le bien de la cause», il est clair que c'est du bien de l'affaire qu'il s'agit, une affaire de contrebande lucrative. Percy, O'Hara, Salmon, et les faux Van Gogh, tout cela, en accord avec la symbolique centrale, est trituré ensemble par l'auteur en un amalgame habile et fort malhonnête, pour former et peindre un secteur social où toutes les formes du faux et du mensonge sont privilégiées et où évidemment l'huile de ricin fera merveille.

Percy, on le repêchera. Il prépare son salut, au fond, depuis la première page, par ses accès de franchise intempestifs («c'est plus fort que lui», dirait-on). Il le fera, ce salut à la frontière espagnole. Une conversation entre lui et l'aubergiste contrebandier conspirateur Mateu est le moyen un peu laborieux de le mener par un cheminement à lui-même obscur à la prise de conscience. On a fait de lui l'instrument de ce complot dont un innocent serait la victime. Encore une fois ne nous faisons pas d'illusions sur les vues de l'auteur: si Percy était encore un bon communiste, perinde ac cadaver, il trouverait tout cela sans importance pourvu que les armes arrivent aux Rouges. Mais Percy est devenu un mauvais communiste qui se pose des questions. Il a laissé partir Stamp, mais il suivra Margot; il se retrouve en prison assez mal traité, et le livre se clôt sur l'honnête larme qu'il laisse tomber sur le sol crasseux, donnant au livre une belle forme parfaitement circulaire dans laquelle s'inscrit une histoire. Laquelle, au premier chef? Qui sait, peut-être celle de ce salut même, de cette accession à l'humain.

Dans cette vision à dominante satirique les personnages connaissent un développement très inégal: il y a pantin et pantin. Nul n'a de ressorts aussi simples que Jack Cruze à qui il suffit de dire: jupon, pour qu'il entre en érection. La plupart sont entièrement contenus dans l'écriture qui les porte; or ne peut-on dire que tout personnage mémorable s'étend dans une zone de silence autour des mots? Reste le cas des Stamp. C'est un bon portrait de raté que celui de Victor, fils de l'inculture australienne qui, comme il advient de tous les pays neufs, a rêvé trop vite de culture. Doué mais pas assez, le voici passé au vieux monde avec ses grosses mains de primitif, un je ne sais quoi de fruste et d'inachevé répandu dans toute sa personne, et, au coeur, la conscience de son échec qui le fait, le jour que nous faisons sa connaissance, se cramponner au sommeil avant qu'il retrouve le courage de réfléchir à son coloris, qui, lui étant ce qu'il est, apparaît absurdement joli: à «ses orangés vulgaires, ses bleus savonneux, ses violâtres nauséabonds», qu'il oppose à la sévérité «quasi-monochrome» des Français. Alors il peint furieusement, contre lui-même et sa nature, une toile violente et simple, une toile rouge, qui se trouve être bonne. Mais il sait que c'est en vain, qu'une bonne toile ne fait pas un peintre, si elle est contre sa nature; qu'elle ne peut le faire reconnaître, même s'il y avait un public pour connaître les artistes. Que ce public n'existe pas, ce qui nivelle pratiquement les bons artistes et, parmi les mauvais, ceux qui se cherchent, dans la même incompréhension, cela embrouille quelque peu l'argument. L'auteur veut grouper trop de significations critiques autour d'un seul personnage. Laissons le public. Victor se sait voué à l'art de second main, dérivatif, fait de souvenirs et non d'invention. Sentir en soi ce creux de création, c'est la pire condition pour endurer le creux de la faim et de la misère non seulement pour soi mais pour sa compagne. Victor est mal dans sa peau. Bourru jusqu'à l'éclat, il est *en fuite*. Peut-être les instincts de mort installés en lui déterminent-ils aussi bien ses acceptations que ses explosions.

C'est comme par un de ces châtiments infernaux appropriés au péché qui les a provoqués que Victor se trouve acculé à la fabrique de faux tableaux, assis à son chevalet, un bonnet de fourrure sur la tête et un bandage sur l'oreille, faisant d'après lui-même un auto-portrait de Van Gogh «ce sentimental rat rose venue de l'hystérique Nord», «avec ses yeux de furet bordés de rouge». «Il ne l'avait jamais beaucoup aimé comme peintre». A coup sûr, Wyndham Lewis non plus, car une des plus mauvaises pages du livre suit, qui évoque avec un humour massif et pâteux sa crise et son oreille coupée. A travers son personnage Wyndham Lewis, comme faisait Hogarth, se livre non seulement à une critique des mœurs mais à une critique du goût, et on n'est pas surpris que le désordre expressionniste de Van Gogh n'ait pas été du sien; mais on voit aussi que s'il a creusé de façon si variée le cas Stamp, c'est que les problèmes du peintre sont tous près de son cœur: même ceux du mauvais peintre s'il se cherche.

Ce misogyne qu'est Wyndham Lewis, Margot l'a intéressé sans le faire céder, de sorte qu'elle est à mi-chemin de la caricature, et même cruelle, mais qu'elle résiste à la malveillance de son créateur et qu'elle a cette dimension humaine, plutôt encore cette faculté d'expansion en nous, qui la distingue, par exemple, de la Bertha de *Tarr*. Prenons-y garde toutefois: le ton de Lewis pour parler d'elle la met sévèrement à distance, et dès lors ce qu'elle pense ou dit lui appartient, et fait un angle plus ou moins aigu avec l'auteur. Or le titre, *The Revenge for Love*, Revanche sur l'amour, lui appartient à elle. A son réveil, «elle s'était dit que l'amour était vain et sans pouvoir, que les Dieux haïssaient l'amour.» Tous leurs malheurs, c'était une revanche du destin sur l'amour. Pauvre petite créature romantique et romanesque, elle rêve de s'immoler pour conjurer le sort qui les persécute. Le lecteur est je crois invité à mettre tout cela en question, amour, destin, masochisme, sacrifice. Peut-être faudrait-il mettre au titre un point d'interrogation.

Elle agace, et Wyndham Lewis la veut agaçante, par excès de sentiment conjugal-maternel—elle est pour son mari non seulement la femme-enfant mais la mère-enfant. L'obsédante préoccupation, à la soirée O'Hara, de nourrir son homme, comme une compensation au creux mental qu'il éprouve, renforcé par sa conversation avec le cruel Pete; la collision, l'assiette renversée, la persévérance comique qui en remplit tant bien que mal une seconde pour le pauvre cher époux qui ne mange pas tous les jours, tout cela est au moins aussi grotesque que touchant. Cela n'empêche pas Margot d'être moins obtuse que Victor, cela ne l'empêche pas dans cette maison à double paroi d'éprouver un intense malaise, le sentiment d'une menace: de se sentir comme un Christ de Bosch cernée de ricanements, entourée non d'humains mais «de grandes, d'imposantes poupées de cire»—les pantins de son créateur devenus maléfiques. Faudrait-il alors présenter cette femme—une femme! —comme lucide face à l'opacité masculine? Ce serait scandaleux. En fait il s'agit moins de lucidité que de voyance, plutôt «extra-lucide,» et Wyndham Lewis peut concéder cela à

la Femme, enfant malade et douze fois impur!

Cela en effet se passe à un degré d'émotivité anormal, hors de tout contrôle rationnel, et sans doute *à cause de cela*.

La succession des scènes n'est pas ordonnée ici comme chez Flaubert avec de savants effets de contre-partie ou de parallélisme. Elle obéit pourtant à la préoccupation de placer quelque chose, de rappeler un point de vue, de faire sinon un pendant, du moins un contrepoids, dès que possible. Bientôt après la soirée O'Hara, nous en avons une qui est, elle aussi, à un degré bien sûr très atténué, satirique. Elle rassemble Margot et son amie Agnes Irons, joueuse de golf quasi-professionnelle, indéniable pantin, qui parle une langue automatique inepte et badine, située entre l'écolière et le militaire. Mais le grotesque de l'entretien rejaillit sur Margot. Certaines formules («a park of one's own») rappellent que derrière les sentimentalités de Margot nous devons entrevoir la figure tutélaire de Virginia Woolf. Cette ridicule Agnes, c'est peut-être un peu la Sally sur qui le souvenir de Clarissa s'attendrit au début de *Mrs. Dalloway*. Ce qui doit ressortir, c'est le côté infantile et sentimental lié à l'image plus amoindrissante qu'attendrissante, essentiellement fausse, elle aussi, de la «petite ermite», qui doit nous poursuivre. Au reste pour mettre sa cervelle dans le coton, dans l'illusion, dans le faux, toujours dans le faux, Virginia Woolf ne suffit pas. Ne voit-on pas Margot, dans ces Pyrénées truquées comme les Alpes de Bécassine, et dont le double fond va l'engloutir, chercher la sécurité culturelle dans les inanités sonores du Ruskin de *Sesame and Lilies*, cet anti-Lewis qui proclame que les femmes sont des Reines!

Elle n'a fait que changer, lors du dernier et fatal épisode, de gentil surnom. Elle est maintenant pour Victor, toutes les fois qu'il veut diminuer la tension en elle avant qu'elle ne craque, Honey Angel, mon Ange tout en miel. Et c'est le titre de cette partie, et qu'est-ce que cela veut dire? Est-ce Margot-objet annulée par son rapport de femme trop femme avec un Victor fruste et idéalisé?—annulée par l'incompréhension de Victor abîmé dans son morne égotisme. Ou bien est-ce vraiment sa nature et sa foncière irréalité? L'auteur joue plus subtilement son jeu de distanciations et d'ironies ici que partout ailleurs.

Si quelques scènes pouvaient faire d'un roman l'un des chefs-d'œuvre de la littérature romanesque, celles qui viennent alors ajoutées à celles du début le feraient. L'Espagne inspire Wyndham Lewis par une sort d'affinité offerte à son art: une expressivité toute extériorisée et terrible comme un des plus subtils caprices de Goya: c'est d'abord la scène du café de Puigmoro. Les nains comme les fous et les simples d'esprit ont là-bas tous les droits. Ce nain-ci, comme les chiens flairent des choses qui ne sont pas physiques, a flairé chez Margot la tension, l'angoisse, le désarroi. Il va dès lors s'emparer de sa présence pour la contraindre à distance à jouer avec lui, pour les délices des spectateurs, contemporains, au XXe. siècle, des cultures primitives, un acte burlesque. Il fait l'enfant qui pleure, ou qui «a envie»—et il l'a choisie pour mère; et par degrés elle bascule dans une sorte d'hallucination suggérée. Elle se voit devenir en effet sa mère, et le tenir dans ses bras. Un visage tordu par une grimace très clairement anormale réveille Victor de la sorte d'absence où il se réfugie habituellement. Quant à elle, elle sait—lucide ou extra-lucide—qu'ils sont très spécialement repérés, et qu'ils devraient fuir ce pays. C'est donc en endormant sa vigilance que Victor passe la frontière avec son chargement; et c'est avec l'habituelle ambiguïté que l'auteur la montre saisie d'une résolution nouvelle, se sentant femme d'action et responsable, décidée à sauver Victor de lui-même et du complot qui l'enserre, et le suivant à Figueiras. Faisons semblant de nous intéresser à la matérialité de l'histoire pour suivre le jeu doux et cruel de l'auteur avec son personnage. Si Margot n'avait pas rejoint Victor à temps pour lui enjoindre de fuir, il eût été arrêté à Figueiras, et le chargement ridicule de sa voiture à double fond découvert; nous le laisserions où nous laissons Percy, dans la prison d'où il serait bientôt délivré par la république populaire—car nous devons être aux derniers jours de la république bourgeoise de Lerroux—quitte à se faire tuer peu de temps après dans une brigade internationale. Rendons grâce à Margot de nous avoir sauvés d'un dénouement dérisoire, et d'avoir été l'agent de leur admirable fuite. C'est là, comme déjà dans l'épisode de Puigmoro, que l'art de Wyndham Lewis «décolle», imaginativement. Somme toute, extériorité ou pas, cet art a été tout au long scrupuleusement réaliste. Mais voici qu'une méthode expressionniste lui vient tout naturellement pour traduire l'état mental de Margot pendant que la voiture fonce, les arbres, les rochers, les poteaux télégraphiques s'abattant les uns sur les autres—une charge folle contre une forêt d'objets. Lorsqu'un de ces objets est, sur la route même, le garde civil qui la barre—rencontre fatale de «l'homme qui était un fusil et de l'homme qui était une voiture»—il faut bien l'aplatir avec le reste, et Wyndham Lewis se plaît à décrire le léger délire de cette Margot dont la toute petite tête est peu solide, se raccrochant à des fragments précieusement insignifiants du passé qui nient le présent, à la ridicule Agnes Irons—envahie cependant et possédée par le garde civil parfaitement aplati et devenu une curieuse image de carton. Nous sommes en pleine intériorité, Wyndham Lewis a laissé ses prescriptions en route.[1]

Un grand acteur nous met hors du monde dans une dimension autre. Un grand romancier aussi bien, et de même, par un surcroît d'intensité. Intensité! Il y a de quoi faire retourner Wyndham Lewis dans sa tombe; et pourtant cette sorte d'hyperesthésie de toutes ses grandes scènes, cet excès minutieux—anormal—du rendu, c'est bien ce qui, dirait Baudelaire, distingue dans l'art de la médiocre nature la précieuse surnature. Malgré lui, nous voyons Wyndham Lewis passer finalement à la surnature. C'est un mérite de cette oeuvre, que d'avoir contraint son auteur.

---

1. Il est assez significatif que presque dès le début il se soit laissé porter par la force et la tension du moment. Quand Percy est sur le point de s'évader ses derniers moments dans sa cellule sont marqués par un tel changement de ton, et un tel surcroît. Par la meurtrière qui lui sert de fenêtre il voit la rivière au clair de lune «avec un scintillement huileux semblable au fond d'une boîte de sardines, et il a aux oreilles le bourdonnement d'un moustique... Ce bourdonnement comme la vibration d'un élément de bronze—un grognement mat d'airain...» C'est Wyndham Lewis écrivant comme Faulkner, malgré lui.

RENO ODLIN

INTELLECTUS POSSIBILIS, OR JÊN²

千有餘歲得
志行乎中國
若合符節先
聖後聖其揆
一也

Mencius, IV, ii, I, 3-4

were as the two halves of a seal
      ½S
in the Middle Kingdom
Their aims as one
directio voluntatis, as lord over the heart
    the two sages united

—*Canto* 77

This will be the hardest kind of a piece to read, with great unwieldy blocks of quotation pulled from any number of authors, and I am sorry for that. It is exactly the sort of piece in which I myself most easily lose my place.= What we shall be investigating—under the above rather cryptic heading—is, roughly speaking, politics. I am sorry for that, too, because it seems doubtful whether much credit is to be attached to the mere *ipse dixit* of a part-time littérateur (and compare if you will the fly-weight utterance of your typical "movie star" doing a Deep Think in front of God and everybody)—and dam'd dangerous too! as may be learned from the history of Ezra Pound's "incomprehensible intervention in World War II."[1]

I justify these few remarks on affairs of state by reminding myself, *first*, that what I am mostly doing is commenting on texts—and not recent ones, either; and *second*, that there has long been in the West a tradition of the *Doctus Orator*, the notion that the mastery of civilization's basic texts (not, Heaven knows, that I am laying claim to any such mastery! but Dante might well have done so) produced Cicero's "ideal orator, the ideal of princes and churchmen... an educational model for centuries. ... By his command of language he simultaneously educed order from Babel and imposed it"[2]... such a tradition being, of course, no more than a fashionable antique in an age wherein there is no agreement as to what might constitute civilization's "basic texts"—although, during the boyhood of men still living, the professional qualifications of the various classes of Mandarin were unabashedly literary:

> I went up to the court for examination,
> Tried Layu's luck, offered the Choyo song,
> And got no promotion,
>   and went back to the East Mountains
>   White-headed.

('Exile's Letter,' *Cathay*, 1915);

or from a subsequent dynasty:

> book-bred,
> out-of-date, fame's race foregone.

(David Gordon, *Living in the Stream*:
Poems of Lu Yu, White Pine 13,
[Buffalo, N.Y., 1977], p. 6).

All this clearly differs, it is to be hoped, from what was stigmatized in a former age as "the intellectual's lay sermon" (the phrase comes from the lay sermon of a Canadian intellectual who was then, at Columbia, engaging in taking the bread out of some deserving American scholar's mouth[3]), although what seems lacking, and has since the Reformation, is a set of objective standards comparable to the Chinese.= Not, let me hasten to explain, that I desire to be governed by a literary caste, or that I think the rigidities of the Mandarin system desirable in themselves—but Dante might well have.

And that was my starting-point, namely a friend's wish that a casual remark about Confucian parallels in the *De Monarchia* of Dante Alighieri (an intellectual's lay sermon if ever there was one) should be expanded, with examples.= What I have done is to lay out these Confucian, and indeed Poundian, parallels, in a manner indicative rather than expatiatory. "Poundian" because, despite the denigration of professed sinologues,[4] such esteem as Confucius enjoys in our time in the West has come his way largely because of the admiration of Ezra Pound. Let that be a lesson to all against sneering at great poets in lieu of helping them correct their "errors"—as those errors, once launched on the tide, will float in and out for centuries.

I concede that there are deeply vexing enigmas here for the reader to struggle through, or to pass by—but to explain everything at length would be intolerable, and to tease out all the significance of the things I am going to be quoting would be to go far beyond anything I know of my own knowledge.[5]

By this profusion of citations what I mean to suggest is that we are not dealing with the hopelessly exotic, nor yet with irretrievably "medieval" quiddities, but with what was until tolerably lately the very breath and substance of our civic understanding, East and West alike: and that if it be indeed lost to man's memory, "you got" (as Rev. Eliot said of the playhouse audience's attention) "to get it back QUICK."

It cannot be denied that a great deal of material whose relationships with my ostensible subject are but vague and filmy has slipped in while I was trying to achieve clarity. So be it: the appearance of disorder this imparts may keep the piece from being mistaken for a systematic treatise.= And with that said, let us for Heaven's sake get down to cases:

Satis igitur declaratum est, quod proprium opus humani generis totaliter accepti, est actuare totam potentiam intellectus possibilis, per prius ad speculandum, et secundario propter hoc ad operandum per suam extensionem. Et quia quemadmodum est in parte, sic est in toto, et in homini particulari contingit quod sedendo et quiescendo prudentia et sapientia ipse perficitur;[6] patet quod genus humanum in quiete sive tranquillitate pacis ad proprium suum opus, quod fere divinum est (iuxta illud: "Minuisti eum paulo minus ab angelis"), liberrime atque facillime se habet.

(Dante, *De Monarchia*, I, iv, 1-16, Oxford text, 1897; hereafter cited as *DM*)

(It has been sufficiently shown that the work proper to the human race, taken as a whole, is to keep the whole capacity of the potential intellect constantly actualized, primarily for speculation, and secondarily [by extension, and for the sake of the other] for action.

And since it is with the whole as it is with the part, and it is the fact that in sedentary quietness the individual man is perfected in knowledge and wisdom,[6] it is most evident that in the quiet or tranquillity of peace the human race is most freely and favourably disposed towards the work proper to it [which is almost divine, even as it is said, "Thou hast made him a little lower than the angels"].)

(translation from *The Latin Works of Dante Alighieri*, Dent, 1934)

That is to say, peace as a means, not an end. (No democratic politician ever understood this.) That end having been defined as the realization of the whole of the human potential—and by his "totam" our author marks himself a more serious character than the compiler of the *Nicomachean Ethics*, in the passage (X, vii, 7) so savaged by Mr. Pound,[7] although he, Aristotle, achieves an admirable clarity as to ends and means, in his first book.

天命之謂性
率性之謂道
修道之謂教

What heaven has disposed and sealed is called the inborn nature. The realization of this nature is called the process. The clarification of this process (the understanding or making intelligible of this process) is called education.

(Pound, *Confucius* [New Directions, 1951], p. 99 [*The Unwobbling Pivot*, I, i]; hereafter cited as *C*)

We have in *The Prince* the best ABC of power ever compiled with a view especially to obtaining political and despotic power: the steps that you must take as a *sine qua non* of success and

subjugation. And it is accompanied with an accurate general description of the creatures that it will be your privilege to subjugate. And *what then*? Well, you will ride about on an immense white horse like the young d'Annunzio, or an elephant: you will live in a palace the size of an elephant,[8] you will have more slaves than anybody else: or if not, *What*? But, of course, the end is a pretence, success even is a fiction, since nothing accomplished and terminated is worth considering. It is not the end, it is the doing it, that is the reward of these as of all other activities.
(Wyndham Lewis, *The Lion and the Fox* [Grant Richards, 1927; reprint, Methuen, 1955], p. 107)

The specific applicability of Lewis's argument is somewhat marred by his failure to take into account the last chapter of *The Prince*: that the end towards which all this scheming and rapine was to be directed was *the liberation of Italy*. For all that, has a better question been asked in these three hundred years?

... sciendum quod iustitia de se et in propria natura considerata, est quaedam rectitudo sive regula, obliquum hinc inde abiciens.

(*DM*, I, xi, 10-17)

(... be it known that justice, in herself, considered in her proper nature, is a certain straightness or rule, rejecting the oblique on either side.)

With which compare Mr. Pound at large on the Unwobbling Pivot, as in

故君子和而不流
強哉矯中立而不
倚強哉矯國有道
不變塞焉強哉矯
國無道至死不變
強哉矯

(*Chung Yung*, X, 5)

Considering which things, the man of breed, in whom speaks the voice of his forebears, harmonizes these energies with no loss of his own direction; he stands firm in the middle of what whirls without leaning on anything either to one side or the other, his energy is admirably rectificative; if the country be well governed, he does not alter his way of life from what it had been during the establishment of the regime; when the country is ill governed, he holds firm to the end, even to death, unchanging. His is an admirably rectificative energy.

(*C*, 113)

—and indeed, when Dante continues:

Quantum ergo ad habitum, iustitia contrarietatem habet quandoque in velle; nam ubi voluntas ab omni cupiditate sincera non est, etsi adsit iustitia, non tamen omnino inest in fulgore suae puritatis, habet enim subjectum, licet minime, aliqualiter tamen sibi resistens; propter quod bene repelluntur, qui judicam passionare conantur

(As concerns disposition, then, justice may sometimes find opposition in the will; for, where the will is not pure from all greed, even though justice be present, yet she is not absolutely there in the glow of her purity; for she is lodged in a subject which to some extent, though it be never so little, resists her. Wherefore, they are rightly rebuffed who attempt to inspire the judge with passion)

—are we not irresistibly reminded of that

Not that it were natural opposite but only
Wry'd a bit from the perfect

(La quale aita la contraria via
Nonche opposto naturale sia
Ma quanto che da ben perfett' è torte)

of Cavalcantian song[9] as well as the above Confucian classic?

... Nihil igitur agit, nisi tale existens, quale patiens fieri debet. ... Et hinc destrui potest error illorum qui bona loquendo et mala operando[10] credunt alios vita et moribus informare; non advertens quod plus persuaserunt manus Iacob, quam verba, licet illae falsum, illa verum persuaderent.

(*DM*, I, xiii, 13-25)

(... Therefore nothing can act unless it already

is itself that which the thing acted upon is to become.... And thus may be refuted the error of such as think that by saying well and doing ill[10] they can inform others with life and morals, not perceiving that the hands of Jacob were more persuasive than his words, albeit the former urged what was false, the latter what was true.)

Surely we have here, explicitly applied to the conduct of the Empire, the Confucian Great Learning: as in

是故君子有諸
己而后求諸人
無諸己而后非
諸人所藏乎身
不恕而能喻諸
人者未之有也

(*Ta Hsüeh*, ix, 4)

Whence we note that the prince must have in himself not one but all of the qualities that he requires from others, and must himself be empty of what he does not want from others in reflex. No one has ever yet been able to induct others into a style of conduct not part of his own viscera.

(*C*, 61-3)[11]

or compare:

(I and mine do not convince by arguments, similes, rhymes,
We convince by our presence.)
(Walt Whitman, 'Song of the Open Road,' section 10)

or:

For a man cannot have publick spirit, who is void of private benevolence.
(Christopher Smart, *Jubilate Agno*, xvi, 44)

Citation of Smart does not come entirely off the wall: one need but look at the Spannthology, *Confucius to Cummings* (New Directions, 1964), to see what we all knew in 1957, that Pound was utterly and lastingly charmed by Smart's cat Jeoffry, who "purrs in thankfulness when God tells him he's a good Cat"—encountered first, I think, in a complimentary copy of the Auden-Pearson anthology, *Poets of the English-Speaking World* (which he brushed off *coram* Meacham saying "I'd as soon read a telephone directory":[12] the pathology of this false contempt, this abrupt disclaimer of knowledge gained from some "secondary" and therefore impermissible source, is indeed interesting—I recommend its study to Mr. Herbert Schneidau—but scarcely relevant to my present purpose).= It was in this same anthology, I believe, that he renewed acquaintance with his other wonder of that year, the Ben Jonson lyric containing "the Wooll of the Beauer."

... quod ius in rebus nihil est aliud quam similitudo divinae voluntatis. Unde fit quod quidquid divinae voluntati non consonat, ipsum ius esse non possit: et quidquid divinae voluntatis est consonum, ius ipsum sit.

(*DM*, II, ii, 48-53)

(... that right as manifested in things is nought else than the similitude of the divine will. Whence it comes to pass that whatever is not consonant with the divine will cannot be right, and whatever is consonant with the divine will is right.)

道也者不可須
奧離也可離非
道也也道

(*Chung Yung*, I, 2)

You do not depart from the process even for an instant; what you depart from is not the process.
(*C*, 101)

The parallel here is perhaps less than persuasive, a fault, if there be fault, to be ascribed to the large number of unexamined postulates which swarm in Dante's pages.= Or put it that the quite lexicographic precisions of the Confucian text have no parallel in Dante, who relies on the reader's unthinking acceptance of whatever may lie behind such a phrase as "divine will."

We need not subscribe to the rather obsolete major theses of the *De Monarchia* (roughly, they are: 1. that the form of government most suited to man and pleasing to God is an absolute monarchy; 2. that its legitimacy will correspond to its Romanity; but 3. that the Pope may keep his nose out of it) to find these incidental points stimulating: and to note that the main thrust is the same as Machiavel's, namely *the liberation of Italy*—in each case by means of a lesser evil: with Dante liberation from the Papacy by means of a secular despot, with Machiavel from a foreign by means of a domestic despot.

The lesser evil—! It may not be much, but it is all the choice we will get in this world: and glad we should be for that much. Had it not been for a hatful of dedicated and vocal extremists, from Sam Adams's time to ours, who have preserved for us the minimal necessities for resistance to tyranny, we should long since have followed the path into ancient blackness down which have stumbled that three-quarters of mankind whose choice now is always and only Hobson's: take what is doled out, or nothing at all.= If one remark the nocturnal terror of Russian garrisons in Afghanistan facing a few half-starved Pathan or Afridi *mujaheddin*, with their home-made jezails and SMLEs, and to these latter compare the lot of the peasant in feudal Japan after the Great Sword Hunt of 1588, when he might be decapitated at any time for what the codes described as "unexpected behaviour," I need scarcely elaborate upon this point.

> Not that never should, but if exceeding and
> no one protest,
> will lose all your liberties.[13]
> (*Thrones*, p. 65)

At least these authors do not bore us with the current American shibboleth of "free elections"—another confusion of means and ends, like the Trial by Jury ("We'll give you a fair trial, and then hang you"), or the elaborate disputations over forms (i.e., *methods*) of government with which certain comfortable Athenians busied themselves, at their interminable banquets or loitering in their very public streets, before the obliteration of their commonwealth.

> ... Scimus etiam, quod vicarius hominis non aequivalet ei, quantum in hoc quod vicarius est, quia nemo potest dare quod suum non est. Auctoritas principalis non est principis nisi ad usum, quia nullus princeps seipsum auctoritare potest.
> (*DM*, III, vii, 40-44)

(We also know that no man's vicar is equivalent to the man himself, because no man can give what is not his. Now the princely authority is only the prince's to use, for no prince can confer authority upon himself.)

Compare "No man has a natural right to the trade of a money-lender, but he who has money to lend," Thos. Jefferson as quoted in *Jefferson and/or Mussolini*, p. 118. Or, more aptly perhaps:

萬章曰堯以天下與舜有諸孟子曰否天子不能以天下與人然則舜有天下也孰與之曰天與之

(*Mencius*, V, v, 1-2)

1. Wan Chang said, "Was it the case that Yaou gave the empire to Shun?" Mencius said, "No. The emperor cannot give the empire to another."
2. "Yes;—but Shun had the empire. Who gave it to him?" "Heaven gave it to him," was the answer. (trans. Legge)

天之生此民也使先知覺後知使先覺覺後覺也

(*Mencius*, V, vii, 5)

Heaven's plan in the production of mankind is this:—that they who are first instructed should instruct those who are later in being informed, and they who first apprehend principles should instruct those who are slower to do so. (trans. Legge)

Nemi licet ea facere per officium sibi deputatum quae sunt contra illud officium; quia sic idem, in quantum idem, esset contrarium sibi ipse; quod est impossibile.

(*DM*, III, x, 30-34)

(No one is at liberty to do, in virtue of the office deputed to him, things that are counter to that office, else the same thing in the same capacity would be counter to itself, which is impossible.)

子曰道不遠人
人之爲道而遠
人不可以爲道

(*Chung Yung*, XIII, 1.)

Kung said: The process is not far from man, it is not alien to him. Those who want to institute a process alien to mankind [at variance with human nature] cannot make it function as an ethical system.

(*C*, 119)

Dante's formulation, by the way, was achieved in the course of an exercise proving—200 years before Lorenzo Valla—that the 'Donation of Constantine' upon which the temporal power of the Papacy was based was a forgery. (Perhaps 'proving' should be placed within inverted commas, as we have seen some half-hearted efforts even in our day to prove the contrary.) Again and again he lights up a long-dead dispute in this manner.

And all the above may be things easy enough to see in action on the county- or family-scale, where we can readily learn whether Candidate X or Uncle Z be fool, knave, or poltroon, but which may be obscured in the pseudo-complexities of the "larger view": or perhaps they are not pseudo-complexities, perhaps they are like stamp-scrip, perfectly plausible in a small isolated village like the Wörgl of "credit-crank"[14] legend, but inexorably colliding, in the larger world, with that common sense which drove Henry Hazlitt to characterize the whole scheme thus:

> Gesell had attracted some attention in the economic underworld by proposing a form of money that would automatically lose part of its value every month, like a rotting vegetable. His proposed method of achieving this was to require the holder of every currency note to have it stamped each month, with stamps purchased at the post office, in order to keep it good at its face value. This means, in effect, that people would have to *pay* interest to the government for the privilege of holding their own money. Money held, without being stamped, would lose a fraction of its purchasing power every month. The purpose of all this was to discourage people from saving; to make monetary saving practically impossible; to force everyone to spend his money, for no matter what, before it lost its value. Any one who was wicked enough to wish to put aside money against the contingency of illness in his family, for example, would thus be effectively frustrated.
>
> It is obvious that such money would never freely circulate except in a community of idiots unless it were made legal tender and there was no choice but to accept it. There was in principle nothing original in the proposal. It did not differ essentially from the immemorial practise of coin clipping, except that it would have occurred much more systematically and much more often. It combined nearly all the evils of ordinary paper inflation with some special disadvantages of its own. Its sole advantage as compared with ordinary paper money inflation is that the holder would clearly recognize and identify the government tax, and know precisely what the incidence of that tax was on himself.

(Henry Hazlitt, *The Failure of the "New Economics"* [Van Nostrand, 1959], pp. 352-53)

Or is it not rather that we have grown used to having the least allusion to ancient truths derided as "simplistic," at the hands of the eloquent gentlemen who determine, each day, what tiny percentage of the day's news we are to be allowed—and how we are to react to it? The processes easiest to note are misdirection, and preemption of the *terms* of discourse:

> But their technique is two lies at once
> so there be no profit in conflict

(*Thrones*, p. 69),

in fact, something rather like media coverage of the last two Papal elections: our attention was directed, you recall, almost solely to the pros and cons of those fabricated "issues" which lie below the belt-line.

I am not going to try recapitulating in this brief space Wyndham Lewis's many uproarious cadenzas on the adepts of *What-the-Public-Wants*, but one quotation, surely, may be allowed, after so many. It enshrines, I believe, a profound, and profoundly tragic, truth under its harsh schematic brilliance; and of its *appropriateness* there can be no doubt:

> The working of the 'democratic' electoral system is of course as follows: A person is trained up stringently to certain opinions; then he is given a vote, called a 'free' and fully enfranchised person; then he votes (subject, of course, to new and stringent orders from the press, where occasionally his mentor commands him to vote contrary to what he has been taught) strictly in accordance with his training. His support for everything that he has been taught to support can be practically guaranteed. Hence, of course, the vote of the free citizen is a farce: education and suggestion, the imposition of the will of the ruler through the press and other publicity channels, cancelling it. So 'democratic' government is far more effective than subjugation by physical conquest.
> (*The Art of Being Ruled* [Chatto & Windus, 1926], p. 111)

But no! Having made that point by way of Lewis, how could one better round out this disjointed stroll among coincident high points of civic wisdom than by that paragraph—again from the suppressed *Doom of Youth*—of which the fitness to sum our blighted century can no longer be accorded the least lingering trace of a doubt:

> The conspiracy of power to-day is—as Mr. H. G. Wells has called it—an open conspiracy. It is all fair, square, and above-board. There is no excuse for any one at present not to be politically enlightened. Yet there have never been so many people entirely ignorant of everything that is happening to them. Which only shows that 'openness' is the best policy. If Guy Fawkes had explained publicly to all the citizens of London exactly what he intended to do, then probably the Gunpowder Plot would have been a signal success. (For is it not only 'madmen' who carry out their destructive designs openly?)
> (p. 262)

---

1. Wyndham Lewis, *The Writer and the Absolute* (London: Methuen, 1952), p. 41.
2. Hugh Kenner, *Dublin's Joyce* (London: Chatto & Windus, 1955), p. 14.
3. *Both* sides, look you, can play the "Canadian Culture" game!
4. See, for instance, Mr. George Kennedy's eleven pages in the *Yale Literary Magazine* for December 1958, ending "He is to be saluted as a poet, but not as a translator."
5. It must have been some such consideration which prompted EP's summary, "a life time work," in response to one student's proposed correlation during the Fifties.
6. Samuel Beckett's eschatology starts from this point.
7. "The rift is clear in Rackham's own preface which I have, with persistence, held over for a conclusion.

> 'Hence the tendency to think of the End not as the sum of the Goods, but as one Good which is the Best. Man's welfare thus is ultimately found to consist not in the employment of all his faculties in due proportion, but only in the activity of the highest faculty, the "theoretic" intellect.'

"That leads you plumb bang down to the 'split man' in Mr Wyndham Lewis' *Apes*. That is the schismatic tendency. Therein is the scizophrenia [*sic*] in its almost invisible embryo.

"Everything that is unsatisfactory in mediaeval scholasticism. Looks harmless?" (*Guide to Kulchur*, pp. 342-43)
8. Crowded quarters these, what?
9. The reference is to that deeply and continuously obscure canzona of Guido Cavalcanti, "Donna mi prega..." in which Pound's interest was as intense, and as life-long, as his interest in the Confucian ethic.
10. And of men seeking good,
  doing evil.
In meiner Heimat
  where the dead walked
    and the living were made of cardboard.
("From Canto 115," *Drafts and Fragments* [1968], p. 24) ("Man" in the first line is an obvious misprint for the "men" of the first, or *Paris Review*, publication.)

We may take the fancied parallel a bit further if we indulge ourselves so far as to see "the living" in Dante's *vita*, "the dead" in the sort of reading of *moribus* which gave us "night dogs" for *nocturnae canes* in "Homage to Sextus Propertius."
11. 吾未聞枉己而正人者也，況辱己以正天下者乎
Mencius, V, vii, 7. "I have not heard of one who bent himself, and at the same time made others straight;—how much less could one disgrace himself, and thereby rectify the whole empire?" in Legge's translation.
12. *The Caged Panther* (Boston: Twayne Publishers, 1967), p. 147.
13. If that be found obscure, the plain prose sense of it is explicit in the *Paris Review* interview (No. 28, Summer–Fall 1962, 44): "What I was right about was the conservation of individual rights. If when the executive, or any other branch, exceeds its legitimate powers, no one protests, you will lose all your liberties." (Reprinted in *Writers at Work*, 2nd series [New York: Viking, 1965], pp. 35-59.)
14. The term is Lewis's, who explains (in a book suppressed in the U.K., *Doom of Youth*): "Now, I do not recommend you to regard all farmers as courteous, open-handed gentlemen, and all 'Credit-kings' (or 'Emperors of Debt') as diabolical villains—since in fact all men are fairly unpleasant, and normally there is not much to choose between them. But if it is six of one and half a dozen of the other in the matter of greed, brutalism and low cunning, it is by no means the same thing when it comes to the *power* to do mischief or to do good. It is not true to say that a man with a lump of dynamite or a cylinder of poison-gas is no more harmful than a cave-man with a flint-axe. And the technique of Credit is an instrument of destruction in comparison with which every other known weapon of offence shrinks into insignificance." (New York edition, 1932, p. 35.)

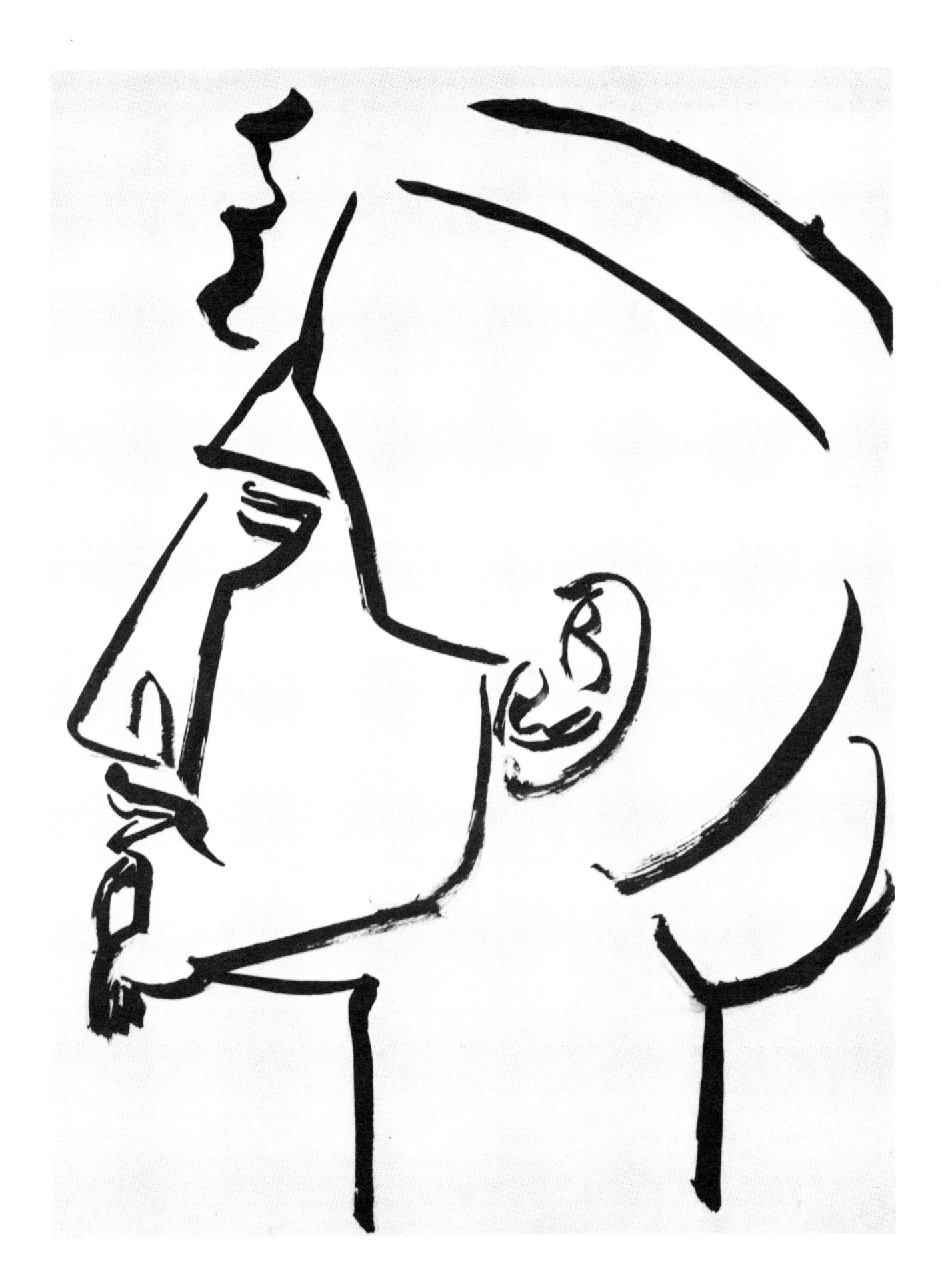

PORTRAIT OF EZRA POUND, 1914
HENRI GAUDIER-BRZESKA
INDIA INK. 49.5 x 37 cm
COURTESY ANTHONY d'OFFAY

BRYANT KNOX

EZRA POUND ON WYNDHAM LEWIS'S RUDE ASSIGNMENT

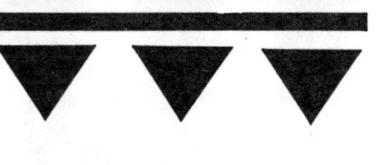

INTRODUCTION

In the autumn of 1908 Ezra Pound arrived in London with little more than his personal belongings and a few copies of *A Lume Spento*, his first book of poems. By mid-1909 he was well on his way to being a celebrity in London's world of letters. *A Quinzaine for This Yule* had been published in December 1908, *Personae* in April 1909. He had lectured at the British Polytechnic; he had made friends with T. E. Hulme and Hulme's circle of poets and writers; and in June 1909 his first contribution to Ford Madox (Hueffer) Ford's *English Review*, "Sestina: Altaforte," was published in the company of such notables as Joseph Conrad, H. G. Wells, and a promising writer named Wyndham Lewis. By then, Lewis had undoubtedly heard of the ebullient American poet.

They first met in 1909 in the Vienna Cafe, the hangout of the British Museum set. Laurence Binyon, whom Pound had known for a number of months, introduced him to Lewis, who was in the company of Sturge Moore. Noel Stock describes the meeting:

> Binyon and Moore stood back and urged each his respective "bulldog" into the fray, or at any rate stood back and watched. This was not a good start and although they saw one another occasionally during the next three years I know of no evidence that they played any part in each other's career during this time.[1]

By 1913, however, Pound was perceiving "analogies to his own hard verse" in Lewis's Timon of Athens drawings.[2] But the crucial year in the development of their relationship was 1914, when Pound and Lewis combined forces under the artistic banner of Lewis's Rebel Art Centre. Although Lewis's institution was designed primarily to promote the principles of avant-garde painting, Pound was regarded as a comrade in spirit and contributed a sign for the Centre's Walls which read "End of the Christian Era."[3]

Pound's friendship with Lewis strengthened at this time and the two men turned their attention to the founding of a new art and literary school, Vorticism, and its publication, BLAST. Lewis and Pound contributed generously to the two issues of the magazine (June 1914 and July 1915). Lewis, however, was dissatisfied with Pound's contributions, as he explained in *Rude Assignment*, thirty-six years after the event:

> At this distance it is difficult to believe, but I thought of the inclusion of poems by Pound etc. in *Blast* as compromising. I wanted a battering ram that was all of one metal. A good deal of what got in seemed to me soft and highly impure.[4]

We will later see that Pound was annoyed with these remarks (see Letter Three), but at the time such criticism was not voiced, and they were active collaborators.

By October 1914 Pound began preparing the prospectus for his interdisciplinary College of Arts in which Lewis was to function on the faculty, along with Gaudier-Brzeska, John Cournos, and others—"practising artists, not... sterile professors."[5]

By the end of 1914, then, Pound and Lewis had become good friends, and in characteristic fashion Pound began promoting Lewis's literary and artistic achievements—a campaign that was to last a lifetime. As well as writing numerous reviews and articles about his work, Pound introduced him to other artists and writers, such as T. S. Eliot, then sub-editor of *The Egoist*, which later published Lewis's first novel *Tarr* (1916–17) and *The Caliph's Design* (1919).[6] Lewis also credits Pound with introducing him to Gaudier-Brzeska, Arnold Dolmetsch, H.D., and Richard Aldington (RA, 121). Also, in March 1915, Pound began praising Lewis to the American art collector John Quinn, in 1917 sent Lewis's *Tarr* to the American publisher Alfred Knopf, and as London editor of *The Little Review* placed "Cantleman's Spring-Mate" in the 1917 October issue.

By 1921 Pound was in Paris, and by 1925 in Rapallo. The two friends now maintained a sporadic correspondence, but Pound's campaign on Lewis's behalf continued. In 1925, for instance, hoping to elicit financial assistance for Lewis as well as for other artists and writers, Pound wrote to Simon Guggenheim regarding the possibility of grants from the latter's recently announced Memorial Foundation. In 1927 Lewis publicly acknowledged Pound's effort on his behalf:

> Once toward the end of my long period of seclusion and work, hard-pressed, I turned to him for help, and found the same generous and graceful person there that I had always known; for a kinder heart never lurked beneath a portentous exterior than is to be found in Ezra Pound.[7]

When it came to Pound's literary talents and methodology, Lewis was not as easily moved to kind remarks. In 1927, the same year he acknowledged Pound's kindnesses, he took pains to dissociate himself from what he called Pound's "scholasticism." To Lewis, it was a matter of artistic principle (and his harsh condemnations of Pound must be viewed in this regard): "It is the *type* of man that Pound is, or partly is, and the *method* that he advocates, and practises, that sooner or later has to be repudiated by the artist." And earlier in the same passage:

> It is *disturbance* that Pound requires; that is the form his parasitism takes. He is never happy if he is not sniffing the dust and glitter of *action* kicked up by other, more natively 'active' men.... The particular stimulation that Pound requires for what he does all comes from without. (*TWM*, 40-41)

Seven years later Lewis still held the same view and asserted that Pound is "mainly a translator—an adapter, an arranger, a pasticheur...."[8] For Lewis, Pound's "creator-as-scholar" methodology is an emasculation of the artistic spirit.

Although Pound and Lewis saw less and less of each other as the years went by, they came together again, briefly, when Pound visited London in late 1938 to organize the estate of his mother-in-law, Olivia Shakespeare. It was at this time that Pound sat for the well-known oil portrait executed by Lewis now in the Tate Gallery.[9] After Lewis left for North America in 1939 he and Pound were seldom in touch.

Pound, however, did make an effort to correspond with Lewis. In January 1940 he enquired of T. S. Eliot: "Have you got Wyndham's Buffalo address? Why the hell don't the blighter write?" (Pound, *Letters*, 335). And in March he wrote to Lewis through Geoffrey Stone. Lewis's reply, if there was one, has not come to light. During the course of the war they were completely out of touch.

Late in April 1946 Wyndham Lewis read the following words from a letter addressed to T. S. Eliot:

> Now as to ole Wyndham whose address I have not, to thee and him these presents. While I yet cohere, he once sd/ a facefull. & apart from 3 dead and one aged [word?] who gave me 3 useful hints. ole W is my only critic—you have eulogized and some minors have analysis'd or dissected—
> all of which please tell the old ruffian if you can unearth him. (Lewis, *Letters*, 394n.)

Pound's greeting, care of T. S. Eliot, was posted from St. Elizabeths Hospital, a mental institution in Washington, D.C., and marked the renewal of their correspondence. On June 30, 1946, Lewis replied. His letter opened with a tongue-in-cheek jibe at Pound's predicament: "I am told that you believe yourself to be Napoleon—or is it Mussolini? What a pity you did not choose Buddha while you were about it, instead of a politician" (*Letters*, 394). Lewis continued in a more serious vein and commented upon the brisk sale of Pound's books in London, the potential of the artist in America, and Pound's concern over personal finances. All in all the letter was chatty and somewhat mundane, and in subsequent letters to Pound it becomes apparent that Lewis frequently suffers from an inability to incorporate matters of substance: "I never know what to say to you when I sit down to write you as I am doing now" (*Letters*, 403).

Pound, nevertheless, was happy with the renewed correspondence. It afforded him the opportunity to campaign for publication of Lewis's work, to promote the kind of intelligence which Lewis represented and to deluge him with myriad books, pamphlets, and articles which he hoped he would read. Such men as Brooks Adams, Agassiz, Benton, Blackstone, Confucius, Del Mar, Frobenius, Kitson, and Morgenthau, to name only a few, were recommended by Pound. He also encouraged Lewis to write articles on some of these men and hoped that he would countenance this formidable array of intelligence. In 1948 Lewis promised to contribute, at Pound's insistence, to Dallam Simpson's *Four Pages* (*Letters*, 436). But by July of that year, Lewis was obliged to set Pound straight: "My dear Ezz. The writing (and reading) you would have me do is impossible. It takes me all my time to keep alive. I have none on my hands at all" (*Letters*, 453). By the end of 1948 Lewis was exasperated with Pound's persistence and complained to D. D. Paige, who was then editing Pound's letters: "Have no wish to read more economics—have something better to do. However many times I say this he [Pound] returns to the charge" (*Letters*, 462).

The pace picked up in 1951 when Pound heard through his son, Omar, that Agnes Bedford had renewed her acquaintance with Lewis. Bedford was Pound's lifelong friend and musical amanuensis, who arranged many of Pound's musical endeavors, including the *Five Troubadour Songs* of 1920 and his operas *Le Testament* (1921) and *Cavalcanti* (1932). When Lewis was beginning to go blind Bedford sometimes acted as his secretary, and after his death assisted Anne Lewis in arranging his papers (a herculean task for which Pound thought Bedford might be able to secure a Fulbright).[10] D. G. Bridson, the BBC writer and producer and close friend of Lewis, has spoken of the latter's friendship with Bedford:

> [She] was seeing a lot of Lewis when we [Bridson and Lewis] became friendly. That, of course, was shortly after he had gone blind—and she was helping him with his correspondence &c. She was a very kind and lovable person, and Lewis was much indebted to her for her goodwill and devotion over the years. I gathered from him that at one time there had been talk of his marrying her (in the late twenties) but he had decided against it, and married Anne W. L. instead. I think you may presume that there was a break between him and Agnes at that time—though whether it lasted until his departure for America in 1939, I don't know. I should not be surprised if it was not his going blind in 1950–51 which brought them together again. Anyhow, from then on they worked together a lot. Relations between her and Mrs. Lewis, for the most part, were very good. I attended Lewis's funeral with both of them. (Letter to Bryant Knox from D. G. Bridson, 8 March 1978)

Pound was soon writing to Bedford, regretting his lack of close contact with Lewis: "Had to leave Sodom [i.e., England and France] in the 1920s/ but possibly cd/ hv/ maintained closer connections. However, no retrospects/ its whaaar do we go frum here?" (5 May 1951). By the end of March 1951 Pound began to think of Bedford as an auxiliary force not only capable of inducing Lewis to read the authors he recommended, but of convincing him to set pen to paper in defence of cultural standards. "Nacherly," he wrote Bedford, "the quicker WL starts on certain 1951 ideas, the sooner the quicker" (5 May 1951).

The three letters that follow were written by a man whose struggle for the improvement of the intellectual and cultural milieu was waged from behind the walls of St. Elizabeths Hospital. From these confines Pound conducted a voluminous correspondence; established, with the aid of various editors, "Poundian" magazines and pamphlets; published poetry and prose; and contributed myriad articles and reviews to international journals and newspapers. His visitors included some of the twentieth century's most prominent poets and writers —T. S. Eliot, William Carlos Williams, George Santayana, e. e. cummings, Robert Lowell, Charles Olson, Conrad Aiken, Hugh Kenner, and Marianne Moore.[11] The letters here printed were written in March 1951 and were prompted by the arrival at St. Elizabeths of Lewis's *Rude Assignment*, possibly sent to Pound by Bedford.[12] Within a month he was asking Bedford if there was "ANY sign of WL taking in Ez VOLuminous notes on Rude Ass/ ?" (5 May 1951). By early July Pound still had not received a response from either Lewis or Bedford regarding these letters into which he had put so much effort: "Naturally difficult to direct W.L.'s thought to useful channels, or even find if yu hv/ read him the notes on Ru/ Asst/ and got any scintillas" (8 July 1951). Lewis apparently never did reply to Pound's comments.

Nevertheless, Pound continued to promote Lewis's work. He asked Bedford: "Cd/ Hutchinson, either at W.L.'s request, or otherwise be purrsuaded to send review copies ASSIGNMENT RUDE to a few continental critics? hand picked or Ezpikt or whatso" (30 March 1951). And in another letter: "SEE that a copy of W.L. 'Rude Assignment' gets to Verlag der Arche, Zurich..." (27 April 1951). Pound's promotion of Lewis's writings did not stop with *Rude Assignment* but continued as a campaign for the total corpus of Lewis's work. He wrote Bedford: "AIM to git WL/ to new generation that hasn't read him. Still want 'I presume [*America I Presume*]' back in print" (8 July 1951).

By 1953 Lewis was totally blind, a fact which Pound at times found difficult to accept. In many of his letters to Bedford he wrote snippets of verse or enclosed material for Lewis—these he would ask Bedford to read to him. But on one occasion he caught himself writing as if to the old Lewis and in a moment of poignant anger expressed the futility of the gesture: "Vide verso fer Wyndham, but yu may as well read it, as he gawdamnit cant" (26 August 1953). Yet despite Lewis's blindness Pound's indefatigable attempts to get him to bless or blast various causes and specific ideas continued; "must be some way for W.L. to knock off an article on the birth of intelligence in murkn university system. Git it in somewhere," he urged Bedford (28 May 1953).[13]

Many of Pound's comments on and recommendations for the improvement of *Rude Assignment* were probably extremely distasteful to Lewis. Indeed, the very nature of Pound's commentary would tend to compromise Lewis's artistic and philosophical credos.

The letters, for example, abound in references to Blackstone, Agassiz, Del Mar, Major C. H. Douglas, and others—men whom Pound recommends that Lewis read in order to write a "proper" autobiography. But were Lewis to accept Pound's entreaties, he would be practicing that for which he criticizes Pound—namely, the "creator-as-scholar" methodology.

When we consider some of Pound's specific remarks in the letters we see, again, that he and Lewis were often on opposite sides of the fence. In Letter One, for example, Pound intimates that Lewis might benefit from considering Major C. H. Douglas, the Social Credit economist, as a "sound" man, one of the "positives" recommended by Pound earlier in the same letter. Pound praised Douglas because he was the "first economist to include creative art and writing in an economic scheme, and the first to give the painter or sculptor or poet a definite reason for being interested in economics."[14] But in 1939 Lewis had expressed a contrary opinion, referring to Douglas as a "credit crank"[15]

Similarly, Lewis's praise of Roosevelt as the "arch-centraliser," whose methods, he says, brought him to "an understanding of the vanity of regional isolationism" (RA, 94), is strongly opposed by Pound (see Letter Three, where Pound condemns centralized governments for knowing little about local needs). Pound regarded Roosevelt, with his policy of centralization, as an enemy of civilization and made him the target of some of his most scathing vituperation.

Another issue on which they disagreed was Mussolini. Although both men had praised Fascism, Lewis's support of Hitler and the National Socialist Party, which he displayed in *Hitler* (1931), did not extend to Mussolini.[16] As late as 1952 Lewis scolded Pound for his "incomprehensible intervention in World War II (when in some moment of poetic frenzy he mistook the clownish Duce for Thomas Jefferson)."[17] Lewis had always regarded Italian Fascism as "political futurism" and unworthy of serious attention (see Wagner, p. 74).

The reader who picks up *Rude Assignment* in the hope that Lewis will disclose little-known facts regarding his life and work will be disappointed. To be sure, the book is an autobiography, and its subtitle, "A narrative of my career up-to-date," is certainly appropriate. But the intemperate "Rude" of the main title forecasts more than a rustic compilation of a lifetime's events. Foremost, *Rude Assignment* is the autobiography of a retaliatory personage; and the "art" of retaliation had no more exuberant a practitioner than Wyndham Lewis. When confronted with hostile criticism which he thought slandered his character or questioned his literary and artistic motives, Lewis would often adopt an aggressive manner. He would turn what a gentler writer might structure as a defense into a scathing offensive. As Lewis put it, "I have made it my habit never to go to law, but to shoot back when shot at" (RA, 52). *Rude Assignment*, written near the end of a lifetime which produced an incalculable number of defensive and retaliatory remarks, is Lewis's final effort to set the record straight:

> As everywhere else in the present work I have, in this part, one engrossing object: namely to meet and to destroy unjust, prejudiced, and tendentious criticism—past, present, and future. It is my object to dispel misconceptions (about myself, or about my work) whether they derive from ill-natured and tendentious criticism, or some other cause. (RA, 141)

Rude Assignment is Lewis's book of counter-polemic; and as Pound remarks in Letter One, it is certainly a "good clearing of cloacae."

Pound, however, really has little to say about Lewis's main thrust in *Rude Assignment*. He is often more concerned with airing his own prejudices than with responding to specific statements made by Lewis. In a sense, Pound is writing to himself—the letter as echo-chamber. The importance of the letters, then, lies more in what Pound has to say about himself than in any specific insights they provide into Lewis's life or thought. Letter One is particularly illuminating in this respect. Seventeen lines into the letter Pound begins to drift from Julien Benda, the topic at hand, into self-congratulation on his early noting of the "FLOP of froggery"; proceeds to defend the type of Fascism in which he believed; and continues with references to his own concerns: Juan Ramon Jimenez, Mussolini, and politically motivated distortion of news reports. Not until line 37 does Pound cite the passages of *Rude Assignment* about which he purportedly writes—and then he gets it wrong: "all this ref/ p. 54 and thaar abouts." But page 54 and thereabouts have no connection with Pound's remarks, and even when we guess he meant to type "34," the connection remains vague. What does emerge is that Pound wants Lewis to engage in the propagation of sound ideas, not merely in the destructive analysis that is all that Lewis's chapter VI offers.

Many of Pound's major statements and ideas in the letters concern matters which had preoccupied him for years: politics, economics, usury, Fascist ideology. Such subjects are typical of his concerns in the early fifties, and have been well documented by Pound scholars. The letters repeat well-worn ideas, yet the particular mode of expression is stimulating, and Pound's casual remarks often illuminate little-known areas of his thinking, or qualify in some way those already known. In the latter category, for example,

Pound's well known admiration for Ford Madox Ford materializes as a profound respect. His praise of Nietzsche's rhetoric in *Thus Spake Zarathustra*, the value he finds in Henry Morgenthau, Sr., and his condemnation of the Italian philosopher Benedetto Croce are all casual remarks yet constitute news for Poundians.

The following letters are presented in facsimile to preserve the unique flavor of Pound's actual typescripts. The editor's transcriptions are meant to facilitate reading and are in no sense presented as definitive. Emendations have been kept to a minimum: paragraphing and some spacing has been regularized, the corrections for a few obvious typing errors have been enclosed in brackets, and only the most unambiguous spelling errors have been corrected silently (otherwise spelling has been left as in the original).

The letters on *Rude Assignment* that are printed here are part of the Ezra Pound–Agnes Bedford collection held by Simon Fraser University Library, Burnaby B.C. The letters take Pound's commentary about halfway through *Rude Assignment*. Three further letters continuing Pound's commentary exist in the Cornell University Library. They appear in the Black Sparrow edition of *Rude Assignment* (1984).

I wish to thank the following people for their generous assistance in the various stages of this manuscript: Ralph Maud, Seamus Cooney, James Laughlin, D. G. Bridson, Percilla Groves, and Linda Knox. The letters herein are used under the auspices of Special Collections, Simon Fraser University Library, and with the permission of the Ezra Pound Literary Property Trust.

---

1. Noel Stock, *The Life of Ezra Pound* (New York: Pantheon Books, 1970), p. 158.
2. Hugh Kenner, *The Pound Era* (Berkeley: Univ. of California Press, 1971), p. 236.
3. William C. Wees, *Vorticism and the English Avant-Garde* (Toronto: Univ. of Toronto Press, 1972), p. 69. Pound was to use the concept in 1921 upon Joyce's completion of *Ulysses*—see Letter Two.
4. Wyndham Lewis, *Rude Assignment: A Narrative of My Career Up-to-Date* (London: Hutchinson, 1950), pp. 128-29. Subsequent references to this work are given parenthetically as RA followed by page numbers in the text and notes.
5. Ezra Pound, *The Selected Letters of Ezra Pound 1907–1941*, ed. D. D. Paige (New York: New Directions, 1971; first pub. 1951 as *The Letters of Ezra Pound*), p. 47. Paige includes most of Pound's prospectus on pp. 41-43n. Subsequent references will be made parenthetically to "Pound, *Letters*."
6. Geoffrey Wagner, *Wyndham Lewis: A Portrait of the Artist as the Enemy* (New Haven, Conn.: Yale Univ. Press, 1957), p. 15.
7. Wyndham Lewis, *Time and Western Man* (London: Chatto & Windus, 1927), p. 38. Subsequently cited as TWM.
8. Wyndham Lewis, *The Letters of Wyndham Lewis*, ed. W. K. Rose (Norfolk, Conn.: New Directions, 1963), p. 224. Subsequent references will be made parenthetically to "Lewis, *Letters*."
9. See Walter Michel, *Wyndham Lewis: Paintings and Drawings* (Toronto: McClelland & Stewart, 1971), Plate VII.
10. Ezra Pound, Letter to Agnes Bedford, 13 April 1957, Simon Fraser University Library, Burnaby, B.C. Subsequent references to the Pound-Bedford correspondence are cited by date parenthetically in the text.
11. For accounts of Pound's myriad activities and intellectual excitement and frustration during the St. Elizabeths years, see the St. Elizabeths issue of *Paideuma* (1974, 3:3); Catherine Seeyle, ed., *Charles Olson & Ezra Pound: An Encounter at St. Elizabeths* (New York: Grossman, 1975); Eustace Mullins, *This Difficult Individual, Ezra Pound* (New York: Fleet Publishing, 1961); and Louis Dudek, ed., *Dk/ Some Letters of Ezra Pound* (Montreal: DC Books, 1974).
12. At Pound's request Bedford had sent other things: "Wyndham did 2 books—lively, in 1940— *V.[ulgar] Streak* & '*America I presume*' —I want any others" (16 April 1946). Bedford kept sending material to Pound until Lewis's death in 1957.
13. And in other letters: "Whether he now haz leisure to KICK some sense into some of 'em [newspapers] I dunno / Agassiz and Blackstone need reBOOST" (7 April 1951); 'Sabotage of chinese studies alZO might interest W.L." (9 December 1952); "W.L. might take up theme of danger of world governed by chipmunks and prairie dogs" (27 February 1953); "W.L. meditate that Jefferson saw ALL debt not repayable in 19 years as tax without representation/ shoved onto unborn and minorenni" (27 February 1953).
14. Ezra Pound, *Selected Prose 1909–1965*, ed. William Cookson (New York: New Directions, 1973), p. 232.
15. Wyndham Lewis, *The Hitler Cult* (London: Dent, 1939), p. 26.
16. Wagner, pp. 73-74, cites Lewis's constant ridiculing of Mussolini in the late twenties and early thirties. Lewis later renounced his support of Hitler in *The Hitler Cult*.
17. Wyndham Lewis, *The Writer and the Absolute* (London: Methuen, 1952), p. 41.

EZRA POUND

LETTERS ON RUDE ASSIGNMENT

TRANSCRIPTION, NOTES AND FACSIMILE LETTERS

[LETTER ONE]

W.L.

ASSIGNMENT, hv/ impression it is best of yr/ theoretico-dogmatics. but not yet finished, and "theo-dog" may apply only to first part. Cert/ good clearing of cloacae/ interim notes as I read// too fatigued to wait, holding stuff in what's left of head/

Naow az swell az kicking them goddam punks/[1] wot about noting the few ideas that Ez has occasionally set down/ as Ez never did fall for any of them punks that got a great deal too much attention BEFORE W.L. fetched out his tardy insecticide. (Incidentally can't remember having translated Benda's "La Traison," but believe am first to mention or boost the dratted little negative (Dial time) and sent first copy of La Traison to London... BECAUSE of the desolation and lack of anything much better in Paris/[2]

credit fer noting the FLOP of froggery at fairly early date.

***wd/ be timely in view of PRESENT circs/ and Fascist lable to note the KIND of Fascismus Ez talked of (sticking to K'ung and Johnnie Adams, and providing a DAMsite better historic view than Toynbee[3] and NEVER falling fer the Fabian concrete mixer. ///

What about a W.L. analysis of the SOUND ideas, the positives during the past 40 years/ submerged by the crap/ and of course the crap DES CLERCS providing the Rothermeres[4] etc with the avalanche material which has damn well submerged/ most everything else. Note Jimenez title "Animal di Fondo" not exactly with this bearing, but not rotten.[5]

la mas triste palabra: habria podido ser... waal, wot bout picking up the IDEAS that WOULD have been useful if every time, let us say, purely fer example, Muss said he needed PEACE. fer the London Slimes[6] to report it as "WAR Speech"

or Ian Monro[7] saying he had to watch EVERY pair of words in his news, cause IF it wuz posbl/ they wd/ take out a phrase, twist the meaning and use it as headline. (all this ref/ p. 54 and thaaar abouts.)[8]

Also the TIMEliness of certain sentences in my Studio Integrale AT the date that trans/ of K'ung was printed in chink and wop bilingual. I spose I ought to have INSISTED more on that text/ but we were not in geographic vicinage in 1927 or whenever I got the first VERY poor version into print.[9]

Previously unpublished letters by Ezra Pound, Copyright© 1983 by the Trustees of the Ezra Pound Literary Property Trust; used by permission of New Directions Publishing Corp., agents. These letters are held in the Contemporary Literature Collection, the Library, Simon Fraser University.

Also look at the Analects/ if Hudson Rev/ hasn't sent it to you, I'll ax 'em to.[10]

O.K yu shd/ HAVE read all that crap, and got out the bug-powder, but what about reading a few serious authors? Blackstone, Agassiz, and especially Del Mar[11] (ask Swabe[12] for copies on loan, or see what is in the British Mouseum.) Alexander Del Mar, almost everything except the "Science of Mon"/ that was a bit off his beat.. and in the less competent part of his mind... bothered by mistranslation of Ari/ etc. I spose, incidentally, that Frobenius was the bloke Gaudier had been reading in the Bib / Nat /[13]

anyhow, time W.L. started looking for solid stuff. another distinction: what one CAN believe, vs all this crap, the curés deguisés[14] try to hoax people into thinking that *they* believe W.L. having at one time EATEN a lot of wind and dust, might have edged rancour over time wasted. Even the fat man,[15] with all his fuzz, had a few right lines/ too bad he never got to Doug/ who was good diagnostician, but not sufficiently anti-bugrocrat. Hence POST-gesellite ratiocination.[16]

Might say ENG PASSANG/ that ole Santayana gave ground on proposition: no philosophy in the occident since gorNoze when, only philo-epistemology.[17] K'ung's four *tuan*, [ideogram drawn in] superior to Aristotl (even before the disciples castrated him, but [by] removing *teXne* from his list. Drop from Nic/ Ethics, to Magna Moralia (which whalo-Morely didn't want to add to Kulch, saying wd/ do me no good at Cowslip (no, that is spelled Oxford.[18]

Incidentally it took a Chinee to look up the EXACT spot in Erigena where he plugs fer right reason as source of authority. wot we need is more COLLYboRation.

Important item in Meridiano d'Italia 11 Feb/ re Idea Luce per L'Europa.[19] dunno how to get copies of whole series. BUT sometime W.L. might reflect that woptalia was the ONLY place where one COULD print certain facts. Ole Meridiano di Roma stopped in U.S. post, for economic ideas.///[20] which is how close the MUZZLE wuz on is [in] Roosenpoops hellhole.

"The state is organized fear" that is anti-fascist. or at least anti M's "lo stato è lo spirito del popolo".[21] Certainly LESS fear in Rapallo over 25 year period than any where else, unless up in the Bunter's Persia.[22] or some such./ If I ever git another edtn/ of Pivot thru the press, kindly ref/ the two or three comments by the translator.[23]

esprits purs/ sorry yu missed (if yu did) Jo Adonis or Costello "whadda I wanna see iz th' guy that 'ud turn down $60,000."[24] **Ez gittin ready to KICK some of them az has sposed he never THOUGHT anything of interest, merely because he refrained from emitting general statements before he had collected enough specific data to know what a general statement might mean. finger (or nose) exercise: List some of the shysters (past and recent) whom Ez never did fall for. Including Neitsch (save fer rhetoric in Zar/a) Bergson, Sorel, Pascal.[25]

A lot of false dilemma in all this occidental crap. and Mencius met, I shd/ say, about ALL the main varieties of nit-wit, and classified 'em.

demur, re/ p. 41 Assignment/ suggest W.L. insert word "BEFORE 1914" (after 1917 at least there wd/ seem to hv/ been considerbl attention to war as product of economic stink, a designed activity.[26] Alex the Gt/ paid his soldiers debts, and died QUITE bloody dam soon after, less than six weeks if I remember rightly, from MYS(ehem)sterious causes.[27] Try the test cui bono BOTH to war and to that greatest of fakes Original sin. (the idea of org.s.) After all W.L's first sketch for first portrait of Ez/ was a Holbinian cine-star,[28] and W.L. cdn't stand it, tho he prob/ forgets the eggspesiion on his mug as he destroyed it (in fact how CD/ he hv/ knowd the eggspression as there warnt no wall mirror, and he cdn't hv/ held a pocket glass while operating on that delicate water colour.

ad interim
and strictly anonymous communique

prob/ more to follow
az I procede thru deh woik.

[LETTER TWO]

W.L.

FOR the Wreck-ord (re/ p 52) I recall Yeats re/ WL/ "PoWWnd'z evIL genius"/ both he and Orage trying to separate or save Ez/ [29] FORD never (let me say NEVER) made any such etc/ and, of course, no such KIND of machination could have entered his occiput. Orage argued on point of philosophic coherence/ and our opposite directions at the time. Fact that mind better be ALIVE than dead, didn't convince him.

What is "Cakes and Ale"?[30]

Shd/ think Joyce's mind was formed in Dublin/ unlikely to hv/ been influenced by Dung when so far thru Ulyss/ [31] Did J/ ever read any Whitehead/ ? Did yu evr hear him mention anyone but Dujardins, Vico, Svevo and Mr Dooley?[32] not that it matters a dam/ Book had to be PUT over, fer practical reason/ but cert/ I sd/ it was an END not a start/ P.S.U. after that FINISH/ period of rot, p.t.c what he may have absorbed later, when he READ nothing gornoze/ american slang via his children.[33]

Pity de Angulo hasn't left (so far as I kno) any orderly statement re Dung (spell it wiff a Y, milorrr)[34]

WL seems to hv/ lured the J/ into serious discussion of something.[35] Can't recall that I EVER did/ tho must have approached it at times/ prob/ because I never rose to his mention of names such as Vico orn [?or] Dujardin/ etc/ One up to Humb/ Woof.[36]

been trying to get a BR/ highly respected stud/t legal "philos" to do a condensed Blackstone/ [37] all the parts containing principles or necessary history/ blighter hedges/ or proGODDAMcrastinates mebbe WL could do it/ Ez simply not got physical force/

purpose of law: to prevent coercion either by force or by fraud.[38] fer garzache[39] start putting some of the essential concepts into circulation.

civilization NOT a one man job.

ef I cd/ purrsuade yu to give some serious attention to PIVOT . . . . not think of it as merely heathen chinoiserie.

mania for having so many laws that they cannot be executed without crushing taxation/ hiring cops to protect people from themselves.

wash up the puppytician// That detritus Em/ Ludwig at Hauptman's talking about LLard George.[40]

(parenthesis, ever read the elder Morgenthau's "Amb/ Morg's Story"?[41] very clever lubricator. also what he does NOT include. identical zones of ignorance in Leahy, MMe de Chambrun, Hull, and even Stilwell.[42]

Has WL/ ANY excuse for the existence of a smear like Croce??[43] on any grounds save that "gawd made him, having nothing else to do"? (o.k. Ez iz a emotional, or dont cheat his own nose.)

NOTE/ a faculty of the olfactory sense is that it does not have to come into direct contact with a thing, in order to discern certain properties of it. Thanks for them kind words re/ Plat and Heg. p. 62 feetnut.[44]

keep down the taxes and the central govt/ cannot become a goddamned nuissance BOTH at home and abroad.

for "credit"/ ref/ Ez/ necessary both trust AND mistrust.

had never thought about Low: a great and dirty criminal, tho possibly sincere in his ignorance.[45] P. 65. pp/1. O.K. first Confucian statement so far in WL.[46] (? or hv/ I missed one?) AND nobody but Orage ever seemed to twig wot Ez/ wuz at in 'Studies in Contemporary Mentality.' even tho Flaubert had started it.[47]

p. 65 pp/ 3 as sd/ Mencius.

J. Adams: "nothing more dangerous than preventing a war".[48]

GET a review copy to Eva Hesse, Munich-Schwabing, Bauerstr/ 19.iii probably most intelligent reviewer on the continent.[49] Do yu see 'Ecrits de Paris?' Also rev/ cop. to Camillo Pellizzi 12 via di Villa Albani. Roma and why not to D.D. Paige, casella 30, Rapallo. it wd/ also reach Gabriella Mistral via DDP/ as she is in Rap/[50]

weren't both Shaw and Wells stinking fabians? and Bennett (Arnold) a better mind? at least when he wrut Old Wives (french derivative but . . .) Did either Sh/ or Wl/ criticise fabianism, with ALL its filth? Pore ole Fordie did NOT swallow it, or milk Burrns and Oats.[51]

Neither did the bgrs/ S & W crit/ the REAL rulers, tho Dizzy had already pointed to them.[52]

Partisans both/ split minds, Shaw and Bertie Rsl[53] never having tied up to the missing halves.

mebbe Wells was split above the midriff/ horizontal not perpendic/ split??

Dont believe serfs had much or ANYthing to do with it. (p. 75 [*i.e.* 73]) Shaw and Wells-bellz merely of the rising, not of the slopping-down party. WL. might ref/ the Leopoldine Reforms mid xviii th.[54]

YU damn well measure the times yu are right against Mencius and the other 3 of the 4 Books.[55]

no it is NOT fascism/ it may be (p. 75 bottom) nazism or Berlinism, but it was neither theory nor fact in Italy. where Croce and that Cambridgified mutt Einaudi, esp/ the latter had a publishing house and nasty britified publications. just DUMB. but tolerated.[56]

fascism rising out of guild ideas, and of balances mixed economy etc/ etc/ and Farinacci very true in saying putt the 25 top gerarchs together and each one will be found with a different idea of [*deleted*: what fascism is] of the corporate state.[57]

and of course D. Low never disagreed with his owners. newspaper caricature per nesessita, the voice of a large herd, herded by the owners.

when a little squirt like Max DOES a caricature contra corrente it stays privately on Orage's wall.[58] which aint fer suppressin' Low but for giving someone a chance to talk back/ which they do NOT get in Shitain. (birds nest in the shrubbery on the dung-heap, or perhaps we shd/ say "once nested".)

Mr Orwell, a LOUSE. Neruda noticed this also. physically diseased (extenuation. . . .)[59]

turning backward to Fordie again. accepted him as delayed preraph/ son of bloke wot wrut on Troubs/[60] who had curious theatric letch to dress up as a tory WITH a large income. None of us ever had any mercy on the hang over from his earlier nerve brakdown or then had faintest understanding of what that meant.[61]

Pow-wowers (why didn' yu say it first?) yu can hv/ it.⁶² I aint in position to shoot it. Most of these observations are in past works, whence WL at lib/ to take 'em for any useful purpose. WITHOUT perusing sd/ scripts/ and wop-print.

The beastly Bullitt, by the bay, had, incidentally, been woke up but not disinfected by the spurloss verschwindet of 5 intimates some time before 1939. The perfect pus-sack.⁶³

Hv. yu read Col Murray's "At close quarters"?⁶⁴

Why dont yu send a copy of Rude to Alice?⁶⁵

> strictly anynonnymouse
> ad interim.

not obsession, but to keep it together/ re Fordie AGAIN/ in perspective/ measured against the successful fakers? some decent ideas are THERE in his books/ NOT out of date. in fact his politica vs/ Shw/ Wel/ Bertie/ and the goddam lotuvum before, contemporary or since?

cert/ much more intelligent than Joyce/ reach excede grasp

man too weak to FINISH certain jobs, but not so swinish as to pretend they dont exist.

[LETTER THREE]

W.L.

p. 92 IN-NO-Vation, me foot/ ⁶⁶ return to pre 1914 when passports only needed for sloughs such as Rhoosia and Turkey. post 1919, how many Ez letters to the Paris Tribune, denouncing the first step toward universal bondage/ well, not the first but a dirty one.⁶⁷ And COULD Ez/ get ANY highbrow support, or make people see ANY disuse in pissports, visas (at $10) and the bank-stoodge Woodie-cod-face)⁶⁸ also coin (same coins) good in Frog/ Baviere, Swiss, Ausstria and Woptalia. The eggstent to which the occident has rotted in 35 years vurry amazink.

Benda, forget in which rotten frog sheet/ must be six years ago saying: Yourup does not WANT to be united. [*deleted*: W.L. also note enc/ printed 4 points.]⁶⁹ Earl Godwin⁷⁰ / got to seeing Am/ inkum snoopers only one step from police state/ due to ROT of police, due to laws to prevent people being themselves. and inkum. ONLy mechanism left to govt/ to get taxes WITHOUT honest money system.

what yu can do is to stimulate COMMUNICATION between intelligent men in different places/ did the O.M.⁷¹ ever git over feeling that anything from E. of Suez is something out of a zoo?

World State no enemies?⁷² nuts/ And for why/ because a son of pig at 3000 miles remove knows less of what any local need is/ and gets more and more abstract with the distance/

Si quieren un goberno di usureros, por lo menos un gobierno di usureros Bolivianos, y no un gobierno di usureros internacionales.⁷³ yan a l'il realism, please, re the U.S.

or specify/ world state AFTER and without. senza/ power. IF Local control of local purchasing power cd/ be guaranteed against monopoly of the press by archswine.

WL didn't notice END of U.S. consterooshun on Dec 23/ 1913.⁷⁴ almost no news of the event leaked to europe, and not much to the yankoboobs?

Oh goRRRRd/ I didn't mean to mention F/ again, 'ow cd/ yu disturbe the ghost. YU hv/ spelled Madox wiff TWO DDs.

I dont mind. and he was indubitably born to suffer, that being his A.1. series A. corn.

P. 128/ pp/ 1 last line: AN' thaaar'z whaar yu're or were wrong. and mebbe hook up on the other end of W.B.Y's bumbusted Bhuddism "withering into".[75]

next pp/ and pp/ 3 O.K.

ov course it AIN'T "difficult to believe", fer anyone whose memory goes back that far. Yr/ eggspression re/ Gaudier was "the Lavery of sculpture",[76] all of which purity was highly stimulating to such of yr/ contemporaries as cd/ take it. (possibly not a very heavy force at the polls.) Gaudier re my mantelpiece glass box: "Museo für orientalsiche Kunst".[77] Ever looked at Pier della Francesca's De (something or other, probably Proportione) Pingendi?[78]

132/ well well, here is some real fascismo/[79] using the term not as pejorative, but simply in ref/ historic fact as to what DID happen and happen with considerable amelioration of product. IN ITALY.

and may add that the last dhirty Biennale I was inveighled into looking at showed the damned Hun pavillion as the decent one/ all other furrin exhibits a mess/ sub Brodsky etc. really diseased.[80] And be it said the wops pampered a lot of rats but what of it, the general level of technique improved and a considerable amount of sincere effort went into it on part of qualified non-painters who worked at the selection. Damn sight better than Bun-Pips and Omega am'mosphere.[81] The favoured did NOT appreciate, having had no eggsperience fuori d'ITalia,[82] and the omitted nacherly squealed, or mumbled. And a few efficient blokes with a market suffered not at all from the competition (stimulus). Results cert/ much better than in Frogland de nos jours/[83] crit/ shd/ observe chronology/ i.e. when one place rots and another sprouts.

Good deal in Vlaminck's: intelligence is internat/, stupidity, national and art is LOCAL.[84]

did I say that Marinetti asked my op/ re/ something on his wall about 5 ft by 7. Pointed out that yu cd/ shift various chunks from here to there, in short introduced subject of COMposition. His Eccellenza quite surprised, a new view of the subject not previously in his etc.

Yet he was useful. [added: &] Went, at advanced age, off to combat[85] like various other big pots. Got no credit, as his "friends" sd/ it was just fer advertisment. all'o'wich relates to the Kulchurl level.

coterie/state. QT': a membership card in this party does NOT confer literary and artistic genius on the holder. Doubt if marinetti was millionaire. Shd/ think Picabia must hv/ had nearly as much.[86] Yus, yus, a vurry useful work, or shd/ be if some of the points can be rammed into the bleating booblik.

133/ might NAME whom they wanted to keep poor.[87]

composer in worse box than the performer, tho latter a dog's life and few bones. almost closed to anyone not tough enough to be able to DO IT anywhere, any time, no matter what state of digestion or fatigue. Other problm the disproportion, enormous fees and prices at one end, and starvation for anything good that dont fit.[88]

can yu furnish connection with Ll. Wright? Hiler re/ Stewed EEl: "at any rate they give you walls."[89]

tears/ re Joyce in Penguin. or whatever. booHOO, only sold 200,000: can't make any money unless they sell 250,000?[90]

The nu Shitsman/ naturally wd/nt face a CIVILIZED country like Italy/ take example from incult mujik, where capital has been enthroned on the ruins of property.[91] of course the great bleeding is having nation pay rent on its own credit/ believe greece was paying 54% of its taxes to meet debt interest. a few millyum to governors and presidents of Cuba, is a mere flea bite.

p/ 137, minor error: Kibblewhite, not Heppelwhite. (I beleev)[92]

and woTTErbaht the MONETARY sense.?? birth notice of which possibly to be printed privately[93] and just fer a Wyndham studio, ½ hour meditation, consider Gesell/ the monthly tax on UNUSED and therefore not absolutely at the moment needed paper certificates of debt (i.e. of what is due the bearer).[94]

Anatole (i.e. Asiatic) France end of L'Isle des Ping/ quoted by Ez/ HAS WL really thought about it/[95] Chesterton said "yes, partly" when I asked if he stayed off it in order to keep in touch with his readers. Fordie got to agriculture and trade-routes.[96]

Suppressed books can't be copyright in this country? or were rights sold here also.?[97]

The "Hitler" prob/ only unbias'd account of THAT period[98] Hv/ recd/ 40 pages of a Tirolese diary, possibly only fair account of THAT recent scene early 1940s.[99]

wonder if any use in speculation re/ dicotomy: WL conditioned by being riz in the rotting/ Poss O.M. choosing the sinking, and Ez sticking to the rising (however Holly-Luced crass and etc/)[100] but with some clean sprouts in the middan. waaawkk, 'ear deh eagul sccream.

on the other hand wasn't that Webb-itch, england's winding sheet, partly murkn??[101]

142. yes Ottoman, vid Ambas/ Morgenthau's story. toward the end.[102]

*** p. 143/ objective truth/ / mayn't yu hv/ to include this in action? Doubt if yr/ total exclusion of "truth" from action is a happy phrase, even if yu were driving AT something needing illustration.[103] Gourmont, L'Homme Moyen S/, Veneson. anti-pink. antag/ O.K. mr cummungs uses the phrase "canaille litteraire"/ probably this INCLUDES the dam lot, lables or no lables.[104]

Malraux is no damgood??[105] (this is a queery, not an assertion, but shd/ hardly expect good chick from bad egg, . . again queery?

The clear definition of ANY pt/ of view is useful TO them az is capable of defining a pt/ of view.

p 145/ oh the GAWDDDam hrooshunz, always a bore, and now a universal pestilence.[106] Czar's aunt (and Mr Proust. damn the pair of 'em.)[107] Can't at moment recall frogs *talking* of women. wonder if it was all *printed* in the old 1 fr/ edtns?[108]

curious that Rebecca cd/ be so perceptive[109] (then, at least,) and NOT be better.) or get better.

surely Max Ernst was the fount/ or do yu take him as grandad of Dada not of sur-real.[110] clue in v. early study of NATURAL forms. WL ever read any Agassiz (esp/ re/ Classifications?) 25 years ago Max must hv/ painted better than Dali (less commercial acumen.) Did the novel end with Ernst' "Femme aux cent tetes"?[111] vurry interestin' in nanny case.

1. In chapter VI of *Rude Assignment* Lewis attacks (among others) Barrès, Bloy, Maurras, Péguy, and Sorel as intellectuals who venerate action and militarism above reflection and reason.

2. Pound did not translate Benda's *La trahison des clercs*, nor did Lewis suggest he had done so. Pound's "boost" was a review he wrote of Benda's *Belphegor* (1919) for *The Atheneum* (9 July 1920, p. 62). *Belphegor* was later serialized, probably on his recommendation as Paris editor, in *The Dial*, Sept.–Oct. 1920.

3. "The heritage of Jefferson, Quincy Adams, old John Adams, Jackson, Van Buren, is HERE, NOW *in the Italian peninsula*" (*Jefferson and/or Mussolini* New York: Liveright, 1933 [1970 reprint, p. 12]). In a letter to Bedford (14 October 1954), Pound complains of Toynbee's parochialism and remarks that "he ignores the whole of the Orient."

4. Lord Northcliffe and his brother Lord Rothermere, owners of England's largest chain of newspapers, including the conservative *Daily Mail* and the popular *Evening News*.

5. Juan Ramon Jimenez (1881–1958), Spanish poet and Nobel laureate in 1956, whose book of poems, *Animal de Fondo* (1949), Pound refers to in Canto 90. The Spanish phrase means "The saddest saying: it might have been...."

6. I.e. the London *Times*, then the organ of establishment views.

7. Ion S. Munro, Scottish journalist, Rome correspondent for the *Morning Post*, and author of a number of books on Italy, including *Through Fascism to World Power: A History of the Revolution in Italy* (1933).

8. The progression and context of Pound's letter would suggest that p. 34 is meant.

9. *Studio Integrale* (Rapallo, 1942) is the Italian translation by Pound and Albert Luchini, with facing Chinese text, of Kung's *The Great Digest*. Pound's "first VERY poor version" was published in Seattle in 1928.

10. Pound's translation of the *Confucian Analects* appeared in the *Hudson Review*, 3 (Spring and Summer 1950): 9-52 and 237-87.

11. The Pound-instigated Square Dollar Series, run by T. D. Horton and John Kaspar, published *Gists from Agassiz* and Del Mar's *Barbara Villiers or A History of Monetary Crimes* in Washington, D.C. in the early 1950s. A volume of Blackstone was projected but never appeared.

12. Rev. Henry Swabey, a long-time correspondent of Pound's and a friend of Lewis's.

13. Henri Gaudier-Brzeska, the French-born sculptor and Pound's close friend and Vorticist colleague from 1913 till his death in 1915, frequented the Bibliothèque Nationale in Paris before he moved to London in 1910. In 1953 Pound recollected that it might have been Gaudier who first told him of Leo Frobenius, the German anthropologist. (See Guy Davenport, "Pound and Frobenius" in *Motive and Method in the Cantos of Ezra Pound* [New York: Columbia Univ. Press, 1969].)

14. (French) disguised curates. Cp. "'Un curé déguisé' sd/ Cocteau's [*sc.* housekeeper] of Maritain" (Canto 77).

15. An affectionate reference to Ford Madox Ford.

16. "Doug" is Major C. H. Douglas, the originator of Social Credit, which Pound advocated as the only sane economic system. (See Kenner's *The Pound Era* for further details.) Silvio Gesell, German economist, was the inventor of "stamp scrip," a device intended to insure the circulation, not the hoarding, of currency.

17. Pound put the proposition to the American philosopher George Santayana in a letter of December 1949. Santayana replied, "That is true of English and even in part of German speculation, but not of the traditional philosophy which has never died out, in the Church and in many individuals" (*Letters of Santayana*, ed. Daniel Cory [New York: Scribner's, 1955], p. 393).

18. Kung's "four tuan" are the four fundamental principles of Confucianism—love, duty, propriety, wisdom. (Thomas Grieve, "The Seraphin Couvreur Sources of Rock-Drill," *Paideuma* 4 [1975]: 400). In a 1952 addendum to his *Guide to Kulchur*, Pound writes of its first edition:

> While "Kulch" was still in the press E.P. noticed that "before pore Ari was cold in his grave" the compilers of the so-called "Magna Moralia" had already omitted TEXNE ["skill in art, in making things"—*Guide to Kulchur* (New York: New Directions, 1968), p. 327] from the list of mental faculties given in the Nichomachean Ethics. E.P. wished to include this observation but a member of the British firm of Faber thought "it would do him no good at Oxford."

The Faber director referred to was F. V. Morely whom Pound dubs "whalo" because of Morely's habit in the thirties of signing on with whalers for his summer holidays (letter to Bryant Knox from D. G. Bridson, 1 Oct. 1980).

19. Unidentified.

20. The Fascist daily to which Pound contributed many articles from 1939 to 1943.

21. Cf. Lewis's summary of the views of Edouard Berth: "A State is... a society organized for war" (*RA*, 35). The Italian means "The state is the spirit of the people."

22. Basil Bunting lived for a while in Rapallo in the early thirties where he first began studying Persian. He continued his researches into Persian poetry and folklore while in Iran during the Second World War.

23. Ezra Pound, trans., *Confucius: The Unwobbling Pivot & The Great Digest* (Norfolk, Conn.: New Directions, 1947). Pound's comments can be found on p. 95 of the 1969 New Directions edition *Confucius: The Great Digest: The Unwobbling Pivot: The Analects*.

24. Lewis quotes Berth's attack on democracy as "anti-traditional, anti-physical,... anti-realist, idealist: it will only recognise *des esprits purs* [pure spirits], a detachment from all historic and natural links... (*RA*, 35).

Jo Adonis is an alias of Jo Doto, the gambling syndicate boss indicted in 1951. Frank Costello was dubbed "the boss of the New York underworld." When in 1946 the State Harness Racing Commission threatened to close the Roosevelt Raceway on Long Island because of bookmaking operations, the Raceway's head, George Levy, paid Costello $60,000 to "take care of" the Commission's complaints. Asked by a Senate Committee if that wasn't a little like "taking candy from a baby," Costello replied, "I want to meet the man that would turn down $60,000" (*New York Times*, 18 March 1951, Sec. IV, pp. 1-2E).

25. All discussed by Lewis. *Zar/a* is Nietzsche's *Thus Spake Zarathustra*.

26. Pound is taking exception to Lewis's remark: "For none of these three writers of remarkable genius [Eliot, Joyce, Pound]... was war a question that ever particularly exercised their minds, I believe I am right in saying." Elsewhere, for example in his biographical sketch for the New Directions *Selected Poems* (1949), Pound insists that his thoughts were turned to economics and the causes of war as early as 1918.

27. Pound regarded the empire of Alexander the Great as a primary achievement of Western civilization (*Guide to Kulchur*, 229). *Cui bono* (Latin): who benefits?

28. Probably a sketch for the portrait (now lost) exhibited at the Goupil Gallery in 1919. (See Michel, plate 45.)

29. Lewis (*RA*, 51-52) says that W. B. Yeats "showed much appreciation" for his satire but "told me that I would be *stopped*, for in England that was what had always happened." A. R. Orage, editor of *The New Age* from 1908 to 1922, tried to "save Ez" from Lewis's philosophical influence: "[Lewis] is for Vorticism; I am for idealization of the actual. It is worth quarrelling about" (Wallace Martin, *"The New Age" Under Orage* [New York: Barnes & Noble, 1967], p. 247).

30. Somerset Maugham's novel (1936), which Lewis called "a little masterpiece" (*RA*, 52).

31. Lewis quotes (*RA*, 55-56) from Harry Levin's *James Joyce* (1941) a passage about the influence on Joyce of the analytical psychologist Carl Jung, whose movement had its headquarters in Zurich during the years Joyce was writing *Ulysses* there.

32. All names familiar to Joyce students, except possibly "Mr. Dooley," a comic Irishman created by the American humorist

Finley Peter Dunne.

33. In the Spring 1922 issue of *The Little Review*, Pound marked "the end of the Christian era" and proclaimed the birth of a new pagan period, "YEAR 1 p.s.U" (post scriptum *Ulysses*, presumably). Pound had little regard, however, for Joyce's later writings. "P.t.c" is unexplained. [Perhaps it stands for *post tempore Christi*, after the Christian era.—*Ed*.]

34. Jaime de Angulo, physician, anthropologist, and writer, was a keen student of Jungian analytical psychology. For his contact with Pound see Raymond L. Neinstein, Letter, *Paideuma* 5 (1976): 499.

35. Alluding to Lewis's exchange with Joyce about the aesthetics of Rouen cathedral (*RA*, 56). Joyce enjoyed its "multiplication of detail," adding that he did "something of that sort" in words.

36. Lewis quotes Humbert Wolfe (*RA*, 56) as telling him "I *admire* what you write. I do not like it."

37. Sir William Blackstone's *Commentaries on the Laws of England* (1765–69), commended as a cultural "sextant" in *Guide to Kulchur*.

38. "Huntington Cairns did an article fifteen years ago in the *Michigan Law Review* and he said Blackstone was of interest and if you read Blackstone you'd get an idea that the real aim of law is 'to prevent coercion either by force or by fraud'" (Pound, quoted by D. G. Bridson in *New Directions 17* [New York, 1961], p. 174).

39. For God's sake.

40. Gerhart Hauptmann, the German dramatist, spent several months a year in Rapallo. It was probably at a gathering in his home that Pound heard Emil Ludwig, the prolific popular historian, talking about Lloyd George.

41. Henry Morgenthau, American ambassador to Turkey under Woodrow Wilson, wrote his recollections of the post in *Ambassador Morgenthau's Story* (Toronto: McClelland, Goodchild & Stewart, 1918).

42. Pound has been reading four sets of memoirs: (1) *I Was There* (New York: Whitlesey House, 1950) by Admiral William Leahy, Roosevelt's Chief of Staff and ambassador to Vichy France; (2) *The Making of Nicholas Longworth: Annals of an American Family* (New York: Long & Smith, 1933) by Clara Longworth Comtesse de Chambrun, whose husband was French ambassador to Rome from 1933 to 1936; (3) *The Memoirs of Cordell Hull* (New York: Macmillan, 1948), Secretary of State from 1933 to 1944; and (4) the *Stilwell Papers* (New York: Sloane, 1948) of General Joseph Warren Stilwell, Chiang Kai-shek's Chief of Staff and commander of U.S. troops in China and Burma, 1942.

43. Benedetto Croce, the Italian philosopher, historian, and literary critic, was a member of the Italian Liberal Party and an opponent of Fascism. Lewis (*RA*, 61-62) cites an excerpt from Croce's *Politics and Morals* (London: George Allen & Unwin, 1946).

44. The footnote in question (*RA*, 62) reads as follows: "For many eminent thinkers the State is of course everything—in Hegel's system it is a metaphysical absolute, conditioning the individual. Plato was by far the most illustrious exponent of this barbarous doctrine. Such a type of thinking is that of men in love with Power—Hegel, the slave of the idea of the Prussian State, Plato an unusually embittered member of the Athenian aristocracy."

45. A cartoon by David Low of the *Evening Standard* appears in *RA* following p. 64. It shows Mussolini politely asking Chamberlain for a match to light a bomb he had just hidden under Chamberlain's chair.

46. In paragraph 1 of p. 65 Lewis speaks of his having come to recognize that "government and force are commutative terms, that *all* government reeks of force" and of his now appreciating "what is good, without being painfully disturbed by what I regard as bad.... The amount and quality of the good is the main thing: of badness no State has a monopoly."

47. Lewis writes (*RA*, 65), "I cannot understand the indifference of people to what happens to the inhabitants of England." In *Selected Prose* (p. 332) Pound remarks: "Moral filth, in print, poisons the reader; intellectual filth can be toxic to a whole race.... Flaubert published his *sottisier*. But half a century later the study of what was actually printed and offered for sale on the bookstalls was considered eccentric on the part of the present writer. I made an analysis in eighteen numbers of *The New Age* ["Studies in Contemporary Mentality," 16 Aug. 1917–10 Jan. 1918], but no publisher wanted to reprint the series...."

48. Lewis writes, in paragraph 3, p. 65, "If you see a man about to step over a precipice you warn him of the danger, if there is still time." He goes on to add, speaking of his activities in the years between the World Wars, "I am one of those persons who, hearing the war-drums beating in a hysterical crescendo, seeing his tribe working itself up into its customary delirium, would violently intervene, shouting *Count Your Dead—they are Alive!* Such a man would be very lucky not to be cut down by the frenzied warriors."

49. Now an internationally known Pound scholar.

50. Pellizzi, president of the Fascist Institute of Culture, was a friend of Pound's for some twenty years (see Charles Norman, *Ezra Pound* [New York: Minerva Press, 1969], p. 387). Paige edited Pound's *Selected Letters* (1951). Gabriella Mistral won the Nobel Prize for Literature in 1945.

51. Lewis had mentioned Shaw and Wells as representative of social critics "belonging as a rule to no Party"; Pound reminds him they were Fabian socialists. Arnold Bennett, author of *The Old Wives' Tale* (1908), criticized Fabianism under the pen-name Jacob Tonson in the pages of *The New Age*. Burns and Oates Ltd. is the London Catholic publishing firm.

52. Benjamin Disraeli (Prime Minister from 1874 to 1880), whose political novels *Coningsby* (1844), *Sybil* (1845), and *Tancred* (1847) had diagnosed "the condition of England" and denounced those responsible for the rise of the national debt.

53. Bertrand Russell, philosopher and left-wing social activist.

54. Lewis writes "had the Tsars suppressed Count Tolstoy and all those who with considerable impunity criticised the regime and petted the serfs, that might have been better for *them*. It would have been less good for *us*:"—since we would not have had Russian nineteenth literature.

Leopold II (1747–1792), grand duke of Tuscany from 1765 to 1790, effected reforms in economics, land laws, and ecclesiastical jurisdiction and generally augmented the cultural level of Tuscany.

55. That is, *The Book of Mencius* and the three Confucian books, *The Great Digest, The Unwobbling Pivot*, and *The Analects*.

56. Lewis had applied the label "fascism" to totalitarian control of critical thought and expression. Luigi Einaudi, later to become president of Republican Italy, published anti-Fascist periodicals such as his *Rivista di storia economica* (Turin), which the Fascist regime tolerated (see Charles F. Delzell, *Mussolini's Enemies* [Princeton: Princeton Univ. Press, 1961], p. 96).

57. Roberto Farinacci was Secretary of the Fascist Party in 1925 and Minister of State in 1938. "Gerarchs" are top officials of the Fascist Party.

58. Max Beerbohm did a number of drawings for *The New Age*. *Contra corrente* (Italian): against the current.

59. Chapter XV, "Libel and the Game of Libelling," gives Lewis's indignant retort to a remark of Orwell's in one of his London Letters to *Partisan Review* (Summer 1946). Orwell wrote that he was "credibly informed" that Lewis had become a Communist and was "writing a book in praise of Stalin to balance his previous books in favour of Hitler." Orwell had contracted tuberculosis in 1938. The Communist Chilean poet Pablo Neruda was a political enemy of Orwell's, but his comment has not been located.

60. Ford's father, Francis Hueffer, wrote *The Troubadours: A History of Provençal Life and Literature in the Middle Ages* (London: Chatto & Windus, 1878). "Preraph" = Pre-Raphaelite.

61. Ford suffered a breakdown in 1916 when a shell exploded next to him.

62. Lewis's Chapter XVI discusses Four-Power meetings in the post-war world; Pound offers his pun.

63. Lewis derides (*RA*, 85f.) the belated awakening of many public figures in the West to the true totalitarian nature of the wartime

171

Soviet ally. Among them he mentions the former U.S. ambassador to the Soviet Union, William C. Bullitt. *Spurloss verschwindet* (German, properly *verschwinden*): disappearance without trace.

64. Arthur Cecil Murray (Lord Ellibank), *At Close Quarters* (London: John Murray, 1946), a work illuminating the close associations that existed for war-making purposes between the heads of the British and American governments during the First World War.

65. Alice Roosevelt Longworth, daughter of Teddy Roosevelt and wife of Nicholas Longworth (see note 42 above). Pound "wanted to get through to her," feeling she had political power (letter to Bryant Knox from James Laughlin, 30 January 1979).

66. Lewis wrote (*RA*, 92), "It is worthy of note that the present British Government is attempting to obtain the consent of other governments to the abolition of visas: this would be a great liberal innovation."

67. Thirteen such letters (February 1921 to September 1930) are listed in the Gallup *Bibliography*, section C (Donald Gallup, *Ezra Pound: A Bibliography* [Charlottesville: The University Press of Virginia, 1983]).

68. Woodrow Wilson, President of the U.S. from 1913 to 1921, whose 1913 banking and tariff reforms were responsible for the Federal Reserve Act, which Pound denounces later in this letter.

69. Pound's enclosure (if any) is not found in this correspondence.

70. White House correspondent for the *Washington Times* in the thirties and forties.

71. T. S. Eliot, who received the Order of Merit from King George VI in 1948.

72. "The idea of a World State has no open enemies, that I know of" (*RA*, 94).

73. (Spanish): If you want a government of usurers, at least let them be Bolivian [i.e., local] usurers rather than international usurers (source unknown).

74. On December 23, 1913, the U.S. Federal Reserve System was created and all national banks were compelled to join. The United States, rather than issuing its own money, now had to borrow from the Reserve Bank and pay interest—provided from tax money—on the loan. This, Pound maintained, was a direct infringement of the Constitution, which stipulated that "The Congress shall have power . . . to coin Money [and] regulate the Value thereof" (see Pound, *Impact: Essays on Ignorance and the Decline of American Civilization*, ed. Noel Stock [Chicago: Henry Regnery, 1960], p. 51).

75. The paragraph concludes: "And where I am saying that in the midst of war 'serious interpretation' is not possible, I have a good saying—expressing something that is echoed everywhere in what I have written, at all periods. It is: 'Truth has no place in action.'" Pound had written in 1937 that "A 'movement' or an institution lives while it searches for truth. It dies with its own curiosity. *Vide* the death of Moslem civilization. *Vide* the very rapid withering of Marxist determinism. Yeats burbles when he talks of 'withering into the truth' ["The Coming of Wisdom with Time" (1910)]. You wither into non-curiosity" (*Selected Letters*, p. 76). In a letter which Lewis quotes on the previous page of *RA*, Yeats assigns a certain "feeling, almost Buddhist," to Lewis's novel *Tarr* (1918).

76. "At this distance it is difficult to believe, but I thought of the inclusion of poems by Pound etc. in 'Blast' as compromising. I wanted a battering ram that was all of one metal. A good deal of what got in seemed to me soft and highly impure" (*RA*, 128-29). In the previous paragraph Lewis wrote of feeling that Gaudier was "a good man on the soft side, essentially a man of tradition—not 'one of Us.'" Sir John Lavery was a British portrait painter and member of the Royal Academy.

77. (German): Museum of Oriental Art. The "glass box" is unidentified.

78. Pound's query is sparked by Lewis's comments (*RA*, 129-30) on the nature and style of his paintings. "Vorticism," Pound remarked to Donald Hall, "as distinct from cubism, was an attempt to revive the sense of form—the form you had in Piero della Francesca's *De Prospettive Pingendi*, his treatise on the proportions and compo-

sition" (Interview in *Writers at Work*, 2nd series [New York: Viking, 1965], p. 44).

79. Lewis writes (*RA*, 131-32) that the artist in England is a "craftsman who has been largely superseded by the machine." But as for remedies, "not today but long ago, the State should have stepped in. It is not our place to organise private relief: that is the function of the State. . . . "

80. Pound praised the German pavilion at the Venice Biennale in a 1942 radio broadcast (see Leonard Doob, ed., *"Ezra Pound Speaking": Radio Speeches of World War II* [Westport, Conn. and London: Greenwood Press, 1978] p. 194). Horace Brodzky was a London-based Australian painter whom Pound regarded as an "ambiable bore with some talent" (Reid, *The Man from New York* [New York, 1968], p. 248).

81. The Omega Workshop was created by the Bloomsbury critic and painter Roger Fry. Lewis joined the group in 1912 but left within two years to found the Rebel Art Centre. He asserts that Fry's workshop created an "economic atmosphere" in which only "a favoured few could survive" (*RA*, 131).

82. (Italian): outside of Italy.

83. I.e., contemporary France.

84. Pound more than once quotes this epigram of Maurice Vlaminck, the French Fauve painter and disciple of Cézanne.

85. Pound met Marinetti, the founder of Italian Futurism, on a number of occasions and, like Lewis—who attacks Marinetti's "anti-passeisme, and dynamism" (*RA*, 129)—grew opposed to his principles. Marinetti fought on the Russian front in his late sixties.

86. A propos of Lewis's "The coterie is—like the sovereign state—exclusive and competitive. It claims for its proteges often a position they do not merit . . . " (*RA*, 132). Lewis cites Marinetti's alleged wealth in connection with the fruits of coterie mutual publicity. Pound's quote (QT) is from Mussolini and is found also in *Jefferson and/or Mussolini*, p. 76. On Picabia, see Andrew Clearfield, "Pound, Paris, and Dada," *Paideuma*, 7 (1978): 113-40.

87. Attacking the public's unwillingness to support art, Lewis writes that "I have even heard them say 'keep him poor'! about an eminent contemporary, on the grounds that that was a guarantee of good work . . . " (*RA*, 133).

88. On p. 134 Lewis has regretted that he was not familiar enough with the world of music to include it in his survey of the economic conditions of the arts. Pound is filling the gap.

89. Lewis writes (*RA*, 134) that even "Lloyd Wright, the most famous architect not only in America but probably in the world, far from being a busy builder of houses has for years had comparatively little to do, except instruct others in his school, who can scarcely expect to be busier than he has been." Hilaire Hiler was a painter and London friend of Pound's. "Stewed EEl" is no doubt the Rooseveltian New Deal.

90. Prompted by Lewis's remark (*RA*, 134) that literature has "suffered fearfully" as a result of "mass-production of books and the decay of values attendant upon modern publicity techniques." Joyce had not in fact been published in Penguin Books at this date.

91. Lewis (*RA*, 135) quotes V. S. Pritchett in the *New Statesman* on the dangers of State support of literature in Russia: "State censorship is a danger, but not the greatest danger: the modern State does not censor, it directs. And State direction, like paid publicity, is fatal." Pound implies that Fascist Italy would provide a better model than the land of the "incult mujik" or uncultivated Russian peasant.

92. Pound is accurate in his correction. Mrs. Kibblewhite's home was the meeting place of a circle including Pound, Lewis, Gaudier, Aldington, Herbert, Read, and Hulme. (See William C. Wees, *Vorticism and the English Avant-Garde* [Toronto: Univ. of Toronto Press], 1972, p. 44.)

93. Lewis's Chapter XXV is entitled "The Birth of a Political Sense." Pound may have in mind one of the Del Mar monographs which T. D. Horton (note 11) was about to publish.

94. This is the stamp scrip referred to in note 16 above, "requiring the bearer to affix a stamp worth up to 1 per cent of its face value fon the first day of every month. Unless the note carries its proper complement of monthly stamps it is not valid. This is a form of tax on money... and provides a medium and measure of exchange which cannot be hoarded with impunity" (Pound, *Selected Prose*, 295-96).

95. Lewis writes (*RA*, 138): "On the battlefields of France and Flanders I became curious, too, about how and why these bloodbaths occurred—the political mechanics of war. I acquired a knowledge of some of the intricacies of the power-game, and the usurious economics associated with war-making." The passage from Anatole France's *Penguin Island*, trans. A. W. Evans (London: John Lane, 1909) was quoted by Pound in "America and the Second World War" (1944; see *Impact*, pp. 184-96) and prefaced with the remark that "even before the previous war, Anatole France, in *L'Ile des Pingouins*, ironically informed his readers of the workings of commercial wars." The passage runs:

> "Certainly," replied the interpreter, "there are industrial wars. Nations without commerce and industry have no reason to go to war, but commercial nations are forced to adopt a policy of conquest. Our wars, must, of necessity, increase in number as our industrial activity increases. When one of our industries fails to find an outlet for its products, we must have a war to open up new markets. This year, in fact, we have had a coal war, a copper war, and a cotton war. In Third Zealand we have massacred two thirds of the natives to force the remainder to buy umbrellas and braces."

96. Pound is referring to Ford's *The Great Trade Route* (New York: Oxford Univ. Press, 1937).

97. "Three of [my] books were suppressed—one was even smothered during its birth, before it actually saw the light, although printed and bound and already a book. The true story of these suppressions would be worth telling" (*RA*, 139). Lewis is referring to *Doom of Youth* (1932), *Filibusters in Barbary* (1932), and *The Roaring Queen* (1935); for details of the suppressions see Bradford Morrow and Bernard Lafourcade, *A Bibliography of the Writings of Wyndham Lewis* (Santa Barbara: Black Sparrow, 1978), pp. 65-67.

98. Pound is referring to Lewis's *Hitler* (London: Chatto & Windus, 1931), written, says Lewis (*RA*, 78), "when he first appeared on the scene... before he came to power and revealed what a lunatic he was.... [It] was 'in favour': though that was not the Nazi's view of the matter...." Lewis's later *The Hitler Cult* (London: Dent, 1939) had not yet been read by Pound.

99. The diary is that of his daughter Mary de Rachewiltz, who lived in the Italian Tyrol during the war (letter to Bryant Knox from D. G. Bridson, 1 October 1980). See her autobiography *Discretions* (Boston: Little, Brown, 1971).

100. The "rotting" is the Notting Hill area of London, where Lewis grew up and lived most of his life. (Pound called it "Rotting Hill" and Lewis used this title for his novel of 1951 about the cultural and political decay of England.) The "sinking" is also England, chosen by the Possum, T. S. Eliot. Pound himself chose the "rising"—presumably *not* Fascist Italy (where, despite his admiration, Pound kept American citizenship and never acknowledged that he had withdrawn allegiance from his homeland) but the United States, despite its corruptions by journalism (Henry Luce, publisher of *Time* and *Life*) and Hollywood. Hence the "eagle" of the next sentence. Lewis had remarked that "Our politics share with the Hollywood cinema industry a cynical mass-technique: they cater for the extra-silly" (*RA*, 142).

101. Beatrice Webb, wife of the Fabian Sidney Webb, was American born. Lewis mentions her fleetingly (*RA*, 141). Pound is referring to Blake's lines from "Auguries of Innocence":

> The harlot's cry from street to street
> Shall weave old England's winding sheet.

102. Lewis writes (*RA*, 142): "The fellow travelling intellectuals, comprising a solid majority, who put me under a curse—because I spoke of communism as practised by the bolsheviks as inhumane and too like the jesuit or ottoman disciplines—these partisans who have controlled the literary world for a quarter of a century would not have gained acceptance for their crypto-communism in the West without a liberal flavouring of christian morality." The end of *Ambassador's Morgenthau's Story* (see note 41 above) is devoted to a condemnation of the Turkish (Ottoman) Empire's persecution of its subject people, especially the Armenians and Greeks.

103. Of the "crypto-communists" and fellow-travellers who are now "repainting themselves some other colour than the old sentimental pink," Lewis writes (*RA*, 143): "these people are all too deeply committed ever to change anything but their labels. They are not interested, it must be remembered in an objective truth: they inhabit a verbal world of labels and slogans. However they may modify the terms of their political ritual, or I may in the future modify my views in detail, the antagonism must remain, even if for the moment our policies happened to be identical."

104. A dense tissue of allusions, generally sympathizing with Lewis's remarks about his "pink" enemies. Remy de Gourmont was for Pound "a great man of letters" and a source of intellectual clarity (see Richard Sieburth, *Instigations: Ezra Pound and Remy De Gourmont* [Cambridge, Mass.: Harvard Univ. Press, 1978]). For Pound's satirical poems "L'Homme Moyen Sensuel" and the "Poems of Alfred Venison," see *Personae* (New York: New Directions, 1971). The cummings remark—"literary rabble"—is probably quoted from conversation.

105. Lewis (*RA*, 143) scoffs at his opponents as time-bound: "For *time* for them is still and always the reality: and a thing that is true today was not necessarily true yesterday." He cites André Malraux, the French novelist, art historian, and politician, as defending "his recent change from communism to Gaullism" with the remark, "It is not I who have evolved, but events."

106. Lewis (*RA*, 144-48) devotes several paragraphs to extolling the "great novelists of Tsarist days" in whose "world" he lived while in Paris, reading all their books in French translation.

107. To show how much of "an arch counter-revolutionary" Dostoevsky was, Lewis cites (*RA*, 147) from his letters "that he thought of postponing a journey owing to the news, which had greatly upset him, of the death of the Tsar's aunt." Proust (not mentioned here by Lewis) is associated in Pound's mind as "an insignificant snob, with no deep curiosity as to the working of modern society, apart from his own career in it" (*Selected Prose*, p. 272).

108. Lewis mentions the observation made by Ivan Karamazov that young men in Russian taverns discuss "Nothing but universal problems...." He adds, "And what do young Frenchman discuss? Undoubtedly women..." (*RA*, 147). Pound may be speculating that instead of *talking* about women, the French *printed* all their talk in cheap books (old one-franc editions).

109. Lewis cites the perceptive comment of Rebecca West (novelist and critic who contributed to BLAST 1) on the similarity of Otto Kreisler in his *Tarr* to Stavrogin in *The Possessed*, adding that she "was by far the best book-critic at that time" (*RA*, 148).

110. Pound is demurring from Lewis's remark that Dali and Chirico are the "two main exponents of surrealism" (*RA*, 153).

111. *La Femme 100 têtes* (1929) is one of Ernst's pictorial novels consisting of over a hundred collages.

ASSIGNMENT W.L. , hv/ impression it is best of yr/ theoretico-dogmatics.
but not yet finished , and 'theo-dog' may apply only to first part.
  Cert/ good clearing of cloacae/ interim notes
as I read // too fatigued to wait, holding stuff in what's left
of head/
Naow as swell as kicking them goddam punks/ wot about
noting the few ideas that Ez has occasionally set down/
as Ez never did fall for any of them punks that got a
great deal too much attention BEFORE W.L. fetched out his tardy
insecticide. (Incidentally can't remember having translated
Benda's "La Traison," but believe am first to mention or boost
the dratted little negative (Dial time) and sent first copy
of La Traison to London... BECAUSE of the desolation and lack
of anything much better in Paris/
credit fer noting the FLOP of froggery at fairly early date.
*** wd/ be timely in view of PRESENT circs/ and Fascist lable
to note the KIND of Fascismus Ez talked of (sticking to K'ung
 and Johnnie Adams , and providing a DAMsite better historic view
than Toynbee / and NEVER falling fer the Fabian concrete mixer.
///

  What about a W.L. analysis of the SOUND ideas , the positives
during the past 40 years/
                         submerged by the crap /
and of course the crap DES CLERCS providing the Rothermeres etc
with the avalanche material which has damn well submerged/
most everything else.   Note Jiménez title " Animal di Fondo "
not exactly with this bearing , but not rotten.

la mas triste palabra ; habria podido ser ... waaal , wot bout
picking up the IDEAS that WOULD have been useful if
every time , let us say , purely fer example , Muss said he
needed PEACE. fer the London Slimes to report it as " WAR
Speech "
or Ian Monro saying he had to watch EVERY pair of words in his
news , cause IF it wuz posbl/ they wd/ take out a phrase, twist
the meaning and use it as headline. (all this ref/ p. 54 and
thaaar abouts.)
                     Also the TIMEliness of certain sentences
in my Studio Integrale AT the date that trans/ of K'ung was
printed in chink and wop bilingual.   I spose I ought to have
INSISTED more on that text/ but we were not in geographic vicinage
in 1927 or whenever I got the first VERY poor version into print.
     Also look at the Analects/ if Hudson Rev/ hasn't
  sent it to you, I'll ax 'em to.

2/ O.K yu shd/ HAVE read all that crap , and got out the bug-powder,
but what about reading a few serious authors ? Blackstone,
Agassiz, and especially Del Mar (ask Swabe for copies on loan , or
see what is in the Brish Mouseum.) Alexander Del Mar, almost
everything except the " Science of Mon"/ that was a bit off his
beat .. and in the less competent part of his mind...   bothered
by mistranslation of Ari/ etc.   I spose, incidentally, that
Frobenius was the bloke Gaudier had been reading in the Bib/Nat/

                anyhow, time W.L. started looking for solid stuff.
another distinction : what one CAN believe, vs all this crap, the
cures deguisées try to hoax people into thinking that they believe
W.L. having at one time EATEN a lot of wind and dust, might have
edged rancour over time wasted. Even the fat man, with all his
fuzz , had a few right lines/ too bad he never got to Doug/ who
was good diagnostician, but not sufficiently anti-bugrocrat. Hence
POST-gesellite ratiocination.
Might say ENG PASSANG/ that ole Santayana gave ground on proposition :
no philosophy in the occident since gorNoze when , only philo-epistemology. K'ungs four tuan, superior to Aristotl (even before the
disciples castrated him, but removing teXne from his list. Drop
from Nic/ Ethics, to Magna Moralia (which whalo-Morely didn't want
to add to Kulch , saying wd/ do me no good at Cowslip(no, that is
spelled Oxford.
Incidentally it took a Chinee to look up the EXACT spot in Erigena
where he plugs fer right reason as source of authority. wot we
need is more COLLYboRation.

Important item in Meridiano d'Italia 11 Feb/ re Idea Luce per l'Europa.
dunno how to get copies of whole series. BUT sometime W.L. might
reflect that woptalia was the ONLY place where one COULD print certain
facts. Ole Meridiano di Roma stopped in U.S. post , for economic
ideas./// which is how close the MUZZLE wuz en is Roosenpoops hellhole.

  " The state is organized fear " that is anti-fascist. or at least
anti M's " lo stato e lo spirito del popolo ". Certainly LESS
fear in Rapallo over 25 year period than any where else, unless
up in the Bunter's Persia. or some such./ If I ever git another edtn/
of Pivot thru the press, kindly ref/ the two or three comments
by the translator.

esprits purs/ sorry yu missed (if yu did) Jo Adonis or Costello
" whadda I wanna see iz th' guy that'ud turn down $60,000. "
** Ez gittin ready to KICK some of them az has sposed he never THOUGHT
anything of interest , merely because he refrained from emitting
general statements before he had collected enough specific data to
know what a general statement might mean. finger (or nose) exercise
  List some of the shysters(past and recent)
                                       whom Ez never did fall
for. Including Neitsch (save fer rhetoric in Zar/a) Bergson, Sorel, Pascal.
        A lot of false dilemma in all this occidental crap.
and Mencius met, I shd/ say about ALL the main varieties
of nit-wit, and classified 'em!

3/ demur, re/ p. 41 Assignment / suggest W.L. insert word " BEFORE 1914" (after 1917 at least there wd/ seem to hv/ been considerbl attention to war as product of economic stink, a designed activity. Alex the Gt/ paid his soldiers debts, and died QUITE bloody dam soon after, less than six weeks if I remember rightly , from MYS(ehem)sterious causes. Try the test cui bono BOTH to war and to that greatest of fakes Original sin.(the idea of or/.s.) After all W.L's first sketch for first portrait of Ez/ was a Holbinian cine-star , and W.L. cdn't stand it, tho he prob/ forgets the eggspesiion on his mug as he destroyed it (in fact how CD/ he hv/ knowd the eggspression as there warn't no/ wall mirror , and he cdn't hv/ held a pocket glass while operating on that delicate water colour.

        ad interim ,
    and strictly anonymous communique

prob/ more to follow
azI procede thru deh woik.

W.L.
    FOR the Wreck-ord (re/ p 52) I recall Yeats re/ WL/
" PoWWnd'z evIL genius " / both he and Orage trying to separate
or save Ez/ FORD never (let me say NEVER) made any such etc/
and , of course, no such KIND of machination could have entered
his occiput. Orage argued on point of philosophic coherence/ and
our opposite directions at the time. Fact that mind better be ALIVE
than dead , didn't convince him.
    What is " Cakes and Ale" ?
Shd/ think Joyce's mind was formed in Dublin/ unlikely to hv/ been
influenced by HHH Dung when so far thru Ulyss/   Did J/ ever read /(but
any Whitehead /? Did yu evr hear him mention anyone but Dujardins,
Vico, Svevo and Mr Dooley ?   not that it matters a dam/   Book had to
be PUT over, fer practical reason/ but cert/ I sd/ it was an END
not a start/   P.S.U.   after that FINISH/ period of rot , p.t.c
what he may have absorbed later, when he READ nothing gornoze/
american slang via his children.
        Pity de Angulo hasn't left (so far as I kno) and
orderly statement re Dung (spell it wiff a Y , milorrr)

WL seems to hv/ lured the J/ into serious discussion of something.
Can't recall that I EVER did/ tho must have approached it at
times/ prob/ because I never rose to his mention of names such as
Vico or Dujardin/ etc/   One up to Humb/ Woof.

been trying to get a BR/ highly respected stud/t legal"philos "
to do a condensed Blackstone / all the parts containing principles
or necessary history/ blighter hedges/ mebbe WL could do it/
 Ez simply not got physical force/   (or proGODDAMcrastinates)
purpose of law : to prevent coercion by either by force or by fraud.
fer garzache start putting some of the essential concepts into
circulation.
civilization NOT a one man job.   HH
ef I cd/ purrsuade yu to give some serious attention to PIVOT ....
not think of it as merely heathen chinoiserie.

mHHMH mania for having so many laws that they cannot be executed
without crushing taxation/   hiring cops to protect people from
themselves.

wHHH wash up the puppytician// That detritus Em/Ludwig at
Hauptman's talking about LLard George .
(parenthesis , ever read the elder Morgenthau's " Amb/Morg's Story " ?
very clever lubricator. also what he does NOT include.

  identical zones of ignorance in Leahy , MMe de Chambrun, Hull, and even
Stilwell,
Has WL/ ANY excuse for the existence of a smear like Croce ??
on any grounds save that " gawd made him , having nothing else to $
do" ? (o.k. Ez iz a emotional, or dont cheat his own nose.)

177

p/ 2
NOTE / a faculty of the olfactory sense is that it does not have to come into direct contact with a thing , in order to discern certain properties of it. Thanks fer them kind words re/ Plat and Heg. p.62 feetnut.

keep down the taxes and the central govt/ cannot become a goddammed nuissance BOTH at home and abroad.

for'credit'/ ref/ Ez/ necessary both trust AND mistrust.

had never thought about Low : a great and dirty criminal, tho possibly sincere in his ignorance. P. 65. pp/1. O.K. first Confucian statement so far in WL. (? or hv/ I missed one ?) AND nobody but Orage ever seemed to twig wot Ez/ wuz at in ' Studies in Contemporary Mentality.'
 even tho Flaubert had started it.
p.65 pp/3 , as sd/ Mencius.
J.Adams : " nothing more dangerous than preventing a war".

GET a review copy to Eva Hesse , Munich-Schwabing , Bauerstr/ 19.iii probably most intelligent reviewer on the continent. Do yu see'Ecrits de Paris ?' Also rev/ cop. to Camillo Pellizzi 12 via di Villa Albani.
                                                                            Roma
and why not to D.D.Paige , casella 30, Rapallo. it wd/ also reach Gabriella Mistral via DDP/ as she is in Rap/

weren't both Shaw and Wells stinking fabians ? and Bennett(Arnold) a better mind ? at least when he wrut Old Wives(french derivative but..)

Did either Sh/ or W/l/ criticise fabianism. with ALL its filth? Pore ole Fordie did NOT swallow it , or milk Burrns and Oats.
                  S+W
Neither did the bgrs/ crit/ the REAL rulers, tho Dizzy had pointed
 to them.   already
 Partisans both / split minds , Shaw and Bertie never having tied up
to the missing halves.   Rsl
mebbe Wells was split above the midriff / horizontal not perpendic/ split ??
Dont believe serfs had much or ANYthing to do with it. (p. 75)

Shaw and Wells-bellz merely of the rising, not of the slopping-down party.
WL. might ref/ the Leopoldine Reforms mid xviii th.
 YU damn well measure the times yu are right against Mencius and the other 3 of the 4 Books.
no it is NOT fascism / it may be (p. 75 bottom) nazism or Berlinism,

but it was neither theory nor fact in Italy. where Croce and that Cambridgified mutt Einaudi , esp/ the latter had a publishing house and nasty britified publications. just DUMB. but tolerated.
         fascism rising out of guild ideas , and of balances
mixed economy etc/etc/ and Farinacci very true in saying putt the 25 top gerarchs together and each one will be found with a different idea of WHHHHHHHHHHHHHHHHH of the corporate state.
     and of course D.Low never disagreed with his owners.

newspaper caricature   per nesessita , the voice of a large
herd , herded by the owners.
when a little squirt like Max DOES a caricature contra corrente
it stays privately on Orage's wall.   which aint fer suppressin' Low
but for giving someone a chance to talk back/
                                                    Which they do NOT
get in Shitain. (birds nest in the shrubbery on the dung-heap ,
or pershaps we shd/ say " once nested ".)
Mr Orwell , a LOUSE. Neruda noticed this also. physically
diseased (extenuation ....)
turning backward to Fordie again   accepted him as delayed preraph/
son of bloke wot wrut on Troubs/ who had curious theatric letch
to dress up as a tory WITH a large income. None of us ever
had any mercy on the hang over from his earlier nerve brakdown
or then had faintest understanding of what that meant.
Pow-wowers (why didn' yu say it first ?) yu can hv/ it. I aint
in position to shoot it.   Most of these observations are in
past works , whence WL at lib/ to take 'em for any useful purpose.
WITHOUT perusing sd/ scripts/ and wop-print.
The beastly Bullitt , by the bay , had, incidentally, been woke up
but not disinfected by the spurloss verschwindet of 5 intimates
some time before 1939.   The perfect pus-sack .
Hv. yu read Col Murray's " At close quarters " ?
  Why dont yu send a copy of Rude to Alice ?

                                    strictly anynonnymouse
                                        ad interim.

not obsession, but to keep it together/ re Fordie AGAIN/
 in perspective / measured against the successful fakers ?
some decent ideas are THERE in his books/ NOT out of date
in fact his politica vs/ Shw/ Wel/Bertie/ and the goddam lotuvum
before, contemporary or since ?
cert/ much more intelligent than Joyce / reach excede grasp
man too weak to FINISH certain jobs , but not so swinish as
to pretend they dont exist.

W.L.
p. 92 IN-NO-Vation, me foot / return to pre 1914
when passports only needed for sloughs such as Rhoosia and Turkey.
pbt 1919. how many Ez letters to the Paris Tribune, denouncing the
first step toward universal bondage/ well, not the first
but a dirty one. And COULD Ez/ get ANY highbrow support, or
make people see ANY disuse in pissports, visas (at $10) and the
bank-stoodge Woodie-cod-face) algse coin (same coins)
good in Frog/ Baviere, Swiss, Ausstria and Woptalia. The eggstent
to which the occident has rotted in 35 years vurry amazink.
Benda , forget in which rotten frog sheet/ must be six years ago
saying : Yourup does not WANT to be united. Wh. also note
end printed 4 prints.   Earl Godwin/ got to seeing Am/ inkum
snoopers only one step from police state/ doe to ROT of police, due
to laws to prevent people being themselves. and inkum. ONLY mechanism
left to govt/ to get taxes WITHOUT honest money system.
   what yu can do is to stimulate COMMUNICATION between
intelligent men in different places/ did the O.M. ever git over
feeling that anything from E. of Suez is something out of a zoo ?

World State no enemies ? nuts/ And for why / because a son of pig
at 3000 miles remove knows less of what any local need is/ and
gets more and more abstract with the distance/
Si quieren un goberno di usureros , por lo menos un gobierno
di usureros Bolivianos, y no un gobierno di usureros internacionales.
van a l'il realism , please, re the U.S.

                                        IF
or specify / world state AFTER and without. senza/. Local control
of local purchasing power   power
cd/ be guaranteed against monopoly of the press by archswine.
WL didn't notice END of U.S. consterooshun on Dec 23 / 1913.
almost no news of the event leaked to europe , and not much to
the yankoboobs?
Oh goRRRRd/ I didn't mean to mention F/ again , 'ow cd/ yu
disturbe the ghost. YU hv/ spelled Madox wiff TWO DDs.
   I dont mind. and he was indubitably born to suffer,
that being his A.l. series A. corn.
                                               or were
P. 128/ pp/ 1 last line : AN' thaaar'z whaar yu're wrong.
and mebbe hook up on the other end of W.B.Y's bumbusted Bhuddism
" withering into ".
next pp/ and pp/ 3 O.K.
ov course it AIN'T "difficult to believe" , fer anyone whose
memory goes back that far. Yr/ eggspression re/ Gaudier was
" the Lavery of sculpture ". , all of which purity was
highly stimulating to such of yr/ contemporaries as cd/
take it. (possibly not a very heavy force at the polls.)

Gaudier re my mantlepiece glass box : Museu für orientalsiche Kunst,
ever looked at Pier della Francesca's De(something or other, probably
                              Proportione) Pingendi ?

132/
well well, here is some real fascismo/ using the term not as pejorative, but simply in ref/ historic fact as to what DID happen and happen with considerable amelioration of product. IN ITALY.
and may add that the last dhirty Biennale I was inveighled into looking at showed the damned Hun pavillion as the decent one/ all other furrin exhibits a mess/ sub Brodsky etc. really diseased. And be it said the wops pampered a lot of rats but what of it , the general level of technique improved and a considerable amount of sincere effort went into it on part of qualified non-painters who worked at the selection. Damn sight better than Bun-Pips and Omega am'mosphere. The favoured did NOT appreciate , having had no
eggsperience fuori d'ITalia, and the omitted nacherly squealed, or mumbled. And a few efficient blokes with a market suffered not at all from the competition(stimulus). Results cert/ much better than in Frogland de nos jours/ crit/ shd/ oobserve chronology/
i.e. when one place rots and another sprouts.
Good deal in Vlamincks's : intelligence is internat/ , stupidity, national and art is LOCAL.
did I say that Marinetti asked my op/ re/ something on his wall about 5 ft by 7. Pointed out that yu cd/ shift various hhh chunks from here to there , in short introduced subject of COMposition .
His Eccellenza quite surprised , a new view of the subject not previously in his etc.
Yet he was useful. Went , at advanced age , off to combat like various other big pots . Got no credit , as his " friends" sd/ it was just fer advertisment. all'o'wich relates to the Kulchurl level.
coterie/state. QT' : a membership card in this party does NOT confer literary and artistic genius on the holder. Doubt if Marinetti was millionaire. Shd/ think Picabia must hv/ had nearly as much.
Yus, yus, a vurry useful work, or shd/ be if some of the points can be rammed into the bleating booblik.
133/ might NAME whom they wanted to keep poor.
composer in worse box than the performer , tho latter a dog's life and few bones. almost closed to anyone not tough enough to be able to DO IT anywhere, any time, no matter what state of digestion or fatigue. Other prob/m: the disproportion , enormous fees and prices at one end, and starvation for anything good that dont fit.
can yu furnish connention with Ll. Wright ??
Hiler re/ Stewed EEl : " at any rate they give you walls ".

tears / re Joyce in Penguin. or whatever. booHOO , only sold 200,000 ; cant make any money unless they sell 250.000?
The mu Shitsman/ naturally wd/nt face a CIVILIZED country like Italy / take example from incult mujik , where capital has been enthroned on the ruins of property.
of course the great bleeding is having nation pay rent on its own credit/ believe greece was paying 54% of its taxes to meet debt interest. a few millyum to governors and presidents of Cuba , is a mere flea bite.

3/

p/137 , monor error: Kibblewhite , not Heppelwhite. (I beleev)

an woTTErbaht the MONETARY sense.?? (birth notice of which) possibly to be printed privately and just fer a Wyndam studio, ½ hour meditation, consider Gesell/ the monthly tax on UNUSED and therefore not absolutely at the moment needed paper certificates of debt(of what is due the bearer) i.e.

Anatole(i.e Asiatic) France end of L'Isle des Ping/ quoted by Ez/ HAS WL really thought about it/ Chesterton said " yes, partly" when I asked if he stayed off it in order to keep in touch with hh his readers. Fordie got to agriculture and trade-routes.

Suppressed books can't be copyright in this country ? or were rights sold here also.?
The "Hitler" prob/ only unbias'd account of THAT period. Hv/ recd/ 40 pages of a Tirolese diary, possibly only fair account of THAT recent scene early 1940s.

wonder if any use in speculation re/ dicotomy: WL conditioned by being riz in the rotting / Poss O.M. choosing the sinking , and Ez sticking to the rising(however Holly-Lucéd crass and etc/) but with some clean sprouts in the middan. waaawkk , 'ear deh eagul sccream.
         on the other hand wasn't that Webb-itch , england's winding sheet, partly murkn ??
142. yes Ottoman , vid Ambas/ Morgenthau's story. toward the end.

*** p.143/ objective truth// mayN'ot yu hv/ to include this in action ? Doubt if yr/ total exclusion of " truth" from action is a happy phrase, even if yu were driving AT something needing X illustration.

Gourmont, L'Homme Moyen S/ , Veneson. anti-pink . antag/ O.K.
mr cummings uses the phrase " canaille litteraire"/ probably this INCLUDES the dam lot , lables or no lables.

Malraux is no damgood ?? (this is a queery, not an assertion , but shd/ hardly expect good chick from bad egg , .. again queery ?
p 145 / oh the GAWDDDam hrooshunz , always a bore,and now a

The clear definition of ANY pt/ of view is useful TO them az is capable of defining a pt/ of view.

universal pestilence . Czar's aunt (and Mr Proust. damn the pair of 'em.) Cant at moment recall frogs talking of women.

wonder if it was all printed in the old lfr/ edtns ?
curious that Rebecca cd/ be so perceptive(then w, at least ,) and NOT be better .) or get better.
surely Max Ernst was the fount/ or do yu take him as grandad of Dada not of sur-real. clue in v. ff early study of NATURAL forms.
WL ever read any Agassiz (esp/ re/ Classifications ?)
25 years ago Max must hv/ painted better than Dali (less commercial acumen.) Did the novel end with Ernst' " Femme aux cent tetes "?
vurry interestin' in nanny case.

SEAMUS COONEY

EZRA POUND ON WYNDHAM LEWIS'S THE HITLER CULT

As a pendant to his commentary to Lewis on *Rude Assignment*, we print here two additional later letters from Pound on an earlier Lewis work, *The Hitler Cult*, 1939. These letters too were located by Bryant Knox in the Contemporary Literature Collection at Simon Fraser University. I have transcribed and lightly annotated them for publication here, chiefly by the citation in the notes of the relevant passages of Lewis's text that Pound is responding to.

Bryant Knox's introduction to the *Rude Assignment* letters above sketches in the situation of the two men at the time of this one-sided correspondence, with Lewis carrying on writing in the face of encroaching blindness in the "Rotting Hill" of socialist-ruled England and Pound from his insane asylum indefatigably working for the dissemination and publishing of key texts and the correction of what he saw as radical misunderstandings of history and economics. Whether it was Agnes Bedford on her own initiative or Lewis acting through her who sent Pound a copy of *The Hitler Cult* cannot be known. But given the fact that Lewis's first book on the Fuhrer, his *Hitler* of 1931, had done so much to ruin his literary career and had indelibly branded him, however inaccurately, with the pro-Nazi label, it can hardly have failed to alarm him to read Pound's comment on that recanted book as "prob/ the only unbias'd account of THAT period."[1] It seems highly probable, then, that Lewis himself took the initiative in sending the corrective 1939 volume.

Like the *Rude Assignment* letters, this commentary too represents an extraordinary and disinterested degree of attention on Pound's part. The two letters here printed are the first and fourth of what must have been a series of five, providing a page by page response to Lewis's prewar book.[2] How far Pound's famous epistolary style, his *idées fixes*, his scornful and passionate sobriquets, and his anti-Semitism were well calculated to engage the sympathies and win the assent of Lewis may well be doubted; how far these traits represent a Pound at this stage as much the prisoner of his own mannerisms as of the federal authorities would be challenging to define. What *is* remarkable is how particularized Pound's attention is—how little he repines, how absent the note of nostalgia, how constructive, for all the occasional vituperation, the spirit in which he writes. "Not arrogant from habit," he was to distinguish in a late Canto, "but furious from perception": and when we focus, in reading these letters, not on his hatreds but on his zeal for propagating particular perceptions of historical causation and for getting due attention paid to important neglected writers, his selfless energy cannot fail to impress us.

---

1. See Letter Three of those on *Rude Assignment* above.
2. *The Hitler Cult* is a book of 255 pages. Pound's first letter here comments on pp. 18 to 82; the other letter, numbered "iv," covers pp. 184-205. It seems likely that a fifth letter completed the commentary.

EZRA POUND

LETTERS ON THE HITLER CULT

TRANSCRIPTION, NOTES AND FACSIMILE LETTERS

[LETTER ONE]

W.L.

Lack of communications a nuissance/ of course yr/ Hit/ Cult came out too late to reach Rap/ pre-war.[1] / p. 18 war for own sake/ no, but war for DEBT'S sake. Oh YUSS.[2]

first impression is the bk/ shd/ go into Penguin, as wedge for sales of expensiv edtns/ of other bks/

"western" science/ might also appear to be partially "nuts" esp/ when it comes to the marketing.[3]

Xt/ why be polite to Gunther ////[4]

p/ 27/ german bogie/[5] BUT idiotic creation of the axis, from cadishness and failure to use Italy as BALANCE. stopped the Anschluss once/ france flopped three times running. Ignorance. idiocy of american politicians/ identical facts UNCONSIDERED by so various a line up as Leahy, Stillwell, Hull, Mme Chambrun.[6] total filth at the top inflated by Weenie [*in margin*: (Frankfurter)].[7]

Weenie and Winnie were messes, gawd ow they did stinGK.[8]

England the socialism/ u.S. the militarism/ all due to anti-Wopism, old school tie/ "But, Mummie, HOW is he italian? why isn't he black?" (favorite qt/ of blond eyetallyann, looking rather like Sinclair the player, ov Abbey teeYater.)[9]

38/ Hindenburg and the postage stamp wise crack.[10]

As to Baldwin/ the sucking swine/ I dare say any of that band shd/ be regarded with max/ expect/ of the basic perfide/ but england's winding sheet and yr/ damn hard luck that old Jenny didn't have that miscarriage six months sooner.[11]

and yu bleed for Rufus Isaac.[12]

Of course if yu wanna intimate that yu CHOSE Tony and Winnie,[13] it wd/ be a fair argument for genocide vs/ ces chers brits/

curious how yu avoid the "SINEWS" of waaarrrrr. The financing of Adolf/ the financing of the rearm.

Gt/ pity yu never were druv to analyze that particularly foul mass of SLOBism inflated by Weenie. a total non-necessity/ having NONE of the excuses or decent motives that ran to excess in Berlin and Roma. Yu do git somewharr on p/ 46.[14]

But yu are a plain fool re/ M/ as the diary after he was copped might show yu/ if someone will translate it for yu.[15]

as to the latin WEST/ [16] Landor possibly the last english LATIN ??? or do we exaggerate.

184

Damn all yu just CANT look at the map of Europe/ yu got to Iberia but not to the Mediterranean.

p/ 52/ [17] cf/ a very experienced congressman re/ the Swelltoad: "War is his only out."/ meaning his internal politics had made such a mess in the U.S. that only by getting a war going in order to get into it, cd/ he keep his mendacity in power. The drivveling political imbecility of the republicans/ the travesty of himself Wilkie, etc. gorsh / / / drivveleria.

Neitzscczhe/ tiresom pollok/ and german music was on the way out. yr/ pt/ that Adolf recalled it. cd/ be.[18]

On that next metaphor, he dam nigh bust the bloomin' win'mill. felo da se/ but wot a smash at the windmill/ which as a matter of fact he rather protected, or wanted to.[19]

Chapter IV/ [20] K'ung has the ANSWER/ superiority of Confucian thought to occidental epistO-splitology/ K'ung got the answer. like 2 and 2 make 4. Occident argues 2 and 2 do NOT make five, 2 and 3 do *not* make four / / / all negative, basicly negative, bother about errors, when it saves time etc/ et BLOODY cet/ to get the right answer and STICK to it.

IF the answer had NOT been known AND *stated* 400 b.C, there might be reason to go of [*i.e.* on] floundering. but the answer WAS got and stated. WL/ neednt giv way to Gugg Faber's anti-chinkismo.[21]

(blighter has confessed to turning down Buck's "Good Earth".[22] (biszchintz' sense? OR?)
cf/ Talleyrand on Aussstria/ and WickHAM Steed [23] on Austria.[24] HAM/
NO/ Marx goes in for ambiguous terminology/ FRank Harris notes "dealing in things the value of which is unknown." NOT antidotes to each other. p. 73[25]

75/ desire for wise crack. even if yu sd/ painting, it wd/ be more accurate to say "some kinds of". and "cunning" is a sort of intelligence.[26] If yu said: ethical guts, that might be closer. Nacherly Arnold of Rugby got stuck in yr/ craw and yu shun his backwash like pizon.[27]

Why the HELL limit the term artist: plasmatour, surely the common basis of the artS (plural) is that they arrange or compose something. As I told yu, Marinetti, hadn't thought of the composition in XYZ's painting.[28]

admit H/ was no clucking Rembrandt (but. dont so bloody much like Hjr Remb/) German pavillion in last Biennale that I got into was preferable to the others. Not all smear and distortion, DEcomposition, ROT. Bolos/ (if true) claiming Bach shows Joe more intelligent (if Joe knows it, I mean if he KNOWS they are claiming Bach.)[29] Must hv/ sense of humour if giving peace prize to Bish who refuses it/ and the old ass of Canterbug. Dean). who probably will if permitted. or do I wrong Spewlett Jnsn?.[30] AT ANY rate, all of 'em better than Eden, Churchill, Ooozesmelt, as human values.

O.K. a bloomink seismograph. And only us had sense enough to suppose he was REGISTERING something, registering SOMETHING.

The spewheads and blubheads tried to suppress it, instead of investigating WHAT caused the tremors.

Incidenatall what stiff was brit/ bumbassador to Rome just after Rennel Rodd/ / I can't remember damBit.

waaal that lot has suicided its self. As Charlie Ricketts[31] may have prayed.

H/ sent back the body of L'Aiglon.[32] and too bad yu cdn't see the french surrender when he did a sort of dance kick, and snapped his fingers. as finale.[33]

Yeats used to mention that the bards of hengland threw their pens into Spenser's grave/ LAST continental "geste" before the dirty Crumwellians Bismarked the country. AND, of course, the aristos had started farming their tithes in time of Gt Liz. Rothschild better man than Gentz.[34]

wot he (H) had was capacity to perceive, sensitivity. Licked by Marconi, who had a rather mean fyce.

Of course outside England, there must be very little information re/ several highly placed stinkers. (I take it Holy Fox[35] is, or was, a poor job)?? this a mere guess.

To be CONstructiv/ has WL/ noticed ANY signs of intelligence and decency in ANY of the cohabiters of his Island? Any uv 'um now over 40 who had even the sense to be partially honest?

Damn all, at least git three or four young and hammer a little sense into their noddles. I cant beleev Pollit wd/ refute much of anything.[36] (am I wrong?)

Blubbery econ/ always as excessive as Mohammed. Del Mar: "teleologically interest is due to increase of DOmestic animals and plants."[37] distinguish usura and a share out of what IS there.

[LETTER TWO]

[Numbered by Pound as "IV," indicating that two letters
in the series provoked by *The Hitler Cult* are missing.]

WL   iv.

Darwin NOT respectable/ [38] a fad/ vide Gourmont. Agassiz WAS respectable and has disappeared from the U.S. universities, which are damn cloacas and obstacles. lousy endowments/ nets of usurocrats.

even now as agenda/ if yu know any labour MP not a louse mention nationalizing diamond mines and stored emeralds. OR honest currency.

what about the corridor thru the corridor?[39]

of course no means of knowing what facts were available TO W.L. in '39.[40]

"Studies in contemporary mentality" did NOT arouse interest. the Pos O.M. didn't see etc . . . and saw no reason to reprint 'em. Flaubert's dictionaire just out in a cute li'l edtn. 1950.[41]

188 minor comment "If blood be the price of empire"
                                                              Rud Kip[42]

item, the seicento Portagoose no sooner got into Goa than he started uprooting spice trees to keep up the price of pepper etc.[43]

the diseased mania of wanting to be industrial at all, needs explaining, or offers field to same. What is it, maccoshism,[44] letch for a novelty that is no longer novel? Romantic queery? or plain horse sense? or dont the bgrz know what UNindustrialized implicates?[45]

of course some people want industry to get MONEY/ that is pig ignorance and lack of historic knowledge.

anyhow Hit/ didn't build Krupp, tho Krupp and sims/[46] may have made Hitler.

minor queery/ aint the sentimeng/ re Rhine land, and Tirol?[47]

naturally hv/ never penetrated into either prussia, rhoosia or Pologne. why wd/ anyone go there?[48]

as a dambrit of [*i.e.* or] ½ brit/ yu neglect fact that area of civilization in occident, is area more or less civilized by Rome/ esp/ mediterranean area. which brit. swine turn back to messy Abyssinian savage. etc. same for east side of Adriatic.

where there is NOW civilization there was Rome. and the density proportional to duration of Roman overlordship.

Serbs/ agreeable??[49] I dont think yu got much kulcl creation from serbs ??? or did yu

and the frogs more civilized in proportion as nearer Roman privincie, and the Slimes is the Slimes,[50] nothing will cure the basic leprosy of THAT Anschauung. and yu cant divorce Scandinavia from the odorous Hambro.[51] and as to wot happned re/ Nickle in Finnland.[52]

p. 203/ zamatr of curiosity: WHEN did G.B. *ever* defend a small state?[53] Of course La Pologne aint (past tense) so small. Now I suppose it just aint at ALL.

The Jew S/ calls it "open door"/ Japan, Perry, that aint defence either. the TWO measures: that has been brits/ code in all (? all or what %) of her forign dealings. Vid recently Iran.[54] Perhaps the U.S. shd/ be considered as three systems, of three periods. 1776/ 1865. '65-1913, and swill pail from Wilson to Ooozenstink. (1) The assertion and maintaining/ (2) the slip/ (3) the END of constitutional govt. with successive moralities for each stage.

and god curse Warburg-Oooze and their swinefellows, Lehman, Dewey, Spewey and the lotuvum.

as a matter of curiosity, being ignorant of details, DOES W.L. know of ANY eggzampl where Brit/ upheld ANY small state save as catspaw or portugal or wottell ? a pawn. I want particulars before I swallow a generality, let alone one that looks so improbable.

That a saner britian tried to maintain a balance of power, and USED small states, perhaps astutely, at least not to [*i.e.* so] smearingly idiotic as during the past 50 years. O.K. NO/ I dont accept it. The brits/ have a female jealousy of any strength. mebbe arising from basic cowardice, tho praps not. Fear leads to a lot of nastiness. Anyhow WL noted that Sanctions were not a coup de genie.[55]

wot about the yeomanry legend? Basil[56] once sd/ "cant do anything till yu get rid of the gent." Hun lieut/ re/ brit prisoners: "decent chaps, a shame we got to fight 'em."

Wop sd/ "hell those aren't germans, they're gente per bene."[57] must base general statements on particular cases. Hard to get enough par/c/

I dunno bout that 2nd. rate power being till so recent. p 203[58] Hen. viii was fairly sizeable in cf/ europ/ powwers. Of course France under them damn, them goddam stinking Louisssss/ xiv xv etc was a stink, a great stink intensively and extensively/ and disporportioned to yourup az a hole.

Possibly the least tolerable period of european history. Almost any other place or european time has in it something that can be admired if yu'r the admirin type. The bully is only the villain when he's a furriner? well praps that is a exaggeration. Mr L/ of Rugby.[59]

the conquered brit/ the ruling class since Dizzy,[60] a gang of foreign invaders, some of whom have moved on, to the befoulment of the vargin forests of murka.

Any theory re/ brits eager acceptance of these vermin IN ALL categories from Brunner to Horeb, to Schloss, alias the Brit. Museum. a continuous underground inflow/ I take it at least ½ yr/ present govt is no more english than their dear Negus.[61] almost a pity the american unflux wasn't tough enough to putt up a sharper resistence.

No, No N O. No moral reaction to Dec 23/ 1913. yu were still ('39) under delusion that this country is governed by elected delegates of the electoRAT.[62]

I take it vurry few hv/ heard of Mr Canham (Canan? or whence) and if WL falls for Lippman, or anybody who bootlicks Lipp/n. . . . Yu'll be taking Sprague or [*i.e.* for] an intellect next.[63]

187

some time since Santayana wrote "the LAST puritan".⁶⁴ come to date. send over a research party to hunt for some moral fibre/ mebbe under the Aztek ruins????

Benda, post bellum: Europe does not WANT to be united.⁶⁵ aint yu rushing things just a bit?

Yu'v got yr/ stinking Unesco. Printing House, LOUSE sq/⁶⁶ ingrandito? or wottell? viler than Geneva?? (get out yr stinkometer, and hire a few dozen Maritans.⁶⁷)

is the remedy for a stinking centralization, which puts the control so far from the controlld area, that every idiocy functions, to be cured by putting the centre still further from the governed, and having high paid pimps magnify ignorance, and prevent Swabe⁶⁸ from planting his bean row? Westminster bad ENOUGH but Lake Suck-cesspool⁶⁹ wusser.

---

1. Lewis's *The Hitler Cult* was published by Dent in London in 1939. References to it hereafter will be identified by *HC* and the page number in parentheses.
2. Writing of Germany after the defeat of 1918, Lewis says: "But of course, in so far as the Jew entered into political life directly, he was bound to pursue a policy of sensible accommodation with other countries, seeing that war, for its own sake, is a doctrine that has no meaning for him, and to military defeat no mystical disgrace is attached, in his eyes, as is the case with the German pure and unadulterated" (*HC*, 18).
3. Quoting (*HC*, 18) from his earlier book, *Hitler* (London: Chatto & Windus, 1931), Lewis imagines the Jew's "answer to the 'destroyer of the Aryan ethos' charge": "... He might ... protest that it was not *he* at all, but the great 'Aryan' inventors and technicians, who have been responsible for all the destructive 'modernism' of the Western world. Western science is to blame, in short."
4. Lewis refers to the "thousands of books about Hitler" that followed his own of 1931. The writers "have been in every case either newspaper reporters, or else politicians in a small way, like Heiden, or itinerant gossip-writers, like Gunther" (*HC*, 20). John Gunther, a popular journalist of the thirties and forties, published *Inside Europe* (New York: Harper, 1936).
5. Lewis writes: "Germany is blusterously imperial once more; nothing it seems should keep Hitler from the Black Sea; and what German, educated in the Kaiser-tradition, could possibly resist the Baltic-to-Baghdad dream, once he had reached the Black Sea? That, however, would spell the downfall of England. England would become a small minor power. The English people would never be heard of again upon the world stage. (This sombre picture haunts me...)" (*HC*, 27).
6. See note 42 to the *RA* letters, above.
7. Presumably Felix Frankfurter, Associate Justice of the Supreme Court of the U.S.A., 1939-62.
8. Cp. "Frankie and Johnny were lovers, Lord how they did love."
9. The Irish actor Arthur Sinclair, who acted at the Abbey Theatre from 1904 to 1916 and later had his own company. He died in 1951.
10. Pages 37ff. of *The Hitler Cult* discuss "Herr Hitler's Personal Appearance." I do not know what the "postage stamp wise crack" about Hindenburg that Pound is reminded of is—presumably something about Hindenburg's statesmanlike appearance, as though fit for appearing on a stamp. Hindenburg is not mentioned here by Lewis.
11. Hitler's unimpressive appearance, writes Lewis, deceived him in his 1931 *Hitler*; and he adds: "In this age of 'Unknown Soldiers,' or of 'cosy,' common-place, Mr Everyman-statesmen, it is with the Stanley Baldwins we should be on our guard, rather than with the 'brilliant' and spectacular Churchills. The latter are innocuous in comparison" (*HC*, 41).

For "England's winding sheet," see note 101 to the *RA* letters, above.

"Old Jenny" is Winston Churchill's mother, an American citizen. Six months earlier Churchill would have been born in the United States and thus not eligible for English political life.
12. Rufus Isaacs, First Marquis of Reading (1860-1935), was Viceroy of India from 1921 to 1926 and later Foreign Secretary in Ramsay MacDonald's National Government in 1931. He is not mentioned by Lewis in *The Hitler Cult*.
13. Anthony Eden and Winston Churchill. Lewis writes (*HC*, 42): "...I should say that they [the Germans] had chosen their leaders far more truly than we have chosen ours, and are more responsible for them; for their vices as well as for their virtues. Take for instance our *Führer*. I have *inherited* Mr Chamberlain, I feel: whereas I should have had some hand in the creation of Herr Hitler, if *he* were my *Führer*."
14. Lewis describes (*HC*, 46) how "long ago those who regarded him as a handy antidote to a corrupt and savage version of the Socialist dream of the West have had enough of Hitler."
15. Lewis remarks (*HC*, 46-47) that Hitler is not "blessed with the cynical detachment of his fellow-tyrant at Rome." The "diary" Pound mentions may be Mussolini's apologia written about his removal from office by the King and replacement by the government of Marshall Badoglio; it was published in Italian under the title *Storia di un Anno* in the Milan newspaper *Corriere della Sera* beginning in June 1944 during the Salo Republic when Pound was in Northern Italy, and as a book in Verona later the same year. It had in fact been translated and published (edited by Max Ascoli) in New York in 1948, as *The Fall of Mussolini: His Own Story* (Farrar, Straus).
16. For Lewis, Hitler embodies peasant, Gothic Germany, cut off from "the Latin West" (*HC*, 47). Walter Savage Landor was often praised by Pound for his verse and for his *Imaginary Conversations*.
17. On p. 52 Lewis quotes "The Australian economist-journalist, Mr Stephen Roberts" as having asserted "that 'Hitlerism cannot achieve its aims without war; its ideology is that of war.'" Pound offers a parallel with Roosevelt.
18. Nietzsche, writes Lewis (*HC*, 59), so disliked some aspects of German culture that "When he was staying in Venice [he] preferred to be regarded as a Pole, not a German...[and] he dwelt upon his Polish patronymic." After quoting Nietzsche's attacks on Wagner, Lewis points out that Hitler "is the slave of Wagner"; "In listening to Wagner he feels in his element.... He lives with the Nibelungen...[and] sees Mr Chamberlain and his

Umbrella, M. Bonnet and his Nose, Mussolini and his Sword of Islam, in terms of Scandinavian mythology"—in this respect resembling the deluded Don Quixote. "We English are one of this deluded man's biggest and most dangerous windmills—alas! for this knight is differently armed from him of La Mancha" (*HC*, 61-62).

19. See preceding note.

20. Chapter IV, entitled "Race" (pp. 66-72), is a critique of Hitler's racial ideas as expounded in *Mein Kampf*.

21. I.e., Geoffrey Faber, head of the London publishing firm that employed T. S. Eliot.

22. Pearl Buck's *The Good Earth* was published to popular acclaim in 1931; she was awarded the Nobel Prize for Literature in 1938.

23. Wickham Steed was a well-known English journalist and editor of the *Times* between the wars. He was author of *Hitler: Whence and Whither* (London: Nisbet, 1934).

24. On p. 73 Lewis discusses the importance of Hitler's Austrian birth.

25. On p. 73 Lewis writes that "a Nationalist is a man who worries very little about social inequality, except where race is the cause of it. So it comes about that the Jew is the almost perfect antidote to Marxian infection. . . ."

26. The wisecrack is probably Lewis's remark, "Yet of course politics and art have much in common. Both are occupations that demand very little intelligence and no training to speak of. . . ." A little further on he speaks of Hitler's having early learned "duplicity" (*HC*, 75).

27. Wyndham Lewis attended Rugby.

28. Mentioned above in Letter Three and note 85 on *RA*. Pound is perhaps responding to Lewis's remark that "Hitler is what is commonly called the 'artist-type.' This does not make him an artist, in any effective sense; for, as has often been remarked, no great artist conforms to the 'artist-type' . . . " (*HC*, 78).

29. Bolos = Bolsheviks. Joe = Stalin.

30. Dean Hewlett Johnson of Canterbury, known as the "Red Dean." Episcopal Bishop Arthur W. Moulton of Utah was awarded the Stalin Peace Prize in 1951, but refused to accept it.

31. British painter, sculptor, and art critic.

32. L'Aiglon was the exiled son of Napoleon Bonaparte who died at Schönbrunn in Austria in 1832.

33. A scene preserved on newsreel film.

34. I.e., the gentlemen or aristocrats.

35. Unidentified.

36. "The British Communist, Mr Harry Pollitt, is 'answering Hitler,' it is announced, in a book shortly to be published. He is taking Hitler's text [*Mein Kampf*], and confuting him step by step" (*HC*, 82).

37. Alexander del Mar, whose *Barbara Villiers or a History of Monetary Crimes* (1899) Pound had had republished in the Square Dollar Series (Washington, D.C., n.d.).

38. "The present enemies of our nation are philosophically the disciples of nineteenth-century scientific thought, and their stupid doctrine of force is respectable, if you consider Darwin respectable" (*HC*, 184).

39. Perhaps referring to the Danzig Corridor, although there is no mention of this subject at this point in *The Hitler Cult*.

40. Lewis's Part IV, Chapter III (*HC*, 186ff.) is entitled "Empire-Building in 1939."

41. Flaubert's *Dictionnaire des idées reçues* is the "sottisier" which Pound refers to in Letter One on *RA* above, where he also discusses his "Studies in Contemporary Mentality." The 1950 edition in question—presumably a French edition—has not been identified. An English translation by Jacques Barzun was published in New York and London in 1954.

42. "The ethics of being big, for a state, consist of precepts of force. . . . We, the Anglo-Saxons, got big in the most natural way in the world. We were seamen, we wandered about the earth . . . and before we could say Jack Robinson we had an empire on which the sun never sets (*see* Kipling)" (*HC*, 188). I have not located Pound's quoted phrase in Kipling.

43. "There will be no 'Spice Islands'—no 'Spanish Main'—to disinfect with their romance the stink of the slaughterhouse, in German twentieth-century imperialism, as it bombs and bludgeons its way into its neighbour's house. . . . [The British Empire] was more adventurous than acquisitive. . . . [T]he 'Spice Islands' were its goal, not petrol: it was pure personal romance, before it became Big Business" (*HC*, 189-90).

44. I.e., masochism.

45. "The question . . . arises whether Germany ever had any right to be an industrial nation at all. It would be right and proper for Russia or the United States, with their great natural resources, great climatic range, and so forth, to be industrial nations of the first order. But the Germans, in view of their limitations in the matter of natural resources, should, as the Machine Age came into being, have played a more modest role. . . . They should, it could be argued, have remained a pastoral and agricultural people" (*HC*, 194).

46. Perhaps Siemens, the large German industrial company.

47. "[T]he Germans are the last people you would expect to feel sentimental about their country. For it is not much of a country according to Latin standards" (*HC*, 196).

48. "Prussia is the least appetizing country that I know. It is the only country through which I pass in the train without troubling to look out of the window, or if I do look out involuntarily I turn my head away" (*HC*, 197).

49. "The Adriatic is an Italian lake, more or less, which there are some grounds in equity for the Italians to claim the right to bottle up, if they want to, provided the Serbs are agreeable" (*HC*, 197).

50. Lewis quotes from an editorial in the London *Times* (*HC*, 197-98).

51. Carl Joachim Hambro, Norwegian political figure active in the League of Nations and in opposition to the Nazi take over of Norway.

52. Pages 198-99 take up the issue of Scandinavian neutrality.

53. "But to-day the defence of the *small* state against other monsters like itself had become almost an obsession with Great Britain" (*HC*, 203).

54. In 1951, after Prime Minister Mossadegh nationalized the Iranian oil industry, the Anglo-Iranian Oil Company withdrew from Iran and brought that country to the verge of economic ruin. Mossadegh was overthrown by a coup in 1953.

There is no mention on p. 203 or thereabouts of the "open door" policy which the United States, by means of a naval force led by Commodore Matthew C. Perry, forcibly imposed on Japan in 1853–1854. "The Jew S/" is unidentified.

55. French: a stroke of genius. Lewis had written in an earlier chapter of the sanctions imposed against Italy in condemnation of her policy in Abyssinia: "It was the Baldwin-Eden 'Sanctions' policy which enraged and frightened Mussolini so thoroughly that he swallowed a German hegemony of Europe, made of the Brenner a public highway—or rather a private road, for Axis use only, instead of a dam against the Teutonic flood: it caused him to accept a subordinate role in the Fascist concert" (*HC*, 140).

56. Bunting, no doubt.

57. Italian: respectable people.

58. "Until a century and a half ago, England, an island of moderate size, was a 'second-class power,' as it is called" (*HC*, 203).

59. ". . . the English, in spite of their famous empire, still feel and think as a small nation. . . . And to the simple, average Englishman, remaining a good deal of a schoolboy, 'the Bully' is the villain of his piece, just as he is of the school playground" (*HC*, 203-04).

60. For Disraeli, the first Jewish Prime Minister of Great Britain, see *RA* Letter Two and note 52 above.

61. Negus = Emperor of Ethiopia (Abyssinia). Haile Selassie, the Emperor in whose defence the League of Nations imposed sanctions on Italy following the Italian invasion of Abyssinia in 1935, had returned to his throne in 1941 and was still alive as Pound wrote. He died in 1975.

62. See Letter Three on *RA* and note 68, above.
63. Lewis quotes from the London journal the *Spectator* an article by an American correspondent, Edwin D. Canham, about the state of American public opinion on joining the war. Canham writes, "As Walter Lippmann (who is an acute student of our thought-ways) recently pointed out, when there seems to be a moral differences between the Powers in Europe American public opinion is bound to be allied with the group that has the moral edge" (*HC*, 205). Sprague is unidentified.
64. Quoting Canham, Lewis writes: " 'The American mental attitude, as everybody knows, is fundamentally Puritan and incapable of remaining morally detached.' And, 'as everybody knows,' the British mental attitude is just the same" (*HC*, 205). George Santayana's novel *The Last Puritan* was published in 1936.
65. Mentioned in Letter Three on *RA*, above.
66. Printing House Square is the location of the offices of the London *Times*.
67. Presumably Jacques Maritain, the French philosopher.
68. Rev. Henry Swabey, Pound's long-time English correspondent mentioned in *RA* Letter One, above. The "bean row" echoes Yeats's "Lake Isle of Innisfree."
69. Lake Success, New York, was the location of the United Nations Security Council headquarters from 1946 to 1951.

W.L.

lack of communications a nuisance/ of course yr/ Hit/ Cult
came out too late to reach Rap/ pre-war. / p. 18
war for own sake / noW but war for DEBT'S sake. OH YUSS.
    first impression is the bk/ shd/ go into Penguin, as
wedge for sales of expensiv edtns/ of other bks/

" western " science/ might also appear to be partially " nuts"

esp/ when it comes to the marketing.

Xt/ why be polite to Gunther ////

p/ 27 / german bogie / BUT idiotic creation of the axis , from
cadishness and failure to use Italy as BALANCE.
stopped the Anschluss once/ france flopped three times running.
Ignorance . idiocy of american politicians / identical facts
UNCONSIDERED by so various a line up as Leahy , Stillwell , Hull ,
Mme Chambrun. total filth at the top inflated by Weenie.

Weenie and Winnie were messes , gawd ow they did stinGK.

England the socialism / u.S. the militarism / all due to anti-Wopism ,
old school tie / " But, Mummie, HOW is he italian ? why
isn't he black ? " (favorite qt/ of blond eyetallyann, looking
rather like Sinclair the player, ov Abbey teeYater.)

38 / Hindenburg and the postage stamp wise crack.
As to Baldwin / the sucking swine / I dare say any of that band
shd/ be regarded with max/ expect / of the basic perfide / but
england's winding sheet and yr/ damn hard luck that old Jenny
didn't have that miscarriage six months sooner.
and yu bleed fer Rufus Isaac.

Of course if yu wanna intimate that yu CHOSE Tony and Winnie ,
it wd/ be a fair argument for genocide vs/ ces chers brits/
    curious how yu avoid the " SINEWS" of waaarrrrr. The financing
of Adolf/ the financing of the rearm.

Gt/ pity yu never were druv to analyze that patricularly foul
mass of SLOBism inflated by Weenie. a total non-necessity /
having NONE of the excuses or decent motives that ran to excess
in Berlin and Roma. Yu do git somewharr on p/ 46.

But yu are a plain fool re/ M/ as the diary after
he was copped might show yu / if someone will translate it
for yu.

as to the latin WEST / Landor possibly the last english LATIN
??? or do we exaggerate. Damn all yu just CANT look
at the map of Europe/ yu got to Iberia but not to
the Mediterranean.

p/ 52 / cf/ a very experienced congressman re/ the Swelltoad :
" War is his only out. " / meaning his internal politics
had made such a mess in the U.S. that only by getting a war
going in order to get into it / cd/ he keep his mendacity

W.L.

2/

a war going in order to get into it, cd/ he keep his
mendacity in power. The drivveling political imbecility
of the republicans / the travesty of himself Wilkie, etc.
gorsh /// drivveleria.

Neitzscczhe / tiresom pollok / and german music was
on the way out. yr/ pt/ that Adolf recalled it. cd/ be.

On that next metaphor, he dam nigh/ bust the bloomin' win'mill.
felo da se / but wot a smash at the windmill / which as a matter

of fact he rather protected, or wanted to.

Chapter IV/ K'ung has the ANSWER / superiority of Confucian thought
to occidental episto-splitology   / K'ung got the answer.

like 2 and 2 make 4. Occident argues 2 and 2 do NOT make
five, 2 and 3 do not make four ///   all negative, basicly
negative, bother about errors, when it saves time etc/ et BLOODY cet/
to get the right answer and STICK to it.

                              IF the answer had NOT
been known AND stated 500 b.C, there might be reason to go
of floundering. but the answer WAS got and stated. WL/ neednt
giv way to Gugg Faber's anti-chinkismo.

                         (blighter has confessed
to turning down Buck's " Good Earth ". (biszchintz' sense ? OR ?)

cf/ Tallevrand on Aussstria / and WickHAM Steed onAustria.

HAM /

NO / Marx goes in for ambiguous terminology / FRank Harris
notes " dealing in things the value of which is unknown. "
NOT antidotes to each other.   p. 73

75/ desire for wise crack. even if yu sd/ painting, it wd/ be
more accurate to say " some kinds of ". and " cunning " is
a sort of intelligence. If yu * said : ethical guts, that might
be closer. Nacherly Arnold of Rugby got stuck in yr/ craw
and yu shun his backwash like pizon.

Why the HELL limit the term artist : plasmatour, surely the
 common basis of the artS (plural) is that they arrange
or compose something. As I told yu, Marinetti, hadn't thought
of the composition in XYZ's painting.

3/ admit H/ was no clucking Rembrandt (but , dont
so bloody much like Hjr Remb/) German pavillion in last
Binennale/was preferable to the others. Not all smear
/that I got into
and distortion, DEcomposition , ROT . Bolos/ (if true)
claiming Bach shows Joe more intelligent (if Joe knows it , I mean
if he KNOWS they are claiming Bach .) Must hv/sense of humour
if giving peace prize to Bish who refuses it / and the old ass
of Canterbug. Dean). who probably will if permitted. or
do I wrong Spewlett Jnsn ?. AT ANY rate , all of 'em
better than Eden , Churchill, Ooozesmelt , as human values.

O.K. a bloomink seismograph. And only us had sense enough
to suppose he was REGISTERING something , registering SOMETHING.

The spewheads and blubheads tried to suppress it , instead of
investigating WHAT caused the tremors.
Incidenatall what stiff was brit / bumbassador to Rome just after
Rennel Rodd // I can't remember damBit.
waaal that lot has suicided
its self . As Charlie Ricketts may have prayed,

H/ sent back the body of L'Aiglon. and too bad yu cdn't see the
french surrender when he did a sort of dance kick, and snapped
his fingers . as finale.
Yeats used to mention that the bardSof
hengland threw their pens into Spenser's grave / LAST
continental " geste " before the dirty Crumwellians Bismarked
the country. AND , of course, the aristos had started farming
their tithes in time of Gt Liz. Rothschild better man than
Gentz.
wot he had was capacity to perceive, sensitivity. Licked by
Marconi, who had a rather mean fyce.
Of course outside England, there must be very little information
re/ several highly placed stinkers.(I take it Holy Fox
is, or was, a poor job)?? this a mere guess.

To be CONstructiv/ has WL/ noticed ANY signs of intelligence
and decency in ANY of the cohabiters of his Island ? Any uv 'um
now over 40 who had even the sense to be partially honest ?
Damn all, at least git three or four young and hammer
a little sense into their noddles. I cant beleev Pollit wd/
refute much of anything. (am I wrong ?)
Blubbery econ/ always as excessive as Mohammed. Del Mar : "teleolog
ically interest is due to increase of DOmestic animals and plants."
distinguish usura and a share out of what IS there.

WL. iv.

Darwin NOT respectable / a fad/ vide Gourmont. Agassiz WAS
respectable and has disappeared from the U.S. universities, which are
damn cloacas and obstacles.   lousy endowments/   nets of
usurocrats .

even now as agenda / if yu know any labour MP not a louse
mention nationalizing diamond mines and stored emeralds. OR honest
currency.

what about the corridor thru the corridor ?

of course no means of knowing what facts were available TO W.L.
in '39.

"Studies in contemporary mentality" did NOT arouse interest.
the Pos O.M. didn't see etc... and saw no reason to reprint
'em. Flaubert's dictio/nnaire just out in a cute li'l edtn. 1950.

188 minor comment " If blood/ be the price of empire"
                                                   Rud Kip.
item , the seicento Portagoose no sooner got into Goa than he
started uprooting spice trees to keep up the price of pepper etc.

the diseased mania of wanting to be industrial at all, needs
explaining, or offers field to same . What is it , maccoshism ,

letch for a novelty that is no longer novel ? Romantic queery ?
or plain horse sense ? or dont the bgrz know what UNindustrialized
implicates ?

of course some people want industry to get MONEY / that is pig ignorance
and lack of historic knowledge.
anyhow Hit/ didn't build Krupp , tho Krupp and sims/ may have
made Hitler.
minor queery / aint the sentimeng/ re Rhine land, and Tirol ?

naturally hv/ never penetrated into either prussia, rhoosia or Pologne.
why wd/ anyone go there. ?

as a dambrit of ½ brit/ yu neglect fact that area of civilization
in occident , is area more or less civilized by Rome / esp/
mediterranean area. which brit. swine turn back to   messy
Abyssinian savage.   etc. same for east side of Adriatic.

where there is NOW civilization there was Rome. and the
density proportional to duration of Roman overlordship.

    Serbs/ agreeable ??I dont think yu got much kulcl creation
         from serbs ??? or did yu

194

WL iv 2

and the frogs more civilized in proportion as nearer Roman privincie, and the Slimes is the Slimes , nothing will cure the basic leprosy of THAT Anschauung. and yu cant divorce Scandinavia from the odorous Hambro. and as to wot happned re/ Nickle in Finnland.

p. 203/ zamatr of curiosity : WHEN did G.B. ever defend a small state ? Of coursexLa Pologne aint (past tense) so small. Now I suppose it just aint at ALL.

The Jew S/ calls it " open door "/ Japan, Perry , that aint defence either. the TWO measures : that has been brits/ code in all (? all or what %) of her forign dealings. Vid recently Iran. Perhaps the U.S. shd/ be considered as three systems , of three periods. 1776/ 1865. '65- 1913 , and the swill pail from Wilson to Ooozenstink. ① The assertion and maintaining / ② the slip / the END of constitutional govt. with / successive / moralities for each stage.

and god curse Warburg-Oooze and their swinefellows, Lehman, Dewey . Spewey and the lotuvum.

as a matter of curiosity , being ignorant of details , DOES W.L. know of ANY eggzampl where Brit/ upheld ANY small state save as catspaw or portugal or wottell ? a pawn . I want particulars before I swallow a generality , let alone one that looks so improbable.

That a saner britian tried to maintain a balance of power, and USED small states , perhaps astutely , at least not to smearingly idiotic as during the past 50 years. O.K. NO/ I dont accept it. The brits/ have a female jealousy of any strength . mebbe arising from basic cowardice , tho praps not. Fear leads to a lot of nastiness. Anyhow WL noted that Sanctions werent a coup de genie.

wot about the yeomanry legend ? Basil once sd/ " kk cant do anything till yu get rid of the gent. " Hun lieut/ re/ brit prisoners : decent chaps , a shame we got to fight 'em. ".

Wop sd/ " hell those aren't germans, they're gente per bene. " must base general statements on particular cases. Hard to get enough par/c/

I dunno bout that 2nd. rate power being till so recent . p 203 Hen. viii was fairly sizeable in cf/ europ/ powwers. Of course wl IV, 3   xv/ HH

France under them damn, them goddam stinking Louisssss/ xiv/etc
was a stink, a great stink intensively and extensively/ and
disporportioned to yourup az a hole.
Possibly the least tolerable period of european history. Almost
any other place or european time has in it something that can

be admired if yu'r the admirin type. The bully is only the

villain when he's a furriner? well praps that is a exaggeration.
   Mr L/ of Rugby.

the conquered brit/ the ruling class since Dizzy , a gang of
foreign invaders , some of whom have moved on , to the befoulment
of the vargin forests of murka.

Any theory re/ brits eager acceptance of these vermin IN ALL
categories from Brunner to Horeb , to Schloss , alias the Brit, Museum.
  a continuous underground inflow/ I take it at least ½ yr/
present govt is no more english than their dear Negus.
almost a pity the american unflux wasn't tough enough to
putt up a sharper resistence.

No, No N O.   No moral reaction to Dec 23/ 1913 .
yu were still ('39) under delusion that this country
is governed by elected delegates of the electoRAT.
I take it vurry few hv/ heard of Mr Canham (Canan ? or whence)
and if WL falls for Lippman, or anybody who bootlicks Lipp/n. ....
Yu'l be taking Sprague or an intellect next .
some time since Santayana wrote " the LAST puritan". come to date.
send over a research party to hunt for some moral fibre / mebbe
under the Aztek ruins ????
Benda , post bellum : Europe does not WANT to be united.
aint yu rushing things just a bit ?
Yu'v got yr/ stinking Unesco . Printing House , LOUSE sq/
ingrandito ? or wottell ? viler than Geneva ?? (get out yr
stinkometer. and hire a few dozen Maritans .)
is the remedy for a stinking centralization , which puts the
control so far from the controlld area, that every idiocy
funtions, to be cured by putting the centre still further from
 the governed , and having high paid pimps magnify ignorance, and
     prevent Swabe from planting his bean row ? Westminster bd ENOUGH
        but Lake Suck-cesspool wusser.

196

WYNDHAM LEWIS, 1955
MICHAEL AYRTON
CRAYON ON PAPER. 36 x 28 cm
FROM THE COLLECTION OF D. G. BRIDSON

RENO ODLIN

FROM THUS TO REVISIT: LEWIS IN 1956

Since memoirs are in vogue...

> I have had this week THREE requests for chit-chat re/ deceased writers. I am WAITING for some recognition of SYstematized pusillanimity. -/-/
> NONE of the requests that I waste my time and waning energy indicated ANY interest in the CONTENTS of the dead men's writing or shows the least velleity toward a curiosity as to whether their writing can be of use, or in ANY way enlighten the young.
> —Ezra Pound, 1959

I have sought in vain for a binding principle for these fugitive reminiscences, one less arbitrary or private than that they happened in my presence, or remain in my head: the more so, in that neither I nor those remembered will command that automatic respect which guarantees, and even rewards, the auditor's interest.= Of one thing our shattered civilization may be fairly accused, that there is no unanimity as to *what things matter*: a Pindar can no longer devote his attention to the conduct, say, of an athletic contest with any assurance of having the question understood of what drove him to notice such things.

There is, to be sure, "gossip value," the interest slaked malice can always evoke, that at least is a constant: the main theme, as it seemed to me, of a certain long-unpublished memoir concerning *Lewis in Toronto*. The essay's Great Discovery, it seems fair to say, concerned WL's famous "persecution complex," surprise surprise! and by suppressing the appropriate narrative links it made shift to convey its author's (and, by implication, Canada's) marvelous moral superiority over such a poor driven thing as had washed up on his doorstep.= Small wonder, indeed, that "Canadian" remained, to the end of Lewis's days, a cuss-word and a burning-glass!

I am not going to rehearse, thus long after the fact and without access to the correspondence on the subject, the reasons this exercise in envy and denigration failed of publication: but I must say it still washes over me, the old anger, at a man who could confess to sitting in Lewis's parlor spilling defamatory back-chat about his late host Pound, and then complain that Lewis found his tongue loosely hung. Of such things was this essay confected.= And many another: I open a current magazine (*Enemy News*) to find a book-review saying: "He [Derek Stanford] draws on Roy Campbell for a particularly nasty canard about Lewis and tells a slightly dubious story about meeting him in the buffet of Notting Hill Station. The Enemy on that occasion supposedly wore a black eye-patch and insisted he was a Captain Brown." This in an issue whose cover depicts the Lewises, T. S. Eliot, Michael Ayrton, and some others at the *vernissage* of the great Tate Gallery show *Wyndham Lewis and Vorticism*, in 1956—in itself a full-dress pretext for the airing of ancient spites and grievances such as could happen only in a cozy little country like England, where they all know each other.= Now, during that photographic session we mere mortals were kept out of the exhibit; while the lions sat for the camera, I was being confidentially informed, with a smirking reference to "the Wild Body, old boy," that "all London knew" Lewis's blindness and Froanna's troubles with her teeth were caused by syphilis.= Right? Plain malice!

The problem comes in distinguishing that sort of thing from whatever may have been motivating Pound when, the next year, he referred glancingly to "Wyndham's bastard"—so glancingly in fact that I cannot recall more than the bare reference, uttered as he swept imperiously on to the point of his discourse. (But further clarification—which may be undesired, *causa dedecoris*—comes from the late Hollis Frampton:

> "Wyndham's Bastard" ...? I can contribute a little to the tableau. The other parent was alleged to be Naomi Savage. EP referred to the kid in question as a "lively infant.")

"The point of his discourse"? If I have not confused two occasions it may be summed up in five words: "WynDAMN had a LOUSY philosophy."= He went on to explain that WL, who had not been to "college" like all his playmates, thought himself obliged in consequence to *have* a philosophy, in order to keep his end up: a judgment, and an explanation, which may be true or not true, but which has in either case little to do with envy or malice.

Regarding the Tate *vernissage* there is little enough to add, save concerning people met: Gladys Hines, for example—who had read proof for *The Red Priest*—remarking: "Well. Ezra was always terribly... *eccentric*," in a tone which suggested she thought he, Pound, from his cell over the ocean, might yet overhear her; or Bridson (D. G.) alarmed at hearing his 1934 review of *One-Way Song*—"If Mr Lewis had chosen to versify his earlier brass-bound prose instead of his latter wobble," *à peu près*—quoted aloud not ten feet from Lewis's ear: or Froanna herself, still disturbed over difficulties met in bringing WL up via the freight lift, and over his visible fatigue—slumped, he was, in a seat before *The Inferno*, where a henna'd scarecrow had been fifteen minutes bending his ear over what a *Naughty Boy* he was in 1914, if you please.

A word might be added concerning events almost unrelated: as, that on his way to the Tate, Peter Russell (who was still, if only just, "*Nine*-ing and dining," in Keidrich Rhys's phrase) stopped by Chatto & Windus for what may have been the last copies of *The Art of Being Ruled*, still in print after thirty years and a War! Or one's memories of seeing the West End saturated in effigies of *Mr W.L. as a Tyro*, which the Tate was using for a poster.

And above all must be stressed the persistent feeling that, blind and dying though he palpably was, London was still the center of the Universe because Lewis still lived there.= I daresay that quality in a man which elicits such frank hero-worship is itself the quality which evokes the sniggering calumny and outright lies which were the standard accompaniment of Lewis's career.

It is suggested that explanations are due a generation which knows not *Nine*. Very well: one of the more persistently intelligent of post-War British literary magazines, *Nine* began publication the year of Lewis's Redfern Gallery Retrospective Exhibition, 1949, with an editorial board of almost alarming breadth and brilliance, Peter Russell, D. S. Carne-Ross, Iain Fletcher, G. S. Fraser and I know not what others. Having bit off vastly more than any journal could decently chew, *Nine* suffered the attrition one might expect, until by its last issue (which came out in the spring of 1956, the year of the Tate Gallery retrospective remembered here) its editorial staff had been reduced to the solo voice of Peter Russell, a poet of remarkable talent, but not a man ruthless enough to carry on successfully as an editor.

Keidrich Rhys? Editor of *Wales*, mainstay of the York Minster Pub, and husband of Lynette Roberts who owned the most interesting, in many respects, of all Lewis's thousand-odd drawings, *Three Men from the East* (you will seek it in vain in Michel's book).

I have found no way, in the body of this piece, to be more explicit in Froanna's—Mrs Lewis's—regard. The period of our correspondence, during the most harrowing part of her early widowhood, was not one in which great lightheartedness could be expected, but even then her astonishing generosity of spirit (I had to tear up and return that sheet of letterhead on which she had written no more than her signature, suggesting I should compose, in her name, some suitable response to one of WL's posthumous tormentors: but I treasured what her gesture showed), her exactness of recall (a remark made in 1958 about my appearance in 1956 would seem mere vanity to quote now, fat and gray as I now am, but it indicated that at a time of great trouble she was thoroughly aware of the world around her), and the prodigality with which she showered oddly enlightening details ("Wyndham... used to row a great deal, and the sea was his cup of tea, but he did not like eating fish I'm afraid": which you would have the devil of a time extracting from his books), were every bit as important in her letters as the—entirely justifiable—self-pity ("I never see anybody who comes to England. They always bypass me and I cannot say I particularly blamed them. A creature with but one idea in her bonnet is no fun for anyone"), or the high seriousness of the quotation with which I propose to conclude this note: "If I can only bring a little bit of sanity and truth as regards W.L. into the world, I shall be as happy as I can be without my very dear W.L., who gave me more happiness than I ever had the right to expect."

▼ ▼ ▼

BERNARD LAFOURCADE

CREATIVITY EN FAMILLE:

A STUDY IN GENETIC MANIPULATIONS

This is a rough diamond, but in a sense all the more Lewisian because of its very roughness. Rarely did The Enemy exhibit such systematic aggressiveness as in this exploration of deliberate caddishness leading—in an atmosphere of madness—to the explosion of the innately absurd. One may be repelled by such an unpleasant display, yet there is something fascinating in its inexorable brutality. *The Red Priest*, a close relative, soon becomes boring; "Creativity" has no time to do so.

The imperfections of the manuscript suggest that the author abandoned this story in the middle stages of its composition, having probably no intention of publishing it.[1] However, it remains readable and sheds much light on Lewis's last period, method, and themes.

One of the reasons why Lewis did not go on with this story was probably that it was basically conceived as a play. In spite of all his externalism Lewis had never been much of a dramatist, and here for one thing he must soon have realized that his "Frankenstein" of a dog would be beyond any stage director. As to the fictionalized version, it retains from the dramatized version a descriptive paucity which makes it somewhat stilted. Yet "Creativity" has the primeval density of a volcanic manifestation and an impulsive logic which must have recommended it to Lewis to the extent of his attempting two different media to materialize it. But surely there was in all this something more intractable than an enormous dog, as is suggested by an examination of Lewis's only straightforward dramatic attempt,[2] *The Ideal Giant* (1917), which bears a resemblance to "Creativity." Its incompetent philosopher-hero, Kemp, a writer too, begins where Simon starts (when casting various objects out of a hat in his search for "The Right Way"): "Life for some people is full of the nuisance of symmetries and forms. When you put your pen down, do you worry about its position in relation to the inkpot? . . . This meticulous sense . . . is the famous generic madness at the bottom of genius." This diagnosis is followed by the same application to "action," and the "symmetry" turns out to be just as fearfully murderous (and vaguely incestuous) as in "Creativity," with the "diabolical" *malgré lui* Kemp unwillingly driving his "pupil" and Doppelgänger, Miss Godd, to kill her father. The pattern is the same in "Creativity" which ends up with a similar "ludicrous scramble of bodies."[3] Yet there is a difference, probably due to Lewis's failing powers and possibly to his failure to introduce a Doppelgänger: Simon's initial metaphysical attempt to shape his life into a novel soon turns out to be a mere personal homicidal/suicidal quest. Even if the abominable Fritz can be seen as an apt symbol of Simon's libidinal thanatos, the accidentalness of the final catastrophe blurs the issues with too Freudian a veil; the initial promise of a play-within-a-play somehow peters out; the incestuous theme (Simon's destructive handling of mother/sister) takes over; and, though the initial accidentalness is ultimately reiterated (the things coming out of the hat versus the dog coming in), no clear ironic circularity is achieved, as it had been in "Cantleman's Spring-Mate" for instance. Surely all this fell short of Lewis's long-lived belief in the superiority of "the dead arrangements by the tasteful hand without" over "the instinctive organizations of the living will within." There is a vulgar streak in "Creativity."

A near miss possibly, an archetypal belch certainly —no wonder "Creativity" should have been the mute eye of a fictional storm, and acted as a turntable for a redistribution of fascinations. This at least is what is suggested by a number of echoes which must be inspected in chronological order, as much as possible, since here accurate dating is subject to many uncertainties.

Originating in Lewis's acquaintance with the Reverend Willis Feast (coming after the ecclesiastical experience of Assumption College during the war), the typical post-war clerical theme makes its first appearance in "The Bishop's Fool," the opening story of *Rotting Hill* (1951). According to Jeffrey Meyers (*The Enemy: A Biography of Wyndham Lewis*, p. 289), Lewis was already at work on that story in December 1949, that is to say certainly before he started on "Creativity," which was written when he was blind. Yet a number of details suggest that, in the final stages of composition, possibly early in 1951, the two stories may have been worked on conjointly. First a small but striking coincidence: Rymer's wife is called Eleanor, the very name of Simon's sister and Roderick's fiancée in "Creativity." Rymer is a combination of the two antagonists of "Creativity": he has Simon's stature and rudimentary fighting technique, and Roderick's calling. Though it has not yet grown to terrific proportions, "The Bishop's Fool" also has its aggressive dog. The disposition of the ideological levels shows a definite symmetry: politics prevails in "The Bishop's Fool" whereas it is totally absent from "Creativity"; on the other hand, sex (rampant in "Creativity") is only hinted at in "The Bishop's Fool" when Rymer is kicked in the genitals by an epigone of Jack Cruze (of *The Revenge for Love*) and attacked by "the dog," precisely named Jacko ("First Jack—then Jacko!" *Rotting Hill*, p. 75). As to the esthetic level, or rather "mock-creativity" if one can call it that, it is equally present in both stories, with Rymer acquiring "a Wyndham Lewis" and then being revealed as an incompetent poet ("the noiseless canticle of a cephalopod," p. 13; note also Rymer's name) whose dreaminess proves fatal—just as Simon's literary pretensions and confusions seem to pave the way for his violent death.

These correspondences and divergences are made more striking by the presence of yet another rival system offered by "The Man Who Was Unlucky With Women," a story twenty pages long, also written in the early fifties, and first published in *Unlucky for Pringle* (1973). It is impossible to determine with certainty whether it was completed before or after "Creativity," but everything suggests it cannot have been long before or after. More polished but definitely less ambitious than "Creativity," it completes the battery of themes met with so far, and its plot can be systematically paralleled with that of "Creativity." Compared with "The Bishop's Fool," the pugilistic theme asserts itself with Richard Dean who, like Simon and Rymer, is an Oxford man and just as huge, though at first equally vulnerable because he is not trained in the noble art. The political and clerical themes are absent this time, but the sexual theme prevails, and above all a new theme, that of the absurd—not explicitly present in "The Bishop's Fool" but running through "Creativity"—finally emerges in the dénouement. Richard Dean rejects his wife on the same grounds of infidelity as Simon when he discards his fiancée Val (clearly an echo of *Snooty Baronet*), though in the latter case the charge of infidelity remains rather vague (as do all the motivations in "Creativity" for that matter). Richard Dean is ignominiously beaten up by his wife's lover, a diminutive but remarkably efficient pugilist (on the same model as Roderick, though the corresponding bout between Rod and Simon remains inconclusive). Following his double humiliation, Richard practices boxing (like Rod and, later, Augustine Card, an Oxford blue) and acquires a real competence of which he takes advantage in numerous wild encounters he provokes (indeed comparable to Simon's conversational assaults). Once more faced with the lover of an unfaithful mistress, he knocks him down, but is then attacked by "a very large wolfhound" (already comparable to the monster of "Creativity," which is "as large as a horse"), an impromptu yet terribly symbolical "Baskerville" pouncing out of the blue on his gesticulating figure. Not concerned with a family galaxy and focusing on a puppet-like character, "The Man Who Was Unlucky With Women" presents a simplified version of "Creativity," with its inner and outer fascinations credibly colliding in a conclusion which, though absurd, has, as well, the satisfactory quality of an epitome. In spite of its impressive savagery, the conclusion of "Creativity," because of all the unanswered psychological problems the story poses (Simon's so-called madness, his relationship with his sister Eleanor, etc.), could only leave the reader with an impression of incompleteness. However, it must be stressed again that all the themes (except political) found in this group of three stories converge in "Creativity."

More distant echoes have also been noticed by the critics.

About *Self Condemned* (1954), Mary F. Daniels remarks (*Wyndham Lewis: A Descriptive Catalogue*, p. 6) that it shows "some thematic relation" with "Creativity." She was probably thinking of Simon's and René's relationship with their family (with their mother especially, a secondary but by no means minor theme), and above all of the pugilistic theme again so brilliantly exploited in the Beverage Room brawl, when René is floored by "a medium-sized... dancing engine rather than a man, a man who was so highly trained that his personality was submerged"

(Ch. XVI, pp. 227-29). Fox and Chapman also noticed the correspondence between this scene and the encounters of "The Man Who Was Unlucky With Women" (*Unlucky for Pringle*, p. 145). The contrast between the antagonists is identical but the superb energized style of *Self Condemned* makes "Creativity" (and also "The Man Who Was Unlucky With Women") pale into insignificance—and this alone would dispose of the theory of a complete decline of Lewis's stylistic acuity consecutive to his blindness.

One last example of canine aggression could be read by analogy in the ferocious treatment inflicted on Madam Carnot by a pack of goatish Yahoos in *Malign Fiesta* (Ch. 3, pp. 371-72)—here retribution, gratuitousness, sex, and murderous assault bang together more stridently than ever before.

Last of all, but closer to the maelstrom of this vortex, the points of contact between "Creativity" and *The Red Priest*, as noted again by Mary F. Daniels, are so obvious and telling that there is no need to expatiate: Anglo-Catholicism, the discarding of old lovers (section 2 in "Creativity" and Chapter 9 in *The Red Priest*), fighting parsons, etc. Only dogs are absent from the scene in Lewis's last novel.

By their raging violence—alternating the punching fist and the bared teeth of dogs—this family of scenes and stories singles itself out by a common atmosphere, which one might be tempted to interpret as illustrating the tensions affecting Lewis in his last period—even perhaps as a projection of the author's wrestling with his tumor and deepening blindness. But then one should conclude that from the start there had been something "cancerous" in Lewis's vision (a notion which, though much too vague in the present state of knowledge, may not be untenable), since the violence and absurdity of his last works are in fact found to revisit old obsessions, even if new themes (such as clerical life) give a special tension to the fictional cluster of the fifties. Surely, in the deeper sense, Lewis was a man who does not change.

Let us only consider the most striking of these "new" themes—canine aggression. It was present as early as 1916 in "The French Poodle," where, below a pathetic crust, the same delirium made itself felt when "the dog," a mild brute this time, was butchered by his incompetent suicidal yet loving master, when he made up his mind to kill it before going back to the Front and certain death. This brooding atmosphere of canine madness gloriously asserted itself in the opening of "Sigismund" (1920), a slapstick burlesque of aristocratic decadence and insanity, in which a decadent bulldog is seen to plant its fangs in the aristocratic buttocks of the decadent hero's dense fiancée, when it finds them locked up in a suspicious embrace it interprets as an assault on its master—the same visual motivations are offered to explain the murderous dog's choice of its victim in "Creativity." "Sigismund," in my opinion Lewis's best story along with "Cantleman's Spring-Mate" (in which animal life offers the same ironic counterpoint to sexual activities of an essentially deadly nature), is animated by a remarkable trepidation which is faintly mirrored in "Creativity."

To make a pretence of leaving this archipelago of reminiscences and psychoanalytical phantasms so harassingly objective as to become absurdly iconic, let us turn to the perverse vortex of the rather enigmatic "Creativity." Simon, both intelligent and, we are told, limited, yet forcefully intuitive and systematic in his destructive urge (fiancée, mother, sister, brother-in-law, himself... such seems to be the platform of his domestic holocaust), Simon is recognizably one of Otto Kreisler's last avatars (René Harding and Augustine Card, to varying degrees, will soon join the family gallery). Simon is *a mad beast*, a man of commotions and collisions, moved by the same contradictions as Kreisler. He is an artist, a novelist, and as such (according to the Lewisian creed, though this is not clearly stated in "Creativity") he should keep out of life, out of the impressionistic accidental, but like all artists he is in life, "evidently"—and his world like Kreisler's and that of the "effigies" of *The Wild Body* appears to be one of expulsions, trespassings, dangerous thresholds and forbidding staircases. More precisely, in both cases the original fatal frustration seems to be the abduction of a family "object" (a sister for Simon: a fiancée pinched by his father for Kreisler) resulting in an obvious mental block.

It should now be clear that the greatest merit of "Creativity" lies in its ambiguous title. Artists, insofar as they participate in life, are likely, when they are creating, to become destructive. Most readers will probably feel that Simon could have made a tolerable novelist, even if his "life-novel" eventually turns out to be a bad melodrama. "Creativity" reprints the central irony of "Cantleman's Spring-Mate"—its title is perhaps a pun taking advantage of the colloquial English meaning of "to create," e.g., "to create trouble," a lot of trouble—creation is a murderous affair. (Cp. Eleanor's remark about Simon: "when he is creating he can be exceedingly tiresome.") This paradox is central to Lewis's vision, and "Creativity," with the haunting "smiling ... gory mask" of dying Simon, presents one of the clearest—though not highest—expressions of a creed that ideally aspires to "elements taking on new and extremely destructive shapes for the extermination of man" ("The Cornac and his Wife," 1927). "Creativity" is a tentative domestic holocaust looking forward to *The Human Age*.

---

1. This edition is based on the final typescript now in the University of Cornell, which also has in its possession holograph versions (some in the hands of Mrs. Lewis) as well as a dramatized version entitled "The Right Way" (a title inspired by the first section of the story). "Creativity" was written when Lewis was blind and the typescript is hardly revised. It bears only a few hand-corrections on the first pages, and its second half is definitely more faulty than the first. Some of the mistakes suggest that it was dictated to the typist ("he even knows" for "Heaven knows," or "topthumping" for "tubthumping," for instance). I confine the corrections mainly to the spelling and to providing a uniform punctuation. Reinterpretations affect only a few isolated words, for which manuscript readings are noted, and one manifestly excrescent sentence has been eliminated.

2. *Enemy of the Stars*, originally a prose poem, is in a class of its own, and *Tyronic Dialogues* is a Socratic piece.

3. Robert T. Chapman. *Wyndham Lewis: Fictions and Satires*, p. 65.

4. *Tarr*, "A Jest Too Deep for Laughter."

WYNDHAM LEWIS

CREATIVITY

I

Number Five Paxton Crescent, Chelsea, was a large Victorian Home designed for a big rich Victorian family. Mrs Richards was rich, but her family consisted of a son and a daughter only, Simon, Richards and Eleanor Richards. The son and heir, Simon, was seated between the bay windows, the sunlight falling on his celtically dark head which was bent forward as he rapidly wrote upon a pad placed on his knee. He stopped now and then to think, irritably; once he flung himself back in the chair for a moment, with a rebellious sigh. It was while in this position that his sister entered, halloing as she caught sight of him, and marched firmly towards the largest of the Richards' armchairs. She was dark like her brother, a very mature twenty-nine, with a fervent beauty which flashed absent-mindedly upon the world at large. As she reached forward to pick up her book she fastened her gaze upon her brother, and said "How is the letter going?"

"I am writing to young Jack Pritt."

"I thought that from your expression," she laughed.

"Oh? I must have a very tell-tale countenance. Just a minute and it will be finished." He scribbled a little quicker and in about a minute sprang to his feet; holding several sheets in his hands and crying, "There it is now," he came across the room and placed the sheets on his sister's knee, and sat down in front of her. "I'm afraid he won't understand. Jack is not very bright, is he?"

"Oh, I don't know," Eleanor said. "He's too young yet. You know, Syme, you would have seemed rather dumb at the age of sixteen—to a stranger, I mean."

"To write a poem at sixteen is all right. But a novel . . ." Simon rubbed his face. "Has his voice broken yet?"

Eleanor began to read the letter: Simon lighted a cigarette, gazing away into the fireplace. Eleanor read in silence except for the loud tick emitted by the clock. She did not take long; she placed the sheets on a small table, looking approvingly over at Simon. "Yes, that is all right," she said.

"Good," Simon commented.

"Jack Pritt is an only child . . . , and Mrs Pritt is not only, as you know, a great friend of Mother's, but the person she is closest to . . . Jack seems to admire your writing. He has sold a number of copies of your book at Marlborough."

"Oh yes. He is a praiseworthy brat." Simon appeared to have something on his mind. He sat with his eyes on the floor, then quickly looked up at his sister. "I find that letter you received from Mother, this morning, very unsatisfactory. I have been thinking about it. She does not seem at all well."

"I agree," said Eleanor. "But the climate of Berwick does not suit her at all. It is much too severe."

"Even so, as soon as she gets back," said Simon, "I really do think we should look for another doctor."

"Well, Stokes is certainly one of the best cardiac specialists in England. I must confess that I have felt once or twice that he was not treating Mother quite as he should. But she swears by him."

"I know that," Simon nodded. "But I think we ought to try and induce her to consult another specialist—Sir Clifford Janes, for instance."

"I will see what I can do," said Eleanor doubtfully. "You had better broach the subject this time. But she is very, very obstinate."

There was a pause, Eleanor looking a little annoyed; she picked Simon's letter off the table. "What do you mean, Simon, exactly, by '*the right way*'?"

"'The right way'? Well, in a novel—because it is a time form—it is a little difficult to survey as a whole. But in the completed novel the characters are placed in relation to one another just as much as the objects on a table—in a right way or a wrong way. For the Novelist to achieve the maximum of reality, his characters must look, not as if they were in a book, but as if they were in life. If the author could look down on them, as he can look down upon a table, he then would be able to see certain things. But he cannot. Therefore he must devise some sort of conspective vision in his way of viewing the whole action of the book."

"Yes." Eleanor frowned. "But I do not understand what is the right way for objects to lie upon a table. Do you mean the fun of their arrangement, as it were? For instance, if there is a blotter on the table, since a person sitting down to write usually sits facing the middle of the table, then the blotter should be placed in the middle, and if there is an inkpot, since we must assume he is right-handed this inkpot should be placed to the right of the blotter, provided the inkpot is all by itself," she added with a laugh.

"No, it is not that."

"Oh." Eleanor looked a little displeased.

"That is a Right Way, but it is not the kind of rightness I am speaking of," Simon continued dully.

"No?"

"There is a fatality which must be respected," Simon insisted rather solemnly. "Don't you ever feel you are offside? Life is a game, and the rules are, unexpectedly perhaps, rigid."

Eleanor tapped her fingers on the arm of the chair, a flat drumming. "Wait a moment. It sounds as if I ought to understand it; but I don't think I do."

"Well...?" Simon looked at her.

"In a case of this kind, Syme, a woman is usually very averse to admitting that she does not understand. She bluffs her way out of it. I, for instance, could very easily say, 'Have I ever felt offside? I have been offside all my life!' Everyone would laugh, admire my aplomb. They would assume that I understood perfectly what you mean... Well, I will not do that."

"It is better not to say that you understand something when you don't," Simon agreed. "Conversation becomes like a traffic-jam, when a lot of people pretend to understand something, but in fact do not."

"It is because I realize that that I never say I understand something when I don't."

Simon smiled. "Darling, I thought it was because you are the most conscientious person I know."

"No, it is because I have the temperment of a traffic-cop."

"I think that is another way of saying the same thing."

"It is not because a policeman is conscientious that he is alert about the traffic," Eleanor said then. "But never mind. Please look at the watch upon your wrist, and tell me the time. It is always Greenwich time upon your wrist."

"Thank you," Simon bowed. He looked at his wrist-watch. "Eighteen minutes past four. Why do you want to know?"

"Because Roderick is coming soon."

"Oh, is he?"

Eleanor picked up the letter again, and began frowningly.

"As I do not understand exactly what you mean, I am sure that poor old Jack will not." She leant towards him, holding the letter up, running her finger along two lines especially. "Explain. This bit here, will you, Syme."

"There is no mystery. I merely made use of a simile which can present no possible difficulties. What I am getting at is the same as what the Painter says..."

"What Godfrey says," smiled Eleanor.

"Godfrey is not the only Painter in the world," Simon told her with a faint sneering laugh. "I wish he were. I know thousands of Painters. There are more Painters in the world than there are any other kind of man."

"I apologize," said Eleanor. "So let it be *as the Painter says*—remembering, oh my Simon, that the problems of the Painters are very different from those of the writer."

"You do not have to remind me of that. I wish sometimes I had become a Painter; what he does is so direct, isn't it? He *shows* you the bonhomme. All *we* can do is to describe him—to say he was fat, or that he was thin, that he strutted or was lame (though there we have the advantage of the Painter) that his suit was greenish or blueish. But, the actual *degree* of fatness or thinness, of greenness or blueness, that only the Painter can give you."

"But *you* can make him *speak*. What animals we should be if we could not speak."

"All right. But the Painter has his uses." Simon got up, and walked briskly to a neighbouring table, and placed himself behind it in the manner of a conjurer. He looked down at it. "This is a full table, there are a lot of things on it. Let us ignore what you have called the *functional* part of it ... Now, the Painter says that there is no way of arranging this table, with the *naturalness* that the table derives from ... well, from the hand of nature."

Eleanor wrinkled up her brows. "I am sorry. I don't understand how the objects on that table have any analogy with the characters in a novel. How can you compare inanimate objects with human beings? Can you class me with a paperknife or a piece of blotting paper?"

"Well." Simon was very fond of saying *Well* and no more—as an indication that he was thinking how best to answer a rather slow-witted person, or else he used it as a noise to spare himself from answering. "What in most cases the novelist desires to do is to achieve the maximum of realness. To make people feel that his characters are alive and kicking—not products of Mr. So-and-so's brain. Naturalness is a great asset. Now, there is, in life, a way in which persons arrange themselves—a predestinate way. Given any character, there are laws which control it. These are the laws of attraction and repulsion. If it is a *play*, instead of a *novel*, you see at once, the moment they begin to act upon a stage, whether the given characters are arranged properly (according to natural laws) or not. But in a novel there is no test of that kind. The novelist has to sharpen his sense of what is *right*."

Eleanor shook her head. "Again, I ought to understand, but I do not. Or, to be more exact, I do and I don't."

"Well." At this point Simon hurried out of the room, and shortly returned with a hat; he again placed himself behind the table, affecting to roll up his sleeves. "Observe this hat." (Holding the hat upside down, he placed in it half a dozen of the smaller objects upon the table. He ostentatiously shook the hat, then reversed it, and emptied it out. He looked up at his sister). "A Painter may cause them to take up a natural position in *that* way. At least the objects will have arrived at their position *accidentally*. But a novelist cannot put his characters in a hat and empty them out onto a table!"

"I suppose he can't," Eleanor laughed.

"Yet his characters have to group as naturally as the objects upon the table must lie (to satisfy the Painter). It is that accidental inevitability that the novelist must aim at. Now the Painter..."

"Oh damn the Painter—damn Godfrey!" While Eleanor was speaking the door opened, and a young clergyman entered.

"Hullo. Very strong language," exclaimed the Reverend Roderick Powell, smiling.

"The air must be blue," Eleanor laughed.

"What on earth is Simon doing?" Roderick enquired. "Is he performing a conjuring trick?"

"Something of that kind," smiled Eleanor.

"It is no use you standing there like that, Rod. I shall not produce a rabbit from my sleeve." Simon remained standing behind a table, as if his demonstration were not concluded.

Roderick was a thomistic anglo-catholic—almost intelligent enough to be a roman catholic. Eleanor and he were engaged to be married. He now sat down near her, pulling a pipe out of his pocket. "Do you mind if I smoke?" he held up the pipe.

"Of course not...," his fiancée told him. "Rod, my little brother is being somewhat mysterious. What he is doing over there is demonstrating how all the objects on the table have *a right* position. A Painter..., Godfrey... has told him how, for the Painter everything in the world arranges itself according to some law. Its rightness for the Painter depends on whether (one), someone has placed it there, or whether (two), it has reached that position according to the will of nature... Something like that. What do you think about that?"

"I wonder what he means by right? I know what is *right* for the Priest..., but what the Painter may mean...?"

Simon picked up his hat from the table. "I was demonstrating with my hat," he smiled a twisted smile. "I filled it with some small objects and emptied them out on the table..., to enable them to achieve the natural look."

"The *accidental*," Roderick corrected.

"That is one way of putting it."

"Ah," Roderick objected. "I am afraid to regard the accidental as synonymous with *the right* represents a way of thinking which is diametrically opposed to my own."

"Yes," Simon paused in thought. "The Painter I am thinking of is not a Classicist. He is an Impressionist."

Eleanor laughed. "He is Godfrey," she told him.

Simon, tall, well dressed according to pre-war standards stepped out from behind his table and replaced the hat upon it. Then he came forward and took up a position between the young clergyman and his sister.

"The Impressionist's world," Simon said, "is the accidental."

"That is what is the matter with it," Roderick smiled.

"Well," Eleanor imitated her brother.

"Nothing," Simon retorted.

"You are going to reconsider your theory?" his sister asked.

"Not that. But there is one question I propose to put to the test."

"When it comes to men and women, instead of objects on a table..., you didn't explain, darling, how the *rightness* in that case was determined," Eleanor gazed at her brother.

"I shall have to make one or two experiments," he said.

"Your trial and error methods of attaining to the *right*...!" Roderick laughed.

"It would be much simpler, Rod, I agree, if I knew the answers to all the questions, as you do, without being obliged to resort to experiment." Simon got to his feet again. He went back to the table, and picked up the hat. He stood gazing at them for a moment.

"Now, ladies and gentlemen, I am about to leave you. You are familiar with my theory that the novelist has a live novel going on all around him—a novel of which he is the hero. You know my view of the obligations of the novelist towards his real life hero. He has constantly to be seeing that the hero does not act beneath his status of hero. I allow Simon Richards a good deal of freedom. There are times, however, when he behaves with great carelessness. Recently, I believe he has slipped up. I have to go and look into that."

"I feel quite sorry for Simon Richards," his sister confided.

"Well. It is the grouping trouble. I think I see Simon in danger of grouping himself *unreally*." Simon stood looking down at them.

"What is an unreal association, please?" asked Roderick.

"One accepted lazily, at a moment when not possessed of one's full reality," the hero laid it down. "For the hero must live up to his intenser reality."

"And how is the hero able to recognise when he is real?" Roderick enquired smilingly.

"When everything around him tingles," Simon chanted. "When he wishes to create."

"I see." Roderick was dubious.

"For instance, I now have the impulse—or, if you like, I am impelled—to do some work on Simon Richards," Simon declared. He began to stroll towards the door.

"You alarm me a little, Simon," his sister told him. "I belong to the main group in Simon Richards's novel—I am naturally a little anxious."

"So do I!" Roderick exclaimed laughing.

Simon moved out of the door as the maid, bearing the tea-tray, entered.

Roderick lowered his voice, and leaning towards Eleanor, said, as the maid approached, "What is he up to? Very mysterious, isn't it?"

Eleanor equally confidentially answered, "I think I know. I should not like to be a certain person of my acquaintance. He will visit her first I think. When he is creating he can be exceedingly tiresome."

"Has he 'created' before?" Rod asked.

"Oh yes; for some time now, he has from time to time, done what he calls 'create'."

"To have a novelist creating in and around one is not very comfortable, certainly," Rod assented. "Your brother, I feel, fancies himself as an Intellectual. To occupy that role, he ought to be a little clear-headed. I have noticed sometimes that when Simon gets in a muddle he kind of hews his way out of it."

"Yes, I have seen him do that. He gets awfully angry if you find him out in some mistake." Eleanor looked serious. "He knows how awful his mistakes can be."

"I hope I'm not being offensive, but I feel that Simon has a good deal of the child in him. He is too ambitious—he should sit down and think things out, instead of plunging head first into argument, which he is not really equipped to carry through to the end."

"My dear Rod, you have said far better than I could something I have felt all along." Eleanor began pouring out tea.

"We must not be too hard about Simon. He is an awfully interesting chap." Rod half-looked over his shoulder towards the door, for he felt that this Childish Man was one of those quite capable of eavesdropping.

II

To be specific, Miss Valerie Fisher lived quite near the Boltons. She was twenty-five years old, three years younger than Simon Richards; brunette, dark brown hair, and dark hazel eyes, tallish, a big smiling girl.

Almost two hours after he had left his mother's house, Simon knocked at the door of Valerie's exiguous flat..., indeed one room, with expansions, a closet, an alcove, and cupboards. When she let Simon in, this tall romantic personable dandy, he sat where he usually did, only with unexpected severity, and she, facing him, made the gesture of hugging herself as if to keep warm, laughing at him over the rampart of her folded arms—screwing her eyes up, and injecting into them much irrelevant mischief. She was extremely surprised when, they having both assumed the sitting position, his first words referred to these peculiarities of hers, of which she was hardly conscious.

"Am I funny?" he began by asking.

"Funny? How do you mean?" she was still smiling at him.

"What I mean is that whenever I arrive, you hug yourself and rock with mirth as if I stimulated you comically." Valerie looked less amused.

"That is a social mannerism I developed somehow or other. It doesn't mean anything. Does it irritate you?"

"Perhaps I am oversensitive."

"Syme—sweet one! Why are we, after a short absence, coming together again in this way? What is all this rot about your looking funny?"

"Nothing really. I thought someone was laughing at me today: then when I came in just now, *vous vous tordez*, you see, and I said to myself, '*She laughs too!*' And then I remembered that you usually go into fits of laughter whenever we meet. So I said to myself, 'Syme, you are a comic cut, you naturally provoke laughter!'"

"I can see I must be careful what I say," Valerie said soberly. "I didn't think you were serious at first. I am sorry I made a fool of myself... I'm just awfully pleased to see you. I overdo it, I expect, as I overdo everything. Look at this lipstick! It is a good colour and it suits me. But it is too strong. I must learn to restrain my enthusiasm."

Simon was observing her coldly, but, as she spoke, he warmed towards her.

"I am sorry Val," he said. "I was finding fault with my honey-pot."

Valerie stopped him. "Allow me to find fault with that expression. *All* women are honey-pots. Can't you find some more personal epithet for me? I hate being just a honey-pot."

"Well," Syme looked at her.

"Very well, my dear, with your famous *Well*. Don't overstrain your imagination. If it is the honey-pot you come here about, I must not be tiresome..., sweetest Syme!" She sprang up and embraced him. He returned the embrace with *brio*. She slipped back upon her chair. Simon sat still for a moment. Then he smacked his lips.

"How soft. How warm. How delicious. Is that what one marries for, d'you think Val?" He fixed his eyes upon hers.

"If you decide there is nothing but softness and warmth, I shouldn't marry, if I were you," she said with growing displeasure.

"Let me see; you went to a good school," he mused aloud.

"An expensive school..., not a good school."

"The Fishers are a good family," he nodded, as if he were ticking off points.

"No. The Fishers aren't much of a family, I agree. But the Richards are very much average people... So far we have softness and warmth, associated with an expensive school." She spoke with a finality equal to his.

Simon smiled. "A certain intelligence..."

"Perhaps not enough for so intelligent a man." She played up well. "But I feel I have improved a little since I knew you."

"No money, except what she gets from the South Kensington Museum."

"Not a bean." She pulled her mouth down at the corners.

"The softness and warmth have been expanded on at least two others." He held up two fingers, the index and the middle finger. "I have *seen* them—so it was not much use denying them. She has been twice on appro. Perhaps that pair got sick of the laughter. Don't blame them."

Valerie looked very serious. "I say, Mr. Richards, how far are we going? I didn't like the last one. A poor girl has her feelings."

"If a doll has, so has a guy," he barked.

"If so, then the guy should recall that the doll is tender here and there. Imagine yourself a mere honey-pot."

"One must be a cad..., oh, sometimes. The honey-pot is so misleading."

She spoke, as if for the first time, on a civilised level. "I realise I am a mousetrap, because all women are. But the softness and the warmth is not of my making. I can see how men must regard it..., as drugged sweets. The mind that planned things out that way was no gentleman, I agree. But what can we do about it?"

"The dirty cad who thought it all up..."

"Hush, darling," she interrupted, "someone might be listening."

"Eavesdroppers," he remarked, "hear no good of themselves. Besides, to go snooping around like that is so unspeakably nasty." Simon shook himself. "What nonsense I am talking," he protested. "That was your doing."

"I won't take the blame for that, I'm damned if I will," she exclaimed. "If we discuss what you call the 'honey-pot,' one is apt to drift into banalities."

Simon remained uncomfortably still for a few moments, taking counsel with himself. Valerie lighted a cigarette and sat puffing smoke up in the air.

"Have you thought how any group of people is a novel in the making? And the laws that govern a novel also govern them in life," he said. "I am naturally my own hero: it is the story of the Adventures of Simon Richards that I live."

"Yes," she answered smoothly, "I see how that must be."

"And I direct my life, just as I should *write* the life of Simon Richards, making the story as interesting as possible."

"That is obvious."

"Well, reviewing this life-novel of mine, you came under review at once."

"*I see.*" A sick pallor spread over Valerie's face. He thought she was going to be sick.

"Of course, I had to think quite cold-bloodedly about the 'girl' I had provided my hero with. What I felt at once was that you were too experienced, not frank and impressionable enough to be the mate for so original a hero . . . You say you are twenty-five years old. But no woman has ever been known to give her correct age. Perhaps you are twenty-seven or twenty-eight . . . Or thirty?"

"Why not say forty, while you're about it? In your novel that would make an awfully interesting situation. Brilliant—but rather simple—young writer is lured into marriage with middle-aged woman. She is reaching her menopause when he is still a dewy young creature of thirty-something."

Simon laughed his applause. "Well played, sir!" he cried.

"What game are we supposed to be playing, Syme?"

"Sex is what it is called. But I must push on. Well, in my novel, of course, the hero puts down his fiancée's age the same as his own. He regards her as a great big leering woman-of-the-world—a potential mother rather than a wife."

"I don't think you can have *her* for your interesting young hero!" she said quickly. "Could you force that idea into your conceited pate?"

Simon smiled to himself. "Perhaps Simon is the sort of fellow who is best suited with the *mother* type?"

"Oh I don't think so, not so spirited a young genius as Simon!"

Simon gave her an appreciative smile. "I think it is quite possible that the adult Simon may prefer an adult woman," he mused.

"A great big leering female?" she enquired incredulously.

"Something like that. Although of course in a few years I might find it difficult to whip up an interest in that, in the hardening arteries of that sardonic old leer."

"That is that." Valerie's smile looked less confident. Simon rose and stretched.

"There are a few other points, I have to work out," he continued. "But they are rather painful, and I will deal with them in my own private mind."

"What, more painful than the items we have just run through?"

Simon remained silent, looking at the ground for a moment. "Yes. More . . . disagreeable."

"Do I smell," she enquired sombrely. "Have I the stink of age?"

"Er . . . no," he dismissed that absent-mindedly. "Good-bye—it's no use my stopping now . . ."

Valerie rose frowning. "No, that would not be wise. I have been behaving absurdly under your insulting cross-examination. Let me make up for that by telling you a truth or two. *You are not* everybody's cup of tea, as you seem to think. I am not a very particular woman, or I would have shrunk long ago from something disagreeable about you—something that suggests *madness* tucked away under your boyish jollity. One comes up against *a glare* in you, and one shivers. You will, I believe—yes, the more I think about it, I believe that curious mind of yours will run away with you. You will end in a madhouse. So . . . , I don't want you to come round here anymore. I'm sick of your rubbishy little mind—

and that nature of yours which wishes to scratch and hurt . . . , at the wrong moment, you know. Now take off your little bag of trifles—I have seen them all and I do not want to see them anymore." She saw his eyes fixed upon something. "No no, that melon is not for you. I am a good-natured woman. I did buy that melon for *us* tonight. But I just cannot imagine myself eating it with you, or anyone else for that matter. I could not conjure up an appetite to sup with a man who might at any moment require a strait jacket." She moved forward briskly, with a touch of hysteria, and opened the front door. "Now go, please. Take your little self off, and don't bring it back again. D'you hear me?"

"Yes, darling, it was very fine indeed," He spoke in a low voice, without any expression.

"Do not be rude to me anymore, Mr. Richards, or I will strike you in the face." Her chest had begun to heave. He watched it in the same way as he would watch a firework, to which he had set a match, a little pensive.

"I did not mean to anger you . . . ," he said thoughtfully.

"But you *have*. Now get out quickly or I shall hurl you out—I shall throw you out through that door!"

Simon turned his broad back upon her, shutting her out from his view. "I would rather walk out," he almost whispered. "Good night." He walked out, a fixed, almost a somnambulic look on his face. He was so quiet that Valerie was afraid, and banged the door upon his heels.

III

The handsome dutch table in the Richards' drawing-room, which Simon had chosen for his demonstrations, was usually appropriated by his sister for work. A week had passed: she now sat at it, copying something into an exercise book out of a massive volume propped up open, on the table at her side. She was absorbed in this way when she heard the door opening and closing behind her.

"Who is that, who is so stealthy?" Hooking her arm on the back of the chair, she turned round, and found her brother sitting quietly down near the fireplace.

"Don't move, El darling, I will wait peacefully here until tea arrives."

Eleanor rose and joined her brother near the fire, which he was energetically poking.

"Yes, I am glad you are doing that," she said as she sat down. "It is frightfully cold—somewhat unseasonable."

"You should not have knocked off, El."

"I should have done so in any case. Rod will be here in a few minutes."

Simon threw himself back. "Since we last met I have been thinking about Mother. I think she should be *obliged* to change her doctor."

"Oh." His sister looked a little confused. "Obliged? I hardly think . . ."

"It is a pity that she is stopping up there till the end of the week. Why did you not suggest that an earlier return would be advisable, in view of her indisposition?"

Eleanor flushed. "Mother is not amenable to dictation. However, I did, as persuasively as possible, advise her to step up a little the timetable regarding her return. I should like as much as you to see her return earlier than she intended. I feel uneasy . . ."

Simon grunted. There was a heavy pause, during which, with both, the subject of the mother appeared to claim their attention.

Simon yawned viciously. He sat up and fixed his sister with a censorious eye.

"Why are you going on with that exam?" he enquired. "Aren't you and Rod getting married as early as you thought?"

"Yes. But having got as far as I have...," she shrugged.

"Sometimes fiançailles abruptly end." He sat dully looking at the floor. Eleanor looked enquiringly at her brother.

"That is so, have you heard of any fiançailles terminating just of late?"

Simon nodded. "I am no longer affianced myself, to go no further."

"Do you mean to say that you and Valerie, Syme...?"

"Even so." He looked very uncommunicative.

"That surprises me a little."

A short silence ensued.

"I was expecting before long to have a bloody God-expert for a brother-in-law," he spoke quietly and unemotionally. Then, before she could answer, he added, "Is there anything I could say to you, El, which would displease you so much that you would refuse to see me again?"

Eleanor laughed angrily. "After what you have said, in speaking of my fiancé, I doubt if it is worth the trouble to answer you. But you are my brother. You say some extremely unpleasant things, even for a brother... However. Has what you tell me about Valerie anything to do with 'creativity'? I *can* imagine people resenting that—I mean, of course, Valerie."

"I should not have thought that anything of a pseudo-scientific nature," he said loftily and lazily, "could be very disruptive. But I am glad I have broken that engagement. To translate into marriage something which begins in the bed of a middle-class woman who loves too easily is absurd."

"I think so too," Eleanor emphatically agreed. "How does that leave your personal novel? And is your 'creativity' now assuaged, Simon?"

Simon shook his head. "No... No."

There was something about the way in which Simon had said "No" that caused Eleanor to look at him sharply. "No? Where do you now find an opening for your 'creativity'?"

"Can you not guess?" He was eyeing her in so curiously cold a way that she felt uncomfortable. An angry fear looked out of her eyes as she sat watching her brother, who pursued a tactic, the object of which was to create uneasiness.

"I cannot, no," she said. "Why should I be able to?"

But Simon did not answer. Keeping his eyes deep down, and his face seeming to go dead in a curious way, Simon had locked himself in.

There was a brief silence; then she spoke in a strained voice. "Simon, what on earth do you mean?"

"Well...," Simon paused. "We have paid no attention to *your* private novel, have we?"

Eleanor's embarrassment deepened. "*My* private novel? Don't be ridiculous! In any case there is no Valerie Fisher in *my* life to excite the creative urge."

"No?" Simon coughed. "No Valerie Fisher?" he asked pointedly.

"What on earth are you talking about?" Her angry irritability sharpened his sister's voice.

Simon had raised his head, and as his eye fastened upon her it glittered a little. She shrank from him.

"It is of course Rod I mean," he said.

Eleanor turned very pale. "A joke's a joke, Simon..."

"Oh, I know that at your age you might not find another man, attractive as you are. I know all about that. But marriage is not the be-all and end-all of life, even for a woman..." He sat with a strange muted glare in his eye, which held her.

"Will you please stop talking nonsense," she said to him severely. "Have you been drinking? What is the matter with you?" She stared at her brother now in amazement rather than anger. Then she burst out laughing.

"Laugh, Eleanor," Simon said, "but listen. Can you make any pretence of being Christian? I know exactly what you feel about Christianity—we have talked about it often enough."

"Roderick says that doesn't matter. He has not made the slightest effort to alter my views. He says it does not matter in the least what I think," she said rapidly in a somewhat lowered voice, as though the door might open at any moment.

"That is because Rod, like all anglo-catholics, is a phoney: a sort of religious smart-aleck," Simon said loudly and emphatically.

"It's you who are the frivolous smart-aleck, Simon," his sister's voice had risen. "We have always got on very well, but I have never taken you *seriously*. You have always remained the undergraduate. You believe in *nothing*—you could not now, however hard you tried. That is what Oxford did for you. I saw you trying once..."

"Very well. I do not believe in Christianity—nor do you... And you never will. And of course Rod will be considerably embarrassed if you take a fancy for going to Church..."

Eleanor became very red. "We shall be good friends no more if you continue to talk like this. And I would rather that you took yourself off now. Roderick may be here at any moment."

"This is my house as much as it is yours Eleanor...," he protested.

Eleanor sprang up violently. "I will never speak to you again unless you leave this minute. Go! And if you meet Rod outside, say you have a date for tea..."

The door opened and Roderick, smiling broadly, entered. "You look like a tragedy queen, Eleanor. Superb!" Roderick came towards them, still smiling.

"You have been listening at the door, Rod. You found it damn funny, didn't you?" Simon laughed. "Come and join us. It won't be any less funny with you here."

Eleanor rushed out of the room.

"I am afraid your sister is dreadfully upset," Rod said, his amiable jocosity entirely gone. "I have never seen her so disturbed. What has been going on, Simon?" Roderick's gravity deepened as he observed Simon's hostile demeanour.

"You heard what I was saying. I have been telling my sister that you are not a good man to marry. I like you personally: but she is scornful of Christianity. I cannot see how she can marry a clergyman."

"That makes no difference, no difference at all," Rod assured him, speaking emphatically. "I should not dream of attempting to influence her."

"That is because you are not a serious man."

Rod looked profoundly disturbed. "I wish I could convince you that I am sincere. I understand very well what you mean, but you are mistaken. Missionary action is of course imposed on me, but I regard myself as exempted in this private and personal matter."

"You expect to have children. Well, they would be as much her children as yours. They would receive religious instruction, would they not?"

"It would be my wish, yes. But if Eleanor was very much against it, it would be her will which would prevail."

"What an extraordinary husband." Simon affected great surprise. "And what an accommodating clergyman!"

"If we had children," Roderick told him, "I should pray for their ardent adherence to the Christian Religion. But I should not loose the Hound of Heaven on my children's heels, even if it seemed to you unmanly and laodicean not to do so."

"Yes. Yes. You can't help it, Rod: it is your profession to be double-faced."

Roderick burst into an exasperated laugh. "You have strangely old-fashioned ideas. Because I do not go about with a face as long as a wet week, because I allow myself a modest amount of geniality, you say I am a humbug!"

"The uninhibited catholic merriment, as practised by Belloc's followers, is not very up-to-date," Simon told him. "I should not rely on you for fashion-tips. Your untiring catholic jollity is at least twenty-five years behind the times. Your smiling nothing-to-hide approach is a 1925 model."

"It is very enjoyable debating with you, Simon . . . and, while you were speaking, I was maturing a smashing retort," Rod laughed. "But I must postpone my triumph until a more peaceable moment. I must see what is happening to the unfortunate Eleanor." He jumped to his feet. "I think I will take her out to dinner . . . , unless she is too crumpled up to do anything." He moved briskly towards the door.

"To lure my sister . . ."

But Roderick was hurrying out of the door. His voice could be heard calling, "Eleanor! Eleanor!"

From his chair Simon shouted, "Reverend Sir! Do not disturb my sister. Please. Be off! Take yourself off!"

IV [1]

Six hours later Simon was seated in the armchair favoured by his sister, reading a book. When his mother entered he felt for the moment that this was a character in the story he was reading. He started heavily, and adjusted his mind to the reality. The book on his knee tumbling to the floor, he sprang up and went quickly towards Mrs Richards.

"Mother! What has brought you back tonight? You do not feel worse? But I am overjoyed to see you."

Mrs Richards was a tall, grey-haired, rather willowy old lady. Her face was extremely pale.

"Oh, you are here, Simon."

Simon, almost hysterically, his mother clutched round the shoulders, kissed her on the cheek with great tenderness.

"How pale you are, Mother! Is there anything the matter?" (She shook her head). "I do hope nothing has happened. Come and sit over here, and tell me all about it."

He took her arm and led her towards the grandiose chair he had just vacated. Her gait was not very brisk, and quite obviously she was immensely fatigued. He assisted her, levering her down, and only leaving her when she was comfortably settled. Then he took up his position not far way in a more austere seat.

"Oh I am so thankful to be home," Mrs Richards murmured. "Where is Eleanor?"

"Eleanor has gone out with Roderick."

"When did she say she would be back?" Mrs. Richards enquired.

"I did not see her before she left. I had better say there has been a disagreement earlier in the day. I told Eleanor what I thought about her marriage. I told her she ought not to go on with it... Rod is not a suitable man to marry. He—Rod—has taken her out to dinner, to remove her from my influence."

The old lady sank back in the chair, with an understandable gesture of dismay, looking a little wildly at her son. She drew her handkerchief out of her bag and lifted it to her mouth.

"Simon, what *have* you been doing. Do you not realise what you are doing? Eleanor may never again bring herself..."

"Yes, mother. But she might as well be marrying a nephew of the Pope. She..., Eleanor!"

"And what if she were! There are many worse husbands one could think of than an intelligent young gentleman. It was very wrong of you, Simon, to..., to..."

Simon sat quite near to his mother, and began to stroke her arm.

"Mother, darling. Please look at this objectively. If you do so, you will see at once that this situation left me no alternative but to step in and do all I could to stop my sister going on with this marriage."

"But what is the matter with Roderick Powell?" his mother asked.

"Nothing," Simon said, "except that he is a clergyman, and my sister is a woman of thirty years old, who knows her own mind, and up till now has had an aversion for the religion of which Rod is a priest. She does not realize all the implications of marriage with a clergyman. If she has children..."

Mrs Richards swung herself over towards him, with an exclamation of impatience. "My dear Simon, when you are a little older you will have outlived the anti-clericalism of youth. We do not go to Church, we regard ourselves as 'modern people.' Often I have thought that I should have proved myself a wiser woman if I had continued to go to Church on Sundays, as some of my friends do..."

"Mrs Hutchinson," Simon exclaimed, "I think of her as an old woman, clinging to the superstitions of her youth, I do not respect her for her church-going habits, in any way. On the contrary, I despise that inferior intelligence—and that fear-ridden spirit, who wishes to hide herself from death behind the furniture of her church, and in the sympathetic warmth of a human being like her, who has taken holy orders, and so has acquired ascendancy over a number of old women like herself. Whereas, I have always deeply respected you for your fearless intelligence. I should not like you to take that away from me."

The old lady released a painful sigh, as she looked appealingly towards her son.

"All that is hysterical prejudice, my dear Simon. You call 'superstition' all that you believed in early life, which is only another superstition, surely you must see that—the superstition fastened on one in the act of growing up."

He laid his hand upon hers. "You cannot, my darling Mother, by a sort of tu quoque alter the fact that certain beliefs which are fastened upon us in childhood, we learn to regard, as we grow up, as ideas with no logical foundation..."

"And we learn a little later, do we not, that these new and contrary beliefs are, themselves, superstitions... However do not let us argue with one another. Let me only say that it is cock-sure undergraduatism for you to ask your sister to give up her first serious love, because it happens to have fallen upon a man who has beliefs you do not share. If Eleanor followed your advice and said good-bye to Roderick, she would probably not find a second man that she was inclined to marry. It is very cruel of you not to consider more closely, and sympathetically, the destiny of your sister."

Simon threw himself back in his chair, and clasped his hands together. "You would drive me, Mother, if you could, from all those severities from which you naturally shrink. For instance I have given up my fiancée, as unworthy, and whatever you said, I should adhere to that decision. I also must adhere to my decision to attempt to drive my sister away from her engagement to an unsuitable man."

The mother and the son gazed at one another, an intellectual combat seizing hold of both, and separating them minute by minute. A frown cut deep vertical lines into his forehead; Mrs Richards rather painfully held herself in. She kept looking up at him, as if intending to say something, but each time she looked down again, exercising a good deal of will. At last words forced their way out.

"Simon . . . , do not be angry with me, but this is not the *first* time you have stepped in and exerted all your great influence with her to prevent your sister from marrying . . ."

Simon's face grew red, he turned his eyes away from his mother, his two hands flew together, and the fingers locked them in an hysterical embrace. He shook his head.

"Dearest Mother, you are quite wrong there. What you refer to was an utterly different case. Is it not natural that I should be attached to my sister . . . ?"

"Of course, Simon. But . . ."

"There are no *buts* about it, Mother. For a quite different reason I intervened in the case of Lionel Prescott. You yourself did not approve of Lionel, partly for the same reasons as myself. It is absurd to compare these two cases with each other. They are so utterly different!"

Mrs Richards quickly held a handkerchief to one of her eyes. "I am sorry I referred to that, Simon. Please forgive me; only . . ."

Simon was still angry and embarrassed. He was about to aim at her some harsh remark, when the telephone, which stood upon a desk placed midway along the inner wall, began to ring. Mrs Richards rose and stalked a little unsteadily towards the instrument. She removed the receiver. "It is I, darling—yes, I got back a short time, a very short time ago . . . ; yes, dear . . . ; yes, yes, dear . . . ; at the Markham Hotel? . . . ; very well, dear, I will come at once." Mrs Richards hung up, and returned across the room, where she was met by Simon. "Your sister is at the Markham Hotel."

"What is she doing that for?" Simon asked angrily.

Mrs Richards shrugged her shoulders. "You are more able to answer that, Simon, than I am. I am going there at once. She wants me to take her night things, and so forth . . ."

"Does she want her little brother?"

"No."

"Well, I shall sleep here. Should she ask for me, I can be found here," Simon said, greatly annoyed. "Do not allow the Reverend Roderick . . ."

"Please put your toys away for the moment, Simon. I feel appallingly tired. I have been in the train for a good many hours. If only I could go straight to bed!"

"Why the devil *don't* you?"

Mrs Richards did not answer, but moved, quickly for her, out of the room.

Her son followed her, and, opening the door, called after her, as she mounted the stairs.

"Mother," he said, "Shall I come with you? You should not go alone."

"Why not, Simon? I am quite capable of taking myself a short distance in a taxi-cab."

"It is as you like, Mother," Simon answered. "I would rather you let me come with you; but if you don't want me, very well. I will call round at the Markham Hotel tomorrow morning."

V

It was not long after midnight that Mrs Richards climbed into a showy but fairly comfortable bed at the Markham Hotel, propping herself up upon several pillows at its gorgeous centre. She then picked up the telephone and asked to be put through to her daughter's room. Eleanor's voice answered immediately, and her mother said, "Thank God I am in bed..., a very luscious bed indeed... Of course darling," she answered when her daughter enquired if she might now come up.

The furnishings of this room suggested Paris rather than London. It was predominantly blue, gilt patterned with much lace, an immense dressing-table mirror, a large bed with cupids appearing to spring up from behind the billowing pillows, one bambino appearing to rest his head beside Mrs Richards sinking into the same feather-charged expanse.

Eleanor's room was in the same labyrinth as her mother's, and almost immediately she appeared at the door, and came and sat down at the side of the bed.

"At least it's comfortable, isn't it, my darling Mums?" She squeezed Mrs Richards's hand.

There was a knock and, in response to the *Come in* of both women, Roderick appeared. He drew himself up just beyond Eleanor.

"Well, here we are, pleasantly settled for the night," Eleanor exclaimed with cheerful heartiness. "There is only one thing we have to worry about. My demented brother!"

"I shall not leave till one," Rod assured them. "He is bigger than I am, but I can box, and I don't expect *he* can. If he begins to throw his weight about in this hotel, I recommend him to do it stripped. He shall not meddle with Eleanor!"

"How gladiatorial you sound, Roderick," said Mrs Richards faintly. "But do not hurt poor Syme. At bottom he is a very nice boy. He has had these fits[2] of crankiness as long as I can remember."

Roderick laughed. "It is I, probably, who will get hurt! Your son is a very big chap."

"I shall not require protecting," cried Eleanor, producing a revolver from her pocket, and displaying it belligerently. "I have brought this with me, and I shall use it without hesitation if he tries to play the fool with me!"

"But darling, what can he do? He is only dear old Simon. Box his ears, perhaps..., but do not wave that beastly thing about in the air. I hope I shall be all right in the morning, in which case I shall give him a talking-to."

"Remember your Mother is not well," Rod spoke in a low and earnest voice. "Do keep that ugly toy out of sight, El."

"Of course, darling Mums, if you were *well*, between us we could keep Master Simon in his place," Eleanor held her mother's hand with one of her own, and with the other, the right, she obeyed her fiancé and put her gun back in her pocket. You must stay here and rest, darling. You ought never to have gone up to Scotland. Our Simon can be a very tiresome fellow, when he gets upon his hobby-horse."

"He is a charming fellow," Rod said, "but he has accesses, a frenzied pasquinade when an undergraduate irresponsibility possesses him. His present 'creativity' is inexplicable." And turning to Eleanor, "For two pins hé would turn his attention to your mother."

"Oh yes, he would think nothing of accusing her of being the wrong mother. He might order you to vacate your house!"

Mrs Richards's voice grew more and more feeble. "I should have to consult my solicitor," she smiled tremulously.

"I know I shall have to see mine," Eleanor said with great conviction.

"I have a proficient lawyer," Roderick intervened. "The best thing we could do would be to get married, darling—we should both be under his protection then."

The telephone rang on the bedside table. Eleanor seized it violently. "How dare you ring at this time of night! Are you mad? I shall stop here until you leave the house... Then in that case I shall go into chambers... If you try and move Mother from here, I shall appeal to the Police... You are my junior. You are out of your mind, and I shall know how to treat you... This 'rag' of yours looks as though it were going to cost us all quite a little money..., ..., ..., go to Hell..., ..." She replaced the telephone receiver.

"Darling! Is this necessary?" asked Mrs Richards, measuring her fierce daughter with her faded eyes.

"No, it is not," Eleanor picked up the telephone again. "Is that the night clerk? Please put no more calls through Mrs Richards. She is under doctor's orders, and must not be disturbed... Yes, until you hear to the contrary. Good night."

"We should have done that before. I think, darling, your Mother is longing to get to sleep," Rod softly reminded her.

Mrs Richards still more faintly said in a faltering voice, "I should like to try to get to sleep."

Eleanor stooped over the bed, and kissed her Mother. "Mums darling. What brutes we all are! Sleep well. If you need anything, ring down to the office. I shall steal in from time to time—I shall be very quiet, darling!" and Eleanor, signalling to Roderick, left the room with dramatic noiselessness, followed by Roderick, tiptoeing.

VI

At eleven o'clock the next morning, Mrs Richards was in the same position exactly, but her pallor had developed so much that she now looked almost another woman. A nurse at her side administered oxygen. Simon knelt at the bedside, beside the nurse. Roderick approached the bed on the opposite side, fell to his knees and began praying in a loud and impassioned voice. Simon rose roughly to his feet, and left the room, with an inappropriate noisiness. In a chair near the window, Eleanor sat crouched and sobbing.

The doctor came into the room quietly; but his entrance was heard by the nurse, who stepped aside and the doctor took her place. She fitted herself in beside the doctor, still engaged in administering the oxygen.

After a brief examination, the doctor in a low voice spoke for a moment to the nurse. As he left the bedside, he noticed Eleanor still crouched by the window;[3] he went up to her, bent down and spoke gently, whereupon Eleanor moved around the bed and knelt down beside Roderick, but nearer to her mother. She wept convulsively. The door opened twice, first allowing the doctor to pass out of the room, and then (as if having something to do with the passage of the doctor) Simon re-entered, glaring at the still murmuring Roderick. He placed himself once more upon his knees at the side of the bed.

For a short time there was a deep silence, except for the muttering of the clergyman.

Occasionally Simon would lift his head and glare at the mutterer. But when the doctor returned, placing himself in his usual position, Simon, speaking across the nurse, said to Doctor Ritchie, "That clerical exhibition is not very good for my mother, is it? He is an intruder. Is there no way of stopping him from showing off?"

His sister raised her head angrily. The dotor examined Rod, who went on muttering, only a little louder, so that everyone could hear it was latin.

"You see," Simon loudly protested, "it is not even in his own language. It is obviously quite unnecessary for him to speak in the language of Julius Caesar." And with growing indignation, "As the whole thing is so artificial, it is inexcusable, while my mother is dying for this fellow to conduct a charade...!"

["..."] 4

"This is outrageous!" These words in a dead language appeared to rouse Simon as no other utterance could. *Calamitate* sounded to him far more challenging than if he had said *Guttersnipe* or *Cad*.

The embarrassments of the doctor were put a stop to, however. Mrs Richards's body was suddenly convulsed. Everyone fixed their eyes upon her. Then she seemed to drop her head backwards upon the pillow. The doctor's fingers were upon her wrist; and after that he raised them to her eyelids. After that he turned to the nurse and his lips moved; whereupon the nurse removed the oxygen apparatus, and moved with it to the other side of the room.

"Is my Mother dead?" Eleanor almost shouted, and the doctor bowed his head in assent. Almost immediately a perfect broadside of latin was discharged by the clergyman.

"Subvenite, Sancti Dei, occurite, Angeli Domini, suscipientes animam ejus, offerentes eam in conspectu Altissimi."

Simon sprang up and left the room, signalling to the doctor to follow him, which the latter did.

Eleanor clutched her mother's dead hand and seemed momentarily to give herself up to grief, muttering and sobbing hysterically. Meanwhile Rod's voice rose also in an emotional chant; the latin words seeming to acquire an emphasis which no familiar words, in the tongue of the speaker, could have done. In about ten minutes Simon returned glaring at his sister and Rod, but again kneeling down at the side of the bed. It was not long before the young clergyman rose and moved towards the door. As he was stooping forward to turn the handle, Simon, who had risen to his feet, came up behind him and violently slapped his face.

"Take that for insulting me at my mother's deathbed, by making that beastly noise!" His voice was hollow and husky. Roderick continued on his way out of the room, with his head bowed, without looking up at his assailant. The door closed, Simon turned towards the bed, but his sister, who had left her side of it, met him and swung her hand around onto her brother's cheek, exclaiming, "Aren't you ashamed to behave like that—have you lost all sense of decency? I will go and apologise..., for the *family*..., to the man you have insulted!"

Eleanor rushed out of the room, Simon standing dazed and bewildered gazing at his Mother with an expression as it were of appeal. But the nurse now seemed to have taken command. She pulled the sheet up over the dead face. Simon's expression as his Mother's face was blotted out, changed completely, his mouth screwed down at the corner as if he were about the cry. His head hung down as he turned towards the door, and slowly walked out of the room.

VII

A week later, at eleven thirty in the morning, Simon was standing in the centre of the Richards' drawing room, with an animal about as large as himself. This was an enormous dog, which he held by the leash; he also dangled an exceptionally heavy whip. A mildly distorted smile on his face, he was gazing at it, as if it had been an even stranger animal than it was.

This great dog advertised its ferocity in every movement. With a guttural snarl, and a periodic explosion of rage, it protested at its muzzle. It followed the whip with its glaring eyes.

"You may learn to love me, Fritz, but you seem determined to learn the hard way."

"Hhu hughhjk!" said the dog.

"All right, criminal," and Simon sat down.

A man-servant entered, and said, "A lady and gentleman to see you, sir; Miss Richards, sir, and Mr Powell."

"Yes," said Simon, getting up, "but this dog has to be removed. Give me a hand, will you! You are not afraid of dogs, are you?"

"I am not afraid of dogs, sir," said the man, "but with this one, sir, I had better have a whip."

Simon handed his man the whip. "He is solidly muzzled. He can only make a noise. His teeth are locked up."

"Yes, sir."

Simon's sister and Roderick Powell had entered, and stood among the chairs in the neighbourhood of the fireplace. Simon led the dog to the door and then handed him over to his new man. As he was leaving the room, the enormous animal heard voices down in the hall. He filled the staircase with the most primeval sounds—the war-cry of the wolf. Simon went quickly outside the door. He placed his hand on the dog's neck.

"There is no occasion to threaten everyone in that way. Until you have good reason to believe that they are inimical, remain silent. I know you *won't*."

The man smiled. "I should be surprised if he did, sir."

Simon went to the head of the stairs. "Who is it?" he shouted down. But at that moment he reached the top and said, "Oh, it's you Harry."

"What is that terrifying monster you have up there, Syme?" cried the young man, looking up the stairs.

"It's my new dog. Let me introduce you," Simon said, pulling the growling dog forward by the collar.

"Gosh, I can dispense with an introduction, I think. Do not let me interrupt your family life. Will you be round at the pub at the usual hour?"

"Yes, I will. Who have you got there with you?"

"Only a woman," Harry shouted, and he and the anonymous female hurriedly left.

Simon then went back into the room and closed the door. "Good morning," he said.

"What a dragon!" said Eleanor.

"He wishes to understand that he is a Second Cause, as much as we are," Roderick observed.

"That is the idea." Simon nodded at some abstract person. "But it should be illegal to put on sale such an uncivilised beast. I shouldn't like the job of putting a muzzle on him."

"It ought never to have been admitted to these peace-loving islands." Roderick addressed himself to a flesh and blood person, not necessarily named Simon.

"Please sit down." Airily identifying himself as the host, Simon waved his hand... "Why don't you install yourself here, Eleanor—back in your old room—until you have decided what you are going to do?"

After a pause, Eleanor spoke, "Are you staying on here, then, Simon?"

"For a short while," answered her brother. There was a silence. Then he continued. "I have a proposition to make" (he looked at both his visitors). "Mother was richer than we realized; practically one hundred and fifty thousand pounds is what I find I inherit... Now, even after taxation, I do not need all that. Leaving nothing to you, because you are soon to be married, was rather extraordinary. But I suppose Aunt Margaret's windfall, she may have regarded as enough, in view of your marriage."

"Simon, although I was left nothing directly, I was recommended to your brotherly care. And much of the furniture in this house is mine, you will recall." She looked at him with an attempted neutrality.

"Of course," he said, "I shall not be here for very long; you may come and pick out whatever you want when I go." (Eleanor wiped her eyes and blew her nose). "But I said just now that I had a proposition to make. Here it is. I will give you fifty thousand pounds—or whatever works out as a third of the estate. You, on your side, agree *not* to marry our Reverend friend. What do you say?... I should hand you a third of my money. I should in any case have passed over to you some such proportion of our mother's estate. There is only one thing, I could not do that so long as you adhere to your intention to marry our friend here."

Roderick, very pale, rose to his feet. "Eleanor, our marriage must not stand between you and this fortune," he said firmly. "You know what I feel. But I would not marry you under the circumstances. I think I had better go." Roderick bowed, and turned towards the door.

Eleanor sprang to her feet, and lifted her hand commandingly. She stared at Simon, her face distorted with rage. "Keep that dirty money in your pocket. I hope it brings you to your ruin! Ugh! You crazy beast!" She rushed after Roderick, caught him up, and seized him by the arm.

Grasping her hand, and removing it gently from his arm, Roderick protested, "No, you must really allow me to leave. It was foolish of me to have come."

Simon, who had risen, swiftly intercepted them, and stood with his back to the door. "I will not allow you both to leave me like this." His voice was hard and cold. "It is *you* who are crazy..., not me. I have only made a *proposal*. Come back here, both of you, and let us discuss this."

"Eleanor, do as your brother suggests," Roderick was genuinely persuasive. "Come back..., come along. Simon is not a totally unreasonable man."

"You do not know him as well as I do." She violently shook her head.

"The man you knew is probably... oh, not the same," Roderick told her.

"Come along, Eleanor." Simon spoke amiably. "I have a new look. Roderick is right." Whereupon they all moved back to their chairs; the ice appeared to be melting. "I am quite sincere when I say that I like Rod, I realise how difficult it must be for both of you to believe that."

"Not for me," Rod burst in warmly. "I have always liked you, Simon, and why should you not feel the same towards me? It is usually that way."

"Well!" Simon left it at that.

"You have a bee in your bonnet about my cloth," Roderick gently insinuated. "But suppose I was some blackguardly stockbroker, *that* I suppose would be all right?" He smiled.

"I am afraid, Rod, you are right in your assumption. If my sister were marrying a stockjobber I should not mind—nor an auctioneer, nor a bookie."

"I dislike a majority of religionists as much as you do," Rod assured him. "I heard a scottish minister on the radio a night or two ago. He nearly made me sick."

"Well, *that* is what your religion is like!" Simon insisted disagreeably. "Did they sing 'Hallelujah Amen'? A beautiful hymn!"

"I could tell you of many worse than that." Rod was sternly peaceable. "A great deal of our religion gets distorted and animalised."

"I see what you mean," Simon said aggressively. "Yours is Christianity for the uppercrust—God for the Public School product. But was not your religion originally a proletarian creed? Was it not designed for the most elementary type of citizen? So is not a Salvation Army performance much nearer to authentic Christianity than the kind of service cooked up in anglo-catholic churches?"

"Emperors as well as slaves became adherents of this teaching." Roderick looked rather tired as if he had taught enough for one night. "However I am not trying to convert you, only to point out that Christianity is a name for a half-a-dozen different cults. You did occasionally encounter persons in holy orders, divinity dons, and so on, up at Oxford. You must have noticed that these distinguished people were not the kind of tubthumping Salvationists for whom you have so great an antipathy."

"Oh yes, and even in this house I have encountered genially smiling, well-tailored, pleasant-mannered gentlemen, who were clergymen. But they are merely Salvation Army Captains disguised." The host glowered sullenly at the guest.

"I do assure you Simon, that you are rating these men, on the whole, too high. I am the genuine article; but nine out of ten of this dark-suited tribe need not embarrass you. They are not much more Christian than you are!" Rod gave his host a tired beam—for he now had no further belief in the efficacy of his beam.

"Well, now," Simon grew facetious, "if you were a man of that kind, a self-confessed idler, who, beyond a short masquerade in church on Sunday, does next to nothing for his fat living..."

"You are wrong, not at all a fat living."

"Well, were you one of that crowd, one could treat you as a small-time businessman."

Roderick helped a sigh on its way with a heave of the shoulders. "I am sorry. There does not seem to be any excuse for me."

"Look, Roderick," Simon was coaxing. "Have you a call? Could you not be a Christian ponce[5] to the woman of your choice? Would you give up your career as a clergyman?"

"Of course not," Roderick objected blandly. "You are a peculiar fellow."

"I do not see where we are wandering to," Eleanor said in a dispirited voice.

"I am afraid," Rod told her, "that your brother will next be proposing that he organises a well-appointed bordello, and appoint me as Manager—on the understanding that I do not wear my dog-collar, and cease to be a parson."

Simon laughed. "That is very near to what I was about to propose."

"I think you should consult a psychiatrist, Simon." Rod pointed towards his head.

"Had it occurred to you that a mental overhaul might be the solution of your present difficulties?" Simon retorted.

"A tu quoque? Have we reached those depths!"

Simon's face took on an increasingly disagreeable expression. "Look, Your Reverence, I have gazed upon that sleek, slimy, clerical face searching this way and that for a weak spot in my defences long enough."

"And I have listened for quite long enough to your coarseness," Eleanor explained as she stood up. "Come, Roderick, let us leave this brute to his own devices."

Simon pressed a bell. The clergyman was sighing. "Very well. There is nothing else for it."

"No, I am afraid there isn't." Simon was now even more final. Diplomacy was at an end.

The man-servant entered the room, and stood, without speaking, just inside the door. Simon turned towards him, saying, "Show these people out, please."

"You got us here in order to insult us, you swine." Eleanor turned on her brother in a spasm of family fury. "You are not insane, but simply a dirty piece of work! If I had a cane in my hand I would slash you across your ugly face!"

Simon, remaining magisterially in his chair, bawled new orders at the man-servant. "Black, I have listened longer than I should to that ill-bred bitch. Please, take her by the shoulders, Black, and run her out." The man approached Eleanor.

"Lay a finger on that lady," Roderick threatened the servant, "and I will knock the head off your shoulders."

Disliking this mode of address, the man went immediately into action; stepping quickly towards Eleanor, and putting his hand under her arm, he grasped her firmly. The behaviour of this new, dark-faced myrmidon of her brother's enraged Eleanor beyond anything which had ever happened to her in her life. With a bound she flung him off, crying, "How *dare* you! Take your filthy hand...!"

But already the man was not there. He had been dragged away with a speed and muscular competence which must have surprised the servant, starting from the moment that the menial hand first dived down insolently beneath the arm of his fiancée, by the knight-errant in clerical grey, beside himself as he saw what was beginning to happen. He no longer thought of this young madman as the *Simon* who was the brother of his Eleanor. That was not the situation; they had quite clearly entered a wild event, in which everything would be decided by the mental convulsion of someone who would probably soon be in the hands of the doctors.

Having dragged the servant away from his fiancée, Roderick stepped back and directed a blow at the proper spot for the purpose of laying an antagonist out at full length on the floor. Down went the servant and, obviously in no mood to fight his master's battles for him, the man lay peaceably where he had fallen. Roderick gave him a glance or two, but was soon convinced that that was all the hired man would do in the present conjuncture.

"Oh my god, a fighting parson!" Simon shouted, laughing.

Eleanor seemed in some way attuned to her brother's hysteria. His laughter incensed her as if it were responsible laughter. She denounced him as if he were the Simon of everyday.

"Stop laughing!" she cried. "If Rod did not know how to defend himself—and defend me—your new fangled footman would be putting me outside the front-door."

Simon stretching his leg out, kicked the recumbent man-servant.

"Here, get up, you cowardly animal," Simon growled. "You will receive no salary for lying on the floor."

The man-servant, without moving, answered his employer without looking up. "You shall hear from my lawyer, Mister Clever."

"You hear that, Eleanor?" Simon turned towards his sister. "Why don't you get *your* little legal bloke to bombard me with a letter or two? I could compare the literary style of his lawyer and of yours."

"I may yet have to resort to the Law," Eleanor warned him.

"Now that we are on these terms, Eleanor," Simon's voice was friendly and confidential, "I want you to tell me something, which I have always been curious about. Does Rod kiss you first, and cross himself afterwards, or the other way round?"

Looking very black indeed, Rod said, in a low voice, "I shouldn't continue, if I were you!"

"Excuse me, is it the Fighting Parson speaking?" Simon politely enquired. "Dear, dear. I see I shall have to smack you, or rather kick you down the stairs."

"What a loathsome individual you are!" Eleanor exclaimed.

Simon smiled. "You never answered me about the clerical kiss. When did he first imprint a kiss upon your bright red lips? Did he shyly steal his professionally smiling lips near to the mole on your left cheek, daring to place a hand on your heaving waist...?"

Roderick sprang at him and struck him blow after blow. But as Simon had run his two forearms up over his face—his two eyes glittering with mischief from between this barricade—Rod did not succeed in landing his blows nearer to a vital spot than the very muscular arms of his young host.

The assault appeared to excite and amuse Simon, who darted out at him, squealing in a strange excited voice (as the blows permitted—the voice being interrupted and, as it were, thudded on). "Obviously... the dark... mysteries... of your sexual life... oh that, you really keep... keep down... out of sight."

Roderick grew more and more infuriated as this voice jeered at him from between the protective barriers of muscle. The openings, from which Simon peered and jeered, easily contracted and expanded. Rod aimed blow after blow at the skulking face, but he was unable to reach it. The sparkling eyes continued to tease him, and the voice to squeal at him insults and pornographic jokes.

"Stand up and fight, you double-dyed cad!" Rod panted.

But the double-dyed cad simply died with laughter within his fortress and squealed with delight. Simon could be coherent too. "Run away, you big bully," he taunted the perspiring Rod. "I am not going to be assaulted in my own house. I shall telephone the police and have you marched off to the Station."

While Simon was saying this, he scored a heavy kick upon Roderick's thigh: a burst of shrill hilarity followed this success. "Saucy little parson," Simon lisped. "I am getting sick of holding these arms up here. I shall get up and kill you if you don't vanish. I will break your arms and break your head." This battle tore along with great speed. To translate anything breathless, words are too sluggish a medium.[6]

There are some things that men see out of the backs of their heads, or feel through a hobnailed boot. Of that class was the appearance in this mad room of the mad face of a vast dog, with its muzzle hanging loose under its chin. So, with an icy suddenness, the blood congealed in everyone's veins, except in the veins of the man. Simon saw the dog with glee. The man-servant upon the floor shivered, for his body was flat, much too flat; at one moment four paws were tensed upon his body. He felt pinned down completely, though [7] a shivering alarm was excessive.

The gargling roar which burst into the room and filled it did not at once still the fists of the Fighting Parson. They continued to hammer—long enough to attract the canine policeman, for was not this the emotional centre for which he was always looking? The tremendous body stood for a moment rigid at the doorway, but once he had spotted where the trouble was, he hurled himself through the air, and his great face was glaring at Simon's twinkling eyes, mocking him from between his forearms.

The dog did not see what men saw, but a cringing figure in front of it attempting to arrest it—what they had taught him at the police-school, the ideal human target,[8] he had literally discharged himself at, and now had much more success than Roderick in unmasking the playful Simon. He fixed his teeth in one of the arms, and tore it away from the face. Simon smelt the hot rancid breath of the dog, and a flavour of blood, which was his. The dark snout, unbelievably unlovely, surmounted the teeth and obscured his view. He looked at it with smiling horror, full of comic reproach.

At this point Eleanor rushed to the telephone, which was not very near, tore the receiver out of its socket, and dialed the classic trio, nine, nine, nine, the number of high emergency. Roderick had followed her across the room, and stood not far away as she breathlessly informed the Police of what was going on in this room.

"No," she cried, "not mad. It is my brother who is mad... No, I have a young clergyman..., no, he is *not* a clerical milksop..., there is a man-servant, but he is on the floor..., no, the clergyman knocked him down..., yes, yes, yes."

She turned to Roderick. "They are awful! They talk such nonsense! Heaven knows what they will do."

"They will come all right," Rod assured her, "but..."

Simon had flung the dog away from his face, had leapt up, and trampling upon the man-servant, he staggered, smiling, across the room, the dog growling at him like an earthquake, his great teeth bared a foot or so from Simon's mouth. Man and dog moved quickly towards the door, and there Simon attempted to push the Frankenstein outside, but Frankenstein preferred to stop inside. Apparently it was a bright idea of Simon's to lure the monster outside by going there himself. But what resulted was that *both* went outside, and Simon was pinned against the wall with the dog at his throat.

In spite of the shrieking woman at his heels, Roderick raced through the door, and seized the dog by the collar, throwing all his weight into the pull. He succeeded in deflecting the monster from its prime target (not by weight of course) only to have the teeth of the dog fixed in his shoulder as it bore him floorwards with a primeval snarl. Simon, still smiling, had taken a step forward, both hands clutching at his gory mask. The dog shook Roderick up and down, then, apparently catching sight of Simon out of the corner of its eye, leapt away from Roderick, and barred the road to Simon, who was about to descend the stairs, with a swelling diapason which was certainly the most thrilling growl ever heard, ending with a snarling crack. That was the situation when Eleanor saw her opportunity. Coaxing and pulling she slid her little hero through the door, and slammed it in spite of his protests.

"You see how things are! You have done all and much more than you need, Rod. You can do nothing with that wounded arm. Take your coat off—if you can—and let me attend to you."

He climbed reluctantly into a chair, and she began pulling his jacket off the uniformed arm.

"Eleanor, so long as I have the strength to lend a hand, I will not be put in a sick-bay..."

The turmoil from the other side of the door caused the young clergyman to stiffen and complain, "I say!"

"I know, darling, it is perfectly awful, but please let us get this jacket off. I must do something about that gash..."

A terrifying crash froze both of them at this moment, the man and the dog had crashed into the bannisters—something of that sort was conveyed to the listeners by the very expressive sounds. Roderick sprang to his feet and actually had his hand upon the handle of the door when she turned the key and removed it.

Roderick was really white with indignation and frustration.

"You shall not lock me up and prevent me from doing my duty, Eleanor," he glared appealingly at her; he was a martyr to her instinct to preserve her husband-to-be.

The man-servant appeared, emerging from behind a cottage piano, rising to his feet, and showing certain signs of intending to join them. They both gazed at him with as much surprise as disgust, Eleanor curling her lip in a very marked manner.

"You miserable cur!" she exclaimed. "Are you not ashamed to show your face, after your performance on the floor?"

The servant looked at her for a moment, getting a little red. "How about what you are doin', lockin' this gentleman in! I'm a servant, see? If you wanted me to play with your mad dogs you would have to pay me a bit more money than your brother does. See, Miss Clever!"

Roderick was again rising from his sitting position, in spite of the serious condition of his shoulder, Eleanor dissuading him.

"Look here, my man!" he spoke with clerical authority. "If you do not keep a civil tongue in your head, I will knock you back onto the floor on which you should have remained."

The man laughed insultingly. "Come and try, though a clergyman like you shouldn't parade your cloth..."

The most infernal noise broke out from a point half-way down the staircase, a prolonged shriek of pain making it particularly terrifying. This was the great crisis, and Roderick rushed to the door, vainly attempting to open it.

"Let him out, Miss," it was the man's voice, "let the little parson kill the dog."

Something broke against the wall, with a startling impact; it was a vase which Eleanor had thrown at the man-servant.

"Thank you, Miss, but it's a good thing for you that it didn't hit me. That would have cost you a tidy bit!"

After the maximum outburst from the stairs, there was a dead silence. Roderick stamped, his eyes flashed. "Open that door! Do you hear me? This is abominable." He appeared to be menacing his fiancée, the veins standing out on his forehead. There were three rifle shots, downstairs, as it seemed. After two or three minutes' silence there was a commotion of voices in the hall, which in its turn, was followed by a heavy step upon the stairs. At this sound Eleanor ran to the door and unlocked it. The servant advanced until he was standing immediately behind the young clergyman. When the door opened, and a police constable entered, it was the man-servant whose voice was first heard.

"These people 'ere, Officer, 'ave been keepin' me locked up in this room."

"You liar—you dirty liar!" shouted Eleanor, threatening to strike him.

"Excuse me, ma'am," said the policeman brusquely. "Are you Miss Richards..., Miss Eleanor Richards?"

"Yes, that is my name." Eleanor stood quite straight and immovable.

"I have some news..., some very serious news for you, ma'am..., extremely serious..."

"What!" She seemed unable to say anymore. Then it was with a gasp that she asked, "Is he... dead?"

"Yes, Miss Richards, I am sorry to have to tell you we found your brother dead, Miss. It is our opinion he was so savaged by that dog, which is as large as a horse..."

Eleanor flung herself into a chair, sobbing with a crazy abandon.

"You have, of course, had no time, Officer, to make any investigations?" Roderick enquired.

"No, sir, not just yet, sir."

"The first thing, I suppose, you will wish to know is who unmuzzled the dog?"

"I noticed how its muzzle hung loose," the policeman agreed. "That hung down under his chin..."

"That fellow there," Roderick said, pointing to the man-servant, "he was in charge of the dog. He left this room with it..."

"Look 'ere, mister, don't you try and pin nothin' on me, or I'll 'ave something to say to..."

"Close your ugly, lying mouth...!" Roderick was unable to control himself.

"Now, none of that, you gentlemen..." the policeman warned.

"Oh I know, I beg your pardon. But that is how all this began..., the dog..., but no muzzle! It suddenly entered the room..." Roderick pointed over at the man-servant. "That fellow got here just before..."

"An' if I did, you bloody little creepin' Jesus..."

The policeman turned angrily towards the man-servant. "A little bit less of you...!"

Roderick, as white as his shirt, and trembling as he spoke, addressed the policeman. "Have you a doctor downstairs?"

"No, sir, not a doctor, sir."

"One must be sent for...," Roderick swayed a little.

The constable approached him, some first-aid material in his hand. "Let me fix that arm of yours, sir," he said, "a nice cut that was, sir."

Eleanor sprang to her feet, unsteadily, her face disgusting with the stains of tears, and the distortions of her grief.

With an exclamation, Roderick rose and flung himself towards her. Seizing her arm, he cried, "Darling, you will fall!"

"Please, Rod, sit down." They swayed about almost in one another's arms. She got her arm covered in blood in the process. She pushed away from him, almost knocking him over. He steadied himself against the back of a chair, his head thrust out towards her.

"What is it...," he asked rather wildly. "Where are you going?"

"I am going to my brother," she answered, staggering towards the door.

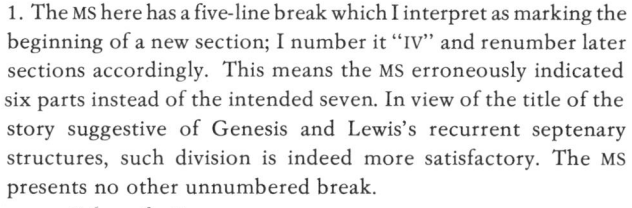

---

1. The MS here has a five-line break which I interpret as marking the beginning of a new section; I number it "IV" and renumber later sections accordingly. This means the MS erroneously indicated six parts instead of the intended seven. In view of the title of the story suggestive of Genesis and Lewis's recurrent septenary structures, such division is indeed more satisfactory. The MS presents no other unnumbered break.
2. MS: "three fits"
3. MS: "door"
4. A break in the MS indicates that Lewis intended to add here a prayer for the recommendation of the soul. Perhaps he intended "Libera, Domine, animam ancillae tuae ex omnibus periculis inferni et de calamitate aeterna." The next prayer by Rod ("Subvenite... Altissimi.") is the one to be uttered just after death.
5. MS: "pounds." Ponce (English slang): a pimp. In the typescript of the dramatized version, this sentence reads: "Could you not be a Christian without being a priest? Supposing I gave you fifty

thousand pounds to the woman of your choice?"

6. This sentence is garbled in the MS, with "unless you" in place of "words"; it is corrected here from the TS of the dramatized version.

7. MS: "thought"

8. MS: "tardy." The typescript of the dramatized version has "tardet."

▼ ▼ ▼

THE STARRY SKY, 1912
WYNDHAM LEWIS
PENCIL, PEN AND INK, WASH AND GOUACHE. 46.5 x 62 cm
COURTESY ARTS COUNCIL OF GREAT BRITAIN
MICHEL 86

MINA LOY

"THE STARRY SKY" OF WYNDHAM LEWIS

who raised
these rocks of human mist

pyramidical survivors
in the cyclorama of space

In the
austere theatre of the Infinite
        the ghosts of the stars
perform the "Presence"

Their celibate shadows
fall
upon the aged radiance
of suns and moons

—The nerves of Heaven
  flinching
  from the antennae
  of the intellect
—the rays
  that pierce
    the nocturnal heart
The airy eyes of angels
the sublime
experiment in pointillism
faded away

The celestial conservatories
blooming with light
are all blown out

Enviable immigrants
into the pure dimension
immune   serene
devourers of the morning stars of Job

Jehovah's seven days
err in your silent entrails
of geometric Chimeras

The Nirvanic snows
drift— — —
to sky worn images

Reprinted from *The Little Review*.

SEAMUS COONEY

NOTES ON THE COLOR PLATES

None of the accompanying illustrations has been published in color reproduction heretofore. Two of the items are not listed in Walter Michel's authoritative *Wyndham Lewis: Paintings and Drawings* (Univ. of California Press, 1971). As a group, these illustrations give a brief survey of the development of Lewis's visual style, ranging from his early experimentalism, through his major Vorticist period, to his later, mellower "dreams of beauty." Especially when viewed in conjunction with the drawings and designs reproduced elsewhere in this volume, they well represent the varied work of a major artist.

In the following brief notes, "Michel" refers to the work cited above, "Farrington" to Jane Farrington's catalogue of the travelling exhibition recently originating at the Manchester City Art Gallery, published by Lund Humphries, London, in 1980; and "Cork" to Richard Cork's *Vorticism and Abstract Art in the First Machine Age*; (Univ. of California Press, 1976). My debts to these authorities will be self-evident. Measurements are given in centimeters.

PLATE 1 *Lovers*, 1912. Pen and ink, watercolor. 25.4 x 35.6 cm. (Private collection.) Michel 74 (pl. 12); Farrington 17. This belongs to the year when Lewis said he came to maturity as a painter (Michel, p. 43) and to the first creative upsurge. In an overall articulated surface of sweeping curves modulating at the periphery into straight lines and angles, the "wild bodies" partake of the energy of the formal picture plane: the eye's rhythmic restlessness and unending circling analogize the movements of the dancing lovers. Farrington calls the composition "reminiscent of Futurist lines of force." Compare *Creation* and *The Dancers*, both also 1912 (Michel 46 and 48).

PLATE 2 *Centauress*, 1912. Pen and ink, wash. 30.8 x 36.8 cm. (Courtesy Cecil Higgins Art Gallery.) Michel 41 (pl. 6); Farrington 10. Incongruously, the organic mythological figure is surrounded by and seems aghast at the strict geometric forms that fill the picture plane and even seem to encroach on her forelegs, which are more like tripods than legs. Farrington sees "A fragile mythological creature confronted by the harsh and threatening forms of the modern industrial world."

PLATE 3 *Composition III*, 1914–1915. Pencil and watercolor. 27.9 x 26 cm. (Courtesy Anthony d'Offay.) Michel 180 (untitled; not reproduced); Farrington 40. One of the designs from the "Vorticist Sketch-Book," this piece captures the excitement and assurance of the Vorticist aesthetic and Lewis's creative use of "the theme of the city," which, as Cork writes, "engaged most of Lewis's attention at this period. He returned to it incessantly, and the twenty pages of his so-called 'Vorticist Sketch-Book' bear witness to an obsession with the kind of quintessential industrial structures recommended as the artist's true subject matter in *Blast No. 1*'s manifestos." Cork writes of the present piece, "The series of repeated rectangles ascending the upper half... can, for example, easily be read as the windows of a modern office block; and yet they are so intermingled with less identifiable fragments of geometry that it would be inadvisable to pin them down to such a specific descriptive function." And he cites Lewis writing in BLAST 2:

> A Vorticist, lately, painted a picture in which a crowd of squarish shapes, at once suggesting windows, occurred. A sympathizer with the movement asked him, horror-struck, "Are not those windows?" "Why not?" the Vorticist replied. "A window is for you actually A WINDOW: for me it is a space, bounded by a square or oblong frame, by four bands or four lines, merely." (Cork, pp. 338-40)

PLATE 4 *The Psychologist*, 1917. Also called *The Great Vegetarian*. Pen and ink, watercolor. 16.5 x 13 cm. (Courtesy Victoria and Albert Museum.) Michel 257 (pl. 32); Farrington 45. Farrington associates this

233

with the 1909 drawings *Anthony* and *The Green Tie* (Michel 11 and 12), but clearly the rendering of the face has moved well beyond their relatively naturalistic style, though not here as "Vorticist" as in other 1917 drawings. Farrington sees a debt to German Expressionism, especially perhaps Nolde about whom Lewis had written favorably in BLAST 1.

PLATE 5 *Walking Wounded*, 1918. Pen and ink, crayon, watercolor. 25.4 x 35.6 cm. (Courtesy Imperial War Museum.) Michel 322 (pl. 33); Farrington 48. This is Lewis, the War Artist, at his most powerful. Farrington remarks that "The high viewpoint and metallic gleam of the bodies make the figures resemble struggling insects." The threateningly outward-exploding shellburst at upper left pushes the eye down to the three men cowering from its force, averting their faces as they painfully struggle to escape. Ahead of them, two stronger and more determined figures seem, with their staffs, reminiscent of pilgrims fleeing the City of Destruction. Above their heads and perhaps continuing off to the right—their ultimate destination?—is a calm but ominous dark blue void.

PLATE 6 *Figure Composition*, c. 1921. Pen and ink, watercolor, pencil. 34.6 x 44.5 cm. (Courtesy Anthony d'Offay.) Michel 456 (pl. 79); Farrington 86. This is one of those works that Hugh Kenner refers to as being "like pictures of pieces of sculpture, fully imagined three-dimensional forms" (in Michel, p. 28). The totem-pole figures occur in many Lewis works of the period and also in the *Tyro* designs. Farrington remarks that "The frieze-like grouping of the forms suggests figures on a stage."

PLATE 7 *Archimedes Reconnoitring the Enemy Fleet*, 1922. Pen and ink, watercolor. 33 x 47.6 cm. (Courtesy The Vint Trust.) Michel 519 (pl. 81); Farrington 95. Archimedes devised engines of war to hold off the Roman fleet besieging his home city of Syracuse. The drawing resembles *Abstract Composition*, 1921 (Michel 441, Color Plate IX) and *Abstract Composition*, 1921 (Michel 442, pl. 81) in its use of space left blank on the paper. All of these, like PLATE 8 below, have moved away from the Vorticist style. As Farrington puts it, "Forms are more complex and curvilinear compared with the Vorticist grid-like shapes." The style here is better seen as a development from the *Tyro* drawings. Michel has high praise for the present piece:

> A final surprise of this period is *Archimedes Reconnoitring the Enemy Fleet*. The vertical structures are spaced to a pulse beat, increasing to the right, interrupted, phased, and finally mounting to a crescendo. To this expansion toward the right, the contraction of the contour provides a counter-movement. Both phrases terminate in an almost blank band. The eye, following their sweep, may be drawn to examine the course of the upper contour which now appears like a vast basin against whose inner surface a sky may be discerned, as if projected by a lantern on a curved surface.
>
> The intricate details of the verticals, characteristic of 1921-3, are now suddenly seen in a three-dimensional space, like guard towers, accenting the depth of the sky.
>
> The composition is full of suggestions of gay flags and shapes of boats and ocean, yet it is truly abstract. (Michel, p. 102)

PLATE 8 *Vorticist Composition*, 1922. Gouache, India ink and pencil. 33.2 x 49.7 cm. (Courtesy Anthony d'Offay.) Not in Michel or Farrington. Title as furnished by Anthony d'Offay. This impressive design, with its mainly curvilinear and organic shapes, would appear related more to PLATES 6 and 7 above than to the work of the Vorticist period. The totem-like figure on the left, now more voluptuously contoured than in PLATE 6, is balanced by a more geometrically composed group on the right, where the ink triangles provide the only reminiscence of Vorticist style.

PLATE 9 *Figures in the Air*, 1927. Also called *On the Roof*. Pencil, pen and ink, watercolor. 29.2 x 16.5 cm. (Courtesy The Vint Trust.) Michel 635 (pl. 85); Farrington 105. An inert-looking recumbent figure seems yet to support a pole on which a group of three others appear to balance. The surrounding volumes are architectural in suggestion, whence perhaps the alternate title. Farrington comments, "The skewered figures and tilting perspective produce a sinister and disturbing composition. A reclining mannikin-like form with stunted limbs occurs frequently in imaginative drawings of the period. . . . "

PLATE 10 *The Immortality of the Soul*, c. 1933. Pen, ink, watercolor. 24.4 x 35 cm. (Courtesy Seamus and Katy Cooney.) Not in Michel. Farrington 123. The inscription, "Athanaton ara e Psyche," translates as "Immortal therefore the soul." The same inscription appears on Michel 626 (pl. 90), 1927, to which it also serves as title; *Creation Myth No. 1*, 1933 (Michel 787, Color Plate II) has the word "Athanaton" inscribed. Farrington remarks, "The latter is the closest to this drawing with the same floating pin-head figures and a glimpse of a calm blue sea"; hence she dates it c. 1933. It may well, however, be closer to 1927, the date assigned by its former owner, The Fine Art Society Ltd.

Uterine shapes are surmounted by a sea-like passage and bounded at the left by an area of calm green and at the right by the white of the paper. Within, balancing on a fire-red column, a busy activity of voluptuous female forms, among them some tiny spermatoid shapes. Two defined faces stand out: a half-smiling figure gazing into the distance to the left, her long hair leading to a supporting tubular column; and on the right, much smaller, a pertly modern female profile with eye and nose treated in the Egyptian style—a humorous touch, surely.

PLATE 11 *Red and Black Principle*, 1936. Also known as *Two Figures*. Oil on canvas. 116.9 x 61 cm. (Courtesy Santa Barbara Museum of Art: gift of Wright S. Ludington.) Michel P62 (pl. 112). Two warriors in a suggestion of Roman armor. The almost featureless heads suggest helmets, with the background to the one on the right evoking a crest. Below, the black suggests cloaks. Farrington's comment on the next item, PLATE 12 below, is apposite here: "Lewis was fascinated by the warrior explorers of past civilizations and their various forms of battledress."

PLATE 12 *Landscape with Northmen*, c. 1936–1937. Oil on canvas. 67.3 x 49.5 cm. (Courtesy Penelope Allen.) Michel P66 (pl. 112); Farrington 131. See the com- the delight of the student of Lewis's *œuvre*" (p. 123). painting to *The Armada* (Michel P70) and *Newfoundland* (Michel P67) as well as to a lost painting called *Christopher Columbus*. She adds: "The sea is invariably present in Lewis's imaginative compositions, and although *Landscape with Northmen* appears at first to be a landscape of undulating hills, the Viking ship's prow indicates that the figures stand on a shore." One might add that the shore is more like a quay or dock, and with the tower in the right background, the suggestion is of a Viking fortified town.

Michel writes of this oil: "If [it] were partially covered, to expose only the upper quarter, we should hardly be able to identify the painter of such a Chinese landscape. Even the whole upper half would be recognized as Lewis's by its controlled richness and daring of the imagination rather than by specific stylistic features. This scene of invented trees and clouds and oriental palaces, an unexpected background for Lewisian stock figures, is another of those imaginative feats, out of the blue, which are the delight of the student of Lewis's *oeuvre*" (p. 123).

PLATE 13 *Mexican Shawl*, 1938. Oil on canvas. 63.5 x 76.2 cm. (Courtesy City of Bristol Museum and Art Gallery.) Michel P84 (pl. 114); Farrington 139. "Lewis's only surviving nude study in oil," writes Farrington. "The bowl of oranges has a Cézannesque precision and acts as a kind of focal point. . . ." The model is Anne Lewis ("Froanna"), the artist's wife. The beautifully restful, gently rocking curves of the composition extend from the tiers of the table and bowl, through the figure in every detail, including fingers and eyelids, to the treatment of shade and color in the pillows. Michel calls this (though it is probably, like the preceding oil, one of the works Lewis painted in a conscious attempt to be commercial) "one of Lewis's finest works, for its luscious reddish-browns, highlighted in the shawl with rich red and green, present a contrast of soft flesh and abstract patterns, which is pulled into a composition of the utmost subtlety" (p. 124).

PLATE 14 *Day Dream of the Nubian*, 1938. Oil on canvas. 76.2 x 101.6 cm. (Courtesy Naomi Mitchison.) Michel P78 (pl. 114); Farrington 138. The present owner of this oil, Naomi Mitchison, posed for the figure it centers on. Farrington quotes from her autobiography, *You May Well Ask* (London, 1979), her description of the painting as a "resting Ethiopian, a beautiful ebony woman lying on a cushion with one hand out above the blue stream in front of her across a corner of the picture. 'What is she doing?' I asked. 'Picking a dream out of the river.' 'Oh, do put it in!' So he paints in the shape of a dream and the background of the picture has a Greek temple front cutting into a strong pattern of white: this too for me." Michel illustrates a detail of an earlier version of the hand, changed at Naomi Mitchison's request.

From Michel we learn that "In 1936, finding no market for his work, Lewis persuaded himself that he must make a deliberate effort to produce works that would sell. He writes to his dealers: 'To hell with these experimental "difficult" contraptions. . . . I will do no more for six months, or until I am solvent. I will really do dreams of beauty, which will sell themselves . . .'" This and the next item, says Michel, "are perhaps the most likely of the thirties paintings to be called 'dreams of beauty'. But the first, except for the head, is a highly abstracted study in blues and greens . . ." (Michel, pp. 123-24).

PLATE 15 *Stephen Spender*, 1938. Oil on canvas. 100.3 x 59.7 cm. (Courtesy City Museum and Art Gallery, Stoke-on-Trent.) Michel P86 (pl. 132); Farrington 141. A worthy representative in our mini-gallery of one of Lewis's greatest strengths: the portrait, especially the literary portrait. His sitters included the giants of the age—Ezra Pound, T. S. Eliot, James Joyce—as well as minor figures like Edith Sitwell and Spender. The self-consciously "proletarian" and would-be modernist character of Spender's work in the thirties accounts for both the costuming and the background of abstract painting, as Hugh Kenner hints. Kenner also remarks how "Spender's [hands] express dangling tension, one forefinger self-consciously raised in a nervous bridge. (Try that pose. Feel the strain on the forefinger)" (in Michel, p. 38).

PLATE 16 *The Island*, 1942. Oil on canvas. 55.9 x 78.7 cm. (Courtesy Black Sparrow Press.) Michel P104 (pl. 161)—detail only. A painting done during Lewis's time in Canada. Akin to such drawings as *Bathers*,

1942 (Michel 992; Farrington 151), or *Allegresse Aquatique*, 1941 (Michel 964, pl. 159). Michel writes: "A group of drawings of 1941-2 introduces new and diverse variations of a theme Lewis had drawn many times before: nudes and bathers . . . [many] inspired by a collection of paintings by Etty, in the house of a Toronto industrialist. . . . His imagination is now more vivid, and lighter and deeper than it had ever been" (p. 143). Something of the air of an earthly paradise inheres in this scene of bathing, wrestling, dancing, and conversing groups of nudes, with the couple at lower right seeming engaged in amorous play. But the contrasting group in right middleground, clothed unlike the others and spatially isolated from them, seem different too in being absorbed in something other than the here-and-now, intently listening to a narrator's account—presumably of the island in the background towards which he is gesturing. Paul Edwards has suggested in a letter that this island (its importance emphasized by Lewis's picture title) is to be read as a reminiscence of Böcklin's *Die Toteninsel* (*The Island of the Dead*—5 versions dating from the 1880s). That Lewis knew this painting is confirmed by a reference to it in *Tarr*, and the island in the present work does markedly resemble Böcklin's, at least in its left half. If the allusion is accepted, the topic of the listening group's preoccupied interest can readily be divined.

▼ ▼ ▼

A PORTFOLIO OF ▶
WYNDHAM LEWIS
COLOR PLATES ▶

LOVERS, 1912
PEN AND INK, WATERCOLOR, 25.4 x 35.6 cm
PRIVATE COLLECTION

CENTAURESS, 1912
PEN AND INK, WASH, 30.8 x 36.8 cm
COURTESY CECIL HIGGINS ART GALLERY

COMPOSITION III, 1914-1915
PENCIL AND WATERCOLOR, 27.9 x 26 cm
COURTESY ANTHONY d'OFFAY

THE PSYCHOLOGIST, 1917
PEN AND INK, WATERCOLOR, 16.5 x 13 cm
COURTESY VICTORIA AND ALBERT MUSEUM

WYNDHAM LEWIS PLATES 3 & 4

WALKING WOUNDED, 1918
PEN AND INK, CRAYON, WATERCOLOR, 25.4 x 35.6 cm
COURTESY IMPERIAL WAR MUSEUM

FIGURE COMPOSITION, c. 1921
PEN AND INK, WATERCOLOR, PENCIL, 34.6 x 44.5 cm
COURTESY ANTHONY d'OFFAY

ARCHIMEDES RECONNOITRING THE ENEMY FLEET, 1922
PEN AND INK, WATERCOLOR, 33 x 47.6 cm
COURTESY THE VINT TRUST

VORTICIST COMPOSITION, 1922
GOUACHE, INDIA INK AND PENCIL, 33.2 x 49.7 cm
COURTESY ANTHONY d'OFFAY

WYNDHAM LEWIS PLATES 7 & 8

FIGURES IN THE AIR, 1927
PENCIL, PEN AND INK, WATERCOLOR, 29.2 x 16.5 cm
COURTESY THE VINT TRUST

THE IMMORTALITY OF THE SOUL, c. 1933-4
PEN, INK AND WATERCOLOR, 24.4 x 35 cm
COURTESY SEAMUS AND KATY COONEY

RED AND BLACK PRINCIPLE, 1936
OIL ON CANVAS, 116.9 x 61 cm
COURTESY SANTA BARBARA MUSEUM OF ART,
GIFT OF WRIGHT S. LUDINGTON

LANDSCAPE WITH NORTHMEN, c. 1936-7
OIL ON CANVAS, 67.3 x 49.5 cm
COURTESY PENELOPE ALLEN

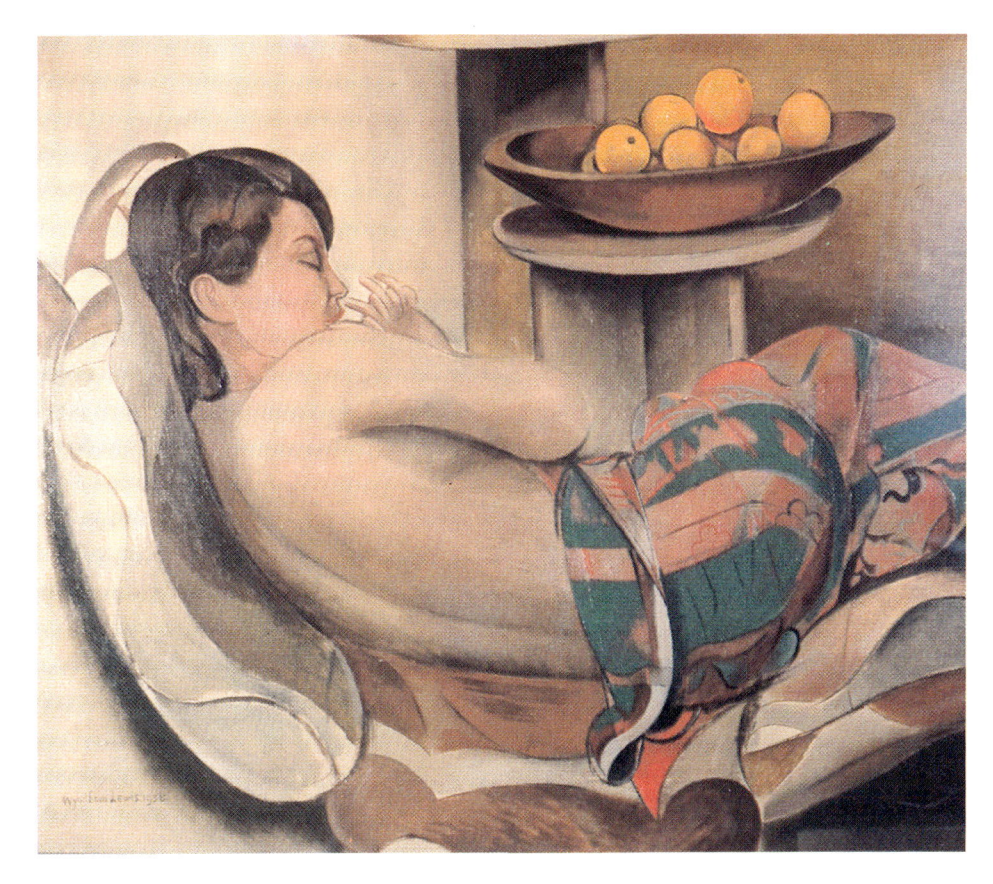

MEXICAN SHAWL, 1938
OIL ON CANVAS, 63.5 x 76.2 cm
COURTESY CITY OF BRISTOL MUSEUM AND ART GALLERY

DAY DREAM OF THE NUBIAN, 1938
OIL ON CANVAS, 76.2 x 101.6 cm
COURTESY NAOMI MITCHISON

WYNDHAM LEWIS PLATES 13 & 14

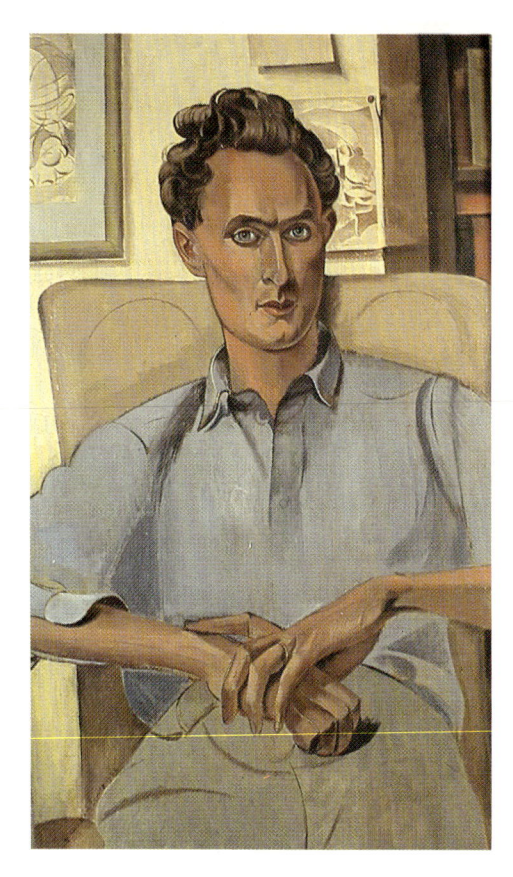

STEPHEN SPENDER, 1938
OIL ON CANVAS, 100.3 x 59.7 cm
COURTESY CITY MUSEUM AND ART GALLERY,
STOKE-ON-TRENT

THE ISLAND, 1942
OIL ON CANVAS, 55.9 x 78.7 cm
COURTESY BLACK SPARROW PRESS

WYNDHAM LEWIS PLATES 15 & 16

JOYCE CAROL OATES

FRISSONS

A HYPOTHESIS

At the age of three months he suffered from tuberculosis of the spine. (If "suffered" is the proper term since, as an infant, he had not yet developed his fastidious sensitivity—he could not have melodramatized himself as "Constantine Reinhart, who suffered.") The spinal tuberculosis led to a severe curvature of the back which in turn affected the shoulders, so that the right shoulder jutted up two inches higher than the left. The arms, legs, and neck were unnaturally thin. The head appeared overlarge on that stunted body though in fact—in fact?—it may have been of normal size. Everyone remarked upon his high broad pale intelligent forehead, however. (He looks so grown-up! And is he frowning—is his forehead creased like that?) And his silky blond hair. (Which was soon trained to fall foppishly across his brow.) His eyelashes were scanty, and so pale as to appear colorless. His large eyes were a faint frank washed-out blue, not unattractive. Rather near-sighted. But that could be appealing: the child stared, he blinked, he raised his thin arched eyebrows. Because of his weak chest he was, of course, highly susceptible to colds—he rarely got through a winter without succumbing to bronchitis—he was always in danger of catching pneumonia. (Which he did catch at the age of eleven, almost fatally. But that was later.) His voice was high and wispy; when tormented by other children he screamed as though he were being killed—which was *very* funny, because his screams were so high-pitched, far sharper than any girl's.

Mere survival, he saw, would require genius. But even then—and this too he saw, he understood, for the child Constantine was nothing if not precocious—even then survival would not be *guaranteed*.

THE VICTIM

Constantine hurries to find a seat, half-crouching. He stoops over instinctively because of his height. He is late—the first of the films is being shown—a girl's face shimmers on the screen—Constantine gropes his way to an empty folding chair, stumbling over someone's legs—he murmurs an apology—he manages to sit down, greatly relieved. (He has been running in the rain for several blocks.)—The girl, that uncanny face? Does he know her?

There is no sound. The image is static. Hair-fine cracks in the print flicker, and the girl's heavy, hooded eyelids twitch now and then, and her nostrils—which are dark, very dark—widen and contract and widen again. Otherwise one would not know whether she is alive or dead.

The girl? Lisel? Whom he has met—whom he has *almost* met—in Myron Falk's entourage? Constantine leans forward in his seat, staring. He is still out of breath—he is still apprehensive.

The camera, stubborn and unmoving, is fixed upon the girl's vacant overexposed face. A close-up, uncomfortably intimate. Though gradually—very gradually—quarter-inch by quarter-inch—the camera is moving back. The girl is about twenty years old. She is "beautiful" but her expression is utterly blank. There is moisture on her forehead—perspiration?—rain?—and her hair, which appears to be wet, has been skinned back brutally from her face. One can see the hard bone of the forehead, the ridge behind the eyebrows (which are thicker and darker than is fashionable at this time). —Lisel? Constantine recognizes her, though he knows that, for the purposes of art, he should not "recognize" her. She is not a human being at the moment, or not primarily a human being: she is an image: an arresting image in a black-and-white film called *The Victim*, one of a dozen or more "experimental" films Constantine Reinhart has agreed, against his better judgment, to review.

As the seconds pass slowly into minutes the idea of "beauty" vanishes; the idea of a "beautiful face" vanishes. Perhaps that is not a face after all?—since it registers so little. It is the girl's queer stuporous immobility that mesmerizes the audience. That, and the idea, the intuition, the *certainty* (quite apart from the film's title) that something invisible is happening: something is being done off-camera.

Constantine cannot settle back in his seat. He is reacting crudely—he knows he shouldn't be *feeling* anything—he is hardly a novice at this sort of thing, after all—but it greatly stirs him, and alarms him, that a girl named Lisel (he doesn't know her last name, though he had asked her companions: no one seemed to know) should be represented on that small shabby screen, her face overexposed (as if in a dream?—a nightmare?), her expression so blank. *The Victim. Film by Myron Falk. 16-mm. 18 min.* It is a provocatively "amateurish" film—Myron Falk is not commercial, of course, or even professional—and if it appears to be pornographic (and Constantine has guessed that of course it will be—it must) Falk has only experimented with the genre: he has not *really* made a pornographic film.

Just as Lisel is not *really* present on the screen. Only her face, only the image of her face. And, in the end, only an image: glaring white, with those heavy eyes, the dark nostrils and eyebrows, the outline of the head obscured by the shadowy formless background.

Slowly, by degrees, slowly the camera moves back, and one can *almost* grasp—something. Or see something. It is invisible, yet it assumes a shape in the viewer's mind. It *does* exist. Though the girl acknowledges nothing—the face registers nothing, not pain, not distress, not even boredom, not even self-consciousness.

Constantine scribbles notes on a pad. He is highly trained, he is wonderfully verbal, but at the same time he is perspiring uncomfortably. How long will this wretched film last? —He examines his watch, he sees with disgust that only six minutes have passed.

LITTLE FREAK

He is terrified that the boys in the locker room will seize him and take off his clothes—he always changes into his gym trunks in a lavatory, he's very shrewd—they'll seize him and strip him and roar with laughter at his skinny twisted torso, his caved-in chest, his bluish skin, the little pink worm flapping between his thighs. Grab it! Yank it off! The normal-sized boys, their faces flushed with health, they eyes shining—the gang of normal-sized boys—including his two older brothers Frank and Gordon—and the girls from Miss Osborne's class will tiptoe in to watch—giggling behind their hands—What a funny little cripple!—funny little dwarf! What's that worm between his legs? It never ceases to amaze them, how his spine twists, and his right shoulder juts up higher than his left shoulder; but without his clothes he is funnier than ever.

Little freak! the children shout. You can't hide inside your clothes!

He is terrified too that on the way home from school they will shove him into a snowbank—drag him out onto Lake Michigan, on the ice—or onto the precarious ice of a deep ditch near the railroad yard—but this *did* happen, didn't it?—and he crashed through the ice into five feet of freezing water—he is terrified that the biggest of the boys (Ron Ormsby) will jump onto his back and try to drown him. Cripple! Dwarf! Freak! The girls will run up, their eyes glittering. Is that Constantine Reinhart in the water?—is that him?—is he drowning?—oh maybe you hadn't better do that—maybe you better pull him out—is he drowning?—is that him bawling?—maybe you better pull him out before the police come—

Constantine wakes in the twisted bedclothes, his heart pounding. He can't remember—is he seven years old, is he eleven, or fifteen, or twenty-six, or thirty-five?—is he really drowning in that ditch of freezing water? But the nightmare (in contrast to his daylight self—his daylight "Constantine Reinhart") is oddly consoling. It is very real, after all. It is authentic—it is his own. *Little freak*, he murmurs, his heart still hammering.

THE BRIDEGROOM

Jayne, half-dressed, her pale brown hair wild about her face, is sobbing with anger. When Constantine tries to touch her—tries hesitantly to embrace her—she pushes his hands roughly away without looking at him. "Why doesn't the fool take better care of himself! Now he knows! Let's hope he learns! The fool! The idiot! Smoking worse than ever—three packs a day, she said—he tried once to give up and couldn't last a week—I hate that coughing—he works too hard and he never *listens*—he's such an idiot—now he knows—I hate him—*I hate him*—my German exam is at eight Monday morning—"

She is throwing things into a suitcase, snatching clothes from hangers, letting them fall to the floor. Constantine tries to help but she pushes him aside. "He's an idiot! They're all idiots! I hate them!" Jayne screams. "I don't care if they all die!"

Constantine drives Jayne the forty miles or so to Bloomfield Hills, to the hospital to which her father, stricken with coronary thrombosis, has been taken. He is twenty-one years old, a senior at the University of Michigan, and Jayne is exactly his age. Until that day—until that terrible morning when the telephone rang in Jayne's little apartment on State Street—it had not occurred to Constantine that he might be in love; still less had it occurred to him that he might be a husband.

A bridegroom, immense with love. Deeply moved by his own magnanimity.

Driving north along I-75 from Ann Arbor. Speaking softly to Jayne, whose rage has now shaded into alarm; squeezing her hand; his heart swelling with love. He suspects—he seems to know—that Jayne's father is already dead.

Driving north along I-75, and then exiting, heading east. That December morning. The hilly landscape of eastern Michigan is austere, achromatic—the grass bleached colorless, the trees denuded of leaves, the previous night's snowfall already melting.

Suddenly she begins again, hoarsely, accusingly: "There isn't any history of heart trouble in our family! Everyone lives to be old—ancient—my grandfather is in perfect health—they're in Florida—there's *nothing* wrong with them. But *he's* such a fool, he never listens— Now—"

Constantine says softly, squeezing her hand again: "I'll take care of you."

"*Now* he'll have to listen, won't he! And those clients of his, calling the house at all hours, bawling over the phone!—the shits!"

"I'll take care of you," Constantine says.

Jayne isn't listening; but perhaps she has heard.

He glances at her covertly—she seems to be staring sightlessly out the window. He can hear her quick shallow breath. Her face is a white knot, almost ugly. Her colorless lips look as if they have been gnawed. Is this Jayne Freiling whom everyone admires and halfway fears—is this Jayne Freiling who is *almost* as acclaimed as Constantine Reinhart himself? She isn't even pretty now. Her skin is mottled, she sniffs and wipes her nose with the back of her hand, crude as a child, made stupid with terror. And the death, the actual death, Constantine thinks, shivering, is still ahead.

That December morning, speeding along the expressway, speeding into the future. The sky is perpetually massed with enormous gunmetal gray clouds through which, nevertheless, the sun's rays pierce at the most unexpected moments. Constantine Reinhart, twenty-one years old. A young bridegroom, revelling in his own strength; his newly discovered manhood. Constantine Reinhart, who has halfway invented himself as a sort of midwestern dandy, a Baudelairean misfit, his deformities—certain of his deformities—proudly on exhibit: but examine him now, study his expression now! He is stunned, like the young woman beside him. He is flooded with relief that life should be—suddenly—irrevocably—so simple.

THE IMPOSTOR

McMahon knows him. McMahon stares rudely at him, in study hall. Sometimes he winks.

Kevin McMahon. English and Drama. The director of the Theater Program. He has a teaching certificate from the State of Michigan, like the other teachers; but he also has (so it is rumored) a master's degree in Anglo-Irish literature from Trinity College, Dublin.

McMahon, it is, calling to him across a tar-splotched corner of the asphalt parking lot of the Sullivan Avenue A & P. One darkening November afternoon. "Con? Con Reinhart? That you—?" His throaty voice lifting as if in surprise.

Constantine pretends for a moment not to hear. It embarrasses him—it rather disturbs him—to be greeted by his teachers outside school.

He glances around. "Hello," he says, not very clearly. "Oh hi, Mr. McMahon."

"Hello, Con."

Hesitation. Clumsiness. He wonders if he should continue walking—if he should escape—or does Mr. McMahon expect him to trot over, maybe to help him put his groceries into the trunk of the car?

"Gets dark earlier all the time, doesn't it?" McMahon calls out cheerfully.

Constantine murmurs a vague answer. He stands with both hands in his jacket pockets, resisting the impulse to slouch. (He is six feet one inch tall, at the age of sixteen. Already two inches taller than his father. And thin. Not exactly skinny—he is in terror of *that*, he has been lifting weights with his brothers to avoid *that*—but thin, and uneasy in his bones. He is partway contemptuous of McMahon's stocky build, his round freckled moonish face, and partway envious—McMahon walks so firmly on the ground, McMahon knows with certainty who he is.)

"Do you want a ride somewhere, Con? Where do you live? —Out High Street, right?"

"I'm not going home," Constantine says.

"—long walk, isn't it? Looks like snow."

"I'm not going home yet, Mr. McMahon," Constantine says, embarrassed.

He is on his way downtown, to the public library. That summer he managed to coerce the head librarian into giving him adult privileges: he can take any book he wants out of that library, including "restricted" material. It seems to have come about that Constantine's reading these days consists almost exclusively of this "restricted" material.

"Well—look—what's the problem?—I don't mind going out of my way," McMahon says.

So Constantine has no choice but to trot over, like an eager young dog. Though his face is burning. Though his heart has turned sullen.

McMahon unlocks the trunk of his car and the door swings dramatically up and Constantine helps with the groceries. Inconsequential chatter, silly questions, the faint odor of beer on McMahon's breath, Constantine's distant voice, which never fails him. . . . Yes, Mr. McMahon. No. Maybe. I don't think so. I suppose so. Laughing at the man's strained wit. Shaking his head as if profoundly amused.

Alone, walking along Sullivan Avenue, Constantine had known himself arrogantly alive, and incontestably Real: trapped now in this meandering conversation, forced to respond and even to initiate remarks, he knows himself Unreal. It is always the same, it has been like this all his life. Alone he is Real, with others he is Unreal. He detests the Unreal Constantine but cannot do without him.

But his uneasiness is compounded, in McMahon's company. For McMahon is one of Con Reinhart's champions at school.

(Constantine is, to put it mildly, a controversial case. He has the highest average in the junior class; he was recently elected vice-president of the class (and next year he will be president—that won't be denied him); he holds offices in the Camera Club, the Journalism Club, the Science Club, and the Boys' Glee Club; he is managing editor of the yearbook and associate editor of the school newspaper, *The Beacon*. And more: he is even a fairly good basketball player, on one of the intramural teams. And even more: he has a girl friend this year, Sandra Mason, who is very pretty . . . and "popular" too. But there is something sly about him, something disruptive and unreliable. He cannot resist making jokes behind his teachers' backs. And sometimes not *quite* behind their backs. Even his champions are not safe from his razorish wit.)

McMahon drives slowly along Sullivan Avenue, continuing his innocuous chatter.

Constantine's cheeks burn unaccountably.

McMahon, one of the best-liked teachers. Despite his bad temper. He must be no more than thirty-five years old but he has more authority than Mr. Skelton, the principal: when his good-natured freckled face goes white with rage everyone, even the boldest of the boys, is terrified. Except perhaps Constantine—who takes it all fairly lightly.

Though—to be honest—Constantine might be apprehensive of McMahon. For a reason he can't quite explain.

241

Kevin McMahon, about whom there are intriguing rumours. The wife, and the drinking. Loud quarrels on weekend nights. (The McMahons don't live in a house like everyone else, but in an apartment building. They have no children. Mrs. McMahon is never seen around school. She is rumored to have been a beautiful woman but Constantine, who had a glimpse of her once, fleetingly, rather doubts it. From time to time there is talk that McMahon has resigned his position and is going to Ireland to live—or Majorca—or Rome—or New York City: he will have a novel published, he will have a play produced: he can't leave Commerce City, Michigan, fast enough! But the next school year rolls around, and there he is, standing in the doorway of Room 19, his hands in the pockets of his baggy tweed coat, his jowly cheeks creased with smiling. For—the really weird thing, as his students say—the *really* weird thing: Kevin McMahon likes it here.)

He pulls up to the curb by the library, and Constantine opens his door. Eager to escape.

He says, chuckling, as if "chuckling" were altogether natural in such a situation: "Just who the hell do you think you're fooling, Con, my friend? *Who do you think—*" he says, squeezing Constantine's arm with mock disapprobation, "*—you're fooling?*"

THE PRIG

Myron Falk was the most wildly successful of the "noncommercial" Soho artists. He burst into celebrity (as the expression went) in the early sixties, with his enormous sleek hard-edge paintings; within a few years these canvases were selling for upward of $50,000. (Despite the well-substantiated rumour that the paintings were partly executed by Falk apprentices— young art students who were part of Falk's entourage.) Then he experimented for a brief while with photo-realism; and then with trompe l'œil sculptures in vinyl; and then with short films in black and white, without sound. From the very first his work was controversial—it was widely and rather angrily discussed. Was Falk a genuine artist, or was he a poseur—was he serious or playful—was he Duchamp's most gifted heir, or simply another opportunist? Lengthy analyses of his work appeared in intellectual journals. There were references to Artaud, Genet, Sade. He appeared on the cover of the *New York Times Magazine*, stocky and arrogant, his bald head tanned and gleaming, his ham-sized arms folded; he wore one of his most arresting costumes—a striped Dacron shirt, a checked sports jacket with wide lapels, a bowtie, and oxford shoes, brown and white, with shiny pressed-tip laces. *Art Violates the Boundary Between Invention and "Real Life,"* the caption read.

The Victim, Auto Wreck, and *Psychosis*, though cruel and witty, were hardly the most discussed of his short films: the really provocative one was of the (alleged) death on camera of a young street person, as a consequence of a heroin overdose. The film was twenty-five minutes long and followed the heroin user from the corner of Eighth Street and Sixth Avenue to a nearby apartment where he collapsed. The photography was in stark black and white, the hand-held camera was leisurely and sinuous, circling about the victim. Or the actor. Falk naturally declined to answer questions about the film (which was called *O.D.*), but members of his entourage insisted that the film was just that, a film: the young man (or was it a young woman?—thinning hair pulled back into a ponytail, eyes gutted, cheekbones painfully sharp, a sleeveless and evidently filthy t-shirt hanging on the bony chest) was an actor and not "real." An amateur, a gifted amateur: but an actor nonetheless. However, no one could locate the young actor and there was no information provided about him or her— not even the name.

Constantine Reinhart, barely thirty years old at the time, was the only "intellectual" to question Falk. In his lengthy and rather passionate review of Falk's films he used words like "vampiristic," "banal," and "bankrupt." He seemed rather angry about something: he failed even to make references to Artaud, Genet, and Sade, among others: the piece was not thought to be particularly persuasive, and for months afterward there were people who would not speak to him, as if fearing contamination. (It was not true, however, that Constantine was dropped by all his friends. His most intimate friends—some five or six people whom he had known for years—were naturally embarrassed at his behavior, but chose to ignore it.)

Constantine thought it ironic that, as the rumors spread, overlapping one another, deepening, it should come to seem that he, Constantine Reinhart, was puritanical and priggish, a voice for censorship, and that Myron Falk and his associates were victims—persecuted artists. He *was* dropped from one or two journals, temporarily. He suspected that people made jokes about him at parties. And all because he had fallen in love—he had become infatuated—with the girl Lisel of *The Victim*, whom he had met only once (under very hectic circumstances) and could not seem to meet again....

He was compared, in print, to the most fanatic of the Prohibitionists. An essayist for the *Village Voice* compared him to the "later" Tolstoy.

FIRST DEATH

Perhaps it is a dream, a long lazy looping dream: driving back from the cemetery in his father's blue DeSoto, along the slow narrow dusty road ... staring dry-eyed at the bleached grass of late August and the abandoned wrecks of houses ... not thinking about the grave, the hard chunky earth, the black coffin with its bright handles ... not listening to his father's low steady pleading voice.... (His father is talking to his grandmother Reinhart, who sits beside him inert as a stone. Constantine is embarrassed in his grandmother's presence now that his grandfather has died and there is something wild and spiteful about her. She isn't the way he remembers her. Secretly he stares at the wavering white part at the back of her head which reminds him of something he can't name. She has fixed her hair in that style for fifty years, Constantine's mother said, and it's so much work for her, just lifting her arms like that, and plaiting the braids, and it isn't at all attractive: the dead-white part at the back of the head, showing too much of the scalp, the gray hair braided (but braided clumsily—she works blind) and brought around to the front of the head to be fastened with oversized hairpins. A crown gone askew. The poor woman looks almost tipsy as a consequence; and of course she is too stubborn to allow her daughter-in-law to tidy her up.)

What does it mean, Constantine thinks, that his grandfather Reinhart is *dead* ...? He stares at the hilly countryside, at the telephone poles that lean as if bracing themselves against the wind, and cannot see any explanation: any connection between the world out there (which is exactly the same as always) and the little world inside his father's car, being transported back to Plover Hill, back to his grandparents' house. Has nothing changed? A few crows fly out of the road, startled by the car: they might be the same crows Constantine saw less than an hour ago, picking in the remains of a groundhog or woodchuck.

Has nothing changed?

He is embarrassed for his grandmother—that nothing *has* changed.

Ruined houses ... collapsed barns ... the boarded-up buildings of the Plover Hill

Mining Company... the old watertower, covered with vines. Constantine and his brothers have explored all of Plover Hill: they have prowled in every house that has been abandoned, in the warehouses (where machinery remains, still, its oiled surfaces thick with dust and chaff), in the railroad yard (where thistles grow between the tracks, as high as twelve feet), in the old grammar school (where, shrieking with laughter, Constantine's brothers ran up and down the aisles of desks, kicking books and papers, wrenching lighting-fixtures from the walls, trying to overturn the teacher's squat wooden desk). They have even crawled through the first-floor windows of the enormous barn housing the mine hoist, though it is pitch-black inside, and said to be dangerous; and their father has particularly warned them against it. Of course they have played for years in the railroad yard and along the river and in any of the old houses that are not boarded up against trespassers. Who would care? Why would anyone care? Yet there is always the sense of violation—the risk, the excitement—the knowledge that they *are* trespassing.

Where have you boys been all afternoon, what have you been doing? their father might ask them suspiciously, seeing their feverish faces, the bits of chaff that stuck to their skin; but of course they only murmured replies. Down by the river, they said. Out in Grandpa's field.

Constantine has asked why everyone moved away from Plover Hill. He has asked his father and his grandfather. (For *he* would happily have moved there—it is so much more interesting than Commerce City.) His grandfather shrugged his shoulders. The mines played out, he said. But what did that mean, Constantine wondered, the mines *played out*...? He asked his father who said, sighing, Well—a man has got to move where there's work. A town can die too, just like a person.

But why does it have to happen? Constantine asked stubbornly.

Along Main Steet only a few stores remained still in business. One of them was Kohls' Hardware whose owner, Buzz, had gone to school with Constantine's father. But that was a long time ago: now the school building was a wreck, every window was broken, the desks tipped into the aisles, books and papers shredded. —Yes but why does it *have* to happen? Constantine is asking petulantly.

Perhaps it is a dream, that long dusty afternoon. Constantine finds himself staring as he always does at the marquee of the old Plover Rialto—the single remaining letters S A O—which will be there for years, in exactly the same position, the O tilting as if it were about to fall to the sidewalk. Surely the letters have some meaning? Surely there is a word, a secret word, for Constantine to discover?

(Many years later, in another part of the country, when Constantine might reasonably claim that no part of the child Constantine remained in him—drop by drop he had squeezed that boy, that son, out of his veins!—he is to wake with the memory of a dream raw and harsh in his mind's eye: something to do with his grandfather in that shiny black coffin with the brass handles; something to do with the ugly part in his grandmother's hair; something to do with those letters on the marquee of the Rialto. He draws in a deep mortified breath. Never to be free—! He would like to weep but of course he cannot: for one thing, he isn't alone in bed.)

Constantine's father is asking Constantine's grandmother when she will come "south" to live with them. (They are in the house now—in the kitchen.) Constantine's grandmother says irritably that she isn't going anywhere. She's going to stay right here in Plover Hill, in this house, for the rest of her life. "Move south! Why would I move south!" she says. "It wouldn't be worth the fuss, my boy—do you know what I mean?"

Constantine's father stares at her. After a long moment he says: "Momma, I won't stand for that kind of talk."

But they drive back without her. They drive back early the next morning, without her. Constantine's father is crying—incredible as that seems. (It *is* incredible. Constantine is greatly embarrassed. He hopes he won't catch his brothers' eyes, and all three of them burst into laughter. But no one says a word. Constantine's mother complains of the heat, fanning herself with a magazine. Constantine's older brother, Gordon, tells a somewhat incoherent story about a hermit who lives back of the railroad yard, in a hut made of packing cases.

Constantine's father continues driving the car as if nothing is wrong, and after a while nothing *is* wrong—he has stopped crying, he is himself again, pointing out things of interest along the road, tapping his horn as he comes up behind a farmer on a tractor. Perhaps it *is* a dream, Constantine thinks sleepily. The shiver of death, the way his stomach felt when he saw the old man—the almost unrecognizable old man—lying with his head on a white satin pillow (a silly white satin pillow like something in a doll's carriage!)—the way he felt when his father turned aside, gulping for breath. Certainly nothing else has changed.

THE FLAMES

He lies in bed, in the high hospital bed with the ungiving mattress, and then in his bed at home, as the flames lick silently about him. Across the floor, along the walls, silent and colorless, a pale cold mass of flames.

Four weeks in the hospital, desperately ill. It was not to be believed—angry Mr. Reinhart could not believe it—that a son of his might die of pneumonia, in 1949!

Flames lightly licking over surfaces: even faces. His mother's face with the small secret fold of flesh beneath the chin. His father's face—ruddy, blotched, aggrieved.

Days and nights and days again. He was at rest, floating. He was half-conscious. The flames flickered but could not touch him. More alarming were the nightmare-cartoon figures—among them Jacky Meyer and himself—who cavorted on the raw insides of his eyelids.

He is eleven years old. His birthday came and went while he sucked greedily at the "air" pumped against his face.

Constantine Reinhart, Joseph Reinhart's youngest son. Skipped ahead to seventh grade but this long bout of pneumonia will ruin everything. Suppose he dies! Suppose his brain is affected! He cannot hear—he certainly cannot hear—adults whispering many rooms away: Suppose his brain is affected! (There is . . . someone's cousin's wife's brother . . . out in South Dakota, maybe . . . or Montana . . . thirty-nine years old . . . kept in a back room . . . never learned to talk . . . gulps and wheezes and eats like a horse . . . it's a mercy, at least, he *did* get toilet trained. They're Catholic. Not the cousin or his wife, but the brother. The thing . . . the thing with the destroyed brain . . . is the brother's son. Thirty-nine years old and never spoke a word in his life and the priest comes to bless him. . . . Isn't that a pity! Isn't that *something*! He had measles when he was four years old, they said, and ran a high fever, and they couldn't bring it down, and that was *it*. . . .)

Constantine's secret, the cold pale flickering flames. He sees them everywhere: on the walls, the windowpane, the curtains, his father's anxious knotted face, the playing cards shuffled in his brother Gordon's fingers. His mother raising the blind. Dr. Van Noy's hornrimmed glasses.

Cream of chicken soup. Campbell's minestrone. Oyster crackers—his favorite. Stewed apricots, stewed prunes. Poached eggs. (Unless the whites were runny. If they were runny he gagged and pushed his tray away.)

Is he going to die? one of his brothers whispers to the other.

Shut up, you asshole, the other says.

Though they are rooms away. On the far side of the house. Surely Constantine cannot hear.

He *isn't* going to die.

Though he deserves to die.

Mr. Reinhart of McCullough's Iron Works, now owner of the company, negotiating to borrow a substantial sum from the Commerce City Savings & Loan to build a new warehouse out on the highway to Escanaba. Telephone calls, luncheon meetings at the Rotary Club (he loves their dining room—the high dome, the "velvet" drapes, the parquet floor), dictating letters and invoices to his wife, who cannot type quickly enough to please him. Mr. Reinhart, shouting at Dr. Van Noy in the hospital corridor while the nurses listened in horror. This is 1949! What the hell are you telling me! If anything happens to him—if anything happens to him—I'll slap a malpractice suit on you and on this hospital so fast you won't know what happens—

Unless, of course, feverish teeth-grinding Constantine has imagined it all. Which is entirely possible.

(Many years later, visiting Commerce City on his way back to New York from a conference in Los Angeles, Constantine will allude rather sentimentally to the day his father threatened old Dr. Van Noy with a malpractice suit. In the hospital, with everyone listening. But Mr. Reinhart will shake his head, puzzled, clearly remembering nothing. Your father never shouted at anyone, Constantine's mother will say, shocked.)

(Many years later, drawn to a pale flat-bodied young woman—or is it a young man?—at a party in Myron Falk's loft on Spring Street, many years after he fell through the ice and nearly drowned and caught a cold which turned into pneumonia which nearly killed him—which *should* have killed him—Constantine will find himself thinking, suddenly, of Jacky Meyer. Whom he hasn't seen since 1954. Whom he has been inventing, in his imagination, as a child still—a pale malicious child of eleven.)

The colorless flickering flames, the fever-hot writhing of the air, the glasses and glasses of orange juice. When he is feeling stronger some of his classmates will visit. Embarrassed, somewhat sullen. Herded into the room by their mothers. (But not Jacky Meyer. He has not asked for Jacky Meyer and his mother doesn't know Mrs. Meyer—doesn't know a thing.)

Playing gin rummy and sheeps'-head with his brothers. Slapping the cards down. Sailing a two of hearts off the bed and into a corner of the room. You shit-head Con, you little fuck-face Con, Gordon whispered furiously. Too bad you didn't die.

But he isn't going to die. They love him too much—the father especially.

Harsh gulping sobs. Ridiculous. As if there was any danger of the little freak dying!

Plans for a new building, a marvelous new showcase, out on the Escanaba Road. McCullough's Iron Works. (Fences of all kinds, specializing in chain-link.) Full-page advertisements in the *Commerce City Journal*. A wine-colored Cadillac with soft gray upholstery. A terracotta-lined swimming pool behind the High Street redwood ranch, "designer-built." All-night sessions with the Escanaba tax accountant, the two of them keeping awake on black coffee. Mr. Reinhart poking his head into Constantine's room, through the shimmering wall of flames. The love in his face—the fear, the apprehension—for what if his son *should* die?

The ice cracking beneath his rubber boots. Dark freezing water. In one of the dreams something has fallen through—a dog, a deer?—a boy—and Constantine has to rescue it. He doesn't run away in a panic like Jacky Meyer. Whatever has fallen through the ice is clawing at the edge, whimpering, gasping for breath. Here, grab hold! Can't you grab hold! Hauled out of the freezing water, a stunted little creature, evidently a boy, with a badly twisted back and a raised shoulder—a dwarf, a freak—with Constantine's blond hair and Constantine's sly dirty grin—

They had been fooling around, Jacky and Constantine. Not for the first time, exactly. Pushing each other—squealing and giggling—calling each other names—wrestling—grunting. Their faces glowing, their eyes bright with tears. Saliva on their lips. Constantine wanted to throw Jacky down, and Jacky wanted to throw Constantine down. Despite their bulky winter clothing. Despite the cold. Their breaths steamed, their eyes shone. A sharp teasing sensation began in Constantine's groin. He wrestled with Jacky, and Jacky grunted and hugged him, trying to knock him off balance, and Constantine cried aloud with surprise—or delight—or sudden panic—and then he began to fight, using his fists, and Jacky fought back, and suddenly Constantine was falling—pushed into the ditch—and the ice cracked beneath his boots—and the dark freezing water engulfed him—and he couldn't get enough breath to scream and scream and scream.

For many weeks afterward, the noiseless flames.

Burning everyone—everything—clean. Invisibly. Without heat.

Constantine, who should have died, is living still, so skinny his ribs jut out, tight against his dead-white skin; the sockets of his eyes are prominent. He has been watching for weeks the flames that lick at everyone and everything. The universe, he hypothesizes, is made of fire, which burns ceaselessly and invisibly, devouring everyone and everything from within. His mother—his father—his brothers—his classmates—his teacher Mrs. Sjöberg—Dr. Van Noy. Nothing matters, nothing is real. Except perhaps the terror he had felt, falling into the ditch. Or the astonishing sword-like sensation in his groin, in the instant before Jacky began to beat him.

THE CARESS

In Myron Falk's famous Spring Street studio-loft there is an exercise bicycle, but it is not a work of pop sculpture: it is a real bicycle, really used. On the floor around it are mats of a kind Constantine remembers from gym class, back in Commerce City High.

Falk asks Constantine (who has been, at last, invited to the loft—in fact, summoned) if he would like to use the bicycle. Constantine tries to show no surprise as he declines the offer.

"People reveal themselves in such interesting ways on my bicycle," Falk says with a broad disingenuous smile. "Especially if they suspect their performance is being filmed."

"Is it being filmed?" Constantine asks, glancing around.

Falk laughs airily, waving his arm, indicating a space some yards away. Constantine looks but sees nothing. Perhaps there would be a camera set up in that position? Or is there a camera, hidden behind a pile of stacked canvases against the wall?

"If you suspected we are on film, at this very moment," Falk says, "you would take everything more seriously, wouldn't you?—yourself as well as me?"

Constantine looks around, refusing to be intimidated. He is a tall handsome intelligent-looking man—he is not a freak—he is not even nervous despite the fact that he and Falk appear to be alone in the studio. (But no one ever sees the master alone!—he has been told. Not even the master's wife of many years.)

An enormous loft, larger than any Constantine has seen in Soho. And not very attractive. Winter sunlight falls through the fifteen-foot windows and gives to the least significant object—even to Falk's imperious simper—an air of intense meaning.

Constantine says softly: "I wouldn't take it seriously at all in that case."

His answer must be satisfactory because Falk laughs immediately, with robust abandon. It is amazing, as everyone says, to watch the man laugh: he appears to enjoy laughter so thoroughly: the bullet-shaped head thrown back, the slightly stained teeth bared, the hilarity coursing through him in spasms—yet clearly feigned. For no sooner does the space ring with his laughter than he stops; no sooner has Constantine (who should know better—who does know better) begun laughing along with him than he falls silent, revealing the outburst of mirth as wholly simulated.

So Constantine is left feeling like a fool. He *is* a fool.

Behind the tanned "healthy" face—behind the relentlessly cheerful, gregarious, ebullient public character of Myron Falk—a pair of gray eyes watches coldly, refusing even to make an aesthetic judgment. Falk is said to see only gradations of light—in literal fact: he is color blind—and to assess the world, even the world of human beings, simply in terms of composition. Constantine, blushing, sees again the uncanny image of the beautiful victim Lisel, and sees at the same time his own image—overexposed, enlarged into "art"—on a screen, a matter of light and shade. *Would* Falk have the slightest interest in him, if he hadn't published that passionate attack . . . ?

He wonders when he will have the opportunity to inquire about Lisel. If he will have the courage, the utterly banal, conventional courage, to ask Falk for a telephone number. . . .

But Falk is eager to show him about the studio, talking loudly, making jokes Constantine doesn't quite catch. Canvases—human figures in vinyl—barrels of what appears to be trash—battered old furniture—an aluminum desk—a filthy fake-Oriental carpet. Constantine hasn't even time to ask polite questions; Falk doesn't register his presence at all. The master is striding about his kingdom, pointing, at times nearly shouting, in a pretense of enthusiasm.

It is Falk's style, Constantine realizes, to simulate certain "normal" emotions—amusement, distress, concern, awe, anger, enthusiasm—but to exaggerate them, and then to recall them abruptly, so that his companions are left behind: are left, in a sense, clumsily human: mere dupes. Constantine had heard this of Falk but hadn't comprehended it, though it is surely nothing more than an extension of his practice as an artist. (Is he consciously in the tradition of Alfred Jarry, Constantine wonders. Will he commit suicide?—and will he take others with him?) Falk does not trouble to make his quick breezy grins plausible—he wants to illustrate (or so it is theorized: Falk does not lack for eager intellectual theoreticians) the grotesque temporary nature of all *affect*.

A theory of the avant-garde as art in rebellion against sanity: Constantine can feel the attraction. But he has taken his stand against Falk (and "for" morality)—he has made a public commitment.

Falk strides through the loft, a short barrel-chested heavy man. The old floorboards creak beneath his weight.

In an overwarm cluttered back room—his "office"—he invites Constantine to sit down, and share a pot of tea. (Tea! Constantine smiles warily, suspecting a joke. But it is no joke.) Falk snaps on a transistor radio and continues to talk, with an almost amphetamine ebullience, his voice raised above the din of rock music. He is cordial, genial, "warm," open. He appears to be utterly sincere. Now and then he runs his big hands over his head, quickly, caressingly, or scratches his chest (he is wearing bib-overalls with no shirt beneath—his graying steelwool-like hair protrudes), or leans forward to poke Constantine's arm for emphasis. He might be a truck driver. He might be—if he troubled to dress up—an automobile salesman. It disturbs Constantine to think that he might be his own father: a successful fencing salesman grateful to be working a twelve-hour day. It is all salesmanship—it is all uphill. And very American. Isn't that right?

Surely he is telling the truth, surely he is sincere, when he fixes Constantine with a hurt look, and tells him that most dismissals of his work are made by philistines whose opinions have no value; but when someone of Constantine Reinhart's stature attacks him. . . .

Constantine blushes, raising a chipped teacup to his lips.

For, after all, he had read that little book of poems Constantine published a few years ago, and of course he had seen the play . . . what was the name of that play . . . and they had innumerable acquaintances in common. . . .

Constantine cannot think of a suitable reply. He knows that Falk is lying, yet the words, the intonation, the wounded expression are extraordinarily convincing. His face burns exactly as if he *had* wronged Falk; he is flooded with guilt.

And so on, and so forth. Falk chatters above the din of the radio. (It is a Hispanic station, turned up high.) Constantine smiles and says something appropriate and nods and shifts uncomfortably in his chair and cannot think, simply cannot think, why he is here—why he accepted Falk's invitation. He wants only to manipulate me, Constantine thinks, but the man's voice is hypnotic, his good-natured mask of a face is so convincing, perhaps he *is* sincere . . . ? Constantine stares at him, narrowing his eyes as if he were looking into a bright light. He can nearly feel—he *can* feel—the man's energy. The radiant shimmering waves of his strength. It was said of him that he tanned himself by sunlamp, even his bald head, and that he sometimes slapped on theatrical makeup, even rouge, which he didn't trouble to use discreetly; but so far as Constantine can judge his skintone really *is* high-colored and rich and "healthy." And he isn't ugly, as his enemies say. He is really quite attractive.

As if by accident Falk lets his hand fall on Constantine's knee, which he then squeezes and caresses, for conversational emphasis.

Constantine pushes his hand away, laughing uneasily.

But Falk moves his hand back. He smiles, baring his strong stained teeth.

Frightened as a schoolgirl, blushing, Constantine draws back. "I—I don't—" he stammers.

Falk lifts his hand—but then allows it to fall again, heavily. This time he slides it along Constantine's thigh. Which he squeezes hard, like a hearty teasing old uncle.

Constantine, in a dream, shoves at him—spills the tea—stammers an apology—tries to get to his feet. His heart is kicking in his chest. "I didn't mean—I—You can't—" he says.

A long minute passes. Someone is shrieking a commercial in Spanish.

Constantine looks down, paralyzed, and sees that Falk is gripping his thigh. He hasn't moved. Neither of them has moved. Constantine didn't push him away—didn't say a word.

Who are you fooling, Falk whispers.

Constantine stares, unable to move. Falk's broad lips are stretched in a grin, a dreamy grin, but he hasn't spoken.

Who do you think you're fooling, he whispers.

THE DARK ANGEL

She has black frizzy crinkly electric hair that flies out from her head, shoulder-long. Her eyes are black as well, sly and almond-shaped. Her breasts are small and hard and yet wonderfully soft: it hardly seems possible to Constantine, their softness. Yet the flesh is hard. Even unyielding. And her belly and thighs—creamy-white—are strong, compact, lean. Her dancer's legs are almost *too* strong: Constantine has kneaded and massaged the muscular calves, kissed the moist backs of the knees, cupped the feet in his hands, marvelling. (Sometimes she winces with pain. She hurts herself dancing—the exercises are so strenuous, and so protracted—her feet are beginning to scar with calluses.)

A dark angel, who will rescue him. He loves her, he is sick with love for her, yet even as he holds her—too tightly, she is drawing breath to protest—it seems to him that he can see ahead, as if through a tunnel, to the time, the space, in which he will be alone again in this very bed.

"I feel so lonely. Hold me. I feel so lonely," she says in a small still child's voice. She buries herself in Constantine, and Constantine buries himself in her. My love. My angel. — And then he feels her thoughts flying away. Simply flying away. She tenses, her muscles go stiff with thinking, planning, plotting—sometimes her mouth works as if she were actually speaking—rehearsing dialogue, or perhaps recalling it—she has even laughed, silently, at some droll recollection, her eyes innocently closed. If the telephone rings when they are in Constantine's apartment (and it frequently does, even late at night) she fairly jumps and shakes her hair out of her face and says, in a voice that contradicts her words: "Well—thank God—that *can't* be for me."

Constantine at the age of forty, divorced for many years, socially active—*very* active—in Manhattan, has innumerable acquaintances and persons who might be called friends; and persons who are intimate friends. In fact he has a network of three or four or five people, including two women, who are, in his own words, necessary for his life. They constitute an informal circle, and though they are all "successful" people in their thirties or forties, the jealousy they commonly feel for one another, and their rather touching dependence upon one another, suggests nothing so much as early adolescence. But this time around, Constantine has thought, adolescence will not hurt nearly so much.

So the telephone frequently rings when Vera is with Constantine, and even if the call is personal rather than professional—*especially* if it is personal—Constantine cannot say more than a few hurried words; otherwise Vera will be offended. Once when he was trapped in a conversation with Kirk Rodman—though "trapped" is an unfortunate word, Kirk was distraught and badly needed Constantine's advice—Vera shoved on her knee-high leather boots and grabbed her coat and simply walked out the door, and Constantine, distracted by his friend's babbling, was too astonished to pursue her.

Constantine must be in love, he feels so edgy, so comically despairing, he examines his face (lines?—wrinkles?—they seem to be caused by grimacing he does during the night) with uncommon anxiety in the morning, trying to imagine what Vera sees. Married too young (he was only twenty-two!—a baby), for a very long time defined by his marriage (he was a "husband"—he was even, for a while, "loyal" to his wife), and then for an even longer time defined by the fact that he *had* been married (he was considered a "divorced" man—a condition not without some glamour), Constantine has been forced to realize in recent years that he "isn't" anything at all. He would like to define himself as Vera Jakobson's lover; there is the rightness of the sound, the old-fashioned gallantry of *lover*, and a certain bright modishness as well; and the fact too—a not inconsiderable fact—that Vera Jakobson is beginning to acquire an excellent reputation in the city. He would *like* to think of himself as her lover soon to be her husband... her second husband.

(What of the first? She doesn't like to talk about the first.)

In fact she shies away, almost literally shies away, like a frightened colt, from "serious" subjects. She can talk for hours about her work—her lessons—her professional contacts—her agent (about whom she can't decide: does he really care about her career?)—her friends in the theatre and elsewhere; only when she is exhausted, or melancholy, or has had several drinks, is she willing to talk with Constantine about her family, or her former lovers, or her apprehension about the future. But even then she clearly dislikes to talk about *their* future.

Nevertheless Constantine must be in love, he feels so precarious, so unreal. Of course his friends have withheld their approval of Vera: they insist she isn't intelligent enough for him (Constantine is, after all, "brilliant"); she isn't deep enough, or reliable enough; and is she *really* so attractive, with her odd crackling hair and her fashionable make-up? Constantine defends her, stubbornly. He has seen that other men are envious of him—it is hardly a secret that other women are envious of her. In any case he is in love. In any case it has become painfully difficult for him to imagine living without her.

His dark angel. His beauty. His prize.

Who will rescue him.

Transported by passion he sometimes says wild, incoherent things, burying himself in her body, pressing his overheated face against her neck. At such times—though only at such times—his flamboyance does not embarrass her.

"My lovely girl," he has whispered. "My angel...."

Once she rolled away from him, stricken by a fit of laughter: she simply couldn't help herself, like a young girl, all knees and elbows and giggles. Oh she hoped he would forgive her—but something struck her as funny—it had nothing to do with him—it was just—just—oh the idea of being an angel— And she collapsed in laughter, her cheeks wet with tears, her lovely eyes narrowed to slits, her fists pounding against the mattress. How very funny, how *very* funny!—how hilarious!—poor sweating staring Constantine Reinhart in love.

SUICIDE

Over Kirk Rodman's elegant and completely successful dessert—*pots de crème au chocolat:* Kirk had studied cooking in Paris, some years ago—they found themselves talking about suicide. Afterward Constantine could not remember how the subject came up.

The first person Nola Peck knew who had committed suicide was her freshman roommate at Wellesley. ("She never came back from winter break," Nola said slowly. "I still find it hard to believe. I still can't think she was *serious*.") The first person Meredith Flint had known was an uncle—an alcoholic uncle—who had gone to live in Hawaii after being discharged from the army in 1945. No one in Meredith's family told the children what had happened but somehow Meredith knew: and the image of his uncle hanging from a beam (where?—a garage, most likely), his neck broken and his face a ghastly bruised color, had stayed with him for years.

Rachel Schiller leaned her elbows on the table and finished her dessert with quick deft movements of her spoon. She had—as they all knew—how could they help but know?—written in great detail on the subject—in her first novel—the death by suicide of a very unhappy young man she had known at the University of Chicago—she hadn't any more to say about him, or about the subject: in writing about it she had completely exhausted its possibilities in her own imagination. "And subsequent suicides," she said, in a voice devoid of all irony, "subsequent suicides haven't meant as much."

Kirk Rodman, animated and wonderfully articulate, told them a lengthy tale of a former student who had killed himself in a most macabre way; Kirk had been in his mid-twenties at the time, a young lecturer at Harvard. (These were the years before Kirk began to publish his poetry, and to publish it to such acclaim.) And the Stalkers—Catherine and Fred—told of a woman who had lived in their apartment building, in Philadelphia, when they were first married: she had taken an overdose of barbiturates, she had washed them down with a pint of gin, *and* she had turned on the gas oven. Oliver Grant said shyly—glancing at Constantine, whose close friend he was at this time—that his first experience with suicide wasn't with suicide as such but only with the threat of it—*only!*—emotional blackmail exacted by a friend—a young Italian artist he had known in Rome while he was there doing a monograph on the architect Antonio Sant'Elia. (Nola Peck said, with a curious vehemence: "The ones you wouldn't exactly mind losing—they're precisely the ones who won't do it! They live and live and live, don't they?—as a form of revenge.")

It was Constantine's turn to speak. He drew breath, they turned to look at him, perhaps anticipating something very interesting—for Constantine had a flair for making personal statements that were also "cultural"—he had the gift, if not intoxicated, of speaking cleverly modulated prose. But he sat for a moment or two, half-smiling, hesitant, and then he murmured with uncharacteristic chagrin that he hadn't anyone significant to offer at all, not even himself. Most of the suicides he had known in his lifetime were hopelessly dull people; and the first he had known he hadn't really known at all, face to face: she was the wife, rumored to be the alcoholic wife, of a high school teacher of his named—but did the name matter?—McMahon. No one ever committed suicide in Commerce City, Michigan, or at least they hadn't in the 1950s, but this poor woman had, by slashing her wrists. Why, Constantine never learned. But he had to apologize—it really wasn't very interesting—it *really* was quite dull. "I can't even offer myself as a candidate," he said, laughing nervously. "My suicide attempts have never moved beyond the point of sheer luxurious speculation."

"But this woman, your teacher's wife," Rachel Schiller asked, leaning around to stare at Constantine, "you don't know *why*? No one knew why?"

Constantine turned away from Rachel, whom he thought unusually unattractive that night. "You heard what I said," he murmured.

THE FLAMES

Licking silently across the shadowed wall, across the ceiling of hammered tin. Running along the pinewood table Constantine uses for a desk—across the books on his shelves—the high stark curtainless windows. A pale noiseless delirium, burning the world clean. Faces, gestures. His father's exuberant smile—his mother's look of baffled concern.

Mr. Reinhart's "condition."

But he's always cheerful on the telephone—always busy, gregarious, "philosophical" (I can't complain, he cries, That's the way the world is, he says), defiantly himself.

For a week or ten days, one ignoble season, Constantine tried to avoid his apartment in order to avoid the telephone because—as he clumsily explained to his friends—he was terrified of the news from home.

Is someone ill? his friends asked.

I don't know, Constantine said.

They stared at him, not knowing if he was joking. (For Constantine Reinhart frequently jokes—his cruellest jokes are about himself.)

One of your parents? Your father, your mother—? they asked.

I don't think so, exactly, Constantine said.

It was all very clumsy. He couldn't explain. He blushed beet red, a tall gangling fool.

For years, for years—how many years!—he telephoned Commerce City or (less frequently) flew out to visit, usually for a weekend; or a few days at Christmas. And Mr. Reinhart was always the same. Wonderfully, indefatigably, the same. In high good spirits—bristling with ideas for McCullough's Iron Works—remembering to ask Constantine about *his* work—giving every impression of listening closely though at a certain moment he would squeeze Constantine's shoulder, in an involuntary gesture of love, and say, "Well look—I knew all along—I knew—*you* were the brains of this family from the start!—just ask your mother—I predicted it, right?—didn't I?—even when you were a little kid!"

As Constantine reports to him one or two or three bits of "news"—his new play in rehearsal, an offer of a visiting professorship in California, a query from the International Communication Agency in Washington (would Constantine be interested in travelling abroad, in Scandinavia, lecturing on "contemporary American culture"). Mr. Reinhart listens impatiently, and interrupts him to say, "Good! Right! It's about time they're catching on! You deserve all that—and more. *I* knew all along, just ask your mother, it was no secret to *me*, the way you learned to talk so young, how fast you caught on with the—what was it—the multiplication table—or fractions—whatever the hell—I drove down to the school, remember?—that hag you had for third grade making you copy things from the blackboard ten times, remember?—no?—Miss Tice her name was—*I* remember—I had a good long talk with her and with the principal too—got a few things straightened out—as if my son Constantine was an ordinary kid, with nothing better to do than—"

The flames licking noiselessly about his beefy perspiring face.

O love, Constantine thinks, sick, O Father, will you let me go?

Years. Years. Mr. Reinhart took the divorce equitably enough—of course Jayne wasn't good enough for Constantine—though naturally he did regret—well, he must regret—not having a grandson. (A grandson, that is, from Constantine. Constantine's brothers Gordon and Frank were doing very well for themselves—they were presumably "normal" men.)

Constantine has tried to explain to his friends his love-sickness for the past. Not only for Commerce City and his family, but for the northern peninsula, the old copper mining region, where his father's parents lived—but his eloquence fails him and he falls silent. Impossible to communicate his love, his hurt!—his loss!

If he had not been pushed through the ice. A stunted little freak, eyes popping out of his head, a secret lust swelling between his thighs—certainly he deserved to be pushed through the ice, he deserved to drown—but of course he didn't drown—the ditch was shallow—Jacky didn't jump on his back as he should have. And, afterward, weeks and weeks of fever, delirium, his lungs impacted: during that time (though it had not felt like "time"—there was no sense of its flow) he had witnessed the flames that constitute the universe, he had seen the transitory nature of all things, all personalities (his "mother," his "father," the child "Constantine" himself) and *he was never quite right again*.

Unless—and this was a very real possibility, knowing Constantine—he was exaggerating it all. Inventing it all.

"You make too much of things," Jayne once said. Her eyes ringed with fatigue, her voice flat. They were married but Constantine was no longer her husband. She continued to be his "wife" for a while—until it became clear that Constantine didn't want a wife.

"You make too much of things, you're too intense, I feel as if my skull were being squeezed out of shape by you looking at me and thinking about me and—well—loving me—*loving me* the way you do—" Vera said, laughing in exasperation. Swiftly and deftly she was braiding her unruly hair, this time into a single thick braid. It was very thick—perhaps too thick. Constantine stared at it, feeling dizzy. It was *too* thick. He reached out to grab it—he would jerk her backward, he would snap her slender neck—but of course he only touched it—stroked it—felt with awe and some distaste the dry tight hair, hairs—woven together—held tightly together like artificial hair. "I think love was just an idea people had," Vera said absently, examining herself in the mirror, "I mean—you know—like the Church—one single united Church for all the world—and women having babies—baby after baby—and men trapped as *men*—" and he saw how the flames licked over her, cupping her taut clever body, enhancing the self-love that shone in her face; and he knew that he had lost her; he could not even convince himself that he had wanted her.

He begins to shudder, remembering. Suddenly he is very weak.

The shudders course through him, one after another. He must be cold—his teeth are chattering—but his face is very warm. His eyes burn as if he hasn't slept for days.

Am I going to be ill, Constantine thinks, frightened, angry, am I going to be ill, over nothing at all—?

MCMAHON

Ingenious Constantine Reinhart has worn his $400 tailor-made suit (it was one of his few self-indulgences: but it came with a vest and two pairs of trousers) to the retirement party at Commerce City High for old Kevin McMahon. How very nice of him to come, everyone exclaims, how very thoughtful! Mr. McMahon will be so pleased.... Constantine cannot bring himself to say that he is really in town to visit his parents—to see his father in particular, who hasn't been well; he cannot say that he heard of the party only accidentally, and has dropped by out of a kind of perverse curiosity which he suspects he will regret. How *very* thoughtful, they say, shaking his hand, leading him across the cafeteria to the guest of honor, a stocky bald near-elderly man Constantine would never have recognized. Mr. McMahon, look who's here, do you recognize him? Constantine Reinhart—who went to New York—

Constantine chose his costume with great care. The handsome gray suit disguises his ugly curved back and his jutting shoulder; even his caved-in chest, flounced out by the gray-striped silk-and-wool vest, looks almost normal. And the trousers, of course, can be relied upon to hide his painfully thin legs. —Mr. McMahon?

But Mr. McMahon is deep in conversation with a large-busted woman and her husband. He doesn't always hear everything *exactly*, Constantine is told.

Constantine is given fruit punch in a Styrofoam cup. Hawaiian punch, it is; and quite sweet.

Does he remember Glen Bixby, someone asks, does he remember Sandra Mason?—Ron Ormsby? (Ron Ormsby! What a character! A state congressman from their district, and *quite* controversial. But he does a good job, really. Speaks out on certain touchy issues: illegal immigration, misuse of welfare funds, abortion on demand.) Constantine sips his Hawaiian punch and says yes, yes he does remember, it is all coming back to him.

Constantine, freakish Constantine, is taller than anyone recalls. His manner is fastidious and controlled—even "debonair." (Which might mean effeminate.) He seems to have worked some sort of magic on himself over the years. Perhaps living in New York City did the trick? (He has had some sort of success there—he's a playwright, or a poet, or a novelist—wasn't there once a flattering piece on him in *Time* or *Newsweek*?) —And how very charming he is tonight, mingling with old classmates, and with a dismaying number of people (most of them younger than he) whom he has never seen before in his life.

Quite by accident Constantine has stopped by the high school, to honor old Kevin McMahon. He flew to Commerce City from Des Moines (where he gave a lecture on contemporary art, or theater—he hurries past such explanations as if sensing that his companions might resent them) to visit his parents. And how is your father? someone asks. Good old Joe Reinhart.

Fine, says Constantine.

In the hospital for a while, wasn't he—?

He's fine now. Has to watch his diet, of course—his blood-pressure is high—and he isn't supposed to work as hard—

Oh you can't stop them, men like that! They *live* for their work!

Glenda, Bill, Sam, Irene, Sally, Ray.... Flames licking about their pleasant, really very pleasant American faces. These are good people, after all. Fine people. And why, Constantine wonders, isn't he one of them?

At home, as soon as he stepped through the door, Mrs. Reinhart clutched at him and said: "Constantine, I've got to talk to you. I never can, on the phone. *He* listens in on the extension. It isn't the way you think—how he talks on the phone, or the letters he writes—it isn't that way at all—he puts on a good show, he's always so cheerful and good-hearted—always has a good word for everyone—you and the boys and his friends and customers—then to me, here alone, in the house alone, to me he's like a crazy man—so angry—flying into a rage—going red in the face and choking if his toast is cold—if the newspaper's wet—Constantine it's hell to live with him and see him so changed—lying like he does on the telephone—saying everything is fine—but business *is* fine—it's never been better—that's the strange thing, it's never been better—profits have never been higher—but he can't rest—he can't slow down—he's a madman—he hates me—he shouts at me and calls me an old hag and he goes so red in the face, what if he *should* die, right here at home? What can I do? What can I do?"

Constantine swallows a large mouthful of his Hawaiian punch. It *is* spiked, though not substantially, with vodka.

How's your father, Constantine? Better now?

Much better, thank you.

You do remember me, don't you?—Jack Meyer?

Oh yes, yes certainly, yes, Constantine says, shaking a proffered hand.

And my wife Sheila—

Yes—Sheila—

Constantine Reinhart, who went to Ann Arbor—didn't you?—then to New York— Is your wife here?

No, says Constantine.

You *did* get married, didn't you? I thought I remembered—

Actually I've been divorced for ten years, Constantine says.

Mr. McMahon is wearing a blue gabardine suit with a white shirt, open at the collar, and a red knit tie, its knot comfortably loose. His handshake is brisk and friendly; he cups his right ear to hear Constantine's name. Yes? What? Oh *yes!*

Nothing to say. Nothing to say. But they chatter amiably just the same. The high school, the old days, wasn't Constantine the one who engineered that fool business—the stuffed bobcat in the tower?—no?—but Constantine was the brains behind a lot of mischief, wasn't he?—just too smart for the rest of the pack. And then he thumbed his nose at them all and went off to Harvard on a full tuition scholarship.

Not exactly, Constantine says shyly, not *Harvard*—

Then made a big name for yourself in New York—

McMahon makes a chortling noise; his small eyes narrow to slits as he laughs. He gives off a beery odor though he is drinking the scarlet-orange punch. Shorter than Constantine recalls, with a fat sagging belly that strains against his white shirt, greatly aged—alarmingly aged—but cheerful just the same. Wonderfully cheerful. What the hell? The weird thing is, old McMahon has always liked it here.

Constantine wants to ask: How did your wife die?—your sad "beauty" of a wife. Did she in fact die at all? Did you ever have a wife?

Instead he murmurs how amazing it is, the passage of time, he himself is now the age (i.e., 40) Mr. McMahon was when—when—when Constantine was his student in English and drama twenty-five years ago. How is it possible! It might have been only—

McMahon is wheezing with laughter, nearly spilling his punch. Just too smart for the lot of them, he says, for us, he says, winking at Constantine, slapping his hand on Constantine's arm and squeezing it hard. Once, twice, a third time. Hard but playful.

Constantine breaks off in the middle of his sentence, having forgotten what he is saying. Time? Something about time? Why on earth is he babbling about—time? He hasn't the faintest idea if time even exists.

He stares down at the old man's hand gripping his arm, as if for support. Odd, he hasn't shivered—it must feel quite natural—or perhaps the vodka is stronger than he believed. Why is McMahon squeezing his arm and leaning against him in this noisy crowded room? The gesture must, like most gestures, mean something.

▼ ▼ ▼

NUDE (SEATED), 1919
WYNDHAM LEWIS
PENCIL, WATERCOLOR, AND INDIA INK. 38.2 x 28.2 cm
COURTESY ANTHONY d'OFFAY
NOT IN MICHEL

CLAYTON ESHLEMAN

LEMONS

These lovely freaks, skins
pulled tight about inner disturbance,
a kind of vegetal lava—a one eyed
face looks out of a slightly blackened
yellow cowl, an eye held in its tensile
puckered mouth

▼▼▼

as if I held in my fist a creature
that was not my hand, a head on
the end of my arm, a head twisted
with wrath, whose soul spills into
the air as I ungrip—

▼▼▼

some are peaked like elves' shoes,
Aladdin's slippers, as the arabesque
of cosmic charge tips
    instead of curling on
    into a seamless sphere—

▼▼▼

one I know has a small aperture
with which it gently grips one's
    distended finger—
        a kind of vegetale mouth,
    the suck we feel
in the presence of lemons

▼▼▼

    place the lemon on the warped block,
        sensation of knife
        slitting through peel and juice
        is good, the lemon glistens
        halved, heard, it hails

        whoever then squeezes
        its blood into a prayer—

▼▼▼

one said: "to dangle here,
        all belly
        on the stem
        of another mind—"

        nun face,

little religious figure, with so much
god contracted,

          navel face

could I but think with my navel
would I see each being's aura
as a palace of umbilical corridors?

▼▼▼

        In the palace of the lemon babies
a music never ceases,
the harmony of rock
that which has no roots
like us

▼▼▼

it is good to be on earth
the two freshly cut halves
draw my heart out

of its heart space hiding
to be a heart man
a hurt man, heard
in vein

▼▼▼

enter into the mind of a lemon,
see how sour
is an ore

a match
by which we ignite
sweetness—

the sweetness of rock
the soul of things that speak
only in the interface of us and them

▼▼▼

In the palace of umbilical corridors
a divided lemon stands for
the heart
          jism
the fullest amplification of the heart,
the whitened heart of generation

▼▼▼

And so I branched
and was hung with glass lemons,
duplex hearts,
a circulation within the greater
circulation

and life then seemed essentially
vegetal core, coeur,
a core that was hollowed,
a chord of whitened arteries,
a music of arteries,
whitened floss of the air.

—February, 1983

AIMÉ CÉSAIRE

LAY OF ERRANTRY
TRANSLATED BY CLAYTON ESHLEMAN AND ANNETTE SMITH

        Everything that was ever torn
has been torn in me
everything that was ever mutilated
has been mutilated in me
in the middle of the plate stripped of breath
the cut fruit of the moon forever on its way
towards its other side's contour to be invented

and yet what remains with you of former times

    little more perhaps than a certain urge
to prick up my ears or to tremble in the night rain
    and whereas some sing the return of Christmas
    to dream of stars
    astray

this is the shortest day of the year
the order given all has collapsed into all
the words the faces the dreams
the air itself has become infected
when a hand advances toward me
I barely infer its intention
I have this so lachrymose season well in mind
the day with a taste of childhood
of something deep of mucus
had evilly turned toward the sun
iron against iron an empty station
where—no trains to be taken—
the same arm always moaning grew hoarse to no avail

Exploded sky flayed curve
of flogged slaves' backs

grief treasurer of the trade winds
shut book of spells forgotten words
I question my mute past

Island of blood of gulfweed
island remora's bite
island cetaceans' hind-laugh
island last word from a risen bubble
island great heart overspilling
high the most distant the best hidden
drunk weary exhausted fisherwoman
drunk beautiful bird caught hand
ill-joined island disjointed island
every island beckons
every island is a widow
Benin Benin oh stone of embittered ones
Ife which was once Ouphas
a mouth of the Zambezi
will we always stretch out our hands toward
an Ophir without an Albuquerque?

long ago oh torn one
in bits and pieces She
gathered her dismembered one
and the fourteen pieces
took their triumphant place in the rays of evening

I invented a secret cult
my sun is the one always expected
the fairest of suns is the nocturnal sun

Woman's body island on its back
woman's body full freighted
woman's body foam born
woman's body recovered island
which is never carried away enough
oh ranunculated night
not to carry its polypary secret to the sky
woman's body palm tree gait
coifed by the sun with a nest
in which the phoenix dies and is reborn
we are souls of noble birth
nocturnal bodies lively with lineage

faithful trees spouting wine
I a flebile sibyl.

Inert waters of my childhoods
into which the oars barely sunk
millions of birds of my childhoods
where if ever was the fragrant island
illuminated by great suns
the season the region so delicious
the year paved with precious stones?

Dismembered in the perturbations of the zones
a tenebrous mixture at the height of its scream
I saw a male bird founder
the stone is embedded in its forehead
I am looking at the lowest point of the year

Garbage soiled body skillfully transformed
space wind of deceitful trust
space fake planetary pride

slow unpolished diamond cutter prince
might I be the sport of nigromancy?
Meanwhile more skillful than Antilia or Brazil
a milestone within the distance
the sword of a flame that racks me
I fell the trees of Paradise

— from *Lost Body* (1950)

ED DORN

"THE PARTY"*

It always ends with a party

It is appalling that anyone
Should seek to be the agent of Shock
But only appalling as a proposition.
Farmed by action, it is amazing
or vulgar. Amazing is a rendering
Free from *everything*, and therefore
It is amazing.   Vulgar, well, vulgar.†

It is the interdiction of meat
and therefore not light and
therefore not good for anybody.
We must resist this dictum
With our whole will,
Should it acquire the status of a real threat.

25 December 1977

---

*By E.S. & Co.
†"Those of you who wish to leave will not be given a refund," or,
"You can check out any time you want, but you can never leave."

TOM CLARK

WAR AND OTHER POEMS

WAR

The desert moves like a museum made out of light.
Its mighty magnitude goes on and on.
It blasts the sleeping woman in her bed. It
Blasts the sleeping man. They are made clean.
Then the wind moves off to Afghanistan.

These are millennial figures.
The tank sits upon the white sand.
The men are away from home for the first time.
Beyond them the great lonely peaks glisten.
They will hear familiar songs in the night wind.

Over to the east the great fires will burn
and burn. Something moves restlessly along the sand.
The wind picks it up and blows it away over the desert.

It is gone into another dimension.
It is like a memory or an artifact in a museum.
The desert washes everything clean.
A bright dog runs from Kabul to Albuquerque.

LIFE IS GREAT

I

Is there any limit to the accumulation of disgrace
In a waste of shame, I guess not, well
There is no relief in quicksand here in Erie
Anyway. How to go on? By keepin' on
Keepin' on and so achieving an enormous loss of integrity.

A great noise as of a tuba comes down out
Of the mountains. A broad wave pattern hum
Follows it down the canyon. Then in
The morning light a number of Asiatics
Appear. They number in the hundreds
Of thousands. Their fingers are pointed to eternity.

II

The blue sky is full of lions. An eagle wheels over.
There are ancient petrogylphs in the sand.
We have been dead for a thousand years.

The winged lions glory in the radiance
Of the sun. They move across the sky like great maned boats.
Their eyes are grave, clear and unendearing.

They nod slightly, knowing what we did wrong.
A painful quiet falls over the scene.
Lions never say "I told you so."

REAL ESTATE

She owns the soft
impeachment of her ways,
and all the rest—
her sweet smile seems to say—
is mere real estate.

OAKS & ENTROPY IN SANTA BARBARA

The antique oak *sobre la veranda*
has to lean on one elbow
to exist: but so does almost
everything here. At least the tree has
an excuse, it is over a
hundred years old. But still grows slowly...
here, in Ojai, in Paso Robles,
the shade it creates is noble, artful
and especially in the afternoons
gives the gardens a light-checkered
repose that is shapely and not torpid.

So select this land.
No wonder the Spanish stopped.

So select these ocean-lying hills,
bowers of lemons and oranges, and
old oaks thickening and making
the land cohere around themselves.
It's a coherence that's proudly
undemanding of water or attention;
as personable as shade, or good
conversation; rooted, firm
and dry-leaved, with beams
that leak through to the foundations
like quick sun rays.

So select this land.
No wonder the Spanish stopped.
No wonder the professionals
supplanted them. Dying
painlessly over years can
be a way of life;
it can provide meanwhile
and nobly for everything around it,
like the oaks do and did;
or it can use everything up
and disappear into the end
of history, without taste or care,
a style that's much more modern.

A POLYESTER NOTION

We have reached the other side of the harbor
the sails of the yachts are slapped against the sky
like acrylic colors straight out of the tube
equally thoughtless and simple is the deep
lavender backdrop against which the ochre
mountains are flatly & theatrically stacked

We can keep on continuing along this line
as far as the grave of Ronald Colman or we
can double back and visit Ross MacDonald's
locker at the swim club though I seriously doubt
Robert Mitchum will be there what with
the polo season opening this week & all that

DEAR CUSTOMER

Quit your gripes about the bad air
being the dead end
of civilization as known

According to Rédiffusion du Sud
it's only a serious case
of dissolution by aerosols
in Le Cimetière Tropique
where invisible particles corrode
the anti-frontiers
and leak a desert music
into the marine band

An advancing state
(in other words)
of post-Club Med tristesse
expressed thru the business end
of a Porsche exhaust pipe

LINES COMPOSED AT HOPE RANCH

Twist away the gates of steel
—Devo

O wide blossom-splashed private drives
Along which sullen mouthed little guys
In motorized surreys
Ride shotgun over spectacular philodendra!
O paradise of zombies!
O terminal antipathy to twist
And shout!
O hotel sized garages
Inside which smoothly tooled imported motors
Purr like big pussies under long polished hoods!
O fair haven of killjoys
United to keep surfers off
One of the great beach breaks
Of the West Coast!
O floral porticos, flowers
Of de Kooning, de Chirico
Châteaux! Estates where jokes
Aren't funny! What secret meaning waits
Behind your stone & steel gates
Your walls of bougainvillea
Your date palm lined roads
Your quiet oak shaded lake
Like a European protectorate in Tanganyika?
Surely nothing disorderly, nothing disarrayed
Nothing at all except the great Pacific swell
Of money!

PILOT TO TERMINAL

Light in a box came too late to rescue
Temporary booty of the wet plasm splitting
Divided up into the dry greed of offspring
It grew hungry to exist at whatever cost
And to encourage this, on the Sony in the cellblock
Something sings from Tokyo to Ossining
And what it sings is Hold still and devolve
The animal's last gasp is simply the beginning
Of life in the machine whose singer's a chip
Honed like an atoll till cutting edge distribute
Translucent surface into phosphorescent husks
Which float on soft waves across that calm bay
Of retinal assent, where crystal blue persuasion
Sucks all thought into an undertow-like coma

"I DRIFT..."

I drift, out of reach of infinite Idiot Monkeys
who wrote the Life Script as a joke for money
(these are the writer-monkeys of the cosmic
Tonight Show etched on my brain by dreams), and yet
not really out of their reach
                              A Mondo Tremendo
beckons from beyond the benign mask of fog
but vanishes too swiftly into a policy
of scorched earth pursued from the mundum tremendum
not yet visited by the magellans of atari
who took six thousand years to discriminate "X"

ENTROPICAL QUESTION

Is the universe nostalgic about itself
as it runs down
or is entropy an essentially
unsentimental process
I believe the latter
and all around I see
a visine synapse
as beautiful as a sunset in baja
eyes drying in the wash
of decaying detail

ROBERT LOWELL

Was born under the shadow of the Dome of the Boston State
House
Was a Pisces
Was born on March 1, worst-fated of birthdays
Came from a family of bankers and Harvard presidents, though his
    father was a naval man
Hated his mother
Was a loner at school
Was called Caliban there, later shortened to "Cal"
Read the Bible, Homer, Shakespeare, Wordsworth & Keats
Ate health food on Nantucket
Hated Harvard
Carried a suitcase of poetry to Nashville to live on Allen Tate's
    lawn in a Sears Roebuck tent
Followed Ford Madox Ford to Boulder
And John Crowe Ranson to Kenyon
Refused to be inducted in the armed forces in 1943
Wrote a letter to President Roosevelt stating his crisis of conscience
22 years later wrote a similar letter to Lyndon Johnson
Protesting America's presence in Vietnam
In between wrote many tight, fist-like, self-revealing poems
Eventually went mad
Wrote to Theodore Roethke that their generation of poets had "a
    flaw in the motor"
Talked often about Hitler and the Blessed Virgin
Created much strain for each of his three wives
Repeatedly renounced his past and announced he was beginning a
new life
Died

CREELEY/OLSON LETTERS

[Banalbufar, Mallorca]
April 8, 1953

Dear Charles,
      Feeling much your own impatience, about all the damn distance. And just now when all this comes up, and hopeless fact of how long it will take to get back to you. To hell with it. Leave us be stoic, etc. Voila.

Re the poem to hand[1]—I get, and damn well respect, your premise. And think, in fact, this is precisely your method, either now or in the past. Or at least that is how the poems have read. The "forms" you've effected in their own fact of the speed & apposition of all facts or detail, etc., have had to be just this "form as present," or else they could never have made it. That is, junking the whole via of "form" as an external discipline (sonnets, etc.), either one can effect the coherence just by means of a like tension between all substances dealt with—and/or, sufficient to keep all in play, etc.—or else they, and the poem, fragment into the state they'd had prior to use of them.

I also see what you mean about "music," i.e., can I take this to be the "swelling" usual to that verse which maintains a "rhythm" irregardless of the closer & more pertinent intervals called for—or one which does go, da/dum, da/dum, etc. And ignores the closer demand of any aspect of a sense just then occurring in the poem's going on.

Anyhow the battle against the iamb & all, seems to me dull primarily because it is a digression, both from the whole problem of rhythm and likewise from a sense that all things are relevant to the use which can be made of them. Which is too general, but no matter. But to fight the fact of iambic pentameter, etc., implies the search for an alternative means to form—and this, at least, doesn't worry me, and should hardly worry you—who gave me the solution. To think of the poem as a "field" means, beyond anything else, that one think of the poem as a place proper to the act of conjecture—and to effect conjecture in form, can only come to—total assertion. If it is a poem. It would strike me that the only possible reason for this iambic pentameter line taking on the weight it seems to, is because, like they say, it might be felt as a general sign of the common rhythm of speaking, in English. I.e., that the stress pattern, generally, is weak/strong, etc., and that the breath, generally, can handle a five-stress line—more or less. The "more or less" is the dullness, and the fact that it is all a

---

These letters will appear in their chronological place in *The Complete Correspondence* of Robert Creeley and Charles Olson, a ten-volume project being published by Black Sparrow Press. Five volumes have appeared since 1980 and are currently in print.

"general" practice, etc., the final one. Or, why the hell bother with it, beyond that. The practice, in any case, of any man either of us could read, would so alter this "general" aspect of a rhythmic structure for poetry, etc., that it would not be at all "iambic pentameter"—or here comes in, I'd guess, all the problem of caesura, and the like. In any case, it does not interest me. As for Williams—here, say, is one case where the iamb is probably at the root, no matter the "five feet," etc., but also where the rhythms which then prove *particular* come to over-ride any such simplicity as this one:

> Liquor and love
> when the mind is dull
> focus the wit
> on a world of form
>
> The eye awakes
> perfumes are defined
> inflections
> ride the quick ear
>
> [*Added in pencil*:]
> What he does here
> goofs me!
>
> Liquor and love
> rescue the cloudy sense
> banish its despair
> give it a home.[2]

Viz, it is somewhat ridiculous, for the man who wrote that, to worry about alternative "forms," etc. Or the answer, in terms of rhythms, for the iambic pentameter line. In fact, when anyone can read that, and comprehend the rhythmic structure thereof—and why it is so damn fine—then the whole thing is no longer a problem. But the problem of each poem, as it comes. Well, call it "theme & variations," etc. [*Added in margin*: P(ound) or P(arker)'s constant & variant.[3]] I have felt that if, say, in any poem I can manage the rhythms of one line, and feel their necessity, actually, then I have made the way altogether for all the lines subsequent. Anyhow—the above strictly in point of rhythms, i.e., that's what just now I would lean on, here—that such rhythm can be held in a poem. The second & third verses are all the "proof" one needs.

Well, for christ sake, you might likewise examine the rhythmic structure of THE KINGFISHERS. Which is the wildest I know of. Can you tell me, for example, how else you could have got to that last part—and why, there, the rhythms are so christly exact. And why, also, you are allowed the whole swell (god knows this is another kind) of that, "With what violence..."[4] If the steam is up—which is nothing other than, this hot world, etc.—then rhythms come to declare it. And these rhythms must, of necessity, and their own, be particular to that content which they issue from. What else.

I only bug at the poem now here, because I think you run it too slow—or, isn't the damn mnemonic the headache, and doesn't it have the kind of rhythm pertinent to memory— "Without power, and only a poor oar..." I think that is the sound of memory, etc. The headache is, for me reading, that there exists a split, in force, between that which rides up as a detail out of memory, and that which is more properly *now*. I.e., I think the memory acts, here, do not exist on a like ground as the other things got to. Well, the lead-off: you're in hot water by line two I think—that once the "depth" is declared, as what it is, etc., then how much longer can you continue with qualifications, even those which bear the sound of the act of memory—i.e., won't the reader bug, as I do, that he has to inhabit this revery finally proper to yourself. Viz, too much like sitting at a table with a man who has gone, if only slightly, to sleep. Which is no damn kick, but that I think it isn't properly in the poem. Likewise—I mean because of this same savoring—you get a problem beginning, "I had made the mast...," in the *form*. For example, think of this usage:

> And I twist,
> in the early morning, asking
> where
> does it stop[5]

And then of that in this poem now to hand. I.e., does this pulling in, here, actually declare a tension in hand—or is it "formal"? It hits me, anyhow, as the latter.

It's a hard one to nail. My sense is, that the present, of the poem, is not of sufficient tension to involve the past actively—i.e., in a proper state of tensions. So it is, that the second mention of "Cabbage" is lost in the first, etc. Or not enough, it seems, more. I have the sense, likewise, that the *purest* part of the poem is, finally, that section beginning "that channel/ would be bluer...," to "...the years..."

That here is the least "formal" usage. And that, otherwise, other acts of this same memory are too glossed with almost a feeling of "symbolism." Viz, do not take on that straight throw, back. [*Added in margin*: And so, forward.] Likewise, that, in the opening, say, there is too much the tone of an "explanation"—which, for example, differs entirely from either the kind of "explanation" you get in the opening to AN ODE ON NATIVITY, or THE K/s.

Well, I think you are right, in short. That a poem must be this "total assertion," and that same is possible only when there is sufficient cause, to provoke it. And what same cause can be sufficient, is so much a matter of just the present, and what there is, there, that how the hell can we ever damn well lay down "general" rules of practice. At least we know *what* we want—which seems the gain necessary.

The "technical equals obedience" is damn useful statement. Obedience to the nature of what is to hand, and it takes the "technical," to deal with it. I had thought, last night, that just here came in that old thing of Bird & all, i.e., Charley Parker—and wonder if I have seemed too silly with all that. I.e., I am dead serious, and want sometime to do a gig on this whole area. (I had hoped to when Bud was here, to help me with notation, etc., likewise with examples, etc., but wasn't time or the place.)

Bird, and the few others equal, are almost the only present relevance, in rhythmic structure, available. Viz, that only Williams is of this order. That, a poet can look to this usage for an analogy to his own—and, if he is not a literal goof, etc., can comprehend that Bird's premise for structure in terms of the musical (or harmonic) line, is or can be, his own.

The same thing is actual in flamenco, but this comes finally to another "classicism," i.e., it is worn to that extent—and tho it can provoke me, it is not of the same use that Bird is, and was. For example, I am more influenced by Charley Parker, in my acts, than by any other man, living or dead. IF you will listen to five records, say, you will see how the whole biz ties in— i.e., how, say, the whole sense of a loop, for a story, came in, and how, too, these senses of rhythm in a poem (or story too, for that matter) got in. Well, I am not at all joking, etc. Bird makes Ez look like a school-boy, in point of rhythms. And his *sense*, of how one rhythm can activate the premise for, another. Viz, how a can lead to b, in all that multiplicity of the possible. It is a fact, for one thing, that Bird, in his early records, damn rarely ever comes in on the so-called beat. And, as well, that what point he does come in on, is not at all "gratuitous," but is, in fact, involved in a figure of rhythm which is as dominant in what it leaves out, as what it leaves in. This, is the point. Only one other man, up to this—viz: the Dr. Like this:

> If I
> could count the silence
> I could sleep, sleep.
>
> But it
> is one, one. No head even
> to gnaw. Spinning...[6]

It's what they call *doubles*, in the other area, but here ok! I.e., that doubling on the, "sleep/sleep" and "one/one." That Williams hears this way, is the fact. And note where it falls, and rides off—to "even." Likewise the "Spinning..."

You are the only other, viz:

> And the too strong grasping of it,
> when it is pressed together and condensed,
> loses it
>
> This very thing you are[7]

Listen to Bird on, All The Things You Are. Too much! (Well, seriously, do sometime hear: Chasing The Bird, Buzzy, April In Paris, etc., etc. I wish to god I had my own with me, I miss them more, finally, than any other one thing—and sit here some evenings turning the damn dial on this damn radio up & down, just for even a fucking imitation, of what this is.)

I think we can afford the casual, to the extent, that for us there can't be any usage but that peculiarly of the moment, instant, or what to call it. Gratuitous equals fortuitous, etc. Tho not at all that simply. But rhythm is where the most work now comes in, that, if we can manage the declaration of rhythms more exact than those now in use—the iamb, etc.—we clean up. Likewise that rhythm is a means to "going on" far more active than any "thot," etc. And that sound is rhythm in another dimension.

Bach & Bird & Williams ought to be enough for any "poet"—and he might do worse than not bothering to read anyone after Shakespeare, etc. Who I honestly, like they say, can't now read myself.

On this last—it is a constant damn embarrassment, that S/ at least in the books I can get, the forms of them, etc., is so slow on the page I get bugged, and don't make it. That, say, whereas Melville, Lawrence, Crane, Cervantes, Williams, yourself, Pound (in his prose), Parkman, Stendhal, and Homer—are all of a particular relevance, immediately & unavoidably clear to me,—S/ is not. I'd be an idiot to say he was, etc. I cannot get into his content, or dig it, enough, to move me to a proper study.

I can't read, or won't, anymore, what doesn't damn well involve me. I don't go stiff, viz not try, etc., but will no longer read with that self-consciousness I had growing up, when the Great Books, etc., seemed damn far away from Acton, Massachusetts. And, of course, were. I have no damn wish to stay a provincial, etc., really the last two years have hoisted me out of that damn viciously. But there is nothing but what is—like you sd, all there is, is, etc. I have to see what there is for myself.

I don't think Rabelais is funny... I can't make Donne... I think James is a horrible old bore... think N/ West's Day Of The Locust, in parts, is better than anything Faulkner or Valéry ever wrote... I hate Beethoven, and get to hate Mozart... I think that Bird, Bach, and a few others are all the music one needs... Well, the sun is shining, it's a fine day, etc. Or leave us cry, etc.

> Liquor and love
> *rescue* the *cloudy sense*
> *banish its despair*
> give   it   a   home.

Write soon, tell us how you all are. All our dearest love to you all.

Bob

[Black Mountain, N.C.
ca. 10 April 1953]

Bob: Damn well *value* that job of yrn just in on the mast. Very damn big help, & just here where i very much am—on these *maxies* (that, the mnemonic is—every line—the danger: the "win," like you say, to reach straight back, and have it in, right now

i'm terribly nervous abt all these damn things—that book. Just on this score. And I am quite aware i am just beginning to come to grips with what such "past" involves. In fact, wish i might do the whole fucking thing *first*—and publish afterwards. But just the publishing (can't thank you enuf, like they say) has jumped the whole thing forward.
                        And tho i keep putting off to make final copies, because new stuff comes on, I'll have to let it out, for now, and figure to catch the failures as I republish (no?)

Not that I'm not trying to see those damned 1,2,3 fresh. But it buggers one, to go back over, yes?

  Anyhow, I take it you are *impeccable* on this score (at least you get me on what i seem to be about, keeping to such material—not leaving it alone, as any Englishman might
      (was burned up anew over all that Lavender Hill Mob's going on abt
      re-orientation, & consolidation:[8]
                 still
    damn well figure that a man's own
    warp is where "tradition" is—at
    least where he'll find how he got
    to this present
        that it is not cultural
       in any previous verbal sense alone—
       aesthetic sense (to cut the arts in)
               viz yesterday, tried all day to see
what i cld do with a crazy biz of Smith's (Capt John)[9]
                   he entered into my picture at 12, when three of us were crawling around Tablet Rock at our usual game, of stalking each other: bang-bang. When suddenly out from behind a bush, comes this voice crying, "Tragabigzanda! Tragabigzanda." And big—like I'd only heard some barker, or a traveling Jesuit come for hell-week to the church, use. Yes, and one other: an old ham had played "Lightning" for twenty years, and gave it the juice, whatever the line was. Well, here, in our own preserve, altogether private to ourselves (except for couples necking, or screwing, we'd stumble on, in same bushes—and be all put out) was something real crazy, real—new, this guy hollering this word)
           We dropped to the ground like the trained Indians we were, eh? And came up to the bush on our bellies, real smooth. And parted same as deftly as Henry Ware or Paul Cotter[10] had taught us to
         And by god if there wasn't John Smith all got up in ruff & armor, a bristling bastard (more Captain Shrimpe, that quondam

drummer, as Morton had it Standish was,[11] than the Admiral of New England, quite another man than that little Pricke from Plymouth), and Smith supporting some swooning Turkish Princess on his arm (she also dressed, a moth-eaten Elizabeth, from a bad movie)
                                            and the two of them taking instruction from a third bird in modern clothes, the director, we found out, of the Tercentenary Pageant (we later got jobs as part of the townspeople, with square shoes, and that damned collar, etc.)
                      but it was that noise, repeating itself—he didn't have it right—
                              "TRAG...
                                       a BIG
                                                ZANDa,
                                                        all over the top of the rock, and the echoes (which we had good control of, and he didn't) slopping out to the sea
                    It was a bizness, to have "history" come bang into the midst of our own game!

A very sad feller, this Smith. Was another of those lads I was getting at in that thing off to you a couple of days ago, got ground out of the N.E. deal because he was Old England, not the on-coming Commonwealth, even tho it was he named it Masschusetts, even, for that matter, named her New England first—and as well made (in his several books) the only solid sense about the difficulties, as well as the virtues of, that coast. His accuracies (this supposed liar, who told such tales of wars in Bohemia, and winning such a fair lady as Tragabigzanda he named Cape Ann as her cape, until Prince Charles reduced that, along with all the Algonquin names Smith had so scrupulously recorded (also for the first time, getting the orthography down in English)—he pegged the difference between the Maine coast and Mass Bay so rightly (1616) that you read it as you know that difference to this day.

Well, he got run over. The Pilgrims refused his proffered help (they took Standish, instead, that squirt). All Smith could get was fishing chances—which were not what he was after: he was after all the economies the situation offered, did want to "plant" a Plantation, found a country. His trouble was, he was wholly secular. And for almost 25 years (the Virginia part of his story lasted 2!) he beat and beat against the Puritan tide, and lost.
                                            In his last year, 1631, he prefaced his last pamphlet with a poem. It is called THE SEA MARKE. And for the life of me, I hate to see it go unused—even if, yesterday, I couldn't give it the rewrite I thought might make it. For it failed then, as now, simply, that that bug, a sea image—wreck, on shoals—won't hold.
    I copy it for you, anyhow, just to let you have it:

Aloofe, aloofe; and come no neare,   (go for this 1st
        the dangers doe appeare;   line!
Which if my ruine had not bene
        you had not seen:
I onely lie upon this shelfe

                    to be a marke to all   (and shelfe &
               which on the same might fall,   selfe)
That none may perish but my selfe.

If in or outward you be bound,
                    doe not forget to sound;
Neglect of that was cause of this
                    to steare amisse.   (& this)
The Seas were calme, the wind was faire;
               that made me so secure,
               that now i must indure
All weathers be they foule or faire

The Winters cold, the Summers heat
                    alternatively beat
Upon my bruised sides, that rue   (& this beaut
                    because too true
That no relief can ever come.   (ha! right here those puritans
     But why should I despaire   win! ho-ho)
          being promised so faire
That there shall be a day of Dome   (doesn't it look fine, speltso?)

Still can't go away from it so easily—in any case, it is wild, that the prose of this struggle, there, the founding (or such verse) is such a sign of the battling went on: Morton & Smith writing so (right out of W. Shax, Gent., etc.) VERSUS that wondrous working word man Bradford (sired out of Lancelot Andrewes by Southampton—or Southhampton's wonder-working lad, W/S)[12]
          (Help me, lad—or wld just some such break into prose as this letter to you be a good ideal for Letter #11 ?????????????)

     By no means meant to get away from that carefully argued letter of yrs on the Bird, Bill, yrself, and the business of our common trade. For of course it is just this rhythm thing which is
          (it did occur to me that the
          reason I may have been sent by Bill—
          as Bill—on the iamb,
               is this fucking headache of
                    a long go:
maybe Bill was puttering with it fr some such post-Paterson push (((like Desert Music[13] raises. To be straight, I think it's as good as Bill ever: took me big—sometime, let's argue that one, for I remember your throwing of it down)))
                         In any case, without turning it at all on such a single poem, the problem stays, of some founding of a language fit to work over longer stretches than such lyrics (I honor the lyric, in this instance) as Bill's several
          Or yr own
               That is, such a loop as you get in the stories (by Bird,

you say) is the headache—to get a loop in long verse, put it

                                       Nor let this sound like
any either-or, no setting yr attack against, or down fr, like problem. Not at all. In fact, what
you are doing by what's left out (that way you have it there, over Bill on counting silence—or
the Bird) still comes to me like a validity I wish I knew more of

                                         All I am throwing in, is
that just such tension as you have also put yr finger on (as of the mnemonic, or any variation
of, the constant of a poem—its present) comes increasingly to seem to involve this question
of where quantity is back in business (as against stress, that is "sound-stress"

                      that the quantity of the sounds restores stress in more than even
                      line & field, drops stress into just such silences as you are saying
                      are the context as

                             well as, when you follow stress to where
              quantity is taking one, it gets down to this base of language, the
              language itself, its "state"

(I started yesterday to have a go with you on more of stuff ten days ago—that is, to try to say in
what way the rise of the subordinate parts of speech (and the consequent return of rime-as-
pun) does put the quantitative in, despite the fact that there is less inflection now in the
language than ever

But today you send me—goof me—with this ride of yr own, on the Bird. It's beautiful. And I
shall try to hear him—have kept asking, but never come on same. Much obliged, for the
titles. Will seek.

            OK. Am still, obviously, inside the present job too much to be clear abt
what's larger than that.
                (And ask you to fuck those Grove people—did have that letter—was
it Donald Allen,[14] or something?—and thot, from his signature, god help us—so much like
those Hudson Review people's handwriting—no balls—no engagement—all this tidy little
school-boy renaissance—Christ, I want to rear up and heave em all, London, and the Village,
or the Universities
            the shits.

OK. Keep me on to everything.
                (((Just reread the stumblings above—and strikes me it is
QUANTITY you are yrself so much engaged on, not only in the poems but in such an analysis
of rhythm as you herein offer
             ok, my mind drifts quickly on to something else, this
morning—no use
        too much beer last night, plus a bad movie
                      plus a bad book (can't freshen
myself, hereabouts after a day's bad work
              Can see why you have a boat! Wild, to hear the
tales of it—tell us more

All well—Kate & I have only a punt & this lake—"pond." But it's all right, some days: she is, like you say, balances   C

[Black Mountain, N.C.]

Robt: Put it down: Friday, July 17, 1953. Yesterday: CREELEY, all afternoon, and then, 11PM–2 AM; and in between, from 8:30–11:00, WC WILLIAMS' A Dream of Love, read by six people in a circle in front of the rest of us!!!

By god, Robt: POETS! Just that damn pleasure of, same. The two of you—and my lad Tudor right in there, talking, as i had talked in the afternoon, of (he) Bach Boulez Parker, I, Bach, Boulez, you, Bill. (And the pleasure of, that such as Vicente, Wolpe, Cunningham, Jalowetz, to speak of the ones most alert themselves, perhaps, plus this Barab (and the "contemporaries": viz, Jack Rice (the "Leader" lad), Dawson (that pitcher, from Kirkwood, Mo), Lafarge (ex-dancer).[15] And the jazz men.

And all "accident," like they say. The afternoon, & midnight sessions, on yr letter of Apr 8, just came about (intended as they were). And I had nothing to do with the production of Bill's play.

Well, to tell you. For the "double" is one of those things, (how often?

Yr own thing is only half done (Tudor was rehearsing, so cldn't make the afternoon session. But set up the midnight one, for Cunningham & himself. And was fine, on Parker—& Boulez. And the lads, in the afternoon, were fine on yr verse & stories—poking it right up to these musicians (who turn out—why Tudor is the exception—to be altogether "academic," by god, on both music & rhythm!
            The next go, I shall not hold until Tudor is through his heavy rehearsing. So that he can tell 'em what he found out, from Parker, and from what must have been his big breakthrough: his task to play B's 2nd Sonate. He'd told me the story before, but I listened to it again, just because it is the story of a man's discovery that the notional, and not the relational, is the law of, reality.
            (A lovely ending, he quoted, of an article of B's—which helped him to figure out what this music was: after a studied attempt to analyze composition now, and unable, of course, to say so exactly how he composes himself, therefore forced to talk of others, to use their work, he ends, something in this fashion, "You may wonder why I make this search for complexity, and I must stop it, for it's aesthetics, and I should go back to my ruled paper!" He ends by saying that music, to him, must go in the direction Artaud has set for art, not so much that aspect of Artaud which would reconstitute things in an exotic civilization, but that music should be ["]*envutement* & hysterical"[16]

(The verb is *envouter*—& above shld be envoutement—and means "to cast a spell," and

281

exactly by sympathetic magic, that is, "by transfixing a waxen image representing the person whom one wants to charm"; and if the root is *vouter*, it comes out to arch over someone (or, i suppose, to draw a circle around them?

Anyhow, magic.

Tudor felt certain that Artaud & Boulez mean hysteria in the sense of the wildness of the instant as giving birth to life (and i don't, for a minute, think he knows that *istera* in Greek is womb!)

SO; *cast spell, & be, instant*. Which seems all right, no? (though this spell-casting remains, I'd take it, for uzamoricans, not so easy a question as, for Frenchmen!) ((That is, it still strikes me, as it did in *Ishmael*, that M[elville] was damned right to investigate the magic question—[17]

and that a great deal of "American power" has to do with appropriation fr nature, of same. Therefore, *any* magic, is to be damned finely questioned—more carefully (& I'd, of course, say "largely") than Bill does, in D of L

BUT, by god, I rush on to say, that the very fact that Bill does get it in there, is, for me, only another evidence to what a very damn great play it is. I tell you, Robt, I don't know *a thing* which is *as close home* as this play. And I was so moved, fr the 1st instant of it, that I understood completely why Con wldn't even go, stayed home instead—and tells me this morning that just because it was going on, up the hill, was too much—that she cldn't sleep, and went finally to sleep writing a letter to Bill in her mind on why she takes it Desert Music does do one thing A Dream of Love doesn't!

Of course it is for her Myra—and, o.c., for me, the Doc (both Danny, of the play, and hisself, he so does stem the thing on his own literal autobiography. E.g., exact stuff here in the Build-Up etc.)

Let me go on a little abt it. You 1st told me of the play, but I don't think (when I did read it) we ever got to it, did we? And I'm not sure it isn't the greatest Williams to me, simply, that I sit, before it, in the presence of reality flawlessly given its dimension for two acts, and, except for the two big speeches of the Doc in Act 3, flawless to the very end—and the end (the Doc's return, home, to his bed) great, GREAT: the end of Myra's hell of one week, that, for that week, she does not love, because he went and died in a hotel bed with some other woman, with big legs!

That is, it's crazy, to say this is the best play an American ever wrote. It's one hell of a lot more. He's right, himself: the only comparison is, those Greeks, the business of reality is so thoroughly here got in—doom, home.

God, the speech! Like when the Doc says to Myra, "Nuts"! Or Josephine, & Mrs. Harding, sing—that hymn! Or the Milkman, on money! on business men. And Myra. (In fact, again, the only place where I don't think the language does the play's job is, those two speeches I sagged to: the speech abt Lizzie, Delia, the mind first, then sex, the streets of Philly as a young man, and the women; and the other, the big one, abt the poet's vision, of beauty as—like the atomic physicists—always, the shape of, a woman.

It's crazy to me, but just exactly the poet is (the thing one might say a man might know best) is where Bill lets it come out statement, and loses that accuracy of everyone in his play's talk, including the Doc's, at all other points.

> (I shld, actually, if i had a copy, go back & read these speeches. For it may be that the guy who read them lost some of the bitterness, & the bite, of them, as they are on the page. Maybe. Tho I do remember some questioning of this 3rd act, reading it. And this may be it.

Anyhow. I was struck by Con's saying she sd the same thing in her imaginary letter: that it is his self which gets free in Desert M, as against its loss in love in Dream. No. That's not—or sd that flatly—not exactly what she was after. But let me put my own way: that the self, in D of L, is the core of the onion Doc says he takes himself as; that that is the self of him which is homogenous to the selves of all these others there; and as onion, he is also a full creature of love, of the dream of it.

But the other subject—love "a little false," the man of him who can't, as Myra can, and all the rest, stay unbored by its objectification in a "one"—no no no

this *is* the onion man; this is the beauty of the differentiation, that he alone has to get the lens of the microscope wiped clean, that he can't say, except in the instant of his excitement, "love you"

It's this other guy—the talker, whose talk Myra & Dot go for, just the most when he does go off as poet (and they go to sleep! or Myra does!)

—it's this guy who, in the 3rd act, feels forced to push his gab into those explicitnesses of (1) how mind & sex fucked him up; and (2) how the Greeks had an advantage on him in presenting "a play"....

that is (let me try this out): that his dream of love is only false in that he

(((that it is a little false for Myra, too, or any of them, simply, that the object is not—even to the sentimental Milkman—will not be the equal of the, emotion

that is, every instant, eh?

but that the women *know*—or so want the *permanence* of it—that they don't need the lens rubbed clean (or at least they don't need a new object to wipe it clean—that the Doc's talk, the man of him, is enough to do just that

(And Con sd a thing seems it, that "mortality," ain't on women's minds

(certainly Myra means it, let me die, right in the middle of the night, like Doc says Mrs Tenant probably will, in the next 24 hrs, he says!)

But mortality is on Doc's mind, damn well is, as it's on any man's. And what i am seeking to say is, that this "self" of him, or any man, does *change* the dream, of love—in fact, so instantly,

283

or *previously*—has changed it, that the vision he talks about is (and I'm not questioning that Bill doesn't see it so) is, in fact, *a dream of, self* (if that is understood to be a dream of, life or, of man)

That is, suddenly, in those two places in act 3, there is a confusion, by explicitness, of self with love—and that the poet, suddenly, of Doc (the talker, not the onion) is unsupported except by outward *reference* to the writing of, sd play—or the other element of the play, sex, by outward reference to, the society—and specifically, the American
(It is at just the moment of the 1st of these two speeches that he sacks the whole question of "other women" by throwing it at Myra that he goes to them to renew his love for her!—which I think is baloney, even if all of us say this, one time or another, mixed up as to why we do do it, forgetting that we damn well know—and Doc shows, in the Dot scene—that it ain't love. It ain't even sex (in the sense of that speech abt himself, up through the streets of Philly—or behind the water-tower, on top of the old French hospital, with the nurses). It's—oh shit, olson, let it go, let it go.

Ok. It's Bill's, anyway. And it's wonderful, the damned best—the only fucking tragedy anybody's written, really, since those who—says he, sound like horses, neighing! (Ain't that wonderFUL: MEN KAI HOOION etc. etc. "They say you were some Buster, in yr day, too"

We talk abt rhythm—and you say Bill's—and by god this play, all all (but those two speeches) IT, right there, making it, what it is, reality, without a hemidemisemiquaver of its flatness lost, to get its dimension.
I am still involved, kept in it. And—
o, yah, wanted to say that i damn well figure the play came from just this quarrel in himself, abt this finagling—and if it isn't flawless, well, shit, who has touched him, who????

Ok. Will come back on, when fresh, to our own businesses—at least start you in to these continuing matters of, Parker, & with-him.

Hell, Back again. And why don't I go all the way (on D of L). Like this:

(prefacing it, that, what Bill's done, there's no use to do any more; that here, the refusal to take any other way than the vocabulary in use—to make all these words fit the events—"a dream(!) of Love (!)" is the best, the damned best possible. No one else wants to, do it!)

(I) that the dream of self (which I think is the fair phrase to cover what the Dr-Poet, in distinction from Dan-the Onionman (no different from Tenant, the Milkman) has its own peculiar issue

& (II), that the vocabulary for it (as flat as the vocabulary of love & sex) won't yield to that other vocabulary that when Myra says early in the play, what you want, is to be free is IT (& not just to fuck some other)

and that when a man is free, it isn't the image of a woman (as the Poet there says it is—and compares himself to the physicist)

in fact it's no image of any object of reality which does fit it—that all those images are stages of freeing, not of, the free thing
(that the very damned problem is, that it *can't* objectify itself—
(((not so different, it suddenly strikes me, than I earlier sd Boulez, or any of us, can't "analyze" his own damn composition)))

and why god is used—all he is (his two attributes are): (1) he is non-existent; and (2), he is free

which a man knows he is, when he is, free: (1) non-existent, in the object sense, however much from that moment all objects, including himself are, because he is free, absolutely *intense*—"vivid," I'd rather say, to avoid any *pressure* ((there is none)); and (2), free: the self, is *known* as free

((((that it ain't, as i sd it was, in Cold Hell, a coat, which we try to turn inside out[18]/ it's not that either/or; it's neither in nor out but *live*: the self is engaged in one act, to—not to discover itself so much as to come to recognize the freedom of the self, to find out that that it burns is its act

To pile it on: that the girl in the pink shower isn't (dazzled as I am too) even if she is the dream of love, the dream of self

Ok. Love love O   Charles

[Black Mountain, N.C.]

Robt—(fri jly 18)—merely to keep you current to this real nervous thing has come up over yr letter of April 8. That is, the place happens to be running over with jazz men! Even including Wolpe, who taught most of the new crop now at Birdland (tho Wolpe is the one excluded fr the conversations, simply, that he has been mauled too often by these very ones he taught, who have moved, and he's left, as a square—but as, for that matter, several of the 20 yearers as well, are ((and why I aren't, I don't know, all of these (except Tudor) seem to me so falsely knowing. And I hit 'em, just that I don't think they do know what they are talking about, they got such gab. And a listlessness (even a stomach, on a pianoplayer, been a job man around Philly, so far as I can figure out since he was a kid)
still the letter hasn't been

read, because Tudor, & Barab, have been caught in rehearsals all week of a new piece (for cello & piano) by this guy Cooper[19]—who damn well does talk most intelligently abt the whole biz, being himself principally a jazz piano

but last night, again, a table session happened, and I quoted yr para:

"I think we can afford the casual, to the extent, that for us there can't be any usage but that peculiarly of the moment, instant, or what to call it. Gratuitous equals fortuitous, etc. Tho not at all that simply. But rhythm is where the most work now comes in, that, if we can manage the declaration of rhythms more exact than those now in use—the iamb, etc.—we clean up. Likewise that rhythm is a means to 'going on' far more active than any 'thot,' etc. And that sound is rhythm in another dimension."

Also, yr marginal note "P(ounds) or P(arker's): constant & variant" ((the latter idea, as you know, the one which the Max things have most moved me in on, led me to question that "constant" as, to what extent more of the "vein of art"[20]—meaning, of course, as P-1 means it, not, because I do not know, P-2's, as you say it, here

—that is, the "field" biz has, in that run fr April 1 to abt July 1, got forced down, I take it—or perhaps the existence of a "long go" is the factor—but i have the sense that at least I don't any longer understand the "constant" in, say, the way the Wilderness Battle[21] was (somehow) the same in Cold Hell; that I feel the thing much more now (and what I mean by a *lower* field) as a rhythm which is being behaved to, in any given unit ("Letter"). How much the existence of, say, "Gloucester," as the "tune"—as "April, in Paris"!——and not at all as "subject-matter"——place as me, & anyone (((did i yet get to you the one starting, "Trolley-cars/ are my inland waters"?[22]))), assumed as known, and then composed *into*

it comes out offense in depth, call it. And I was struck by Coop saying, "Parker bounces it off three walls, rhythm, harmony, & melody"—and going on, just like Mr Eliot!, abt how the "historical" is nothing you can make explicit, yet, the way every other jazz man has, and does treat April, in Paris, is also a thing in Parker's given ride any given night

(which is what i mean abt how i'm not sure these guys do know more than what, in verse say, any bright one might)

But it don't matter. For what I am getting is a fill-in. And simply because you said, "I am more influenced by Charley Parker, in my acts, than by any other man, living or dead." And that—like they say—is good enough, for me!

I myself wldn't know where (taking it, you say I do, every so often) I do pick up, except—from my feet!

One thing did occur to me (a propos yr own language in above para—and pointing out to assembled cats, that just yr word "gratuitous" is wild, and the way a poet damn well does talk (not abt augmented 8ths, triplets, etc. etc.—that tho we are too are a time-art, we have no more words than such a[s] iambs, and they're so broad all one is talking about is the same as a "measure," bar—and such as odes, strophes, antistrophes, no more than codas, etc.

And still stay as amazed as I probably told you I was, when I turned to Dante's Vulgare Eloquio, figuring here, at least, I'll hear talk of the *insides* of the job—and all i got was, that 5, 7 etc. are harmonious and the even weights are flat![23]

And even once, four or five years ago, figuring there must be an ars poetica in EP, starting to put together all I cld find he had said, over the various, including the Treatise, on Harmony[24]—and again, that actually no *vocabulary* exists, sufficient to make real talk!

Not, of course, exaggerating this, taking it that the things themselves are the place, anyhow. But again, just now, just to understand what you are about better—and what this craving in myself is, for more inner music, like i sd, I also crave some gab. (So this present gig, here, is perfect, for my purposes—as, last year, that Boulez was, I shipped to you —still haven't had the chance to get together with Tudor on B's new stuff. But will.)

Also: that just that our sounds ain't from signs, but from words—and that the signs are the sounds as well as that they are names for things & actions, processes & states of being— plus that the instrument for their making is silent silent silence, this is so immense a difference, that such a vocabulary as musicians' is never possible (???

tho i had the strong feeling, last night, that just now cld damn well be the time when a body of words & definitions—a veritable ars poetica—can come

And that yr letter above referred to is root (Crazy, suddenly remembering, that I'd sd "The Operation"[25] cld lead me to such a thing too! How abt that? What's going on here? By god—look out, ahead!

Did the wildest thing yesterday (instead of reading yr letter over, wanting to be as new to it, read aloud, as the others, so that the ride of it wld catch me again, as well)—read, instead, Shelley's A DEFENCE OF POETRY!!!

And tho it is a tract, and he not Keats by a long shot, in such matters, there were some sentences I wanted to put over to you:

"all expression being subject to the laws of that from which it proceeds"

"The distinction between poets and prose writers is a vulgar error"

"those who cannot distinguish words from thoughts"

The two good sections are (1) on language in its primes; and (2), a fine job on the Provençal, traced by Christianity & chivalry, and so on Love, as, there, Dante:
"Galeotto fu il libro, e chi lo scrisse."[26]

The latter section is not quotable, and maybe nothing from the language passage will come out & over, but the identity of some of the things he says abt language "in the infancy of society" are straight Fenollosa! Even if, of course, S finally feed [*i.e.*, fed] it all *up* to Plato!

"Their (that is, poets') language is vitally metaphorical; that is, it marks the before unapprehended relations** of things and perpetuates their apprehension, until the words which represent them become, through time, signs for portions or classes of thoughts instead of pictures of integral thoughts; and then if no new poets should arise to create afresh the associations which have been thus disorganized, language will be dead to all the nobler purposes of human intercourse."

> (** it is this "relations" business—and always worked out, in this "Defence," by way of that bloody image of "reflections," in a mirror[27]—which fucks up this whole piece (as, of course, it fucked up and continues to fuck up, verse—even, i'd say now, to this "associations" thing as well
>> ((my own present mood says this associations shit is what we ought to dig imagism's grave for... without knowing enuf yet, i surmise that it is just this last trailing veil of "relation" which does fug imagism (????????

I damn well clot, and the blood cries, rhythm—rhythm alone, alone, is what does it / and we are back with what you do cry, Parker, Parker!

And suddenly that damned dream—and those words, dreamt—still says what I believe:
       of rhythm is... [28]
              and that the rest *only* comes *after*
that there are no walls (not three, or any
                   there is this slot, which reaches all the way back, is under, has to be got in, or there is nothing there but construct—"he has fine ideas," the boys tell me, one says, of certain players—and they may, or may not, make for such improvisation as, P's

And if Shelley only "thought" a little, he'd not have left this thing he interests me very much for being interested in—that *the grace* & truth, he says (in Hymn to Intellectual Beauty), is inconstant, visits us spasmodically—he'd not have made us so much nightingales, legislators, and whose very words are "burning atoms of inextinguishable thoughts" (bah)

What is so damned fine is, that it is rhythm he is talking abt. But he fugs it, being so goddamned metaphysical.—That rhythm is inconstant, and is a pisser to *always* have in there (as it goes, & comes, daily, as toward *anything*
      —why "love" is also to be thrown down, that
      vision of
      continuity (not the family, as
      Rimbaud/ Or extremes,
      sought. But
      this inconstant made
      (a poem, anyway) a
      constant

The constant (By god, does EP *mean* just that ?????????
And has the misunderstanding been my own?)

It was a damned joy, anyway—never being able (nor shall I) to forget that scream of yrs once, recently, that, so far as writers go (Martin, was yr example, at the moment) that *grace*, by god (writers & non-writers!) is what it is[29]—to find this lovely Shelley at least saying it, however metrically!

> In H I B:
>> that this "Ghost" he's talking abt, and what he dedicated himself to— "O awful LOVELINESS"
>
> "Gives grace and truth to life's unquiet dream"

(Wish to christ I had got off to you a letter went to Mason[30] in which, provoked by something he'd sd—or merely that he is, at 40, still too fucking respectful of the past, and not attentive to his own damned present—for which read, self—on *progression*, in language now

I don't think I ever saw so clearly how a thing does not go toward something except as it proceeds from & by its first instant, and each succeeding one. And because I continue to think of him as an engineer (despite the fact he tells me he is a Revenue Official, and was trained as a lawyer!), I quoted him what the dictionary told me, that progression "is a discrete series that has a first but *no last element*, esp. one in which any intermediate element is related *by a uniform law* to the other elements."[31]

I can't get it back now, but it was strong feeling of laws of composition arising from principles of force which does damn well undo so much of the nonsense of discourse (Shelley, here, of course, an example, and so Adonais useless—as Keats' poems are—for our purposes)

[*Added in pencil*:] Was broken off fr this yesterday (Thursday, not Friday)
& will put it in mails as is,

not sure it adds a fucking thing   But I want to understand these things, & yr own work is the one work I learn from (did you ever do that job on WCW's poems—& where can I get a copy?)

Olson

[Banalbufar, Mallorca]
July 19, 1953

Dear Charles,
Your two damn beautiful letters in this afternoon, and saved my life, i.e., otherwise deluged with half-backbiting business from Cid & somewhat lukewarm reception of book from Paul B/. But, very happily, to hell with that. Ok.

It is very damn fine you were talking with those people about Bird and all. The more any of it comes clear, the more he does damn well seem the key—or one of the most substantial users of what time can do in any business. That thing of cutting an ⅛th off the quarter, etc., is it, and the precision of such rhythms so got is a) the necessary fine-ness of the intention and b) the greater potential of variation then possible. I.e., what bugs either one of us, in the old biz of closed verse, or any such partitioning of potential forms, etc., is the damn loss of variation effected. Not, to grant them the obvious, that infinite variation *within* the given isn't also possible, etc., etc., but that total set is pre-determined. Bird, in any case, first man importantly, call it, to stress the vertical potential of the melodic line, and by vertical I think I mean much of what you have always meant, i.e., that emphasis on the *single* & *total* content of any *one* word or note therein occurring without an overstress on projection-along-a-line, or what they loosely call "sequence," or what you've called horizontalism. What I'm trying to say, in any case: that Bird manages *single* content of the note, call it, in conjunction with total content, and/or its place in the whole structure of the melody, etc., etc. Whereas, say, usual "modern song" goes along, etc., i.e., moves from note to note (and gains our patience or impatience only in same), Bird clears notes one by fucking one, and reasserts a rhythmic structure with *each* note posited. Myself, I think you go back to Bach before you ever find it done quite so clearly.

Well, that is fuzzily put, etc. To hell with it. I know nothing about music more than I can hear, and that is enough for the moment. For example, we have a hell of a headache in just how much weight any one word can carry, either by virtue of its sound & rhythm, or by virtue of its implicated content, or finally by virtue of both these facts then conditioned by the context given, etc. At this point you might insist (I do, etc.) that most poets now writing have as much knowledge of sound weights & rhythmic structures, etc., as Guy Lombardo has of the equivalent in his own business. There are in both places the old devices, etc., and their use (ad nauseam) gets to the same end. Anyhow for one analogy is useful, Bird with his given line, what his rhythm section is doing, the base chords of the melody he is on, etc., and *then* what he does. I would claim that any poet, worth the time, will come back to his own job more clear if he could, without feeling much one way or the other, hear four good choruses by Bird on the *same* base structure. People have the dull notion, all flows the same way, at the same time, and if we assert our own piddling 'individuality' against same, even so we die, die, die, etc. But poem or song is autonomous, or else nothing, so that is not really relevant. (It damn well pleased me to note in Ez' ABC OF READING, biz abt Provençal poets considering use of another man's forms the same kind of plagiary a steal of his content might mean for us now.[32] I.e., When forms are given such emphasis and care as those apparently got, you don't really get an overfineness or mechanical procedure—but actually an insistence on each man finding his own, which will best & most accurately serve him. The same condition obtains in the case of Bird & followers, etc. It would be a like sin. The extent to which padding & like set device is condemned by same, gets evidence in the contempt they feel for any man using what they call "doubles," i.e., repetition of a phrase (1,1). Same is stock in trade with any so-called swing band, etc., etc. And very funny to hear Bird parodies of same, i.e., do de da do—etc., etc., like yawning behind vaguely cupped hand, etc.

What I wd insist on, is that practice & conditions obtaining here have direct parallel in present usage in poetry. When we call for a poetry the direct issue of language in a given instant, i.e., when we say it is possible, and a gain, to make a poem precisely in terms of *all* the words which can occur in it, their rhythms & their sounds, & what each then figure as in terms of a total structure—we argue the same premise that Bird uses when he hangs off the ⅛th of an instant. Because there is another note to follow. And he knows it.

Well, fuck that perhaps. But that it is a usable stimulus. And hearing a line of B/s music, one sees the possibilities of his own. If I write:

>...The unsure
>
>> egoist is not
>> good for himself...

same is my own extension of what sd Bird has taught me is possible, more than any other man I can honestly think of, offhand. Bird's effected relation between sound-weights & rhythms is the greatest any man ever got to, or I don't see anyone as having done it any better. This don't mean, sadly, that almost all of so-called BeBop is not dull, dull hash of what B/ does. You should hear German bands (with their talent for precise imitation sans feeling) play what they think they heard. It's what one finally *has* to hear that's interesting.

Also, as Buddy pointed out to me, music played at the corridas is very much Bird's way. And wild fact usual flamenco ends at that precise point you swore it couldn't. It is too much, when it is good. (You should hear what they do with ¼ & ⅛ tones, etc. How, I damn well don't know.)

So. I like yr poems, last one most of all.[33] Ann suggests title of, THE TRAP—i.e., she knows what you mean, and I goddamn well do. Saying "you & me" is damn well my arrogance. I think all that counts is not to care the way some do, i.e., to have it, I would try to, "we who have perhaps, nothing to lose, etc." I don't finally see that I do. I.e., Cid climbing for a reputation, etc., is his business. Luckily over here I am so much out I can get free of that most of the time. I cannot bullshit so much, because there is no one to bullshit. I think kids & wife etc. are conditions of sanity. Fuck them all!

It wd be wild if you cd all come over. I damn well wish you would. Write soon. All our dearest love to you all,

Bob

NOTES BY GEORGE BUTTERICK

1. "The Mast" by Olson now published for the first time following these letters.
2. "The World Narrowed to a Point," in *The Collected Later Poems of William Carlos Williams* (Norfolk, Conn.: New Directions, 1950), p. 20.
3. Pound writes in *ABC of Reading* (Norfolk, Conn.: New Directions, 1951), p. 201: "Most arts attain their effects by using a fixed element and a variable."
4. "... benevolence is bought." See Olson's "The Kingfishers," *Archaeologist of Morning* (London: Cape Goliard, 1970), p. [48].
5. From "Concerning Exaggeration, or How, Properly, to Heap Up" (*Archaeologist of Morning*, p. [104]).
6. Opening lines of Williams's "Song," in *Collected Later Poems*, p. 178.
7. From "The Kingfishers" (*Archaeologist of Morning*, p. [47]).
8. The editors of the London magazine *Nine*, after the gang of thieves in the 1951 movie starring Alec Guinness.
9. See "Maximus, to Gloucester, Letter 11" (*The Maximus Poems*, Berkeley: Univ. of California Press, 1983, pp. 52-55), and Butterick, *Guide to the Maximus Poems* (Berkeley: Univ. of California Press, 1978), pp. 76ff., for identification of references. Tragabigzanda, e.g., was the Turkish princess for whom Smith first named Cape Ann. Olson describes in what follows the tercentenary pageant portraying the successive stages of Gloucester's history, held in August 1923 at Stage Fort Park, site of the original settlement by Dorchester fishermen not far from the poet's boyhood summer cottage. Smith's poem, "The Sea Marke," quoted later in the letter and which was prefaced to his ADVERTISEMENTS *For the unexperienced Planters of New-England, or any where* (1631), is also presented in its entirety in "Maximus, to Gloucester: Letter 15" (*Maximus*, pp. 73-74).
10. Heroes of a series of adventure novels for boys by Joseph Altsheler (see *Maximus*, p. 58, and Butterick, *Guide*, p. 85; also *Maximus*, p. 277).
11. Nickname given Miles Standish by Thomas Morton in his *New English Canaan* (1637). See *Maximus*, p. 53, and Butterick, *Guide*, p. 80.
12. William Bradford (1590–1657), was governor of the Plymouth Colony and author of the *History of Plymouth Plantation*; Lancelot Andrewes (1555–1626), renowned for his sermons, contributed his skills to the King James Bible; while the third Earl of Southampton, Henry Wriothesley (1573–1624), was one of Shakespeare's chief patrons.
13. Williams's poem "The Desert Music," reprinted in *Origin* 6 (Summer 1952), 65-75.
14. Editor at Grove Press; later, editor of *The New American Poetry* (New York: Grove, 1960), and of Olson's *Human Universe and Other Essays* (San Francisco: Auerhahn, 1965; New York: Grove, 1967), as well as publisher of both Olson and Creeley through his Four Seasons Foundation and Grey Fox Press.
15. Pianist David Tudor, painter Esteban Vicente, musician Stefan Wolpe, dancer Merce Cunningham, and voice teacher Johanna Jalowetz, all teaching at Black Mountain that summer, as was cellist Seymour Barab. Red-headed Jack Rice, dream-figure in Olson's poem "The Leader" (*Archaeologist of Morning*, p. [85]); artist and writer Fielding Dawson; and Timothy LaFarge, one of the dancers for whom Olson wrote "The Born Dancer" (*The Fiery Hunt*, Bolinas, Calif.: Four Seasons, 1977, pp. 49-56), were all students at the College.
16. Composer Pierre Boulez concludes his "Proposals," first published in *Polyphonie*, 2 (1948), as follows: "I have, finally, a personal reason for giving so important a place to the rhythmic phenomenon. I believe that music should be collective hysteria and spells, violently of the present time—following the lead of Antonin Artaud and not in the direction of simple ethnographic reconstruction in the likenesses of civilizations more or less remote from ours. But, here too, I have a horror of dealing in words with what is complaisantly called the esthetic problem. I shall therefore prolong this essay no longer; I prefer to return to my staff paper" (*Notes of an Apprenticeship*, trans. Herbert Weinstock [New York: Knopf, 1968], p. 71).
17. See *Call Me Ishmael* (New York: Reynal & Hitchcock, 1947), pp. 52-56.
18. ya, selva oscura, but hell now
   is not exterior, is not to be got out of, is
   the coat of your own self, the beasts
   emblazoned on you And who
   can turn this total thing, invert
   and let the ragged sleeves be seen
   by any bitch or common character?
   —"In Cold Hell, In Thicket," *Archaeologist of Morning*, p. [68].
19. Donald F. Cooper, pianist, who had come to Black Mountain to study with Stefan Wolpe.
20. The phrase is John Keats's, in his letter of 21 September 1819 to George and Georgiana Keats, and used by Olson in a poem entitled "for J/K," first written, apparently, in the margin of Creeley's 8 April 1953 letter.
21. After the Civil War battle fought in May 1864 between Lee's and Grant's forces in the heavily wooded and tangled region in northeast Virginia along the Rapidan River known as the Wilderness. (See *Archaeologist of Morning*, p. [67], "how far, how sufficiently far can he raise the thickets of / this wilderness?")
22. "The Twist," *Maximus*, pp. 86-90.
23. See *De Vulgari Eloquentia*, II. 5-6.
24. Ezra Pound, *Antheil and the Treatise on Harmony* (Paris: Three Mountains Press, 1924; Chicago: Pascal Covici, 1927).
25. Poem by Creeley (*The Collected Poems*, Berkeley: Univ. of California Press, 1982, p. 128), sent Olson in his 27 June 1953 letter.
26. "Galeotto was the book, and he who wrote it"—*Inferno*, V. 137, quoted by Shelley in his "Defence of Poetry."
27. Shelley writes that language "is as a mirror which reflects," and, also in the "Defence," that "poetry is a mirror which makes beautiful that which is distorted."
28. See "ABCs (2)" from 1950 (*Archaeologist of Morning*, p. [51]): "of rhythm is image / of image is knowing / of knowing there is / a construct..." In "Equal, That Is, to the Real Itself" from 1957, the passage is prefaced: "As the Master said to me in the dream..." (*Human Universe*, p. 121). See also *Maximus*, p. 584.
29. Creeley had written, 2 April 1953, concerning English writer Martin Seymour-Smith (b. 1928): "M/ apparently the ONLY englishman with balls,—very tough man, and like him very much. I think he will make it—god knows he is well away from the above [Ian Fletcher, F. T. Prince, G. S. Fraser]. However much forms will be his headache, as of now. But he has *grace*, and that is damn well 9/10ths of it I get to think."
30. Olson had written in a 13 July 1953 letter to Ronald Mason (b. 1912), author of *The Spirit Above the Dust: A Study of Herman Melville*, which he favorably reviewed in "The Materials and Weights of Herman Melville" (*Human Universe*, pp. 109-16): "one can say that progression is now interesting not that it is moving toward a climax or an end (what one might fairly call the law of traditional form, in prose and verse), but that it is *also* moving without allowable loss *from* and *by* each succeeding instant of itself. Force, we have damn well learned from 100 years of non-Euclidean geometry plus the superb physicists, is as much from, as towards, itself. And 'field,' in itself, is—nest is—as the eggs. (The last image is, of course, resting on that magnificent notion, that the law of gravitation and of the magnetic field are one)."
31. *Webster's Collegiate Dictionary*, 5th ed., p. 793 (a mathematical usage).
32. Pound, *ABC of Reading*, p. 69: "There is a tradition that in Provence it was considered plagiarism to take a man's form, just as it is now considered plagiarism to take his subject matter or plot."
33. Unpublished poems "The Knife" and "To Be Thrown to the Wind..." (Literary Archives, University of Connecticut Library).

ABSTRACT FIGURE STUDY, 1921
WYNDHAM LEWIS
INDIA INK AND CHINESE WHITE ON PAPER. 26.7 x 20 cm
COURTESY ANTHONY d'OFFAY
NOT IN MICHEL

CHARLES OLSON

THE MAST

I had to unship the mast or we would have been over, & in, to
the depth just there, the American Channel, the dark blue
as against the brilliance of the lighter color from the sands
of the shallow water closer in to the banks
         I had made the mast,
and it was too big for the boat, too high
& heavy. It wasn't the area
of the sail.
Or anything the matter with the rigging.

          Without power & only a poor oar,
I worked in, over the shallows, to a thing of an island was for birds.
And that day it was no thing more than that—a place to ground,
& figure out how to cross that channel, and get back. When we did,
I was a lather, and lost the pleasure of the evening.

But now, this day, that day jumps
another way: that island
is what I read, or saw—or it is Fisher's Hill
where Cabbage and I . . . it leaps on me
like a man caught boys, & kept them there,
in cinder caves (the harshness,
the holes, the rottenness
of corals

  I am flooded
with a boy's time
     with that going off
to a place of my own
       where Cabbage and I went, where,

294

patently,
I still am

              And waters and islands

                            (but not the boat,
at least not that boat)

              are not Island #9, are not American
Channel

     Or are such
     as I

      are not any chart, any such place
as I then was, almost swamping her, & pulling out (to be cool),
& sweating, to bring her in

That now the island (the grit
that it was—a guano, or a piece of sand a good storm . . .)
should bulk as all my secret self
                        even to this (beside the man)
                        that I am Theda Bara beaten
                        with a poker
                        by a step-mother. Even this trace
                        is one of the edges which scrapes
                        as I am suddenly grounded

                        (as my leg was torn
                        so I still have the scars
                        the day I slipped and it got wedged
                        in that split rock the barnacles
                        had covered both faces of)
all that world
        is not at all
                gone

Yet, like the island, or Fisher's Hill (now one mass of semi-detached
                            houses, the dreariness
                            of yards

I am this master would, today, not take that boat to sea
or enjoy, as he did, that boy, such
revery, yet does all these things,
on new matters, as clumsily, as
happily, as
surely

And am that advantage that
I have all of it,
as he did not have
             (Or what did he have less
than I, now, have?
                 or I, then, Cayo Hueso?

                                What, if I am more, am I?

I am. That would be the insistence, or there is nothing here
but memory—that thing makes the new streets on the edge of a city, & new houses
a scene wind and boys and roofing papers are the only life of

that channel
would be bluer,
would be more seen were I there today.   As that mast
would be right, would be cut and shaped, would not be shipped
no matter how many days . . . (or, in better matters, the years

That this is the difference, for the boy, too, that the fantasy
does not retract, it only
comes home: he knows
who the man is, I know
the wicked step-mother, I go off
without escaping, Cabbage
is me

    And the mast

                                                     —April, 1953

FIELDING DAWSON

GOODNIGHT IRENE

from VIRGINIA DARE

I was waiting to get a haircut and saw him through the window. He glanced in and saw me.
What did you do?
I joined him on the sidewalk!
Well.
How is he? I asked.
Hasn't changed at all: plump at forty, Tony Curtis in slacks and sportsjacket doing the talking.
Is he still bartending?
No.
"I quit there a year ago," he said. Eyes sleepy.
"The joint on upper Lex," I said. "What happened?"
"Do you want to hear?"
"You know."
"I was fired," he grinned. We walked into a place on the corner and ordered, and as we drank I watched Tony trying to find a beginning.
"I made some money, but it was a terrible place."
"They're pretty bad."
"Coffins," he observed. "Smoke?" "No, thanks." Tony lit up a slender green low tar filter saying the clientele was a mix of bums on welfare or unemployment and the usual Lex tough guys and their girls. The owner a bastard you wouldn't believe. His lips thinned.
"No buybacks," I said.
"Yeah, but even so I made my money."
I wondered if that was why he was fired. He chuckled, sipped his drink and blew some smoke over my shoulder.
"You gotta hear this," he said.
Okay.
"I'd been there a couple of years," he began. "It's a miracle I lasted that long. I got to know just about everybody in the neighborhood, so I could spot a stranger, and one night a guy comes in, sits down and orders vodka twister rocks water chaser, no ice in the chaser. Got it?"

I said yes and he said,

"You and me, we've been around, right? Well, nobody will ever figure it out, but after one look at that creep, I hated his guts."

He looked at me.

"You know me," he said. "I'm a nice guy, right? Sure I am, I mean it, am I wrong? Tell me!"

I punched him in the shoulder and said he was a nice guy. "What happened."

"You always were a good listener."

He could make a martini with his left hand, a tom collins with his right while serving a beer and beginning a bloody mary, he got so hyped he couldn't stop to talk, and it infuriated him when customers didn't pay in his rhythm. "I know," I said.

"Okay," he said, putting his cigarette out, and ordering two more saying, "let me get these. I won at the tracks yesterday," watching the slow bartender make two languid drinks. "I'm even," Tony said, "and that guy sure is slow."

"Maybe he was faster when O. Henry came in. He looks about that old." But Tony was in thought.

"He didn't come in often, twice a week at most, but always with his two cats, around ten, ten thirty at night Jesus he was terrible. Tall, talltall, skinny with a caved-in face, long ratty hair, yellow kind of eyes with the whites that old brown—"

"Sepia."

"Yeah, sepia, and he always sat in the same spot—at the bar—on his barstool, to get smashed out of his skull, and leave around three with a quarter on the bar for my tip."

"Two bits," I murmured.

"Two fuckin' bits," he said, face reddening. "And on top of that, around midnight he starts coming on for buybacks, and you get it. I say look, I can't do that, I'll get fired, right?"

"Right."

"This is store policy, don't you get it? But he *didn't* get it, he kept on well no, over a year and I was beginning to flip—me! even when I *saw* him yeah but but then I began to wonder how I was gonna unload the dirty laundry, right? right and one night, one night I noticed that the last thing he did was to drink the whole water chaser before he left. I noticed it."

"It seemed to mean more than it did."

"Real clear, but everything he did did because he was one of those lush bums who budget themselves down to their last nickel, aw you know. I know you know."

"I know," I said.

"I knew it," he said, "and not long after I'd noticed that last thing he did, one night he came in as usual, cats on his back and his skin like rotten meat, and on the second drink he starts begging me for a freebee, hey come on, please, I'm a poor man, can't you give me just one drink? and I thought I was gonna freak, the owner at the other end of the bar watching *me* say no, if you're broke, go home. I'm not broke, the guy said, I'm poor, buy me a drink, please. Please. Listen, I say, I'm not gonna lose this job over a fuckin' bum like you, or anybody else either, you want a drink, you pay for it, got it? do you want a drink? I want a drink, he says. Free. No way, I said. Case closed. All right, he said, I'll pay, and I poured it and moved down the bar to other customers while he dug seventy-five cents out of his pocket, in nickels and dimes—pennies, too! while he stirred the vodka around until some of the ice melted and it looked like a double is how it went until around three maybe earlier smasherrooney, cats on his shoulders, he went to the pisser, came back, sat down, and while they got settled again, he put two bits on the bar, finished his drink, smiled Goodnight Irene, and knocked back the whole glass of water, held onto the bar and the barstool, stood up, and staggered out the door."

"Nothing new."

"Nothing new except that I knew something had to happen but didn't know what." He finished his drink.

I did too.

"Let me get these," I said.

"I can smell him," he whispered. "I was so sick of that son of a bitch I didn't know what to do. I couldn't just—"

"No."

"You could see the dirt on him, and he smelled of catpiss, you could almost taste him, and when he pleaded with me, begged me—I'll tell you, the nice guy I am, went away, disappeared. Poof! and somebody else came in."

"Why didn't you refuse him? Bars have that right."

"That's true," he agreed. "But the guy did spend his dough, and though he was the worst creep in the place he had plenty of company! The women liked his cats and aw shit I mean that guy and that place give me the *shivers*! Stay out of the Lex bars!"

"I will indeed," I said, paying the bartender, we clinked glasses, and sipped. "Thanks," he said. "What happened?" I asked.

His eyes were hard with a glint: he said, "One night a guy came in, a regular, but who only drank the Russian—Stolichnaya hundred proof—sat next to Cat Man I gave the guy his usual, and they start talking about cats Jesus cats cats cats, the place got crowded, everybody knew each other and because I was so busy I kept the Russian in the speedrack, okay?"

"Okay."

"Okay, the night went on, pimples and whiskers that fuckin' bum talking about his cats, to his cats, customers petting them and something told me tonight was the night. I didn't know what I was going to do, or how—or what would happen, but something was in the air. I went on, as usual, until around midnight I began giving him doubles, working very fast, shifting around so the owner couldn't see me, and around one old Catboy was pretty loaded—ahead of schedule—and by two so wasted he couldn't much talk, or much walk, so when he stood up to take a leak he pointed to his drink and said Goodnight Irene, thanks for being so kind, his eyes almost crossed, seeing those doubles double, maybe, and staggered back to the men's room. But because the guy who drank the Russian had just gone home—smashed—the bottle was still in the speedrack, and I took the pourer out of the bottle, and while filling catcreep's rock glass to the brim with the eighty bar vodka, an easy triple, I emptied his chaser glass of water and filled it with the Russian hundred, put the pourer back in, returned the bottle to its normal place on the shelf behind me, and served other

299

customers until Katzo came back, fished around in his pockets for my two bits, found it, put it on the bar, and stood, weaving around, picked up the rock glass and drank it. His eyes popped open, what a surprise! but he shuddered, breathed deep, found balance, thanked me, said goodnight, raised and drained the other glass."

I a little gagged.

"Unh huh," he said, "that's right. At first he stood there. Then he retched, and a little dribbled out of his mouth, but he wanted to keep it, the hardboiled lushes don't want to lose any of it, and while his stomach heaved, he fought for control, the blood ran out of his face, pale as a corpse. He turned to his right in staggering, jerky motions, and by holding onto backs and shoulders of other customers—they were used to him!—he made his way to the door while the cats adjusted to his lurching, but just in front of the door he stopped, put both hands on his chest and jacknifed, slammed his face on a tabletop and fell sideways onto the floor as the cats jumped free. Somebody helped him up, put the cats back on him, and walked to the door with him, as he bent forward, hugging himself, a guy opened the door, he pitched forward, bounced off the doorjamb, and stumbled outside."

My voice was soft. "Did he die?"

"Who knows? Fuck him. I was fired that night."

"So you never saw him again."

"I never saw him again, that catfucker. Listen, I gotta go. I gotta date and I gotta go home and clean up. Lend me your pen and I'll give you my new address and phone number. Let's get together again, and you do the talking. Okay?"

"Sure," I said, handing him my pen.

▼ ▼ ▼

NUDE (KNEELING), 1919
WYNDHAM LEWIS
PENCIL AND WATERCOLOR ON PAPER. 28.5 x 38.2 cm
COURTESY ANTHONY d'OFFAY
NOT IN MICHEL

KENNETH GANGEMI

SIX POEMS

RECEPTION

At our American cocktail parties
people are standing and highly mobile.
Freedom is the rule: we are free
to move, to stay or leave, to talk
or be silent. I appreciate receiving
the invitation, the expectation,
the surprises, the chance meetings,
the challenging situations, the skills
that are required, the random
combinations of people and subjects.

Forecasting a party from the invitation
is the game we all play.
These gatherings are a glorious
mixture of work and play, an efficient
way to see and talk with many
people at one time. Afterwards I try
to be alone, to think it over,
and to recover from the two hours
of compressed experience. The next
day I contemplate the invitation,
comparing the illusion to the reality.

CAREER GIRL IN A SUPERMARKET

No one can stop me
from examining your cart.
I see lettuce, cottage cheese,
diet soda, lo-cal dressing,

grapefruit, and lamb chops.
Still dressed for the office,
you glare at me
for invading your privacy.
But I see much more, know
all your secrets, you have no
defense against my imagination.

At work you are a computer
hooked up to a cash register.
Making love to you is like
cuddling up to a mannequin.
You dislike the sight of happy
couples, but would never admit it.
The beautiful machine takes
quick showers, eats yogurt in
taxis, worries about shampoos,
the size of her ass, and crowded
laundromats. You are the American
woman so incredible to Europeans.

Your apartment is in a new building,
with plastic plants in a sterile
lobby, and impersonal halls and
elevators where no one says Hello.
You resent the young doorman
because of his class origins,
because you think he is too familiar,
but most of all because he knows
too much about your sex life.

You come home to an empty apartment
with its barren refrigerator
and immediately switch on music.
You know hundreds of people
but are often lonely at night.
Your desire for men is balanced
by a paralyzing fear of involvement.
Thirty years old and no one in sight,
no one who could put up with you.
Emotionally deprived, an expert on
sleeping alone, terrified in your
loveless bed, you wonder again
what will become of you.

JONES BEACH

Sitting on my blanket,
I look out upon the ocean
and the beach pedestrians.
An unattractive girl approaches,
squinting in the glare.
She is one of millions,
with pale skin and poor posture,
sitting on her ass all day,
chewing gum, smoking too much,
drinking sodas, eating junk food,
watching television at night.
Trapped in some fatal office
with a blind-alley job,
soon she will be finished
like the others before her.

But she is still young,
with a pretty face,
and has good bone structure.
Sculpting in my mind,
I imagine her much improved,
with sunglasses, tanned skin,
good muscle tone from exercise,
better hair tied with a ribbon,
a flat belly, no cigarette, ten
pounds lighter, a tasteful bikini,
and taught to walk with grace.

AMERICAN MUSEUM OF NATURAL HISTORY

I have loved this place
since I was six years old.
The bright cafeteria,
filled with schoolchildren,
has animal photos on the walls.
In the hallways are portraits
of the quiet men of science;
one exhibit is labeled
Threat Display of the Spotted Owl;

a diorama shows a golden eagle
perched on a cliff in Montana,
looking out over its domain.

This museum is humbling.
I read that a spiral galaxy
has been discovered,
with over 200 billion stars.
For brief moments I see the world
through the eyes of a Greenland
Eskimo of the Sixteenth Century,
then the eyes of an Egyptian
peasant of the Third Century B.C.
I examine the shapes of leaves,
the collection of tropical butterflies,
admire the beauty of the birchbark canoe.

Exhibit notes say that the four
members of the camel family
in South America are the alpaca,
llama, vicuna, and guanaco;
that during the Ice Age the Sahara
received heavy rainfall;
that an Amazon tribe cannot count
beyond poettarrarorincoaroac,
which is their word for three;
that Humboldt penguins are found
near the Equator in Peru;
that the musk ox inhabits the
bleakest land in North America.

I am grateful to the illustrators.
They depict Manhattan rising
through ice sheets, a portrait
of a Neanderthal family, tyrannosauri
hatching in Wyoming, a view of
the Martian surface, dinosaur
landscapes, a group of wooly mammoths,
giant dragonflies from the Coal Age,
visions of Pleistocene America.

DONUT SHOP NEAR BOSTON COMMON

One time during a morning walk
I traced the smell of fresh donuts
to its busy and glorious source.
I was there at the right time
to observe the morning rush
while sitting at the counter.
Office girls going to work
with sleepy faces and unseeing eyes
ordered donuts and coffee to go,
fumbled for change,
then hurried out with paper bags.
I wondered about them, caught
whiffs of perfume but nothing better.
What had they done the night before,
from what beds had they come,
which ones were freshly fucked?

CANADA

When I was eighteen years old,
during my first college summer,
I worked in a gold mine in Ontario.
It was 1956, the Eisenhower years,
and jobs were everywhere. I was hired
with fifty other apprentice miners.

Gold was mined around the clock,
and every week we had different shifts.
They started at eight o'clock
in the morning, four in the afternoon,
and midnight, the graveyard shift.
The first day was embarrassing with
my new lunchpail, heavy belt,
miner's helmet, and rubber boots.
But soon I looked as grubby
as the rest. Before the "cage"
started taking us down, many groups
of men were speaking the languages
of Europe. I was the only American.

The Kerr-Addison mine was clean and
safe, with whitewashed walls near
the shaft. I worked at the 2500-foot
level, a comfortable temperature.
It was cold near the surface, and
too hot further down. The gold was
microscopic in the rock and seldom
seen. But once I went down to the
6500-foot level, warm and tropical,
and saw the yellow metal, tracing the
vein with my fingers. After a shift
we showered, where I saw numbers
on some of the arms. Then we walked
naked up the stairs past an old man
in a chair, who looked us over for gold.

My partner was a Russian man
who told stories of World War II,
where he was in the German army.
He spoke five languages,
had a wife and three children,
and twenty years in the mines of Europe.
Vasily or "Bill" had survived
because he was careful. He was always
looking at the roof of the "stope"
with suspicion and poking it with
a bar. Yet one time during lunch
tons of rock missed us by inches.

Bill taught me how to use dynamite,
which looked like yellow sawdust.
I admired his skill at blasting:
he would study the rock face
for a long time, and then chalk
the locations of the holes. After
we drilled, he would figure the
percent of the dynamite and the timing
of the fuses. We rolled the ends of
the sticks open, inserted the fuses,
then closed them up. I packed the
dynamite in with a rucksack, walking
down the dark tunnels, opening the
heavy air-doors, avoiding the oretrains.

The mine was 300 miles north
of Toronto, near the Quebec border.
Virginiatown had a frontier look,
with wooden sidewalks and muddy streets.
The countryside was rolling hills
and the beginning of tundra,
the endless Canadian bush.
Fishing was good in the many lakes,
blueberries were abundant,
and I often saw moose beside the road.

The three categories of Canadians
were old, new, and French. The new
Canadians were European immigrants
from many countries. My friends were
a group of young Germans from cities
in the Ruhr, children of the rubble
of Essen and Düsseldorf.
Next stop for them was British Columbia,
then they wanted to go to the USA
and become cowboys in Texas. I slept
in a bunkhouse, sharing a room with
one of the Germans. We ate in a
cafeteria with a sign that said:
Take All You Want/Eat All You Take.
On weekends we drove to Quebec,
where French-Canadian girls, some
of them young and pretty, were available
in the saloons for five dollars.

My girlfriend that summer was an older
woman. Already twenty, she loved it
more than I did. In my 1947 Plymouth
convertible we made excursions
to the woods, where she knew all the
best spots. We had all we needed:
ourselves, a blanket, a six-pack of
Canadian beer, a starry sky. In her
house I felt uncomfortable with
her father. After all, I was screwing
his daughter. But her mother understood,
and was happy for us. When I went
back to the States, she gave me
a kiss and a homemade blueberry pie.

JOHN SANFORD

THE LEO FRANK CASE 1913-1915

THE NIGHT WITCH DID IT

*When children cry out in their sleep, it
means the night witches are riding them,
and you must wake them up, or next morning
you will find them strangled to death.*
—Negro folklore

Mary Phagan was a white girl of fourteen, and the chances are she never heard of cacodemons that rode the young at night, never knew what the blacks all did, that no one was immortal in the dark. Just before she died, therefore, she could hardly have cried out that fiends were upon her, and yet to all seeming they were, even as in the legend. When found, she had a rope of jute around her throat, so tightly drawn that her tongue protruded for half its length. She lay on a slag pile in the basement of a pencil factory, her face tumid and discolored, and from a gash in her scalp, she'd bled until her hair was a nameless shade between blood and brown. Her body, wherever visible through a breading of cinders, was skinned down to the derma, as if she'd been dragged for some way along the splintery floor. Her drawers were stained with urine, her mouth was filled with graphite and cedar sawdust, and some of her fingers were bent back and out of joint. There were two notes lying beside the misused body, and one of them said *The night witch did it.*

Witch it may have been, incubus, rider of the nighttime hours, but even so, no hue and cry of witch was raised: who could bring that kind to book, what law would make it swing? Better, it was thought, to look for guilt where all guilt flourished, in the natural world of man. Better to leave ghosts to the ghastly, the casters of spells—hell's hosts belonged to hell. There was deuce enough in earthly beings, and two such readily sprang to mind.

One of them was foreign to Georgia—Leo Max Frank, a Jew from the state of New York. An engineering graduate of Cornell in the class of 1906, he'd gone to Atlanta to act as superintendent of the National Pencil Factory, owned by an uncle. Soon thereafter, he married a Lucile Selig of the same city, and until the year 1913, the couple resided with her parents, who were said to be cultured and who were certainly rich. Outside the tacit ghetto of Atlanta, Leo Frank had no standing whatever; within it, as a Jew of German descent, he was of superior rank and merit, a leader undisputed by the led. In his physical being, he was unimposing, a man of slight build and median height, with no characteristic more striking than the pince-nez he wore before his prominent eyes. He was in his twenty-ninth year when Mary Phagan went to the factory for the day's pay that was owing to her—$1.20 for ten hours' work.

The other mortal who might've filled the bill was a Negro named Jim Conley, described as short, stocky, and, for what it may have meant, ginger-colored. He was not a Mechanical Engineer, nor had he descended from a family of German Jews in Brooklyn. In and around Atlanta, he was known as a liar and a petty thief, often seen on a chain gang and fined times without number for breaches of the peace. Nervous in manner and never at ease, he seemed to have a liquid essence, and if so, it was whiskey-fed, for he was nearly always drunk. During the two years prior to the death of Mary Phagan, he'd been employed at the pencil factory as a furnaceman and sweeper.

Little Mary Phagan / She went to town one day The day was a Saturday late in April, the Confederate Memorial Day, and early in the afternoon, there'd be a parade through the streets of Atlanta, and many would march behind the Stars and Bars in their old regimentals, behind flags ragged, faded, torn by shot, and all along the way, heads would be bared for the gray who'd fought the blue from First Manassas to Appomattox. *She left her home at eleven / She kissed her mother goodbye* For the occasion, Mary dressed herself in her best, a poor enough showing, true, but she did have a mesh bag that she prized and was proud of, a vivid parasol, and a pretty pair of shoes. *Not one time did the poor child think / That she was a-going to die* No one knows whether she saw the parade or any part of it, a color guard, a military band, a slowly passing line of old soldiers, nor does anyone know whether she caught a glimpse of her doer-in. When her body was discovered by a night watchman, her lavender pongee was a silken ruin, ripped and spattered, and one of her gunmetal shoes was gone. The parasol turned up later at the bottom of an elevator shaft, but the reticule ($1.20 plus carfare home) was never found. *Now little Mary's mother / She weeps and mourns all day.*

Because of the holiday celebration, only a handful of employees were at the pencil factory that morning, and those few had come voluntarily to perform some minor maintenance work on the machinery and would leave at noon or soon thereafter. Leo Frank, however, was writing a series of reports for the company, and save for a lunch-hour recess, he'd remain in his office until the day was well along. On being questioned by the police after the discovery of Mary Phagan's body, he was said to have been in a state of agitation *apparently high-strung, a fluent talker, polite and suave, smokes incessantly.* He was arrested on suspicion of murder, and Conley was jailed two days later when it was reported that he'd been seen trying to wash bloodstains from a shirt.

At Frank's trial, the black man became the chief witness against him. Liar, thief, convict, souse, he swore the Jew's life away with the story he told on the stand. On the day stated, he said, he'd been at the factory at Frank's request, and for one purpose only—to stand lookout while Frank seduced Mary Phagan. He'd been instructed to remain downstairs, he said, and on the girl's arrival, he was to send her up to the second story, where Frank's office was, after which, when Frank stomped on the floor, he was to lock the outer door and await a second signal, a whistle, which would indicate that Frank's purpose had been accomplished. Conley had done as told, he said, but when the whistle came, the girl had not appeared. Instead, Frank was standing at the top of the steps

> shivering, trembling, rubbing his hands.
> His eyes were large,
> and they looked right funny.
> He looked funny out of his eyes.
> He said, "Did you see that little girl

who passed here just a while ago?"
and I told him I saw one come along,
and he says,
"Well, I wanted to be with the little girl,
and she refused me, and I struck her,
and I guess I struck her too hard,
and she fell and hit her head,"
and he said,
"You know I ain't built like other men."
  (the reason he said that was
  I had seen him in a position
  I haven't seen any other man.
  A lady was in his office,
   and she was sitting down in a chair,
   and she had her clothes up to here
    (indicating waist)
   and he was down on his knees,
   and she had her hands on Mr. Frank)
He asked me if I wouldn't bring her
   (meaning Mary)
so he could put her somewhere,
and he said there would be money in it.
I found the lady lying flat on her back
with a rope around her neck.
Cloth was also around her neck,
like to catch blood.
She was dead,
and I came back and told Mr. Frank
she was dead.

Nor was that all that Jim Conley testified to before a judge and a jury and a courtroom crowd; he bore witness to much more to all these and, through the open windows, to the minatory mob outside. Five thousand, there were, and they filled the streets so full that trolleys could not pass, and on sheds across the way, hundreds stood in the sun all day to cheer the black and mock the blackhearted Jew. At Frank's direction, Conley said, he'd written the two notes placed near Mary's body, and for so doing, Frank had paid him $200. And

Mr. Frank looked at me and said,
"You go down there in the basement,
and you take a lot of trash
and burn that package in the furnace."
And I said, "Mr. Frank,
you are a white man, and you done it,
and I am not going down there
and burn that myself."

He said, "Let me see that money,"
and he took the money back
and put it in his pocket and said,
"Why should I hang?
I have wealthy people in Brooklyn,"
And I said, "Mr. Frank, what about me?"
and he said, "Don't you worry about this.
You just come back to work Monday
like you don't know anything,
and keep your mouth shut.
I am going home to get dinner...."

The night witch did it.
It was the law of Georgia that no one charged with a capital crime could testify in his own behalf; a defendant might, however, make a statement to the jury, not under oath, and it would rest with the jury to determine its weight. Frank elected to avail himself of the right, and he prepared the statement himself. It took him four hours to read it, all through an afternoon, to the silent, watchful, sweating talesmen. It was simply written and ably delivered (*Cornell graduate, fluent talker, rich Jew*), it revealed with great particularity each of his doings on the day of the parade, and it ended with

Gentlemen,
I know nothing whatever
of the death of little Mary Phagan.
I had no part in causing her death
nor do I know how she came to her death
after she took her money
and left my office.
I never saw Conley in the factory
or anywhere else on April 13, 1913.
The statement of Conley
is a tissue of lies from first to last,
and as to his helping me dispose of the body,
or that I had anything to do with her
or to do with him
that day
it is a monstrous lie.
The story as to women coming into the factory
for immoral purposes
is a base lie, and claims to have seen me
in indecent positions with women
is a lie so vile
that I have no language
with which to denounce it.
I have no rich relatives in Brooklyn.
My father is an invalid

of very limited means.
Nobody has raised a fund
to pay the fees of my attorneys.
These have been paid by the sacrifice
of the small property my parents possess.
Gentlemen, I have told you the truth.

The night witch did it.
But there was no night witch in it. After a trial that had lasted twenty-nine days, the jury was out for only three hours, including a one-hour intermission for lunch (chitlins and poke sallat? winnies and coke? hot plates with bull-fuck gravy?), and their verdict was Guilty. For the first time in Southern history, a black man's word (liar, thief, jailbird, boozer) had been taken against a white's—that is, if Jews are really white.

In the streets, the crowds acclaimed the verdict, and on Sunday next, it'd serve all cracker preachers as a text. Tom Watson, old Populist editor of the *Jeffersonian (the Jeff*, the rednecks called it), wrote

We Georgians save our kisses
for our wives and children.
Mary Phagan was only a factory girl:
she had no mighty connections.
Frank belongs to the Jewish aristocracy,
a rich depraved Sodomite.
The Jew basks in the warmth;
the child has fed the worms.

Frank's appeals were denied all the way to the Supreme Court of the United States. Thereafter, his sole hope lay with John Slaton, governor of Georgia, and four days before his term of office ended, he issued an executive order

The performance of my duty
under the Constitution
is a matter of conscience:
the responsibility rests
where the power is reposed.
I cannot endure the constant companionship
of an accusing conscience,
which would remind me in every thought
that I failed to do right.
This case has been marked by doubt:
the trial judge doubted;
two judges of the Court of Georgia doubted;
two judges of the Supreme Court doubted;
one of three Prison Commissioners doubted.
Therefore, in accordance with my duty,
it is ordered

that sentence in the case of Leo M. Frank
be commuted from the death penalty
to imprisonment for life.

Tom Watson raged and wrote

The State of Georgia has been raped!
We have been violated, and we are ashamed!
The breath of some leprous monster
has passed over us,
and we are unclean!

One month after Frank was removed from the death cell to a penitentiary at Milledgeville, while he lay asleep, his throat was cut by a convicted murderer who worked in the prison kitchen; the weapon was a butcher-knife. In the *Jeff*, Tom Watson wrote

Kosher!
The knife used on Leo Frank
was also used for killing hogs.
Let the Jews of Georgia beware.

But Frank survived the assault, and within a few weeks' time, he was released from the hospital and returned to the barracks. He lived for one more day. A band self-styled the Knights of Mary Phagan, broke into the prison compound, seized Frank, and drove with him to a place called Frey's Gin, a hundred and seventy-five miles away. There they hanged him from an oak tree not far from the house where Mary had been born. No one was ever prosecuted for the lynching, although photographs of the party were sold all over Georgia for the next fifteen years.
The night witch did it.
Four people swore that Jim Conley had murdered Mary Phagan. Annie Carter, a black woman, knew that he had committed the crime, because he told her so; and the Baptist minister Ragsdale knew; and William Smith, Conley's lawyer, knew; and, name unknown, a fellow convict knew. But the people of Georgia didn't want Conley. They wanted the Jew, the Jew, and they'd've taken Christ Himself and hanged him twice, once to cover the Resurrection.
Was Leo Frank the Sodomite? Or was it Jim Conley, who, in letters to Annie Carter, wrote

Now baby
you have that right hip for me
cause if you hold your fat ass
on the bottom
and make your papa go like a kitty cat
then you have won a good man—
that's me

and he wrote

if you let papa
put his long ugly dick
up your fat ass
and play on your right and left hip,
just like a monkey playing on a trapeze,
then Honey Papa
will be done played hell with you

and he wrote

Give your heart to God
and your ass to me. . . .

The night witch did it.

▼ ▼ ▼

JOHN SANFORD

EUGENE V. DEBS
1855-1926

A SPEECH IN CANTON, OHIO

*Whoever when the United States is at war,
shall wilfully cause insubordination,
disloyalty, mutiny, or refusal
of duty in the military or naval forces,
shall be punished by...*
—Espionage Act, 1917, as amended

From a bandstand in Nimisilla Park, not far from the parallel roadbeds of the Interurban and the Wheeling & Lake Erie, he addressed a gathering of some twelve hundred on a Sunday afternoon in June, 1918. It was a scorcher even for the place and the time of year, hot enough to make the sky shake over the baking tracks and ballast, and nary a jacket could be seen on the twelve hundred shirts being ironed by the sun on the backs of the crowd. But it could've been a heap sight hotter, and still they'd've turned out to hear what Gene had to say. Many of them had never seen him before, but precious few hadn't been told of how he leaned forward when he spoke, of how he'd poke at them with his finger *(I felt as if he was hitting me in the nose with it)*, of how each would feel the words were meant for him alone. What they saw up there on the platform was a tall, bald, string-gutted old specimen of sixty-three, a rail of a man homely enough for two, what with those cupped ears of his and that cute-angle beak, but once he began to speak—*Comrades*, he said—he seemed to change from plain to fair. Something happened to his gaunt face and his flimsy figure, something got into that high thin voice, something made it stay on the air like the sound of crystal—*Comrades*, he said—and for every man below him on the grass, it became a brand-new expression, one coined for them on the spot, and yet somehow they all understood it as an end to divisions. With that, heat or no heat, they pressed closer to where he stood, mingled their sweat and cigar-smoke: they wanted more of what he'd brought them from Terre Haute, more of that good stuff he had in his mouth, and it didn't matter much that their neighbours stank or gobbed on their shoes. Well, he had more, and he gave it to them.

He was there, he said, to speak for labor, to plead the cause of those who toiled, and he felt it an honor to put it forward, to serve those whose very lives were service. But these were hardly the best of times, he said, they were a cold and parlous season in history, imperative, unsparing, a winter of the mind *(Whoever when the United States is at war)*, and it behooved a man to use great care in choosing what to say and how to say it. Still, while he couldn't say all he believed, he'd be damned if he'd say what he didn't believe, which was this, that the war was a just one, fought under flowing banners for the good of all men. He was no suck-up, he said, no licker of spit, and any day, sooner than kiss a jingo's ass, he'd piss on freedom and go to prison.

He said those things. Those were the things he said.

He was born over on the Indiana shore of the Wabash, a good four hundred miles from that bandstand in Canton, and in a frame house not even a little bit better than the ones next door, he lived there still. It had a railed-in porch, and when the weather was fine (he had a bad back, lumbago or something), he liked to sit there in a rocker and chew the rag with anyone who slowed down or stopped, and if they kept on going, he'd wave as they were passing by. There'd be days, though, when he'd see nobody, say nothing, merely sit: he'd be deep in a book he'd read a dozen times before, a book by a Frenchman about a stolen loaf of bread, and for him on those occasions there'd be no sights or sounds outside the pages: he'd be in it with the wretches and their rags. The book, or a fresh copy of it, stayed with him all his life—that there should be both bread and hunger!, he thought. Maybe that's why so many went out of their way to walk his street and go past his door; maybe the things he felt about bread were in the air, and though he was with Valjean and Javert, unaware of them and their greetings, in some way they seemed to improve. The lonely, the lowly, the desperate, none of them knew how it happened, none saw his magic, his particular medicine, but all seemed better than they'd been before.

He'd made some mention of prison, he said, he'd spoken of preferring it to keeping his mouth shut, but there was nothing new in that, because never was there a time in history when a few hadn't put freedom of speech ahead of freedom itself and mouthed their way to jail, the theory being that there was more liberty inside than out. A loony notion, most people held, and maybe they were right, maybe it was true that the few were simply wrong in the head, longing for the Cross and the vinegared sponge and itching to die for the crowd—maybe it was so, he couldn't deny it. But suppose this, he said from that bandstand in the park, suppose no one had ever made that lunatic choice, chosen to speak when speech was a crime, suppose they'd served themselves instead of time—we'd still be wearing skins, he said, and snotting through our hands.

Those were the things he said.

At fifteen, he was firing locomotives for a dollar a day, small pay for burns and scalds and the danger of dying in a ditch. He was as tall then as he'd ever get, six-two or thereabouts, and spare as a spike-maul, and though he liked the work, his mother didn't

A BOILER EXPLODED NEAR VINCENNES ON FRIDAY LAST, KILLING THE ENGINEER

and she made him quit it to become a clerk for a wholesale grocer. It was a dull grind alongside those runs he'd had on the Terre Haute line, it never stirred him, never caught his mind. On the warehouse air, there were spices, teas, and herbs, but what he breathed was steam and smoke: at heart, he stayed a rail. In the evening, when he shut his ledgers, he didn't linger to dwell on cloves and fennel and darjeeling: he made his way to the yards, where other rails were, and there he forgot about firkins and canisters—the talk was of unions, and young Gene listened. They held him in good regard down at the roundhouse; they thought there might be something going on between those cocked ears of his. He read, they noticed, he read all the time, things by Tom Paine about rights and reason, things by some frog about the miserables—he was always gabbing about the miserables. Therefore when the brotherhood organized a firemen's local, they picked a man to lead it who no longer rode the footboard—Gene, six feet two of lean meat. He was twenty years old and on the way to where he ended.

In those days, he said, his grip was always packed. In behalf of the brotherhood, he was always off to somewhere or other, always boarding a train, often as blind baggage, and now and then he was kicked out into the snow, the sleet, the rain, whatever the weather was doing at the time. *I rode on the engines*, he said, *I slept in the cabooses, I ate from the pails of swarthy stokers—* he was twenty-five years old and he was making the union go.

> Some who were there that sunny afternoon say that he kept his coat on all the way through that two-hour speech—he was the spareribbed kind, they said, and he never felt the heat. If so, he must've staved it off with his own, because he was talking against the war in Europe, and he hated it, he said, and hated those who'd brought it on—the Prussians of Prussia and the Prussians of Wall Street. Wherever found, they were one and the same: they spoke different lingos, and they wore different clothes, but the man didn't live who could tell them apart. Who could tell the rich apart? They had one love, one desire, one God, and its name was Plunder.
>
> Those were the things he said.

He'd worked as a scoop for two-three years, four at most, but looking back from that balustered porch, he must've felt that he'd never left the road, that he was still stoking for those cornfield runs, still pitching in chunks of his life along with the chunks of coal. When he wasn't lost in that Frenchman's book, when he was just rocking himself quietly, and no one was passing by, he might've been thinking of fireboxes, of steam domes and ash pans, of sights once seen from rights-of-way, forests, farms, children waving, he might've been remembering the Mollies, the bomb in the Haymarket, the town of Pullman—Pullman, he'd've thought, the workers' paradise, a small and perfect garden in a great imperfect world. He'd not have forgotten its parks and pleasances, its green stone church and its wheel window, the theatre in the Moorish manner, the blocks of flats with a crapper for every two and a tap for every five. How vivid still that feudal Eden, where the pay was cut a nickel from 20ᶜ an hour! Sitting there and rocking gently, he'd've clearly heard Mr. Pullman say *There is nothing to arbitrate*, clearly seen a strike begin that he knew the union could not win. But he'd led it all the same, because the men had desired it, and for a matter of days, it'd gone well: no train entered or left Chicago, the rails grew rust, and there were naps of dust on the palace cars and the cold engines; in stalled reefers, food went bad, and no mails got through with bills and bundles and *billets-doux*. In the end, though, the soldiers were sent in, and the strike was lost—to wedding invitations and postcards with pictures of the Falls. That wasn't enough for the railroads and the rich, for the Government and that Pullman son-of-a-bitch: they had to put Gene in a cell for six months to show the people who really ran the planet Earth.

On his Eighth Street porch, he sat looking away through those gold-rimmed specs he wore, as if his pale blue eyes could see the past. If so, he saw the reading-room of the Woodstock jail, where a photo was taken of him with a book in his hands. Only he ever knew whether it was the volume of Shakespeare he'd brought along, or the speeches of Ingersoll, or *Wealth Against Commonwealth*, or that favorite of his wherein he read of Fantine, Cosette, and a fateful loaf of bread.

> And he said that all through the ages, wars had been waged for wealth, not for the commonwealth, for spoils, not for the good of man. The masters had always declared such wars, he said, and the serfs had always fought them, lost their lives while the others won the world. To the crowd, to the white-shirt glare spread out before him that Sunday afternoon, he said this—that their real enemies were those who, in the name of liberty, sent them off to be slain. They were our own Junkers, he said, full brothers to the Prussian kind, and their only god was Gain.
>
> He said those things to the people. Those were the things he said.

Four days after delivering the speech, he was indicted by a Federal grand jury, and on being tried, he was found guilty of having intended to subvert the armed forces of the United States. He offered nothing in extenuation, he made no plea in abatement: he'd known that his words were being taken down, he said, and he denied none of them. In fact, he'd go even further: war was odious to him, he said, and he'd spoken against it because in his view it impeached the social order and shamed the Christ the Christians vaunted. He was listened to in silence, and when he'd finished, he was sentenced to ten years in the penitentiary, first at Moundsville in West Virginia (*I never met a kinder man*, Warden Terrell wrote. *He is forever thinking of others, never of himself.*), and then at Atlanta, where he became Convict #9653.

Whoever when the United States is at war shall wilfully, etc., he shall be clad in prison gray, a blue shirt, and canvas sneakers, and he shall sleep one of six in a cell of springless bunks, and he shall eat mush in the morning, slum at noon, and beans at night. He shall be limited to one letter a week, and that to his wife, but on Independence Day, he shall have the privilege of writing to the person of his choice. (*There are six of us in one cell. My five companions are the finest, and I love them all, a German, a Jew, an Irishman, and two Americans. I have no complaint. I am in perfect health. All's well.*)

It was to his brother that he wrote on the Fourth of July, but he didn't tell him that he couldn't eat the slubber he was given, the hash, the liver, the mutton stew, he didn't let on that his heart was arrhythmic and wearing out, that he could hardly breathe in that cell for six with those he loved so well, his Germans, his Jews, his Micks, and nary a word did he say of the stink or the heat, the weakness he felt, the pains in his back, the loss of weight. He merely said *The prisoner to whom we sent a little money for tobacco two years ago has been very kind to me*; he merely said he was quite serene.

But when a visitor journeyed from afar to see him, the serenity she found was that of coming death. She raised such a ruckus, there and in Washington, that he was moved to the prison hospital and put into what was called the kick-off room, where dying lags were taken to await the final roll-call, a small enough place with a cot, a table, and a couple of chairs. There was hardly space for the bareboned man and his two-three books, one of which might've been written with him in mind. Somehow or other, he didn't kick off in the kick-off room, and, who knows?, it could've been due to one of those books.

People were always after him to petition for a pardon, but Gene didn't have the right

319

kind of knees for begging or the horns for pulling in, and besides, he had no use for Mr. Wilson, nor had Wilson use for him: *I know that in certain quarters of the country there is a popular demand for the pardon of Debs, but it shall never be accomplished with my consent.* He needn't have fretted: Gene wouldn't've said Uncle even to Uncle Sam. And hell, with Wilson out there, the company was better inside.

For Gene, truly it was better. He loved all those lifers, all those bank robbers and counterfeiters, and he talked to them as if they were still a part of the world, still worth respect, still human, and slowly they came to understand that he meant the things he said, that though they called him Little Jesus, he wasn't made of tin. On his walks through the yard, they simply followed him around, a cloud of hangers-on, and at ball games they vied for a place at his side or anywhere nigh. They asked him for advice, they brought him letters to answer on letter-day and also the Fourth of July. He gave them shares of his tobacco, and when theirs ran out, he left off smoking and threw in his own. He taught English to some, one of them an old wop who said *Mister Debs justa like God*, and what chocolate he came by went to the lungers in the tb ward. Little Jesus, his name was in that house of lowlives. It must've been the lowlife way of saying thanks to someone they'd heard was dead.

They were proud when his Socialist Party sent a delegation to tell him that for the fourth time he'd been nominated for the Presidency, and they were joyous too: they thought that when elected, he'd pardon himself and set them free. He announced that he intended to conduct a front-porch campaign from his residence in Atlanta (laughter); at least, his opponents would know where to find him (laughter). No convict had ever run for the office before—run, so to speak, while standing still—but Gene wasn't fazed by bars and walls: he ran all the same, and for a stationary candidate, he got a slew of votes, some nine hundred thousand, and he'd've gotten two thousand more if those in the pen had had a say.

The election was won by a Mr. Harding, an Ohio man from Blooming Grove and he was nothing like the stroke-struck cove whose place he took. He was cut from different cloth—and cut on the bias. He was a loose one, Warren G., a poker-playing soak, a chaser of the girls, and he no more fit the White House than tits would fit a boar. Even so, dreary, venerean, smoke-stained man, he seemed to know that something was wrong where Gene was in jail and his friends were not—his God damn friends! He gamed with them and drank the same drench, they were his liars and arrangers, they stood guard while he jigjigged with Nan—and then they gave away Wyoming while he looked for his pants. His God damn friends! Something was wrong, he must've thought . . . or maybe there was no thinking to it, just a weakness for an old man who'd lived long and done no harm, a soft spot for one of the few in whose coat there were no holes. Whatever it was, he couldn't rest till Gene was let go. It was the one good act of his life—but how many, he may have thought, how many do more?

On the Day of the Nativity, 1921, the warden sent for Gene and gave him a brown suit of clothes, a winter overcoat, and a five-dollar bill, and then he took him through the corridors to let him say goodbye to his beloved mail-thieves and murderers. What they said back he never learned, because all he could hear as he passed their cells was a storm of sound from two thousand men: it was a walk in the wind! Two thousand voices called out to him in a great and constant roar. They must've called out his name, Gene! Gene!, and on that day of days, how could they not have hailed Little Jesus! *They need me*, he said as he went through the gates, *I hate to leave them*, and for a long way down the road, he could still hear the tumult, and if he grew less sad when it died away, maybe he knew he hadn't really left after all. He had a certain book in his satchel, of course, and that helped too.

Home again in Terre Haute, he sat on the porch, sometimes with the book and sometimes not, and as before he waved at passersby, he rocked his chair, or, if thinking of firemen, Pullman, Nimisilla Park, he sat still for a long time and saw nothing, not even the book he held in his hand. All men were miserables, he may have thought, imperfect but striving, striving and falling short. Some day, though, some day . . . and there he may have smiled.

▼ ▼ ▼

BOWLES/RODITI

OPEN LETTERS TO LE JOURNAL DE TANGER

JANUARY 12, FEBRUARY 2, FEBRUARY 9, 1980

I

AN OPEN LETTER

(TO THOSE INTERESTED IN SURVIVING THE COMING DECADE)

We are aware that this message is addressed to a tiny minority of people who, for one reason or another, prefer to continue their existence during the Nineteen Eighties. The democratic ideal, upon which the civilization of the Twentieth Century is widely believed to rest, demands that any minority, however small, must be taken into consideration. The following suggestions are proffered with the aim of preventing unnecessary suffering.

For those who have already applied to Humanity International for their VQ Tabs (personal cyanide pellets) there is no problem, save perhaps for some who live in the rural areas of the more remote countries. Deliveries are being speeded up, however, and by April it is predicted that every citizen of every country which recognizes our organization can be provided with his own tablet, to be used at his discretion.

A word of warning (which is by no means a digression) is in order at this point. Recently the market has been flooded with a spate of inferior and dangerous brands of cyanide. (Zoffo, Suremort, Hallelujah, Adios and others.) These products are definitely not approved by Humanity International, and we cannot advise too strongly against their use. Death has been known to take a full half-hour in the case of Adios, according to a report issued by the research laboratories at the Attu Branch of Humanity International in November 1979. Those interested in the ideal escape will not find a product equal to our approved VQ Tabs; they are buffered, with added salidehydro-cyanuro-desoxycholic acid. The only safe pellet, the only one guaranteeing instant relief. No coma, no pain. Our service is absolutely gratis, as we constantly attempt to make clear in our thousands of broadcasts carried out in sixty-three languages. Unfortunately, human nature being what it is, suspicion is always aroused by the distribution of gifts; people feel that something paid for must be superior to something handed out free of charge, and this suspicion has been exploited by several unscrupulous pharmaceutical companies eager to profit by the present popularity of cyanide.

Humanity International does not, as has been charged, "recommend" the use of its VQ Tabs; it simply supplies them to those who ask for them. The worldwide response to our offers speaks for itself. In order partially to offset the accusations that have been levelled at the organization, we seize this occasion to address ourselves to the minority, to those hardy individuals who have decided to make the attempt to get through the entire decade without medical assistance.

First let us consider sustenance. It goes without saying that luxuries such as meat, fish, poultry, milk, eggs, butter, sugar, fruit and vegetables will soon be unobtainable. The recently developed protein substitutes such as Protoproxy should be used in quantity. An entirely new attitude toward food must be adopted. The concepts of "edible" and "inedible" must be abandoned. Both are conditioned by preconceived ideas which are no longer applicable to reality. It has been proven, for instance, that cats, dogs and rats will not only sustain life indefinitely if eaten in sufficient quantity, but that truly excellent dishes can be prepared with them by the efficient housewife. With an eye to preserving the gourmet tradition during the coming years, Humanity International has issued three useful handbooks: *Fifty Tasty Kitty Recipes, Man's Best Friend and How to Cook Him* (with list of breeds and the culinary treatment appropriate to each breed) and *The Rat Comes Into Its Own* (with a special chapter on the preparation of mice). For the first time in history these readily available sources of food, formerly used only in extreme situations and totally without scientific supervision, have been studied assiduously by top-flight dieticians and chefs, whose expertise is now within reach of anyone who wishes to profit by it.

The kind of foodstuffs we enjoy today will be in increasingly short supply, due largely to lack of fuel for delivery. We must learn the science of harvesting and preserving all edible plants. Each year billions of tons of weeds go to waste and disintegrate into the soil, only to produce more unused weeds. This great natural reserve must be exploited. It is true that citizens of tropical countries will be likely to have greater access to food, but this advantage will be outweighed by the incidence of disease.

Money will not be a problem, since it will be entirely without purchasing power. In addition, the list of purchasable commodities will rapidly shrink to zero.

Living space, on the other hand, will present intolerable difficulties to those accustomed to personal privacy. Because of the geometric progression in population increase and the impossibility of constructing new dwellings or even repairing old ones, requisitioning of floor-space will shortly be instituted. The target of fifteen cubic meters minimum to be allocated to each adult is admittedly utopian, at least during the coming decade. For the foreseeable future the figure will remain in the vicinity of ten cubic meters. Since people who previously enjoyed the use of an entire house or apartment will now be restricted to one corner of one room, a certain amount of dissatisfaction, even of confusion, may result. A few practical hints here may be useful.

There are ways of making your corner comfortable, even attractive. Cut out a large triangle of thick foam rubber (if you are unable to find any, bags of straw or shavings will do) and fit it into the corner on the floor. On top of that you can pile attractive rags and stuffed sacks. The walls behind can be covered with artistically chosen magazine covers or tasteful advertisements varnished over. If you have time, you can cut them up first and make personalized collages. A screen to provide a modicum of privacy can be constructed out of old crates, and perhaps covered with wrapping paper to give it that soigné look demanded by today's housewife.

The idea that fresh air is essential for healthy sleep was discarded by medical experts fifty years ago. It has been proven that, on the contrary, the instinct of the human species is to burrow deep into a relatively airless spot when sleep is desired. Apart from the possibility of contagious diseases, it is just as healthy to sleep shut into a room with several others as it was to sleep in your own room with the window open. Actually this enforced communal living can prove to be a blessing. It serves as a deterrent to mass attacks on living quarters by bands of starving teen-agers.

Survival in the Eighties will require enormous adaptability to adverse physical circumstances. A new, functional lifestyle is waiting to be created, one which will take into account the future as well as the present rapid deterioration of the situation. This requires a high order of talent, but there will be those who will rise to the occasion. Reduced circumstances need not, and indeed, must not be allowed to result in shabbiness, which comes from a morbid clinging to concepts of style no longer realizable. We must learn that the only consideration of any importance in the matter of clothing is that it should provide the warmth essential to normal human functioning. As the seasons change, the number of garments will vary, and from this simple phenomenon we can evolve a style that will be the very essence of sartorial elegance. Instead of the three sweaters, blanket and mittens of winter, we find that when spring comes, we may have only two sweaters and no blanket at all. It is from such small things that we create the poetry of a truly functional lifestyle. The greatest pleasure comes from the close inspection of ordinary objects, we are told. Those who have chosen to brave it out can reap spiritual profit, if they will, from this unique opportunity.

Your corner need not be in total darkness every night. You can make your own lamps out of rags soaked in vegetable oil, squeezed into interesting shapes and placed in oil-filled saucers. They give a dull, romantic glow. A welcome addition to gala affairs is a set of small alcohol burners to be used as hand-warmers. (Stock all the burning alcohol you can now; during a cold spell it has been known to make the difference between life and death). The ideal garment for winter corner-sitting is a large woolen blanket with a slit in the center for the head. Your corner can be made cozy, and you can be comfortable in it. It is up to you to decide whether you want to make the effort.

We at Humanity International believe firmly that if it is worthwhile living at all (and a few of those who read this will be of the opinion that it is), then it is also worthwhile to spend the effort necessary to transform what could otherwise be a humdrum existence into a meaningful life, a life of joy created, not in spite of hardships, but thanks to them. This is Humanity International's New Year message to the courageous.

Remember, VQ Tabs are always yours for the asking.

Paul Bowles,

Director of Public Relations,
Humanity International.

II

L'ASSOCIATION AVATAR ET HUMANITY INTERNATIONAL

Monsieur le Directeur,

C'est avec le plus grand intérêt que j'ai lu la très remarquable lettre ouverte que l'éminent écrivain américain Paul Bowles adressait, en tant que directeur des Relations Publiques de l'Association bénévole Humanity International, aux lecteurs du *Journal de Tanger* du 12 janvier dernier. Tout en étant d'accord avec l'essentiel de ce qu'il y propose, j'aurais néanmoins lieu de lui reprocher d'avoir négligé de faire allusion au très important appui logistique que notre Association Avatar apporte déjà aux activités de Humanity International.

Dans l'inévitable disette que provoquera bientôt l'explosion démographique dont nous constatons déjà les sinistres effets dès que nous nous voyons obligés de faire la queue à la Grande Poste pour y envoyer un télégramme, Paul Bowles propose ainsi aux lecteurs du *Journal de Tanger* d'avoir recours à des sources encore inexploitées de riches protéines animales; et il explique, à ce propos, que son Association Humanity International a déjà publié, dans un but non-lucratif, trois excellents manuels où le lecteur intéressé trouvera un grand choix de recettes culinaires lui permettant d'accommoder à son goût la chair des chats, des chiens, des rats et même des souris.

Paul Bowles semble toutefois sous-estimer l'importance de l'appui que notre Association Avatar apporte dans ce domaine aux activités de Humanity International. Sans cet appui, il n'y aurait en effet bientôt plus de chats ni de chiens, tous également morts de faim. Après quoi, l'humanité serait de même destinée à succomber à la même famine.

Consciente de cette grave lacune qui nous menace, telle l'épée légendaire de Damocles, dans la chaîne alimentaire, notre Association Avatar a donc entrepris une campagne internationale pour alerter le public contre les abus et le gaspillage du recyclage de nos chers défunts que nous confions, selon des traditions encore primitives et en quelque sorte artisanales, à des cimetières ou des Tours du Silence où leurs dépouilles mortelles n'alimentent que des vers ou des vautours estimés à juste titre peu comestibles; ou bien, à des fours crématoires où nos chers défunts sont transformés en une pollution de l'air qui a déjà inspiré au poète Paul Valéry ce vers prophétique:

«Je hume ici ma future fumée».

La campagne internationale que notre Association Avatar, dernière née parmi les multinationales, a ainsi entreprise ne constitue toutefois qu'un premier pas dans ses activités humanitaires. Notre but essentiel consiste en effet à recycler tous nos chers défunts de façon à combler cette catastrophique lacune dans la chaîne alimentaire qui menace notre planète de la disparition totale de toute vie animale ou humaine. Nous avons donc déjà contacté les plus grands producteurs de conserves pour chiens et chats afin de transformer les riches resources de protéines animales encore disponibles et inexploitées en Ronron et Canigou ou bien en farine d'ossements propre à alimenter nos élevages industriels de rats et de souris. Menacés, à mesure que s'amenuisent leurs sources de matières premières traditionnelles, d'une crise de plus en plus grave qui provoquerait d'abord des licenciements massifs de leur personnel avant la fermeture définitive de leurs usines et la liquidation ou la faillite de leurs industries, ces capitalistes clairvoyants ont accueilli fort chaleureusement nos propositions tout en nous assurant qu'ils sauront obtenir des autorités gouvernementales intéressées à la lutte contre le chômage l'aide financière nécessaire pour la reconversion de leurs installations et pour une campagne publicitaire adéquate auprès du grand public.

Pour une somme d'ailleurs tout à fait modeste, les familles des défunts pourront en effet s'assurer que le portrait du cher trépassé sera reproduit sur l'étiquette de chaque boîte de conserve qui contiendra de ses dépouilles; et ceci, en un monde de plus en plus surpeuplé, offrira l'avantage d'éviter d'une part le gaspillage de l'espace vital qu'entrainent les concessions à perpétuité et d'économiser d'autre part les frais d'investissement et d'entretien des monuments funéraires. Il va sans dire que tout un chacun aura en tout cas le choix, selon ses préférences personnelles et ses propres dispositions testamentaires, de léguer ses dépouilles mortelles aux chiens ou bien aux chats et de même aux souris ou bien aux rats.

Notre Association Avatar assurera de cette façon à tous nos chers défunts une véritable survie, en somme la seule que puissent nous promettre nos connaissances actuelles de la biochimie. Loin de chercher, selon les mots du poète Jules Laforgue, une impossible *«métamorphose des lys en roses»* ou une transmigration plus strictement métaphysique des âmes que la science risquerait un jour de démentir, nous garantirons dorénavant à tout un chacun que ses dépouilles mortelles alimenteront d'abord des chiens, des chats, des rats ou des souris qui, à leur tour, alimenteront par la suite notre propre postérité humaine en une chaîne alimentaire ininterrompue et aussi économique qu'éternelle; et nous nous félicitons d'avoir ainsi réussi à mettre l'immortalité tout à fait démocratiquement à la portée des petites bourses.

Edouard Roditi

Président à vie de l'Association Avatar.

Expert consulté par l'Organisation
de l'Alimentation et de l'Agriculture
des Nations Unies,
Membre du Club de Rome.

II

AVATAR ASSOCIATION AND HUMANITY INTERNATIONAL

[TRANSLATED AND ADAPTED BY THE AUTHOR]

Dear Sir,

I read with great interest the very noteworthy Open Letter which Paul Bowles, one of America's most eminent writers, recently published in your pages, for the benefit of the readers of your *Journal de Tanger* and in his own capacity as Director of Public Relations of Humanity International, a non-profit organization. Though I agree fully with the lofty humanitarian ideals and aims that inspired his proposals, I nevertheless have good reason to criticize Mr. Bowles for his failure to refer at all to the very important and efficient logistic support which our Avatar Association already supplies to the activities of Humanity International.

In the inevitable shortage of foodstuffs that must very soon be caused by the disastrous demographic explosion which we can already witness whenever we find ourselves obliged to stand in line at the Main Post Office here in Tangier for several hours before we can send a telegram, Paul Bowles proposes to your readers that they avail themselves of some sources of rich animal proteins that still remain unexploited; and he explains, to this effect, that Humanity International has already published, as a philanthropic initiative, three excellent handbooks in which an interested householder can find a broad range of cooking recipes for the preparation, according to his or her personal tastes, of the meats of cats, dogs, rats and even mice.

Paul Bowles appears, however, to underestimate the importance of the support which our Avatar Association brings in this field to the activities of Humanity International. Without this support, there would no longer be, within a short while, any more cats or dogs, or indeed rats or mice, to cook according to his excellent recipes, since all these animals would soon succumb as victims of famine; in fact, a shortage of rats and mice, exterminated by starving cats and dogs, would in turn decimate our household pets, leaving us finally without any animal proteins for our own sustenance.

Fully aware of the disastrous gap in nature's alimentary chain that threatens us like the legendary Sword of Damocles, our Avatar Association has therefore launched an international campaign in order to make public opinion finally conscious of the criminal abuses and waste involved in our obsolete failure to recycle our dear departed ones when we entrust their mortal remains, according to traditions that are still somewhat primitive and not yet fully integrated in our modern industrial economy, to mere graveyards or Towers of Silence where they can feed only worms or vultures which, quite properly, are considered to be scarcely edible; or else, to crematoria from which our dear departed ones finally emerge as vapors and soot that further pollute the atmosphere in a manner that inspired the poet Paul Valéry to compose one of his finest lines:

Je hume ici ma future fumée...

The international campaign which Avatar Association, the youngest among the Multinationals, has now undertaken after consulting the appropriate divisions of the United Nations Food and Agriculture Organization in Rome, remains however but a first step among our many proposed humanitarian activities. Our basic purpose is indeed to recycle all our dear departed ones in such a manner as to fill at long last the above-mentioned catastrophic gap in nature's alimentary chain which now threatens our planet with the total disappearance of all animal and human life. We have therefore contacted some of the more important producers of canned pet food in order to transform these vast unexploited reserves of animal proteins of human origin that are still available into popular brands of pet foods or into bone-meal that would then be suitable as feed for industrial rat-farms and mouse-farms; in addition, we have undertaken research in the production of new synthetic hormones whereby we hope to be able to produce, within a normal period of growth, mice of the size of an elephant and rats of the size of a whale. These will be bred mostly in special National Parks in Africa for the convenience of authorized big-game hunters, wild-life photographers and disciples of the late Ernest Hemingway.

As enlightened capitalists, these pet-food producers already realize that their traditional sources of raw materials are rapidly dwindling and that their traditional markets are likewise threatened with extinction. They thus find themselves facing an increasingly serious crisis that would first lead them to reduce drastically their personnel and finally to close down their plants and go into voluntary liquidation if not into actual bankruptcy. They have therefore expressed great interest in our proposals and assured us that they will be able to obtain, from government authorities interested in maintaining a high level of employment, the necessary financial subsidies or fiscal facilities for a reconversion of their industry and for an adequate publicity campaign to educate public opinion.

Among other facilities, the families of the departed will then, for a relatively modest sum, be able to make sure that the portraits of their loved ones will be reproduced on the label of each can that contains any of their remains; and this, in an increasingly overcrowded world, will offer the advantage, on the one hand, of avoiding the present waste of valuable living space that is entailed by grants in perpetuity in cemeteries and, on the other hand, of also economizing on the cost of investment and maintenance of expensive grave-stones, family vaults and other such monuments. Everyone will, of course, remain free to choose, according to his or her personal tastes and to appropriate clauses in a last will and testament, whether to bequeathe his or her remains to cats, dogs, rats or mice.

Our Avatar Association will thereby ensure, to all our dear departed ones, a real afterlife, in fact the only one that our present knowledge of biochemistry can truly promise us. Far from seeking, according to the words of the French poet Jules Laforgue, an impossible "metamorphosis of lilies into roses" or a more strictly metaphysical transmigration of souls that science might well disprove sooner or later, we would henceforth guarantee to all and sundry that his or her remains will first feed dogs, cats, rats or mice and then, in turn, our own human posterity in an uninterrupted alimentary chain as eternal as it is economical. We can indeed pride ourselves on having thereby made immortality available to the modest means of the average citizen of a true democracy.

Sincerely Yours,
Edouard Roditi

Life President of the Avatar Association,
Honorary Consultant to the United Nations Food and
Agricultural Organization, Member of the Club of Rome.

III

Dear Sir:

I read with the greatest interest the encouraging message from Monsieur Edouard Roditi, President of the Avatar Association, published in your issue of February second. Any responsible survey of the present situation with regard to scientific planning to meet future nutritional needs would of course dwell lengthily upon the crucial role being played by Avatar's recently developed recycling plans. Clearly the Avatar Association is in a position which gives it the capability of bringing immeasurable assistance to the human race.

Nevertheless, Monsieur Roditi's admirable optimism, with its beatific vision of the establishment of an "alimentary chain, as economical as it is eternal", remains, for the present at least, largely unjustified. What Monsieur Roditi neglected to state in his letter (perhaps from an understandable desire not to add to the general atmosphere of uncertainty and gloom prevailing at present) is that recycling can be carried out with safety only in the case of those individuals who have succumbed to natural deaths or as a result of accidents. But, inasmuch as this recyclable material accounts for only 44% of all recorded deaths, it must be assumed that the remaining 56% of the material will be tainted with cyanide.

In our Maldive Islands experimental laboratories, Humanity International researchers have demonstrated that recycled human material containing even minimal amounts of cyanide will destroy dogs, cats and rodents alike, thus eliminating the very creatures upon whose flesh we propose to subsist. In view of the rapidly increasing popularity of cyanide tablets, the problem is obviously one of grave importance, and one whose solution must be implemented on a worldwide scale. This implementation involves strict international controls. The commercial manufacture of cyanide must be halted. (Note: All the tablets sold by the pharmaceutical firms render the material unfit for recycling. These include the newer and much touted brands such as Sayonara, Godspeed and Laserquik, none of which is instantaneous in its effects, and all of which make successful recycling impossible, thus wasting more than half the available potential).

To Humanity International's VQ Tabs our chemists have now added something startlingly new: a marvelous substance which, without in any way diminishing their instant efficacy, forms, on contact with the stomach, a hermetic container by freezing the mucous membrane into a tight, hard ball enclosing the cyanide. And now the miracle! Deep inside this small leathery pod chemicals are at work disintegrating the particles of cyanide, transforming the poison into a tiny mass about the size of the head of a pin. This is easily extracted during processing, with the result that even the petrified stomach wall is rendered fit for recycling.

Let me stress, however, that only if VQ Tabs, the sole product embodying this sensational new discovery becomes *the one cyanide available on the world market*, can we be assured that the animals being bred in our experimental collectives will be properly nourished. This legislation must be pushed through at all costs.

If recycling were as simple a matter as the Avatar Association would have us believe, then indeed our nutritional worries would be considerably lessened. Unfortunately a tremendous amount of work must be accomplished before this state can be reached.

Meanwhile, for your own peace of mind, if and when you make the decision to depart, and in order that those who have chosen to stay behind may be assured of adequate and regular food, use only the new Improved VQ Tabs. Spread the good news to your friends. New Improved VQ Tabs are an essential adjunct to every responsible person's home. Don't be caught without them.

In the hope of serving you,
I remain Sincerely,

Paul Bowles,

Director of Public Relations,
Humanity International.

▼ ▼ ▼

GERARD MALANGA

EDWARD ALBEE'S EAR
IN THE MANNER OF ALLEN GINSBERG

*(o Po-ets, you
should getta
job*

—Charles Olson,
from "Maximus, to Gloucester"

*I used my mental illness like an emblem,
like a flag.*

—Antonin Artaud,
from a letter to Jean Paulhan

Poor Jimmy Schuyler?
FUCK JIMMY SCHUYLER!!!!!!!!
is what I want to say to Ted [Berrigan]
who rings me up asking if I know anyone
close to Edward Albee who cld speak to him
regarding his speaking to Howard Klein
[Pres., the Rockefeller Fdn] on behalf of
Schuyler receiving grant
(Ted saiz he can't approach Allen [Ginsberg] as he's
gotten a Rocky two months ago and it wldn't
look good his requesting one for friend
so soon after) because he doesn't
want to see Jimmy in position he was
two years ago nearly out on the street
(that's when he got the Pulitzer + Nat'l
Inst. of Arts & Letters) and it's not like
he's poverty-stricken :
"he's got a contract with THE NEW YORKER

for 'first refusal' on any poem he writes
and," also according to Ted, "nearly 7 grand
in the black right now (I'm in the black
too, what's called the dark night of the
soul) what with two trust funds! (1) from
Kenward Elmslie 5 grand a year and (2)
the other from Fairfield Porter
Estate for undisclosed amount and Christophe
De Menil wised up and stopped giving him money
at the time he received NEA (1979), Guggie (1980),
and CAPS (1981)," so it's not like
the guy's eating beans and tuna sandwiches
and I'm saying to Ted *But can he get a job?*
[Remember the Central Soviet vs. Joseph Brodsky]
"Oooh, nooo," Ted replies. "Jimmy's on medication
because of anxiety attacks [frankly a suppository
the only cure-all he needs] and what with
his rent at Hotel Chelsea and part-time sec'y
[male, no doubt] his expenses add up to about
20 grand a year." *Poor Jimmy.* And here I am
with 7 cents to be exact (one nickel + 2 pennies)
and I can't believe my ears what Ted's
telling me and nobody thought about my situation
on November 10, 1979—before or since (I refuse
to be victim, I'm driven by love of life)—
and I'm still trying to recover
and you can be sure I'll never
disclose the *one* person close to me "who has
Edward Albee's ear."

9:vii:82 nyc.

▼▼▼

PRESS RELEASE

FOR IMMEDIATE RELEASE **CONTACT: HENRI COLE**

JAMES SCHUYLER AWARDED $10,000 ACADEMY OF AMERICAN POETS FELLOWSHIP

New York, April 26, 1983——Announcement was made today by Mrs. Hugh Bullock, President of The Academy of American Poets, that the Chancellors of the Academy have named James Schuyler the 44th recipient of the $10,000 Fellowship for "distinguished poetic achievement."

James Schuyler was born in Chicago in 1923. He was formerly on the staff of The Museum of Modern Art and an associate editor of *Art News*, to which he continues to contribute articles. Aside from his poems, collected in *The Morning of the Poem*, for which he received the Pulitzer Prize in 1980, *The Crystal Lithium, Hymn to Life*, and *Freely Espousing*, he is the author of three novels, *Alfred and Guinevere, What's for Dinner?*, and, with John Ashbery, *A Nest of Ninnies*. James Merrill has written of his work, "All six senses are at play, plus those of tone and form, in these marvelous poems. One had almost forgotten that 'reverence for life' doesn't need to be a deadly bore." Mr. Schuyler makes his home in New York City.

The Fellowship of The Academy of American Poets was the first award of its kind in the United States. Past recipients have included Robert Frost, William Carlos Williams, Ezra Pound, Marianne Moore, and Elizabeth Bishop. Fellows are nominated and elected by the Academy's Board of Chancellors, a group currently comprising Robert Fitzgerald, Anthony Hecht, Daniel Hoffman, John Hollander, Stanley Kunitz, William Meredith, James Merrill, Howard Nemerov, May Swenson, David Wagoner, Robert Penn Warren, and Richard Wilbur.

The Academy of American Poets, now in its 49th year, is a non-profit organization devoted to stimulating interest in the poetry of the United States. In addition to its Fellowship, the Academy sponsors the Lamont Poetry Selection, the Walt Whitman Award, and the Harold Morton Landon Translation Award. The Academy also sponsors prizes for student poetry in more than 125 American universities and colleges, as well as readings, symposia, and walking tours in the New York City area.

(0837)

THE ACADEMY OF AMERICAN POETS 177 EAST 87 STREET N.Y. 10028

K. R. CAMPBELL

A NECESSARY SUPPLEMENT TO "THE MAKER OF THE SOUND"

I

There is the feeling of stark, raw existence in the making of a sound. If a man smacks a hammer across a bell the resulting sound "is" and speaks, in that vibrant instant, of the man's "being." Sound is an immediate physical sensation. But music is polysemous; while keeping the power of the fundamental sonority, it moves through time, imagining a past and anticipating a future. In doing so it mirrors man's life and reflects his various attempts to explain existence. In the old world, music's polysemy was confined to the particular stage for which the work was composed (opera house, concert hall, chamber work, etc.) or the type of genre it was composed in (symphony, opera, sonata, rondo, etc.). The fact that this music was heard in fixed contexts led to the illusion still rampant today—that a work of art must "stand on its own," i.e. be entirely self-sufficient, and give no reference either to the circumstances in which it was produced or the channel through which it is heard. This is insufferably naive and simplistic in an age of electromechanical reproduction, where a musical composition might be found as easily behind a TV commercial as in a recital hall. A new self-reflective art is needed which can function globally and still retain its integrity.

In this colliding matrix of information channels, the critic/interpreter is increasingly powerful because he has influence over how and where the art work is heard. The artist, aware of the critic's power, must usurp his techniques. Criticism, rather than playing the passive role of just assigning category and significance, must become an active shaping force in the art work. Wilde speaks of criticism that "treats the work of art as a starting point for a new creation." The artist should push this further until the creative subsumes the critical text and something new appears—a hybrid which has criticism's self-conscious language and penchant for supplemental interpretation, but retains art's unpredictability and life energy. These new hybrids are necessary as we find ourselves being echoed endlessly through technology's information-disseminating windows.

> These birds whose lambent calls
> once reconstated outside
> now flap and rollick hysterically
> in circuitry
>
> wire birds (not Saint Helen's plovers
> in wire grass)
> with video wings
> that make the audio moan

and I, the circuitor
inquietude, and coming from outside the body
click the tongue to her words
and resist.

Looking back to when I began working on *The Maker of the Sound* (the title of the whole work is the same as this first section—a song for voice and concrete tape) I see myself as being remarkably innocent of the complexity and the broader implications of what I was attempting. I thought I was making a piece for theatre, and included stage directions which read: *The auditorium is dark. On stage only one small light just bright enough to illume a man sitting at a table with a tape recorder. Behind him and to his side is a cluster of four speakers stacked together and beside these speakers a trumpet player and a pianist barely visible on the dark stage. The singer begins intoning*: "Born of bone I make the sounds that speak to bone..." In order to help the performer achieve a more exact performance, I sang and recorded the piece on magnetic tape with the desired intonations, rhythms, and pitches. This tape was meant to help the performer learn the piece but I soon found myself wildtracking it against the concrete music sounds played on another tape recorder. In this way I could demonstrate to interested parties how a stage performance might sound. Soon the success of these "household performances" convinced me that "realized composition," composition which exists like a painting, as a single object in the world, would be preferable to some distant and tentative (how often is new music scheduled?) theatre performance.

I envisioned a music written for the individual collector/entrepreneur, who would ferret out a work's particular meaning and become an expert on, and aesthetic guardian to, that work. *The Collector* was written with this musical piece-as-object in mind. It is a piece for trumpet, tape, and a poem which is not sung but exists as a separate entity on paper. The poem and music are referential but independent of each other. The listener, being aware of the poem, listens to the music making his own meanings and correspondences. The action is shifted from the "stage in the world" to the "stage of the mind." As a result the effect of the piece is determined by the individual listener's mood and degree of participation as compared to theatre's collectively imposed spectacle. The poem *The Collector* came from an advertisement:

> ANCIENT AIR COLLECTOR LOOKING FOR ANCIENT AIR... am looking for old wells or mines unopened for decades, also tombs, ancient bottles and barrels or any place old air can be found.

II

THE COLLECTOR

clank

the sound of the Venus de Milo's arms falling off

a sonic artifact

enter the collector
speaking like a poet reading...

"The white-eyed boy
The water-stained building holding promise
The snow-blind sneaking home
away from the grey-brick citadel"

consumed by that which he was nourished by

(when the light fails
collectors panic
in the dark we discover
that some paintings actually make sound
these works become the most prized)

an ancient-air collector appears
and the painter cries;
"ears, ears what will you give me for my eyes?"*

(when the light is restored
men will be seen with their hands in the air
gesturing violently ...
as if making something)

||:renoirdegasmanetmonetlatour:||
moon-soaked sounds
I dream the dream
of the man who searched for ancient air

After finishing *The Collector* I once more found myself wildtracking—this time the trumpet part against the concrete sounds. Again I felt a certain dissatisfaction with the arena (in this case the listener's mind) for which the piece had been written. The reasons for this dissatisfaction are unclear to me. Perhaps it was the lack of collector-entrepreneurs of the sonic artifact in my neighborhood, or the fact that leaving the piece's final form and meaning to the caprices of another's mind was anathema to me.

I decided to concentrate on language and leave behind the ideas of a "stage in the world" and a "stage in the mind." I called the third piece *Is There Anything There or Just a Noise?* Again, as in the first piece (*The Maker of the Sound*), the voice part was sung. This time, however, the action takes place at the level of the vowels and consonants sounding against the tape sounds. If listeners (including myself—how often does the artist really "know" what he's done?) are unable to hear the composition's subtleties or derive a meaning, at least I would know that meaning was there, at the language level, to be discovered at some future date. "Sounds go by with a life you can't hear... THE PIECE HAS GONE ON FOR SOME TIME NOW! WHERE WERE YOU?"

* source unknown

The reader of this supplement might at this point ask as Charles Ives does in his prologue to *Essays Before a Sonata*:

> ... How far is anyone justified, be he an authority or a layman, in expressing or trying to express in terms of music (in sounds if you like) the value of anything, material, moral, intellectual, or spiritual, which is usually expressed in terms other than music?

I would answer as Ives does further down in the prologue " ... is not all music, program music—is not pure music representative in its essence?"

To have documented the search for context as I did in the first three pieces was certainly programmatic. But at the completion of the third section I looked back at the work and saw a new all-encompassing, yet amazingly simple programmatic structure. This new program corresponded to a *Peanuts* cartoon I remembered. Lucy, after being nagged by her brother Linus to "read me a story," picks up a book, opens it, and says "a man was born, he lived and died, the end." This is funny because it reduces a complex situation to such an absurdly simple point that complexity again rushes in.

"A man was born" ...... *The Maker of the Sound*
"he lived" .... *The Collector*
"and died" .... *Is There Anything There or Just a Noise?*

But the outline above did not account for the last words of Lucy's story, "the end." I decided a fourth section was needed that would escape from both this new reductive program and the "search for a context" program outlined earlier. I decided the final section would be about the preceding sections.

> ... the supplement supplements. It adds only to replace. It intervenes or insinuates itself *in-the-place-of*; if it fills, it is as if one fills a void ...
> (Jacques Derrida, *Of Grammatology*.)

The title of this final section was taken "tongue in cheek" from a line of William Carlos Williams: *We Play the Piano We Don't Fall into the Strings*. I see this final section as a "deconstruction" of the preceding section's fragmented, concrete music sounds set against a melismatic, rhetorical (and to my ear romantic) song style. The piano, playing romantic music fragments, vies with the tape in ways that keep this section from falling prey to the homogeneity and delimitation of "a work." The listener is denied the passive comforts of a pre-programmed experience and finds himself confronted with a "text." "The logic that governs the text is not comprehensive (seeking to define what a work means!) but metonymic; and the activity of associations, contiguities, and cross-references coincides with a liberation of symbolic energy." (Roland Barthes, *From Work to Text.*) It took me three years to compose *The Maker of the Sound*. All the sounds in the piece are concrete (recorded with a microphone). These sound fragments were laboriously assembled together to form the complete piece. More efficient ways of making electronic music exist but none of these has the psychological depth ("fundamental sonority") of concrete sound. Furthermore, the form of the piece follows the characteristics (or content) of the various sounds gathered for the piece.

At this point I thought *The Maker of the Sound* could rest. But that "oh so exomatic world" intruded. I was asked to include the piece in BLAST. This meant the "wildtrack" performances in my house had to be reduced to a vinyl disk. Like taking a polaroid photograph of a painting, detail and life were lost in going from six tracks on three-quarter inch tape to a needle in a groove. However, the piece profited enormously by having Michael Ingham sing the voice part. Putting the music into a printed medium has created the hybrid you hold: *The Maker of the Sound* and the *Necessary Supplement*.

[A phono-disc recording of "The Maker of the Sound", sung by Michael Ingham accompanies each copy of BLAST 3.]

STILL LIFE WITH MASK OF SOPHIE BRZESKA, 1912
HENRI GAUDIER-BRZESKA
PASTEL 33 x 56 cm
COURTESY ANTHONY d'OFFAY

GILBERT SORRENTINO

JOHN GARDNER: RHINESTONE IN THE ROUGH

John Gardner is of the puppeteer school of novelists. He moves his characters in ways vaguely imitative of "real" people, puts stagy, pseudo-authentic dialogue in their mouths, and dresses them in costumes direct from the Wardrobe Department. The reader is to suppose that he is looking at Life. One can almost hear the numbing rhetoric about how if it was good enough for Dickens, for Tolstoy, and so on *ad nauseam*. That it was not good enough for Nashe, or Cervantes, or Sterne, or Austen, or James is quite apparent, but Mr. Gardner works in the aberrant mode of realism or naturalism, that upstart of imaginative writing, and to such writers this *arriviste* mode is the only mode.

He is the darling of reviewers, some of whom occasionally complain mildly of the "toneless" quality of his prose: they mean "styleless" but have difficulties with that word because of their enormous problems in the recognition of style. His work is taken seriously because his mirror-up-to-life routines reflect the images that his ill-read audience takes to be important: Look! There we are! Relentlessly descriptive of the fragmented quotidian (on which he imposes "order," *à la* Robert Frost), he is understandable and quite wonderful to readers to whom Jane Austen and Henry James are radical and difficult (they don't *say* anything). That these latter writers are these things to such readers is because of their departure from the mimetic, a departure that dates back at least to *Le Morte d'Arthur*.

In his "On Style or Writing," Rémy de Gourmont notes that "there are two kinds of writers: writers who can write and those who cannot write." In the latter camp may be placed those writers with a contempt for, or aversion to, style, the writers of "ideas," of substance, of the famous *content*, that odd ingredient that exists like the man on the stair: one meets it but it isn't there. Mr. Gardner, with a great stack of wooden books that he has sedulously inflicted on the public over the years, is one of those writers who cannot write, one for whom, or so the published evidence seems to show, style appears to be analogous to the effete, the frivolous, the "literary." He is a writer who goes about his business doggedly pretending that Flaubert never existed, or, if he did, that he was a realist, a kind of Gallic Tolstoy. He gouges his paralyzing books out of *ideas*. It seems that he wants to tell us ... the Truth!

October Light, a recent Gardner novel, seems to me to be an excellent subject for a cursory examination of the author in bloom.[1] It may, or so I propose, stand as the quintessential Gardner approach to fiction. A look at this work may make it possible to locate and isolate the virus that informs the canon. This canon has, depressingly, taken its place as the focus of a new trend in American fiction: the "think" novel for the reader ready to graduate from Harold Robbins, a genre much like the painting of Andrew Wyeth or the music of Aaron Copland. Art Without Tears. *October Light*, then, may be read as a guide to the author's *oeuvre*. It is amazing in its witlessness, using the language with a carelessness hardly ever found outside the idiocies of the consumer goods perpetrated by the hack robots grinding out Good Reads. It is rich in solecism and cliché, crammed with characters who Walk Off the Page and with dialogue that reads like the speech we hear daily, unchanged and unselected, without design, dialogue that is, in Valéry's phrase, utilitarian.

We are given an old, crusty, bigoted Yankee farmer, James Page. He chases his old, somewhat sensitive and refined sister, Sally Page Abbot, into her bedroom after smashing her television set. There ensues a war of wills when Sally refuses to come out of her bedroom. Neighbors, relatives, and friends are summoned from Central Casting to help, but they fail.

The Past is dredged up in all its Mystery.

We discover certain Skeletons in the Closet.

At the close, both James and Sally have Strange Experiences and Insights into Truth and Reality.

Sally finally emerges, Wiser and Better. As is James.

Both have been Cleansed in the Purifying Fires of Self-Examination.

Music up and Credits. All this is seen, as you surely will have guessed, through a haze of soap bubbles floating iridescently on blasts of hot air rising, ever rising, from the churning narrative. One can imagine Dickens (to cite a misnamed realist) doing this at twelve.

But, enter Literary Experiment. Sally, while in her room, reads a tattered copy of a trashy paperback novel, *The Smugglers of Lost Souls' Rock*, which is presented to us in counterpoint to the Real novel. It does not work as counterpoint (or gloss), but since nothing else in this book works, its inclusion is a perfection of ineptitude. There seem, on occasion, to be tenuous connections or slippery correspondences between the Real novel and the Trashy one, but Mr. Gardner cannot make them work as commentary, correlative, or irony. The niceties of technique of that wild, avant-garde movement, Symbolism, are ignored, lost in the same limbo in which dwells Flaubert. Mr. Gardner sits stunned before his own materials.

But to be specific: a small catalogue of exhibits drawn from *October Light* will surely be of more use than general condemnation. I assure the reader that these fragments are absolutely representative and have many counterparts throughout this work. From the Trashy paperback:

> Mr. Nit struggled to find words, bit his lips together, and squinted.

–and from the Real novel in which this Trash resides:

> He said nothing, biting his lips together and not meeting her eyes.

and:

> She bit her lips together, watching him pour the whiskey....

What are we to make of this? What is Mr. Gardner doing? Why is he doing it? Does he know or care what he is doing? Possibilities present themselves. 1. Trashy novels are as good as good novels; 2. Trashy novels are no worse than good novels; 3. Mr. Gardner's Trashy novel is on a level with his Good novel; 4. All writing is to be considered as sets of data to which style is inconsequential; 5. *The Smugglers of Lost Souls' Rock* is the Real novel, and *October Light* its prophet. The last is interesting to consider, since it implies that Mr. Gardner thinks either that writing which is patently rubbish is not so, or that he has no measure by which to gauge his own writing, since it is demonstrable that the writing in "both" novels is equally wretched. Can this all be a joke? Is the author giving us *two* parodies, one of the world of garbage fiction and one of the world of Gardner fiction? This idea is not defensible, however, in the light of Mr. Gardner's other novels, all of which flounder as hopelessly as *October Light*. We are stuck, it would seem, with the fact that Mr. Gardner is one of those "writers who cannot write," a Robert Bly of fiction.

The curiously machined mental processes of the hack are at work in the above fragments. When arriving at a problem of description, the true hack turns briskly into the celebrated Path of Least Resistance, and, rather than *looking* at what is before his eyes, the veteran laborer rummages in his bag of scraps and finds, ready to hand, a phrase, a simile, an analogy, an image, from which every ounce of energy has long since been siphoned. The reader will surely recall the famous corpse: "He looked at him as if seeing him for the first time," a construct that I have come across in at least fifty novels. Of course, Homer nods. But this particular Homer is comatose. The above quotations reveal a mind working in smooth grooves of banality, a brain worthy of claiming kinship with that of Monsieur Bouvard. The wonderful foolishness of those bitten-together lips! And given us, not once, but three times! It is delicious. I asked myself how else those lips might be bitten: separately? one after the other? And it will be recognized that in the world of mimesis, it is *de rigueur* to deal with more than one aspect of a "closely observed" face, hence, the effortless move to the eyes, the process of seeing. Conventional practice, or, how it really is in *life*.

More wonders: in the Trashy novel, we read this idiotic degradation of the simile:

> The lines of the houses were as clean and precise as the hands of clocks, and the streets moved over the hills like well-planned arguments.

Those "lines" might well be "as clean and precise" as the blades of knives; those "streets" very comfortably move "over the hills" like perfectly delivered lectures. (Or, the reader may insert his own comparisons.) This is known as Vivid Description, or, The Return of the Blob. But it may be protested that this excerpt is from the Trashy novel. What of the Real novel?

> ... in the middle of the valley, the village sat like a village of toy houses, a Christmas village waiting for fake snow and lights.

—a triumph of cliché from the Warehouse of Hackneyed Phrases, to be found on the same floor as the cartons filled with the Clouds that Sail Across the Sky Like Great Ships.

We might look closely at the following, again, from the Real novel:

> She stared at the wall for a time, thinking nothing, at first with an expression of sadness and compassion, then with a sterner expression. Her jaw became firmer, her eyes more fierce.

Disregarding the graceless, installation-manual prose of the whole, what is the *matter* with it? Why is it so blurred? We find the answer in the useless comparative "sterner." The prose is saying that an expression "sterner" than the expressions of "sadness" and "compassion" appears on the face described, but are "sadness" and "compassion" ever "stern"? Then, the poison at work, Mr. Gardner blusters into two more useless comparatives, "firmer" and "more fierce." Her jaw is "firmer," her eyes "fiercer" than they were—when? When she had "an expression of sadness and compassion" on her face, a time when, apparently, her jaw was only *firm*, her eyes but *fierce*. The prose, because of this endemic carelessness, simply decays. The grammar, the syntax, have no bones, and the sentences they should support collapse.

This inattention leads to unconscious howlers, as in (from the Real novel):

> He had a curious, boyish habit, with which she never interfered, of chewing little pieces of the newspaper while he read it.

—a glorious sentence: I see this man assaulting the paper, nibbling on a corner of the editorial page, gnawing the box scores. We assume, of course, that the author *means* something else, but he does not tell us what he means. His language obfuscates as does that of the advertising copywriter.

There are also displayed, throughout *October Light*, flashy similes worthy of fiction-workshop students with poor instructors. I give three as *exempla*. The first uses the Crippled-Analogue Shuffle:

> She remembered when his hair, snow-white, had been as brown as shoe polish.

(precise, in a world devoid of all other colors of shoe polish).

The second employs the Garbled-Comparison Hop:

> By the whitewashed post six feet away, the cats sat watching, soft and tame-looking as pillows on a couch...

(excellent if one thinks of pillows as possessing the qualities of living creatures).

The third is the tried-and-true, local-color, Down-Home Two-Step:

> His faith in laconic truth cracked and gave way like the wall of a haybarn...

(that, past the bucolic ornamentation of that collapsing barn—which functions like our clock-hands and well-planned arguments—leaves us with the problem of meaning as to "laconic truth." Brief truth? Pithy truth? A truth sparing of words? The truth known by our friend whose mouth is full of newspaper? Whatever, "laconic truth" is certainly a no-nonsense truth, it is a part of Country Wisdom.)

The preceding are all from the Real novel, as is the last, and my hands-down favorite fragment, clearly an example of *furor scribendi*:

> DeWitt... moved to the head of the stairs... a wide, shy grin on his red-headed, freckled face...

Cursed as he is with this monstrous deformity, DeWitt had *better* grin.

There is no point in going on with this. My point has, I hope, been made. Where there is no style there is no fiction, or, as Williams remarked of the sonnet, "Who cares what the line 'says'?"

In an astonishing interview with Mr. Gardner, published soon after the appearance of *October Light*, the author is quoted as saying: "Writing is not in its best phase right now. I think I'm lucky—I'm one of the best there is."

He is incorrect in his assertion.

He goes on to say: "I have to write all the time because I write very slowly and I throw away an awful lot."

He does not throw away enough.

---

1. The reader should know that this essay was written before Mr. Gardner's death. The author is not in the habit of savaging the deceased. *De mortuis nil nisi bonum.*

ALAN MUNTON

FREDRIC JAMESON: FABLES OF AGGRESSION:

WYNDHAM LEWIS, THE MODERNIST AS FASCIST

Fredric Jameson, *Fables of Aggression: Wyndham Lewis, the Modernist as Fascist*. University of California Press, Berkeley, Los Angeles and London, 1979. 190pp. $11.95 and £7.25.

The difficulty with recent literary criticism based on Marxist interpretations of structuralism has been shortness of breath. This criticism has rarely consisted of more than brief and suggestive essays, which cannot deal with the whole of an author's work. Fredric Jameson's study of Wyndham Lewis shows that such theories can deal successfully and provocatively with a lifetime's span of creativity, and it is welcome for that reason. Jameson also gives us some of the most powerfully intelligent criticism of Lewis that we have; previous criticism is surpassed by this suggestive and sympathetic discussion, when it is at its best. When it is not at its best, however, we have something quite different: criticism that is unscholarly, speculative, damagingly eclectic, and insufficiently informed about Lewis's work.

Professor Jameson is primarily interested in *Tarr*, "Cantleman's Spring-Mate," *The Childermass, The Revenge for Love, Self Condemned, Monstre Gai*, and *Malign Fiesta; Time and Western Man* is the only critical work considered in any detail. Already an emphasis is apparent: Jameson is not interested in Lewis's own theoretical writings. Yet one would expect a political study of this kind to deal with *The Art of Being Ruled*; and BLAST and *Enemy of the Stars* are not even mentioned. Lewis's own theoretical preoccupations are set aside, and what remains is operated upon by an array of recent critical methods. Jameson sets himself the difficult task of simultaneously discussing Lewis's work as if it had never before been discussed, and of making fresh theoretical developments of his own in the fields of ideology, psychoanalysis, and the analysis of narrative. It is an enormous project for a book of 190 pages, and as a result the writing is dense, the theory compact and the discussion of texts is glancing and briefly illuminating rather than sustained.

The book is in three parts: a Prologue on theory is followed by four chapters which are an expansion of an article first published in the *Hudson Review* in 1973; these are succeeded by five chapters of new material, and an Appendix on Lewis's *Hitler*. This is gathered under a title which Jameson admits is provocative, and which does not describe the book's real concerns. "Aggression" turns into the psychoanalysts' "aggressivity," and "fascist" into "protofascist," both less advertisable products. The title ingeniously incorporates the book's three themes, however; for by "fables of aggression" Jameson means that Lewis's fictions ("fables") are the working out of a psychic aggressivity in narrative forms that express an ideology of modernism. "Protofascism" refers to a complex of historical elements which emerge in Lewis's texts as a petty-bourgeois and anti-Marxist critique of capitalism. Lewis's psychic aggressivity is identified, not in the man himself but in his texts, by means of the concept of *libidinal apparatus*, a term from psychoanalysis which is here given social and historical potentiality.

The wider purpose of *Fables of Aggression* is to provide a theory of modernism which is "a critique and synthesis all at once of the two great rival theories of modernism current today" (p. 13). The first is Lukács's apologia for nineteenth-century realism, which involves a rejection of modernism, and the second a view of modernism which would produce the argument, for example, that *Finnegans Wake* is valuable because it breaks up the sentence and the word, and in doing so destroys bourgeois expectations of what a novel ought to be like. The critique and synthesis of these positions "all at once" creates further difficulties in an already difficult book. Nor is it clear why they need to be synthesized; except that Jameson can never leave a theory alone—everything he uses is reworked, resynthesized, reinterpreted. This limits *Fables of Aggression* in one important respect: for although it is, as I have said, a

345

welcome attempt to apply recent theory to literature, none of these theories is applied in its original form. Everything suffers a sea-change. Jameson's own reformulations, and his alone, are set to work upon Lewis's fiction; the theory is validated, but it is simultaneously rendered useless, for it is now in such a form that nothing else can be done with it.

Since Jameson writes as a Marxist, he has a distinct political purpose. This is to dispute the predominance of Henry James, James Joyce, Ezra Pound and Marcel Proust as representatives of modernism in departments of English Literature in Britain and America. It was easy to institutionalize this modernism because its "strategies of inwardness" reflected, and did not oppose, the social disintegrations of capitalism. By contrast, Jameson argues, Lewis's externalizing and expressionist writing could not be assimilated so easily; and this is fortunate, for Lewis's work retains the vitality to act as an alternative modernism which shows up the accommodation that has taken place between the institutions and what were once meant to be radically new departures. We should notice that Jameson's political strategy is limited to the university and to the question of what has been defined as "literature"; whereas Lewis's enterprise was an attempt to take hold (not that he succeeded) on the whole of Western culture. Jameson's methods prevent him from dealing with anything wider than this, but this is obscured by his range of theoretical reference.

Jameson's first chapter shows how "Cantleman's Spring-Mate" is a "demystification of the organic," a critique of the natural world which refuses to allow nature to go its own way, unobserved. As the observer in this case, Lewis uses metaphor with such intensity that his prose exposes itself for the activity of production that it is, and creativity itself is demystified. Further acts of demystification or defamiliarization are identified, and Jameson argues that Lewis's prose is an attack on the organic forms favored by a dominant culture. Lewis's sentences, by contrast, are produced as if by a machine: they are democratic and make no pretence at being a crafted whole; for them, beauty is impossible.

Here, Jameson is arguing from the second of his two definitions of modernism. Lewis's novels belong to the dialogic tradition of the novel (the term is from Bakhtin), and this means that rather than being concerned with an individual organic consciousness, such as Bloom's in *Ulysses*, Lewis's characters always show themselves conscious of the relationship they have with others, and constantly make allowances for this in their speech and actions. At the same time, Lewis's characters are infected by the received ideas and clichéd language of the world around them, yet despite this oppression a more authentic life still persists. The result is that "a kind of 'double articulation' or surcharged text" (p. 41) is written, which shows both the corruption of language and gesture, and the authentic life struggling beneath it. Jameson gives as an example the well-known passage from *Tarr* where the growth of the Restaurant Vallet is described like a speeded-up film ("But perpetual scenes of unbridled voracity... gradually brought about a change in its character"). Here, nothing is natural or given; the objects of reality are transformed in accordance with the demands of a narrative that shows a radical dissatisfaction with the commonsense view of the real. The same transformation is applied to what used to be known as "character" and "human nature" (which Joyce and Proust's modernisms were able to retain), and *Tarr* provides persuasive examples of this process. There is no longer "a single unified character, held together by a proper name" (Jameson follows Propp here), but instead a set of functions in which human objects with names are observed to take part.

The Childermass extends these processes. Jameson introduces the concept of the *pseudo-couple* from Beckett's *The Unnamable* ("I naturally thought of the pseudocouple Mercier-Camier"); it is the most brilliant of his borrowings. The pseudo-couple of Satters and Pullman

> remain legal subjects who nonetheless lack genuine autonomy and find themselves thereby obliged to lean on one another in a simulation of psychic unity which is little better than neurotic dependency. (p. 59)

They are related to Hamm and Clov, Bouvard and Pécuchet, Faust and Mephistopheles. Pullman's identity is disintegrated because he is corrupted by the *Zeitgeist*; he therefore makes the mistake of choosing to support the Bailiff in the afterworld. But Lewis offers no Jamesian ethical judgement on this. Instead, his prose foregrounds the problem of making any ethical judgements at all. The existence of the pseudo-couple makes narrative possible where the individual subject and the language that define him have disintegrated. These figures, Jameson argues in his third chapter, "The Epic as Cliché, The Cliché as Epic," are produced by the *bricolage* of a degraded culture:

> The collage-composition practiced by Lewis thus draws ... on the warehouse of cultural and mass-cultural cliché, on the junk materials of industrial capitalism... that systematized network of cultural code and representation which preexists, speaks, and produces the individual subject by means of the ruse of a belief in individuality itself. (p. 73)

Lewis's artificial epic, as Jameson calls *The Childer-*

mass, "takes as its object of representation not events and actions themselves but rather the describing of them" (p. 76); this language is related to the culture of which it is a critique because it shows "a passionate revulsion for that great automobile graveyard which is the 'modern mind' " (p. 80). A brief chapter on *The Revenge for Love* concludes this part of the book, which establishes a very valuable understanding of the relationship between Lewis's prose style and the culture of which he was part.

Jameson now turns from style to narrative, and the remaining five chapters are an attempt "radically to historicize the gap between style and narrative" (p. 7). Lewis's style is radical in its implications, but the narrative structures of his fiction are not. They are negative and contain a "sequence of rape, physical assault, aggressivity, guilt and immolation" (p. 8). Narrative requires a different kind of investigation from style. The libidinal apparatus is brought forward; this is a means of articulating a narrative structure so that it can be filled with history: "we will see that it is the diplomatic system of the pre-War nation-states which provides a narrative apparatus" (p. 11). In this operation it is only the text of a Lewis novel that is worked upon; not Lewis's psyche, not the culture of his time, not any empirical real which the novel may be said to be about. The text is opened up to criticism by means of the signifier-signified distinction, drawn from linguistics; Jameson follows Lacan in this: "the signifier is what represents the subject for another signifier" (p. 91), or in other words the subject is constituted in a network of signifying practices, and is not what conventional literary criticism knows as "character." The novel is a series of relationships between signifiers. It is the novel's *form* which carries its larger meanings; one such form is allegory, which "opens up that specific and uniquely allegorical space between signifier and signified" (pp. 90-91). In this way the signifier-signified relationship produces a narrative form, allegory. To join the historicized narrative structure to the novel's form, Jameson now offers the concept of *national allegory* and applies it to *Tarr*. The nationalities of Tarr, Kreisler, Bertha and Anastasya "figure those more abstract national characteristics which are read as their inner essence" (p. 90). The effect is seriously reductive:

> The allegorical signified of such narratives is ultimately always World War I, or Apocalypse: not in any punctual prediction or reflection of this conflict as a chronological event, but rather as the ultimate conflictual "truth" of the sheer, mobile, shifting relationality of national types and of the older nation-states which are their content. (p. 91)

This means that the form of *Tarr* is not a reflection of an actual event (World War I), but shows instead a "truth" about the relations between national types who stand for their countries. But who would be so foolish as to think *Tarr* was about the First World War? Why the fierce rejection of a reflection theory held by no one? (And what is the status of a "truth" between quotation marks? Presumably that it is not truth at all.) Despite Jameson's stress on "historicity," actual history is present here in only the vaguest way. The relationships between nation states are naively transferred to the relations between characters, so that Kreisler, the failed German artist in Paris "tells the story of a national inferiority complex," while in cultural terms "Kreisler's fury reenacts the humiliation of Germany" (pp. 91, 92). This is, to put it mildly, a distinctly disappointing outcome from such a massive theoretical effort.

There are further difficulties in Jameson's position. If everything depends upon the text upon which the critic works, then it is advisable to use the right text. Jameson appears not to know that *Tarr* exists in three different versions. All his quotations are from the revised edition of 1928, though he thinks he is dealing with the first publication of 1918. He is evidently unaware of the existence of the serialized version which appeared in *The Egoist* between April 1916 and November 1917. The existence of this version, probably completed in November 1915, makes almost impossible (if we did not doubt it already) the belief that *Tarr* is about "World War I or Apocalypse." *Tarr* was begun in 1908, and its essential outlines were present, as Lewis's correspondence shows, from an early stage. These simple facts cause the collapse of great tracts of Jameson's argument about *Tarr*, and not least the suggestion that the first sentence ("Paris hints of sacrifice") refers to the "heroism and agony of France in the trenches" (p. 122). If this is true, then Lewis was very punctual indeed! The most notable victim of the collapse is the concept of the *epistemological break* caused by the First World War, which is put forward to explain the difference between the narratives of *Tarr* (1918) and *The Childermass* (1928): for the text which Jameson is quoting was written after the break is supposed to have occurred, and yet is supposed to prove its existence. This is one of the dangers to which an operation upon the text alone is open—the failure to apply the ascertainable facts of scholarship.

This failure is part of a wider one, Jameson's peculiar sense of history. His earlier book, *The Prison-House of Language*, injected historicity into the ahistorical categories of structuralism. But Jameson's history is rather like a peon in *The Childermass*—it dissolves if looked at too hard. Here too ascertainable facts are a difficulty. It is literary texts which are the real events

347

of the past, Jameson believes, and it is in them that history lives on; but it is history of the most generalized kind, huge undifferentiated entities like The General Strike, The Second World War, The Cold War, that Jameson finds inscribed in Lewis's fiction. If Althusser's anti-empiricist attitude to history lies behind this, then the arguments of E. P. Thompson's brilliant polemic "The Poverty of Theory" (1978) apply equally to Jameson's denuded historical landscape.

A second dubious category is Jameson's "strong personality," which is generalized from *The Childermass*: the weak personalities of the peons dissolve, the stronger are more real. The discussion of ideology is centered upon this concept, and to justify it Jameson assumes that it is an ideal to which Lewis himself held, rather than being a fictional device. Jameson quotes on p. 105 a passage from *Time and Western Man* in which Lewis asserts the importance of the self, and this leads him to discuss the "ideological value of individual identity" in Lewis. But the quoted passage is not all Lewis has to say about identity; for he did not believe that he was himself exempt from those very stresses and strains upon the self that he made his subject (and which Jameson is so usefully concerned with). Jameson omits to quote, from the same page of *Time and Western Man*, the question Lewis asks himself: "How do you propose to avoid the contradictory factors of empirical life?" and his answer:

> I have allowed these contradictory things to struggle together, and the group that has proved the most powerful I have fixed upon as my most essential ME. This decision has not, naturally, suppressed or banished the contrary faction, almost equal in strength, indeed, and even sometimes in the ascendant.... the dominant one is never idle or without criticism. (U.S. edition, pp. 136-37)

This is not the ideal of a unified ego, and it is quite wrong for Jameson to pretend that this is what Lewis believed.

Upon this basis—which is no basis at all, in fact—Jameson erects his theory of ideology. We notice here too the way in which he sets aside, or brackets, almost the whole of Lewis's critique of his time. Everything Lewis says is ideological, "the desperate response to a contradictory situation":

> The ideal of the "strong personality"—too complex to be resumed under the current term of "elitism"—is in fact the central organizational category of Lewis'[s] mature ideology, and the primary "value" from which are generated all those more provocative, yet structurally derivative ideological motifs and obsessions of racism and sexism, the attack on the Youth Cult, the disgust with parliamentary democracy, the satiric aesthetic of Otherness, the violent polemic and moral stance of the didactic works, the momentary infatuation with Nazism as well as the implacable repudiation of Marxism. (p. 110)

Even this presents problems of interpretation. The contradictory situation that Lewis endured, we are told in the Prologue, was "between his aggressive critical, polemic and satiric impulses and his unwillingness to identify himself with any determinate class position or ideological commitment" (p. 17)—a view which I accept[1]—yet the immediate commentary on the passage quoted above is said to signify Lewis's "group adhesion" (p. 111). Was there no ideological commitment, or was there group adhesion? Is this contradiction or explanation? In any case, the discussion of ideology is intended to demonstrate Althusser's proposition that art gives us a "view" of ideology, "an *internal distantiation*" which exposes to the reader the ideology in which the writer is gripped. In Jameson's view Lewis provides a particularly "scandalous" (p. 21) example of this process at work; and I accept that this is so, particularly in Lewis's weaker works. My objection is that Jameson attempts no detailed working out of this process of distantiation; his proposition remains an assertion.

I have disputed the validity of two of Jameson's primary terms, national allegory and the strong personality, neither of which, I believe, has substantial existence. Both terms are essential to the next stage in his argument: that they can in some way fill the empty matrix of the concept of libidinal apparatus, and that this in turn can be applied to *Tarr* and *The Childermass* in the form of a psychologized version of Greimas's semiotic rectangle. The terms with which Jameson sets out—epistemological break, national allegory and strong personality—are so damaged that the diagrams we are offered of this rectangle (and lozenge) have no meaning. They are in any case absurd diagrams. One might as well fill the little boxes with terms like Earth, Air, Fire and Water, or the bodily Humours. Although we are jostled by Marxist terms, these diagrams represent an abandonment of all that is social, everything that is felt and known about what it means to live under capitalism. It is a tragic and pathetic abandonment of the critic's responsibility.

It is in Chapter 7, "The Jaundiced Eye," that Jameson deals with Lewis's critique of culture. *Time and Western Man* is described as a critique from the Right, in that it "takes as the basic object of its diagnosis the consciousness of *other people*" (p. 130) rather than the transformation of self proposed by liberal critiques. Lewis, the intellectual, believes that other intellectuals are the source of social and cultural corruption; hence the attack on Bloomsbury. But this is a misunderstanding. Lewis attacks Bloomsbury in *The Apes of God* as the agents or conduits of a corruption originating in the requirements of political and cultural action: power in its different forms. Jameson does not discuss Lewis's major political and cultural study *The Art of Being Ruled* (1926; here misdated 1925), and as a result gives only part of the argument. *Time and Western Man* is too narrowly based to provide a full understanding of Lewis's critique of culture. As its title suggests, *The Art of Being Ruled* is intended to be a critique from below, and is both a discussion of other intellectuals, and of the ways that cultural and political control is exercised in the western democracies. It deals with the press, communism, fascism and anarchism, feminism, "masculinism," homosexuality, the family, and a multitude of other subjects. It also discusses such intellectuals as Proudhon, Sorel and Fourier. Jameson's endorsement (p. 116, n. 4) of Geoffrey Wagner's discussion of Lewis's relationship to early twentieth-century neoclassical thought (to which Lewis had no relation at all) suggests that he has not examined these questions very closely. Yet one would have thought that as a Marxist Jameson would turn first to this book, and I find it impossible to understand why he has not discussed it at all. It does have the disadvantage of showing that Jameson's notion that Lewis adhered to a "great man theory of history" (p. 30) is untrue, and that he did not project an image of the state as "an arbiter above the social classes" (p. 17), and also shows that he was by no means a consistent anti-feminist and sexist. It is an awkward book, but it is too easy for Jameson to bracket the difficult matters it raises as "ideology," and to assert Lewis's sexism as a means of declaring his own radical credentials. The refusal to confront *The Art of Being Ruled* makes the ingenuities of this chapter appear largely beside the point.

The following chapter discusses *Self Condemned, The Revenge for Love* and the two final volumes of *The Human Age*. Here as in Chapter 4, *The Revenge for Love* provokes some of Jameson's best criticism; by now the reader is able to sift out such sentences as "If Harding marks the final destiny of the Tarr-ego in Lewis'[s] post-World-War-I narrative system, then Victor must be seen as the equally unexpected avatar of the old Kreisler-id" (p. 147), and pay attention instead to the valuable discussion of satire and of cliché. Here, at last, the reactionary Lewis begins to satisfy the Marxist Jameson, for in *The Human Age* "Lewis'[s] system of representation approaches something like a genuine dialectical consciousness of itself" (p. 157) and this fiction offers "something like an immanent awareness of its own historicity" (p. 158). We arrive in Heaven just in time to witness "a repetition of the same dismal process of cultural corruption that it [Lewis's imagination] had denounced on earth" (p. 159). In the final chapter, "How to Die Twice," one necessary repetition is discussed: death. "The attempt to imagine death is at the ideological and instinctual center of *The Human Age*" (p. 160). How can death for these puppets be real if life is unreal? We are taken through a long exposition of what Freud, Lacan and Sade have to say about the "second death" (but what of Lacan's aside "Like Dylan Thomas, I don't want there to be two"?). Freud's *Beyond the Pleasure Principle* demonstrates the relationship between aggressivity and the death instinct, though since we are dealing with fictional texts, the second death in the afterworld can only be imagined, not enacted. Lewis is a satirist, whose business is to kill with the word, but he only kills what is imaginary. The initial reality (the process of cultural corruption on earth) "projects itself into a phantom and transcendent realm beyond its own material remains, in order there the more surely to die a second time" (pp. 170-71).

But Jameson is not satisfied with this imaginary satirical killing. He has to insist on making it real, and the business of breaking out from the structuralist world into the real world proves difficult. We now reach "the ultimate crisis in Lewis'[s] narrative system" (p. 172). After reading a study of Lewis's narrative which has bracketed all questions of his actual engagement in the history of his times, after struggling through an analysis which makes the signified-signifier distinction its means of opening out the texts with which it deals, and which concludes with an account of the "second death" which Jameson admits is "essentially ahistorical" (p. 171), we are asked to believe that quite suddenly the whole of Lewis's narrative effort opens out onto the real world:

> For if the second death is an imaginative possibility, and death can become real after all, then the satirist bears final responsibility for what are now real victims, and the guilt inherent in his aggressivity must at last be confronted undisguised. (p. 172)

We have early been warned that "the private psyche of the biographical individual, Wyndham Lewis" (p. 11) is not available to us; yet is turns out to have been there all along, its head under a sheet at the back of the stage, waiting to be unmasked and condemned for creating *real victims*. The situation is preposterous. This is not a resolution but a collapse of argument. What Jameson wants to do—and it runs against the anti-empirical bias of the whole book—is to get into a position in which he can mention the liberal intellectuals' responsibility for the Vietnam war. He wishes to say that the intellectual has responsibilities: "For was not Lewis himself just such an intellectual, whose endless and enthusiastic pages ... could be invoked to legitimize the most mindless forms of brutality and institutionalized lynching?" (p. 176). Two points need to be made: first, that of course Lewis had such responsibilities (and knew he had them), but such a question is not prepared for by the discussion in this book; second, the reader should notice the words "could be invoked"—this phrase neatly avoids the empirical question of whether they *were* invoked in this way, in actual historical situations. This is another question this book is not equipped to answer, and to raise it at this late stage points to the great drawback of Jameson's method: he cannot sustain it to the end. Just as this method makes empirical questions impossible, it should do the same with aesthetic questions and all questions of value; yet Jameson evidently feels under intense pressure to introduce these matters. In the final lines of the book he smuggles in from *The Revenge for Love* an aesthetic and idealist entity, "the realest tear in all literature" (p. 177), which can only be legitimately present if all the methodology that precedes it is abandoned.

The massive eclecticism of this methodology presents many problems, though it has the advantage that since Lewis's work has never been appropriated as "literature" by the universities it can here be placed all at once into an active relationship with a whole network of critical positions. However, Jameson is clearly worried by the extent of his own eclecticism, and I cannot accept his invitation (p. 6) to ignore its problems:

> The methodological eclecticism with which such a project can be reproached is unavoidable, since the discontinuities projected by these various disciplines or methods themselves correspond to objective discontinuities in their object (and beyond that, to the very fragmentation and compartmentalization of social reality in modern times).

In other words, although Jameson objects to capitalism because it fragments social reality, it is somehow legitimate for a Marxist critic to repeat that fragmentation in his own work. This is both circular and damages his claim to be a Marxist.

My objection to the first part of this justification is that though it is an undoubted fact that there are objective discontinuities in Lewis's work, this does not explain why any particular critical theory should apply to any particular point in it. Why Sartre here, and Gilles Deleuze and Félix Guattari there? Jameson does not explain; though the reader of *The Prison-House of Language* and the essay "Criticism in History" (in *Weapons of Criticism*, ed. N. Rudich, 1976) will recognize many of them. There seems to be a remarkable conjunction between what Jameson chooses to survey, purely theoretically, in those two places, and the theories which find their application in Lewis. Evidently Jameson values certain disciplines or methods out of the set available to him, and proceeds to apply them as "correspondences." This is not an objective process, for contrary to what the above quotation attempts to suggest, there can be no such correspondences before they are projected by Jameson himself.

If we look at the actual relations of some of the critics and theorists whom Jameson uses, we find that E. P. Thompson has conducted a fierce polemic against both Althusser and Terry Eagleton; Althusser and Lacan are in disagreement with Sartre; Deleuze and Guattari's *Anti-Oedipus* is a critique of Freud, who is the ultimate source of Jameson's psychoanalytical materials; Guattari has criticized the relationship existing between Lacanian and Althusserian structuralism, and has described Lacanian analysis itself as "the prototype of new forms of power." Samuel Beckett, source of the concept of the pseudo-couple, could have no place amongst these theorists except as mocker. Finally, E. P. Thompson and Christopher Hill are historians who belong to a quite different Marxist tradition from Althusser and the rest; and this brings me to the point at issue: when Jameson detaches an idea and puts it to use in his own system, does it not bring with it something of its origins? For example, detaching Althusser's definition of ideology from the essay "Ideology and Ideological State Apparatuses" in *Lenin and Philosophy*, Jameson writes: "two features of this definition need to be retained" (p. 12). No criterion of *need* is given. Similarly, his description of the origins of a central term, libidinal apparatus, appears to be a reversal of the meaning given to it by its originator, J.-F. Lyotard (see p. 10, note 8). If the criterion of need is the usefulness of a definition when it is applied to Lewis's work, then Jameson has merely arranged his terms in advance, just as bourgeois criticism does. There is no necessity in his choice of method.

One reason for this eclecticism may be that Jameson wishes to prevent his methodology being absorbed by institutions. It cannot be swallowed whole (who could believe in the truth of all these theories?), but would require too many individual acts of appropriation for all the small particulars to be taken over. It is impossible for any individual to read this book properly,[2] because any one person will not know, or cannot believe, all the theories it draws upon. Every reader therefore is forced to read parts of it in bad faith: only *as if* they were true.

This unrepeatable methodological structure ensures Jameson's place as an avant-garde critic, but the reader is wrong-footed so often that it seems he has no wish to be *followed*: there is a fear of repetition. This ensures the critic's dominance over the reader, but if Lewis's method is democratic, then Jameson's is tyrannic.

The difficulties persist if Jameson is read alongside his sources. Reading Deleuze and Guattari's *Anti-Oedipus: Capitalism and Schizophrenia* makes us aware of a lack in Jameson's text. *Anti-Oedipus* is comic and amusing, whereas *Fables of Aggression* is tense and reserved. *Anti-Oedipus* has a feeling for the liberating and pleasurable possibilities of literary texts, whereas Jameson's discussion of the manic growth of the Restaurant Vallet in *Tarr* does not recognize that Lewis's writing is exhilarating. This question of pleasure indicates a point of similarity between the two French writers and Lewis. Lewis's prose and thought refer back to what can be called the illegitimate tradition in nineteenth-century European writing: to Fourier, Saint-Simon, Max Stirner, Proudhon, Nietzsche and Dostoevsky. They all understand excess and their writing shows it. It is hardly surprising that in *Self Condemned* René Harding should throw into the Atlantic a copy of *Middlemarch*. Deleuze and Guattari also refer to an illegitimate tradition: Büchner, Nietzsche, Samuel Butler, Beckett, Artaud, Ginsberg, Wilhelm Reich. Jameson calls Lewis a petty-bourgeois; and we recall that Marx said the same of Proudhon, who greatly interested Lewis.

But Marx also said this of Proudhon's *What Is Property?*

> Provocative defiance, laying hands on the economic "holy of holies", superb paradox which makes a mock of bourgeois common sense, withering criticism, bitter irony, and, betrayed here and there, a deep and genuine feeling of indignation at the infamy of what exists, revolutionary earnestness—. (Marx and Engels, *On Literature and Art*, Moscow, 1976, p. 110)

This describes the oppositional spirit in which a great deal of Lewis's work was done. Placing him into relation with these illegitimate groupings makes it possible to grasp the transgressive and pleasurable nature of Lewis's work. This provides a reason for reading Lewis that is not available to Jameson, who finds Lewis "embarrassing" and underestimates the importance of satire in his work.

Jameson's book is intensively theoretical, synthesizing, rule-making rather than rule-breaking. It lacks the sense of pleasure. Nevertheless it has transformed the study of Lewis's style, and has provided an analysis of narrative that does not succeed but which cannot wholly be evaded. However much its author may want to avoid assimilation by the institutions, with this book the study of Lewis enters decisively the world of criticism.

---

1. See my essay "The Politics of Wyndham Lewis," *Poetry Nation Review* 1 (1976).

2. In writing this review I have benefited from discussions with Edward and Kate Fullbrook, Paul Edwards, and Steve Crook.

NOTES ON CONTRIBUTORS

MICHAEL AYRTON (1921–1975), the distinguished British painter and sculptor, was Lewis's staunchest friend and supporter during the difficult but rewarding years at the end of Lewis's career.

PAUL BOWLES is an expatriate American writer and composer living in Tangier, Morocco. His latest book, *Points in Time*, is being published by Ecco Press, which is also re-issuing *Their Heads Are Green and Their Hands Are Blue*. A book of translations, *She Woke Me Up So I Killed Her*, is being published by Cadmus Editions.

GEORGE BUTTERICK is Curator of Literary Manuscripts and Lecturer in English at the University of Connecticut, and lives with his wife and sons in the nearby mill city of Willimantic. He is currently editing Charles Olson's unpublished prose and poetry and is writing a biography of the poet.

K. R. CAMPBELL studied with Vladimir Ussachevsky in Utah. He now lives and works in Santa Barbara, California.

ROY CAMPBELL (1901–1957), South African poet, went in 1919 to study at Oxford. A rather Byronic figure, his poetry is often strongly satiric as in *The Georgiad* (1931), an attack on Bloomsbury culture. Among his finest works are translations from Baudelaire, St. John of the Cross, and Calderon, and a short study of Lorca. He wrote two autobiographies, *Broken Record* (1934) and *Light on a Dark Horse* (1951). He was an intimate of Lewis for many years and appears as a character in *Snooty Baronet* and other works by Lewis.

AIMÉ CÉSAIRE was born in Basse-Point, Martinique, in 1913. After completing a degree at the Sorbonne, he returned to Martinique; in 1945 he became the Martinique Deputy to the French Assembly and later the mayor of the capital, Fort-de-France, as a member of the Communist Party. He broke with the Party in October 1956 and was re-elected in 1958 as a member of the Martinique Progressive Party. He was recognized early as a major poet in the surrealist tradition, and is the author of six collections of poetry, several plays, numerous articles and historical essays, the best-known in English being his *Discourse on Colonialism*.

GIOVANNI CIANCI is Professor of English Literature at the University of Genova, Italy. He is the author of *La Scuola di Camridge* (on the literary criticism of I. A. Richards, Empson, and Leavis; Bari, 1970) and *La Fortuna di Joyce in Italia* (Bari, 1974). He edited *Quaderno* No. 9 (a special issue on Futurism/Vorticism; Palermo, 1979) and the international collection of essays in *W. Lewis, Letteratura / Pittura* (Palermo, 1982). He is currently writing a book on the impact of Futurism on the early English avant-garde.

TOM CLARK's *Paradise Resisted: Selected Poems 1978–1984* will appear early in 1984 from Black Sparrow Press. His previous books include *Who is Sylvia?* (novel), *The World of Damon Runyon, Writer: A Life of Jack Kerouac* (biography), *The Last Gas Station and Other Stories* (stories), *The Great Naropa Poetry Wars* (polemic), and *When Things Get Tough on Easy Street* (poetry).

SEAMUS COONEY was educated at University College Dublin and at Berkeley. Now Professor of English at Western Michigan University, he has published articles on Scott, Byron, Henry James, and Austin Clarke, among others. He has edited the poems of Charles Reznikoff and co-authored the Black Sparrow Press *Bibliography*.

ROBERT CREELEY's most recent books are *Collected Poems, 1945–1975* and *Mirrors*, with *Collected Prose* to follow in early 1984. Recently he has been living in Berlin on a DAAD grant, and is now David Gray Professor of Poetry and Letters at SUNY/Buffalo.

REED WAY DASENBROCK teaches English at New Mexico State University. A confirmed Lewisian of many years' standing, he wrote his Ph.D. dissertation on Lewis and Pound under the direction of Hugh Kenner at Johns Hopkins. Since then, he has published articles on Lewis in *Enemy News* and has contributed a brief survey of Lewis's work to the *Critical Survey of Long Fiction* (Salem Press, forthcoming). His forthcoming book *Literary Vorticism: Towards the Condition of Painting* will be published by Johns Hopkins University Press.

GUY DAVENPORT: A short story writer (*Tatlin!, Da Vinci's Bicycle, Eclogues, Trois Caprices, Apples and Pears*), poet (*Flowers and Leaves, Cydonia Florentia, Goldfinch Thistle Star*), critic (*The Intelligence of Louis Agassiz, The Geography of the Imagination*), translator (*Archilochos, Sappho, Alkman; The Mimes of Herondas; Herakleitos and Diogenes*), and illustrator, Guy Davenport is the

Alumni Distinguished Professor of English at the University of Kentucky. He won the Zabel Prize for Fiction awarded by the American Academy and Institute for Arts and Letters in 1981.

FIELDING DAWSON, turned 53 in '83, a prolific writer and artist, lives in New York. Most recent publication November 1982: *Krazy Kat & 76 More, Collected Stories, 1950–1976*. Due in 1984: *Virginia Dare, Stories, 1976–1981*. Both from Black Sparrow Press. And from Duke University Press, *Tiger Lilies, An American Childhood*. Fall 1984.

EDWARD DORN's book-length poem, *Captain Jack's Chaps, Houston/MLA*, was published autumn, 1983. He teaches at the University of Colorado, Boulder.

PAUL EDWARDS was born in Colchester, England, in 1950. He attended Cambridge University, and later studied the work of Wyndham Lewis at the Universities of Birmingham and London. He is an editor of *Enemy News*, the journal of the Wyndham Lewis Society.

CLAYTON ESHLEMAN's many books include *What She Means, Hades in Manganese* (Black Sparrow Press, 1981), *Fracture* (Black Sparrow Press, 1983), and a translation (with Jose Rubia Barcia) of Cesar Vallejo's *Complete Posthumous Poetry* (Univ. of California Press). The latter book won the 1979 National Book Award. Eshleman is currently the editor of *Sulfur*, "A Literary Tri-quarterly of the Whole Art," published by the California Institute of Technology, Pasadena, where he teaches. He is also a regular reviewer for the *Los Angeles Times Book Review*.

KENNETH GANGEMI's most recent books are *The Volcanoes from Puebla*, about living and travelling in Mexico, and *The Interceptor Pilot*, a cinematic novel. A new paperback edition of *Olt*, his first novel, was published in Spring 1984. He is working on a second book of poetry.

HENRI GAUDIER-BRZESKA (1891–1915) began working as a sculptor in Paris in 1910. With Wyndham Lewis and Ezra Pound, the young French artist was one of the founders of Vorticism.

JEAN GUIGUET was born in France in 1913. He studied at the Universities of Lyon and Lille and at the Sorbonne. He taught in London and successively at Kenyon College, the University of Washington in Seattle, California State University at San Diego, at the Universities of Grenoble, Aix-en-Provence, and Nice. He wrote novels, critical studies—on Virginia Woolf, Hart Crane, Theodore Dreiser—a book on American civilization, and articles in various scholarly journals. He enjoys retirement away from a decaying (French) academic world.

MICHAEL INGHAM has performed in many major European festivals and specializes in singing music of the twentieth century.

BRYANT KNOX is a former high school teacher, college and university instructor who holds a Master's degree in English from Simon Fraser University. He has written previously on Ezra Pound and Charles Olson and is working on a pictorial presentation of "Charles Olson's Yucatan." He has also studied and travelled extensively in Mexico and lectures professionally on pre-Hispanic art and culture. He lives with his wife and two daughters in Burnaby, British Columbia.

BERNARD LAFOURCADE was born in 1934 in Grenoble, France. He is a lecturer in English literature at the University of Savoy in Chambéry. Co-author of *A Bibliography of the Writings of Wyndham Lewis* (Black Sparrow Press, 1978), he has written a number of articles on Lewis and has translated "Cantleman's Spring-Mate" (Paris, 1968), *Tarr* (Paris, 1970), *The Revenge for Love* (Lausanne, 1980), and *The Wild Body* (in collaboration, Lausanne, 1980).

WYNDHAM LEWIS (1882–1957) was a novelist, painter, essayist, poet, critic, polemicist, and one of the truly dynamic forces in literature and art in the twentieth century. He was the founder of Vorticism, the only original movement in twentieth-century English painting. Of his many books, several works of fiction (*The Apes of God, The Complete Wild Body, Snooty Baronet,* and *Self Condemned*), a travel book (*Journey Into Barbary*), his intellectual autobiography (*Rude Assignment*) and the epoch-making periodical BLAST 1 and 2 are currently in print in authoritative editions from Black Sparrow Press.

MINA LOY (1882–1966) was a brilliant experimental poet, designer, and painter. Her biographer, Virginia Kouidis, writes "It is as a precursor of postmodernism that Loy's place in the modernist vortex becomes clear. She belongs in the Stein-Pound-Williams-Moore current of modernism, the current that by generating postmodern poetry became the most vital force in American poetry."

GERARD MALANGA: Besides his current book with Black Sparrow Press, *This Will Kill That*, Malanga's most recent books are *UPTIGHT! The Velvet Underground Story* written with Victor Bockris (Omnibus Nooks, U.K.), *The Legacy of Gaile Vazbys*, a collection of new poems and photos from AUsRA in a limited signed A-Z edition, and in Spring of 1984 Lustrum Press will be bringing out his collection of voyeurism poems and photos *Autobiography of a Sex Thief.*

TIMOTHY MATERER is the author of *Wyndham Lewis the Novelist* (Detroit, 1976) and is presently working on a book entitled *Modernist Alchemy: Pound, Yeats, and Eliot*. His edition of *Pound/Lewis: The Correspondence* will be published by New Directions in the fall of 1985.

JEAN-JACQUES MAYOUX, French author of books on Melville, Joyce, and Shakespeare, taught for many years both in England and France (at the Sorbonne). He served in the French Navy and in the French Resistance in World War II, and later in the French Consultative Assembly and Unesco until 1951. He now resides in Paris.

BRADFORD MORROW is editor of *Conjunctions* and has published a number of critical articles about Ezra Pound, Italian lyric poetry, and Vorticism. He is a rare-book and manuscript dealer, now living in New York City.

ALAN MUNTON was born in England in 1945. He completed his doctoral dissertation on Wyndham Lewis's theory and fiction at Cambridge University in 1976. He is currently Senior Lecturer in English at the College of St. Mark and St. John in Plymouth, England. He has edited the *Collected Poems and Plays of Wyndham Lewis* (1979, revised 1981), and with Alan Young has compiled a bibliography, *Seven Writers of the English Left*, published by Garland in 1981. He has published critical essays on Wyndham Lewis in collections edited by Jeffrey Meyers and by Giovanni Cianci. He writes on poetry and criticism for the Manchester-based periodical *PN Review.*

JOYCE CAROL OATES is a novelist, short-story writer, critic, and essayist. Her most recent novel is *Mysteries of Winterthurn*. She is on the faculty of Princeton University and is a member of the American Academy-Institute of Arts and Letters.

R. W. ODLIN: By turns egyptologist and swine-herd, Mr. Odlin may be seen in the pages of various computer-oriented magazines as often as elsewhere.

CHARLES OLSON verified the gains of Vorticism while extending them. His epic *Maximus* poems have recently been issued in a single volume by the University of California Press, and his collected poems, including more than 300 previously uncollected poems not in the *Maximus* series, is forthcoming. His *Complete Correspondence* with Robert Creeley is being published in ten volumes by Black Sparrow Press.

MICHÈLE POLI was born in 1937. She is a lecturer in English literature at the Sorbonne.

EZRA POUND (1885–1972) was one of the great poets, translators, and editors of the Modernist era. He was an early friend and supporter of Wyndham Lewis, with whom he launched the Vorticist movement in London prior to World War I, and he retained a lifelong interest in Lewis's writing and painting.

B. W. POWE lives in Toronto. His essays, articles, and stories have appeared in magazines and journals in the United States and Canada. He has just finished his first novel and his book of critical essays on Canadian writers *A Climate Charged: Essays on Canadian Writing*, is published in the United States by Flatiron Books.

EDOUARD RODITI was born in Paris in 1910. He has published extensively in American, English, French, and German periodicals in the areas of literary criticism and art history. He is also a poet, and has translated works from French, Dutch, German, and Turkish.

JOHN SANFORD is the pseudonym of Julian Shapiro, a New York lawyer and the author of thirteen books of fiction and nonfiction. The work printed here is from his latest, *The Winters of That Country*, soon to be published by Black Sparrow Press.

DANIEL SCHENKER is presently completing a book on religion and modernism entitled *The Quality of Unbelief: The Sacred Texts of James Joyce and Wyndham Lewis*. He lives and works in Syracuse, New York.

C. H. SISSON is a poet, translator and critic. He was born 1914 in Bristol, England, and presently lives in Somerset. His *Collected Poems* will appear in 1984.

ANNETTE SMITH, born in Algiers, teaches at the California Institute of Technology. Her critical articles have appeared in *Women's Studies, Claremont Quarterly*, and elsewhere. Other translations of Césaire's poetry by Eshleman and Smith have appeared in *Sulfur*, nos. 1 and 5, *Montemora*, nos. 6 and 7, and *Bachy*, no. 18.

GILBERT SORRENTINO was born in Brooklyn, New York, in 1929, and lived in that borough and in Manhattan most of his life. He was the editor of *Neon* in the 1950s and one of the editors of *Kulchur* in the 1960s. From 1965 to 1970 he worked as an editor for Grove Press. His published work includes more than a dozen volumes of poetry and fiction, as well as many critical essays and reviews. He currently teaches at Stanford University and lives with his family in Palo Alto, California.

E. W. F. TOMLIN is the author of a number of books on philosophical and literary subjects, including *Living and Knowing, Simone Weil, The Oriental Philosophers*, and *Man, Time, and the New Science*. He has held professorships at the Universities of Nice and Southern California. In the British Government cultural service, he was Representative and Cultural Counsellor in Ankara, Tokyo, and Paris. *Wyndham Lewis* (1955, revised 1969 and 1984), *Wyndham Lewis, an Anthology of His Prose* (1969), and an essay in *Wyndham Lewis: a Revaluation*, ed. Jeffrey Meyers (1980) are his main contributions to Lewis studies.

WILLIAM C. WEES is an Associate Professor of English and Director of the Film and Communications Program at McGill University, Montreal, Canada. He is the author of *Vorticism and the English Avant-Garde* (Univ. of Toronto Press, 1972), and is currently working on a study of avant-garde film.

Printed August 1984 in Santa Barbara & Ann Arbor for Black Sparrow Press by Graham Mackintosh & Edwards Brothers Inc. Typesetting by Eildon Graphica of Toronto. Color reproductions by The Paget Press of Toronto. Designed by Barbara Martin & Peter Sibbald Brown. This first edition is published in paper wrappers & 426 deluxe numbered copies have been handbound in boards by Earle Gray.

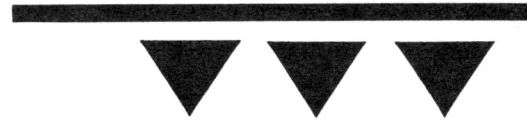